Science and Philosophy
in the Indian Buddhist Classics

COMPENDIUM COMPILATION COMMITTEE

Chair

Thamthog Rinpoche, Abbot of Namgyal Monastery

General Series Editor

Thupten Jinpa, PhD

Advisory Members

Geshe Yangteng Rinpoche, Sera Me Monastic College
Geshe Thupten Palsang, Drepung Loseling College
Gelong Thupten Yarphel, Namgyal Monastery

Editors

Geshe Jangchup Sangye, Ganden Shartse College
Geshe Ngawang Sangye, Drepung Loseling College
Geshe Chisa Drungchen Rinpoche, Ganden Jangtse College
Geshe Lobsang Khechok, Drepung Gomang College

SCIENCE AND PHILOSOPHY

IN THE

INDIAN BUDDHIST CLASSICS

VOLUME 3

Philosophical Schools

CONCEIVED AND INTRODUCED BY

His Holiness the Dalai Lama

Developed by the
Compendium Compilation Committee
Edited by Thupten Jinpa

Translated by Donald S. Lopez Jr. and Hyoung Seok Ham
Introductory essay by Donald S. Lopez Jr.

Wisdom

Wisdom Publications
199 Elm Street
Somerville, MA 02144 USA
wisdomexperience.org

A translation of *Nang pa'i tshan rig dang lta grub kun btus, vol. 3.* Dharamsala, India: Ganden Phodrang Trust (Office of His Holiness the Dalai Lama), 2019.

Library of Congress Cataloging-in-Publication Data is available.
LCCN 2017018045

ISBN 978-1-61429-789-5 ebook ISBN 978-1-61429-813-7

26 25 24 23 22
5 4 3 2 1

Designed by Gopa & Ted2, Inc.
Cover art by Getty Images.
Set in DGP 11/14.

Printed on acid-free paper that meets the guidelines for permanence and durability of the Production Guidelines for Book Longevity of the Council on Library Resources.

Printed in Canada.

Contents

Preface

General Editor's Note

Classical Tibetan texts often refer to ancient India as the Land of the Noble Ones, rightly admiring it for its rich spiritual and philosophical traditions. Recognizing this dual aspect of India's heritage—spirituality and philosophy—Tibetan writers praised the Land of the Noble Ones as the source of both Dharma (spirituality) and "the sciences" (*vidyā*). The Dharma the Tibetans admired most, and devoted maximum effort toward to bring it to their homeland, was the Buddhadharma, especially the tradition of India's great monastic university of Nālandā. But the Tibetan translators also conveyed India's other knowledge disciplines: grammar and linguistics, poetics, civility and governance, logic and epistemology, Ayurveda medicine, and the astro-sciences. As part of this largescale importing of knowledge, the Tibetans inherited the philosophical writings of great Buddhist thinkers like Nāgārjuna, Āryadeva, Bhāviveka, Asaṅga, Vasubandhu, Dignāga, Dharmakīrti, Candrakīrti, Śāntideva, and Śāntarakṣita, and institutions based on the study of their major works were established in Tibet. The Tibetan admiration for Indian knowledge was such that the very script that the Tibetans would develop as the medium for this ambitious cultural transference was modeled on the Indian Devanāgarī script of the seventh century.

As a translator myself, rendering classical Tibetan texts into English, I have often wondered what considerations might have led individual Tibetan translators in their choices of what to translate when faced with the enormity of the body of literature representing the long history of Buddhist thought in India. Were the choices determined primarily by circumstances, such as the popularity of a given text at the time or the preferences of an influential contemporary Indian teacher? Or was there, at least on occasion, a more systematic approach, an effort to present a spectrum of particular subjects, genres, and authors? For it was only in the thirteenth century, several centuries after the first phase of Tibetan translation, that the vast body of texts the Tibetans inherited from India came to be compiled into the two canonical collections—the Kangyur (translations of sacred words) and Tengyur (translations of treatises).

Be that as it may, among the over five thousand Indian texts that came to be translated into Tibetan over several centuries is the genre of *siddhānta*, doxographical works that present a kind of history or encyclopedia of philosophy. As noted by His Holiness the Dalai Lama in his introduction below and underlined in the introductory essay, the earliest known text of this genre is Bhāviveka's sixth-century *Essence of the Middle Way* (*Madhyamakahṛdaya*) and its autocommentary *Blaze of Reasoning* (*Tarkajvālā*). That such an early encyclopedia of Indian philosophy was authored by a Buddhist thinker is no coincidence. Thanks to the travel writings of Chinese pilgrims, especially Xuanzang, who studied at Nālandā in the seventh century, we know that the curriculum at major Buddhist educational institutions included an array of disciplines. Students at these monastic universities would study, in addition to Buddhist thought, the philosophical systems of Sāṅkhya, Vaiśeṣika, Nyāya, Mīmāṃsā, Vedānta, and Jaina as well as the views of the materialist Cārvāka school, often in a format that we might today call "comparative philosophy." *Siddhānta* texts like those of Bhāviveka clearly demonstrate the value and power of such a comparative and critical engagement with the key tenets of these diverse systems of thought.

In addition to Bhāviveka's seminal works, the Tibetan traditions also came to admire a second encyclopedic work authored by another Buddhist thinker. This is Śāntarakṣita's eighth-century *Compendium of Principles* (*Tattvāsaṅgraha*)—running to some 3,646 stanzas—together with its commentary by the master's disciple Kamalaśīla. These two works provided a rich resource for the Tibetan tradition to develop its own indigenous *siddhānta* literature. Some of these indigenous Tibetan texts are voluminous, such as Jamyang Shepa's famed *Great Exposition of Tenets*, while others like Könchok Jikmé Wangpo's *Jewel Rosary of Tenets* are short primers for young students. Typically, once the student has gone through the elementary debate training through study of the Collected Topics (*bsdus rva*), they engage with such a primer on Indian philosophy alongside two other primers, one on the typology of cognitions (*blo rig*) and the other on the science of reasoning (*rtags rigs*). This is how I received my own training at Ganden Monastery.

This volume is the third in the four-part *Science and Philosophy in the Indian Buddhist Classics*, conceived by and prepared under the personal supervision of His Holiness the Dalai Lama. Within the Dalai Lama's threefold categorization of the subject matter of classical Buddhist texts into science, philosophy, and Buddhist religious practice, the first two volumes focused on science, or the nature of reality. This and the final, fourth, volume are devoted to philosophy, with the current volume presenting the diverse systems of Indian philosophy and the fourth focusing on six major areas of inquiry. The vision behind this special compendium the reader can learn from the Dalai Lama's introduction below.

The approach of the present volume is characterized by three key features: (1) All presentations are grounded in classical Indian sources. (2) Unlike traditional *siddhānta* literature, the views of each school are presented from the perspective of the schools themselves rather than from the perspective of the Buddhist critique. And (3) special attention has been made to present not just specific views but the arguments behind these views. That said, it is important to note that the primary source used by the editors of this volume was the Tengyur, so the views of non-Buddhist schools are presented as described in *siddhānta* texts authored by Buddhist philosophers. Even so, efforts have been made to ground the views attributed to the specific schools in the key works of the traditions themselves.

It is truly a source of joy to see in print this special volume on the philosophical systems of ancient India. As generations of students and scholars have enriched their minds, sharpened their intellects, and deepened their contemplations through their engagement with the key tenets of diverse Indian philosophical systems, especially through the *siddhānta* literature, today contemporary readers in English will share in that opportunity. It has been a profound honor to be part of the creation of this volume, as the general editor for both the original Tibetan version as well as this English translation. First and foremost, I offer my deepest gratitude to His Holiness the Dalai Lama for his vision and leadership of this most valuable initiative of bringing the insights of ancient Indian tradition to our contemporary world, especially through the creation of the four-volume compendium *Science and Philosophy in the Indian Buddhist Classics*. This volume is blessed to have a lengthy introduction from His Holiness himself.

I thank the Tibetan editors who worked diligently over many years to create this compendium, especially for their patience with the substantive changes I ended up bringing to the various stages of their manuscripts. I would like to thank the two translators of this volume, my friend Professor Donald Lopez and his colleague Dr. Hyoung Seok Ham, for their monumental achievement in creating a masterful translation. Professor Lopez's deep familiarity with the Tibetan tradition (including translating the famed Tibetan *siddhānta* work Changkya's *Beautiful Adornment of Mount Meru*), his remarkable ability to always situate specific ideas within their broader context, and his natural skill in rendering Tibetan sentences into lucid English and Dr. Ham's expertise in non-Buddhist Indian philosophical systems make them a perfect team to bring this challenging volume to the contemporary reader. Readers of this volume are especially fortunate to have in the Professor Lopez's introductory essay a comprehensive yet a clear synopsis of the vast world of Indian philosophy, thus preparing the reader to engage with main body of the text in an efficient and focused way. That essay, a veritable treasure, truly enhances the richness of this volume. At Wisdom Publications, I must thank David Kittelstrom and Brianna Quick for their incisive and diligent editing of the English translation. Finally, I express my deep gratitude to the Ing Foundation for its generous support of the Institute of Tibetan Classics, which made it possible for me to devote the time necessary to edit both the original Tibetan volume and this translation.

Through the publication of this volume, may the insights and ideas of the great Indian philosophical systems become an inspiration, sharpening the intellect and deepening the contemplation of contemporary readers across the boundaries of language, culture, and geography.

Thupten Jinpa

Translators' Note

In 2019, Donald Lopez's translation of *Beautiful Adornment of Mount Meru*, the famous text on Buddhist philosophy by the renowned Geluk scholar Changkya Rolpai Dorjé (1717–86), was published in Wisdom Publications' *Library of Tibetan Classics* series. It was therefore natural that he would be asked to translate the present volume, which covers the same philosophical schools. Changkya's text is renowned for its penetrating engagement with specific philosophical issues in the course of its survey of the Buddhist schools, differing in this way from the much longer, more comprehensive, and quotation-laden *Great Exposition of Tenets* by Jamyang Shepa (1648–1721).

The respective strengths of these two famous works are reflected in His Holiness's *Science and Philosophy in the Indian Buddhist Classics* volumes. The present volume is the first of two on Indian philosophy. It adopts the traditional Tibetan approach of setting forth the most important tenets of the great Indian philosophical schools in the traditional order, starting with the non-Buddhist schools and then proceeding through the Buddhist schools. The second volume will revisit the tenets of those same schools, but from a thematic perspective, comparing their positions on such foundational issues as the two truths, the valid means of knowledge, and the nature of the self.

Although the present volume is thus traditional in format, it differs from earlier Tibetan works of the tenets genre in its more detailed presentation of the non-Buddhist schools of classical Indian philosophy: the Hindu schools, the Jaina school, and the Lokāyata or "materialist" school. This is a major contribution, providing for the first time an opportunity for students of Tibetan Buddhism to recognize the interconnections and influences among the Buddhist and non-Buddhist schools of Indian philosophy over the course of more than a millennium.

Because of the substantial chapters on the non-Buddhist schools, many of whose most important works are preserved in their original Sanskrit, Lopez invited Hyoung Seok Ham to join the translation project. He is a distinguished scholar of Sanskrit and an expert on the non-Buddhist schools, especially the Mīmāṃsā, the most formidable of the Buddhists' opponents in India. To produce the initial draft translation, Ham concentrated on the non-Buddhist chapters and Lopez on the Buddhist chapters. We then both went through the entire text together, with much time devoted to the consistent translation of technical terms. When the Sanskrit for a specific quotation was available, we tended to translate from the Sanskrit, sometimes making modifications to also reflect the Tibetan. Sanskrit texts that were consulted are listed in the bibliography in the final section, after the lists of Tibetan translations in the Kangyur and Tengyur.

The schools of classical Indian philosophy, both Buddhist and non-Buddhist, share much of the same vocabulary. In some cases, however, they give very different meanings to those terms. We have noted those differences in the glossary.

The translators would first like to express their sincere thanks to His Holiness the Dalai Lama for conceiving and planning this important series. We are honored to make this small contribution to its success. Second, we would like to thank Thupten Jinpa for his own role in bringing the series to fruition and for his support and advice throughout the translation process. Third, we would like to thank the members of the Compendium Compilation Committee for their prodigious efforts in compiling the present volume, one that honors the Tibetan tenets genre while contributing to it in new and important ways. Fourth, we would like to thank Geshe Yeshi Lhundup of Loseling Monastic College for offering many helpful suggestions during the translation process. Finally, we would like to thank David Kittelstrom and Brianna Quick of Wisdom Publications for their meticulous editing of the volume, which added greatly to its clarity.

Donald S. Lopez Jr. and Hyoung Seok Ham

Introduction

The Dalai Lama

Nearly a decade ago, I suggested to a group of monastic scholars that it would be wonderful if a presentation could be developed in which the subject matter of the entire Tibetan canon, the Kangyur and Tengyur—the teachings attributed to Buddha Śākyamuni and the commentarial treatises—were differentiated in terms of three broad categories. If such a presentation could be developed, it would facilitate a comprehensive presentation of the essence of the entire collection of key Buddhist treatises. More importantly, this could help bring about a new educational resource for our human family of over seven billion, regardless of their religious beliefs or lack thereof. The three categories I proposed were: (1) the nature of reality—the parallel of science in the classical Buddhist texts, (2) the philosophical views developed in Buddhist sources, and (3) based on these two, Buddhist spiritual or religious practice. My introduction to volume 1 of this series, *Science and Philosophy in the Indian Buddhist Texts: The Physical World*, explained the nature of each of these three categories and indicated their unique features. As volumes 3 and 4 on philosophy in the classical Indian sources are nearing publication, I offer this essay in the form of an introduction.

The Difference between Science and Philosophy

There is a range of opinion on what exactly the term *science* means. I understand it to be a system of investigation with unique methods of inquiry and the body of knowledge derived from such investigation. When science explores a question, it does so with a hypothesis based on observations, experiments to test whether the hypothesis holds true, and verification of those results through replication. When results are replicated by other researchers, such findings are incorporated into the body of scientific knowledge, and they become part of what subsequent researchers must engage with in their own research. It is this system—a method of inquiry, a body of findings, and associated theories and explanatory principles—that is called *science*. Defined in this way, a scientist may hold a specific philosophical view, but this does not mean that that view has been proven scientifically.

Philosophy, on the other hand, is a system of views about the deeper or ultimate nature of reality developed by thinkers on the basis of rigorous observation, rational inquiry (often in the form of argument), and the authority of past thinkers. Thus philosophers are those whose minds, not content with immediate sensory data, probe deeper by asking the question "What hidden reality underlies the diverse everyday world we experience?" Thus we could say that it is philosophers who seek to open doors to the understanding of the world's more hidden dimensions. Historically, a great diversity of philosophical views has appeared, employing diverse methods of critical inquiry. These philosophical views continue to the present day, serving as resources to help human thinking evolve.

The Development of Philosophy in India

Tibetan treatises on philosophical traditions as well as contemporary historians of Indian philosophy agree that the Sāṅkhya school is among the earliest philosophical schools in India. Modern scholars date the origins of Sāṅkhya to around the eighth century BCE. Sāṅkhya developed a profound and comprehensive philosophy, with all three elements of a system of thought: a *view* of the nature of reality; a *path* consisting of psycho-spiritual practices; and a *result*, a salvific state that such a path leads to. Sāṅkhya presents the nature of reality in terms of twenty-five categories and, more specifically, describes all effects as manifestations of an underlying principle called *prakṛti* (primal substance, primary nature). The person or self, called *puruṣa*, is an experiencer but not the agent of actions. Proponents of Sāṅkhya philosophy assert that one attains salvific freedom when, through meditative concentration, one sees the nature of the true self. Within Sāṅkhya, one branch asserts Īśvara (God) as the creator, saying that since primary nature itself is a fixed potency and devoid of intent, it alone cannot be the creator of the world. It maintains that it is a combination of God's intent and primary nature, the grand universal from which all manifestations appear, that creates everything in the world—the cosmos and the natural environment and all the beings therein.

Regarding the self (*ātman*), although ancient Indian non-Buddhist schools by and large share with Sāṅkhya the basic standpoint that the self is the *experiencer* and is eternal, they diverge on its specific attributes. In fact, the various Indian philosophical schools engaged in extensive debate over their views on the self and on the nature of the world. For example, chapter 4 of the *Brahmasūtra*, an authoritative work for the Vedānta school, explicitly states that all views of the self apart from the view of self as *brahman* are untenable. Chapter 2 of this same text extensively refutes the Sāṅkhya view of ultimate truth as well as the views of the Buddhist Cittamātra and Madhyamaka schools. Similarly, chapter 3 refutes Sāṅkhya's denial of a self that is independent from matter.

Like this, both Buddhist and non-Buddhist classical sources engaged in extensive debate over their philosophical positions, and these debates helped advance the views of these schools of thought. The most consequential non-Buddhist Indian philosophical schools are those of Sāṅkhya, Vaiśeṣika, Nyāya, Vedānta, Mīmāṃsā, and Jaina, and their views are set forth extensively in Buddhist texts such as Bhāviveka's *Blaze of Reasoning* and Śāntarakṣita's *Compendium of Principles*. They present other schools as well, but fearing length, I have touched on only the most important ones. The Buddhist systems of thought are among the newer philosophical schools in India, but they evolved side by side with non-Buddhist schools for well over a millennium. Despite important differences, it is undeniable that Buddhist thought shares many ideas and concepts with the non-Buddhist schools that were part of the cultural sphere of ancient India, including the concepts of karma and rebirth, types of rituals, and the approach to ethics.

Buddhist Philosophy

Buddhist philosophy evolved from the teachings of Buddha Śākyamuni. Unlike other Indian traditions of his time, the Buddha taught the concept of no-self (*anātman*), which became the hallmark of Buddhist thought. The Buddha first taught his philosophy of no-self in a cultural milieu where belief in self was so widespread as to be almost universal. He therefore knew that he would face substantial challenges. In fact, the Buddha was compelled to declare:

> Profound, tranquil, free of elaboration, luminous, and
> unconditioned—
> such an ambrosia-like truth I have found.
> Were I to reveal it, none would comprehend,
> so in a grove in the forest I will silently remain.[1]

I speak often about the philosophy of no-self, so there is no need for an extensive explanation here. But in brief, when we speak of the philosophical view of no-self, we are not speaking of total nonexistence; we are identifying an important disparity between our perception and reality—the reality that things do not exist the way they appear to. If things existed as they appear, then by following an appearance, we would reach reality. There would be no instances of delusion, where what we perceive is not real. Furthermore, afflictions like attachment and aversion arise based on the appearances that we superimpose onto actual reality. That reality is that things are devoid of self-existence; they exist only through mere dependence. When this truth is seen, attachment, aversion, and all the other delusions find no place to reside and thereby cease. *No-self* refers to this absence of independent intrinsic existence. This view of no-self, which means that things are dependently originated, is the heart of Buddhist philosophy. Without a clear understanding of this truth, there simply is no definitive understanding of Buddhist philosophy. Nāgārjuna's student Āryadeva said that the best way to generate conviction in the Buddha is to cultivate an understanding of the meaning of emptiness.

The criterion for a system of thought to be Buddhist is acceptance of four axioms that were declared by the Buddha himself:

> All conditioned things are impermanent.
> All contaminated things are of the nature of suffering.
> All phenomena are empty, devoid of self.
> Nirvāṇa is true peace.

Based on differences in how they interpreted these four axioms, especially the third one on no-self, four distinct schools of Buddhist philosophy emerged. Since those philosophical schools and their unique views evolved over time, I do not think that they were present during the Buddha's own time.

More specifically, since one finds in Nāgārjuna's *Root Verses on the Middle Way* explicit refutations of many views of the Vaibhāṣika school, there is no question that Vaibhāṣika was established before the composition of the *Root Verses*, which most likely appeared in the second century CE. If, as is often argued, Sautrāntika emerged from one of the eighteen śrāvaka schools, this school must also have been quite early. Some of the tantras mention the four Buddhist schools explicitly. Among the classical treatises, one of the earliest to refer explicitly to the four Buddhist philosophical schools is Āryadeva's *Compendium on the Essence of Wisdom*. Formal differentiation of Madhyamaka and Cittamātra as philosophical schools could not have occurred prior to their respective founders, Nāgārjuna and Asaṅga. As some contemporary scholars have observed, the earliest systematic and detailed presentation of the four Buddhist schools with their distinctive views is in Bhāviveka's (ca. sixth century) *Essence of the Middle Way* and its autocommentary (*Blaze of Reasoning*), which contain, in addition to the views of the Buddhist schools, clear presentations of non-Buddhist Indian schools. We can therefore surmise that the tradition of the "four Buddhist philosophical schools" was established by the sixth century. The master Vasumitra states that "the schools emerged just as diverse opinions emerge among people," and so, since different schools of thought emerge owing to the diversity that exists among people's mentalities, who could prevent their appearance?

In Bhāviveka's *Essence of the Middle Way* and its autocommentary, in Nāgārjuna's analytical treatises, and later, in Śāntarakṣita's *Compendium of Principles*, one finds debates with extensive refutations even among Buddhist philosophers on such topics as real entities, reflexive awareness, intrinsic arising and cessation, and, in particular, epistemology. These debates helped to foster the refinement and advancement of Buddhist philosophy.

Treatises on the Philosophical Schools

Judging from extant literary evidence, Bhāviveka's *Essence of the Middle Way* and its autocommentary are the earliest works presenting the various schools of Indian philosophy in the form of a compendium. Śāntarakṣita's eighth-century *Compendium of Principles* and its commentary [by his student Kamalaśīla] are the most extensive Indian presentations of the various schools of Indian philosophy, with systematic refutations and arguments, and they also supply the philosophical views that emerged after Bhāviveka. Many Buddhist texts, especially in Nāgārjuna's analytical corpus, refute specific philosophical views of both Buddhist and non-Buddhist schools without surveying the views of those other schools in a compendium. Finally, I find Jetāri's *Distinguishing the Sugata's Texts* to be an important doxographical work, with its explicit refutations of non-Buddhist views and clear differentiation among the views of the four Buddhist schools.

Treatises presenting systems of Indian philosophy became popular and abundant in Tibet. Among the earliest of these are those by Rongzom Paṇḍita (eleventh century), Chapa Chökyi Sengé (twelfth century), and Üpa Losal (thirteenth century). The fourteenth century brought Sakya Paṇḍita's *Excellent Discourse on the Systems*, which should be recognized as a work on philosophical schools, and the omniscient Longchenpa's *Treasury of Tenets*. Among texts that appeared in the seventeenth century and later, the most extensive are Jamyang Shepa's *Great Exposition of Tenets*, Changkya's *Beautiful Adornment of Mount Meru*, and Thuken's *Crystal Mirror of Philosophical Systems*. These three are the works on tenets I am most familiar with. Interestingly, Jamyang Shepa's work shares important similarities with Taktsang Lotsāwa's fifteenth-century *Complete Knowledge of Tenets*, including the overall framework for presenting the various schools and key distinctions between Buddhist and non-Buddhist schools. Taktsang's text also contains his critiques of Jé Tsongkhapa's views, what Taktsang calls "eighteen heavy burdens of contradiction."

Jamyang Shepa's *Great Exposition of Tenets* seems to be the most extensive Tibetan text on philosophical schools. This work grounds the presentations of the views of the individual schools in citations from the works of the schools themselves and from other important classical Indian texts. Furthermore, Jamyang Shepa offers new explanations of aspects of the views of non-Buddhist Indian schools that were not previously accessible to the Tibetan reader. Thus this work is of great benefit to those with an interest in understanding Indian philosophical systems. Furthermore, Jamyang Shepa presents an extensive rebuttal of Taktsang Lotsāwa's eighteen heavy burdens of contradiction, building on the earlier rebuttal by Jamyang Gawai Lodrö (1429–1503). Generally speaking, because the eighteen heavy burdens of contradiction leveled by Taktsang were based on critical inquiry by a learned intellect, becoming familiar with them offers an opportunity for followers of Tsongkhapa to deepen their understanding of the latter's treatises. Also, judging from a statement Taktsang makes toward the end of his text to explain his reason for enumerating the eighteen heavy burdens of contradiction, it is clear that his argument was not motivated by attachment or aversion.

Changkya's *Beautiful Adornment of Mount Meru* contains a more manageable number of classical text citations [than Jamyang Shepa's text]. Changkya offers original insights in his treatment of the Cittamātra view, showing how one gains insight into the truth of consciousness only. And, in the concluding section, he gives a detailed list of all the texts available in Tibetan that he used as his sources. This work by Changkya is a key treatise of the tenets genre, offering an easy way to engage with the subject while being quite comprehensive in its scope.

Thuken's *Crystal Mirror of Philosophical Systems* goes into detail on the views of the Tibetan schools, especially the four main traditions of Sakya, Geluk, Kagyü, and Nyingma, including the tenets of subschools when those exist. The work also presents Bön and Chinese systems of thought. Given these, the text is unique among the tenets genre.

Concluding Points

Scholars compare the four Buddhist philosophical schools to steps on a staircase, understanding the views of the lower schools as steps leading to the views of the higher schools. The Vaibhāṣika rejection, for example, of an eternal universal, an eternal creator, and so on paves the way for accepting the Sautrāntika rejection of unique particulars as the referents of words, its denial of substantial existence of permanent entities, and its positing of general characteristics as mental constructs. Similarly, the Sautrāntika assertion that cognitions of perceived objects are generalized mental constructs whose instantiation may include unique particulars, and their rejection of a self of persons, pave the way to accepting the Cittamātra view of the selflessness of phenomena. Finally, the Cittamātra rejection of true existence for external objects could pave the way to accepting the

Madhyamaka rejection of true existence for even subjective awareness. Understood like this, the views of the preceding school can become steps leading to the views of the subsequent school.

In any case, knowing the numerous philosophical views that exist in the world, especially the essential points of the four Buddhist philosophical schools, can open our intellect and enrich our resources for critical reflection in other domains. In particular, the study of the profound philosophical topics presented in the Buddhist sources—such as the Cittamātra argument for constant dual cognition and its theory of emptiness, and the Madhyamaka understanding of emptiness in terms of dependent origination—can benefit us now in this life, regardless of whether we believe in future lives. It can broaden our perspective, dismantling the mental afflictions that blind us from seeing things in a comprehensive way, that keep us narrowly fixated; it can stop us from planting the seeds of unhappiness for ourselves and others. These are benefits I can attest to from personal experience.

In light of these points, I am happy that today, just as I had expressly wished, the two volumes on philosophy compiled from Indian Buddhist sources are now complete. Of these two philosophy volumes in the *Science and Philosophy in Indian Buddhist Classics* series, this one, the first, introduces the views of the main Indian philosophical schools. To that end, it presents their views on the nature of reality, including their logical arguments, using sources that the schools themselves consider authoritative.

One important difference compared to the traditional Tibetan tenets genre is that this volume only presents views about the nature of reality; it does not include the schools' presentation of their path and results. The reason is that the purpose here is to help open the intellect of contemporary readers, especially their critical faculties; it is not to benefit exclusively the adherents of these Buddhist and non-Buddhist schools.

Volume 4, the second volume on philosophy, selects some major topics that have been the object of critical inquiry since ancient times, such as the two truths, the nature of self, logic and epistemology, and the relation between words and meaning. My objective and my hope for these two volumes on philosophy is that many discerning minds of our time will be able to gain an understanding of the deep philosophical insights of ancient India.

In conclusion, I pray that these two volumes on Indian philosophy, volumes 3 and 4 of the series, will benefit many interested readers.

The Buddhist monk Tenzin Gyatso, The Dalai Lama
Introduction translated into English by Thupten Jinpa

Introductory Essay

Donald S. Lopez Jr.

This is the third volume in His Holiness the Dalai Lama's *Science and Philosophy in the Indian Buddhist Classics* series, the first to be devoted exclusively to philosophy. Before turning to the Indian philosophical tradition, we might quickly dispense with a question frequently posed: "Is Buddhism a philosophy, a religion, or a way of life?" The answer obviously depends on how one defines *philosophy* and *religion*. In the West, the first is easier to define, or at least describe, generally assumed to mean a tradition of discourse that began in ancient Greece and that continues to the present day, addressing questions of ontology, epistemology, logic, and ethics. The term *religion* is far more elusive, with much discourse on how it might best be defined. It is the case, however, that the various traditions counted as religions have much to say about the creation of the world and its inhabitants and about what happens to those inhabitants when they die. From that perspective, it might be most accurate to say that Buddhism is a religion that encompasses philosophy—indeed, a long and rich tradition of philosophy, a tradition that this volume embodies.

The Tibetan title of this book is *Compendium of Philosophy* (*Lta grub kun btus*). Here, "philosophy" is the translation of *lta grub*, literally "established view" or "proven view." It is a hybrid of two traditional terms, both Tibetan translations from the original Sanskrit: *lta ba* ("view") and *grub mtha'* ("tenets"). The term translated as "view" is *darśana* in Sanskrit and is the term traditionally used for the six schools of classical Hindu philosophy—Sāṅkhya, Yoga, Nyāya, Vaiśeṣika, Mīmāṃsā, Vedānta—five of which receive a full chapter in this volume. Hindu expositions of philosophy also discuss non-Hindu schools, which because they deny the authority of the Vedas are called *nāstika* (those who say, "it is not"). These typically include Buddhism, Jainism, and the materialist Lokāyata school. The term *darśana* thus clearly has the sense of a philosophical view or a worldview.

However, it also has a somewhat more mystical sense of a vision, often used to describe the experience of seeing a sacred image or a saintly teacher, whereby in modern parlance one is said to "receive *darshan*." Thus the term *darśana* may encompass what is meant by "philosophy" in English but with the implication that such philosophy leads to a higher state and, as we will see, to knowledge that transcends discursive thought.

The other element of the Tibetan term *lta grub* is *grub mtha'*, the translation of the Sanskrit *siddhānta*, literally "established end," in the sense of a proven conclusion or philosophical position; it might be translated as "doctrine," "dogma," or "tenet." In ancient India, texts on a range of topics carried the word *siddhānta* in their titles; one thinks immediately of works on astronomy, such as the *Sūryasiddhānta* (literally "tenets about the sun"), or schools of theology, such as the *Śaivasiddhānta* ("tenets about Śiva"). More often, however, *siddhānta* refers to what might be called technical philosophy, with much attention paid to ontology, logic, and epistemology.

Modern translators have sometimes translated *siddhānta* as "doxography," a term coined by the German classicist Hermann Alexander Diels (1848–1922) literally meaning "the description of an opinion," to describe Greek works, including those by Plato and Aristotle, that describe the positions of earlier philosophers, especially philosophers whose works are no longer extant. In this sense, "doxography" is an appropriate translation of *siddhānta*, a genre where we find the positions of schools that have not survived to the modern period. The term used to translate *siddhānta* and its Tibetan rendering *grub mtha'* in this volume will be "tenets."

The term is used in Tibetan Buddhism to refer to the four major schools of Indian Buddhist thought—Vaibhāṣika, Sautrāntika, Cittamātra (or Yogācāra), and Madhyamaka—sometimes (as in this volume) adding chapters on various non-Buddhist schools. As will be discussed below, the tradition of collecting the tenets of various schools of Indian philosophy into a single volume has a history of over fifteen hundred years in India, represented in works of well-known authors, both Hindu and Buddhist. That the positions and arguments of these schools remain important to the present is evidenced by the volumes in the *Science and Philosophy in the Indian Buddhist Classics* series as well as by the substantial body of scholarship about each of the Hindu and Buddhist schools. Among the many English-language works that might be cited as examples, we find Surendranath Dasgupta's *History of Indian Philosophy*, published in five volumes between 1922 and 1925, and Karl Potter's *Encyclopedia of Indian Philosophies*, published in twenty-five volumes.

As we will see, works in the tenets genre are not mere descriptions of the various schools' doctrines. They are often also polemical, with the author, typically an adherent of one of the schools, first presenting the positions of each school and then critiquing those positions from the perspective of his own. In this case, the opponent is not there to defend himself. However, as is so often the case with Indian texts, what is written likely derived from something oral. There are famous accounts of public debates, sometimes rather fabulous in nature, to be found in both Hindu and Buddhist sources. In the Hindu sources the Hindus tend to win, and in the Buddhist sources the Buddhists tend to win. The stakes were said to be high. Often, a condition of the debate was that the loser as well as all his disciples had to convert to the winner's religion. Thus, in Tibetan paintings of the great Buddhist logicians, one sees in the background Hindu yogins weeping as they cut off their dreadlocks to become shaven-headed Buddhist monks. According to the accounts of the famous Chinese pilgrims to India, many of those debates took place at Nālandā Monastery.

THE NĀLANDĀ TRADITION

His Holiness the Dalai Lama often refers to Tibetan Buddhism as the Nālandā tradition. Why does he do so? Nālandā is located in what is today the northeastern Indian state of Bihar, so named because it was once the home of so many Buddhist monasteries (*vihāra*). The largest and most important of these was Nālandā. According to the well-known Chinese pilgrim Xuanzang (602–64), it was founded by King Śakrāditya, sometimes identified as Kumāragupta I (r. 415–55). The fifth-century date is confirmed by archaeological evidence. This was almost a millennium after the passing of the Buddha. However, the Buddha spent much time in the vicinity, with the village of Nālandā mentioned in many stories of the Buddha and his immediate disciples. Close by was the city of Rājagṛha, capital of King Bimbisāra, who is said to have first met the Buddha shortly after he, still Prince Siddhārtha, had left the palace in search of enlightenment. Bimbisāra and, later, his son Ajātaśatru would become two of the Buddha's most loyal patrons. Outside the city and not far from Nālandā is Vulture Peak, where the Buddha delivered so many famous sūtras, including the

Lotus Sūtra, the *Heart Sūtra*, the *Tathāgatagarbha Sūtra*, and the *Sukhāvatīvyūha Sūtra*. It was in the shadow of Vulture Peak that the Buddha would take his afternoon stroll. It was in a cave near Vulture Peak that the First Council took place, when the teachings of the Buddha were collected and recited after he had passed into nirvāṇa. On the grounds of Nālandā is the stūpa of the Buddha's wisest disciple, Śāriputra, his interlocutor in many sūtras. Thus, long before the founding of Nālandā Monastery, its region was a rich site of Buddhist teaching and practice.

The most detailed accounts of the monastery come from the descriptions of Chinese monks who studied there, especially Xuanzang, who spent almost five years studying there, and Yijing (635–713), who spent ten years there. Xuanzang describes a campus of eight monastic complexes, each with as many as three hundred cells; Yijing reports that there were three thousand monks. Both praise the high level of learning and the strict adherence to the monastic code; Xuanzang says that no monk had been expelled for misconduct for seven hundred years. Other sources report that there were ten thousand students and fifteen hundred teachers. Monks came from as far away as China, Korea, Tibet, Central Asia, and Indonesia to study there. Its famous nine-story library is said to have held hundreds of thousands of texts.

Xuanzang's travel journal and his biography (composed by one of his disciples) describe the curriculum at Nālandā, where the tenets of the eighteen schools of Buddhism (described in chapter 10) were set forth, along with the Mahāyāna schools of Yogācāra and Madhyamaka. In addition, there was instruction in the four Vedas (which would have been well known by the many Buddhist monks who came from the brahmin caste). In addition to Hindu and Buddhist philosophy, Xuanzang himself is said to have studied astronomy, geography, medicine, and divination. Among the Hindu schools, he seems to have focused especially on Sāṅkhya and Vaiśeṣika, gaining sufficient mastery to defeat their proponents in debate. His chief teacher was Śīlabhadra, whom he describes as the most learned monk at Nālandā. Śīlabhadra was the disciple of the well-known Yogācāra scholar Dharmapāla, who was himself a student of Dignāga, considered the father of Buddhist logic; he is cited often in the pages that follow.

Thus Nālandā was a major center for the study of Indian philosophy and science, making it a fitting inspiration for His Holiness the Dalai Lama's series *Science and Philosophy in the Indian Buddhist Classics*. He has compiled a list of seventeen Buddhist masters (literally, the *paṇḍitas*, or "scholars," and *siddhas*, or "adepts") of Nālandā and composed a poem extolling them. Because all but one of the seventeen appear in the pages that follow, we provide a short sketch of each.

The first is Nāgārjuna, the most famous of all Buddhist philosophers. He is considered the founder of the Madhyamaka school and the eloquent proponent of the doctrine of emptiness (*śūnyatā*), derived primarily from the Perfection of Wisdom (*prajñāpāramitā*) sūtras. He is known for his Six Collections of Reasoning, the most famous of which is his *Root Verses on the Middle Way*, a work that was widely commented upon in India, China, and Tibet and that continues to be translated and retranslated into many languages. He was also the author of several influential hymns of praise to the Buddha, each with important philosophical themes. He is regarded as the first major proponent of the Mahāyāna; according to legend he retrieved the Perfection of Wisdom sūtras from the bottom of the sea. Scholars tentatively place Nāgārjuna in the second century of the Common Era and in South India, thus some centuries before and many miles away from Nālandā Monastery. However, according to Tibetan hagiographies, he lived for six hundred years, providing him many years to travel the many miles to Nālandā. Regardless of whether he actually visited the site of the monastery, his works were a major presence there.

Nāgārjuna's most famous disciple was Āryadeva, the author of the well-known *Four Hundred Verses* as well as the *Hundred Treatise* (*Śatakaśāstra*), preserved in Chinese as one of the three treatises of the Sanlun, or Three Treatise, school, the most influential Madhyamaka school in China, Korea, and Japan. Tibetan hagiographies also place him at Nālandā despite his early date. The works of Nāgārjuna and Āryadeva would provide the textual foundation for the subsequent schools and subschools of Madhyamaka and were considered authoritative by them all.

Five of the principal figures in those schools and subschools are counted among the seventeen masters of Nālandā. Three of these are linked by a controversy over how to present and defend the Madhyamaka position in debate, and the philosophical implications of the chosen form of argumentation, a controversy discussed in chapter 14. Proceeding chronologically, the first is the early fifth-century scholar Buddhapālita, who, in his commentary on Nāgārjuna's *Root Verses on the Middle Way*, used a logical form called the *consequence* (*prasaṅga*). In the sixth century, Bhāviveka, in his own commentary on Nāgārjuna's text, criticized Buddhapālita, arguing that the Mādhyamika should instead use the syllogism (*prayoga*). Then, in the seventh century, again in a commentary on the first chapter of Nāgārjuna's *Verses*, Candrakīrti came to the defense of Buddhapālita and attacked Bhāviveka, arguing that the consequence was the proper medium for proving emptiness and that there were philosophical problems in the use of the syllogism. Based on these opposing views, Tibetan authors would call the school of Buddhapālita and Candrakīrti the Prāsaṅgika or "Consequence" school and the school of Bhāviveka the Svātantrika or "Autonomous [Syllogism]" school. These were not, however, the only contributions of these masters, with Bhāviveka composing one of the two most important Buddhist compendia of Indian philosophy, entitled the *Blaze of Reasoning*, and Candrakīrti composing a foundational text for Mahāyāna thought and practice, *Entering the Middle Way*.

The other two principal expositors of the Madhyamaka subschools both lived in the late eighth century, Śāntarakṣita and his student Kamalaśīla. They were major figures in what is called the Yogācāra-Madhyamaka synthesis, in which doctrines of the two major Mahāyāna philosophical schools, whose founding figures had critiqued each other, were combined in interesting ways. Śāntarakṣita (725–88) was ordained at Nālandā and taught there. He is the author of two works that are crucial to this volume. The first is his *Ornament of the Middle Way*, where he delineates a progression through the various meanings of no-self, including the Mainstream (that is, non-Mahāyāna), Yogācāra, and Madhyamaka positions. In the realm of Buddhist logic, he presents one of the most well known and commented upon of the several proofs of emptiness, called "the lack of being one or many." Śāntarakṣita is more famous in the domain of Indian philosophy for his massive survey and critique of the philosophical schools of the day, both Hindu and Buddhist, called the *Compendium of Principles*, which remains a major source for the understanding of Indian philosophy of the medieval period. Here, in 3,646 verses in twenty-six chapters, he considers a wide range of Buddhist and non-Buddhist schools.

His disciple Kamalaśīla (ca. 740–95) wrote commentaries on his teacher's works and composed his own exposition of Madhyamaka thought called *Illumination of the Middle Way*. Both Śāntarakṣita and Kamalaśīla would eventually travel to Tibet, living there until their deaths. Kamalaśīla took part in the famous Samyé Debate against a Chan monk, Heshang

Moheyan, on the question of sudden versus gradual enlightenment, holding and, according to Tibetan sources, successfully defending the gradual position. While in Tibet he composed at least one, and perhaps all three, of his works called *Stages of Meditation*, which set forth meditative practices from the development of the aspiration to buddhahood up to its achievement. These texts were precursors to the well-known Tibetan *bstan rim* ("stages of the teaching") and *lam rim* ("stages of the path") genres.

The next two masters of Nālandā are the only brothers (or half-brothers) in the group: Asaṅga and Vasubandhu, whom scholars place in the fourth century (before the monastery's founding), both hailing from what is today the city of Peshawar in Pakistan, quite far from the monastery's eastern Indian locale. Regardless, their philosophical works were among the most influential in the history of Buddhism. Asaṅga is regarded as the founder of the Yogācāra school, its extreme subjectivist position leading it to also be called Cittamātra ("mind only") and Vijñaptimātra ("cognition only"). He was the prolific author of a wide range of works on Buddhist thought and practice, forming the foundation for the Mahāyāna in India, East Asia, and Tibet.

His brother Vasubandhu began as a monk of a Mainstream school, composing the most influential work on Abhidharma in the history of Buddhism, the *Treasury of Abhidharma*, which both critiqued the Vaibhāṣika school and set forth the position of the Sautrāntika school. This text would become the foundational work for Abhidharma studies in China, Tibet, and Japan (where it had its own school named after it, the Kusha school). Vasubandhu would later be converted by his brother to the Mahāyāna, of which he became an eloquent proponent, setting forth the Yogācāra position in both verse and prose in a series of important works.

The next two masters are the foundational figures in the field of Buddhist logic: Dignāga (sixth century) and Dharmakīrti (seventh century), both of whom made major contributions to one of the central debates in Indian philosophy, the nature of valid knowledge (*pramāṇa*). As will be seen in the pages that follow, non-Buddhist schools listed as few as one and as many as six sources of valid knowledge, the latter list including "speech," which includes the Vedas, regarded by its adherents as an eternal source of truth. Dignāga, both building upon and critiquing the Hindu schools, especially Nyāya, limited the valid means of knowledge to two: direct perception and inference. His most famous work is entitled

Compendium of Valid Knowledge. He also made significant contributions to philosophy of language with the concept of *exclusion* (*apoha*). Dharmakīrti both expanded and deepened the work begun by Dignāga, rather modestly entitling his major work *Commentary on [the Compendium of] Valid Knowledge* (referred to in the pages that follow as the *Exposition of Valid Knowledge*), the best known of his Seven Works on Valid Knowledge.

Among the seventeen masters of Nālandā, these eleven made the most important contributions to Indian philosophy in the strict sense of that term. The remaining six made signal contributions to related domains of Buddhist thought. The "three trainings" of Buddhism are ethics, meditation, and wisdom. With an elaborate code of conduct for monks and nuns, there are extensive discussions of what constitutes an ethical life, what does and does not constitute a transgression, and what penalties should be imposed upon those who transgress. The monastic code of the school followed in Tibet, the Mūlasarvāstivāda, evolved into a huge and unwieldly work, far more than a single monk could memorize. Guṇaprabha (ca. seventh century) and Śākyaprabha (ca. eighth century and said to be a disciple of Śāntarakṣita) wrote more manageable works, eliminating many of the stories that illustrated various transgressions. In the monasteries of Tibet, Guṇaprabha's *Vinaya Sūtra*, or *Discourse on Discipline*, became the major text on monastic discipline in their curriculum.

Of particular interest to Buddhist thinkers is the structure of the Buddhist path. For the Mahāyāna tradition of India, a central text in this regard is the *Ornament of Realizations*, attributed to the future Buddha, Maitreya, and one of the most commented upon of the Indian Buddhist treatises, its commentaries devoted to unpacking its tersely cryptic verses. Among these commentaries are those of Vimuktisena (ca. sixth century) and Haribhadra (ca. eighth century), the latter said to have been a disciple of Śāntarakṣita.

The next two masters are particularly beloved in Tibet, not so much for their philosophy, although both were formidable philosophers of the Madhyamaka school. The first is the eighth-century Nālandā monk Śāntideva, author of one of the most celebrated of all Mahāyāna works, *Entering the Bodhisattva Way*, a work that many Tibetan monks have memorized over the centuries. Renowned for its inspiring poetry, its ninth and penultimate chapter is devoted to the perfection of wisdom. Here Śāntideva presents dense argumentation (in verse) for a variety of Madhyamaka positions and critiques of a range of opponents, both Buddhist (including Yogācāra) and Hindu (including Sāṅkhya). He is counted as a Prāsaṅgika. His other well-known work, the *Compendium of Training* (*Śikṣāsamuccaya*), is an anthology of passages from various sūtras organized thematically to set forth the practices of the bodhisattva.

The final, and chronologically the last, of the seventeen masters of Nālandā is the Bengali scholar Atiśa Dīpaṃkara Śrījñāna (980–1054). After repeated invitations, he finally agreed to leave India (he was living at the monastery of Vikramaśīla at the time) to travel to Tibet, arriving in 1042 and living there until his death. He is a major figure in the revival of Buddhism in Tibet in the eleventh century, composing his famous *Lamp for the Path to Enlightenment* there. He was also a renowned proponent of Madhyamaka, writing works on the topic and overseeing the translation of important Madhyamaka works from Sanskrit into Tibetan.

From this brief survey, it is easy to see why the Dalai Lama refers to Tibetan Buddhism as the Nālandā tradition. Three of the seventeen masters traveled to Tibet and played key roles in its history, with Śāntarakṣita founding Samyé, the first monastery in Tibet, and serving as the first abbot. After his death, Kamalaśīla traveled to Samyé to debate Heshang Moheyan. After the fall of the Tibetan empire and the "period of fragmentation," Atiśa came to Tibet and played a leading role in the restoration and the revitalization of Buddhist thought and practice.

The works of the seventeen masters are also centerpieces of the monastic curricula. In the Dalai Lama's Geluk school, for example, the "four topics" of the *geshé* curriculum—Madhyamaka, Pramāṇa, Vinaya, and Abhidharma—are based on the works of Candrakīrti, Dignāga, Dharmakīrti, Asaṅga, Vasubandhu, and Guṇaprabha. Four of its well-known "five books" are by Candrakīrti, Dharmakīrti, Vasubandhu, and Guṇaprabha, with the works of Nāgārjuna, Haribhadra, Vimuktisena, and Śākyaprabha extensively studied. The curriculum at Nyingma monasteries such as Dzogchen and Shechen is based on thirteen books, eight of which were by one of the seventeen Nālandā masters.

And many more than seventeen Nālandā monks are key figures in the history of Tibetan Buddhism. Among the most famous of these were Nāropa and Virūpa, whose tantric teachings were especially important to the Kagyü and Sakya sects. The works of the Yogācāra scholar Sthiramati are widely studied. In 1204, in the wake of Muslim raids on Nālandā and other monasteries in the region, Nālandā's former abbot Śākyaśrībhadra traveled to Tibet with a group of nine other Indian and Nepalese monks, giving extensive teachings on a variety of philosophical topics. Among his disciples, Sakya Paṇḍita (1182–1251), whom he ordained, would go on to become one of the most influential figures in the history of Tibetan Buddhism. He composed a work on Buddhist logic, the *Treasury of Valid Knowledge and Reasoning*, renowned as the only Tibetan work to be translated into Sanskrit. According to a well-known story, it caused sufficient stir in India that six Hindu scholars made the long trek to Tibet to debate with its author, only to be defeated and forced to become Buddhist monks. Despite these famous visitors from India, it is important to note that the traffic between Nālandā and Tibet was not one way, with many Tibetans making the arduous journey to India to study at the famed monastery, so many that a dormitory for Tibetans was eventually established.

There is ample evidence that the doctrines of all of the philosophical schools discussed in this volume, both Buddhist and non-Buddhist, were studied at Nālandā. Why was this the case at a Buddhist monastery? There was likely a conviction that all of the philosophies and sciences of the day should be represented there. But there were also more quotidian reasons. Despite its international fame today, throughout its long history in India, Buddhism was a minority religion, constantly fighting for (and eventually losing) patronage and thus needing to defend itself against the Hindu schools.

The Buddhist monastic community began as an itinerant group, only later developing permanent dwelling places. As these institutions became larger, it was impossible for the entire community to be fed by monks begging from door to door each day, as had been the previous practice. Royal patronage was required, with kings often donating villages and their lands to monasteries to provide for their sustenance. As the largest monastery in India, Nālandā required substantial support; Yijing reports that it was supported by two hundred villages. However, royal patronage waxes and wanes. Some Indian monarchs were ecumenical in their support of all the religions of their realm, others were devoutly Buddhist, others were devoutly Hindu. Among the latter, some were inimical to Buddhism, going so far as to chop down the Bodhi Tree, where the Buddha had achieved enlightenment centuries before.

One of the ways that philosophical schools competed for patronage was through debate. It was therefore important that Buddhist monks know the texts and the tenets of their Hindu opponents. Nālandā Monastery is said to have established gatekeepers at the several entrances of the monastery whose responsibility was not to decide who could and could not enter but to debate with the Hindu philosophers who arrived to challenge the Buddhists. Thus only the best scholars were appointed gatekeepers. According to his biographer, one of the signs of the expertise and eminence that Xuanzang achieved during his time at Nālandā is that he, a Chinese monk, was called upon to debate with a Sāṅkhya philosopher, whom he of course is said to have defeated.

THE STUDY OF INDIAN PHILOSOPHY IN INDIA

As discussed above, the doxography or tenets (*siddhānta*) genre originated in India, where we find both Hindu and Buddhist exemplars. Among Hindu texts, the most well-known are the *Collection of All Views and Tenets* (*Sarvadarśanasiddhāntasaṅgraha*), falsely attributed to the Vedānta master Śaṅkara (ca. 700–50), and the *Compendium of All Views* (*Sarvadarśanasaṅgraha*) by the Vedānta master Vidyāraṇya (1296–1391). The former consists of twelve chapters, beginning with three non-Vedic schools—the materialist Cārvāka (a.k.a. Lokāyata) followed by Jainism and Buddhism (with Buddhism divided into Vaibhāṣika, Sautrāntika, Yogācāra, and Madhyamaka)—followed by six Hindu schools, culminating in his own Vedānta. The latter work considers sixteen schools presented in ascending order, beginning with the three non-Vedic schools—the materialist Cārvāka, followed by Buddhism and Jainism—and then thirteen Hindu schools, again culminating in the author's own Vedānta. Among Jaina works, the most famous *siddhānta* text is the *Compendium of the Six Views* (*Ṣaḍdarśanasamuccaya*) by the eighth-century scholar Haribhadra Sūri. Here, the "six views" are Buddhism, Nyāya, Sāṅkhya, Jaina, Vaiśeṣika, and Mīmāṃsā, with a seventh, Lokāyata, discussed in a postscript.

Among Buddhist doxographical works composed in India, two are of signal importance. The first is the *Blaze of Reasoning*, Bhāviveka's prose autocommentary on his *Essence of the Middle Way*, written in the sixth century. He deals with six schools, four Hindu—Sāṅkhya, Vaiśeṣika, Vedānta, and Mīmāṃsā, as well as Jaina (discussed in passing)—and two Buddhist: Śrāvaka (by which he means the non-Mahāyāna schools, which he deals with as a group) and Yogācāra. These are bracketed by chapters in which he presents his own Madhyamaka position on a range of topics. Thus the first three chapters deal, respectively, with the aspiration to enlightenment (*bodhicitta*), the vows of the sage (*munivrata*), and the knowledge of reality (*tattvajñāna*). After his chapters on the various opponents, he concludes with two chapters, one on the proof of the Buddha's omniscience (*sarvajñasiddhi*) followed by a chapter of praise of the Buddha (*stutilakṣaṇa*). Among the chapters on his opponents, the longest is devoted to the Mīmāṃsā.

The second Buddhist work is the massive *Compendium of Principles*, composed some two centuries later by the eighth-century Madhyamaka scholar Śāntarakṣita, one of the seventeen masters of Nālandā discussed above. It contains 3,646 verses, in which the views of the major philosophical schools of the day are presented and critiqued: atheistic Sāṅkhya, Śaiva, theistic Sāṅkhya, Lokāyata, followers of Brahmā or Grammarians (Vaiyākaraṇa), followers of the Vedas, Vaiśeṣika, Nyāya, Mīmāṃsā, Nirgrantha (Jaina), and followers of the Upaniṣads (Vedānta). Among the Buddhist schools, the Vātsīputrīya, the so-called "proponents of the person" (*pudgalavādin*) who asserted the existence of an "inexpressible person," are also subjected to critique. Śāntarakṣita's disciple Kamalaśīla provided a lengthy prose commentary, where the names and positions of various proponents of these schools are identified. As such, the work offers detailed insight into the philosophical landscape of eighth-century India, providing a sense of which schools the Buddhists saw as their opponents. It is noteworthy that over 40 percent of Śāntarakṣita's 3,645 verses are devoted to the critique of Mīmāṃsā, meaning that Buddhist thinkers over the course of several centuries regarded them as their primary rivals.

If the attribution of the *Collection of All Views and Tenets* to Śaṅkara were correct, by the eighth century, we have a Hindu master dividing the Buddhist philosophical schools into the four that would be known in Tibet: Vaibhāṣika, Sautrāntika, Yogācāra, and Madhyamaka. As noted in the introduction to chapter 10, this list also appears in a Buddhist philosophical treatise and in a tantra, both of unknown date. This fourfold list, and its hierarchy, are so familiar from the Tibetan context that it is easy to forget that it was not always the case. We know from the account of Xuanzang that Yogācāra was the dominant school at Nālandā during his time there. Dharmapāla, a Yogācāra scholar whose works would be influential in China, had recently been the abbot, and his disciple (and Xuanzang's teacher) Śīlabhadra, was the leading scholar at the monastery, at least according to Xuanzang's account.

The four schools of Buddhist tenets in Tibet were seen as a hierarchy, in the sense that the Sautrāntika position is more sophisticated than, and therefore can defeat, the Vaibhāṣika tradition. Cittamātra can in turn defeat Sautrāntika, and Madhyamaka can defeat Cittamātra. However, this is not simply a case of philosophical bragging rights. As discussed in chapter 15, the conclusion, the movement through the four schools is regarded as a progression, in the sense of a ladder or stairway, with each school seen as a step to the next, the profundity and subtlety of each level only evident by having understood and appreciated the prior level. This approach has a long history in Buddhism. In the Pāli tradition, we find reference to *anupubbikathā*, or "step-by-step instruction," in which the Buddha would begin by teaching the karmic benefits of generosity and morality, including rebirth in heaven, before explaining the dangers of attachment to the objects of the senses. He would then teach the benefits of renunciation, before setting forth the four noble truths and the peace of nirvāṇa.

The Study of Indian Philosophy in Tibet

Despite the almost complete absence of Hindu philosophers in Tibet, and with no concerns about losing patronage from a Hindu king, the tenets of the Hindu schools continue to be studied and debated in Tibetan monasteries to the present day, with particular distinction accorded to those with the forensic skills to successfully defend a Hindu position against a Buddhist opponent. One such figure was the well-known debater of Labrang Monastery Gendun Chöphel (1903–51), who gained the admiring sobriquet "Sāṅkhya abbot." Tibet also has a long tradition of scholars composing works on Indian Buddhist philosophy, both in the form of commentaries on important Indian Buddhist treatises and in the form of texts on tenets, where the positions of both Hindu and Buddhist schools are presented. The Dalai Lama mentions some of the most famous works in this genre in his own introduction; several other works can be discussed briefly here.[2]

Buddhism is said to have entered Tibet in the seventh century, with Samyé, the first monastery, being founded in the late eighth century. It was during this latter period that the translation of Buddhist texts from Sanskrit into Tibetan began, a process that would continue over the next six centuries. It is interesting to note that some of the first works composed by Tibetans were works on tenets, including *An Explanation of Different Views* (*Lta ba'i khyad par bshad pa*) by Yeshé Dé and *Explanation of the Stages of Views* (*Lta ba'i rim pa bshad pa*) by Kawa Paltsek, both of which date from this early period of the late eighth and early ninth centuries.

After the fall of the Tibetan empire in 842, there was an interregnum of a century and a half during which the translation of Indian works seems largely to have ceased. This ended with a revival of translation in western Tibet, led by the Tibetan monk Rinchen Sangpo (958–1055) and the arrival of Atiśa in 1042. A number of important texts on tenets would appear in the eleventh and twelfth centuries, including Rongzom Paṇḍita's *Memoranda on Various Views and Tenets* (*Lta ba dang grub mtha'i brjed byang*) and Chapa Chökyi Sengé's *A Summary of Presentations of Buddhist and Non-Buddhist Tenets* (*Phyi nang gi grub mtha'i rnam bzhag bsdus pa*). In subsequent centuries, important tenets texts would be composed by the Sakya lama Sakya Paṇḍita and the Nyingma lama Longchen Rabjampa. Beginning in the sixteenth century, the tenets genre would become a particular interest of the Geluk sect, with the Second Dalai Lama, Gendun Gyatso (1475–1542), composing the evocatively entitled *Ship that Sails the Ocean of Tenet Systems* (*Grub mtha' rgya mtshor 'jug pa'i gru gzings*).

In his introduction to this volume, His Holiness mentions four well-known tenets texts composed by Tibetan authors. The first is the *Treasury of Explanation of Tenets* by the thirteenth-century scholar of the Kadam school Üpa Losal. He had taken part in the organization and redaction of the Tibetan canon, the famous Kangyur ("translation of the word of the Buddha") and Tengyur ("translation of the treatises"). These efforts provided him with an extensive knowledge of a wide range of Indian Buddhist texts from which to draw in his own work; his book on tenets is renowned for its ample citation of Indian sources. Previous Tibetan texts on tenets had only presented the Buddhist schools of India. Üpa Losal's *Treasury* was the first to also present non-Buddhist schools, including Lokāyata, Sāṅkhya, Śaiva, Vaiśeṣika, and Jaina; four of these are discussed in the present volume.

The other three works discussed by His Holiness are by Geluk luminaries. The first is *A Presentation of Tenets: The Song of the Five-Faced [Lion] that Relinquishes Confusion* (*Grub mtha'i rnam gzhag 'khrul spong gdong lnga'i sgra dbyangs*), a work in verse completed in 1689 by Jamyang Shepa (1648–1721), an important author, abbot, and founder of monasteries during the tumultuous period after the death of the Fifth Dalai Lama. Ten years later, he would complete a lengthy prose commentary called *Sun of Samantabhadra's Land* (*Kun bzang zhing gi nyi ma*). Both because of its length and because of its scope, the work is better known simply as *Great Exposition of Tenets*.[3] As His Holiness notes, the text is quite long (673 small print pages in one edition) and is filled with often difficult quotations from a host of Indian sources; he presents thirteen non-Buddhist schools in addition to the Buddhist schools, offering a detailed discussion of the traditional eighteen Mainstream schools. For these reasons, it is a text that is more often consulted than read in its entirety.

A more succinct, but still quite substantial, text was composed by a young incarnate lama that Jamyang Shepa had helped identify. Its full title is *Clear Presentation of Tenets, a Beautiful Adornment of the Meru of the Sage's Teachings* by Changkya Rölpai Dorjé (1717–86), a Geluk polymath and preceptor to the Qianlong emperor. It is sufficiently famous to be simply known as *Changkya's Tenets*.[4] Noting that it has a more manageable number of citations from Indian sources than Jamyang Shepa's text, His Holiness describes it as "an important treatise of the doxographical genre, offering an easy way to engage with the subject while being quite comprehensive in its subject matter."

His Holiness also mentions a Tibetan text included in the tenets genre that adopts a different structure from its predecessors. This is the *Crystal Mirror of Philosophical Systems* by Thuken Losang Chökyi Nyima (1737–1802), a student of Changkya. Although it briefly surveys the classical Indian schools, its focus is the religious systems of Tibet, including Bön, and it even goes on to consider the Buddhist and non-Buddhist Chinese schools as well as other religions, including Christianity.[5]

About This Volume

This volume is very much part of this long and venerable tradition of Indian and Tibetan doxography. However, it differs from its Tibetan predecessors in a number of important ways. As mentioned, there were no Hindu philosophers in Tibet and thus no non-Buddhist opponents to debate, with no stakes in terms of conversion or loss of royal patronage. The classical Hindu schools, together with Jaina and Lokāyata, were therefore hypothetical. So while they were studied and their positions debated,

Tibetan tenets texts tended to leave the non-Buddhist schools out entirely or deal with them in only a relatively cursory way. Different schools were sometimes grouped together in a single chapter, and their positions were divined from the works of their Indian Buddhist opponents that had been translated into Tibetan rather than from the original works themselves.

This volume is very different. One of the many consequences of the Tibetan diaspora that began in 1959 has been a renaissance of Sanskrit studies by Tibetan Buddhist monks, who, for the first time in centuries, have been able to study Sanskrit with Indian scholars in India. Much of this study has taken place at Banaras Hindu University in Vārāṇasī, not far from the Central Institute of Higher Tibetan Studies in Sarnath, the site of the Buddha's first teaching. As part of their studies and under the tutelage of Indian scholars, Tibetan monks have translated from Sanskrit into Tibetan a number of important Indian philosophical works that were not previously known in Tibet. Drawing on these translations, and often citing them directly, as well as benefiting from the extensive scholarship on the Hindu schools that is available in Hindi, this volume presents a more detailed and complete view of seven major non-Buddhist schools of Indian philosophy than has appeared in the long history of Tibetan doxographical literature. The rich description of the non-Buddhist schools that appears in the pages that follow thus offers a perspective on Buddhist philosophy that previous works composed in Tibetan have often lacked, and that is how much the Buddhist and non-Buddhist schools share. It is of course the case that the Buddhists part company with the Hindu schools on the authority of the Vedas and part company with the Hindu schools and the Jains on the question of the existence of a permanent self. Yet even with these important distinctions, the reader will find that the schools of Indian thought, both Buddhist and non-Buddhist, share the same philosophical universe and much of the same philosophical vocabulary, a vocabulary they employed over many centuries in spirited philosophical debate.

In Tibetan doxographical literature, the great majority of the pages over the centuries have been devoted to the Buddhist schools. That is also the case in this volume. Those schools have traditionally numbered four: Vaibhāṣika, Sautrāntika, Cittamātra, and Madhyamaka. However, even among the presentations of Buddhist schools, the problem of representation by the opponent has been present, especially when it came to Vaibhāṣika. The Vaibhāṣika school is named after its foundational text, the *Great Exegesis of the Abhidharma*, a work so well known that it is simply referred to as the *Great Exegesis* (*Mahāvibhāṣā*). It is one of the most important works, and certainly the longest work, in the history of Indian Buddhist philosophy, presenting, critiquing, and defending a wide range of positions in the vast and complex world of the Abhidharma, the axis of Buddhist philosophy, as presented from the perspective of the Sarvāstivāda school. Despite its bulk, it is but one of a number of important works on the Abhidharma in Sanskrit and Pāli. A number of the Sanskrit works are discussed in chapter 11.

When scholars speak of Buddhist philosophy, and especially of early Buddhist philosophy, they are often referring to the Abhidharma, the third of the "three baskets" (*tripiṭaka*) of the Buddha's teachings. Often translated as "advanced Dharma," "pertaining to the Dharma," or "special Dharma," it is a collection of texts generally regarded as having appeared after the death of the Buddha, although there is a famous story that the Buddha taught the Abhidharma to his deceased mother in one of the several Buddhist heavens, where she had been reborn as a god after dying seven days after the Buddha's birth. According to this story, the Buddha would descend to earth each day to repeat those teachings to the monk Śāriputra. The Abhidharma texts present a wide range of opinions on a wide range of topics that might be classified as cosmology, epistemology, psychology, and soteriology, all presented in a technical vocabulary.

The *Great Exegesis* is important both as a source of Buddhist positions on a wide range of topics and as the opponent of some of the most famous philosophers in the history of Buddhism, including Nāgārjuna and Vasubandhu. For a variety of reasons, however, it has had relatively little influence outside India, where it was likely compiled around 150 CE. It was not translated into Chinese until 659, a process that took Xuanzang and his distinguished team four years. It was never translated into Tibetan. Between the time of its composition and its translation into Chinese, Vasubandhu wrote his *Treasury of Abhidharma*, a much briefer work in which he presents the Vaibhāṣika positions in verse and then critiques them in his prose commentary on the verses, arguing in general that one should look not to the *Great Exegesis* as the authoritative source of the Abhidharma but to the Buddha's statements in the sūtras, hence the name Sautrāntika ("followers of the sūtras") as opposed to Vaibhāṣika ("followers of the *Exegesis*").

It is important to note that Vasubandhu's attack on the adherents of the *Great Exegesis* was not fatal. The monk Saṅghabhadra wrote a lengthy rebuttal entitled *Treatise on Conforming to Reasoning in the Abhidharma* (*Abhidharmanyāyānusāra*); according to Xuanzang (who translated both it and Vasubandhu's text into Chinese), the original title was *Hailstones on the Kośa*. Nonetheless, because of a number of factors, including its manageable size and its well-known author, as well as the absence of the *Great Exegesis* in Tibetan translation, Vasubandhu's work would become the foundation for Abhidharma studies in East Asia and Tibet.

It was stated above that the *Great Exegesis* was never translated into Tibetan. It would be more accurate to say that it was not translated into Tibetan until the twentieth century. It was then that the Chinese monk Taixu (1889–1947) sent a number of his monks to study at monasteries in Tibet. One of these monks was Fazun (1902–80), who translated several important Indian and Tibetan works into Chinese, including Candrakīrti's *Entering the Middle Way* and Tsongkhapa's *Great Treatise on the Stages of the Path* (*Lam rim chen mo*). However, he also translated the *Great Exegesis* from Chinese into Tibetan, completing the translation in 1949; as it did for Xuanzang, the translation took four years. When the young Dalai Lama visited Beijing at the invitation of Mao Zedong in 1954, Fazun presented him with a copy of the translation. Portions of that translation were lost during the Cultural Revolution, but it was later reassembled in Beijing and published in 2011 in ten volumes. Fazun's magisterial translation is cited extensively in the Vaibhāṣika chapter of the present work, the first time in the long history of Tibetan doxographical literature that Vaibhāṣika has been presented in the words of its most important text rather than in the critiques of its famous opponents.

Another way in which the present volume differs from the traditional Tibetan tenets text is its structure. Tibetan texts on Hindu and Buddhist tenets are generally synthetic, with the author organizing the various positions of the particular school under three headings: the basis, the path, and the fruition. The section on the basis sets forth the school's positions on a host of questions on ontology and epistemology. Indeed, this section is often divided into two, beginning with the objects of experience (*yul* or "object") before proceeding to epistemology (*yul can* or "subject," literally "object possessor"). The former category would include the school's delineation of the two truths, conventional truths (*saṃvṛtisatya*) and ultimate truths (*paramārthasatya*); the latter would include the school's position on the valid means of knowledge. The next section of the chapter would deal with soteriology, the path to liberation from rebirth. It would typically set forth both the path of the disciple who becomes an arhat and the path of the bodhisattva that culminates in buddhahood. Each of these paths has a number of stages, which can occur over many lifetimes. This is followed by a section on the fruition, that is, the goal of the path. It is here that one finds the discussion of nirvāṇa as well as of the various bodies and qualities of a buddha. Since the focus of the present volume is philosophy, for the most part encompassed under the traditional category of the basis, the path and fruition of the various schools of Indian philosophy, although alluded to, are not set forth in a systematic way here.

Because in Tibetan Buddhism it is asserted that buddhahood can only be achieved via the tantric path, many tenets texts conclude with a brief chapter on tantra. Because it is generally held that Buddhist tantra offers unique practices for progressing on the path, it accepts, or at least assumes, the philosophical positions of the Madhyamaka school or, in some cases, the Cittamātra school. Again, because the focus of the present volume is philosophy, there is no systematic discussion of tantra here.

A final point about how this text differs from more traditional tenets texts: As mentioned above, in both India and Tibet, texts on tenets, whether the author was Hindu, Jaina, or Buddhist, tended to be polemical, with the positions of other schools presented as positions to be refuted and their proponents as opponents to be defeated. Thus Buddhists would seek to refute the idea of a creator deity of several of the Hindu schools. Hindu schools would seek to point out the host of problems with the Buddhist doctrine of no-self, especially its implications for rebirth. And everyone would criticize Lokāyata for its denial of both moral efficacy and rebirth. As also discussed above, there was often much at stake in these refutations, which is one reason why the genre of *siddhānta* flourished in India for so long. At the same time, these critiques served a somewhat more noble purpose, providing their readers with the opportunity to understand the form and content of philosophical disputation and the dynamics of debate, nurturing their own philosophical sophistication and critical faculties in the process. For a variety of reasons, those polemics have generally not been included in the present volume, which takes the more familiar modern form of a detailed survey of philosophical schools.

An Overview of the Text

The volume opens, as we have seen, with an introduction by His Holiness the Dalai Lama. Given that this series is called *Science and Philosophy in the Indian Buddhist Classics*, he begins by offering his thoughts on the difference between science and philosophy, describing a philosopher as someone who is not content with the knowledge that can be gained through the senses and who asks the question "What is that hidden reality that underlies the diverse everyday world of experience?" Turning to Indian philosophy, he identifies Sāṅkhya as the earliest of the Indian schools, going on to note that the non-Buddhist schools assert the existence of a self, although they differ in how they describe it.

Turning to the Buddhist schools, he says that the hallmark of Buddhist philosophy is the doctrine of no-self, which he presents briefly, noting that he has discussed it extensively in his other writings. He notes that the traditional criterion of what constitutes a Buddhist philosophical school is the acceptance of the four seals: (1) all conditioned things are impermanent, (2) all contaminated things are of the nature of suffering, (3) all phenomena are empty and devoid of self, and (4) nirvāṇa is true peace. The various Buddhist schools accept these four statements but interpret them differently. He goes on to identify the most important Indian and Tibetan works that present the various Buddhist and non-Buddhist schools, mentioning several of the titles discussed above, including Bhāviveka's *Blaze of Reasoning* and Śāntarakṣita's *Compendium of Principles*.

Before closing with a brief description of the next and final volume in the series and how it is organized differently from the present volume, he talks about the schools of Indian philosophy as like the ascending steps in a staircase, noting that the study of philosophy is not simply an academic pursuit but is something that can benefit us in our daily lives, as he attests to from his own experience.

Following this introductory essay, the volume continues with an introductory chapter called "The Development of Indian Philosophy." It offers an overview of the entire book. It begins with offering a typology of religions, dividing them into those that do and do not have philosophy, with the latter referring to those religions that worship various natural phenomena, such as the sun. Those that have philosophy can be divided into those that do and do not believe in a creator deity, with the former further divided into those that do and do not accept the existence of rebirth. Those that believe in both a creator deity and rebirth include the Indian schools of theistic Sāṅkhya, Vaiśeṣika, Nyāya, and Mīmāṃsā. Examples of those that believe in a creator but do not accept rebirth are not named but would presumably include Christianity, Judaism, and Islam. Among those that do not believe in a creator god, there are also those that do and do not believe in rebirth, with the former including atheistic Sāṅkhya, Jainism, and Buddhism, and the latter including Lokāyata, the so-called materialist school. Among all the Indian schools, the Buddhists are famous for their denial of a permanent, partless, and independent self.

The chapter goes on to offer an account of the evolution of religions that have philosophy, presenting here the traditional Buddhist creation story that occurs most famously in a Pāli sutta called the *Account of Origins* (*Aggañña Sutta*). Here, after beings are reborn as humans in a newly formed world and human society is established, a group of people renounce that society, begin meditating, and develop supersensory knowledge (*abhijñā*). As the text says, "Those people were called 'sages' (*ṛṣi*). Among them, many attained supersensory knowledge and trained in logic, using their own intellectual analysis to compose treatises that presented the paths for the attainments of high rebirth and liberation and set forth reasons that proved them. Based on that, various philosophies arose."

The chapter then turns to a more historical discussion of ancient India, focusing on the origins of the caste system and the Vedas, explaining that through the study and analysis of various elements of the Vedas, various philosophical views called *tenets* began to appear. Both Hindu and Buddhist authors agree that the first of the Indian philosophical schools was Sāṅkhya, while the Jains give pride of place to their own school. Regardless, by the time of the Buddha, several Hindu schools and the Jaina philosophical school had already been established. It then turns to a discussion of the dates of the Buddha and the different accounts of his teaching in the Pāli and Sanskrit (which in this case means Mahāyāna) sources. The chapter next offers a brief chronology of the four major schools of Buddhist philosophy, mentioning their central texts and major authors, topics that will be expanded upon in the individual chapters on those schools later in the volume.

The chapter turns next to a discussion of meaning and etymology of the Sanskrit term *siddhānta*, translated here as "tenet," citing a number of Indian texts, before considering the difference between *siddhānta* and *darśana*. Next is an interesting discussion of the difference between a Buddhist and a non-Buddhist. We should note in passing that the Tibetan for these terms literally mean "insider" and "outsider," with the latter so called because they are outside the teachings of the Buddha. In Sanskrit Buddhist texts, non-Buddhists are often referred to as *tīrthika*, whose etymology is discussed. This term is sometimes translated as "heretic," which is misleading because a heretic is a person who deviates from orthodoxy, while in this case, the non-Buddhist teachers were not former Buddhists. Although *tīrthika* is sometimes translated as "forder," in the present volume it is left untranslated.

Turning to the substantive differences between Buddhist and non-Buddhist, the text makes a distinction between being a Buddhist or non-Buddhist and being a Buddhist or non-Buddhist philosopher or "proponent of tenets," with the former based on whether one takes refuge in the Buddha, Dharma, and Saṅgha, and the latter based on whether one accepts the four seals mentioned above, with particular emphasis given to the view of no-self. Almost in passing, the text makes the interesting observation that one can be a Buddhist and not be a proponent of Buddhist tenets. It then goes on to briefly consider the problematic case of the Vātsīputrīya sect of the Sāṃmitīya school, one of the eighteen Mainstream schools, that famously asserted the existence of something called the "inexpressible person." The chapter raises the question of whether they therefore do not accept the fourth seal and therefore are not proponents of Buddhist tenets. From here, the chapter offers a number of quotations from well-known Buddhist texts about the four seals before discussing the meaning of each seal.

Next, the chapter makes the important point that despite their many differences, the schools of Indian philosophy, both non-Buddhist and Buddhist, had much in common, from shared vocabulary to shared goals. Although they had disagreements and engaged in spirited debate about those differences, their motivations were noble, seeking to liberate their disciples from suffering; the chapter cites a number of passages warning of the dangers of attachment to one's own views.

The chapter concludes with a lengthy section called "How the texts that collect and set forth the different Indian schools of tenets arose," naming a number of Indian Buddhist texts but focusing on two already discussed above, Bhāviveka's *Blaze of Reasoning* and Śāntarakṣita's *Compendium of Principles*, offering a description of the eleven chapters of the former and the twenty-six chapters of the latter, before discussing the *Compendium of All Views*, also mentioned above, by the Advaita Vedānta master Vidyāraṇya (also known as Mādhava). The chapter then provides a chronological survey of tenets literature in Tibet before closing with a list of the texts, both Hindu and Buddhist, that serve as the major sources for the present volume.

With this general discussion of Indian philosophy concluded, the volume turns to the first of its two major sections, a presentation of the non-Buddhist schools of Indian thought. Seven of these schools are discussed in their own chapters, but the section begins with a chapter presenting an overview of the non-Buddhist schools and sects named in Buddhist texts, where, as we will see, the number greatly exceeds seven.

The lifetime of the Buddha (whenever that occurred) was clearly a time of intellectual ferment and creativity in India. The names of many schools survive in texts; of the very few of those schools that survive to the present day, Buddhism, Jainism, and the Vedānta school of Hinduism are the most prominent. Why these few survived while so many others did not is a fascinating question but unfortunately not one that we can consider here. These schools' proponents are sometimes presented as opponents of the Buddha.

Buddhist texts contain many lists and classifications of these schools and proponents. The most common of the lists is that of six non-Buddhist teachers—Pūraṇa Kāśyapa, Maskarin Gośālīputra, Sañjayin Vairaṭṭīputra, Ajita Keśakambala, Kakuda Kātyāyana, and Nirgrantha Jñātiputra. The first is represented as denying rebirth and thereby the law of karma. The second represents the Ājīvika school, none of whose texts survive. However, he is represented as teaching that purification is assured after enduring a certain (and huge) number of lives; beings have no agency in their own salvation. The third is a famous skeptic, who finds all answers to speculative questions to be somehow inadequate. The fourth represents the Lokāyata school, also denying rebirth and karmic cause and effect. The fifth is also an Ājīvika. The sixth represents the Jaina school and espouses purification through certain restraints. Although the positions that these teachers espouse in Buddhist texts likely existed, they themselves are most often portrayed as stock characters, improbably often traveling as a group, often seeming to provide comic relief rather than serious philosophical disputation. They are always challenging the Buddha and always being defeated by him, most famously by his miracle at Śrāvastī.

This is not to say that there are not interesting philosophical questions raised in the Buddhist representation of their opponents. The most well-known of these are the sixty-two views that appear first in a Pāli discourse called the *Net of Brahma* (*Brahmajāla Sutta*). Here, the Buddha divides the sixty-two into eighteen views about the past and forty-four views about the future, which he then divides further according to particular claims (labeling some "equivocators" or, more literally, "eel wrigglers") before declaring them all to be wrong. In our text, the main source is Bhāviveka's discussion in the *Blaze of Reasoning*. Many important questions are raised here, including whether the self and the world are finite and infinite. Indeed, the most important and enduring of the Buddha's classifications of wrong views is the simple binary called the extreme of existence and the extreme of annihilation. Exactly what these two terms mean became a perennial question in Buddhist philosophy, engaged most influentially by Nāgārjuna.

Space does not permit a complete survey here, but at least one observation might be made. With the exception of the scorned Lokāyata, the other major Indian schools accept the doctrine of rebirth. The existence of past lives (and hence future lives) was generally not a topic of philosophical argumentation (although the great Buddhist logician Dharmakīrti would later provide a proof for rebirth); rather it was something confirmed by meditative experience. It is a general tenet of Indian religions that one can come to remember their past lives through the appropriate practice of meditation. We note in the chapter here that distinctions are made between those who can remember as far back as twenty, forty, or eighty eons (*kalpa*), a unit of time typically described in similes rather than numbers in Buddhist texts but clearly encompassing many billions of years. More pertinent in the context of philosophy is that what they remember becomes the basis for a right or wrong philosophical view. As the classification of religions in the previous chapter made clear, the Buddhists were in a minority on the question of the existence of a creator deity. They were therefore obliged to explain how this erroneous belief arose. In Buddhism there are many gods, but no God; there are many heavens, but no Heaven. One is reborn as a god as a result of various auspicious deeds, from generosity to the achievement of certain meditative states, but rebirth in one of the several heavens is temporary, coming to an end when the karmic cause has been exhausted. Some types of gods have longer lives than others, however. Thus the Buddhists explain that someone was born in a heaven ruled by the god Brahmā, died in that heaven before Brahmā did, was reborn as a human, practiced meditation, and gained the ability to remember their past lives. Seeing that Brahmā was still present in the heaven they had recently exited, they concluded that he was eternal. Therefore God exists. Such arguments are surprisingly common in Buddhist critiques of the views of their opponents.

If sixty-two wrong views are not enough, there are also the 363 wrong views mentioned by Bhāviveka. He only provides the names of about a third of these, but the reconstruction of the Sanskrit from the Tibetan, the meaning of the names, and what they might possibly refer to continue to vex scholars. It seems clear, however, that many of these are not the names of schools in a philosophical sense but are instead the names of often bizarre cults or practices—those who live in a hole in the ground, those who behave like dogs—said to have existed in India at the time.

After listing twenty-two views set forth in a commentary on the *Descent into Laṅkā Sūtra*, the text makes an alarming reference to 570 views before providing various lists from various Indian and Tibetan sources, Buddhist and non-Buddhist, far more manageable in scope, ranging from twelve to five. Several of these are subjects of their own chapter in the pages that follow.

Sāṅkhya

With this background, the individual chapters on seven non-Buddhist schools begin. For those readers who may not be familiar with Indian philosophy, both Buddhist and non-Buddhist, it is important to know that each school tries to provide a comprehensive system, its own theory of everything, accounting for all components of the physical world, all states of mind, and all events. This focus of Indian philosophy, often to the point of obsession, with accounting makes it appropriate that the first school to be considered is Sāṅkhya, which means "enumeration." It is the subject of the longest of the non-Buddhist chapters in the volume, in part because of its priority as the oldest of the classical schools and in part because of its great influence, especially its influence on Buddhist thought, with Buddhist authors writing about it for almost a millennium.

Each of the chapters beginning with this one has a similar structure, opening with a brief history of the school, listing its major figures and its most important texts. This is followed by a definition of the school, a discussion of its other names, and an enumeration of its subschools. This is followed by the heart of each chapter, a discussion of principal tenets and philosophical positions, generally beginning with the external world (however defined) and then turning to consciousness. It is in the latter section where we find a discussion of epistemology as well as the all-important topic of valid knowledge.

Here we learn that the founder of Sāṅkhya was the ancient rishi Kapila, a figure mentioned in the Upaniṣads. He is also considered the founder of the atheistic branch of Sāṅkhya; the founder of the theistic branch is Patañjali, author of the *Yoga Sūtra*, where *yoga* is famously defined as the "cessation of mental activity." Turning to their tenets, we immediately encounter Sāṅkhya's bold attempt to account for everything in their twenty-five categories (*tattva*, sometimes translated as "principles"), presenting the most radical example of consciousness-matter dualism in Indian thought. Of the twenty-five, twenty-four (including mind, intellect, and ego) are matter or primary nature (*prakṛti*), from which everything arises and to which everything returns. Only one is consciousness, the silent observer known as the self or the person (*puruṣa*). Theistic Sāṅkhya adds God (Īśvara) as the agent of change. In this chapter, each of the twenty-five principles is described in some detail, as are the three well-known qualities (*guṇa*) of primary nature: *sattva* (lightness), *rajas* (mobility), and *tamas* (darkness).

Beyond the discussion of the twenty-five principles, several other sections of this chapter are of particular interest. These include the discussion of the three sources of valid knowledge according to Sāṅkhya: direct perception, inference, and reliable testimony. This is interesting in its own right, as well as for the fact that it served as the foundation for the positions of other schools, who in most cases would include additional valid means of knowledge. The Buddhists would subtract one, verbal testimony, leaving only direct perception and inference. Although not philosophy in the technical sense, there is something almost poignant about how Sāṅkhya describes the process of liberation from rebirth. Primary nature and the person have always worked together; according to the famous simile, they are like a lame man (the person) riding on the shoulders of a blind man (primary nature). Over the ages of their association, the person mistakenly comes to imagine himself as the agent of primary nature's actions. Eventually, however, through the practice of concentration, he comes to recognize his error. At this point, primary nature withdraws from the person, and a sequence begins in which the twenty-three material elements that evolved from primary nature, each arising from the one before, begin to slowly dissolve into each other in reverse order, finally leaving just primary nature. The point at which there is only the person and the primary nature—now in the unmanifest state—is called *isolation* (*kaivalya*). This, for Sāṅkhya, is liberation.

Vaiśeṣika

The Vaiśeṣika or "particularist" school is able to encompass everything that can be known in only six categories, categories that both in Sanskrit and in English seem to indicate a move toward philosophical abstraction: substance, quality, activity, universal, particularity, and inherence, with later adherents of the school adding a seventh category, nonexistence. As in the other Indian schools, categories are composed of many elements. The first, substance, has nine, for example, an ostensibly disparate group that includes the four physical elements—earth, water, fire, and wind—as well as space, time, and direction followed by self and mind.

As in the other chapters, each of these is defined. Here, we learn that although the various physical entities composed of earth, water, fire, and wind are impermanent, the individual particles of these four are permanent, a position that the Buddhists would attack. This emphasis on the abstract is evident throughout the six categories and their subcategories, differing from Sāṅkhya, whose twenty-five principles include so many body parts and mental functions. In Vaiśeṣika, we find under *quality* such concepts as size, disjunction, distance, and proximity, each of which is not a description of a state but an active agent that produces that state. *Proximity*, for example, is defined as "a quality that serves as the specific cause of the convention of nearness."

The *self* (*ātman*) that is described in Vaiśeṣika also differs from the remote and passive *person* (*puruṣa*) of Sāṅkhya; it is endowed with the agency and emotions associated with ego in the Western in sense of the term; its qualities are intellect, pleasure, pain, desire, aversion, effort, merit, demerit, and formative force. Indeed, some of their proofs for the existence of self are based on the idea of agency, that on the physical level, there must be something to regulate the energies that flow through the body and that causes the eyes to open and close. On the emotional level, there must be something that serves as the basis of desire and hatred. As the chapter notes, a full description of the nature of the self according to Vaiśeṣika is found in volume 4 of this series.

Among the schools of Indian philosophy, the Vaiśeṣika categories of the universal and the particular would be influential in the field of logic, with *universal* defined as that which serves as the cause for a shared term or concept to apply to a substance, quality, or activity, whether it is something all-encompassing, such as *existence* or something particular like *cow*. It is the universal that allows someone to see a black cow and a white cow and understand that they belong to the same species despite the difference in their color. The category of particularity performs the opposite function, serving as the cause for the ability to observe difference.

Nyāya

The term *nyāya* is generally translated as "reasoning" or "logic." The school by that name is credited with providing a sophisticated system of logic to Indian philosophy. Its foundational text is the *Nyāya Sūtra*, perhaps best translated as *Aphorisms on Reasoning*, attributed to the rishi Akṣapāda, also known as Gautama. His dates are unknown, and how much of the text is his own is unclear. The Madhyamaka master Nāgārjuna, usually dated to the second century CE, provides a critique of the first chapter only. Nyāya would provide the foundation for Buddhist logic, largely through the Buddhist contestation of many Nyāya categories. That contestation, with each party attacking the other, would continue for almost a millennium.

Like the other Hindu schools, Nyāya has its list of categories meant to encompass everything. Its sharp focus on logic is obvious simply from the names of its sixteen categories: means of knowledge, the object of comprehension, doubt, purpose, example, tenet, parts, reasoning, ascertainment, debate, disputation, cavil, pseudo-reason, deceit, self-defeating objection, and points of defeat. This is confirmed when we note that the cosmology, ontology, epistemology, and soteriology that consume most of the categories of the other schools are for the most part dispensed with in just the second of the Nyāya categories, object of comprehension, where we find ātman, body, sense faculties, objects, intellect, mind, activity, fault, future lives, effect, suffering, and liberation. Nyāya and Vaiśeṣika are often paired in presentations of the Indian schools. In the present volume, the Vaiśeṣika position on the forms of valid knowledge is deferred to the Nyāya chapter because of its similarity. More than half of the chapter is devoted to means of knowledge—that is, valid knowledge—holding pride of place as the first of the sixteen categories.

Nyāya is renowned for positing four valid means of knowledge, the standard direct perception and inference as well as analogy and testimony. The Buddhists would accept the first pair, with important modifications, and reject the second pair as sources of valid knowledge. Nyāya was particularly influential in its detailed description of the mechanics of the syllogism and its classifications of various kinds of signs (*liṅga*) or reasons, which are set forth, with examples, at the conclusion of this chapter.

Mīmāṃsā

Mīmāṃsā, "examination" or "investigation," is among the most fascinating of the schools of Indian philosophy, a school that is at once conservative and radical; conservative for its strict adherence to the Vedas, not so much works like the Upaniṣads but the early works on Vedic sacrifice; radical for its firm resistance to concepts like liberation from rebirth that would come to be shared by the other schools, both Hindu and Buddhist. For Mīmāṃsā, emotions like desire cannot be purged from the mind through meditation or any other means, because desire is a natural property of the mind, like heat for fire. The Vedic gods are not deities to be worshiped but are simply the components of properly performed Vedic rituals; the ritual produces the desired boon. Religious practice (*dharma*) is Vedic ritual.

It is Mīmāṃsā that would prove to be Buddhism's most formidable opponent in India, as measured by the pages that major figures like Bhāviveka and Śāntarakṣita devote to refuting them, and to the sophisticated attacks against Buddhist positions mounted by figures like the late seventh-century scholar Kumārila. Among the many factors that led to the decline of Buddhism in India, the sustained critique by the Mīmāṃsaka is often counted.

Mīmāṃsā counts six forms of valid knowledge: direct perception, inference, analogy, verbal testimony, postulation, and nonexistence. The first four are familiar from other schools. The last two would tend to be seen as forms of inference. For Mīmāṃsā, the most important is verbal testimony, which is defined here as "apprehending the meaning of a hidden object of knowledge based on sound." It has two kinds, produced from a sound not made by a person and produced by the speech of a trustworthy person. They assert that because both understand a hidden meaning, they are not direct perception, and because they do not rely on a sign with the three modes, they are also not inference. The key phrase here is "sound not made by a person." This refers to the Vedas, which are regarded as preexistent and eternal sound, spoken by no god or human, but only eventually heard by the great sages of the past. Indeed, the fact that there is no memory of the author of the Vedas is offered by Mīmāṃsā as proof that they have none. The words of the Vedas are valid, reliable, and trustworthy precisely because they are not the products of fallible humans.

The chapter concludes with a section on Caraka, sometimes described as a related school named after a sage associated with the ancient Indian medical tradition of Āyurveda. Although it is therefore mostly known in the context of traditional medicine, it has its own positions on what constitutes valid knowledge, including two that do not appear in the other schools—oral transmission and intuition. The first would be like knowledge passed down in a local community that a spirit resides in a certain tree. The second would be like a sister thinking that her brother will come home on a certain day, and he does.

Vedānta

Among the schools of Hindu philosophy, Vedānta is certainly the best known in the West, the result of efforts of Hindu proponents such as Swami Vivekānanda beginning in the last decades of the nineteenth century. However, as our text notes, the contributions of Vedānta to Indian philosophy in the strict sense, especially in the domains of epistemology and logic, have been less significant than those of the other schools. Our text gives as evidence of this the relative dearth of references to Vedānta in the works of Dignāga. It should be noted, however, that this can be attributed in part to the fact that Vedānta rose to its greatest prominence as Buddhism fell toward its demise in India, a process that Advaita Vedānta, and especially its most famous figure, Śaṅkara, sought to hasten. Śaṅkara's important predecessor Gauḍapāda and his school are the subject of a chapter in Bhāviveka's *Blaze of Reasoning*. The presentation of Vedānta here is drawn largely from Śāntarakṣita's discussion of Vedānta in his *Compendium of Principles*.

As its name "end of the Veda" suggests, Vedānta draws its inspiration not from the early parts of the Vedas on sacrifice, as Mīmāṃsā does, but on the last section, the Upaniṣads. These are its acknowledged and orthodox sources. The chapter here concludes with a discussion of the unacknowledged influence not only of Sāṅkhya but of Madhyamaka and Yogācāra. Indeed, when we read the definition of Vedānta, it would not be surprising to feel that we were reading a definition of Yogācāra, were it not for the phrase "that follows the scripture of the Vedas." That definition is: "a philosophy that follows the scripture of the Vedas and argues that all phenomena are the nature of consciousness, empty of the duality of object and apprehender." That nondual consciousness is eternal and true; everything else, the world and its inhabitants, is an illusion. Liberation is achieved by understanding the identity of the individual self (*ātman*) and ultimate reality (*brahman*). This is the central focus of Vedānta. On those occasions when they discuss valid knowledge, they follow the sixfold system of Mīmāṃsā.

With the conclusion of this chapter, we have reached the end of the presentation of the Hindu schools among the non-Buddhist schools of Indian philosophy. We now turn to the two well-known non-Hindu schools: Jaina and Lokāyata.

Jaina

The Tibetan source text calls this chapter an "Explanation of the Tenets of the Jaina or Nirgrantha." The name Jaina means "follower of the conqueror (*jina*)," and Nirgrantha might be translated as "unencumbered," in this case by clothing, referring to those Jaina monks who go naked.

Among the schools of classical Indian philosophy, Jainism has the most in common with Buddhism. Both reject the Vedas as sources of valid knowledge. Both have orders of celibate monks and nuns, and both have founders who appeared at roughly the same time in ancient India while tracing their tradition back through a series of teachers in previous epochs. The Jaina founder, called Vardhamāna and Mahāvīra, was, like Prince Siddhārtha, a prince of the warrior caste who left the life of a householder in search of enlightenment, practicing asceticism for twelve years (rather than Prince Siddhārtha's six years) before achieving enlightenment. He is counted as the twenty-fourth *jina*, an epithet also used for the Buddha. Indeed, Buddhism and Jainism share much vocabulary although, as the chapter notes, often with different meanings. The two groups had much contact and, as rivals, criticized each other, with Buddhist texts often mocking Jaina monks for their immodesty in going naked and the Jaina criticizing Buddhist monks for eating meat. Buddhism and Jainism are the only two of the non-Vedic ascetic groups to survive to the present day. Buddhism moved beyond the borders of India; Jainism did not. Jainism survived in India; Buddhism, until its rather recent return, did not.

After giving a brief biography of Mahāvīra and mentioning some of the most important works in the prodigious Jaina canon, the chapter turns to the Jaina categorization of the constituents of the universe, enumerated as seven principles and six substances. Unlike some of the categories of the other schools, the seven principles of Jaina—soul, nonsoul, influx, bondage, stoppage, disassociation or destruction, and liberation—are all concerned with the process of achieving liberation from rebirth; two more—sin and merit—are sometimes added. As in other schools, the soul (*jīva*) or self, is eternal; it is said to be the size of the body. Unlike the Buddhists, who hold that there are six classes of sentient beings, the Jaina hold that there are nine, cited in the text as "earth, water, tree, fire, wind, worm, ant, bee, and human," that is, inanimate objects such as earth, water, and wind as well as insects, animals, and humans, with the number of sense faculties ranging from one (touch) to five. Some of the Jaina arguments for why plants have consciousness are presented at the end of the chapter.

Jainism shares some of the themes found in Sāṅkhya about the association of the self with matter and the description of liberation of the soul from matter, hence the presence of terms like influx, bondage, and stoppage among the Jaina principles. Here, however, it is karma that is the culprit, flowing in and binding the soul. The Jaina path involves stopping the influx of karma by a variety of means. This is the philosophical foundation for the well-known Jaina practice of *ahiṃsā*, literally "non-injury," as well as the ascetic practices of Jaina monks. Mentioned here are the "five fires," in which one sits under the sun surrounded by four fires as means of burning off karma. When all karma has been destroyed (the sixth principle, "destruction"), one achieves liberation (the seventh principle).

The Jaina emphasis on meditation is evident also in their description of consciousness, where knowledge gained through the senses, what is called *direct perception* in Buddhism is, although valid, classified as indirect, with direct valid knowledge limited to extrasensory knowledge, knowledge of others' minds, and omniscience. Each of these is defined in the chapter. On the question of inference as a source of valid knowledge, the Jaina express a skepticism exceeded only by the Lokāyata, accepting a proposition as valid only if it is "otherwise inexplicable" (*anyathānupapannatva*). Indeed, the Jaina have a sophisticated epistemology—at odds with and often in debate with that of the Buddhists—centering especially around the terms *anekāntavāda* ("many-sidedness," which they illustrate with the story of the blind men and the elephant) and *syādvāda* ("it may be the case"), neither of which is discussed in this chapter.

Lokāyata

Among the seven chapters on the non-Buddhist schools, the second longest chapter is devoted to Lokāyata (also known as Cārvāka), despite (or perhaps because of) their being the most universally maligned of all the schools of Indian philosophy, labeled as *ucchedavāda* (literally "proponents of destruction"), rendered as "annihilationist" and "nihilist" because they do not believe in karma (or even causation) and they do not believe in rebirth. And yet they survived, being mentioned, almost always negatively, in Hindu and Buddhist texts for centuries. From a somewhat more neutral perspective, they might be called "materialists," "skeptics," or even "secular humanists." Their Sanskrit name Lokāyata is used in Indian philosophical literature to mean "beyond the world" in the sense of "beyond the pale." Their other name, Cārvāka, might be rendered as "hedonist."

The chapter cites a Buddhist text to the effect that the school existed prior to the time of the Buddha but notes that modern scholarship suggests that its texts date from around the time of the Buddha. Among their most famous claims is that consciousness is produced from the body (and not from a prior moment of consciousness, as some Buddhist schools assert). This position alone forecloses both rebirth and liberation from it. Like so many Indian schools, its origin is traced back to an ancient rishi. This, however, immediately raises the question of how a sage could advocate a view that the other schools regard as so obviously false. Hindu texts account for this by saying that the gods of the Heaven of the Thirty-Three on the summit of Mount Meru—the rishi, named Bṛhaspati was their teacher—were once again at war with the demigods (*asura*) who lived on the slopes of the mountain, and in order to send them to hell, he taught them this depraved view. His work known as the *Bārhaspatya Sūtra* is mentioned in a number of Buddhist texts. In listing other Lokāyata works, the chapter mentions a work called *Lion that Devours Principles* (*Tattvopaplavasiṃha*) by the eighth-century author Śrī Jayarāśi Bhaṭṭa. This work, which holds the radical position that there are no sources of valid knowledge, is identified as a Lokāyata text in the chapter, a claim that is questioned by some scholars.

After dealing with their various names and divisions, the chapter turns to their tenets, all of which are based on their central claim that the body, the sense faculties, and the mind derive from the four elements of earth, water, fire, and wind and therefore cease at death. There is no causation and thus no creator deity. Things are produced naturally, from themselves, without depending on causes and conditions. They famously asked: Who made peas round, who sharpened thorns, who painted the colors on the tail of a peacock? For Lokāyata, there is only one form of valid knowledge: direct perception; inference is fallacious. The only causation that they concede is that which can be directly observed, such as a sprout growing from a seed. Their rejection of karmic retribution is based on the observation, confirmed even by those who claim to have the ability to see former lives, that the greedy and wicked are often seen to thrive while the generous and good are often seen to suffer. Thus they conclude, "There is no [effect of] giving. There is no sacrifice. There is no fire ritual. There is no good conduct. There is no bad conduct." What then is one to do? The chapter cites as a Lokāyata text that advises, "Beautiful one, live well and eat. / The supreme body, once gone, will not arise. / This body is just a collection. / Once destroyed and gone, it will not return."

The chapter goes on to describe Lokāyata's often mocking refutation of many religious practices. If it makes no sense to give provisions for a traveler long after they have departed, why would one make offerings to the dead? If the dead depart to another world, why do they not return to their home and their loved ones? If a Vedic priest believes that the cow that he kills during a fire sacrifice will be reborn in heaven, why does he not kill his own father? Thus they conclude, "Therefore these ritual works for the dead

/ performed by brahmins here / are just their means of livelihood. / They are nothing more than that." In a critique more pertinent to Buddhism, they deny the existence of enlightened beings because they deny the existence of the series of lives required for the attainment of that state. In their own version of "A bird in the hand is worth two in the bush," they advise, "A pigeon of today / is better than a peacock of tomorrow. / A doubtless copper coin / is better than a doubtful gold coin."

General Explanation of the Tenets of the Buddhists

The volume now turns to Buddhism, with substantial chapters on Vaibhāṣika, Sautrāntika, Cittamātra, and Madhyamaka to follow. These are preceded by a brief history of Buddhism and of the origins of the Buddhist schools, presented from a traditional point of view, entitled "Overview of the Buddhist Schools of Tenets."

It begins with a brief biography of the Buddha, explaining that he divided his teachings topically into three categories—the well-known Tripiṭaka—corresponding to the three trainings. Thus the section of the Vinaya teaches the training in ethics, the Sūtra section teaches the training in *samādhi*, and the Abhidharma teaches the training in wisdom. Different Buddhist schools and traditions have different canons and different views as to what is to be considered the word of the Buddha. All Buddhist schools accept some version of the Tripiṭaka, with the Mahāyāna schools also accepting the Mahāyāna sūtras and the adherents of Buddhist tantra also accepting the tantras. In the Tibetan tradition, all of these works are considered the word of the Buddha, set forth by him based on the needs and capacities of his disciples. Thus the text says, "To disciples interested in the practice of freedom from attachment, our Teacher primarily taught practices free from attachment; this is the scriptural collection of śrāvakas. To disciples interested in the vast, he taught such things as the ten levels (*bhūmi*) and the six perfections (*pāramitā*); this is the scriptural collection of the perfections or of bodhisattvas. To those disciples especially interested in the profound, he primarily taught practices of desire; this is the secret mantra Vajrayāna."

The term *śrāvaka*, literally "hearer" but often translated as "disciple," refers to the followers of so-called Hīnayāna, what some scholars refer to as the Mainstream schools, those schools that generally do not accept the

Mahāyāna sūtras as the word of the Buddha. From the Mahāyāna perspective, those sūtras are his teaching, and they regard his teachings such as the four noble truths and the eightfold path as intended for those who seek primarily to end attachment to the world. To others "interested in the vast"—that is, a bodhisattva's compassionate vow to free all beings in the universe from suffering—he taught the Mahāyāna sūtras, which set forth such topics as the six perfections and the ten levels of the bodhisattva's long path to buddhahood. To "disciples interested in the profound"—the ultimate nature of reality—he taught the tantras, referred to here as the "secret mantra Vajrayāna" with its "practices of desire," a reference to tantra's sexual elements and the transmutation of negative emotions into the path.

The Mahāyāna sūtras present their own version of what the Buddha taught and when he taught it. Perhaps the most influential of these appears in a sūtra called *Explanation of the Intention Sūtra*, in which the Buddha explains his intention in teaching different things to different audiences. This text describes three different sets of teachings or "turnings of the wheel of the Dharma" at three different places, beginning with the traditional teaching of the four truths in the Deer Park at Sarnath shortly after his enlightenment. Later, on Vulture Peak, he taught the Perfection of Wisdom sūtras, which set forth the doctrine of emptiness that would become the foundation for the Madhyamaka school. Finally, at Vaiśālī, he taught what is called "the wheel of good differentiation," specifying what does and does not exist and how things exist. Although not specified in the sūtra, commentators generally identify its teachings with the Cittamātra school, as the chapter notes.

As this sūtra and others make clear, the Buddha taught different things to different people based on their capacity; not everything that he taught was his final view. It is therefore necessary to organize his teachings based on those capacities. Here, we are told that when we consider the motivations of his disciples and the practices that they follow to reach their desired goal, there are two major categories, the Śrāvaka Vehicle (again, the so-called Hīnayāna, which would also include the Pratyekabuddha Vehicle), which leads to the nirvāṇa of the arhat, and the Bodhisattva Vehicle, the Mahāyāna, which leads to buddhahood. What the Buddha taught can also be organized based on philosophical view, with the various schools regarded as the Buddha's adaptation of his teachings to accord with the philosophical acumen of his disciples. From the Tibetan perspective, these are organized in a hierarchy, beginning with Vaibhāṣika and culminating in Madhyamaka. This is obviously a Madhyamaka description, one to which adherents of the three other schools would not subscribe. The chapter continues with a number of passages that describe the Buddha's pedagogical approach.

After briefly listing the various places where the Buddha lived, the chapter turns to his passage into nirvāṇa and the gathering of monks that occurred shortly after his death. This is renowned as the First Council, with the term *council* borrowed from the Christian term for the various synods of the Church fathers; the Sanskrit *saṅgīti* literally means "singing (or chanting) together." There are many accounts of this all-important gathering; according to some, only the Vinaya and the Sūtra collections were recited; according to others, the Abhidharma was also recited. The account here follows the latter. This is followed by a brief description of the Second Council, and then the Third Council, after which the monks in attendance split into eighteen schools. As noted above, from the Tibetan perspective, both the Mahāyāna sūtras and the tantras are the word of the Buddha. Hence the chapter alludes briefly to how they were gathered.

For the Mainstream tradition, the evolution and organization of the eighteen schools is of particular importance; this is discussed in some detail in the chapter on Vaibhāṣika. The current chapter ends with a discussion of the fourfold division that provides the structure for the Buddhism section of this volume: Vaibhāṣika, Sautrāntika, Cittamātra, and Madhyamaka. After describing the various criteria by which the schools are divided, the chapter concludes by saying, "Those who seek to eradicate [ignorance] completely from the perspective of determining the selflessness of persons should be classified as Vaibhāṣika and Sautrāntika, the two śrāvaka schools. Those who seek to do so primarily from the perspective of determining the selflessness of phenomena should be classified as Cittamātra and Madhyamaka, the two Mahāyāna schools." All of this is explained in detail in the chapters below.

Vaibhāṣika

As noted above, the Vaibhāṣika school is so named because of its reliance on the *Great Exegesis of the Abhidharma*, making it the school among the four Buddhist schools presented here that is most devoted to the vast

Abhidharma tradition. This chapter therefore provides a summary and discussion of many of the main topics discussed in the Abhidharma literature, especially those dealing with ontology and epistemology, with much of the chapter devoted to the topic of causation.

Each of the chapters in the Buddhist section begins with a discussion of how the school arose. In most cases, this section is relatively succinct. Here, it encompasses a fifth of the chapter because it discusses the complicated topic of the eighteen schools. The eighteen schools of the Mainstream, or non-Mahāyāna, tradition have been the subject of much scholarship, seeking to date and organize the schools, identifying the earliest schools and then determining which branched off from which. Many charts have been produced in an attempt to represent this. It is a complicated process for a variety of reasons, including the fact that there are several accounts and they don't always agree. Although the number eighteen is repeated often, there are differences about which schools constitute the eighteen. In what remains the most thorough study of the topic, André Bareau's *Buddhist Schools of the Small Vehicle*, first published in French in 1955, thirty-four schools are discussed.[6]

In this chapter, the eighteen schools are presented as they appear (in three different versions) in Bhāviveka's *Blaze of Reasoning*, with long passages cited verbatim from this text. Much of the discussion is about the sequence in which the schools appeared and their affiliations, but it also provides some brief descriptions of their respective positions on a range of issues. For example, providing a glimpse into the finances of a Buddhist monastery, we learn that according to the Mahīśāsaka, offerings to the saṅgha bring about great karmic effects, while those to the Buddha do not, yet according to the Dharmaguptaka, offerings to the Buddha bring about great effects yet those to the saṅgha do not. There are many fascinating doctrinal points mentioned in passing in this section.

After citing Bhāviveka's discussion, a number of other lists are provided, followed by an explanation of the etymologies of the names of the schools. At the end of this section, we learn that the affiliation of the Vaibhāṣika school, the subject of the chapter, among the eighteen is not clear, but it seems to be with the Sarvāstivāda, which means "those who say that everything exists," an ostensibly odd thing for a Buddhist philosopher to say. In this case, "everything" refers to the past, present, and future. This section ends with a discussion of the major Vaibhāṣika centers in India, drawn from the travel journal of Xuanzang, which was translated into Tibetan by the Mongolian monk Gung Konpo Gyab during the eighteenth century.

The chapter turns next to a discussion of the main texts of the school. Here we find a useful survey of the celebrated seven books of the Abhidharma, their authors, and the sequence of their composition before turning to the *Great Exegesis* that gives the Vaibhāṣika school its name, a work that is intended as commentary on one of the seven books, the *Establishment of Knowledge* (*Jñānaprasthāna*) by Kātyāyanīputra. This section also discusses Vasubandhu's *Treasury of Abhidharma*. It closes with a list of the seven works on Abhidharma of the Theravāda school, mentioning as well Anuruddha's *Compendium of Abhidhamma* and Buddhaghosa's renowned *Path of Purification*, or *Visuddhimagga*.

The remainder of the chapter is the most important, setting out in some detail the tenets of the Vaibhāṣika school, tenets that are important in their own right but also because they provide so many of the foundational categories and terminology of Buddhist philosophy, as well as so many of the doctrines that the other Buddhist schools would seek to refute. Set forth in this chapter are the five aggregates, the twelve sources, the eighteen constituents, the six minds, and the forty-six mental factors that are central to Buddhist epistemology. We also find what are called the "five foundations of objects of knowledge": forms, minds, phenomena arisen from minds, compositional factors not associated with minds, and the unconditioned.

Like the Hindu and Jaina schools considered above, the Buddhists also had their theory of everything. We learn Vaibhāṣika's straightforward definition of the two truths: conventional truths and ultimate truths. If something can be broken into parts with the body or the mind, it is a conventional truth. If it cannot, it is an ultimate truth. This definition of ultimate truth means that Vaibhāṣika asserts the existence of physically partless particles and temporally partless moments of consciousness, a position that other schools would attack. This chapter also includes a discussion of the problematic Vātsīputrīya who, as noted earlier, argued, in a religion known for its claim of no-self, that there exists an "inexpressible person."

Among the many topics considered in this chapter, one is particularly important for Buddhist philosophy, and for Indian philosophy more generally—causation. As we have seen, the various non-Buddhist schools have all tried to account for creation and change, with Sāṅkhya speaking of a primary nature, other schools speaking of a creator god, and

Lokāyata denying the existence of all but the most obvious and organic causation. As a school that believes in rebirth and does not believe in a primary nature or a creator god, causation was a consequential concern for Buddhist thinkers. In general, in Buddhist philosophical works, all of which stress the impermanence of conditioned things, a particular impermanent phenomenon passes through three phases: production, abiding, and disintegration (or sometimes, as in the case of Vaibhāṣika, production, abiding, aging, and disintegration). How and why does this happen? For Vaibhāṣika, very much in keeping with many of the Indian schools considered above, this occurs as a result of an external factor. Thus something is produced through the agency of the principle of production, it abides through the agency of the principle of abiding, it ages through the agency of the principle of aging, and it disintegrates through the agency of the principle of disintegration. These four occur in sequence over time. This position, sensible as it might seem, would be rejected by the other Buddhist schools.

Sautrāntika

The second of the Hīnayāna or śrāvaka schools presented here is Sautrāntika, the "followers of the sūtras." One might assume that all Buddhists are followers of the sūtras or discourses of the Buddha. However, as mentioned above, the sense indicated here is that this school does not rely on works like the seven books of the Abhidharma or on the *Great Exegesis* for its tenets but on the sūtras of the Buddha. Thus they would reject the account of the First Council in which it is stated that the monk Mahākāśyapa recited the Abhidharma that he had heard from the Buddha. For the Sautrāntika, the texts that constitute the Abhidharma Piṭaka are not the word of the Buddha but were composed by arhats or, according to some, unenlightened monks who had the same names as the well-known arhats. Those texts are therefore not reliable or, in the language of Buddhism, "of definitive meaning."

As clear as this distinction is, the origins of the school are unclear, with some authors associating it with the Dārṣṭāntika ("user of examples") scholar Kumāralāta. However, there is some debate whether Dārṣṭāntika and Sautrāntika are two names for the same school, as most Tibetan presentations hold. The name appears in a text composed by the early fourth-century scholar Śrīlāta entitled *Explanation of Sautrāntika* (*Sautrāntikavibhāṣā*). Śrīlāta was the teacher of Vasubandhu, the author of the most famous Sautrāntika text, the *Treasury of Abhidharma*. As noted above, in this text, he presents the Vaibhāṣika positions in the verses and refutes them in his commentary. Another important Sautrāntika text is Harivarman's *Treatise Establishing the Truths* (*Satyasiddhiśāstra*). The two greatest figures in the history of Buddhist logic, Dignāga and Dharmakīrti, are also identified with Sautrāntika, although important elements of their works are clearly associated with Cittamātra.

Although, as will be discussed below, there are important innovations in their theory of perception, Sautrāntika gives particular importance to the objects of the sense consciousnesses, exalting them to the level of ultimate truths, which they define as phenomena capable of performing a function. Thus, contrary to common assumptions about Buddhist philosophy, for Sautrāntika, something as ordinary as a clay pot is an ultimate truth. This is because it can perform a function, because each pot is unique, because it exists independent of language, and because it has the ability to serve as the object of the consciousness that perceives it. Such things are therefore called *specifically characterized* (*svalakṣaṇa*).

In all of these ways, things that can perform functions and are the objects of the five sense consciousnesses are different from the objects of thought. For Sautrāntika, objects of thought are conventional truths, lacking the vivid vitality of the objects of the senses. These objects of thought are described as *generally characterized* (*sāmānyalakṣaṇa*). It is in this context that the important topic of *exclusion* (*apoha*) is introduced, where it is observed that a specifically characterized pot, for example, is not what a thought perceives. Instead, a thought perceives a generic image of a pot formed through a process of exclusion—that is, by eliminating everything that is not a pot. This generic image, the product of a negative process, is in fact permanent in the Buddhist sense that it does not change in every moment. This is only a brief summary of an important topic, discussed at length in this chapter.

Sautrāntika also differs significantly from Vaibhāṣika on causation. As noted above, Vaibhāṣika posited four principles that bring about production, abiding, aging, and disintegration, over four moments in that sequence. For Sautrāntika, this contradicts the Buddhist dictum that everything that is produced is momentary; they argue that all impermanent things are produced, abide, and cease in each moment, that production, abiding, and cessation are in fact three names for the same moment of a given phenomenon: its coming into existence is its production, its lasting for a single moment is its abiding, the fact that it will not last more than a moment is its cessation. This is what they refer to as *subtle impermanence*. They reject not only the fourfold sequence but the Vaibhāṣika assertion that production, abiding, aging, and disintegration are principles that act on impermanent things.

Although Sautrāntika argues that it is these constantly disintegrating things that are the ultimate truths, it makes a number of important contributions to epistemology (in addition to exclusion theory), two of which can be mentioned here. The first is a mental function that might be translated as *reflexive awareness* (*svasaṃvedana*). They argue that for each moment of direct perception, there is another consciousness that takes that direct perception as its object. That other consciousness, reflexive awareness, is not a form of thought but is itself a form of direct perception. Sautrāntika argues that without such reflexive awareness, the subjective element of memory, remembering how one felt when perceiving something with the senses, would not be possible. This form of direct perception, upheld by Sautrāntika and Cittamātra, rejected by Vaibhāṣika and some proponents of Madhyamaka, would be the subject of contentious debate among the Buddhist philosophical schools.

Also in the realm of epistemology is what is called the *aspect* (*ākāra*). While Vaibhāṣika argued that a sense consciousness directly perceives its object in an unmediated manner, Sautrāntika and Cittamātra would argue that consciousness, which is immaterial, cannot directly perceive something that is material. Thus, although sense perception can be said to perceive its object, what it is actually perceiving is the "aspect" of that object, a kind of image that is cast by the object and perceived by the sense consciousness. Thus, when an eye consciousness sees a patch of blue cloth, what it is seeing is the aspect of that blue cloth, like looking at an object under a clear piece of crystal. The topic of *aspect* is only briefly discussed in this chapter; it is discussed more extensively in the next chapter on Cittamātra, where various schools, including one called Half-Eggist, disagreed on how veridical the aspect of the object really is. Despite their agreement on many points, Sautrāntika and Cittamātra would also disagree on this, as is clear from the title of the Sautrāntika text *Proof of External Objects*.

Cittamātra

With Cittamātra (also known as Yogācāra and Vijñaptimātra) followed by Madhyamaka, we move to the two Mahāyāna schools of Buddhist philosophy, so called because, unlike the other schools, they accept the Mahāyāna sūtras as the word of the Buddha and use those sūtras as the textual sources for their defining doctrines. The Mainstream schools deny that the Buddha taught the Mahāyāna sūtras. Thus one of the concerns of the Cittamātra and Madhyamaka authors was to argue that he did. The fact that those arguments can be found in the works of Mahāyāna authors over the course of almost a millennium in India suggests that the authenticity of those sūtras remained a point of contention.

Because Cittamātra and Madhyamaka would spread beyond India in ways that the Mainstream schools did not, they achieved particular fame, with their texts widely read, their founders—Asaṅga and Nāgārjuna—among the best known figures in the history of Buddhism, and their signature doctrines, including emptiness, mind only, and the foundation consciousness (*ālayavijñāna*), the subject of endless commentary. Indeed, as we read in this chapter, Asaṅga is so revered in Tibet, where Madhyamaka reigns, that some there argued that although Asaṅga taught Cittamātra, his personal philosophy was that of Madhyamaka.

There are hundreds of Mahāyāna sūtras, and they say very different things, meaning that the Cittamātra and Madhyamaka authors used them selectively to support their philosophical positions. The Perfection of Wisdom sūtras, with their repeated renditions of emptiness, were the main source for Nāgārjuna and his followers. There are many sūtra sources for Cittamātra, including the passage cited at the beginning of the chapter, "These three realms are mind only." However, as the chapter notes, one Mahāyāna sūtra was foundational for Asaṅga and his followers, the *Explanation of the Intention*. There the Buddha explains, among many pivotal topics, that when he said that everything was empty, he did not mean it literally but intended something different.

The chapter identifies Asaṅga as the founder of Cittamātra and goes on to list his many important works as well as those of his half-brother, Vasubandhu, who seems to have converted from the Hīnayāna Sautrāntika to the Mahāyāna Cittamātra at some point in his life, going on to compose several of the foundational works of the school. Among Asaṅga's works, the chapter identifies his *Compendium of the Mahāyāna* as a particularly important source of Cittamātra philosophy. Asaṅga was also the author of a number of other works, such as the *Bodhisattva Levels*, that would provide much of the vocabulary and categories of the Mahāyāna path to buddhahood for both the Cittamātra and Maḍhyamaka schools. Because the present volume is devoted only to Buddhist philosophy, those works are not discussed here.

Turning to its names, because the school denies the existence of external objects, it is called Cittamātra ("mind only"). Because the doctrines of the school derive in part from the subjective experiences of meditators, it is called Yogācāra ("practice of yoga"). Two different divisions of subschools are described. The first is Cittamātra Following Scripture and Cittamātra Following Reasoning, with the former including Asaṅga and Vasubandhu and arguing that there are eight forms of consciousness (to be discussed below) and the latter asserting that there are the usual six. The second is the division into True Aspectarians and False Aspectarians, divided on the question of the extent to which the aspect (*ākāra*) that appears to the senses is veridical.

Before this long chapter moves to a detailed description of the tenets of the Cittamātra school, its three major positions are listed. The first is that, unlike the other Buddhist schools, it denies the existence of material objects, whether they are composed of partless particles (which some schools assert) or not. Second, those objects that appear to be external to the consciousness that perceives them are in fact not; they are like things seen in a dream, entirely of the nature of consciousness. Third, the consciousness that has transcended duality in that it understands subject and object as the same entity is said to exist ultimately.

Among the topics central to Cittamātra, the first to be presented here is the three natures (*trisvabhāva*): the imaginary (*parikalpita*), the dependent (*paratantra*), and the consummate (*pariniṣpanna*). The *imaginary nature* is described in two ways, one related to sense experience, the other related to thought. Cittamātra concedes that ordinary sense experience is dualistic, with object and subject. They do not deny that there is object and subject, but they assert as false, and hence imaginary, the experience of the object as something that is distant and cut off from the consciousness that cognizes it. In the realm of thought, they note that objects appear to thought as naturally being the bases of their names, when in fact naming is entirely adventitious. Thus external objects that are different in entity from the consciousness that perceives them, and objects that are naturally the bases of their names, are called *imaginary natures*; they are false appearances that in fact have no referent in the external world, a world that does not exist.

The *dependent nature* is that which is produced by causes and conditions. As stated, this seems simple enough, and something that would be accepted by all Buddhist schools, with their emphasis on causation and impermanence. However, in Cittamātra, where external objects do not exist, the dependent nature is essentially consciousness and what appears to consciousness; Cittamātra does not deny that objects appear to consciousness; it asserts that those objects themselves are the nature of consciousness, called "dependent" because it depends on a number of causes and conditions, including past karma or, in the language of this school, *predispositions* (*vāsanā*). As discussed below, these predispositions are like seeds that bear the fruit of experience, with a single seed simultaneously producing both the perceiving consciousness and the perceived object.

The third nature is the *consummate*. This is the ultimate reality for Cittamātra. Like the ultimate reality of Madhyamaka, the ultimate reality in Cittamātra is a form of emptiness. Here, however, it is not the emptiness of intrinsic nature (*svabhāva*), it is the emptiness of the duality of subject and object, or more precisely, of subject and object being different substantial entities. The relation of the three natures is sometimes described in this way: "the absence of the imaginary in the dependent is the consummate" or, as glossed in this chapter, "the consummate is the reality that is the emptiness of the object of negation—the imaginary—in the basis that is empty—the dependent." Although the category of the two truths, conventional and ultimate, is less prominent in Cittamātra than in other schools, they assert that the imaginary and the dependent are conventional truths and the consummate is the ultimate truth.

The chapter turns next to the most famous of the Cittamātra doctrines, the foundation consciousness (*ālayavijñāna*), evocatively rendered into Tibetan as the "consciousness that is the foundation of all" (*kun gzhi'i rnam par shes pa*). Before turning directly to the topic, the chapter provides an interesting survey of Buddhist views on the number of consciousnesses, ranging from one to nine. Those who assert that there is only one consciousness say that it moves from sense organ to sense organ, like a single monkey running from one window of a house to another. Most Buddhist schools say there are six, one for each of the five sense faculties plus a mental consciousness. "Asaṅga and his brother," as the chapter often refers to Asaṅga and Vasubandhu, say that there are eight, the usual six plus the foundation consciousness and something called the *afflicted mental consciousness* (*kliṣṭamanas*), discussed below. The proponents of nine add something called the *unstained mind* (*amalavijñāna*).

The foundation consciousness serves as the depository and repository for the predispositions or seeds that are created by former deeds, remaining there for an unspecified period of time and then fructifying as experience, producing both the subject and the object, as noted above. The foundation consciousness is the passive and neutral observer of all this. Hence we read, "the definition of the foundation consciousness is the primary mental consciousness, which is very stable, serves as the basis for infusing the predispositions, and observes any of the three: the sense faculty, object, or predisposition; its aspect is unobstructed and neutral; although both the sense faculty and the object appear to it, it does not ascertain them." The chapter provides eight different reasons for the existence of the foundation consciousness. The first of these acknowledges the perennial challenge that Buddhist philosophical schools faced in upholding the doctrine of rebirth while denying the existence of the self: "In general, if a consciousness is the kind that takes rebirth, it cannot be the kind that sometimes exists in one's continuum and sometimes does not exist; it must have all the qualities, such as operating uninterruptedly from the moment of conception until death. Because the six collections of consciousness do not have all those qualities, they are not suitable to take rebirth; the foundation consciousness has all of those qualities."

Having described the foundation of the predispositions, the chapter turns to a detailed discussion of the seeds themselves, their types, how they are deposited, how and when they fructify, and so forth. Among the several challenges for a school that denies the existence of an external world is the presence of shared experienced. Here, we learn that one of the types of seeds are "shared seeds," which fructify to produce sensory experience of the environment.

The afflicted mental consciousness observes the foundation consciousness and mistakenly perceives it to be a permanent self. It is defined in the chapter as "a mind that views the foundation consciousness abiding in the same continuum, constantly apprehending it and thinking 'I' and 'mine.'" Like the section on the foundation consciousness, this section presents a number of arguments for the existence of the afflicted mental consciousness. For example, were there no afflicted mental consciousness, there would be no conception of personal agency for actions, whether good or bad: "For example, in all virtuous thoughts such as 'I will cultivate loving kindness,' nonvirtuous thoughts such as 'I will commit murder,' and neutral thoughts such as 'I will eat food,' it is known through experience that the conception of 'I' is present."

With the presentation of the eight types of consciousness complete, the chapter turns to the various proofs of mind only that occur in a wide range of sūtras and treatises. Rather than presenting sustained arguments, this section provides a series of passages from various texts, each followed by a gloss of how it is proving mind only. Of special interest here is the demonstration through quotation that both Dignāga and Dharmakīrti, who did not assert the existence of a foundation consciousness, nonetheless argued that external objects do not exist. This is followed by a section setting forth the positions of the True Aspectarians and False Aspectarians as well as those of their various subschools. For example, for the True Aspectarians there are three: the Proponents of an Equal Number of Subjects and Objects, the Half-Eggists, and the Nonpluralists, each of whom has a different opinion on the nature of sense experience.

The chapter concludes with a discussion of valid knowledge according to Cittamātra. For Asaṅga and Vasubandhu, like proponents of other Buddhist schools, there are the two, direct perception and inference, to which they seem to add a third, scriptural valid knowledge. This last is an important topic unto itself, not pursued in this chapter, on how the words of the Buddha serve as a source of valid knowledge. An important question that the chapter does address is this: If sense direct perception is a source of valid knowledge, as Dignāga and Dharmakīrti famously argue, how can they do so if they are in fact proponents of Cittamātra and therefore hold that all sense experience is mistaken because it perceives external objects that do not exist? How can direct perception be "undeceived" as it is commonly defined? It would seem that a different definition is required, and this is indeed the case. We read, "Because of this important point, in Dharmakīrti's *Ascertainment of Valid Knowledge*, the definition of *direct perception* is posited as awareness that is free from thought and that arises based on predispositions."

Madhyamaka

The description of the schools of Indian philosophy concludes with a chapter on Madhyamaka, the Middle Way school, regarded in Tibet, and especially by the Dalai Lama's Geluk sect, as the pinnacle of Buddhist philosophy. The chapter begins with a lengthy discussion of its founder, the renowned Nāgārjuna, a figure said to have been prophesied by the Buddha himself. The sūtras from which he drew his philosophical positions—both the Perfection of Wisdom sūtras and a number of others—are mentioned. Among these is the *Teaching of Akṣayamati*, which is said to have provided his criteria for dividing Buddhist sūtras, and individual statements within those sūtras, into two categories: the definitive (*nītārtha*) and the provisional (*neyārtha*). In other Buddhist schools, these two terms had tended to refer to whether a particular passage could be taken literally or not. The *Teaching of Akṣayamati* takes a different perspective, declaring that statements about ultimate truths (in Madhyamaka, emptiness) are definitive and statements about conventional truths (in Madhyamaka, everything else that exists) are provisional, needing to be interpreted to arrive at their true nature, which is emptiness. This shift in the meaning of definitive and provisional from what were essentially hermeneutical categories to what were philosophical critique is regarded as a hallmark of Madhyamaka.

The chapter goes on to consider Nāgārjuna's works in some detail, focusing especially on his most famous, the *Root Verses on the Middle Way* (*Mūlamadhyamakakārikā*), also called the *Middle Way Treatise* (*Madhyamakaśāstra*) or, as was common in Tibet, *Root Wisdom* (*Rtsa ba'i shes rab*). The organization of its twenty-seven chapters is described, going on to discuss how his other philosophical works develop themes set forth in those chapters, illustrated by passages from those texts. This section is not simply bibliographic, however. It also discusses the meaning of the *middle way*, a term strongly associated with Buddhism. It appears in the Buddha's first sermon after his enlightenment, delivered to his former fellow ascetics, the "group of five" at the Deer Park in Sarnath. There, apparently speaking from his experience first as a prince indulging in various forms of pleasure, and then later as an ascetic engaging in extreme forms of asceticism, he speaks of a middle way or a middle path between self-indulgence and self-mortification as the path to liberation from suffering.

Nāgārjuna redefines the term in a philosophical sense, describing a middle way between existence and nonexistence. The discussion in the chapter makes clear that by *existence* he means intrinsic existence (*svabhāva*, literally "self-nature") and by *nonexistence* he means utter nonexistence. In his works, he thus seeks to carefully chart a middle way in which nothing intrinsically exists but everything conventionally exists. He does this by focusing especially on the process of causation as set forth by various non-Buddhist and Buddhist schools, pointing out the logical consequences of their positions, in which they seek both to maintain a kind of essence for the elements of their systems while also seeking to present a coherent system of cause and effect. From Nāgārjuna's perspective, this is impossible: once something comes into existence as a result of a series of causes and conditions, it cannot possess some kind of intrinsic nature. Once something is in any sense dependent, it cannot be independent; it cannot intrinsically exist. Indeed, it necessarily lacks any intrinsic nature. This absence of intrinsic nature is what Nāgārjuna calls *emptiness* (*śūnyatā*). To hold that things are endowed with intrinsic existence is what Nāgārjuna would define as an extreme of existence or an extreme of permanence. To hold that something endowed with intrinsic nature ceases to exist is what he would define as an extreme of nonexistence or an extreme of annihilation.

To make his point, Nāgārjuna enlists another term from the basic vocabulary of Buddhism in addition to *middle way*. It is *dependent arising* (*pratītyasamutpāda*), a term that is largely used in the Mainstream tradition to refer to a twelvefold sequence, beginning with ignorance and ending with aging and death, that describes the mechanism of *saṃsāra*, the cycle of rebirth. As he does in other contexts, Nāgārjuna takes this technical term and simplifies it, taking it to mean the simple fact that effects depend on causes. Nothing is independent; everything is dependent. If that is the case, everything is empty of independence. This does not simply include the objects of our ordinary experience; it includes the four truths, nirvāṇa, and the Buddha himself. Thus, as the chapter states, "Thus it is saying that in the final analysis, the very fact that phenomena are dependently arisen proves that they do not intrinsically exist; *emptiness* must be understood as the meaning of dependent arising."

The primary criticism leveled at Nāgārjuna by his rivals was that emptiness was essentially nothingness and that his position was a form of nihilism, essentially negating the world. For Madhyamaka, the power of his argument is that his equation of emptiness with dependent arising allows dependent arising alone to refute both the extreme of existence and the extreme of nonexistence. Because things arise in dependence on causes, they do not intrinsically exist. And because things arise in dependence on causes, they exist. As the chapter notes, "Therefore Madhyamaka does not need two separate reasons to refute the two extremes, and all presentations of such things as actions and effects are tenable for that very basis where a nature of true existence is refuted."

The chapter then turns to the long lineage of Indian masters who devoted themselves to promoting and defending Nāgārjuna's views, composing commentaries on his works as well as writing their own Madhyamaka treatises. These include many of the most celebrated figures in the history of the Mahāyāna, many of whom were masters of the Nālandā tradition, figures such as Āryadeva, Bhāviveka, Candrakīrti, Śāntarakṣita, Kamalaśīla, Śāntideva, and Atiśa. The Madhyamaka authors and their major works are listed in this section of the chapter.

The chapter next turns to the two branches of Madhyamaka: Svātantrika and Prāsaṅgika, sometimes translated as the Autonomy school and the Consequence school. As the text notes, there are no references to these two terms as the names of Madhyamaka schools in the Indian sources; their existence is something that was postulated by Tibetan authors based on their reading of the commentaries on the *Root Verses on the Middle Way* by Bhāviveka and Candrakīrti; the Sanskrit names of these schools are back translations from the Tibetan. The locus classicus for these names is the commentaries of these two masters on the first chapter of Nāgārjuna's text, as discussed above in the context of the masters of Nālandā. Buddhapālita and Candrakīrti are called Prāsaṅgika, and Bhāviveka is called Svātantrika, despite the fact that none of them used those terms to describe themselves or each other.

The difference between the two schools is also drawn from a statement by Bhāviveka when, in discussing the three natures, he suggests that to deny that phenomena are established by way of their own character (*svalakṣaṇa*) even conventionally is to go too far. From this statement, Tibetan commentators argued that he upheld the existence by way of the object's own character conventionally, something that Prāsaṅgika would reject. As the chapter notes, "Therefore, although nothing is established from its own side without being posited by the power of appearing to a nondefective awareness, this does not contradict that there is establishment from the side of the object in this system in general."

This is not to say that Bhāviveka did not make important contributions to Madhyamaka philosophy. The current chapter, for example, cites his glosses of the term *ultimate*, both as it appears in the phrase "ultimate existence" (which is something that Madhyamaka negates) and "ultimate truth" (which is something that Madhyamaka defines as emptiness and upholds). He also argues that Madhyamaka negation of ultimate existence is what is called a ***nonimplicative negation*** (*prasajyapratiṣedha*), meaning that it does not imply anything else.

The chapter then proceeds to present lengthy sections on Svātantrika and Prāsaṅgika. Again, in a Tibetan innovation, Svātantrika has two branches, Sautrāntrika Svātantrika and Yogācāra Svātantrika, the first represented by Bhāviveka and Jñānagarbha and the second by Śāntarakṣita and Kamalaśīla, so called because the former, like Sautrāntika, asserts that external objects exist, and the second, like Yogācāra, asserts that external objects do not exist. The works by Śāntarakṣita and Kamalaśīla are what modern scholars call the Yogācāra-Madhyamaka synthesis of later Indian Buddhism, where elements of what had been two opposing schools were incorporated into a single system of tenets.

Having identified these two branches of Svātantrika, the chapter presents a long section on the positions that they share. This takes the form of scrutinizing particular passages from the authors of the school in an effort to identify their position on the ontological status of conventional phenomena in order to demonstrate that their critique of the conventional was not as thoroughgoing as that in Prāsaṅgika. Here, we find a detailed discussion of the metaphor of the magician's illusion, in which a magician places a substance on a pebble or stick and recites a mantra, causing the audience to see a horse or an elephant. This provides an opportunity to consider exactly what it is that the audience sees and on what basis they see it.

The chapter moves next to Sautrāntrika Svātantrika, surveying its basic assertions on self, no-self, and the status of external objects, citing Bhāviveka's critique of Yogācāra in his *Blaze of Reasoning*. It turns then to Yogācāra Madhyamaka, listing the works of Śāntarakṣita and Kamalaśīla and explaining where they agree with Yogācāra (on such things as the nonexistence of external objects and the existence of reflexive awareness) and where they part company (on such things as the existence of the foundation consciousness and the afflicted mental consciousness). It also describes their endorsement of a progressive realization of no-self, moving from the lack of a self of persons, to a lack of external objects, to the lack of ultimate existence in all phenomena, including consciousness.

The chapter next turns to the Prāsaṅgika branch of Madhyamaka, considered here to be the pinnacle of Buddhist philosophy. Its major author is the seventh-century scholar Candrakīrti, whose major works are listed. In a section called "general explanation of its tenets" we find its position stated succinctly: "The unique feature of this system is that no person or phenomenon is intrinsically established in any way, yet all categories of actions and agents are possible. The ultimate root of the many unique ways of describing the world in this system is that it does not accept own-character even conventionally." The chapter goes on to describe how Candrakīrti, although rejecting the three natures as set forth in Cittamātra, provides his own Madhyamaka reading of them.

The Geluk lama Tsongkhapa composed a work called *Notes on the Eight Difficult Points*, a discussion of eight points on which Prāsaṅgika diverged from one or more of the other schools, describing not so much its refutation of other schools but how Prāsaṅgika, with its radical view of the emptiness of intrinsic existence, provided its own position on the issue. Seven of those are listed here, and three—the status of external objects, the state of disintegration, and the three times—are discussed briefly. Here, as elsewhere, there is a certain simplicity about Prāsaṅgika. Having presented a thoroughgoing critique of the nature of phenomena, we see a tendency to then maintain the ordinary, to affirm the conventions of the world, with the understanding that they only exist conventionally. Prāsaṅgika therefore resists the need for what it seems to regard as unnecessary and superfluous philosophical fixes, especially those of Cittamātra, its primary opponent. It argues that external objects exist conventionally and that consciousness does not have the primacy and the intrinsic nature ascribed to it by Cittamātra. The world accepts the existence of external objects, and so Prāsaṅgika does as well. They also reject the existence of reflexive awareness.

A hallmark of Prāsaṅgika is its claim that the emptiness of intrinsic existence in no way contravenes the viability of the world, especially in the realm of causation. As has been noted throughout the volume, causation is central to the philosophical schools of India in two arenas accepted by all of the schools except Lokāyata (with its rejection of the two being the hallmark of its system): karma and rebirth. Within their commitment to impermanence, the Buddhist schools must find a way to uphold the efficacy of actions in producing future experience, and they must find a way for individual persons to move continuously through time and from one lifetime to the next. One solution set forth in the Abhidharma is something called *acquisition* (*prāpti*), a substance that attaches a particular karmic deed, for example, to the mental consciousness, where the deed continues to exist until it bears its karmic fruit. The solution set forth in Cittamātra is the foundation consciousness, where the seeds of all past actions performed over all past lives can reside, from lifetime to lifetime, until they produce their effect.

Prāsaṅgika rejects both acquisition and the foundation consciousness and yet must be able to uphold rebirth. They do this by their position on what is translated here as the *disintegrated state*. For the other schools, once something has been produced, abided, and disintegrated, it ceases to exist, its state of disintegration being a mere absence that performs no function. However, Prāsaṅgika argues that that state of disintegration is a functioning thing, impermanent like all functioning things, but continuous, with one moment of the disintegrated state producing the next moment over time. This becomes crucial in the context of karma. Once an action, whether virtuous or nonvirtuous, has been performed, that action is complete and comes to an end. Yet it must somehow persist in order to eventually produce its karmic effect. Prāsaṅgika argues that what persists is its state of having disintegrated. This allows them to uphold foundational Buddhist principles like causation and impermanence, while also upholding rebirth, without the invention of things like the foundation consciousness, which for them move dangerously in the direction of self. As the chapter explains, their position on the disintegrated state has implications for how they define the three times: the past, present, and future.

The chapter on Prāsaṅgika concludes with a discussion of what it means to conventionally exist; as the chapter says, "It is most tenable that although nothing exists intrinsically, things exist from the perspective of depending on others and being designations, without being utterly nonexistent." Returning to the meaning of the middle way between the extremes of existence and nonexistence, it notes that the other schools of Buddhist philosophy dispel the extreme of existence or the extreme of permanence with their respective doctrines of emptiness, impermanence, the lack of self, or the lack of external objects. The other schools dispel the extreme of nonexistence or the extreme of annihilation by what is called *appearance*, the observation of the elements of the phenomenal world and their functions.

In Prāsaṅgika, however, the extreme of existence is dispelled by appearance; the very recognition of dependent arising, that things arise in dependence on causes, naturally dispels any conception that they exist independently or intrinsically. The extreme of nonexistence is dispelled by emptiness. As the chapter states, "whatever appears, the very perception of the absence of intrinsic existence of a phenomenon causes it to vividly appear as a mere imputation by thought."

Conclusion

The volume concludes with a discussion of two points. The first follows from what has just been discussed in the Madhyamaka chapter: how the four Buddhist schools of tenets abandon the extreme of permanence and the extreme of annihilation. As Buddhist schools, the four schools of Buddhist tenets all assert that they set forth the middle way between extremes. However, each school does so differently because each defines the two extremes differently. This is not to say that they do not share many basic views. For instance, they all accept that a belief in the existence of a permanent, partless, independent self is a view of permanence. They all also accept that to deny that virtuous actions bring about happiness in the future and nonvirtuous actions bring about suffering in the future is a view of annihilation. The chapter goes on to provide a sentence about each of the four schools and the way in which they reject the two extremes.

The second and more substantial section of the conclusion returns to a topic alluded to briefly before, that the schools of Indian philosophy, in addition to being opponents (which they certainly were), can, when organized into a hierarchy, be seen as steps or a ladder moving to more and more sophisticated positions. Such a claim assumes, of course, that one school represents the pinnacle of this progression, a claim that all but one of the schools would reject. In this chapter, that progression is set forth for the four Buddhist schools in the order in which they appear in this volume: Vaibhāṣika, Sautrāntika, Cittamātra, and Madhyamaka. Thus the two Mainstream Buddhist schools deny the existence of various constituents, most importantly the self, that the non-Buddhist schools uphold. Cittamātra denies the existence of the partless particles asserted by Vaibhāṣika and Sautrāntika. Madhyamaka rejects the truly existent consciousness asserted by Cittamātra. The chapter goes on to give a number of other examples of this, first between the non-Buddhist and Buddhist schools, especially in the context of the philosophy of language, and then among the Buddhist schools, noting how "many unshared assertions of the former are undermined by the correct arguments of the latter."

This, however, is not the stairway that the chapter seeks to present and to which it then turns. It notes that the logical categories and structures for argumentation of the non-Buddhist schools served as the foundation for innovations in Buddhist logic. The category of imputed existence (*prajñaptisat*) in Sautrāntika, in some ways a reaction against the notion of substance (*dravya*) in Vaibhāṣika, becomes central to their philosophy of language, which in turn allows Cittamātra to place the idea that objects are naturally the bases of their names into the category of the imaginary. This in turn allows Svātantrika to examine the role played by the mind, what is called "appearing to a nondefective awareness," in the conventional status of an object, something that Prāsaṅgika in turn critiques. The chapter goes on to illustrate how each of the four schools makes use of the metaphor of the magician's illusion to put forth its position on the status of the objects of experience. All four use the same illusion, all four see something different, drawing their own lesson from it. Thus, "through a careful analysis based on the philosophy of the lower, the higher only becomes more profound."

The chapter and the volume close by arguing for the benefits that accrue from proceeding upward through the schools of philosophy, with each school providing a basis from which to understand and appreciate the philosophical innovations and subtleties of the next, just as each step on a stairway allows one to continue upward, revealing a wider and wider vista. Much of this nuance and depth is missed if one starts at the top. Indeed, starting with the subtlest view is described as potentially dangerous. Instead, if one's study proceeds from the lower schools to the higher, "one will gain the certainty of conviction that these various traditions of tenets that were created by the great masters with discernment and with the intention to benefit others are solely a source of benefit and happiness for disciples of a variety of capacities and interests."

And so concludes the first of the philosophy volumes in the *Science and Philosophy in the Indian Buddhist Classics* series. As noted above, this volume is organized in the traditional way, presenting each school in a similar format, and in a hierarchy. Because this is a Buddhist work, the Buddhist schools hold the higher positions. The next volume is in a more familiar format for the modern reader, looking not at schools but at particular philosophical problems and how different schools address them. Still, there is much to be said for the traditional format, allowing the reader to see each school as a self-contained system, yet one that is in conversation with other schools. The traditional format makes the majesty of the classical Indian philosophy abundantly clear, the equal of the European philosophical tradition in antiquity, sophistication, and profundity. The world awaits their conversation.

1

The Development of Indian Philosophy

In India, non-Buddhist and Buddhist scholars developed a variety of ways to delineate the foundations of their respective systems. A summary of their most important assertions on how reality was presented by Buddhist scholars in general, and by the scholars of Nālandā Monastery in particular, was already explained in the first two volumes of *Science and Philosophy in the Indian Buddhist Classics*. Here in this volume, the most important topics of the many different philosophical positions of the scholars of India—such topics as how the mode of being is delineated through reasoning based on reality, the conclusions drawn from such a delineation, the methods of delineation, and the presentations of the valid means of knowledge—will be discussed in brief. The compendium of philosophy within the *Science and Philosophy in the Indian Buddhist Classics* series is divided into two volumes. The present volume provides summaries of the assertions of the non-Buddhist and Buddhist schools of tenets. The second volume discusses and analyzes, separately and at some length, the most important philosophical topics, such as the two truths, the analysis of self and no-self deriving from the ultimate truth, and particularly, in the context of Madhyamaka and Cittamātra, the valid means of knowledge and the analysis of the meaning of words connected to that.

First, we will present a rough outline of the period when the non-Buddhist and Buddhist philosophies arose. In general, here on earth there are religions that do not have philosophy and religions that have philosophy. Religions that have no philosophy at all consider such things as the sun and fire to be sacred, offering prayers to beings such as gods and nāga serpents. Religions that have philosophy are two types: those that do and those that do not assert the existence of a creator of the world. The first of these can be divided into those that do and those that do not assert the existence of rebirth. Those who assert the existence of rebirth are such systems as the theistic Sāṅkhya, Vaiśeṣika, Nyāya, and Mīmāṃsā. Those who do not assert the existence of rebirth are religions that assert that God not only created the environment and the first beings but that he directly created individual persons in their present lifetime.

The schools of tenets that do not assert the existence of a creator of the world are also of two types: those that do and do not assert the existence of rebirth. The school that does not assert the existence of rebirth is Lokāyata. Those who do assert the existence of rebirth are the atheistic Sāṅkhya, the Nirgrantha, and the Buddhist. [23] The atheistic Sāṅkhya and the Nirgrantha assert that there is a permanent, partless, independent self that experiences pleasure and pain. The Buddhists do not in any way assert that there is a permanent, partless, independent self that experiences pleasure and pain, and they refute it with many reasonings. Thus, in India, the proponents of Buddhist tenets were renowned as the proponents of no-self.

Between the religions that do not have philosophy and religions that have philosophy, the religions with no philosophy spread first. People worshiped the natural elements that provided the foundation of their lives, such as the earth, water, fire, wind, the sky, the sun, and the moon. Such religions seem to have been based on the belief that these elements helped people fulfill their hopes.

Turning to the question of how religions that have philosophy arose, when transmigrating humans first came into being here on earth, crops appeared for their use that did not need to be cultivated or planted. When people began hoarding the crops, farming and labor became necessary. Because of that, some people began to steal, and so a leader was selected to enforce laws to prevent disharmony. At that time, the leader disciplined the people who had committed misdeeds. Some who saw this became discouraged and went to live in seclusion in the forest. They were called brahmins. Among them, some had few desires and were content to live in seclusion. Through cultivating methods to focus the mind, they attained various meditative states. Based on that, some of them attained supersensory knowledge (*abhijñā*) and magical powers. Those people were called *rishis* (*ṛṣi*). Among them, many attained supersensory knowledge and were skilled in logic. Using their own intellectual analysis, they composed treaties that presented the paths for the attainment of high rebirth and liberation and set forth reasons that proved them. Based on those, various philosophies arose. This is set forth in a Buddhist scripture called *Analysis of the Vinaya*.[7]

According to some histories of India, around 2000 BCE, a people who called themselves the Aryans, "the noble ones," appeared in India, and from that point the Vedas gradually became widespread. That became the foundation for various religious vocations, such as making offerings to the gods. At that time, those of Aryan descent put other races into servitude and, based on that, the system of master and servant arose. It is explained that four different castes gradually arose. Among the Aryans, those having a talent for analysis were called brahmins. People who subdued and governed the country were the warrior (*kṣatriya*) class. [24] People who performed basic occupations such as farming and herding constituted the merchant (*vaiśya*) class. Those considered lower class, such as cobblers and barbers, were called the underclass (*śūdra*) or the outcastes (*caṇḍāla*).[8]

The brahmins composed a text that set forth the origin of the classes in which the brahmins came from the mouth of the god Brahmā, the warrior class from his shoulders, the merchant class from his thighs, and the lower class from the soles of his feet, explaining that the brahmin class was supreme among the four classes. This led to great differences of privilege among the class divisions.[9] However, initially, among the four classes, there was no hierarchical difference between the warrior class and the brahmins. Later, because some brahmins held the position of chaplain or priest to the kings of the country, the tradition began of their being venerated even by the king. Then, because the brahmins came to be exalted for their class, their talent, and their position, the practice gradually became widespread to recognize them as the highest of the four.

From the time the Vedas became widespread, they provided the foundation for training in the sciences such as education, conduct, and the arts. Also based on the Vedas, the rituals of sacrifice, the mantras, and so forth spread widely. Brahmin scholars with a vast knowledge of the Vedas analyzed them through study and contemplation and established proofs for such things as the categories of logic, truth and falsity, analyzing whether rebirth exists, the happiness and suffering of this life, and the paths for achieving high rebirth and liberation in the future. Citing the Vedas as sources, they composed many works setting forth their philosophies. Based on those, the different philosophical views of India, both generally and specifically, first came to be called *tenets* (*siddhānta*).

The tenets of the non-Buddhist tīrthikas arose before those of the Buddhists. Their order of appearance is set forth in Buddhist texts such as the *Commentary on Praise of the Exalted* by Prajñāvarman, where it is explained that, "At the time of the first eon, there was a sage named Kapila who composed a treatise on Sāṅkhya. His disciples are called the Kāpila."[10] At the time of the first eon, limitless years ago, there was a sage named Kapila who composed a treatise that sets forth the tenets of Sāṅkhya. It is considered the first text on tenets. [25]

In accordance with that, Candrakīrti's *Entering the Middle Way Autocommentary* explains, "The various tīrthika schools arose among those who accepted Sāṅkhya, based on minor differences."[11] The other tīrthika schools did not directly split off from Sāṅkhya. However, based on a variety of additions and subtractions that differed slightly from the permanent self accepted by Sāṅkhya, the various ways that tīrthikas explain the self emerged. The statement that many different schools split off clearly indicates that this philosophy of Sāṅkhya was the first of the tīrthika schools to appear.

According to an explanation in the Nirgrantha scriptures, the teacher Arhat was the first to appear. Bhāviveka's *Blaze of Reasoning* says, "This is what they say. When the retinue of Arhat assembled, he had already transmitted the tenets that he had investigated with his own mind to tīrthikas such as the Sāṅkhya. After that, he also gave [tenets] to Brahmā, saying, "Mahābrahmā, welcome. You have come very late. I have already handed out all the treatises. Take this Veda."[12] This is thus saying that Jaina asserts that the first teacher of all the tīrthikas was the sage Arhat.

It is explained in the ancient texts that the teacher Kapila, the founder of Sāṅkhya philosophy, appeared when the lifespan was limitless. However, later researchers of antiquity say that he appeared in the seventh century BCE. It is explained in the Sanskrit texts that this sage was born with Kardama as his father and Devahūti, the daughter of the sage Manu, as his mother in Bindusarovara in India.[13] The evolution of the most famous non-Buddhist schools, the names of their primary masters, and the works that they composed will be explained in the chapters on their individual schools below. [26]

Thus the various tīrthika schools of philosophy had already appeared before the coming of Śākyamuni in India. It is explained that when Śākyamuni was alive, there were eighteen tīrthika teachers in India. The *Chapters on the Vinaya* says, "Pūraṇa Kāśyapa, Maskarin Gośālīputra, Sañjaya Vairaṭṭīputra, Ajita Keśakambala, Kakuda Kātyāyana, and Nirgrantha Jñātiputra . . ."[14] The assertions of those eighteen tīrthika teachers appear in rough outline in the Vinaya scriptures in the context of the Buddha replying to questions about them from such monks as Mahākāśyapa and the two supreme disciples [Śāriputra and Maudgalyāyana].

Turning to the chronology of the Buddhist schools of tenets, the founder of the Buddhist schools was born in a place called Lumbinī, the son of his father, King Śuddhodana of the Śākya clan of India, and his mother, Mahāmāyā. His name was Prince Siddhārtha or, as he is known to both non-Buddhist and Buddhist philosophers, Śākyamuni. There are several assertions among the Buddha's followers regarding his dates. According to the tradition of the scholars of the Theravāda, which primarily upholds the Pāli lineage in such countries as Sri Lanka and which is well known today, the Buddha was born in Lumbinī Garden in 623 BCE and passed into nirvāṇa in Kuśinagara in 543 BCE at the age of eighty-one. Based on these dates, there was an international gathering in 1956 to commemorate the 2,500th anniversary of the Buddha's passage into nirvāṇa.

According to the tradition that primarily upholds the Sanskrit tradition, Śākyamuni came into this world and turned the wheel of the Dharma three times. In Deer Park in Ṛṣipatana near Vārāṇasī, he turned the first wheel, the wheel of the Dharma of the four truths, for the virtuous group of five. In the holy place of Vulture Peak in Rājagṛha, he turned the middle wheel, the wheel of the Dharma of signlessness. In places such as Vaiśālī, he turned the final wheel, the wheel of the Dharma of good discrimination. Both the Vaibhāṣika and Sautrāntika schools are primarily based on the first wheel, the wheel of the Dharma of the four truths. The Madhyamaka school is primarily based on the middle wheel, the wheel of the Dharma of signlessness. [27] The Cittamātra school is primarily based on the final wheel, the wheel of the Dharma of good discrimination.[15]

Taking the words of Śākyamuni as their foundation, the traditions of those four schools of tenets came to be established widely. After the Buddha displayed the method of passing into nirvāṇa, the arhats assembled and delineated the seven books of the Abhidharma, which became widely known.[16] In particular, through compiling the *Great Exegesis*

(*Mahāvibhāṣā*), the tradition of the Vaibhāṣika school became widespread. What is known as the *Great Exegesis* or the *Ocean of Exegesis* is a huge text. Although there are several different explanations of how it arose, the preface to the text explains that its compilers take as their root source the statements of the Buddha himself. At many points in the text, the assertions of the four great Abhidharma masters—Dharmatrāta, Ghoṣaka, Vasumitra, and Buddhadeva—are stated. On difficult points, the assertion of Vasumitra is taken to be the correct position. The text's general structure follows that of the *Establishment of Knowledge* compiled by Kātyāyanīputra, one of the seven books of the Abhidharma. In the seventh century this treatise was translated in its entirety from Sanskrit into Chinese by the Chinese translator Xuanzang. In two verses that the translator himself composed in the colophon, it is clearly stated that four hundred years after the Buddha passed into nirvāṇa, during the reign of the emperor Kaniṣka, five hundred arhats were invited to Kashmir; when they commented on the Tripiṭaka, they composed the *Great Exegesis*.[17]

According to the story of Vasubandhu composed by Paramārtha that exists in Chinese translation, the *Great Exegesis* was compiled under the direction of Kātyāyanīputra with Śūra assisting him.[18] It also explained that this great text was compiled right after what is known as the Fourth Council during the time of the emperor Kaniṣka.[19] Vaibhāṣika's own texts that set forth their system are the seven books of the Abhidharma mentioned above, the *Great Exegesis*, and the root text and commentary of the *Treasury of Abhidharma*. [28]

The Sautrāntika tradition became widespread after the Buddha displayed the method of passing into nirvāṇa; its philosophy was disseminated by the famous Indian scholar Kumāralāta. The works that extensively set forth this philosophy are the treatises he composed, such as the *Garland of Examples* (*Dṛṣṭāntapaṅkti*) and the *Compendium of the Piṭaka Master* (*Piṭakadharamuṣṭi*).[20] Not only were these works not translated into Tibetan, but Indian editions of them have also yet to be found. A famous upholder of this philosophical tradition was the Kashmiri scholar Śubhagupta. Among the works composed by him are the treatises *Proof of External Objects* (*Bāhyārthasiddhi*), *Analysis of Exclusion of Others* (*Anyāpohavicāra*), *Examination of the Veda* (*Śrutiparīkṣā*), and *Proof of Omniscience* (*Sarvajñasiddhi*), which are found today in Tibetan translation in the Tengyur. In addition, the seven books of Abhidharma, Vasubandhu's root text and commentary of the *Treasury of Abhidharma*, Bhāviveka's *Blaze of Reasoning*, Śāntarakṣita's *Compendium of Principles*, as well as the Buddhist treatises on valid means of knowledge clearly set forth the Sautrāntika philosophy.

The Cittamātra school of tenets was set forth extensively in the fourth century by Ārya Asaṅga, who composed the five treatises on the levels and the two compendia: the *Compendium of the Mahāyāna* and the *Compendium of Abhidharma*. In the second century, Nāgārjuna composed his collection of Madhyamaka reasoning, distinguishing and spreading widely Mahāyāna philosophy in general and Madhyamaka philosophy in particular.

Thus, over the long history of philosophy in India covering many millennia, many non-Buddhist and Buddhist teachers developed a variety of religions equipped with philosophies that connected the immediate and ultimate desires of humanity with the quest for methods to achieve them. The scholars who were followers of the respective schools of tenets refined their views through refutation and proof as well as reasoned debates about their tenets. Collecting subtle and precise points under the rubric of basis, path, and fruition, they delineated the positions of their schools. [29]

The Definition and Etymology of Tenets

What is the definition of *tenets*? A *tenet* is the full establishment of the mode of being of an object for one's own mind through reasoning, having overcome extraneous factors superimposed by thought. A person who propounds such a view using reasoning is called a proponent of tenets. For example, the *Descent into Laṅkā* says, "Mahāmati, what is a tenet? It is thus. It is that by which yogins stop the misconceptions that appear to their minds."[21]

The term for tenet in Sanskrit is *siddhānta*. It is explained that the Sanskrit term comes from a root that can refer to a treatise, a vow, or a realization of reality. Here, however, it refers to the factor of establishing through reasoning or deciding from the perspective of one's own mind, thinking, "The true mode of being or the nature of things is nothing other than this."[22] *Siddha* means "established" and *anta* means "end"; combining them results in *siddhānta*, "established end" or "tenet." Thus the etymology of *tenet* is refuting through either scripture or reasoning those extraneous factors that are superimposed by thought and then, through a proof or thesis about a reality that is perfectly correct for one's own mind, coming to the decision "there is no route to another conclusion." That which is decided upon is called a *tenet.* As Dharmamitra's *Clear Words: Commentary on the Ornament of Realizations* says, "Your tenets are what is established as your assertions, set forth through scripture and reasoning; because you do not go beyond that, it is an end."[23] In some contexts, *tenet* and *view* (*darśana*) are synonymous. This can be understood from the fact that the non-Buddhist scholar Mādhava's treatise on tenets is called the *Compendium of All Views* (*Sarvadarśanasaṅgraha*). [30]

What is the difference between a view and a tenet? Although there are cases in which they are said to be synonymous,[24] the Sanskrit *darśana* is understood to mean a way of seeing with awareness or a way of viewing with the mind. Therefore a *view* is primarily the way of seeing a particular object with the mind and stating a thesis related to that. *Tenets* are primarily a collection of many assertions and theses, providing a complete presentation of the basis, path, and fruition. Therefore one can say that a way of viewing a particular object is a view, and the complete views of a philosopher, collected in one place, are their tenets.

In brief, views and tenets occur through mental investigation and analysis of a variety of external and internal forms of existence. For example, on a cold day, an ox will stay in the sun. When it gets hot, it knows to stay in the cool shade. Humans are not satisfied with that, turning the mind to such things as how this "sun" came into existence, how hot it is, how many years it has been since it came into existence, and what will happen to it in the future. Taking the state of objects of knowledge seen by one's eyes and heard by one's ears as the basis, one states many proofs based on that and then analyzes and decides, "Ultimately, the subtle mode of being of objects of knowledge is like this." Even when it is analyzed by another person, they will determine, in accordance with their mind, that it is the true nature, without finding fault. Based on such a foundation, one can make inferences about a variety of topics. Having employed a variety of methods of analysis, one presents a philosophy by establishing the conclusion that has been determined for one's own mind.

Sentient beings are two types: those who have not engaged in philosophy and those who have. The first are those who merely seek happiness in this life naturally, without recourse to a scriptural tradition that uses reasoning. The second are those who, not being satisfied with just that, decide what to adopt and what to discard after analyzing the nature of things based on a scriptural tradition that is correct from their own perspective. [31]

A Summary of the Differences Between Non-Buddhist and Buddhist Schools of Tenets

The synonyms for non-Buddhist [literally "outsider" (*phyi pa*)] are "member of another school," "not of this religion," and tīrthika. The synonyms of Buddhist [literally "insider" (*nang pa*)] are "of this religion," "member of our school," "insider," and Buddhist (*sangs rgyas pa*). Because in Buddhist texts, the tīrthikas are outside the Buddhist system, they are outsiders. Because they are other than the Buddhist school, they are members of other schools. Because they are other than this Buddhist religion, they are not of this religion. Because they hold extreme views, they are called *tīrthikas*. However, there is another etymology of *tīrthika* in general. For example, the *Commentary on Praise of the Exalted* says, "Liberation, the path to high rebirth, and treatises that set that forth are *tīrthika*."[25] This is explaining that because they uphold and propagate treatises that set forth the entranceway or path to liberation and high rebirth of their respective systems, they are called *tīrthika*. Furthermore, *tīrthika* is the name of the Jaina religion among the non-Buddhists. Thus there seems to be a way to explain the term in which it does not refer to the non-Buddhist tenet systems in general. Nonetheless, Avalokitavrata's *Commentary to the Lamp of Wisdom* clearly explains that *tīrthika* is a name for the non-Buddhist tenet systems in general: "Tīrthikas are those who reach the shore for their religion, such as Vāsudeva [Kṛṣṇa], Kubera, Mahādeva [Śiva], Brahmā, Kapila, Kaṇāda, Akṣapāda, Śaṅkara, and Jaiminiputra."[26]

On what points do the non-Buddhist and Buddhist schools differ? There are a variety of statements about this in the Buddhist scriptures, the principal of which is that the difference between simply being a non-Buddhist or a Buddhist is made from the perspective of refuge. It is also well known that non-Buddhist and Buddhist schools of tenets are distinguished based on their views.

The difference between non-Buddhists and Buddhists from the perspective of refuge is that a person who accepts that the Three Jewels set forth in the scriptures of the Buddha are the true refuge is of this religion, an insider, and a Buddhist. A person who does not accept those Three Jewels as the true refuge is not of this religion. [32] This differentiation of non-Buddhist and Buddhist by refuge is well known in the statements of Ratnākaraśānti and Atiśa.[27]

The difference between a [non-Buddhist and Buddhist] proponent of tenets from the perspective of the view is that [a Buddhist] not only accepts the Three Jewels as the true refuge, they also accept the four seals that mark a view as the word of the Buddha: that all conditioned things are impermanent, that all contaminated things are of the nature of suffering, that all phenomena are empty and devoid of self, and that nirvāṇa is peace. In brief, a proponent of tenets who accepts that an independent self does not exist is a proponent of Buddhist tenets, and a proponent who does not accept that is a proponent of non-Buddhist tenets of other schools. The *Detailed Explanation Illuminating All the Vehicles* composed by the brahmin master Subhūtighoṣa says, "Regarding the outsiders, our own school sets forth two types of view whose center or essence is the two types of no-self. Those who are outside of that are tīrthikas."[28] This is saying that Buddhists are differentiated from non-Buddhists by accepting either the lack of self and the lack of mine or the selflessness of persons and phenomena.

The need to differentiate non-Buddhist and Buddhist schools through their view is set forth in similar ways in many sūtras and tantras. Therefore the difference between non-Buddhist and Buddhist in general must be from the perspective of refuge. The difference between non-Buddhist and Buddhist schools of tenets specifically must be from the perspective of the view. In that case, if someone is a Buddhist, they are not necessarily a proponent of Buddhist tenets.

Someone might ask, "The Vātsīputrīya school of the Sāṃmitīya accepts the existence of an inexpressible self of persons. Should they therefore not be counted as proponents of Buddhist tenets?" Although they do not accept the Buddhist view of no-self, they are counted as Buddhists because of their practice of refuge, ethics, and so forth. Also, "devoid of self" in the four seals refers to the selflessness that is the lack of a permanent, partless, independent self, and the Vātsīputrīya accept that. Because they assert the existence of a person that cannot be described as either conditioned or unconditioned, this does not contradict the assertion that all conditioned things are impermanent. Therefore there is a tradition of explaining that it is suitable to describe them as accepting the four seals that mark a view as the word of the Buddha. In some texts, there are three seals: all phenomena are selfless, all conditioned things are impermanent, and nirvāṇa is peace. [33] For example, the *Salient Points Commentary to the Treasury of Abhidharma* composed by Śamathadeva says, "The *Four Hundred Verses* in praise of the Bhagavan by Mātṛceṭa says:

> All phenomena are selfless,
> all conditioned things are momentary,
> and nirvāṇa is peace
> are the three seals of your Dharma."[29]

The four seals that mark a view as the word of the Buddha are also called the "four bindings of the Dharma" and the "four aphorisms of the Dharma." For example, the *Questions of the Nāga King Sāgara* says:

> What are the four? Bodhisattva mahāsattvas enter the inexhaustible knowledge of the teaching that all conditioned things are impermanent. Bodhisattva mahāsattvas enter the inexhaustible knowledge of the teaching that all contaminated phenomena are suffering. Bodhisattva mahāsattvas enter the inexhaustible knowledge of the teaching that all phenomena are selfless. Bodhisattva mahāsattvas enter the inexhaustible knowledge of the teaching that nirvāṇa is peace. O lord of nāgās, those who express these four aphorisms of the Dharma express the eighty-four thousand collections of the Dharma.[30]

Ornament of the Mahāyāna Sūtras says:

> For the benefit of sentient beings
> the four bindings of the Dharma
> have been taught to bodhisattvas
> as a cause of samādhi.[31]

The noble Asaṅga's *Bodhisattva Levels* says, "These are the four aphorisms of the Dharma. The buddhas and bodhisattvas teach them in order to purify sentient beings. What are the four? The aphorism of the Dharma

'All conditioned things are impermanent,' the aphorism of the Dharma 'All conditioned things are suffering,' the aphorism of the Dharma 'All phenomena are selfless,' and the aphorism of the Dharma 'Nirvāṇa is peace.'"[32] [34]

Regarding *impermanence* in the context of the four seals, most proponents of Buddhist tenets say that conditioned things are produced having a nature such that they disintegrate due to the power of the same cause that produces them, without relying on a cause for their disintegration that arises later. Therefore it is posited that by nature, having been produced, they do not remain for even a moment. The statement that all contaminated things are *suffering* means that contaminated phenomena are related to the afflictions as either their cause or effect—or else it refers to coming under their power. To be *empty and devoid of self* means that an experiencer of happiness and suffering that is separate from the aggregates does not exist, that there is no self that is the agent of actions, and there is nothing that belongs to such a self. The statement that *nirvāṇa is peace* refers to the peace that is the destruction of the defilements in the mind. This is posited when Dharmakīrti's *Exposition of Valid Knowledge* says, "They are not permanent."[33]

As discussed above, non-Buddhist and Buddhist proponents of tenets had many disagreements about the view. However, all the philosophers of India who asserted the existence of rebirth and karmic cause and effect agreed on a great many points, including such fundamental topics as good and evil and what to adopt and what to discard. There was no debate about shared practices of such things as love, kindness, patience, and contentment. It is important to understand that they all shared the fundamental aim of the present and future benefit and happiness of humanity.

One might ask, "If there were so many practical points of agreement among the schools of tenets, why did the great masters analyze those schools through the lens of debate and refutation?" They did so to liberate from suffering the disciples who believed in the different philosophies. They debated in order to delineate, with correct reasoning, their own philosophy as the basis for the practice of knowing what to adopt and what to discard. They did not debate out of attachment to their own philosophy or out of hatred for other philosophies. As Candrakīrti's *Entering the Middle Way* says:

> Analysis in the treatise is not done out of attachment to
> debate;
> it sets forth reality for the sake of liberation.
> If, when explaining reality, the systems of others are destroyed,
> there is no fault.[34] [35]

Mistaken ideas such as attachment to one's own tenets, hatred for other tenets, and pride in knowing one's own tenets are causes of suffering. As the *King of Sāmādhis Sūtra* says:

> Whoever hears the Dharma and feels attachment
> and hears what is not the Dharma and feels hatred
> is destroyed by pride and haughtiness.
> By the power of pride, one undergoes suffering.[35]

Therefore attachment to and hatred of tenets must be discarded.

Furthermore, one who, with attachment and hatred, is prejudiced toward their own views and against the views of others can never travel to the place that is free from suffering; conceiving the two positions—one to be adopted and one to be discarded—to be truly existent, one will never find peace. That is what it says in Āryadeva's *Four Hundred Verses*:

> If you have attachment for your own position
> and dislike the position of others,
> you will not travel to nirvāṇa,
> and doing these two will not bring you to peace.[36]

Thus many sūtras and treatises describe how, if one does not analyze with an honest mind—one that has abandoned the extreme positions of attachment to one's own position and hatred for others'—then the very act of analyzing tenets will affect one's mind negatively. If one views this question historically, when the Indian schools of tenets debated and analyzed each other's positions through subtle engagement in the three—refutation of the opponent's position, presentation of one's position, and abandoning objections—on such questions as the nature of the minute particles that are the basis of the composition of external objects, the nature of the self or person, the number and definition of valid forms of knowledge, and difficult points of logical reasoning, they expanded each other's minds, thus lifting the level of analysis of the subtle topics of the non-Buddhist and Buddhist schools to new heights.

How the Texts That Collect and Set Forth the Different Indian Schools of Tenets Arose

In general, in *Points of Controversy* (*Kathāvatthu*) in the seven books of Abhidharma of the Theravāda school, the assertions of the Vātsīputrīya, the Sarvāstivāda, and the Lokottaravāda are refuted, and Theravāda assertions are presented. The protector Nāgārjuna in such works as *Root Verses on the Middle Way*, the verses and commentary of his *Refutation of Objections*, and the *Finely Woven* sets forth the assertions of non-Buddhist and Buddhist proponents of true existence, making refutations and presenting his own position. [36] This occurred in the early period. However, the most famous and earliest treatise on tenets that assembles in one place and extensively sets forth the assertions of the non-Buddhist and Buddhist schools appears to be the *Essence of the Middle Way* and its autocommentary, the *Blaze of Reasoning*, by the great scholar of Nālandā Bhāviveka, who lived in the sixth century.

These two texts each have eleven chapters. The first chapter, "Not Relinquishing the Aspiration to Enlightenment," and the second, "Correctly Relying on the Vow of the Sage," set forth the topic of the vast practice of the bodhisattva. The third, "Seeking Knowledge of Reality," sets forth how to seek the profound reality from the perspective of the Madhyamaka system, which for Bhāviveka is the true reality. The fourth chapter, "Entering the Reality of the Śrāvakas," sets forth how reality is asserted by the Buddhist schools of Vaibhāṣika and Sautrāntika. The fifth chapter, "Entering the Reality of Yogācāra," sets forth how reality is asserted by the Yogācāra Cittamātra. The sixth, seventh, eighth, and ninth chapters set forth how reality is entered by the non-Buddhist schools of Sāṅkhya, Vaiśeṣika, Vedānta, and Mīmāṃsā. The tenth chapter sets forth the achievement of omniscience as the goal. The concluding eleventh chapter praises the Buddha for expounding the two truths.

In two works from the eighth century, the Nālandā scholar Śāntarakṣita's *Compendium of Principles* and Kamalaśīla's *Commentary on the Compendium of Principles*, the assertions of non-Buddhists and Buddhists are extensively delineated. Both the root text and commentary were very famous in India, not only among the Buddhists but among all the schools of tenets. The fundamental assertion of these two treatises remains the view established by the protector Nāgārjuna—that is, the Madhyamaka assertion of no-entityness (*niḥsvabhāva*). However, because it emphasizes the topic of the valid means of knowledge and the modes of logical argument that were delineated well by Dignāga and his heir [Dharmakīrti], it is an extremely important treatise that unites Madhyamaka and Pramāṇa.

Throughout the thirty chapters of the root text and the chapters of the commentary, the assertions of the non-Buddhist and Buddhist schools of tenets are extensively analyzed as a means of establishing that the lack of entityness is the nature of reality and that Dignāga's *Compendium of Valid Knowledge* and Dharmakīrti's Seven Treatises on Valid Knowledge are the correct means for proving that. The first chapter explains the assertions of the atheistic Sāṅkhya, who propound that the primary nature (*prakṛti*) alone is the cause of the environment and its inhabitants. The second deals with the followers of Īśvara. The third deals with the theistic Sāṅkhya, who propound that both the primary nature and Īśvara are the cause of the environment and its inhabitants. [37] The fourth deals with the Lokāyata, who propound that the environment and its inhabitants arise naturally, without a divine or karmic cause. The fifth deals with the followers of Brahmā. The sixth deals with the followers of the Vedas, who propound that this world was created by the [supreme] person. The seventh deals with Nyāya and Vaiśeṣika. The eighth deals with Mīmāṃsā. The ninth deals with the followers of Kapila. The tenth deals with the sky-clad Nirgrantha. The eleventh explains the assertions of the followers of the Upaniṣads.

Then the twelfth chapter explains the assertion of an inexpressible self by the Vātsīputrīya of the Buddhist school. The thirteenth chapter, "Analysis of Permanent Things," explains how various non-Buddhist and Buddhist schools of tenets accept the existence of truly established things either explicitly, implicitly, or indirectly. The fourteenth chapter analyzes the relationship between actions and their effects. After that, five chapters explain the Vaiśeṣika assertion of the six categories, the objects of knowledge. The twentieth chapter analyzes the meaning of words. Then, the twenty-first to twenty-third chapters analyze, respectively, the definition of direct perception, the definition of inference, and other valid means of knowledge. The twenty-fourth chapter analyzes the elements. The twenty-fifth analyzes the three times. The twenty-sixth again analyzes Lokāyata, the school that propounds annihilation. The twenty-seventh analyzes external objects. The twenty-eighth analyzes the Vedas. The twenty-ninth primarily refutes those who propound that the Vedas are a valid source of knowledge and analyzes claims of validity based on inherent properties. Finally, the thirtieth chapter analyzes beings who can see objects that are beyond the senses of others. Thus the assertions of non-Buddhist and Buddhist schools of tenets are extensively discussed.[37] Kamalaśīla's *Commentary* analyzes the general and specific meaning of words in separate chapters, making thirty-one chapters. Apart from that, its other chapters are like those of the root text.

Among the works of non-Buddhist scholars, the most famous of the treatises that gather and set forth the schools of tenets is the *Compendium of All Views* (*Sarvadarśanasaṅgraha*) composed by the Vedānta school author Mādhava, who lived in the fourteenth century. The text has sixteen chapters. The first three deal, respectively, with the Lokāyata, the Buddhists, and the Nirgrantha. Beginning in the fourth chapter, he deals with the tenets of the Vaiṣṇava master Rāmānuja; the tenets of the Dvaita Vedānta master Madhva or Pūrṇaprajña; [38] the tenets of the Śaiva Pāśupata of the Nakulīśa system; the Śaiva of southern India; the tenets of Pratyabhijñā, a type of Śaiva; the tenets of the Raseśvara Śaiva; then the tenets of Vaiśeṣika, Nyāya, Mīmāṃsā, the Grammarians, Sāṅkhya, and Yoga. The sixteenth and final chapter deals with the tenets of Vedānta. He gathers the essential assertions of sixteen different Indian schools and explains them. Because Mādhava himself was a proponent of Vedānta, he considered its tenets to be the highest. According to his own view of the Indian schools of tenets, the lowest were, in order, Lokāyata, Buddhist, and Nirgrantha, which he presents as schools that say "no," and he places them earlier [in the text]. He then sets forth the rest from lowest to highest. Because he considered the tenets of the Sāṅkhya and Yoga schools to be closest to those of Vedānta, he places them at the end. Seeing his own school, the Vedānta, to be the pinnacle, he places it last, as the goal.

In Tibet, the tradition of collecting and analyzing the assertions of the non-Buddhist and Buddhist schools in a single text and then studying them was widespread. To survey it quickly, initially, at the time of the early dissemination in the eighth century, the translator Yeshé Dé composed *An Explanation of Different Views*. After that, the translator Kawa

Paltsek composed *Explanation of the Stages of Views*. At the time of later dissemination, in the eleventh century, Rongzom Paṇḍita Chökyi Sangpo composed *Memoranda on Various Views and Tenets*. After that, there were composed, in order, the lord of reasoning Chapa Chökyi Sengé's *A Summary of Presentations of Non-Buddhist and Buddhist Tenets*, Chekawa's *Tenets*, Chomden Rikpai Raldri's *A Flower Adorning Tenets*, and Üpa Losal's *Treasury of Explanations of Tenets*, Jamgön Sakya Paṇḍita's *Classification of Tenets*, the omniscient Longchenpa's *Treasury of Tenets*, the root text and commentary of Taktsang Lotsāwa's *Complete Knowledge of Tenets*, the Second Dalai Lama Gendun Gyatso's *Ship That Sails the Ocean of Tenets*, the root text and commentary of the omniscient Jamyang Shepa's *Great Tenets*, Changkya Rölpai Dorjé's *Beautiful Adornment of Mount Meru*, as well as many shorter works on tenets by Geluk scholars such as the omniscient Könchok Jikmé Wangpo's *Jeweled Rosary of Tenets*. [39] Later, in the last half of the nineteenth century and the first half of the twentieth century, there were such works as Ju Mipham's *Collection of Tenets, A Wish-Granting Treasury* and Drakar Losang Palden's *Lamp Illuminating Jewels: A Summary of the Essentials of Tenets*.[38]

In these texts, when the non-Buddhist and Buddhist schools are explained, it is based primarily on the root text and commentary of Bhāviveka's *Essence of the Middle Way* and the root text and commentary of Śāntarakṣita's *Compendium of Principles*. In addition, such texts as Āryadeva's *Compendium of the Essence of Wisdom* and its commentary composed by Bodhibhadra, the root text and commentary of Jetāri's *Distinguishing the Sugata's Texts*, and works by other Nālandā scholars and adepts are used as sources. The principal sources for the non-Buddhist schools include the *Verses of Sāṅkhya* (*Sāṅkhyakārikā*), the *Bārhaspatya Sūtra*, the *Compendium of Caraka* (*Carakasaṃhitā*), and Mādhava's text on tenets cited above. [40]

Part 1

Non-Buddhist Schools of Tenets

2

Overview of the Non-Buddhist Schools of Tenets

It is not possible to determine the precise number of tīrthika philosophies. Many sūtras and treatises mention various philosophers. For example, the *Chapters on the Vinaya* says:

> Who are the six logicians? Pūraṇa Kāśyapa, Maskarin Gośālīputra, Sañjayin Vairaṭṭīputra, Ajita Keśakambala, Kakuda Kātyāyana, and Nirgrantha Jñātiputra. Who are the six Vedic masters? Brāhmaṇa Kūṭatāṇḍya, Brāhmaṇa Śroṇatāṇḍya, Brāhmaṇa Cogin, Brāhmaṇa Brāhmāyus, Brāhmaṇa Puṣkarasārī, and Brāhmaṇa Lohitya. Who are the six meditators? Udraka Rāmaputra, Ārāḍa Kālāma, the wanderer Subhadra, the young brahmin Sañjayin, the sage Asita, and the fire-worshiper Uruvilvā Kāśyapa.[39]

Thus it lists eighteen tīrthika teachers. Those tīrthika teachers' assertions also appear in a rough form in the Vinaya scriptures when Mahākāśyapa and the supreme pair of śrāvakas [Śāriputra and Maudgalyāyana] converse with those teachers. The *Chapters on the Vinaya* says:

> Then the two young brahmins, Upatiṣya and Kolita, approached Pūraṇa Kāśyapa and said, "O wise one, what is your teaching? What is your instruction to your disciples? What is the fruition of chastity? What is its benefit?"
>
> Pūraṇa answered, "O young brahmins, I see thus and say this. Giving does not exist. Sacrifice does not exist. Fire ritual does not exist. Good deeds do not exist. Misdeeds do not exist."[40]

"Giving does not exist. Sacrifice does not exist. Fire ritual does not exist. Good deeds do not exist. Misdeeds do not exist." These five statements refute the reality of causation. What is said after that, "The effects and fruitions of good deeds and misdeeds do not exist," refutes effects. The five statements after that—"this world does not exist, [41] the next world does not exist, mother does not exist, father does not exist, miraculously born sentient beings do not exist"—refute both cause and effect. In this way, Kalyāṇamitra accurately and minutely elucidated the meanings of the discussions with other teachers in his *Commentary on Chapters on the Vinaya*.[41] The *Jewel Lamp of the Middle Way* by Bhāviveka the Lesser explains that there was a series of 363 views created by those teachers—Pūraṇa Kāśyapa and so forth.[42]

Also, the *Brahmā's Net Sūtra* says, "O monks, some learned wanderers and brahmins speculate about the past and have delineated views about the past. They expound it and discuss it. Some speculate about the future and have delineated views about the future. They expound it and discuss it. All of these are based on the sixty-two views. There are no more than that."[43] Thus it says that all speculations about the past and all speculations about the future are included among the sixty-two views. As to how they are included, Bhāviveka's *Blaze of Reasoning* says:

> What are those sixty-two wrong views? The *Brahmā's Net Sūtra* says that there are eighteen tīrthikas who speculate about the past. Four among them are eternalists. Four are partial eternalists. Four say [the self and world] are finite and infinite. Four are equivocators. Two say they arise without a cause. Thus there are eighteen. There are forty-four who speculate about the future. Sixteen of them say that there is perception [after death]. Eight say that there is no perception. Eight say that perception is neither existent nor nonexistent. Five say there is nirvāṇa in this lifetime. Seven are annihilationists. Thus they are forty-four.[44]

Those sixty-two views are identified in many texts. Here they are described in some detail based on the extensive description in *Blaze of Reasoning*. The four views of the eternalists are those of non-Buddhist meditators: (1) those with dull faculties capable of remembering twenty eons with their supersensory knowledge of remembering former lives; [42] (2) those with middling faculties who remember forty eons, (3) those with sharp faculties who remember eighty eons, and (4) those with the supernatural ability of the divine eye. When they see sentient beings of good and bad appearance die and be reborn as this and that, they say that the self and the world are eternal, as they see them to be.

There are four views of the partial eternalists: (1) Someone in the retinue of the great Brahmā dies and is reborn as a human. He achieves concentration (*dhyāna*) in solitude and attains supersensory knowledge. Seeing that the great Brahmā has not died, he says that the great Brahmā is eternal and other gods are not eternal. (2) The great Brahmā, seeing that the great elements are not eternal but that the mind does not cease, says that the elements are not eternal but the mind is eternal. (3) A god of the desire realm is seduced by play, and through the force of play, his mindfulness and introspection deteriorate, and he dies and is reborn as a human, where he achieves supersensory knowledge. Seeing with his vision that his former companions did not die, he says that those gods seduced by play are not eternal while others are eternal. (4) A god whose mind is agitated dies for that reason and is reborn as a human. As before, supersensory knowledge arises in him, and with that vision he sees that others did not die. He says that gods with agitated minds are not eternal while others are eternal.

The four views of those who say [that the world] does and does not have an end come about when non-Buddhist rishis with supersensory knowledge wish to investigate whether the world has an end. (1) When they remember the eon of destruction, the perception of an end arises. (2) When they remember the eon of formation, the perception that there is no end arises. (3) When they wish to investigate the limit of the physical universe and do not see beyond the Avīci hell below and the fourth concentration above, the perception of a vertical limit arises. (4) When they do not see a horizontal limit beyond everything, the perception of no horizontal limit arises.

The four views of the equivocators: (1) When asked whether the effects of virtuous and nonvirtuous actions exist, some think, "If I answer, 'they exist,' [I would be lying because] I do not know it through direct perception. If I answer, 'they do not exist,' those with supersensory knowledge would expose my faults," and so they equivocate with various words. (2) When asked whether former and future lives exist, some answer as before. (3) When asked what virtue is, some think, "I know, but if I teach 'virtue is like this,' it would benefit them. If I do not teach, I would be defeated by them," and so they equivocate with words. (4) When some who are very stupid are asked, they cannot answer, and so they equivocate with words. [43]

The two proponents of causelessness: The first are the proponents of causelessness based on concentration. When some sentient beings die in the formless realm and come to be born in the desire realm or the form realm, some rishis with supersensory knowledge look for the previous cause for that and do not see it, and so the view arises that the body and mind arise adventitiously. The second are the proponents of causelessness based on logic. They observe that rain and wind suddenly arise and that trees sometimes have flowers and fruit and sometimes do not, and so they say that the self and the world do not have a cause.

Because all eighteen views above are based on speculations about the past and present, they are called speculation about the past. Because the past and present have already occurred, they are the past.

Among [the forty-four] views that speculate about the future, sixteen are views of those who say that there is perception [after death]. Four are the views that: (1) the perceiving self is physical and to say otherwise is deluded, (2) the perceiving self is not physical, (3) the perceiving self is both, and (4) the perceiving self is neither. Four are the views that: (5) the perceiving self has an end, (6) the perceiving self is endless, (7), the perceiving self is both, and (8) the perceiving self is neither. Four are the views that: (9) the perceiving self is pleasurable, (10) the perceiving self is painful, (11) the perceiving self is both, and (12) the perceiving self is neither. Four are the views that: (13) the perceiving self is one, (14) the perceiving self is many, (15) the perceiving self is small, and (16) the perceiving self is limitless.

For the eight views of those who say that the self does not have perception, change "the perceiving self" in the first eight out of the sixteen above to "the self without perception." That is, viewing the self without perception, there are eight views: the self without perception is physical, not physical, both, neither, has an end, is endless, is both, and is neither.

For the eight views of those who say that the self is neither with perception nor without perception, the former eight are changed to "the self that both has no perception and does not have no perception."

For the seven views of the annihilationists, they count humans, desire realm gods, the entire form realm, and each of the four levels of the formless realm individually, and they view such births as suffering before death and completely annihilated upon dying.

For the five views of those who say there is liberation in this lifetime, one view says that liberation is attained in this lifetime by enjoying sensual pleasures licentiously, and four views say that liberation is attained in this lifetime by attaining the four concentrations. [44]

Among those sixty-two views, these latter forty-four are said to be the speculations about the future because they speculate predominantly about the future. Also, the *Descent into Laṅkā* says:

> (1) Mahāmati, some tīrthikas say that by stopping the aggregates (*skandha*), sources (*āyatana*), and constituents (*dhātu*), becoming free from desire for objects, and seeing what is not eternal, the many minds and mental factors do not arise. By not recollecting past, future, and present objects and by extinguishing causes like a lamp, a seed, and the wind, thought does not function. Therefore they think that this is nirvāṇa. However, Mahāmati, one does not pass into nirvāṇa through the view of annihilation. . . . (22) Some think that one achieves nirvāṇa through seeing no difference between nirvāṇa and mundane existence.[45]

Thus it speaks of twenty-two views. The identification of those twenty-two views is set forth here in the order in which they are described in the commentary on the *Descent into Laṅkā*.[46] (1) The assertion that awareness ceases. (2) The assertion that one attains liberation by coursing like an arrow and landing in another realm. One example is the Jaina assertion that there is an abode like an upright white umbrella, 4.5 million *yojanas* wide, for persons who attain liberation. (3) The system of Īśvara that asserts that the permanent self is liberated when the apprehending mind and the object that is known no longer appear as subject and object. (4) The assertion that one attains liberation based on seeing that the self is permanent and the aggregates are impermanent.

(5) The Vedānta or followers of the Upaniṣads (Aupaniṣada) assert that, by seeing thoughts of various signs to be like tumors and thorns and being frightened of them, the permanent self abandons them and achieves nirvāṇa, the abode of supreme joy. (6) The followers of Brahmā assert that

there is an indestructible self during the three times and one who knows that achieves nirvāṇa. Furthermore, the Buddhist Vaibhāṣika assert that one achieves nirvāṇa by understanding the specific and general characteristics of internal and external phenomena and realizing that the three times are substantially established. (7) The assertion that one who realizes and knows that all phenomena are the nature of the permanent self, and thus are indestructible, achieves nirvāṇa. [45]

(8) The theistic Sāṅkhya assert that one achieves nirvāṇa by seeing the difference between primary nature and the person, knowing that the three qualities are in equilibrium, and pleasing Īśvara by knowing that the permanent Īśvara is the creator of the various transformations. (9) The assertion that one becomes liberated by practicing the yoga that perceives the self and completely exhausts the perceptible signs of meritorious and demeritorious karma.

(10) The assertion that one achieves nirvāṇa, the state of abandonment of all afflictions, by attaining the peak of existence (*bhavāgra*) without realizing reality through wisdom. (11) The assertion that to achieve nirvāṇa one must please Īśvara by seeing that he created the entire world. (12) The assertion that one achieves nirvāṇa when the self is separated from qualities such as hatred and desire, understanding that the world originates from sequential evolution: in dependence on the self, its qualities—afflictions such as hatred and desire—arise; by accumulating karma, one takes rebirth; and this does not arise from another cause such as Īśvara.

(13) The Nyāya assertion that one achieves nirvāṇa by realizing the true path, the sixteen categories. (14) The Vaiśeṣika assertion that the self endowed with the qualities is liberated when the nine qualities of self are completely eliminated. (15) The assertion that one achieves nirvāṇa by seeing that all things arise naturally without a cause. (16) The atheistic Sāṅkhya assertion that one achieves nirvāṇa by comprehending the twenty-five principles.

(17) The assertion that one achieves nirvāṇa through deeds like those of a compassionate king who brings about the welfare of others with love and compassion: When compassionately destroying the dangerous, he separates his own [subjects] from the foe and then goes to war to subjugate the other party and does battle with them. If it is not the right time, he waits. He knows how to conquer a fortress. When the enemy is subdued, he makes a treaty. (18) The assertion that one achieves nirvāṇa by seeing that

time is the creator of the entire world. (19) The assertion that one achieves nirvāṇa by merely enjoying the amusements of the desire realm without developing concentration, and the assertion that one achieves nirvāṇa by cultivating the first, second, third, and fourth concentrations. These are the assertions of five worldly paths that are said to liberate one in this very lifetime. [46]

(20) The assertion that one attains liberation not by abandoning the superimpositions of a self of persons and phenomena but by performing sacrifice at the mouth of the Ganges River. (21) The assertion that perfect knowledge of existence and nonexistence is their true reality, Mahādeva [Śiva]; by fully understanding his nature, one achieves nirvāṇa. (22) The assertion that one achieves nirvāṇa by seeing that there is ultimately no difference between mundane existence and nirvāṇa. This is said to be the Mahāyāna system.

Thus, although most systems explained here are tīrthika assertions, the first, sixth, and twenty-second are Buddhist systems. This is clear from the *Ornament for the Essence of the Tathāgata*, a commentary on the *Descent into Laṅkā Sūtra* composed by the Indian abbot Jñānavajra.

Also, Bhāviveka's *Blaze of Reasoning* says:

> Furthermore, there are eighty such root or fundamental [views]. When divided, there are the Buddhists, those who apprehend nothing, the Ājīvika, the Leaf Clad, the Vedic masters, the Vaiṣṇava . . . and those who view earth, water, fire, wind, and space as sentient. Because all these 363 views have been passed down without interruption, everyone would courageously debate for what is praised in passages of their own sacred texts.[47]

He is saying that eighty fundamental views and 363 divisions existed.

Also, Bodhibhadra's *Explanation of the Compendium on the Essence of Wisdom* says, "If someone asks, 'Are all the views of 363 proponents who debate about this teaching derived from ninety-six impostors as well as the division of the four schools of tenets of this [Buddhist] teaching into eighteen set forth here?' 'Yes, that is why it is called the *Essence* [*of Wisdom*].'"[48] Here, this mentions the views of ninety-six impostors and the 363 debaters issuing from them.

Bhāviveka the Lesser's *Jewel Lamp of the Middle Way* also states:

> There is the series of 363 views formulated by Pūraṇa Kāśyapa, Maskarin Gośālīputra, Sañjayin Vairaṭṭīputra, Nirgrantha Jñātiputra, Ajita Keśakambala, Ārāḍa Kālāma, and Udraka Rāmaputra, [47] the sixty-two views, the twenty peaks of the view of the perishable collection (*satkāyadṛṣṭi*), the twelve views of the creator Puruṣa, the twelve propositions on self, the five views, the three views, and the two views.[49]

Thus it says that there are many divisions of views. The great teacher Vitapāda's *Oral Teaching on Meditation on Reality* commentary also says, "Those are the main speculations. They are said to be infinite, summarized as 570 views."[50] This mention of 570 views is cited here simply to illustrate the many types of views mentioned in the sūtras and treatises.

Thus both philosophy in general and the specific philosophies of the non-Buddhist tīrthikas appeared in India. There are many ways to categorize them, to identify their main texts, and to count them set forth in the ancient texts of both Buddhist and non-Buddhist scholars. Here we will mention the most well known among them. First, Bhāviveka's *Blaze of Reasoning* lists nine groups of the non-Buddhist schools with brief explanations of their assertions: (1) Sāṅkhya, (2) Vaiśeṣika, (3) Vedānta, (4) Mīmāṃsā, (5) Lokāyata, (6) Nirgrantha, (7) followers of Brahmā, (8) Vaiṣṇava, and (9) Śaiva. The *Blaze of Reasoning* says:

> This is the supreme Brahman,
> which Brahmā and the others cannot grasp.

"[Gods] such as Brahmā, Viṣṇu, and Maheśvara take pride in seeing reality."[51] It also says, "Besides Vedānta, Mīmāṃsā also asserts that what appears in the Vedas are self-arisen."[52] It also says:

> Now the power in this scripture is to be understood;
> it is not in any other.

"By teaching this, what the Sāṅkhya, Vaiśeṣika, Nirgrantha, Nāstika, Buddhists, and so forth claim . . ."[53]

Stainless Light, the commentary on the *Kālacakra Tantra*, lists tīrthika tenets in seven groups: (1) Sāṅkhya, (2) followers of Brahmā, (3) Śaiva, (4)

Vaiṣṇava, (5) Lokāyata, (6) Nirgrantha, and (7) Persian. *Stainless Light* also says, "*Degenerate tenets* [48] refers to the tenets of Brahmā, the sun worshipers, the naked ones [Jaina], and the hairy ones. These four degenerates are the degenerate tenets."[54] Āryadeva's *Compendium on the Essence of Wisdom* says:

> The Śaiva and so forth assert that there are qualities.
> For Sāṅkhya, qualities do not exist.
> Brahmins assert Brahmā. They abide in three states.
> The Kāpila are the way of empty space.
> Those who withstand the senses are the way of the sky.
> Those who exhaust [their karma]
> strive to worship images of the Jina.
> Those who regard brahmins as supreme
> think that ātman endowed with five senses exists.
> The Lokāyata scripture is evil,
> saying that neither karma nor liberation exists.
> In the teaching of the Śaiva . . .

It also says:

> Those who hold the tenets of the moon
> are always absorbed in venerating Hari.[55]

Thus it sets forth twelve groups of non-Buddhist tīrthikas. (1) The Śaiva. (2) The Vaiśeṣika who say that time is the cause.[56] (3) The atheistic Sāṅkhya, who do not assert that the origination of various things is a quality of Īśvara. (4) Followers of Brahmā, who assert that they are the sons of Brahmā. (5) Some other Vaiśeṣika. (6) The Kāpila, who assert that environments and inhabitants arise from the empty space. (7) Some other Vaiśeṣika who, out of fear of external objects, restrain their senses and assert that sound and so forth are qualities of space. (8) The Nirgrantha, who assert that karma and afflictions are exhausted by bodily mortification and who have faith in the First Conqueror (Ādijina). (9) The Vedāntin, who say that the independent ātman is endowed with the five senses and that Puruṣa, the creator of the world, exists. (10) The Lokāyata, proponents of an evil scripture that says that karma does not exist, thereby denying causes, and says that liberation does not exist, thereby denying effects. (11) Those Śaiva who practice the way of pleasure via sexual intercourse between male and female. (12) The Vaiṣṇava, who assert that one attains liberation by striving to respectfully venerate Viṣṇu, who always steals. [49]

Śāntarakṣita's *Ornament of the Middle Way* explains the non-Buddhists in this way: (1) followers of Kaṇāda, (2) the Jaina, (3) followers of Jaimini, (4) followers of Bṛhaspati, (5) followers of Kapila, (6) followers of Brahmā, (7) the Vaiṣṇava, (8) the Śaiva, and (9) followers of the Upaniṣads. His *Compendium of Principles* lists: (1) atheistic Sāṅkhya, (2) Śaiva, (3) theistic Sāṅkhya, (4) Lokāyata, (5) followers of Brahmā or Grammarians, (6) followers of the Vedas, (7) Vaiśeṣika, (8) Nyāya, (9) Mīmāṃsā, (10) Nirgrantha, (11) followers of the Upaniṣads. He thus divides Sāṅkhya into two, theistic and atheistic. Organizing them into these eleven groups, he then analyzes them. The followers of Bṛhaspati enumerated in *Ornament of the Middle Way* refer to the Lokāyata, the followers of Kaṇāda to the Vaiśeṣika, and the followers of Jaimini to the Mīmāṃsaka. Also, Grammarians have a position similar to the assertions of the followers of Brahmā in that they regard Brahmā as the teacher and they rely on his scripture. Thus some scholars do not count them separately.[57]

It is explained that some include followers of Brahmā and the Upaniṣads under Mīmāṃsā, Vaiṣṇava and Śaiva under Nyāya, and followers of Yoga under Sāṅkhya. Also, some explain that Nyāya, Vaiśeṣika, Uddyotakara, and Aviddhakarṇa are included under the category of Śaiva, and followers of Brahmā, Mīmāṃsā, followers of the Vedas, Grammarians, followers of Caraka, followers of Jaimini, and followers of the Upaniṣads are included under the category of Vaiṣṇava.[58] Grouped in this way, those systems of tenets are labeled as either Śaiva or Vaiṣṇava because, although there are many tīrthika sects that take refuge in the gods Śiva and Viṣṇu and faithfully worship them, these are the primary ones.

Early Tibetan doxographers divided the non-Buddhists into the five schools of logic: (1) annihilationist Lokāyata, which speaks of annihilation, (2) Sāṅkhya, (3) Śaiva, (4) Vaiṣṇava, and (5) eternalist Nirgrantha—that is, one annihilationist and four eternalists.[59] Later scholars counted one annihilationist and eleven eternalist tīrthika groups based on Śāntarakṣita's *Compendium of Principles* and Dignāga's *Compendium of Valid Knowledge* and his commentary on it.[60] [50]

In the tīrthikas' own texts, the classification of the *ṣaḍdarśana*, or six views, is well known. However, it is said that this was primarily used by Vedānta scholars after the twelfth century.[61] Thus Indian philosophy is divided into two—Āstika and Nāstika. Within the former, there are Sāṅkhya, Yoga, Vaiśeṣika, Nyāya, Mīmāṃsā, and Vedānta. Within the latter, Nāstika, there are Lokāyata, Buddhist, and Nirgrantha. This way of dividing them is widespread up to the present. The six Āstika schools are not different in that they recognize the authority of the Vedas, they evolved from a section of the Vedas—the Upaniṣad—and they all say that a permanent ātman exists. However, among them, the views of the first two, the middle two—Nyāya and Vaiśeṣika—and the last two—Mīmāṃsā and Vedānta—are very similar. Therefore, here in this volume, the chapters on the six schools are set forth in the same sequence. As mentioned above, the non-Buddhist master Mādhava's *Compendium of All Views* sets forth the three Nāstika schools—Lokāyata, Buddhist, and Nirgrantha—first. Then, in the Āstika section, it places first the holders of Vaiṣṇava and Śaiva tenets prevalent in his region of South India. After that, it organizes and delineates the earlier schools in the order of Vaiśeṣika, Nyāya, Mīmāṃsā, the Grammarians, Sāṅkhya, and Yoga; it places Vedānta last as the pinnacle of tenets. [51]

3

The Sāṅkhya School

How This School of Tenets Arose

The Sāṅkhya, or followers of Kapila, are generally regarded as the first proponents of tenets in India. Its philosophy originated long ago, and many texts of its ancient masters are no longer extant. Even the famous commentaries on the root text of Sāṅkhya were produced only after the lineage of this system had already ended. For these reasons, we lack the means to describe its history and doctrines in their entirety. Nevertheless, its principal assertions, based on what appears in the texts of the ancient Buddhist and non-Buddhis masters of India, will be briefly explained in three sections: (1) how this school of tenets arose, (2) its definition and divisions, and (3) its doctrines.

According to what is generally known, the Sāṅkhya school originated from the ancient rishi named Kapila. Such things as the period when he lived were explained above in the brief description of the history of Indian philosophy. The teacher Kapila's name is not mentioned in the Vedic hymns, the earliest knowledge system of India. However, this passage appears in the Upaniṣads, produced at the end of the Vedic period: "Kapila, born of the seer, together with his supreme knowledge."[62] From passages such as this, one can infer that this teacher appeared before the beginning of the Common Era.

Modern researchers explain the history of this system by connecting three periods with three ways of explaining the meaning of the Sanskrit word *sāṅkhya*, or "enumeration." When *sāṅkhya* is used as an adjective, the word applies to an enumerated set; it is appropriate to use it in any branch of science, such as mathematics, grammar, prosody, and medicine. When taken in this way, this method of enumeration appears, for instance, in the ancient treatises on statecraft (*nītiśāstra*) and in medical texts. When used as a masculine noun, the word refers to a person who uses the principles of enumeration. When used as a neuter noun, *sāṅkhya* is a philosophical delineation that brings about final liberation by enumerating objects of knowledge, the fundamental components of internal and external phenomena, and understanding the way they exist. [52]

These three explanations correspond to the following three periods. The first is from more than a thousand years before the Common Era. The second starts from around the eighth century before the Common Era. The third is from around the first century before the Common Era. What is widely known today as the Sāṅkhya system of tenets, endowed with a variety of philosophical views, appeared in the third period.[63]

According to the explanations that appear in non-Sāṅkhya texts concerning the lineage of the teachers of this philosophy, the direct disciple of the rishi Kapila was Āsuri, and his direct disciple was Pañcaśikha, who composed many Sāṅkhya texts. According to the *Verses of Sāṅkhya* (*Sāṅkhyakārikā*, a.k.a. *Īśvarakṛṣṇa's Tantra*), which explains the tradition begun by the rishi Kapila:

> The sage who had achieved the peak of purity
> conveyed it to Āsuri with compassion.
> By Āsuri to Pañcaśikha,
> who greatly expanded the tradition.[64]

In addition, that Āsuri was the direct disciple of the teacher and rishi Kapila is clearly attested in the *Commentary on the Yoga Sūtra* composed by the rishi Vyāsa.[65] That the master Pañcaśikha was the direct disciple of Āsuri is attested in the Indian historical texts *Vāmanapurāṇa*, *Jaigīṣavya*, *Voḍhu*, the *Kūrmapurāṇa*, and the *Vāyupurāṇa*.

The names of the lineage of disciples of Pañcaśikha are Āvāḍya, Janaka, Varṣa, Vārṣagaṇya, Vyāḍi, Bhārgava, Ulūka, Vālmīki, Hārīta, Devala, Bāddhali, Kairāta, Paurika, Ṛṣabheśvara, Patañjali, Kauṇḍinya, Garga, Yāska, Āṣṭeṣeṇa, and Īśvarakṛṣṇa.[66] However, apart from the names of those masters who maintained the tradition after Pañcaśikha, details such as their sequence and dates do not appear in the Sāṅkhya texts. After the master Īśvarakṛṣṇa there was a master named Vindhyavāsin, also known as Rudrila, who appears to have been a contemporary of the Buddhist master Vasubandhu. [53]

Buddhist texts state merely that the teacher Kapila first founded this Sāṅkhya system of tenets and that the rishi Arhat, Maheśvara, and the teacher Patañjali appeared after that. There is little that is clear on this system's history beyond this.

The extant root text setting forth the Sāṅkhya philosophy seems to be the *Sāṅkhya Sūtra*, known to be composed by the rishi Kapila. In addition, the *Verses of Sāṅkhya*, composed by Īśvarakṛṣṇa—known as the "Tantra of the Black Lord" to Tibetan scholars—was translated from Sanskrit into Chinese around 600. It was translated into Tibetan in 1974. Since it is explained that this master named Īśvarakṛṣṇa appeared around the fourth century, he was also probably a contemporary of Asaṅga and his brother [Vasubandhu].[67] The text known as the *Sāṅkhya Sūtra* is said to date from a very ancient time, but because it contains refutations of the Jains, Buddhists, and others, it seems it is a compilation by a later scholar.

In addition to those two texts mentioned above, the *Yoga Sūtra* by the teacher Patañjali, the founder of theistic Sāṅkhya, should be counted as a root text of Sāṅkhya. It primarily sets forth how to practice internal yoga and secondarily how to worship Īśvara. It thus appears to be a founding treatise of the philosophy of theistic Sāṅkhya. Moreover, Dignāga's *Autocommentary on the Compendium of Valid Knowledge* says, "Mādhava, the destroyer of Sāṅkhya, transgressing the earlier system of the Kāpila, says. . ."[68] This is stating and then refuting the assertions of a later Sāṅkhya master who transgressed the earlier Sāṅkhya system. Therefore that system [of Mādhava] is also a variety of Sāṅkhya assertions.

The Definition and Divisions of Sāṅkhya

The Tibetan word *grangs can*, "enumeration," is the translation of the Sanskrit *sāṅkhya*. There are various ways of explaining the meaning of that word, and some were explained above. There are also two key explanations related to the sense of "number" specifically. Regarding the first, this philosophy is known as Sāṅkhya because it propounds tenets from the perspective of dividing everything into twenty-five categories of objects of knowledge or principles (*tattva*) and then examining and analyzing them. [54] Regarding the second, the eternal self, or puruṣa, of this system is said to be an eternally changeless entity. It consists of former and latter parts, and in each there exists 4.32 billion fractions of the seedlike puruṣa.

Taken together, 8.64 billion fractions of puruṣa exist. Similarly, they say that puruṣa's consciousness is endowed with exactly that number [of parts]. For this reason, it is called Sāṅkhya.[69] Thus, because this system of tenets asserts the definite number of twenty-five for objects of knowledge and asserts the definite number above for the knower puruṣa or consciousness, there are these two explanations of the meaning of the word *sāṅkhya*.

There are also explanations that are not from the perspective of number: According to the system of the Jaina scholar Somatilaka Sūri, *sāṅkhya* refers to Śaṅkha, a name for puruṣa. Because it is their tenet to accept that puruṣa as reality, it is named after him.[70] This explanation is somewhat similar to the above-mentioned explanation in which the name was given based on the number of [parts of] puruṣa's consciousness.

There is another explanation.[71] As is clear in ancient texts such as the *Mahābhārata*, the *Compendium of Ahirbudhnya* (*Ahirbudhnyasaṃhitā*) and the *Compendium of Caraka* (*Carakasaṃhitā*), *sāṅkhya* is the knowledge of correct understanding. That knowledge refers to a correct wisdom that understands that the twenty-four principles (*tattva*) of the primary nature (*prakṛti*) are different from the person (*puruṣa*). Because their position is to set forth such correct wisdom, they are called the Sāṅkhya. In short, in those texts, [Sāṅkhya] seems to be explained as the knowledge or correct knowledge of the reality of all objects of knowledge.

Turning to the works of Buddhist scholars, Bhāviveka's *Blaze of Reasoning* says, "They are called the Sāṅkhya because they assert that one is liberated by engaging in enumeration or by completely understanding enumeration."[72] This is saying that they are called the Sāṅkhya because they assert that one is liberated through complete understanding of the characteristics of the twenty-five enumerated objects of knowledge. Bodhibhadra's *Explanation of the Compendium on the Essence of Wisdom* says, "Because they say that there is a specific number of causes for the arising of things, they are called the Sāṅkhya; they say that things are produced by causes that are enumerated."[73] This is explaining that because they enumerate—that is, delineate the causes for the arising of things—they are called the Sāṅkhya. [55]

Regarding the synonyms for the school:

> The "followers of Kapila," "proponents of three qualities,"
> "proponents of primary nature," "having consciousness,"

"those who say primal substance is the cause," "upholders of
the thirty,"
and "enumerators." These are the synonyms.[74]

They are called "followers of Kapila" because they set forth tenets delineated by the teacher Kapila. They are the "proponents of three qualities" because they assert that the primary nature is endowed with the three qualities of *rajas* (mobility), *tamas* (darkness), and *sattva* (lightness). They are called the "proponents of primary nature" because they accept the existence of the primary nature. They are called "having consciousness" because they assert that the independent self [or puruṣa] has a nature of consciousness. They are the "proponents of primal substance as the cause" because they assert that the primal substance (*pradhāna*) or primary nature (*prakṛti*) is the creator or the cause of the world. They are called "upholders of the thirty" because they revere the text called *Treatise on the Thirty* (**Triṃśikaśāstra*), said to have been composed by the teacher Patañjali under the protection of Īśvara, and because they assert that there are thirty enumerations of the self. They are called "enumerators" because they assert that objects of knowledge are enumerated in twenty-five principles, as explained above. These are the seven different synonyms.

The Sāṅkhya school is defined as a school of tenets of tīrthika philosophers whose fundamental tenet is that all objects of knowledge are included in twenty-five principles upon which the basis, path, and fruition are delineated.

There are two divisions: atheistic Sāṅkhya and theistic Sāṅkhya. The first sets forth a philosophy in which worldly abodes, bodies, resources, and so forth directly or indirectly arise only from the primary nature, and afterward, having dissolved only into the primary nature, liberation is attained. They do not accept any other agent, such as the god Īśvara, and so are called the "atheistic Sāṅkhya." This is how they are described in Kamalaśīla's *Commentary on the Compendium of Principles*, "According to the followers of Kapila . . . [Śāntarakṣita's] specification 'solely from the primal substance' (*pradhānād eva*) is meant to exclude [other agents] such as puruṣa. The term 'only from' (*kevalāt*) is meant to eliminate the Īśvara imagined by the theistic Sāṅkhya. The word 'arise' (*pravarttante*) means to directly or indirectly produce."[75] [56]

The second are called the theistic Sāṅkhya because they assert that although cause and effect have the same nature, they say that transformation occurs through the control of the great god, Īśvara. This theistic Sāṅkhya emerged after the appearance of the tīrthika teacher Patañjali. Their position is that the primary nature does not have intention and, lacking that, is unable to control or produce environments and inhabitants. Because its inability is permanent, it is not able to produce its own effect. Therefore these various environments and inhabitants do not originate solely from the primary nature. Because it is also inappropriate for puruṣa to be a creator, they assert that Īśvara, in dependence on the primary nature, is the creator of effects. Thus the *Commentary on the Compendium of Principles* says, "Some Sāṅkhya say that these different effects do not originate solely from the primary nature because it is devoid of intention. That which lacks intention lacks control, and so the creation of its own effect is not seen. It is not appropriate for puruṣa to control because it is not conscious at that time [of creation]."[76] The same text says, "Therefore Īśvara is the creator of different effects in dependence on the primary nature, not alone. As it is said, someone named Devadatta does not produce [a child] by himself. A potter does not produce a pot by himself."[77]

In short, according to the *Compendium of Principles* root text and its commentary, Sāṅkhya is divided into two, theistic and atheistic Sāṅkhya, based on whether they assert that worldly abodes, bodies, and resources arise just from the primary nature or from the prior intention of a deity such as Īśvara. Both systems of Sāṅkhya are further divided into two. An effect exists as the same nature as its cause in its unmanifest mode and is made manifest by conditions. One system calls this *production*. The other tradition speaks of *transformation*, like yogurt being the nature of milk at the time it is milk and later turning into yogurt as a result of conditions.

Sāṅkhya Assertions

A Brief Presentation of the Twenty-Five Objects of Knowledge

Regarding the assertions of the Sāṅkhya school, the verse summary says:

> Sāṅkhya includes all objects of knowledge
> under the primary nature and self. [57]
> They say that there are twenty-four primary materials
> and one permanent consciousness.[78]

As it says, this system includes and delineates all phenomena in twenty-five objects of knowledge: (1) puruṣa, the conscious self, (2) the primal substance (*pradhāna*) [or primary nature (*prakṛti*)], (3) intellect (*buddhi*), or the great one (*mahat*), and (4) ego (*ahaṃkāra*). Then the five subtle elements (*tanmātra*): (5) form (*rūpa*), (6) sound (*śabda*), (7) smell (*gandha*), (8) taste (*rasa*), and (9) object of touch (*sparśa*). Then the five sense faculties (*buddhīndriya*): (10) eye (*cakṣus*), (11) ear (*śrotra*), (12) nose (*ghrāṇa*), (13) tongue (*rasana*), and (14) body (*sparśana*). Then the five action faculties (*karmendriya*): (15) voice (*vāc*), (16) hand (*pāṇi*), (17) foot (*pāda*), (18) anus (*pāyu*), (19) sex organ (*upastha*), and (20) the mind (*manas*) that has the nature of both sense and action organs. In addition, there are the five coarse elements: (21) earth (*pṛthivī*), (22) water (*āpas*), (23) fire (*tejas*), (24) wind (*vāyu*), and (25) space (*ākāśa*).

The Sāṅkhya assertion of the twenty-five objects of knowledge is clearly attested, even in Buddhist sūtras. For example, the *Great Sūtra on the Final Nirvāṇa* (*Mahāparinirvāṇasūtra*) says:

> The Bhagavan said, "Is the *primary nature* you speak of permanent or impermanent?"
>
> The brahmin replied, "What I call the *primary nature* is permanent."
>
> "Brahmin, is that primary nature the cause of all internal and external phenomena?"
>
> He replied, "Yes, it is."
>
> The Bhagavan said, "Brahmin, how is it the cause?"
>
> He replied, "Gautama, the great one is born from the primary nature. Ego is born from the great one. The sixteen principles are born from ego. They are earth, water, fire, wind, space, five sense faculties—eye, ear, nose, tongue, and body—five action faculties—hand, foot, mouth, anus, and male and female organs—and the faculty equivalent to mind. These sixteen principles are born from the five principles of form, sound, smell, taste, and objects of touch."[79]

This is clearly set forth in the same way in many Buddhist treatises, such as the *Blaze of Reasoning*.

Among the twenty-five objects of knowledge, they accept that puruṣa, the conscious self, is consciousness and the remaining twenty-four [principles] are matter. All of the Indian Buddhist and non-Buddhist philosophers who accept the categories of cause and effect are similar in asserting that when there is an effect, there is a cause, and when there is no cause, there is no effect. Sāṅkhya asserts that all effects exist at the time of their own causes in a way that is not evident to the sense faculties. This is illustrated by yogurt at the time of milk and a rice sprout at the time of a rice seed existing in an unmanifest way. [58] A rice sprout that is unmanifest at the time of a rice seed becomes manifest as an object of the sense faculties by the power of all the conditions—such as water, manure, heat, and time—being complete. This is called *production*. Because both the rice seed and the rice sprout exist as one in the primary nature in that way, they assert that cause and effect are of the same nature.

Otherwise, they believe, if an effect did not exist at the time that its cause was produced, the fault would ensue that everything would be produced from everything: darkness would arise from a flame and oil would arise from sand. Therefore this school holds that because cause and effect exist as one in the primary nature, they are the same nature. This school's own *Īśvarakṛṣṇa's Tantra* contains many logical proofs for the necessity that whatever is an effect must exist at the time of its cause. These will be explained below.

Turning to how the self experiences objects, when the self or puruṣa wishes to experience an object, the primary nature emits such things as sounds, and their images or shapes appear to the intellect. The image of self also appears to the intellect, and the two images become mixed. This is how the self experiences objects or how the self knows the objects that appear to the intellect. Several of the most important assertions of this system, such as saying that the puruṣa, the conscious self, is permanent, partless, and independent will be explained here.

In general, the twenty-five objects of knowledge are enumerated and are divided into four categories: cause only, effect only, both cause and effect, and neither cause nor effect. (1) The category of being only a nature, or cause, consists of the primary nature alone. It is asserted to be the creator of all transformations or effects. (2) The category of being only a transformation or effect consists of sixteen principles: the five coarse elements of earth, water, fire, wind, and space; the five action faculties of voice, hand, foot, anus, and sex organ; and the five sense faculties of eye, ear, nose, tongue, and body. To these fifteen principles, the mental faculty is added, making sixteen. (3) The category of being both nature and transformation, or both cause and effect, consists of seven principles: intellect or the great one, ego, and the subtle elements of form, sound, smell, taste, and touch. They are effects because they arise from the primary nature. They are also causes because they produce their own effects, such as the five coarse elements. (4) The group of being neither nature nor transformation, or neither cause nor effect, consists of puruṣa, the conscious self. The *Verses of Sāṅkhya* says:

> The primary nature is not transformation.
> The seven beginning with the great one are both natures and
> transformations. [59]
> The sixteen are transformations.
> Puruṣa is neither nature nor transformation.[80]

Many Buddhist treatises, such as Candrakīrti's *Autocommentary on Entering the Middle Way* and Kamalaśīla's *Commentary on the Compendium of Principles*, cite this verse when they discuss the Sāṅkhya assertions. At the beginning of his chapter on Sāṅkhya in his *Compendium of All Views*, the non-Buddhist master Mādhava also provides a summary of this system's assertions based on this very method of classifying the natures and transformations.[81]

The Nature of Each of the Twenty-Five Objects of Knowledge

1) Among the twenty-five objects of knowledge, puruṣa, the conscious self, has many qualities. Because it cognizes objects, it is consciousness. Because it is not composed by causes and conditions, it is unborn. Because it is neither created nor decays, it is permanent. Because it experiences happiness and suffering, it is the enjoyer. Because it pervades all transmigrating beings, it is the pervader.[82] It lacks the primary nature's qualities of *rajas* (mobility), *tamas* (darkness), and *sattva* (lightness). It is not the creator of transformations. Something is said to have activity when it enters a place that is not occupied. However, because there is no place that it does not occupy, it has no activity.[83] Because it lacks parts, it is unitary. It has neither beginning nor end. Candrakīrti's *Entering the Middle Way* says:

> Ātman, imagined by the tīrthikas, is the enjoyer,
> permanent, real, not a creator, without qualities and actions.[84]

The synonyms for puruṣa, the conscious self, are ātman (self), consciousness, awareness, sentient being, and the person.

2) The *primary nature* provides whatever the self wishes, like a servant who fulfills the wishes of his master. It has no consciousness and understands no object, and so, between object and subject, it is only an object. It is the creator of various transformations. Because it is not produced, it is eternal. Because it has no parts, it is unitary. [60] It pervades all causes and effects, all environments and inhabitants. It is asserted to be an object of knowledge in which the three qualities—mobility, darkness, and lightness—are in equilibrium. Thus Bhāviveka says in his *Essence of the Middle Way*:

> The primary nature is unconscious,
> consists of three qualities, and has the nature of creation.[85]

The *Commentary on the Compendium of Principles* says, "The primal substance, the primary nature imagined by the Sāṅkhya, has the qualities of *rajas*, *tamas*, *sattva*."[86]

Among the three qualities, *rajas* causes suffering, *tamas* causes delusion, and *sattva* causes pleasure. When the three qualities are in equilibrium, they do not cause any transformations. However, when the three qualities lose their equilibrium, the quality that is predominant becomes manifest and creates transformations; it is said that the primary nature emanates transformations. For example, in the state of milk, sweetness and sourness remain in equilibrium; when sourness becomes predominant, yogurt manifests. The synonyms of the primary nature are nature, the chief one, and the primary one.

Such a primary nature has these qualities: (1) It has the nature of unconscious matter. (2) It has the nature of the three qualities in equilibrium. (3) It is the creator of all transformations. (4) It is not an effect or transformation. (5) It is cause only. (6) Because its nature was not evident even to the rishi Kapila, it is unmanifest. (7) It has the nature of permanence. (8) It pervades all objects of knowledge. (9) It is unitary. The *Blaze of Reasoning* says:

> The primary nature exists and is not endowed with consciousness. It is also unproduced and permanent. It is the object of experience of the agent (*puruṣa*). It is unitary, all-pervading, and endowed with the three qualities. It is unmanifest because it cannot be perceived by any gods, demigods, or human beings by way of characteristics like color, size, and shape.[87]

3) *Intellect* has the characteristics of determining or ascertaining objects. Like a clear mirror, it is matter in which reflections of both external objects and the internal puruṣa appear. Regarding this, the *Verses of Sāṅkhya* says, "Intellect is determination."[88] Similarly, the Buddhist text *Commentary on the Compendium of Principles* says, "The word 'great' (*mahat*) refers to intellect (*buddhi*). Intellect has the characteristic of ascertaining objects, as in 'this is a pot' or 'this is a cloth.'"[89] [61] To intellect, which is like a two-sided mirror, reflections of internal puruṣa and external objects appear, but puruṣa is changeless. For example, even though a reflection of a face appears in a mirror, the face does not change. Regarding this, the *Blaze of Reasoning* says, "Or, [puruṣa] imitates the acts of comprehension of the object by the intellect, which is transformed like a reflection in a mirror; [puruṣa] is not transformed."[90]

4) *Ego* is the overt pride that clings to such things as having a good lineage and abundant wealth. The *Verses of Sāṅkhya* says, "Ego is clinging."[91] Also, the *Blaze of Reasoning* says, "The conception of 'I' is that which takes pride in 'I' and 'mine.'"[92] There are three different kinds: *sattva*-dominant ego, *tamas*-dominant ego, and *rajas*-dominant ego. These are also called, respectively, ego from transformation, ego from the elements, and ego from energy.

5–9) Regarding the *five sense faculties* such as eye, the *Verses of Sāṅkhya* says:

> Eye, ear, nose, tongue,
> and body are the sense faculties.[93]

The reason they are called *sense faculties* (literally "faculty of intellect," *buddhīndriya*) is because the eye and so forth cognize their own objects such as form, they engage with their objects before intellect does, and they are the doors for the sense consciousnesses to engage with objects. Thus the *Blaze of Reasoning* says, "The five—ear, body, eye, tongue, and nose—are the sense faculties. They are called *sense faculties* because they cognize their own objects, or because they engage [with objects] before intellect, or because puruṣa cognizes objects due to their being the doors [to objects]."[94]

10–14) Regarding the identification of the *five action faculties* beginning with voice, the *Verses of Sāṅkhya* says: [62]

> Voice, hand, foot, anus, and sex organ
> are called action faculties.[95]

They are called the *action faculties* because they control actions, such as speaking words and taking things. Pūrṇavardhana's *Investigating Characteristics: A Commentary on the Treasury of Abhidharma* says:

> Sāṅkhya understands the voice faculty and so forth to be different from the sense faculties such as the eye. The voice faculty is that by which one speaks words. The hand faculty is that by which one takes things. The foot faculty is that by which one moves—that is, walks. The anus faculty is that by which one excretes feces. The sex organ faculty is different from the body faculty. It is that by which one attains the pleasure of complete joy.[96]

Also, the *Blaze of Reasoning* says, "Voice, hand, foot, anus, and sex organ function before actions. Because they remain close to the actions of a person, they are called the *action faculties*."[97]

15) The *mind faculty* has the nature of both the sense and action faculties. The *Verses of Sāṅkhya* says, "Here, mind has the nature of both."[98] Also, the *Blaze of Reasoning* says, "Mind has the nature of both. Being associated with cognition, it is a sense faculty. Being associated with activity, it is an action faculty."[99]

Regarding the difference between the three—intellect, ego, and mind—the *Commentary on the Compendium of Principles* says:

> There [in *Verses of Sāṅkhya* 22 just quoted] the word "great" (*mahat*) refers to intellect (*buddhi*). Intellect has the character-

> istic of ascertaining objects, as in "this is a pot" or "this is a cloth." Ego has the characteristic of overt pride, as in "I am fortunate" or "I am good-looking." Mind has the characteristic of conceptualizing. For example, a child hears that there will be a feast in another village. Thinking, "I will go there," he wonders whether there will be molasses and yogurt or only yogurt. Engaging in such thoughts is called *mind*. This is how the mutual differences between intellect, ego, and mind should be understood.[100] [63]

16–25) In addition, there are the *five subtle elements* such as form and sound and the *five coarse elements* such as earth. Someone might ask, "The five such as form and sound are called *subtle elements*. Why aren't the five coarse elements called that?" The five coarse elements have many different natures, such as being peaceful and wrathful, whereas there are no such distinguishing features in the nature of the five such as form and sound. Therefore they are called *subtle elements* (*tanmātra*, literally "just that"). Thus the *Blaze of Reasoning* says, "Because earth and so forth differ from the subtle elements due to their natures of being peaceful, wrathful, and so forth, they are different."[101]

In short, all Buddhist and non-Buddhist philosophers agree in asserting that, among the twenty-five objects of knowledge, twenty principles—the ten faculties, the five coarse elements, and the five subtle elements—are forms (*rūpa*). Sāṅkhya in particular asserts that even the primary nature, mind, ego, and intellect, or the great one, are material forms.

When those twenty-five objects of knowledge are organized, they can be grouped into two categories—ultimate truths and conventional falsities. The primary nature, the supreme object of knowledge, which is not manifest as a sense object, and puruṣa, the conscious self, are the ultimate truths. The twenty-three principles other than those two—the great one and so forth—are asserted to be conventional or false since they manifest as sense objects and are without essence, like a magician's illusion. A Sāṅkhya text quoted in the *Commentary on the Ornament of the Middle Way* says, "The great rishi Kapila said that the supreme nature of [three] qualities cannot be seen. That which can be seen is unreal, like an illusion."[102]

Another way of organizing the twenty-five objects of knowledge is into the manifest and unmanifest. The unmanifest are the ultimate objects of knowledge explained above. The manifest are the conventional objects of knowledge. The manifest have nine distinctive features: (1) Because they are produced by the primary nature, they are caused. (2) Because they have the quality of being produced, they are impermanent. (3) Because they do not pervade everything, they are not pervasive. (4) Because they are produced, they are not the support but the supported. (5) Because they are observed in many forms, they are many. (6) Because they have a nature of dissolution, they are marks, or *liṅga*. (7) Because they have the activities of intellect, ego, and the eleven faculties, they are active. [64] (8) Because they have parts, such as sound, they are composite. (9) Because they depend on a cause, they are dependent. Therefore the twenty-three objects of knowledge of intellect and so on are the manifest, and opposite of that, the two objects of knowledge—the primary nature and puruṣa—that do not have those features are the unmanifest. The *Verses of Sāṅkhya* says:

> The manifest is caused, impermanent, nonpervasive,
> not a support, many, dissolvable, active,
> composite, and dependent.
> The unmanifest is the opposite of that.[103]

The Stages of Arising and Dissolution of the Twenty-Five Objects of Knowledge

The primordial substance or primary nature and puruṣa do not depend on any cause or condition and are therefore self-arisen. According to atheistic Sāṅkhya, when puruṣa wishes to enjoy objects such as sound, it joins with the primary nature, and through that the primary nature emanates these various objects of knowledge. According to theistic Sāṅkhya, when puruṣa wishes to enjoy form, sound, and so forth, the primary nature emanates various objects of knowledge through Maheśvara's control.

Initially, the primary nature emanates intellect or the great one, which is like a two-sided mirror, for the sake of puruṣa's enjoyment. When puruṣa looks at that, the reflection of puruṣa itself arises. After [puruṣa] observes that, ego, which takes pride in the self, is produced. This is how ego is produced from intellect or the great one. Regarding that ego, from among the three, the first, the *sattva*-dominant ego, produces the eleven faculties, the eye and so forth. The second, the *tamas*-dominant ego, produces the five subtle elements—form, sound, and so forth. The third, the *rajas*-dominant ego, is the nature of the previous two egos.[104] Analogies of these three are, respectively, eleven sons of a brahmin mother and five sons of a *śūdra* mother who are fathered by a single brahmin who is the husband of both. From the five subtle elements, the five coarse elements (*mahābhūta*) are produced. From the subtle element of sound, space is produced. From the subtle element of touch, wind. [65] From the subtle element of form, fire. From the subtle element of taste, water. From the subtle element of smell, earth. This is how the five coarse elements originate from the subtle particles of the five subtle elements. This is described in the *Verses of Sāṅkhya*:

> From the primary nature, the great.
> From that ego arises, from that the group of sixteen.
> From five of those sixteen, the five elements arise.[105]

Avalokitavrata's *Commentary on the Lamp of Wisdom* says:

> From the signless and unmanifest primary nature, the great one, which is slightly manifest and merely transformed, is produced. From the great one, a fully manifest ego is produced. That ego is of three kinds: one consisting of transformations, one consisting of energy, and one consisting of elements. From the *sattva*-dominant ego consisting of transformations, the eleven faculties are produced: eye, ear, tongue, body, mind, voice, leg, hand, anus, and sex organ. Among them, the five beginning with eye are the sense faculties. The five beginning with voice are the action faculties. The mental faculty has the nature of both; it abides in the sense faculties as well as in the action faculties. From the *tamas*-dominant ego consisting of the elements, the five subtle elements originate: the subtle element of sound, the subtle element of touch, the subtle element of taste, the subtle element of form, and the subtle element of smell. The *rajas*-dominant ego consisting of energy is the nature of both. Imagine that a certain brahmin has two wives, one brahmin and one *śūdra*, and the brahmin wife has eleven sons, while the *śūdra* wife has five sons. Ego consisting of transformations is like the

> brahmin wife, and the eleven faculties are like her eleven sons. Ego consisting of elements is like the *śūdra* wife, and the five subtle elements are like her five sons. Ego consisting of energy is like the brahmin man.[106]

Turning to the stages of dissolution, having mistakenly conflated the two—the active primary nature, which is like a blind man with legs, and the inactive puruṣa, which is like a lame man with eyes—puruṣa proudly imagines that the activities of the primary nature are its own. As long as this continues, it cycles in saṃsāra. At some point, puruṣa finds fault with objects and contemplates the nature of the twenty-five principles. When, through achieving superior knowledge (*abhijñā*) based on concentration (*dhyāna*), it realizes that the primary nature and puruṣa are different, the primary nature no longer emanates the manifest [principles] and does not follow puruṣa. [66] Not only does it not join with [puruṣa], it separates from it. At that time, the five coarse elements dissolve into the five subtle elements. Up to the point that intellect or the great one dissolves into the primary nature, the manifest principles dissolve, in reverse order of their production, and finally dissolve into the primary nature. When they become unmanifest nature and puruṣa abides in the state of isolation (*kaivalya*), liberation is attained, so they assert.

In short, just as a dancer, having performed various dances, stops dancing, the primary nature emanates various transformations, such as the great one, for puruṣa's enjoyment. When it shows itself to puruṣa, the transformations dissolve in the reverse order of their production. The *Verses of Sāṅkhya* says:

> A female dancer, having performed for an audience,
> withdraws from dancing.
> In the same way, the primary nature
> shows itself to puruṣa and withdraws.[107]

The Subject, the Cognizing Intellect

Among the twenty-five principles, puruṣa, intellect, ego, the five sense faculties, and mind are asserted to be the subjects. Among these, the assertions on the person or puruṣa will be explained below. The definition of the intellect or great one has already been provided above; we now turn to the assertions about the intellect.

Intellect has eight features. Four are related to *sattva* (lightness), which has the qualities of virtue (*dharma*), knowledge (*jñāna*), nonattachment (*virāga*), and might (*aiśvarya*). The other four are related to *tamas* (darkness), which has the opposite qualities of nonvirtue, ignorance, attachment, and impotence. Intellect has these eight.

Among them, (1) *virtue* refers to the causes of high rebirth such as kindness, ethics, and giving. (2) *Knowledge* is the understanding of external objects of knowledge—that is, the fields of science (*vidyāsthāna*)—and internal objects of knowledge such as the primary nature and puruṣa. (3) *Nonattachment* is the lack of attachment to external desirable qualities and to the internal puruṣa and so forth. (4) *Might* refers to the eight mighty capacities. Because it has the power to move, having taken on a very minute form, might has the quality of minuteness. Because it has the power to pervade the world, having taken on a huge form, it has the quality of greatness. Because it has the power to travel to objects, having become as light as cotton fluff, it has the quality of lightness. [67] Because it has the power to acquire whatever object it desires, it has the quality of attainment. Because it has the power to achieve whatever it desires, it has the quality of acting as it wishes. Because it becomes the master of the three realms—below the earth, on the earth, and above the earth—it has the quality of sovereignty. Because it has the power to control all environments and inhabitants, it has the quality of control. Because it has the power to dwell at will in places from the great (the world) to the small (minute particles), it has the quality of abiding wherever it wishes. Might has these eight capacities. Their opposite has qualities related to *tamas*. The *Verses of Sāṅkhya* says:

> Intellect is determination.
> Virtue, knowledge, nonattachment, and might—
> these are its *sattva*-related natures.
> Their opposite are its *tamas* [natures].[108]

If intellect is divided, there are three: viewing, seeing, and determining. Because the first two observe just the entity of the object, they are nonconceptual perception. Because the third observes the qualities of objects, it is asserted to be conceptual. The five sense faculties engage with present objects; the internal organs—intellect, ego, and mind—apprehend all objects of knowledge of the three times. Thus the *Verses of Sāṅkhya* says:

> The five are asserted to engage in just viewing form and so forth.[109]

The same text says:

> The objects of the external belong to the present.
> The internal organs [function] in the three times.[110]

Regarding how subjects engage with objects, the three internal instruments—intellect, ego, and mind—and the external sense faculties such as eye engage with manifest visible objects either immediately or latently. In the former, if one sees something like a snake, when the external eyes first see the form of a snake, the internal mind thinks "this is a snake." Then, ego thinks "it is coming to harm me." The intellect decides that is the case, and one flees. Because those activities occur without interruption, it is explained that this is called *immediate* engagement. From this example, one should understand that the ear and so forth engage with their objects in the same way. [68]

The second, *latent* engagement, is when, for example, the eyes first see a lump in the distance, and then the mind wonders, "Is that a man over there?" Then, as one gradually comes near and sees the limbs and other body parts, ego determines, "What I saw is definitely a man." After intellect decides that that thing is a man, one engages in activities such as conversing with him.

While the five sense faculties such as eye engage with manifest objects of the present, the three internal instruments—intellect, ego, and mind—also engage with invisible hidden objects. Preceded by direct perception, they engage with objects of all three times successively or simultaneously. Therefore they engage with and ascertain objects in accordance with what was already seen by the sense faculty that induces them. In the same way, they assert that the subjects of hidden objects, such as inference, are preceded by direct perception. The *Verses of Sāṅkhya* says:

> It is taught that, for the visible,
> the four engage latently and immediately.

Likewise, for the invisible,
the three, being preceded by that, engage.[111]

Thus the way that [the internal and external faculties] engage with objects is described in detail.

Valid Means of Knowledge

Like all philosophies, this school also accepts that for something to be an object of knowledge, it must be established by a valid means of knowledge. Therefore they define *valid means of knowledge* as "that which determines the fact as it is." When divided, objects of comprehension are determined to be manifest, hidden, or extremely hidden. Corresponding to these, the Sāṅkhya assert that the valid means of knowledge have three varieties: direct perception, inference, and verbal valid knowledge. The *Verses of Sāṅkhya* says:

> Because direct perception, inference, and trustworthy words
> encompass all types of valid knowledge,
> it is asserted that they are the three kinds of valid knowledge.
> Objects of knowledge are established by valid knowledge.[112]

Also, Kamalaśīla's *Summary of the Opponents' Positions in the Drop of Reasoning* says, "According to Sāṅkhya, there are only three valid means of knowledge: direct perception, inference, and verbal testimony."[113] [69]

1) First, direct perception. When a connection between an object and a sense faculty is established, the operation of the mind that apprehends and perceives the aspect of that object is the definition of direct valid knowledge. Thus the *Sāṅkhya Sūtra* says, "When a connection is established, the consciousness that perceives its aspect at that time is direct perception."[114] Also, in the *Lamp of Reasoning* (*Yuktidīpikā*), the Sāṅkhya master Vārṣagaṇya says, "Direct perception is the activities of ear and so forth."[115] The *Blossoms of Reasoning*, a Nyāya text, identifies an example of direct perception, saying "Direct perception is the nonconceptual activities of the ear and so forth,"[116] explaining that this is the assertion of the Sāṅkhya master Vindhyavāsin.

Similarly, the Buddhist scholar Dignāga's *Autocommentary on the*

Compendium of Valid Knowledge says, "The Kāpila assert that direct perception is the activities of ear and so forth. They say that, empowered by the mind, the ear, body, eye, tongue, and nose engage their objects; that is, they apprehend, respectively, present sound, touch, form, taste, and smell. They call this *direct perception*."[117] This is clear from the Sāṅkhya statements of their position. Regarding the meaning of "empowered," some Sāṅkhya assert that it means the mind and the sense faculty engaging the object together. Others assert that it means awareness by the mind. They assert that mind becomes aware of an object after it is apprehended by a sense faculty; it is determined by the intellect after that.

They assert that there are two types of direct perception: conceptual direct perception and nonconceptual direct perception. Regarding conceptual direct perception, when the sense faculties encounter their respective objects, the intellect that ascertains each object is produced. At that time, because *sattva* outshines the quality of *tamas* belonging to intellect, the nature of *sattva* increases and becomes stronger, producing a thought with a stable ascertainment of each object. That is called *direct valid knowledge*. In short, this is explained as conceptual direct valid knowledge that gains stable ascertainment of an object. Nonconceptual direct perception is posited as the direct perception of the ear and so forth explained above. [70]

2) The definition of *inference* is understanding the meaning of pervasion based on previously comprehending the connection between a sign and that which bears the sign. A person's understanding of the significance based on that is called *inferential consciousness* or *inferential valid knowledge*. The *Verses of Sāṅkhya* says, "It is preceded by a sign and that which bears the sign."[118] In the same way, the *Sāṅkhya Sūtra* clearly says, "Inference is what determines the pervaded fact based on an earlier understanding of the relationship between the sign and that which bears the sign. A person's comprehension of such a fact is inferential consciousness."[119] For example, one states, "The subject, the eye and so forth, bring benefit to another because they are composites." Through understanding the connection of sign, being composite, and that which bears the sign, benefiting another, the intellect realizes that the eyes and so forth benefit others (the pervader) through the observed sign that they are composites (the pervaded). This is called *inference*. Based on such an intellect, the consciousness that realizes

that the eye and so forth benefit others is called inferential consciousness or comprehension of a meaning by a person.

Dignāga's *Compendium of Valid Knowledge* states, "According to Sāṅkhya, establishing something new on the basis of a direct perception of relationship is called *inference*."[120] This is saying that, based on some connection established earlier by direct perception, one realizes a remaining object—in other words, something else that is not obvious, and this is called *inference*. For example, having previously seen the connection between fire and smoke via direct perception, then later, by merely seeing smoke, one infers the remaining object, a fire, that is not obvious.

As the *Summary of the Opponents' Positions in the Drop of Reasoning* says, "For the Kāpila, inference is of two types, *general seeing* and *specific seeing*."[121] Thus there are two kinds of inference, general seeing and specific seeing. *General seeing* is like inferring the existence of fire by merely seeing smoke after having previously recognized the relationship between fire and smoke.

When inference through general seeing is divided, there are two types. *Inference from what is prior* (*pūrvavat*) is to understand the arising of an effect from its cause, like understanding that smoke arises from fire. *Inference from what is left* (*śeṣavat*) is to understand that a cause has arisen after seeing its existing effect, like understanding that a fire has started after seeing existing smoke. They assert that the former can be mistaken, but the latter cannot be mistaken. [71] Inference through *specific seeing* is like, having seen the connection between fire and smoke, repeatedly understanding the existence of a specific fire from specific smoke.

A somewhat different way of dividing inference also appears. The *Verses of Sāṅkhya* says, "Inference is asserted to be of three kinds."[122] The nature of each of the three kinds is not clearly identified in that text, but the various assertions of the later Sāṅkhya scholars can be summarized as follows: (1) inferential valid knowledge from what is prior (*pūrvavat*), (2) inferential valid knowledge from what remains (*śeṣavat*), and (3) inferential valid knowledge from common sight (*sāmānyatodṛṣṭa*).

Among these three, the first is valid knowledge that infers, from seeing a previously existing cause, that its effect arises later, like inferring the effect of rainfall from the sign or reason of dark clouds circling in the summer sky. This is called the inference from what is prior (*pūrvavat*).

The second, inferential valid knowledge from what remains (*śeṣavat*), is inferential valid knowledge that infers, through seeing a quality of one of any effects, that everything that remains that is similar has that quality. It is like inferring, for example, that because a single fruit that one has eaten is sweet, that all the fruit from the same tree that have the same shape, color, and fragrance have that sweetness. Alternately, it is asserted to be when one ascertains that some quality exists in a basis and decides it does not exist anywhere else, ascertaining that that quality exists in what remains of the earlier basis. For example, it is like ascertaining that a smell is based on a substance of one of the elements, and not seeing it in a substance of fire, wind, water, or space, inferring its existence in the remaining element, earth.

The third, inferential valid knowledge from common sight (*sāmānyatodṛṣṭa*), is realizing a specific quality seen earlier regarding a certain basis. For example, it is like seeing a peach tree blossom in a particular country in springtime and inferring that all peach trees in other countries also blossom in springtime. [72]

3) *Verbal valid knowledge* is the speech of a trustworthy person and the valid knowledge produced based on that. The *Sāṅkhya Sūtra* says, "[Valid knowledge of] speech (*śabda*) is the instruction of a trustworthy person."[123] The *Verses of Sāṅkhya* says, "What is heard from a trustworthy person is trustworthy words (*āptavacana*).[124] Thus it is clear that they assert that it is both expressive speech, or valid words, and the valid awareness produced in dependence on hearing such speech.

When verbal valid knowledge is divided, there is (1) the speech of beings who are truthful, such as rishis, (2) the conventions of elders, and (3) terms that have the same basis as well-known words. Based on these, the connection between word and meaning is understood; verbal valid knowledge based on that is posited as three. Examples of these are explained by the Sāṅkhya master Aniruddha. (1) From the speech of a rishi, "This is a pot," one understands what a pot is. (2) From the speech of an elder, "Drive the cow with that white stick," a listener, having seen that action, sees the connection between those words and their meanings. (3) When someone says, "A bird is eating fruit," that speech produces the awareness that what is called "fruit" is edible.

Turning to how they enumerate the valid means of knowledge as three, it is a common tradition among all Indian logicians that the number of forms of valid knowledge is established through establishing the number of objects that can be known. This system also establishes them in this way: (1) The type of objects that can be known by the intellect through consciousnesses based on the five sense faculties is the *manifest*. (2) The type of objects that can be known by the internal faculties, which are beyond the sense consciousnesses, such as the mind in dependence on a sign that shares the mode of being of the thing, is the *slightly hidden*. (3) The type of objects that cannot be known by those means but must be known based only on trustworthy speech is the *very hidden*. Because the objects are enumerated as three, the forms of valid knowledge are proven to be only three: direct perception, inference, and verbal valid knowledge. The *Verses of Sāṅkhya* states:

> Based on inference through the sight of a common
> characteristic,
> that which is beyond the sense faculties is known.
> The hidden that is not established even by that
> is established from trustworthy scriptures.[125] [73]

The Methods for Knowing Objects

Someone might ask: What are the modes of reasoning in this system, and what are its divisions? Recognizing a pervasion through previously comprehending the connection between a sign and that which bears the sign is called a reasoning and is asserted to be insentient matter, a transformation of intellect. Such a proof has three parts: (1) a position (*pakṣa*) that is the existence of a property (*dharma*) to be proven for a subject (*dharmin*); (2) a sign (*liṅga*) that has the three modes: existing in the position, being in a similar class, and not being in a dissimilar class; and (3) an example (*dṛṣṭānta*)—a similar example that is similar to the property to be proven and a dissimilar example that is similar to the dissimilar class.

The *Autocommentary on the Compendium of Valid Knowledge* says, "According to the Kāpila, in order to teach others, there are two kinds of inference: direct inference (*vīta*) and inference by exclusion (*āvīta*). There are five kinds of objects to be stated for direct inference because of the division of the thesis and so forth."[126] Thus, for inference for the sake of proving something to others (*parārthānumāna*), there are two: direct inference and inference by exclusion. They assert that a five-part verbal proof that mainly proves one's own position, like the five syllogisms that prove the existence of the primary nature, is a direct inference. An absurd consequence that proves one's own position by refuting the position of the other is an inference by exclusion.

According to *Māṭhara's Commentary* (*Māṭharavṛtti*) on the root text [the *Verses of Sāṅkhya*], the five parts are identified as: the thesis (*pratijñā*), the statement of the reason (*apadeśa*), the example (*nidarśana*), the application (*anusaṃdhāna*), and the restatement of the thesis (*pratyāmnāya*). It is called *inference for the sake of others* because it causes others to understand a meaning known by oneself through these five parts or methods. However, in enumerating the five branches, the Sāṅkhya master Aniruddha and others list these five: thesis (*pratijñā*), sign (*liṅga*), example (*dṛṣṭānta*), application (*upanaya*), and conclusion (*nigamana*).

This system asserts that *inference for oneself* is realizing an object through seven connections and asserts that there are seven connections between the sign and that which bears the sign. The *Summary of the Opponents' Positions in the Drop of Reasoning* says: [74]

> Sāṅkhya says that there are seven connections between things: (1) the connection between self and its possessions, like that of someone named Devadatta and [his son] Yajñadatta, (2) the connection of nature, like that of clay and a pot, (3) the connection between cause and caused, like that of a potter and a pot, (4) the connection between cause and effect, like that of a seed and a sprout, (5) the connection like father and mother, like that of a branch and a tree, (6) the connection of spouses, like that of mating ducks, and (7) the connection of enemies, like that of a crow and an owl.[127]

Among the reasons that cause one to infer the object to be proven based on those connections, there are two kinds: correct reasons and pseudo-reasons. Just as inferential valid knowledge has the three types explained above, a correct reason that is the basis of that inference also has three types:

1) A correct syllogism with a sign of something prior is like a reasoning that proves that rain will soon fall in a place because, like in a land that has

abundant rain in the summer, there are now dark clouds hovering and the sound of thunder.

2) A correct syllogism with a sign from what remains is a reason that proves, through seeing a quality of one of any effects, that everything that remains that is similar has that quality. It is like proving, for example, that because a single fruit that one has eaten is sweet, all the fruit from the same tree that have the same shape, color, and fragrance have its sweetness. Or it is like a reason proving that a smell that is a quality of a substance of one of the elements, because it is not a quality of fire, wind, water, or space, then it must be a quality of the remaining element, earth.

3) A correct syllogism with a sign of common sight is like a correct reason that proves that flowers blossom in spring in countries one has not seen because, when one has seen a tree blossom in a particular place like Vaiśālī in springtime, the sight of flowers blossoming in springtime must be common to other places. [75]

Regarding proofs for the existence of the subtle objects of knowledge such as the primary nature, the first is the way of proving the existence of the primary nature with an intrinsic sign or a sign of common sight. The *Verses of Sāṅkhya* says:

> The reason it is not perceived is because of its subtlety, not
> because it does not exist.
> It is established based on its effects.
> The great one and so forth are its effects.
> They are similar to and different from the primary nature.[128]

Ordinary direct perception cannot see the primary nature because the primary nature is subtle, not because it does not exist in general. The existence of the primary nature can be inferred from clearly observing the qualities of the primary nature—*rajas*, *tamas*, and *sattva*—in its effects such as the great one. If the three qualities clearly exist in the effects, then the cause, being of a similar type, must also have the three qualities. The unmanifest nature endowed in that way is called the *primary nature*.

The *Verses of Sāṅkhya* sets forth five proofs for the existence of the primary nature, which is the unmanifest cause of those transformations that are its effects.

The unmanifest cause exists
because individual things are finite, because of similarity,
because of the activity of capability,
because of the difference between cause and effect,
and because the diverse world is undifferentiated.[129]

Regarding the meaning of these, Kamalaśīla's *Commentary on the Compendium of Principles* says:

> This means that the primary nature exists (1) because individual things are finite. In this world, that which has a maker is seen to be finite. For example, say that from a lump of clay, a potter makes pots that can hold a finite amount of five quarts, two quarts, and ten quarts. In the same way, the manifest, such as the great one, is also seen to be finite: one intellect, one ego, five subtle elements, eleven faculties, and five coarse elements. Therefore they prove through inference that the primary nature that produces the finite manifestions exists. If the primary nature did not exist, these manifestations would not be finite.[130]

Also, the same text says: [76]

> The primary nature also exists (2) because its particulars are seen to be similar. That which is observed to be the same type arises from a cause that has that nature. For example, just as particular things in the category of clay, like a pot and a bowl, arise from a cause that has the nature of clay, manifest particulars are observed to have types such as pleasure, suffering, and ignorance.[131]

Also, the same text says:

> The primary nature also exists (3) because of the activity of capability. In this world, that which engages with a certain thing has a capability for that. For example, just as a weaver is making cloth, it is proven that the capability of the primary nature to

> produce manifestations exists. That capability is not without a basis. Therefore the primary nature that has that ability exists.[132]

Also, the same text says:

> The primary nature also exists (4) because of the difference between cause and effect. In this world, cause and effect are seen to be different. For example, a lump of clay is a cause while a pot has the nature of being its effect. It also has a nature different from that of a lump of clay; a pot can hold honey, water, and milk; a lump of clay cannot. Thus, having seen these effects such as the great one, they say that the primary nature that produces effects such as the great one exists.[133]

Also, the same text says:

> The primary nature also exists (5) because diverse natures are undifferentiated. "Diverse natures" refers to the three worlds. When they disintegrate, they become undifferentiated. The five coarse elements become undifferentiated from the five subtle elements. The subtle elements and the faculties become undifferentiated from ego, ego to intellect, and intellect to the primary nature. Therefore, when they collapse in that way, the three worlds become undifferentiated. Undifferentiated means indistinguishable. Thus they think that the primary nature into which the great one and so forth dissolve without differentiation exists.[134] [77]

Extensive proofs for the existence of the primary nature, the unmanifest cause, are also clearly presented in the *Blaze of Reasoning*.

There are also five proofs that demonstrate that effects exist at the time of their cause without being manifest:

1) If an effect does not exist in the state of its cause, it cannot be manifested by it. Therefore it is proven that an effect exists at the time of its cause. For example, in the world, an effect that does not exist at the time of its cause is not produced, just as oil does not come from squeezing sand.

2) Those who seek an effect seek a particular effect; they acquire the cause necessary for that effect. Therefore it is proven that an effect resides in its cause. For example, those who seek the effect yogurt seek and take its cause, milk; it is not taken by those who seek earth and stones.

3) It is not possible for every effect to be produced by any cause; what is produced is something that exists at the time of its cause. For example, only barley is produced by a barley seed; a tree is not produced.

4) A cause acts as the cause of only the effect that it is able to produce; it cannot act as the cause of something else. Therefore it is proven that an effect exists at the time of its cause. For example, when a goldsmith makes a gold ornament with a hammer, only gold is the nature of the ornament.

5) Effects are similar to the nature of the thing that serves as their cause. Therefore it is proven that an effect exists at the time of its cause. The effect, a clay pot, comes from clay; a clay pot does not come from a tree. Thus the *Verses of Sāṅkhya* states:

> Because a nonexistent thing has no cause, because people seek
> [a cause],
> because of the impossibility of everything,
> because a capacity is only a cause of what it is capable of,
> and because [an effect is the nature of] its cause,
> an effect exists [in its cause].[135] [78]

They also set forth five proofs for the existence of the unmanifest self, the conscious puruṣa. They will be explained [in the next volume] in the context of analyzing self and no-self.

Someone might ask: Why is it that the primary nature and the self exist, yet they cannot be directly perceived by the senses? In general, there are eight reasons why things exist but are not seen. The *Verses of Sāṅkhya* states:

> Because of great distance and nearness,
> because of faults of the sense faculties, because of a distracted
> mind,
> because of subtlety, because of obstruction,
> because of being outshone, and because of losing what is
> similar.
> Because it is subtle, it is not seen.[136]

This means: (1) It is not seen because of great distance, just as the eyes of an ordinary person cannot see distant stars. (2) It is not seen because of great nearness, just as one cannot see eye ointment smeared on one's eyes. (3) It is not seen because of damaged sense faculties, just as a blind man cannot see forms. (4) It is not seen because of a distracted mind, just as eyes do not see forms when the mind is attracted to pleasant sounds. (5) It is not perceived because of great subtlety, just as the eye cannot see such things as particles. (6) It is not seen because of obstructions, just as one cannot see a pot obstructed by a wall or a curtain. (7) It is not perceived because of being outshone, just as one cannot see stars in the daytime because they are outshone by the sun. (8) It is not seen because chances to see it are lost due to its being mixed with things of similar type, just as one cannot see individual grains when grains of rice are piled together. Here it is asserted that the two—the self and the primary nature—are not seen by the five sense faculties such as the eye because of their great subtlety.

This Sāṅkhya philosophy is one of the earliest schools of tenets to be delineated in India using the path of reasoning. It, together with Vaiśeṣika, Nyāya, Mīmāṃsā, and Vedānta, are the earlier tīrthika schools. It long served as the basis for Buddhist philosophers to engage in analysis using the path of subtle reasoning. In particular, the lords of reasoning Dignāga and Dharmakīrti analyzed it in detail. Therefore, seeing how important it is to understand the principal assertions of the earlier and later scholars of this school, it has been explained here somewhat more extensively than the other non-Buddhist schools, relying on what appears in the texts of both the Buddhist and the non-Buddhist scholars of India. [79]

4

The Vaiśeṣika School

How This School of Tenets Arose

MANY INDIAN BUDDHIST and non-Buddhist scholars assert that the founder of this school of tenets was the rishi named Kaṇāda ("grain eater") or Ulūka ("owl"). Kamalaśīla's *Commentary on the Compendium of Principles* says, "The Naiyāyika are called the Ākṣapāda because they are the disciples of Akṣapāda. The Vaiśeṣika are called the Kāṇāda because they are disciples of Kaṇāda."[137] He identifies Akṣapāda as the teacher of the Naiyāyika and Kaṇāda as the teacher of the Vaiśeṣika. According to the Bengali scholar Prajñāvarman's *Commentary on Praise to the One More Perfect Than the Gods*, the teacher of this school is called Kaṇāda because he relied on the ascetic practice of eating grain. There appear to be many such explanations.[138]

The *Blaze of Reasoning* says, "The rishi Owl (Ulūka), whom they assert to be omniscient, is not liberated."[139] The same text says, "The Owls (Aulūkya), the followers of his scripture . . ."[140] Accordingly, rishi Owl must refer to the teacher and Owls to the proponents of tenets who primarily follow him. There seem to be many explanations of why he is called Owl. He is so called because he composed his treatise during the day and went out for food at night like an owl; because he was the son of the rishi Owl Possessor; and because when Kaṇāda was meditating, the lord Īśvara appeared in the form of an owl and taught the six categories (*padārtha*). Kaṇāda's two disciples, Piṭhara and Pīlu, as well as Śaṅkarapati, are said to be later Vaiśeṣika teachers.[141] [80]

Turning to the texts that set forth this system's philosophy, the root of all the extant Vaiśeṣika texts is the *Vaiśeṣika Sūtra* attributed to the rishi Kaṇāda. The text widely regarded as its earliest commentary is the *Treatise on the Ten Categories* (*Daśapadārthaśāstra*) by Candramati, who lived during the fifth century. Praśastapāda, the famous sixth-century scholar who unerringly penetrated the meaning of the *Vaiśeṣika Sūtra*, appeared later. He wrote the *Compendium of Categories* (*Padārthadharmasaṅgraha*), a commentary on the *Vaiśeṣika Sūtra*, and is known for spreading the Vaiśeṣika philosophy widely. From around the tenth century, the three most famous commentaries on Praśastapāda's treatise were written: Vyomaśiva's *Having Sky* (*Vyomavatī*, ca. tenth century), Śrīdhara's *Deer of Reasoning* (*Nyāyakandalī*, ca. tenth century), and Udayana's *Garland of Moonbeams* (*Kiraṇāvalī*, ca. eleventh century).[142]

The Definition and Etymology of Vaiśeṣika

Vaiśeṣika is defined as a non-Buddhist philosophy that follows the tīrthika teacher Kaṇāda and accepts the objects of knowledge of the six categories (*padārtha*) as its fundamental tenet. It is called Vaiśeṣika ("Particularist") because this philosophy particularly explains categories, because it says much about the differences between the universal (*sāmānya*) and the particular (*viśeṣa*), and because it follows Kaṇāda's sūtra, which elucidates particulars.

Vaiśeṣika and Nyāya are not similar in terms of their origin and history. Nevertheless, their fundamental assertions are known to be very similar. Indeed, in Bhāviveka's early tenets text the *Essence of the Middle Way* and its autocommentary, there is a separate chapter for a refutation of Vaiśeṣika assertions, but there is not a separate chapter refuting Nyāya. However, it seems necessary to differentiate them: Vaiśeṣika primarily emphasizes the delineation of the mode of being of the foundation based on the six categories, while Nyāya emphasizes the method for delineating objects, setting forth sixteen categories of logic. [81]

Vaiśeṣika Assertions

Regarding Vaiśeṣika assertions, the summary verses say:

> Kaṇāda, the supreme teacher of the Vaiśeṣika,
> with the three valid means of knowledge,
> designated the six categories
> to be the reality of objects of knowledge.[143]

This system follows the teacher Kaṇāda and delineates six categories to be the reality of objects of knowledge (the object) based on three forms of valid knowledge (the subject). The *Vaiśeṣika Sūtra* says, "We assert that, due to the qualities or particulars of phenomena, liberation is attained through knowledge of reality born from comprehending the similarities and dissimilarities of the six categories: substance (*dravya*), quality (*guṇa*), activity (*karman*), universal (*sāmānya*), particularity (*viśeṣa*), and inherence (*samavāya*)."[144] The *Commentary on the Compendium of Principles* says, "You do not accept any existent not included in the six categories."[145] As is clearly stated in the *Blaze of Reasoning*, Vaiśeṣika asserts that all objects of knowledge are included in the six categories. The six categories are substance, quality, activity, universal, particularity, and inherence. Some later masters in the lineage of this school of tenets add nonexistence (*abhāva*), making seven categories of objects of knowledge.

Substance

To explain the six categories of objects of knowledge, the first, *substance*, is defined as a phenomenon that has three features—possessing activities, possessing qualities, and being the cause for inherence. Bhāviveka's *Blaze of Reasoning* says, "The general nature of substance is to possess activities, to possess qualities, and to be the cause for inherence; this is the nature of substance."[146] They assert that *being the cause for inherence* means that a substance is the cause of different qualities inhering together in a substance. It is called *substance* because it exists independently and serves as the basis of other phenomena, such as qualities. [82]

When it is divided, there are nine subcategories: earth (*pṛthivī*), water (*āpas*), fire (*tejas*), wind (*vāyu*), space (*ākāśa*), time (*kāla*), direction (*diś*), self (*ātman*), and mind (*manas*).

They assert that the particles of the four elements are permanent while coarse things, which are accumulations of those particles, are impermanent. The *Commentary on the Compendium of Principles*, citing the *Vaiśeṣika Sūtra*, says:

> Regarding the "nine kinds," the sūtra says, "Earth, water, fire, wind, space, time, direction, ātman, and mind are called substances." Four among them, earth, water, fire, and wind, are

> of two types, differentiated by whether they are permanent or impermanent. Here, in order to set forth these two kinds, [Śāntarakṣita's verse] says, "First, these . . ." Those with a nature of particles, such as earth, are permanent because particles are permanent. That which is composed of them is impermanent because they reason that that which has a cause is impermanent.[147]

The *Blaze of Reasoning* also clearly states this.

1) The definition of *earth* is a substance that has the quality of smell. Earth particles are permanent, but an accumulation of many of them is impermanent. Earth is divided into three types: body, sense faculty, and object. For example, body is like the body of a sentient being, sense faculty is like the nose faculty that perceives smell, and object is like a rocky mountain.

2) The definition of *water* is a substance that has the sensation of coolness. Water particles are permanent, but a collection of many of them is impermanent. It also has three types, divided into body, sense faculty, and external object. For example, body is like the body of a water deity, sense faculty is like the tongue faculty that perceives taste, and object is like a river or an ocean.

3) The definition of *fire* is a substance that possesses the sensation of burning. Its particles are also permanent, but an accumulation of many of them is impermanent. It also has three types, divided into body, sense faculty, and external object. For example, body is like the body of the sun, sense faculty is like the faculty inside the black star [pupil] of the eye that apprehends form, and object is like a mass of flame or lightning.

4) The definition of *wind* is a substance that has an invisible form but is an object of touch. Its particles are permanent, but a collection of many of them is impermanent. [83] It also has three types, divided into body, sense faculty, and external object. For example, body is like the world of wind or the body of a wind deity, sense faculty is like the skin faculty that covers the entire body and apprehends objects of touch, and object is like an external wind that moves trees or an internal wind or breath that moves the mind.

5) *Space* is a substance that possesses the quality of sound. Among the nine substances, the substance that has the quality of sound is called space. It is a permanent, unitary, and all-pervading substance.

6) The definition of *time* is a different entity from temporal measurements such as year, month, day, and hour. It is posited as a substance that

is the object apprehended by a mind that thinks thoughts like "it is a long time" and "it is quick." It is also a substance that serves as the cause for conventions like "a long time" and "a short time." It is asserted to have the nature of being all-pervading, permanent, and motionless. The *Blaze of Reasoning* says, "Direction, space, and time are unproduced, all-pervasive, permanent, and motionless."[148] Regarding the reason for the existence of such time, the *Commentary on the Compendium of Principles* states, "The [*Vaiśeṣika*] *Sūtra* says that after and before, simultaneous and not simultaneous, and long and short are markers of time."[149] Time is divided into the three: the past, present, and future. In addition, Vaiśeṣika seems to assert that time is the agent of all activities; the *Commentary on the Compendium of Principles* sets forth the Vaiśeṣika position:

> Time ripens beings.
> Time collects creatures.
> Time awakens sleepers.
> Time is difficult to overcome.[150]

7) The definition of *direction* is a substance that is unitary, all-pervasive, and permanent that serves as the cause for conventions such as "east." For example, east is the appearing object of a mind thinking "This is east." It is divided into ten: the four cardinal directions such as east, the four intermediate directions such as southeast, above, and below.

8) The definition of *self* (*ātman*) is a substance that is different from body, sense faculty, and intellect; it is a substance that pervades all transmigrating beings, as was explained in the previous chapter on Sāṅkhya.[151] [84] It is asserted to be the synonym of *puruṣa* and *pudgala*. It is divided into two: the supreme ātman, like the ātman of Īśvara, and the ordinary ātman, like the ātman of a cow. The details of ātman and its qualities are explained in the second volume of *Compendium of Philosophy* in the section on how the self is asserted in the various schools of tenets.

9) The definition of *mind* is the mental faculty that serves as the cause of experiencing pleasure and pain. It is a permanent substance of unconscious matter and is endowed with motion. It is not all-pervasive because it does not engage with the eyes when engaged with the ears, and so forth. The *Blaze of Reasoning* says, "Mind is permanent, endowed with motion, and limited."[152]

In summary, among the nine substances, five—mind and the four elements of earth, water, fire, and wind—are not all-pervasive substances because they are limited. The four substances ātman, direction, time, and space are all-pervasive because they are not limited.

Quality

The definition of the second category, *quality* (*guṇa*), is that which relies on a substance, does not possess another quality, does not serve as the cause for previously separate things to conjoin, does not serve as the cause for previously conjoined things to separate, and does not depend on a sign. Citing the *Vaiśeṣika Sūtra*, the *Commentary on the Compendium of Principles* says, "As the sūtra says, 'The definition of quality is that which depends on a substance, does not possess another quality, is not the cause of conjunction and separation, and is independent.'"[153] Regarding how the *Vaiśeṣika Sūtra* explains the twenty-four divisions of quality, the *Commentary on the Compendium of Principles* says:

> The sūtra says, "(1) Color (*rūpa*), (2) taste (*rasa*), (3) smell (*gandha*), (4) touch (*sparśa*), (5) number (*saṅkhyā*), (6) size (*parimāṇa*), (7) individuality (*pṛthaktva*), (8) conjunction (*saṃyoga*), (9) division (*vibhāga*), (10) remoteness (*paratva*), (11) proximity (*aparatva*), (12) intellect (*buddhi*), (13) pleasure (*sukha*), (14) pain (*duḥkha*), (15) desire (*icchā*), (16) aversion (*dveṣa*), and (17) effort (*prayatna*)." The word "and" implies: (18) weight (*gurutva*), (19) liquidity (*dravatva*), (20) viscidity (*sneha*), (21) formation (*saṃskāra*), (22) merit (*dharma*), (23) demerit (*adharma*), and (24) sound (*śabda*).[154] [85]

This passage sets forth twenty-four, combining the five intellects or consciousnesses, such as the eye consciousness, into one and enumerating the seven [items] included in the word "and." These qualities are asserted to be different from the substances on which they rely. Bhāviveka's *Blaze of Reasoning* and Avalokitavrata's *Commentary on the Lamp of Wisdom* enumerate the five consciousnesses individually and omit weight and so forth. However, it will be explained here according to the *Commentary on the Compendium of Principles*.

To identify each of the individual qualities briefly:

1) The definition of *color* (*rūpa*) is a quality apprehended only by the eyes. It is divided into two from the perspective of its modes of activity: illuminating colors, like sunlight and lightning, that illuminate both their own and others' colors, and nonilluminating colors, like water, that do not illuminate in that way. It is also divided into seven from the perspective of its nature: blue, yellow, white, red, green, brown, and a variegated color. Because those are qualities, they must rely on other substances. On which substances do they rely? All the colors rely on the earth element. Nonilluminating white relies on water. All the illuminating colors rely on fire.

2) The definition of *taste* (*rasa*) is a quality apprehended by the tongue faculty. It is divided into six: sweet, sour, bitter, astringent, coarse, and salty. They all rely on earth. Only sweetness relies on water.

3) The definition of *smell* (*gandha*) is a quality apprehended by the nose faculty. There are two kinds: fragrant and nonfragrant. They are asserted to rely only on the substance earth.

4) The definition of *touch* (*sparśa*) is a quality apprehended only by the body faculty. It is divided into three: warm, cool, and neither warm nor cool. These rely on any of the four substances: earth, water, fire, and wind. The *Commentary on the Compendium of Principles* says, "Color is apprehended by the eyes and resides in earth, water, and fire. Taste is apprehended by the tongue faculty and resides in earth and water. Smell is apprehended by the nose and resides in earth. Touch is apprehended by the body faculty and resides in earth, water, fire, and wind."[155]

5) The definition of *number* (*saṅkhyā*) is a quality that serves as the cause for conventions like "one" and "two." For example, "one person" is not "a person," nor is it a word for "person"; it is an entity distinct from a person and serves as a cause for the words "one person" to mean a person who is alone without a companion. [86] It is asserted to be the direct object of expression of the term "one person" and is the appearing object of the mind that thinks "That is one person." The numbers two, three, and so forth are to be understood in the same way.

A number relies on all nine substances. They assert that numbers that rely on space and subtle particles are permanent and those that rely on the four coarse elements are impermanent. The number one relies on one substance while the numbers two and so forth rely on many substances. As the *Commentary on the Compendium of Principles* says, "Number is the cause for the conventions one and so forth and is characterized by oneness and so forth. It relies on one substance and on many substances. The number one relies on one substance; the numbers two and so forth rely on many substances."[156]

6) The definition of *size* (*parimāṇa*) is a quality that serves as the cause for a specific measurement of the length or weight of a substance. It is divided into four: large, small, long, and short. Large is divided into two: permanent and impermanent. Permanent large is a quality of space, time, direction, and ātman. Impermanent large is a quality of coarse substances composed of three or more particles. There are also two small sizes: permanent and impermanent. Permanent small is a quality of a minute particle that has the characteristic of appearing to the mind as round. Impermanent small is a quality of the first whole that is composed of two particles. Size is also asserted to rely on all nine substances.

7) The definition of *individuality* (*pṛthaktva*) is a quality that serves as the specific cause of a convention of difference. For example, the individuality of a pillar and a pot is such that neither can be both a pillar and a pot. Individuality is not a pillar and a pot separately; it is a different substance from them, and it does not possess both a pillar and a pot. It serves as the direct object of expression and the appearing object of the word as well as the mind that differentiates a pillar from a pot. They say that without individuality, it would be impossible to distinguish a pillar and a pot. As the *Compendium of Principles* says, "Because of difference, they speak of individuality."[157] It relies on all nine substances. [87]

8) The definition of *connection* or *conjunction* (*saṃyoga*) is a quality that is the appearing object of a consciousness apprehending a connection, or a lack of a gap, between substances; it is the explicit object of the statement, "there is no gap between this and that connected substance." For example, the cause of the mind that apprehends that the threads of a piece of cloth are stitched together and that there is no gap in their connections is the connection of those threads—that is, there is something different from the threads themselves. They say that threads and their connections are different things because a consciousness apprehending threads and a consciousness thinking "the threads are connected" have different objects of apprehension. This relies on all the substances.

9) The definition of *division* (*vibhāga*) is a quality that serves as the cause of the convention of dividing what is assembled in one place. As when a river splits into two channels, it is the appearing object of a consciousness

that apprehends the dissolution of what was once connected or a mutual separation. It is posited as being different from what is divided. If division did not exist, when a thing, previously connected without a gap, later splits, there would be no cause to produce the mind that apprehends the gap. What is the difference between this and individuality? That which is split from the beginning is called individuality. That which was at one time a single substance and is split into two later is division. This also relies on all the substances.

10) The definition of *remoteness* (*paratva*) is a quality of not being near and that serves as the cause of the convention of distance. For example, when a pillar and a pot are placed together, remoteness is the cause of the mind that, seeing a pillar, thinks that a pot is different, and it is the appearing object of the mind that apprehends this. It is a property of the pot and is different from the pot.

11) The definition of *proximity* (*aparatva*) is a quality that serves as the specific cause of the convention of nearness. There is nearness in terms of space and nearness in terms of time. These rely on the five substances: the four elements and the mind.

12) The definition of *intellect* (*buddhi*) is a quality of apprehending objects that serves as the cause that allows all conventions of objects to be known. *Consciousness*, *intellect*, and *observer* are asserted to be synonyms. The *Commentary on the Compendium of Principles*, citing a Vaiśeṣika text, says, "It is explained [in the *Nyāya Sūtra*] that 'Intellect (*buddhi*), observation (*upalabdhi*), and consciousness (*jñāna*) are not different.'"[158] An example is an eye consciousness. They do not assert that an intellect knows itself; it is known by another intellect. [88] The *Commentary on the Compendium of Principles* says, "Others assert that such a nature does not have the nature of knowing itself; it is understood by another intellect."[159]

Intellect has two kinds: one that has the nature of memory and one that has the nature of experience. The first is a consciousness produced from the force of familiarity, for example, a consciousness that remembers a past event. The second is all consciousnesses other than memory and has two kinds: the experience of something as it is and the experience of something as it is not. The former is valid knowledge, and the latter is invalid knowledge. Valid knowledge is asserted to be of three kinds: based on direct perception, inference, and verbal valid knowledge.

13) The definition of *pleasure* (*sukha*) is a feeling that is experienced by

a sentient being in accordance with its own desire. (14) The definition of *pain* (*duḥkha*) is a feeling that is experienced by a sentient being that is not in accordance with its own desire. (15) The definition of *desire* (*icchā*) is being attached to an object of one's desire and to hope for it. (16) The definition of *aversion* (*dveṣa*) is to turn away from an undesired thing. (17) The definition of *effort* (*prayatna*) is the quality of striving to accomplish any activity. Thus, Candrakīrti's *Autocommentary on Entering the Middle Way* says, "Pleasure is the experience of a desired object. Pain is the opposite of that. Desire is hope for the object of desire. Aversion is to turn away from an undesired thing. Effort is the skillfulness of mind to complete what is to be accomplished."[160]

18) The definition of *weight* (*gurutva*) is a quality of relying on a coarse substance to induce something to fall by its own power. It relies only on earth and water. (19) The definition of *liquidity* (*dravatva*) is a quality of melting. It relies on the substances of earth, water, and fire. It has two kinds: that which melts naturally, belonging to water, and that which melts due to a condition, belonging to iron and so forth, which abide in the nature of earth and melt when they meet fire. (20) The definition of *viscidity* (*sneha*) is that which serves as the cause that makes things like powder stick together. It is a quality that depends only on water.

21) Formation (*saṃskāra*) is of three kinds: energy, latency, and elasticity. The first, energy, is produced from a specific action by a person's effort on earth, water, fire, wind, or mind. For example, when an arrow is shot, it serves as the cause for the arrow not to fall in flight and is produced by the power of exertion. This is asserted to be a different substance from the arrow and the exertion of shooting the arrow. [89] The second, latency, is produced from the consciousness that serves as its cause, later producing a consciousness that is its own effect. Its existence is proven by the fact that something seen, heard, or experienced produces a memory later. They assert that if a latency is not deposited by such things as seeing and hearing, one would not remember them later. The third, elasticity, is a quality of a physical thing. Although something becomes different through exertion, when exertion stops, it has a quality of returning to its previous state. For example, although a sharp wire is bent with exertion and becomes a different shape, elasticity is what makes it return to its previous original state when the exertion stops.[161]

22) The definition of *merit* (*dharma*) is a cause for high rebirth and liberation that is produced by an action enjoined in the Vedas. (23) *Demerit* (*adharma*) is that which brings pain, the effect produced by an action prohibited in the Vedas. They assert that nine qualities—intellect, pleasure, pain, desire, aversion, effort, formative force, merit, and demerit—rely on the ātman.

24) The definition of *sound* (*śabda*) is a quality that is apprehended by the ear faculty. It has two kinds: sound that has the nature of tone, like the sound of a drum, and sound that has the nature of speech, like a recited scripture. There are another two kinds: manifest sound, like the two kinds of sound above, and unmanifest sound, which resides in space and is not within the scope of the ears. Because they are qualities that depend only on space, they are asserted to be permanent.

Activity

The definition of the third category, *activity*, is that which has a nature of movement, like walking. It has five kinds: (1) *Raising* (*utkṣepaṇa*), an action of bringing something above from below. It is a different substance from what is lifted and what lifts. (2) *Lowering* (*avakṣepaṇa*), the opposite of that; it is an action of lowering something below from above. It is a different substance from what is placed and what places. (3) *Contraction* (*ākuñcana*) serves as the cause of making something straight crooked. It is a different substance from what is contracted and what contracts. (4) *Expansion* (*prasāraṇa*) is the opposite of that; it makes what is crooked straight. It is a different substance from what is expanded and what expands it. (5) *Going* (*gamana*) is what makes one go to different places. It is a different entity from the destination and the traveler. [90] Citing the *Vaiśeṣika Sūtra*, the *Commentary on the Compendium of Principles* says, "The sūtra says that raising, lowering, contraction, expansion, and going are called *action*."[162] This also appears clearly in the *Blaze of Reasoning*.

Universal

The fourth category, *universal*, is defined as that which causes common terms or concepts to be attributed to things that instantiate a quality.

There are two kinds, pervasive universal and partial universal, which are also called supreme universal and nonsupreme universal, respectively. The first is coextensive with the substance, quality, and activity that are its basis, and it serves as the cause for a shared term and concept for that phenomenon. It pervades all three [substance, quality, and activity] and refers only to what is universal—for example, existence (*sattā*). The second applies to whichever of the three—substance, quality, or activity—is its basis and refers to a universal that is also a particular, for example, a pot's "potness." This is a universal because it is coextensive with particular pots; however, because it is a factor that differentiates its particulars, pots, from what are not pots, it is also particular. Thus the *Commentary on the Compendium of Principles* says:

> Universals are of two kinds: supreme and nonsupreme. Existence is supreme because it is the cause of the consciousness that engages with all three—substance, quality, and activity. It is only a universal and not a particular. The nonsupreme, on the contrary, has the characteristic of substance, quality, or activity. It is called *universal* because it is the cause of the consciousness that engages with the substance and so forth that is its basis. Although it is a universal, it is called *particular* because it is the cause of a consciousness that excludes things of a different type from its basis.[163]

The *Blaze of Reasoning* also says, "There are two universals—the great universal and the partial. Because substance, quality, and activity are said to exist, existence is the great universal. A partial universal is like cowness. It is a partial universal that excludes such things as horses."[164] [91]

This demonstrates how we know that those universals exist. Regarding cows, if a single cause that produces the thought "they are cows" was not necessary, then, just as the thought "they are cows" arises that apprehends a white cow and a black cow as the same species, so the thought that apprehends a cow and a tree as the same species would need to arise. This is because the two cases are similar in that they do not require a shared universal to cause the mind to apprehend a single species. Therefore shared terms and concepts prove universals exist.

Particularity

The definition of the fifth category, *particularity* or *difference*, is asserted to be a quality that serves as the cause for understanding that a basis is different from something else. As the *Blaze of Reasoning* says, "Being different is to have a distinctive feature. Just as white and black are different, substance and quality are also different."[165] Also, they assert that if what is called *particularity* did not exist, nothing could be understood as different from something else.

The three—universal, explained above, particularity, and inherence, explained below—are asserted to be without cause, pervading many, of a permanent nature, one without parts, inactive, and dependent on substance, quality, and activity. As the *Blaze of Reasoning* says, "Universal, particularity, and inherence are unproduced, pervasive, permanent, partless, without activity, and dependent on substance, quality, and activity."[166]

Inherence

The definition of the sixth category, *inherence*, is posited as that which serves as the object apprehended by a consciousness that, having observed the supporting and supported qualities of a single object, thinks "This has that." The *Blaze of Reasoning* says, "Inherence is an object that is understood correctly by an intellect, 'This is how it exists.'"[167] For example, it is the object of apprehension of a consciousness that thinks "The pot has a color." It is the factor that connects and relates the pot and the color. They assert that if inherence did not exist, there would be the fault that even though the pot and the color are connected, the intellect that thinks "The pot has a color" would not be produced. [92] Or, even though they are not connected, an intellect would be produced that thinks "This has that." Inherence is an object of consciousness that is a different substance from both the consciousness apprehending the pot and the consciousness apprehending the pot's color. Therefore they say that inherence is a different substance from both the pot and its color. It has two kinds: the relationship of the support and what is supported, like a tree and a crow perched in it, and the relationship of inherence in which there is not a different place, like a pot and its color.

One might ask what the difference is between the above-mentioned conjunction (*saṃyoga*) and inherence. Conjunction is the cause of a consciousness that apprehends the lack of gap between two connected things. Inherence is different because it is the cause of an intellect that apprehends that the supported exists on the support. Regarding the categories, they assert that a quality does not have another quality; a quality does not rely on anything other than substances; an all-pervasive universal is not coextensive with another universal; activity is impermanent; and particularity and inherence are permanent.

The later Vaiśeṣika sets forth the system of seven categories by adding nonexistence (*abhāva*) to the six categories of objects of knowledge explicitly enumerated in the *Vaiśeṣika Sūtra*. Yet even in the earlier Nyāya-Vaiśeṣika treatises they posit an independent entity called *nonexistence* with four subdivisions, although it is not described as a category. However, the fifth-century Vaiśeṣika master Candramati first set forth a system of ten categories by adding capability, incapability, lower universal, and nonexistence.[168] Based on that, eventually Vaiśeṣika widely counted nonexistence as a seventh category. For example, the *Deer of Reasoning* (*Nyāyakandalī*), composed by the tenth-century Vaiśeṣika master Śrīdhara, and the *Garland of Moonbeams* (*Kiraṇāvalī*), composed by the eleventh-century master Udayana, added nonexistence and made the system of seven categories authoritative in their own tradition. Delineated in this way, that assertion spread widely.

Nonexistence

The seventh category, *nonexistence*, is defined as the object of valid knowledge that perceives the absence of real existence. It has four kinds: prior nonexistence (*prāgabhāva*), nonexistence through disintegration (*pradhvaṃsābhāva*), utter nonexistence (*atyantābhāva*), and mutual nonexistence (*anyonyābhāva*). They can be illustrated as follows. Prior nonexistence, for example, is like the nonexistence of yogurt in milk. Nonexistence through disintegration is like the nonexistence of milk in yogurt. Utter nonexistence is like the nonexistence of the horns of a rabbit. Mutual nonexistence is like the nonexistence of a horse and a cow in each other. [93]

The Formation of Coarse Form from Particles and the Stages of Formation of the Environment and Its Inhabitants

We now turn to what this system asserts about how coarse form is created from extremely subtle particles and about the stages of the formation of the environment and its inhabitants.

First, regarding how a coarse whole substance is created, we can take the example of a coarse whole object such as a pot. When different particles of similar type, such as subtle particles of earth, cohere around the same place, first, a quality called *conjunction* is produced; it is the mutual connection of the particles that is different from those particles. After that, the substance of a whole, which is different from its parts, is produced. They assert, using the example of the pot, that if a whole that is different from the parts of a pot is not produced when the parts of a pot are assembled, then just as the convention of a pot does not apply to the individual parts of the pot, the convention of a pot would not apply to the assembled parts.

From a connection of two particles, the first whole substance, called the *secondary particle*, is produced. Because it is not an object of direct perception, it is called a particle. A part that is produced either from a connection of many particles or two wholes, such as the first whole, is an object of direct perception and is called *coarse*. Only the substances of the four elements can compose a whole substance; other particles cannot compose a whole substance. There are three kinds of parts: individual particles, the first whole composed by a connection of two particles, and the coarse whole composed by a connection of three or more particles.

Among these, the first are only parts. The latter two are both parts and wholes. They assert that the wholes composed of them are also of three kinds: those composed of individual particles, those composed of first wholes, and those composed of coarse wholes. Each single particle is neither a whole nor coarse. The first whole is a whole but does not appear to direct perception and therefore is not coarse. The coarse whole is an object of direct perception in every way and therefore is not a particle.[169] [94]

The stages of formation of the environment and its inhabitants have been briefly explained in the first volume of this series, *The Physical World*, in part 5 on the environment and its inhabitants. Regarding this system's assertions, citing a Vaiśeṣika text, the *Commentary on the Lamp of Wisdom* says:

> A tīrthika Vaiśeṣika text says that when the world disintegrates and becomes empty, the subtle particles of earth, water, fire, and wind remain permanently without dimension. After that, when the world forms, Maheśvara desires to emanate the world. Then, due to the ripening of sentient beings' karma and driven by their merit and demerit, from among those subtle particles of earth and so forth, first, two subtle particles of wind join. That is called a substance of two subtle particles of wind. To that substance of two subtle particles of wind, a third subtle particle of wind then joins. That is called a subtle particle of two subtle particles of wind. That subtle particle of two subtle particles of wind then instantly creates the resulting substance of subtle particles of wind. Then, for the first time, there is a great mass of wind, blowing again and again.[170]

This sets forth how those permanent and partless subtle particles of earth, water, fire, and wind compose the resulting substances of earth, water, fire, and wind. The same text says:

> Then, after that, a great circle of earth, an extremely solid mass, arises. On top of that, a great mass of fire, blazing everywhere, becomes a single tongue of flame that remains burning. Inside the great mass of fire, through Īśvara's desire, the bright and blazing great egg of Brahmā appears. When that bright and blazing great egg of Brahmā ripens and hatches, among the four-faced ones called Brahmā, the ancestors of the cosmos, Śikhin, born from a lotus, arises on the seat of a lotus. That Brahmā, the ancestor of all the worlds, produces all kinds of creatures, and the world is formed and abides. This is what they assert.[171]

This sets forth how the world of inhabitants is formed. [95]

The Subject, the Mind

This system, like Nyāya, asserts that there are three forms of valid knowledge: direct perception, inference, and scripture.

The definition of *direct perception* is a material relation established from the conjunction of ātman, sense faculty, mind, and object. Dignāga sets forth the Vaiśeṣika explanation in the *Compendium of Valid Knowledge*: "Vaiśeṣika says that what is established from a conjunction of ātman, sense faculty, mind, and object is different from them."[172]

It is divided into six kinds based on relation. (1) The *relation of conjunction* is like a connection between the eye sense faculty and a whole pot. (2) The *relation with what is included in conjunction* is like a connection between the eye sense faculty and the color, smell, and so forth included in a pot. (3) The *relation of what inheres in conjunction* is like a connection between the eye sense faculty and the universal of color included in the color of a pot. (4) The *relation of quality and qualified of the conjunction* is like a connection between the eye sense faculty and a place without a pot. (5) The second relation of conjunction among these [relations] is asserted to be the *relation of inclusion*. (6) The third relation of conjunction is the *relation of what is included in convergence*. In summary, they are included in two relations—the relation of conjunction and the relation of inherence. One may ask: What is it that posits a sense consciousness apprehending form? They think it is established by the power of the relation between the eye sense faculty (the dominant condition) and a form.[173]

The definition and subdivision of *inference* and the definition and subdivision of *verbal valid knowledge* ["scripture" above] are similar to those of Nyāya. They can be understood from the presentation of the Nyāya assertions on the valid means of knowledge in the next chapter.

A Brief Explanation of the Proofs for the Categories of Objects of Knowledge

Now to briefly explain the proofs for some subtle objects of knowledge. One might ask: What kind of proofs are delineated for the above-mentioned categories of objects of knowledge, especially for hidden objects? This system, as is the practice of all philosophical schools, delineates the mode of being of things using reasons. [96] As mentioned above, Vaiśeṣika in particular is very similar to Nyāya on the essential points of logical reasons and follows them.

First, to explain their presentation of reason, the definition of a reason is generally said to be the statement of a reason or sign in order to understand what is suitable to be proven. It is divided into correct signs and pseudo-signs. A *correct sign* is a consciousness preceded by a direct perception that apprehends the relation between the sign and the property. In the case of an inference, it appears that a sign in which the relation between the sign and the property is proven and that serves as the basis of an inference must be posited as a correct sign. This has three kinds: reasons with positive and negative pervasions, with only positive pervasion, and with only negative pervasion. Or, as Dignāga's *Compendium of Valid Knowledge* says, "Nyāya says that inference, which is preceded by that, is of three kinds: inference from what is prior, from what remains, and from what is commonly seen."[174] Just as inference is divided into three, the reasons that serve as its basis are divided into three. A reason that infers an effect from a cause is a reason from something prior. A reason that infers a cause from an effect is a reason from what remains. A reason that infers something hidden by seeing another thing is like seeing the moon disappear behind a mountain and inferring that the sun disappears in the same way. In general, for those reasons that involve sight, this system appears to assert what is asserted by Nyāya.

A *pseudo-sign* is a reason different from those above. Regarding its divisions, the *Autocommentary on the Compendium of Valid Knowledge* says, "There are three kinds of pseudo-signs for Vaiśeṣika: reasons that are not established, that are not indicated, and whose existence is doubtful."[175] Thus they assert three kinds of pseudo-signs: signs in which the relation between the sign and the property is not established, is uncertain, and is doubtful.

Second, to explain how they delineate hidden things that are invisible to direct perception, some of the things that appear in the works of Indian scholars will be given as examples. First, to prove the existence of Īśvara, the eternal and self-arisen creator of the world, they say, "The abode, bodies, and resources of the world are preceded by an intellect of a creator because after resting, he acts, like a hatchet; [97] and because they have specific shapes, like a pot; and because they are able to perform a function, like a battle axe." They say that these three reasonings prove the existence of a creator who created everything in the world with prior intention. Such an agent is Īśvara. The *Exposition of Valid Knowledge* says regarding Īśvara:

> Acting after a rest, having specific shapes,
> performing functions.[176]

The evidence provided for the existence of ātman in the *Vaiśeṣika Sūtra* is that the strength of the vital winds that move up and down in the body need regulation. From this, one can understand that there is such a regulator; an entity that exercises such regulation in a way that is suited to the body is the ātman. Also, because there must be an actor to act as one wishes, such as to open and close the eyes, the existence of the ātman is inferred. They have many such reasonings.

One such proof for the existence of an independent ātman is that the word *ātman* refers to a single entity that is not included in the collection of body, sense faculties, mind, intellect, and feelings because it is singular, like the word *pot*. To Vaiśeṣika, this proves that the ātman is independent and does not share the characteristic of the mental and physical aggregates.

Another proof for the existence of the ātman is based on how desire and hatred rely on something because they are effects of an existent thing, like form and so forth. Having established the existence of the basis of desire and hatred with this reason, if the eight other substances—the four elements, mind, space, direction, and time—are eliminated as that basis, then the existence of a basis for desire and aversion that is none of the eight other substances is established. They say that this, therefore, proves that ātman exists.[177] This can be found in detail in other sources.

A reason for the permanence of individual particles of the four elements is that they always remain in their own nature, since they themselves are not caused by any other particle; otherwise, they would become wholes. Therefore they are permanent because they have no cause. This is also stated in [98] the *Commentary on the Compendium of Principles*: "Since it is said that an entity without a cause is permanent, the permanence of particles is established based on their lack of a cause."[178]

The proof that sound is a quality that is dependent on the substance of space is that whatever is produced and disintegrates is necessarily based on a substance, like the light of a lamp. Sound also is produced and disintegrates; therefore it is established that sound relies on a substance. If its dependence on a substance other than space is refuted, it is established that it relies only on space. They refute that it relies on another substance because if it relied on the four—earth, water, fire, and wind—then sound would need to be where its support earth and so forth are, but it is not there. It is also because sound is heard separately from earth and so forth. It is not a quality of the ātman because it is perceived outside by the sense consciousnesses and is commonly perceived by many, both self and other. It is not a quality of direction, time, and mind because it is apprehended by the ears. Thus, the *Compendium of Principles* states:

> For the reason of cessation and so forth,
> sound relies on something.
> It is space.[179]

A logical proof for the existence of mind is that even when the five sense faculties and their five objects meet and remain near at the same time, the five consciousnesses are not produced simultaneouly; they arise gradually. For this reason, it is established that there is a cause for sense consciousness that is not included in either the sense faculties or their objects. They call this *mind*. The *Commentary on the Compendium of Principles* cites the sūtra of the rishi Akṣapāda: "The sūtra says that the fact that consciousness is not produced simultaneously is the mark of mind."[180]

The logical proof that a whole and its parts are different substances is illustrated with the example of the whole of a cloth and its parts, the threads. Because the maker of a cloth is a male weaver and the maker of the threads is a female spinner, they have different makers. Because a cloth can remove cold while the threads cannot, they have different capabilities. Because the threads originate earlier and a cloth arises from them later, they exist in different times. [99] Because the width and length of a cloth are large and small and its threads long and short, they have different sizes. Based on many such reasons including these, it is proven that the two are different substances. Regarding that, the *Commentary on the Compendium of Principles* says:

> In order to prove that a whole and its parts are different, [the root verse says], "just as a cloth and its threads are different." To express this in syllogisms: A cloth is different from the threads, the material from which it is made, because the one who made it is a different person, as in the case of a pot. The threads and a cloth are different because they have different capabilities, like a poison and its antidote; because they originate at earlier and later times, like a father and his son; because their sizes are different, like the fruit of jujube, Indian gooseberry, and Indian

> bael trees. To cover all their concomitance, [the root verse] says, "because they have contradictory properties." The reason that things differ from each other is that they have contradictory properties, like a pillar [from a pot] and so forth. This also applies to the case of a whole and its parts. Thus the maker of the threads is a woman while that of a cloth is a male weaver. Cloth can produce the effect of removing cold while the threads cannot. The threads are seen first because they arise earlier. Cloth arises later because it is seen later when it is made by a weaver. Because each thread does not have the width and length of cloth, they have different sizes. Therefore they think that those reasons are not indefinite.[181]

This concludes a brief presentation of the basic tenets of Vaiśeṣika philosophy and of the reasons delineating them based on what appears in Indian Buddhist and non-Buddhist texts. [100]

5

The Nyāya School

How This School of Tenets Arose

The teacher of this system is Gautama, author of the *Nyāya Sūtra*—the foundational teaching for this school.[182] Early Nyāya treatises by such masters as Vātsyāyana, Uddyotakara, and Vācaspati Miśra say that Gautama and Akṣapāda are the same person. The majority of early Tibetan scholars hold that the rishi Akṣapāda composed the *Nyāya Sūtra*, thus also asserting that Gautama and Akṣapāda are not different persons.[183] The name of the rishi Gautama is clearly mentioned in the *Padma Purāṇa* as well as in the *Mahābhārata*, attributed to the rishi Vyāsa, a follower of the rishi Gautama who lived during the Dvāpara Yuga [the previous cosmic age]. Based on this, both the teacher and tenets of this system are asserted to have appeared during the Dvāpara Yuga or earlier. Among Buddhist texts, the name Nyāya and its philosophy clearly appear in some versions of the *Descent into Laṅkā Sūtra*.[184]

There seem to be many explanations of the meaning of the name Akṣapāda ("one whose eyes are on his feet"). According to an ancient legend in Prajñāvarman's *Commentary on Praise of the One More Perfect Than the Gods*, when Maheśvara [Śiva] appointed him to protect his wife, Umā, the rishi dropped his eyes to his feet to keep the vows. [101] Because Maheśvara was pleased by that, he empowered him to compose the scripture, and so he is known by that name.[185]

What are the texts that set forth Nyāya philosophy? As noted, the foundational text is the *Nyāya Sūtra* composed by the rishi Gautama. Nāgārjuna, in his *Finely Woven* root text and its commentary, identifies the subject matter of the *Nyāya Sūtra*, the sixteen categories (*padārtha*) of logic, and extensively refutes them. Thus it is clear that the *Nyāya Sūtra* had already been committed to writing during the lifetime of Nāgārjuna. However, it is also clear that at that time, only the first chapter of the presently extant *Nyāya Sūtra* existed; the master's treatise does not refute the other parts of the *Nyāya Sūtra*, and the other parts of the extant *Nyāya Sūtra* cite and refute the assertions of Asaṅga and his brother Vasubandhu as well as the assertions of Sautrāntika, which all postdate Nāgārjuna.[186]

Vātsyāyana, the master of this system who appeared during the fourth or fifth century, composed the first commentary on the *Nyāya Sūtra*, the *Extensive Explanation on the Nyāya Sūtra* (*Nyāyabhāṣya*). It contains many refutations of Buddhist philosophy in general and of the works of Asaṅga and his brother Vasubandhu. Later, Dignāga, the great founder of Buddhist logic, refuted that text many times. During the sixth century, Uddyotakara composed the *Commentary on Nyāya* (*Nyāyavārttika*), a commentary on the *Extensive Explanation on the Nyāya Sūtra*. Jñānaśrībhadra's *Commentary on the Ascertainment of Valid Knowledge* says, "The phrase 'others say' refers to Uddyotakara, a commentator on the rishi Akṣapāda's sūtra and a contemporary of Dharmakīrti."[187] This indicates that Uddyotakara lived around the time of the Buddhist scholar Dharmakīrti in the seventh century. [102]

Apart from their titles, most of the texts by Nyāya-Vaiśeṣika masters of the seventh to ninth centuries are not extant. However, the *Compendium of Principles* and its commentary, by Śāntarakṣita and his heir Kamalaśīla, set forth the assertions of Nyāya masters such as Aviddhakarṇa and Śaṅkarapati in detail.[188] It can be inferred from this that Nyāya-Vaiśeṣika tenets continued to flourish during the eighth century. In the ninth century, the scholar Jayanta Bhaṭṭa composed the treatise entitled *Blossoms of Reasoning* (*Nyāyamañjarī*). Also in the ninth century, the master Vācaspati Miśra composed the *Notes on the Meaning of the Commentary on the Nyāya Sūtra* (*Nyāyavārttikatātparyaṭīkā*). In the tenth century, the master Udayana composed the treatise entitled *Purification of the Notes on the Meaning* (*Tātparyaṭīkāpariśuddhi*). Thus it is clear that a series of Nyāya masters flourished, producing many commentaries and subcommentaries on the *Nyāya Sūtra*. In the fourteenth century, the master Gaṅgeśa composed and propagated the famous treatise *Wish-Granting Jewel of Reality* (*Tattvacintāmaṇi*), spreading the tradition of New Nyāya (Navyanyāya). Thus the tradition arose of dividing Nyāya into two: the Early and the New Nyāya.

The Definition and Divisions of Nyāya

The Nyāya school is defined as a school of tenets that follows the rishi Gautama and delineates the mode of being of objects of knowledge with sixteen categories of logic. Those who follow the rishi Gautama's *Nyāya Sūtra* and expound its philosophy are called the Naiyāyika.

They are divided into two: Early Naiyāyika and New Naiyāyika. Those who based themselves on the *Nyāya Sūtra* composed by Gautama and lived up to the late thirteenth or early fourteenth century are known as Early Naiyāyika. In the early fourteenth century, the master Gaṅgeśa composed a Nyāya treatise, and its followers are known as New Naiyāyika.

Nyāya Assertions

A Brief Explanation of the Sixteen Categories

The summary verse says: [103]

> Akṣapāda, empowered by Īśvara,
> imagined sixteen categories of logic
> such as *pramāṇa* and *prameya*.
> The commentators elucidated them.[189]

They assert that one is liberated from suffering through using reason to delineate the sixteen categories of logic, such as the valid means of knowledge (*pramāṇa*) and the objects of comprehension (*prameya*), and then understanding them without error. In the *Nyāya Sūtra*, renowned as the first text on the science of reasoning, the mode of being of objects of knowledge in general is summarized specifically into the sixteen categories of logic, from "valid means of knowledge" to "points of defeat" (*nigrahasthāna*). Nyāya's sixteen categories are enumerated at the beginning of the *Nyāya Sūtra* itself.[190] The *Detailed Explanation Illuminating All the Vehicles* by Subhūtighoṣa, a brahmin monk, also mentions them:

> Nyāya's sixteen categories are (1) valid means of knowledge (*pramāṇa*), (2) object of comprehension (*prameya*), (3) doubt (*saṃśaya*), (4) purpose (*prayojana*), (5) example (*dṛṣṭānta*), (6)

> tenet (*siddhānta*), (7) parts (*avayava*), (8) reasoning (*tarka*), (9) ascertainment (*nirṇaya*), (10) debate (*vāda*), (11) disputation (*jalpa*), (12) cavil (*vitaṇḍā*), (13) pseudo-reason (*hetvābhāsa*), (14) deceit (*chala*), (15) self-defeating objection (*jāti*), and (16) points of defeat (*nigrahasthāna*).[191]

Among those sixteen categories, the first two, (1) valid means of knowledge and (2) object of comprehension, will be explained below. Regarding the others, in sequence: (3) *Doubt* (*saṃśaya*) is confusion about two alternatives, whether something is or is not. (4) *Purpose* (*prayojana*) is a thing for the sake of which one makes an effort toward its cause, as a potter shapes clay for the purpose of a clay pot. (5) An *example* (*dṛṣṭānta*) is something that shares features with the object under discussion. (6) *Tenet* (*siddhānta*) is something that divides debaters as to whether it is right or wrong. (7) *Parts* (*avayava*) are the elements that prove the meaning of a thesis. (8) *Reasoning* (*tarka*) is investigation in order to understand reality. (9) *Ascertainment* (*nirṇaya*) is comprehending an object of investigation. (10) *Debate* (*vāda*) is two opponents holding their own positions and presenting refutations. (11) *Disputation* (*jalpa*, also translated as "discourse") is applying a word to a meaning. (12) *Cavil* (*vitaṇḍā*) is merely refuting another position without presenting one's own position. (13) *Pseudo-reason* (*hetvābhāsa*) is faulty reason. (14) *Deceit* (*chala*) is to spread lies or to cheat. (15) *Self-defeating objection* (*jāti*) or wrong response is the opponent's fallacious refutation of the proponent's reason, property to be proven, thesis, example, and so forth when the proponent has formulated a valid proof that can establish his thesis. (16) *Points of defeat* (*nigrahasthāna*), or *places of destruction*, are places where one is defeated by reasoning either by not stating the parts of the proof to the opponent correctly [104] or not correctly expressing the faults in the proof stated by the opponent.

Object of comprehension (*prameya*) is defined as that which becomes the nature of an object of valid knowledge. When divided, it is asserted that there are twelve objects of comprehension, from ātman to liberation. As Nāgārjuna's *Finely Woven Treatise* says, "If you ask, 'Why do you say intellect is an object of comprehension?' It is because you say that ātman, body, sense faculties, objects, intellect, mind, activity, fault, future lives, effect, suffering, and liberation are objects of comprehension."[192] This system's assertions on the ātman are for the most part similar to those of Vaiśeṣika.

On other objects of comprehension such as the body, Nyāya seems to share the assertions of the other tīrthika philosophical schools.

A Detailed Explanation of the Subject, Valid Means of Knowledge

Valid knowledge (*pramāṇa*) refers to an unmistaken understanding of an object, like understanding that a pot in a certain place exists and knowing that if the pot is not in that place, a pot is not there.

Nyāya asserts that there are four valid means of knowledge: direct valid knowledge, inference, analogy, and testimony. As the *Summary of the Opponents' Positions in the Drop of Reasoning* says, "Nyāya speaks of only four types of valid means of knowledge: direct perception, inference, similarity, and testimony."[193]

Direct perception (*pratyakṣa*) is such things as the eye faculty, which serves as the cause of understanding the object with direct valid knowledge. *Direct valid knowledge* is defined as an unmistaken consciousness produced from the contact between its causes, a sense faculty and an object. It is like an eye consciousness that clearly perceives an object based on the contact between the eye faculty and its object, a color. The *Blaze of Reasoning* says, "In the same way, direct valid knowledge is a consciousness from the coming together of a sense faculty, an object, and the mind."[194] [105]

It has two kinds: direct valid knowledge that is permanent and direct valid knowledge that is impermanent. For example, Nyāya asserts that the direct valid knowledge of Maheśvara is permanent. Because Maheśvara, being the cause, is asserted to be a permanent self-arisen being, his consciousness is also asserted to be permanent in the sense that it does not rely on causes and conditions. The eye consciousness of an ordinary human, however, is asserted to be impermanent because it undergoes change.

Direct valid knowledge is also divided into the nonconceptual and conceptual. The first is posited as direct perception that engages an object without analysis. It is called "without analysis" because it refers to an apprehension or consciousness of just the entity of the object; it does not also apprehend the connection between its general and specific qualities or its substratum and distinguishing features. For example, it is like a sense perception that only apprehends a shape.

The second, the *conceptual*, is posited as a direct perception that engages with its object with analysis. It is "with analysis" because it refers to an apprehension or consciousness of an object through the connection between its substratum and distinguishing features, and so forth. It is like, for example, a sense perception that apprehends that an object with branches and leaves is a tree, that those are branches, and that anything that is different from this is not a tree. It is asserted to be conceptual because it analyzes its object.

The *Compendium of Valid Knowledge* says, "Nyāya says that direct perception is consciousness produced from the contact between a sense faculty and an object that is nonverbal, unmistaken, and has the nature of ascertainment."[195] The contact between a sense faculty and an object in this definition of direct perception is, for example, the coming together of an eye faculty and an external object that has shape; that is, it is their conjunction with no spatial or temporal gap.

The second valid means of knowledge, *inference*, is of two kinds, based on whether it is verbally expressed: inference for oneself and inference for others. A consciousness that understands a hidden object based on a sign or a reason that is preceded by a direct perception that apprehends the relationship between the sign and the property is called an *inference for oneself*. For example, a person knows that if there is smoke in some place, like a kitchen, it is definitely due to its cause, fire. Then, wondering whether there is fire on a nearby mountain, he sees smoke on that mountain. As soon as he remembers that if there is smoke there must be fire, he produces a mind apprehending the sign, thinking "There is fire in that smoky place." This is valid knowledge that understands the existence of fire in that place based on the smoke. [106]

There are three kinds of inference for oneself based on whether it has both positive and negative concomitance, has only positive concomitance, or has only negative concomitance. In other words, the three kinds of inference are asserted to be that which is based on a sign of something prior, a sign of something remaining, and a sign of something commonly seen.

The second kind of inference, *inference for others*, is a cause for inferring a thing that has a sign. This refers to a verbal syllogism that has five parts stated to cause someone else to comprehend a thesis that the proponent understands. The five parts are: (1) the thesis (*pratijñā*), (2) the reason (*hetu*), (3) the example (*dṛṣṭānta*), (4) the application (*upanaya*), and (5) the conclusion (*nigamana*). Take, for example, the syllogism "A pot is impermanent because it is produced, like a cloud. In the same way, a pot is also produced. Therefore a pot is impermanent." Here, "A pot is impermanent" is the statement of the thesis. "Because it is produced" is the statement of the reason. "Like a cloud" is the statement of the example. "In the same way, a pot is also produced" is the application. "Therefore a pot is impermanent" is the conclusion. They assert that based on such an inference for the sake of others, a mind apprehending the sign is produced, and based on that, valid inferential knowledge is produced.

The third valid means of knowledge, *analogical valid knowledge*, is valid knowledge of the exemplified based on an example that is similar to it. The *Compendium of Principles* says:

> When a villager asks,
> "What is a gayal like?"
> A herder answers, "It is like a cow."
> Analogy is known to be this.[196]

For example, a farmer who does not know what a gayal is asks a herder who does, "What is a gayal like?" The herder answers, "A gayal is an animal similar to a cow." It is said that when the farmer is told this, it produces analogical valid knowledge of the gayal, the exemplified, based on the form, shape, and so forth of the cow, the example.

Verbal valid knowledge is posited in the *Nyāya Sūtra* as the words of a trustworthy person.[197] It has two kinds: one that has a visible thing as its object and one that has an invisible thing as its object. The first is like the words of worldly people. The second is like the words of a rishi, such as "One attains rebirth in heaven by performing the horse sacrifice." [107] There are three principal causes for understanding the meaning of such statements: the strong desire of the listener, the listener's ability to understand the meaning of the statement, and the spatial and temporal distance between the words. They explain that based on all three of those causes, a consciousness that understands the meaning is produced.

Logical Reasoning

The definition of a *reason* (*hetu*) is posited as that which is stated as a reason or a sign. It has two kinds: correct reasons and pseudo-reasons. A *correct reason* is defined as that which is coextensive with the property of the position. Something that a person wonders about and wants to know is called the *subject to be known*. When one proves that there is fire on a smoky mountain pass, the subject to be known is a smoky pass. That which proves the pervasion relationship and has the property to be proven is called a *similar example*. For example, when proving the existence of fire on a smoky pass, a similar example is a kitchen. That which does not have a given property to be proven is called a *dissimilar example*. For example, when proving the existence of fire on a smoky pass, a dissimilar example is a river.

Correct reasons are of three kinds based on how they prove the pervasion: (1) that which proves both positive and negative pervasion, (2) that which proves only positive pervasion, and (3) that which proves only negative pervasion. To give examples of these: (1) That which proves both positive and negative [pervasion] is like the statement "Fire exists on a smoky pass because there is smoke." Here, where there is smoke, there is concomitant fire that precedes it, as in a smoky kitchen. Such a statement proves a positive pervasion. Where there is no fire, there is also no smoke, as in a river. Such a statement proves a negative pervasion.

(2) A correct reason that has positive pervasion only is like saying, for example, "A pot is an object of comprehension because it is an object understood by a valid means of knowledge, as is a pillar, for example." That which is understood by a valid means of knowledge is necessarily an object of comprehension; something that is both not understood by a valid means of knowledge and not an object of comprehension is necessarily not established by a valid means of knowledge. Therefore this is asserted to be a reason that has only positive pervasion.

(3) That which has negative pervasion only is like saying, for example, "This living body has an ātman because it is alive." The reason why it is not established by its opponent with a positive pervasion is that there is no similar example other than the subject of the thesis. Therefore positive pervasion is not proven. [108] However, they argue that it is a correct reason that has only negative pervation by stating "That which has no ātman is not alive, for example, like a pot."

Also, when divided in terms of terminology, there are three kinds of inference: (1) the prior, which infers an effect from a cause, (2) the remaining, which infers a cause from an effect, and (3) the commonly seen, which is knowing a very hidden object from seeing some phenomenon. The *Com-*

pendium of Valid Knowledge states, "Nyāya says that inference, which is preceded [by direct perception], is of three kinds: those of something prior, of something later, and of the commonly seen."[198]

Turning to pseudo-reasons, a pseudo-reason is said to be a sign that cannot prove the thesis for the person who wishes to know. It has five kinds: mistaken pervasion, contradiction, dissimilarity, not established, and harmful.[199]

The first, *mistaken pervasion*, is called a sign in which there is no certainty of concomitance in the similar and dissimilar classes. It has three kinds: signs that are uncertain because of being common, being uncommon, and being unincluded. The *mistaken pervasion because of being common* is a reason that applies to an object that lacks the property to be proven. For example, it is like saying, "This mountain has a tree because it is an object of knowledge." Here, being an object of knowledge also applies to a place without a tree and so is uncertain.

The *mistaken pervasion because of being uncommon* is a reason that does not apply to similar or dissimilar cases but only to the basis of the debate. For example, it is like stating that sound is impermanent because it is sound to someone who does not understand whether sound is permanent or impermanent. That person is uncertain about whether sound belongs to permanent or impermanent beings, because the property of being sound exists only in sound.

The *mistaken pervasion because of being unincluded* is a reason that lacks inclusive and exclusive examples. For example, it is like saying, "The subject, all objects of knowledge, are impermanent because they are objects of comprehension." Because "all objects of knowledge" includes everything, there is no basis for delineating an object of knowledge that is not included. Thus, because an object of comprehension is not included in the similar class or dissimilar class, it is called a mistaken pervasion because of being unincluded. [109]

The second, *contradictory pseudo-reason*, is said to be a reason that ascertains what does not exist in the property to be proven. It is like saying, "The subject, sound, is permanent because it is a product." Whatever is a product lacks permanence because it is necessarily impermanent.

The third, *dissimilar pseudo-reason*, is a sign that does not have its own property to be proven; rather, it is a correct sign for proving the opposite about the property to be proven. It is like saying, "The subject, a pot, is permanent because it is a form." It is a correct reason for the opposite position: "The subject, a pot, is impermanent because it is a form."

The fourth, *unestablished pseudo-reason*, is a sign that does not prove the property of the position. It is further divided into unestablished basis, unestablished nature, and unestablished due to lack of the pervaded. A sign that is an unestablished basis is like saying, "The subject, the horn of a rabbit, is a form because it is a horn." It is called *sign that is an unestablished basis* because its basis, the horn of rabbit, is completely nonexistent.

A sign that is an unestablished nature is like saying, "The subject, sound, is impermanent because it is an object of the eye consciousness." It is called a *sign that has an unestablished nature* because the nature of the sign is not established for the subject one wishes to know about.

A sign that is unestablished due to lack of the pervaded is like saying, "The subject, a mountain pass, has smoke because it has fire." Among places filled with smoke, which is the property to be proven, there are cases where there is no fire, the proof. Therefore it is called *unestablished due to lack of the pervaded*.

The fifth, *invalidated pseudo-reason*, is like saying "The subject, a mass of fire, is not hot because it is a substance." It is called an *invalidated pseudo-reason* because what the sign is proving is undermined by another valid cognition, direct perception that apprehends the feeling of heat.

This has been a brief description of the Nyāya system, the great Indian school of tenets that principally delineates its tenets in terms of the sixteen categories of logic. [110]

6

The Mīmāṃsā School

How This School of Tenets Arose

The Mīmāṃsā, or Jaiminīya, school of tenets was founded by the teacher Jaimini. Its original texts are the Vedas, such as the *Ṛg Veda*, renowned as the ancestor of all Indian scriptures and sciences. It is explained that the most ancient Vedic texts spread in India about two thousand years before the Common Era. There are four Vedas: the *Ṛg Veda*, the *Sāma Veda*, the *Yajur Veda*, and the *Atharva Veda*. Each has four parts: the Saṃhitā, Brāhmaṇa, Āraṇyaka, and Upaniṣad. This is a vast textual corpus in terms of both subject matter and terminology, including hymns to individual deities; poetic compositions; rituals of burnt offerings, which are means of attaining rebirth in heaven and liberation; maṇḍala rites and the mantras connected to them; proofs for the ātman; texts on the seasons related to individual planets and stars; and the science of astronomy illustrated by the conjunctions of the planets and stars.

Because Vedic texts are very complex, people found them difficult to use. Seeing the great need to clarify obscure topics and, especially, to prove that the words of the Vedas are a nondeceptive source of valid knowledge, the teacher Jaimini [ca. fourth century BCE] composed his own text called the *Mīmāṃsā Sūtra* or *Jaimini Sūtra*. The sūtra has sixteen chapters; the first twelve are called the texts of twelve characteristics, or the twelve chapters, and the latter four are the divine treatises. It has 2,644 individual sūtras [in the sense of aphorisms].

Thereafter a follower of Jaimini, the second-century teacher Śabarasvāmin, whose real name was Ādityasena, composed a vast commentary on the *Mīmāṃsā Sūtra* called the *Commentary of Śabara* (*Śābarabhāṣya*). During the seventh century, Kumārila Bhaṭṭa, who upheld the tradition of this philosophical school, composed three famous commentaries on the

Commentary of Śabara: the *Commentary in Verse* (*Ślokavārttika*), the *Commentary on Ritual Practice* (*Tantravārttika*, written in prose), [111] and the *Small Commentary* (*Ṭupṭīkā*). He also wrote many other commentaries. Maṇḍana Miśra, the chief disciple of Kumārila, composed such works as the *Ordered Explanation of Mīmāṃsā* (*Mīmāṃsānukramaṇī*). Then, at the end of the seventh century, the master named Viṣṇu composed the *Examination of Īśvara* (*Īśvaramīmāṃsā*) and a compendium of philosophies. The eleventh-century master Pārthasārathi Miśra composed the *Jewel of the Doctrine* (*Tantraratna*) and the *Lamp on the Treatise* (*Śāstradīpikā*). Thus the lineage of Kumārila flourished.

Prabhākara, a disciple of Kumārila, his direct disciple Śālikanātha (ninth century), and Bhavanātha (tenth century) also composed many treatises of this system of tenets, further enlarging the lineage of the gurus. The master Murāri Miśra, who lived during the twelfth century, composed works such as the *Eyes of the Threefold Law* (*Tripādīnītinayana*) and the *Eleven Chapters* (*Ekādaśādyadhikaraṇa*). Based on his works, what is known as the Murāri tradition or the New Mīmāṃsā tradition became widespread; their exegesis is distinguished from the Old Mīmāṃsā tradition.

The Definition and Etymology of Mīmāṃsā

Mīṃāmsā is defined as a school of tenets that follows the teacher Jaimini, accepts six types of valid knowledge, such as direct perception and inference, and asserts that the knowing ātman has the nature of consciousness, is not matter, is partless and permanent, and is a separate substance.

The Mīmāṃsā school is also called Jaiminīya and Mīmāṃsaka. It is called Mīmāṃsā ("examination") because they conduct subtle examination and investigation. They are called Jaiminīya because they are followers of the teacher Jaimini. They are called the Mīmāṃsaka ("practitioners") because they practice the extensive external rites prescribed in the Vedas, such as sacrifice and burnt offerings. There are three lineages: of Kumārila, of the gurus, and of Murāri; sometimes two are given: the Old and New Mīmāṃsā. [112]

THE ASSERTIONS OF MĪMĀṂSĀ

The Basis

Regarding their tenets, Candrahari's *Jewel Garland* (*Ratnamālā*) says:

> Mīmāṃsā says that desire and so forth
> are natural properties of the mind,
> like the heat of fire, and so cannot be abandoned even by
> meditation.
> Thus there is no buddhahood.
> Because the cause and effect of future and former lives,
> virtue and sin, merit (*dharma*) and demerit (*adharma*),
> are established by valid Vedas, they exist.
> Most of their terminology
> is similar to that of Vaiśeṣika.[200]

They assert that there is temporary liberation from suffering. However, because the defilements are the nature of the mind in the way that heat is the nature of fire, they do not assert that there is complete liberation and buddhahood. In their assertions on substances and qualities, and on generalities and particularities, they are most similar to Nyāya and Vaiśeṣika.

Regarding how the environment and its inhabitants are formed, they say that when this world is empty darkness, the particles of the four elements remain separate, unpaired, and isolated, without touching each other. When the time comes for the shared karma of the sentient beings destined for this world to ripen, by the power of that karma two particles join. From that point many particles assemble, gradually forming the foundation, the wind maṇḍala. Then the fire maṇḍala is formed, where there rests an egg of Brahmā, blazing with golden light. Then the water maṇḍala is formed, where Viṣṇu sleeps on the nāga Śeṣa. An egg of golden light emerges from the blossom growing from his navel. Soon that egg grows and hatches, giving birth to the grandfather of this world, the four-faced Brahmā, on his lotus throne. He creates all the abodes, bodies, and resources of the world.

Their philosophers have seven names for that Brahmā in seven eons. The *Blaze of Reasoning* says, "The followers of that scripture say this. He is the fortunate one in different eons. In the first, he is called 'self-arisen.'

In the second, Brahmā. In the third, [113] Prajāpati. In the fourth, 'lotus born.' In the fifth, 'four faced.' In the sixth, 'grandfather.' In the seventh, 'he of the golden matrix.'"[201]

Brahmā created the inhabitants, sentient beings, by creating eight mothers of the cosmos: the sun mother, the mother Diti, the nāga mother, the garuḍa mother, and the mouth of Brahmā, his shoulders, his thighs, and the soles of his feet. The *Blaze of Reasoning* says, "After the appearance of Prajāpati, the eight mothers of the world were created. Then the sun mother gave birth to all the gods. The mother Diti gave birth to the demigods (*asura*). The mother of humans gave birth to humans. The nāga mother gave birth to the nāgas. The garuḍa mother gave birth to the garuḍas."[202] The same text describes how Brahmā created the four human castes: "From the mouth of Brahmā was born the brahmin. From his shoulders, the *kṣatriya*. From his thighs, the *vaiśya*. From the soles of his feet, the *śūdra*."[203] Thus they assert that the four castes of India were originally born from the body of Brahmā.

One might ask: Because this system asserts that karmic effects are not lost, what do they say about the nature of the ātman that is the basis of such karmic effects? They differ from other schools of tenets in their assertions about the ātman. Unlike the ātman of Sāṅkhya, it has the nature of the intellect. It is not physical matter as asserted by the Śaiva but has the nature of consciousness. Unlike the Buddhists, it is not impermanent but is permanent. Unlike the inseparability of body and mind asserted by Lokāyata, it is a separate substance from the body. It is not something that lacks the positive and negative concomitance asserted by Nyāya. Mīṃāmsā asserts that when the ātman experiences happiness it does not experience suffering, and when it experiences suffering it does not experience happiness. For example, when a snake is coiled it stops being stretched, and when it is stretched it stops being coiled, but it does not stop being a snake. Those circumstances stop, but its nature does not stop, and it is partless. Śāntarakṣita's *Compendium of Principles* states Kumārila's position in this way:

> Others assert that the ātman has a nature
> of negative and positive concomitance,
> that it has the nature of intention,
> that it has the character of intentional intellect. [114]
> For example, when a snake is coiled,

as soon as it stops
it becomes straight,
yet its snakeness continues.[204]

This is discussed extensively in the *Compendium of Principles* and its commentaries.

Valid Means of Knowledge

Regarding its assertions on the valid means of knowledge, Kamalaśīla's *Summary of the Opponents' Positions in the Drop of Reasoning* explains in general how this school presents the object of apprehension, its apprehender, how that apprehender engages its object, the effects of that engagement, and the sequence of their production:

> Jaiminīya and others say that, given that in the world what is to be proven and the proof by which it is proven are known to be distinct, it is only logical that the effect [i.e., knowledge] is distinct from the instrument of knowledge; an axe is not what is cut. Thus the truth of this knowledge consists solely of four aspects: the apprehender, the object of apprehension, the valid means of knowledge, and the realization. Among these, the apprehender is a person. The object of apprehension is an object such as a form. The valid means of knowledge is a sense faculty and so forth. The realization is the determination of the object. When only consciousness is a valid means of knowledge, subsequent consciousnesses are effects, and preceding ones are valid means of knowledge. A consciousness of an attribute such as a generality is a valid means of knowledge. A consciousness of an attribute such as a substance is an effect.[205]

When one cuts wood with an axe, the resulting cut wood must be posited as separate from the axe. In the same way, the apprehender, the object of apprehension, the means of apprehension, and the result of that apprehension, knowledge, must be posited separately. First, a mind that sees just the nature of an object is produced, and from that a mind is produced that ascertains its attributes, such as its type. From that, one engages with the object and then acquires the object. From that, happiness and so forth arise. Thus they assert that earlier minds are valid means of knowledge and subsequent ones are results.

They assert that valid means of knowledge that apprehend such objects are of six kinds. The same text says, "The Jaiminīya say that there are only six valid means of knowledge: direct perception, inference, similarity, verbal testimony, inference from circumstance (*arthāpatti*), and nonexistence (*abhāva*)."[206] [115] The first, *direct perception*, is a cognition produced from the contact between a sense faculty of a person and an object. The *Autocommentary on the Compendium of Valid Knowledge* says, "The Mīmāṃsaka say that direct perception is a cognition produced when a person's sense faculty has contact with an existent thing."[207]

In general, direct perception is of two kinds. Nonconceptual direct perception is like that which initially focuses on an object. Different from that is conceptual direct perception, which recognizes the object seen by direct perception, thinking, "This is it." The *Summary of the Opponents' Positions in the Drop of Reasoning* says, "The Jaiminīya say that only the first moment of the consciousness focusing on the object is produced nonconceptually. All subsequent direct perception is conceptual."[208]

The second valid means of knowledge, *inference*, is posited as a consciousness produced from a preceding direct perception. For example, a consciousness that infers the existence of fire by directly perceiving smoke on a mountain is produced from having directly seen their relationship in the past. Also, the knowledge that is produced through an earlier direct perception—like seeing the relationship of the sun and moon and inferring their movement through seeing the movement of another person—is posited as inference. The *Autocommentary on the Compendium of Valid Knowledge* says, "It is because inference and so forth are preceded by direct perception in Mīmāṃsā."[209]

Third, *analogy* for Mīmaṃsā is similar to the Nyāya assertion; please see that explanation above.

Fourth, the definition of *verbal valid knowledge* is apprehending the meaning of a hidden object of knowledge based on sound. It has two kinds, that which is produced from a sound not made by a person and that which is produced by the speech of a trustworthy person. They assert that because both understand a hidden meaning, they are not direct perception, and because they do not rely on a sign with the three modes [of being a property of the subject and of having positive and negative concomitance with the property to be proven], they are also not inference. The *Commentary on the Compendium of Principles* says:

> Śabarasvāmin says that the definition of *verbal valid knowledge* is understanding a given fact through the perception of sound. That which produces the meaning of a hidden object after apprehending the specific characteristics of a sound comes from sound. [116] Therefore it is verbal valid knowledge. It has two kinds, one produced from sounds not made by a living being and one produced from the words of a trustworthy person. Because it has a hidden object, it is different from direct perception. Because it lacks the three modes, it is not inference.[210]

This school asserts that the Vedas, which are uncreated by a living being, are a valid means of knowledge. Therefore it emphatically and extensively delineates proofs for the validity of verbal testimony in general and, especially, of the words of the Vedas. The Buddhist scholar Dignāga proved with reasoning that all expressive sounds have exclusions as their referents, that they engage with their objects by excluding what they are not, and that the meaning of expressive sounds depends on the wish of the speaker. Mīmāṃsā scholars like Kumārila strongly refuted Dignāga's assertions, but it is essential to know that this was because they went to the heart of Kumārila's own tenets.[211]

Fifth, inference from circumstance is posited as the understanding of a meaning unseen by oneself induced by another valid means of knowledge. It is like, for example, realizing that someone is away from home by seeing that the person, who is alive, is not at home. The *Compendium of Principles* says:

> An understanding of another unseen object,
> that is inference from circumstance.[212]

Inference from circumstance has six kinds based on the six valid means of knowledge, direct perception, and so forth, that induce it: (1) *Induced by direct perception* is like postulating the ability of fire to burn by directly perceiving its heat. (2) *Induced by inference* is like postulating the ability of the sun to move by inferring that it has moved to another place. [117] (3) *Induced by analogy* is like postulating the ability of cows to be milked and carry loads by knowing that cows are similar to gayals. (4) *Induced by verbal testimony* is like postulating that a fat person eats at night after hearing that that person does not eat food during the day. (5) *Understanding induced by implication* is like understanding the permanence of the use of a term by implication, as in previously calling a white cow a "cow" and later seeing a black cow and thinking, "This is a cow." This is because if the word originally used were impermanent, it would not come to mind when the verbal convention is used later. (6) *Induced by nonexistence* is like postulating that someone named Devadatta is outside by seeing that he is not dead and not in the house. The *Commentary on the Compendium of Principles* discusses these extensively. Regarding the first two, it says:

> In the verses beginning with "therein" (*tatra*), [Śāntarakṣita] provides examples of inference from circumstance preceded by the six types of valid knowledge, in order. Among them, inference from circumstance induced by direct perception is like understanding the ability of fire to burn after experiencing burning through direct perception. Inference from circumstance induced by inference is like understanding the ability of the sun to move from inferring that it has gone to another place.[213]

Sixth, *valid knowledge of nonexistence* is defined as valid knowledge that understands what is not understood by any of the five other forms of valid knowledge, such as direct perception, mentioned above. The *Compendium of Principles* says:

> When the five forms of valid knowledge
> do not produce knowledge of the nature of an object,
> in order to understand that that object exists
> there is the valid knowledge of nonexistence.[214]

It has four kinds. *Valid knowledge that understands prior nonexistence* (*prāgabhāva*) is, for example, understanding that yogurt does not exist in the state of milk. *Valid knowledge that understands nonexistence through disintegration* (*pradhvaṃsābhāva*) is like understanding that milk, having been destroyed, does not exist in the state of yogurt. *Valid knowledge that understands mutual nonexistence* (*anyonyābhāva*) is like understanding the nonexistence of a cow in a horse and the nonexistence of a horse in a cow. *Valid knowledge that understands utter nonexistence* (*atyantābhāva*) is like understanding the nonexistence of the horn of a rabbit. Thus the *Compendium of Principles* says:

> The nonexistence of yogurt in milk
> is called prior nonexistence.
> The nonexistence of milk in yogurt
> is characterized as nonexistence through disintegration. [118]
> The nonexistence of a horse in a cow
> is called mutual nonexistence. . . .
> The nonexistence of the horn of a rabbit
> is asserted to be utter nonexistence.[215]

To give just an illustration of the reasonings that Mīmāṃsā uses to prove the correctness of their tenets, this is how they prove that the Vedas are eternal and self-arisen valid knowledge: The causes of fallacious words are faults, such as the ignorance and unkindness that reside in humans. Therefore they assert that words that are not produced by humans are necessarily trustworthy. The *Essence of the Middle Way* says:

> Because they are defiled by faults like desire,
> the words of humans are false.
> Because the Vedas were not made by humans,
> they are held to be valid.[216]

Also, they assert that because the author of the Vedas is not remembered, they were not produced by humans. Even the ancient seers, the reciters of the Vedas, merely recited the Vedas that existed before, passed down from one to the other; they did not newly create them. The same text says:

> Because they assert that the author is not remembered,
> the Vedas were not made by humans.
> Because their transmission has not been severed . . .[217]

Also, because Vedic speech was not produced by humans, it only expresses definitive meanings; it does not express different meanings based on the speaker's intention. For example, when one hears the words *agnihotraṃ juhuyāt*, "One who seeks heaven should perform the *agnihotra* ritual," it refers only to the *agnihotra*. In his *Exposition of Valid Knowledge*, however, when refuting Mīmāṃsā, Dharmakīrti wonders whether those words mean "One should eat dog meat" [because, with an author, one cannot know what the Vedas mean].

> Therefore, when one hears "one who desires heaven
> should perform the *agnihotra*,"
> does it not mean
> "One should eat dog meat"?[218]

Debates such as this appear extensively in Dharmakīrti's *Exposition of Valid Knowledge* and *Ascertainment of Valid Knowledge*, and in Bhāviveka's root text *Blaze of Reasoning* and its autocommentary. [119]

This system sets forth many reasonings to prove the existence of the ātman, such as the reasoning that the ātman exists because recognition and memory exist. In doing so, they seek to directly prove that the ātman exists and indirectly undermine Buddhists, who assert that a self of persons does not exist. The *Ślokavārttika* by the Mīmāṃsā scholar Kumārila says, "Therefore recognition is proven to be valid. Thus this recognition, acknowledged by the entire world, undermines those who say there is no ātman."[219] This argument is also stated in Śāntarakṣita's *Compendium of Principles*:

> There is such a soul
> because recognition exists.
> By simply realizing this,
> no-self is utterly undermined.[220]

This has been a brief description of the Jaiminīya or Mīmāṃsā system, which asserts many tenets, such as the proof that the Vedas are valid and the six types of valid knowledge.

The Assertions of the Caraka, a Sect of Mīmāṃsā

To briefly explain the assertions of the Caraka, or "physicians," the master of medicine named Caraka compiled the medical texts composed by the rishi Agniveśa called the *Compendium of Caraka* (*Carakasaṃhitā*). That medical text, in addition to methods for analyzing disease, delineates such topics as definitions of the valid means of knowledge, the meaning of logical terms, past and future lives, and so forth. They are the foundation of this system's philosophy. Some modern scholars say that this master and the Buddhist master Nāgārjuna were contemporaries. Some Indian medical texts say that when Viṣṇu took the form of a fish and restored the Vedas, the nāga Śeṣa took birth as the son of a rishi to pacify the various diseases of the human world; this son was Caraka. There seem to be a variety of descriptions of him, such as this legend.

This system's presentation of the basis is similar to that of Mīmāṃsā. Regarding consciousness, in general, as in the other schools of tenets, whether an object of knowledge is the basis of analysis by the subject, an awareness, is posited from the perspective of whether it is observed by a valid means of knowledge. [120] They assert four ways to examine objects: direct perception, inference, trustworthy statements, and reasoning. The *Compendium of Caraka* states, "Everything is of two kinds; existent or nonexistent. They are analyzed in four ways: trustworthy statements, direct perception, inference, and reasoning."[221]

1) *Direct perception* is asserted to be an awareness that illuminates its object when it engages the object based on the conjunction of the ātman (the support), the mind (the immediately preceding condition), a sense faculty (the dominant condition), and the five objects such as form (the observed object condition). The *Compendium of Caraka* says:

> When engaged through the conjunction
> of self, sense faculty, mind, and object,
> awareness illuminates it;
> this is described as direct perception.[222]

2) *Inference* is, for example, a mind that infers the existence of fire in a certain place because of directly perceiving smoke there. They assert that

there are three kinds of inference for the three times: Inference of a past cause based on the sign of its effect is like inferring previous sexual intercourse from the birth of a child. Inference of a future effect based on the sign of a cause is like inferring the growth of fruit from a seed. Inference of another instance of a present object based on the sign of a presently seen object is like presently inferring fire on the other side of a mountain pass from seeing billowing blue smoke at present. The *Compendium of Caraka* says:

> Inference preceded by perception
> has three kinds for the three times.
> From smoke, one knows there is fire.
> From seeing a pregnant woman, one knows there was sexual intercourse.
> From seeing something similar in the past,
> one knows that a future fruit comes from a seed.[223]

3) *Trustworthy statements* are the speech of excellent people who have destroyed passion (*rajas*) and ignorance (*tamas*). Because they are words that are free from doubt and are great truths, they are trustworthy statements. They assert that the words of those who are not excellent are not trustworthy statements because they are not free from doubt and thus are the words of those who have not destroyed passion and ignorance. The *Compendium of Caraka* says: [121]

> Words of the trustworthy and excellent
> are free from doubt
> and are great truths.
> Why would those without passion and ignorance speak falsely?[224]

Therefore a mind that understands the meaning of a word based on a trustworthy statement is asserted to be verbal valid knowledge.

4) *Reasoning* is like the coming of an abundant harvest in autumn based on water, manure, heat, moisture, plowing, and so forth. It is like pregnancy based on a combination of the six elements: earth, water, fire, wind, space, and consciousness. As is clearly stated in the *Compendium of Caraka*:

> Crops arise from the conjunction
> of water, plowing, seed, and season.
> Pregnancy arises from the conjunction of the six elements.
> This is reasoning.[225]

Whether or not they used the category of the four kinds of reasoning, this is in fact the reasoning of dependence.

This system asserts other forms of valid knowledge that are neither direct perception nor inference. The *Summary of the Opponents' Positions in the Drop of Reasoning* states, "The Caraka and others say that there are other forms of valid knowledge, called reasoning, nonobservation, possibility, oral transmission, and intuition."[226] Thus they assert that reasoning, nonobservation, possibility, oral transmission, and intuition have validity.

Reasoning here is a valid means of knowledge that understands the effect of a phenomenon by reason of its positive and negative concomitance in terms of its existence and nonexistence. Because it is conceptual, it is not direct perception. Because no example can be found for a sign that is the basis of inference, it is not inference. The reason why no example can be found is that if a phenomenon exists, it will belong to the class of existents, so there is nothing that can be shown as an example that is not within such a class. If a category of that phenomenon is used as its own example, it would need another category to be used as its example, and there would be no end. The *Commentary on the Compendium of Principles* says: [122]

> The physician Caraka says that reasoning is understanding that if this exists, its effect exists. Because it is conceptual, it is not direct perception. It is also not inference because there is no example. If an example existed, one would understand its result from its existence, which would require finding another example. Because that would require yet another, there would be no end. Therefore it is a separate form of valid knowledge.[227]

Nonobservation is a valid means of knowledge that understands that something does not exist because it is not observed in that place. It is like understanding the nonexistence of a horn of a rabbit because it is never observed by valid knowledge anywhere. Like the previous case, it is asserted to be neither direct perception nor inference. The *Commentary on the*

Compendium of Principles says, "In the same way, nonobservation is understanding nonexistence due to the absence of observation. It is a separate form of valid knowledge for the reason stated earlier."[228]

Possibility is a valid means of knowledge that understands the existence of a part when one understands the existence of a whole. It is like knowing that there are one hundred when one knows there are one thousand. Because this has no example, it is not inference, and because it is conceptual, it is not direct perception. The *Commentary on the Compendium of Principles* says, "The definition of *possibility* is that which understands a part when it understands the existence of a whole. It is like understanding that there is one hundred and so forth when one knows there is one thousand. Because this also has no example, it is not inference."[229]

Oral transmission is a valid means of knowledge that understands a meaning from an oral tradition passed down from one speaker to another. It is like knowing the abode of a *yakṣa* [a local spirit] based on a speaker passing on the transmission "a *yakṣa* lives in this tree." The *Commentary on the Compendium of Principles* says, "Others assert that oral transmission and so forth are separate forms of valid knowledge. Oral transmission is a transmission of a well-known teaching by a speaker. It is like saying 'a *yakṣa* lives in this tree.'"[230] [123]

Intuition is a valid means of knowledge that is like thinking, without any reason, that something will happen and then it happens. It is like a young girl thinking, "My brother will come today," and then he comes, just like that. The *Commentary on the Compendium of Principles* says, "Intuition is a consciousness that shows that something is or is not suddenly, without determination of the time and place. For example, a young girl thinks, 'My brother will come today,' and then he comes, just like that. Thus this is a form of valid knowledge."[231]

Regarding how this system proves former and future rebirths, the *Compendium of Caraka* states:

> Children who do not resemble their fathers and mothers are born. Even among those born in the same family, their complexion, shape, voice, mind, intellect, and merit are different. Some are born into a high caste, others into a low caste. Some are servants, others are lords. Some are happy, others suffer. Their lifespans are different. . . . Deeds done in previous lives are irre-

> versible and are not lost. This is called *merit*, and one is bound to it. That is the effect of this, and from this yet another effect will occur. From a fruit, its seed is inferred. That is an inference.[232]

As it says, from the same father and mother, children of different dispositions are born. Transmigrating beings of the same family have different colors and shapes. They do things without having created the causes for doing them in this life. Babies know how to suckle without being taught by others. People are born with characteristics of previous lives. Deeds done early in life produce different effects later in life. One's mind is clear about some things and not about others. People remember their past lives. There must be a cause for this, and it is impossible that that cause was established immediately and completely in the present. Thus there is no doubt that a part of that cause was established before, at a previous time. Therefore they assert that from the signs of these effects that are manifest in the present, one can infer, directly and indirectly, their causes: karma and the previous lives in which it was accumulated.

This has been a brief explanation of the Caraka presentation of objects of knowledge and the valid means of knowledge based on the texts of Indian Buddhist and non-Buddhist masters, especially the medical text *Compendium of Caraka*. [124]

7

The Vedānta School

How This School of Tenets Arose

Vedānta is similar to Mīmāṃsā in that they present their tenets having accepted the authority of the ancient Vedic scriptures, such as the *Ṛg Veda*. However, they differ in the fact that Mīmāṃsā primarily comments on the meaning of mantras and injunctions set forth in the most ancient parts of the Vedas, while Vedānta presents its tenets emphasizing the meaning of the Upaniṣads, the final part of the Vedas. Sometimes, the Mīmāṃsā is called Pūrvamīmāṃsā, or the Old Examination, and Vedānta is called Uttaramīmāṃsā, or the New Examination.

The Vedic scripture says, "The Vedas are of two kinds, mantras and brāhmaṇas." The Veda of mantras refers to mantras that are words of praise for particular gods and goddesses and the words that commemorate them. The Veda of brāhmaṇas, meaning "originated from brahmins," are treatises that extensively explain injunctions of burnt offerings and so forth. As mentioned above in the Mīmāṃsā chapter, between these two Vedas, the Veda of mantras is said to have been divided into four groups by the rishi Vyāsa according to their subject matter: the *Atharva*, *Yajur*, *Sāma*, and *Ṛg Veda*. After the the second part of the Vedas, the Veda of brāhmaṇas, the vast textual corpus called the Upaniṣads ("the secret"), the final part of the Vedas, appears. Because the assertions of a variety of the Indian schools of tenets are extensively set forth there, it is considered a common scripture of most of the Indian schools.

The earlier Vedic texts explained above are merely scriptural sources for its tenets; they are not the primary texts that set forth Vedānta's unique assertions. The primary texts that are its original sources are the Vedānta (that is, the Upaniṣads), the *Song of Śrī Kṛṣṇa* or the *Song of Viṣṇu* (that is, the *Bhagavad Gītā*), and the *Brahma Sūtra* (also known as the *Vedānta*

Sūtra)—the scripture of five hundred aphorisms, said to have been composed by the rishi Vyāsa, that delineates in one place a variety of topics from the first two scriptures. [125] Vedānta calls these three the *three objects of engagement* (*prasthānatrayī*).

Among these three, the text that primarily delineates the tenets of this system, the view set forth in the Vedānta (the Upaniṣads), is the *Brahma Sūtra*. However, because it is very concise, generations of scholars composed various commentaries on that treatise, spreading the Vedānta lineages. The modern Hindu tradition is said to be based chiefly on this Vedānta school of tenets. Within Vedānta, the most widespread lineage is Advaita; however, based on how different masters commented on the meaning of the *Brahma Sūtra*, several other lineages of Vedānta also appeared.

The tenets of Advaita Vedānta were extensively delineated by the famous master Śaṅkarācārya, who lived in the late seventh or the early eighth century. However, that the school predates him can be inferred from the presence of a chapter on the proponents of Vedānta in Bhāviveka's *Blaze of Reasoning*, which directly cites passages from the Upaniṣads as well as the *Verses of Gauḍapāda* (*Gauḍapādakārikā*).[233] Śāntarakṣita's *Compendium of Principles* sets forth this school's assertions on the ātman separately, and his commentary on his *Ornament of the Middle Way* cites passages from the *Verses of Gauḍapāda* when explaining assertions from the Upaniṣads. It is clear from this that the master Gauḍapāda should be posited as the founder of the Advaita Vedānta school. It is indisputable that the *Verses of Gauḍapāda* is later than Asaṅga and his brother (Vasubandhu). Śaṅkarācārya calls him "the guru of the guru." Modern historians place him around the late sixth century.

The Definition and Synonyms of This School

The Vedānta school is defined as a philosophy that follows the scripture of the Vedas and argues that all phenomena are the nature of consciousness, empty of the duality of object and apprehender. [126] The followers of the Vedas generally assert that Brahmā expounded the Vedas, and Vedānta asserts that Brahmā taught the Vedas; they follow the Vedic texts and assert that they are valid.

Synonyms for proponents of Vedānta are followers of the Upaniṣads (Aupaniṣada),[234] Vedāntin, New Mīmāṃsaka, Proponents of the True

Existence of Brahman, Proponents of the Best of Brahmins, and Proponents of Puruṣa as the Cause. They are "Secretists" because they follow the secret text. They are Vedāntin, or proponents of the end of the Vedas, because they say that they have gone to the end of the Vedas. They are New Mīmāṃsaka because they are the later between the early and later Mīmāṃsaka. They are Advaita ("nondual") Vedānta because they declare that consciousness of nonduality is the ultimate truth. They are Proponents of True Existence of Brahman because that ultimate consciousness is also called the reality of Brahman. They are Proponents of the Best of Brahmins because they say, "I am the best among brahmins." They are Proponents of Puruṣa as the Cause because they declare that the Puruṣa described in the Vedas is the sole cause of the various environments and inhabitants. Regarding these, Āryadeva's *Compendium on the Essence of Wisdom* says, "We are the best brahmins."[235] Bodhibhadra's commentary on that text says, "The best brahmins are those who declare, 'we are the best among brahmins.'"[236] The *Blaze of Reasoning* says, "A Vedāntin is one who has gone to the end of knowledge."[237] The *Compendium of Principles* states, "They think Puruṣa is the cause of the world."[238] [127]

VEDĀNTA ASSERTIONS

The Basis, the Two Truths

The description of the basis in the Vedānta system here is mainly that of Advaita Vedānta. Like the Buddhist and non-Buddhist philosophical schools in general, they assert that there are conventional and ultimate truths. However, based on statements in the Upaniṣads such as "I am Brahman" (*ahaṃ brahmāsmi*), "that is you" (*tat tvam asi*), and "this self is Brahman" (*ayam ātmā brahma*), they assert that the ultimate nondual consciousness alone is true; all phenomena of the environment and its inhabitants are merely false illusions. Also, there are four states: the waking state, the dreaming state, the sleeping state, and the "fourth state." Among the four states, what is experienced in the first three are the objects of the states of those not liberated from the bondage of not knowing the nature of conventional error. They are asserted to be conventional. The ultimate truth is the fourth state. It is the supreme Ātman and is called the state of abiding alone in the reality of Brahman. The first three states are worldly states that have a nature of conventional error, where one is not liberated from the bondage of ignorance. The fourth state is free from illusion-like appearances. The Ātman of that state is the ultimate truth. They assert that it is called the nondual reality of Brahman.

Such an ultimate truth is called Ātman, Brahman, Puruṣa, and Īśvara. The Upaniṣads explain that Brahman has three attributes: truth (*sat*), consciousness (*citta*), and bliss (*ānanda*). Ātman is also explained to be all-pervading, permanent, nonconceptual, and beyond the realm of intellect. The *Essence of the Middle Way* and its commentary cite the scriptures of the followers of the Upanisads:

> When a yogin meditates
> on the one, all-pervading, permanent
> Brahman, the supreme deathless state,
> he will not be reborn.
> That which is always nonconceptual
> is not within the reach of speech.
> Those whose minds are captivated by division
> use words for it.[239]

They explain that conventional phenomena merely arise by the power of a mistaken mind that makes distinctions and that they are illusions fabricated by ignorance. They assert that conceptions of diverse conventional pheneomena arise as the effects of the ripening of predispositions of beginningless ignorance. They assert that false conventionalities are of three kinds: [128] the mundane, the pure mundane, and the supramundane. The *mundane state*, or waking state, has both an apprehended object and an observing subject and engages in adopting and discarding based on the conception that those two are true. The *Verseṣ of Gauḍapāda* says:

> That which has the two, object and observer,
> is asserted to be mundane.[240]

The state of consciousness that observes although it has no object to apprehend is asserted to be the dream state or *pure mundane state*. The same text says:

> That which observes but has no object
> is asserted to be pure mundane.[241]

The state in which the dualistic appearance of the apprehended object and the apprehending subject has disappeared and does not exist is asserted to be the state of deep sleep or the *supramundane state*. The same text says:

> That which has neither object nor apprehender
> is called the supramundane.[242]

Here we will set forth the principal tenets of Vedānta as collected by Śāntarakṣita, citing Gauḍapāda's text. His autocommentary on the *Ornament of the Middle Way* says:

> The followers of the Upaniṣads say that the supreme Ātman is unitary, is the nature of consciousness only, and is vast like space. By meditating on it, a yogin becomes free from innate and noninnate ignorance; his breath (*prāṇa*) merges with it just as the space inside a pot merges with vast space when the pot is broken. The proponents [of Ātman] give it limitless names such as breath, quality, and element. This world has the nature of illusion and is free from duality, yet various entities appear, like dreams to a dreamer. The text says:
>
> > Just as when a pot is destroyed
> > the space inside the pot merges into space, [129]
> > breath merges into that Ātman.
> > Forms, effects, and expressions
> > are different here and there,
> > yet space has no difference.
> > Breath is certain to be the same.[243]
> > Just as fools think
> > stainless space is stained,
> > the unwise think that the Ātman is stained.[244]
> >
> > Just as a rope not recognized in darkness
> > is imagined as things
> > like a coiled snake,

so is the Ātman imagined.
When the rope is recognized,
the misconception stops.
It is just a rope, nothing else.
The Ātman is recognized in that way.
It is imagined to be limitless things
such as the breath.
That which causes confusion
is the illusion of the gods.
By those who know breath (*prāṇa*)
it is called *breath*,
elements (*bhūta*) by those who know them.
Those who know qualities (*guṇa*) think it is *qualities*,
realities (*tattva*) by those who know those.[245]

Just as there is no doubt that in a dream
the nondual mind appears to be dual,
so there is no doubt that when one is awake
the nondual appears to be dual.
Whether animate or inanimate,
what appears to be dual is the mind.
When Ātman is truly realized,
nothing is realized.
At that moment the mind vanishes;
when there is nothing to grasp,
there is no grasping.[246]

All of these descriptions that view the self as permanent and nondual were refuted earlier.[247] [130]

The verses cited above set forth essential points of this school's unique views of the basis, path, and fruition. The Ātman is like space. The ātmans of various beings appear to be different just as the spaces inside various clay pots appear to be different, yet when the pots are destroyed, those spaces become one. Also, a mind that imagines difference, like mistaking a mottled rope for a snake, produces mistaken appearances that dualistically apprehend difference through the power of ignorance concerning the fundamental basis of confusion, the nondual ultimate consciousness. The permanent Ātman is like the seed of both environments and inhabitants. Just as when one understands there is no snake in a rope, the error that apprehends the snake stops, so too, when one realizes that internal and external phenomena are produced by ignorance from the radiant Ātman that is the basis of error, mistaken dualistic appearances stop, and one abides in the state of nonconceptuality beyond the limits of subject and object.

This Vedānta system is like Vijñaptivāda [Cittamātra] in not accepting the existence of external objects. However, unlike Vijñaptivāda, they assert that the ultimate consciousness is permanent, unitary, and partless. They also seem to assert that, from the perspective of worldly conventions, which are mistaken and like illusions, object and apprehender—that is, valid knowledge and its object—are different substantial entities.

The Subject, Consciousness, and Valid Means of Knowledge

Vedānta masters, like most Indian philosophers, distinguish between the conceptual and the nonconceptual. However, this system must posit the actual reality, called the nonconceptual, to be Brahman, the ultimate state of objects. Such a nonconceptual and nondualistic consciousness is neither subject nor object. Its nature is just to illuminate itself, and it is completely pure, without action or quality. They assert that it is the innate primordial wisdom.

However, when they present valid means of knowledge in accordance with worldly convention, like Mīmāṃsā, they posit six forms of valid knowledge: direct perception, inference, analogy, verbal valid knowledge, postulation, and nonexistence.[248] Among all of these, this school regards scripture or verbal valid knowledge to be primary because, like Mīmāṃsā, it asserts that the Vedic scriptures are valid speech that was not created by humans. In general, Vedānta explains its tenets emphasizing the permanent Ātman, the nature of Brahman, and the ultimate consciousness free from duality. Thus they had little influence on logical argumentation in India. This can be inferred from that fact that Dignāga almost never includes theirs among the opponents' assertions on logic in his *Compendium of Valid Knowledge*. [131] In any case, as explained above, Vedānta refers to the mind that cognizes phenomena of the three states—mundane, pure mundane, and supramundane—as consciousness in the context of positing the valid means of knowledge and objects of comprehension. The objects of those three states are called the "objects of consciousness" in this context. Among those three wisdoms, *outward wisdom* is the wisdom that looks outward to understand various worlds. *Inward wisdom* is the wisdom that is devoid of any object and apprehends reality in terms of the subject, which is real. *Dense wisdom* is the wisdom in which dualistic appearances of object and apprehender disappear and the mind only knows its own nature. These are asserted to be the seed, ground, and essence of all saṃsāra and nirvāṇa. What they call "self-knowledge" is not understood [in the Buddhist sense] to mean consciousness taking itself as its own object. It must be understood simply as having the nature of awareness.

The Influence of Other Schools of Tenets

In general, there is no debate that this Vedānta school of tenets arose based on the intended meaning of the final part of the Vedas (the Upaniṣads), the *Bhagavad Gītā*, and especially the *Brahma Sūtra*'s explanation of them. However, it appears that this school of tenets was greatly influenced by earlier schools of tenets. For example, in this system they explain how the mistaken appearances of conventional illusory phenomena arise by the power of ignorance and that when the Ātman realizes the nature of Brahman, all errors of duality cease and only nonconceptual awareness remains. This is very similar to Sāṅkhya. According to Sāṅkhya, manifestations arise from the primary nature (*pradhāna*, *prakṛti*). When the knowing self (*puruṣa*) understands that, manifestations disappear as if they were ashamed, and the knowing self remains alone, without an object. From the historical perspective, the strong similarity between the two schools of tenets can be roughly inferred from the explanation that the Vedānta master Gauḍapāda wrote a commentary on the *Verses of Sāṅkhya*. The way that this school of tenets presents the valid means of knowledge in general and presents scripture or verbal valid knowledge in particular is very close to that of the Mīmāṃsā school discussed above.

Vijñaptivāda [Cittamātra] texts in general and the *Descent into Laṅkā Sūtra* in particular describe how the error of dualistic appearance arises through the power of ignorance. Vijñaptivāda proves the falsity of objects in the waking state with examples of false objects in a dream and proves the existence of consciousness without external objects. It presents the three natures (*trisvabhāva*), in which the imaginary nature (*parikalpita*) imagines duality in the dependent nature (*paratantra*), and explains that the absence of the imaginary, the object of negation, in the dependent is posited as the consummate nature (*pariniṣpanna*). [132] The three states presented here in the Vedānta school of tenets—the mundane, pure mundane, and supramundane states explained above—seem very similar. Nāgārjuna's Madhyamaka system was a major influence on this school of tenets. When we look at what is called this system's view of nonproduction, proving that things lack production, it is stated in a way that is very similar to Nāgārjuna's refutation of the four extremes of production (*catuṣkoṭi*). For example, the *Verses of Gauḍapāda* says:

> Not self, not other,
> neither true nor untrue.
> Consciousness knows nothing;
> the fourth one sees everything.[249]

Furthermore, how it uses the example of illusion and the example of a rope mistaken for a snake are seen to be influenced by the Madhyamaka reasoning proving the emptiness of all phenomena.[250] However, this system asserts that the ultimate consciousness of nonduality is permanent, all-pervading, and unitary. Thus it is not similar to the foundation consciousness (*ālayavijñāna*) of Vijñaptivāda. Because they assert that such a consciousness is the permanent Ātman, this school of tenets is included among the tīrthika proponents of self (*ātmavāda*). Madhyamaka asserts that all phenomena are not intrinsically produced and are merely dependently arisen; this system's assertion that conventional phenomena are false is partially similar to that. However, because it declares that nondual awareness is ultimately established, the Buddhists correctly classify it as a school that propounds true existence.[251]

The assertions of this school of tenets were fully delineated using the path of reasoning under the influence of the famous Vedānta master Śaṅkarācārya. [133] This master's assertions are not elucidated in the tenets texts in our Tengyur, such as the *Blaze of Reasoning* and its commentary, Śāntarakṣita's *Compendium of Principles*, and Āryadeva's *Compendium on the Essence of Wisdom* and its commentary by Bodhibhadra. Therefore they are not elucidated in Tibetan tenets texts. The most renowned texts of Śaṅkarācārya are the *Commentary on the Brahma Sūtra* (*Brahmasūtrabhāṣya*), which is very extensive, and his explanation of individual Upaniṣads, including the *Bṛhadāraṇyaka*, *Taittirīya*, *Aitareya*, *Chāndogya*, *Muṇḍaka*, and *Praśna*. In addition, there are the *Thousand Teachings* (*Upadeśasāhasrī*) and his commentary on the *Bhagavad Gītā*. These works remain widely known to the present day. Although this master's positions are generally in accord with those of Gauḍapāda, he seems to have created several original assertions. For example, this master divided Brahman into two—*nirguṇa-brahman*, "Brahman without qualities," and *saguṇa-brahman*, "Brahman with qualities." The first is the ultimate abode that is nonconceptual, actionless, and not an object, only a subject. The latter is asserted to be Īśvara, the creator of saṃsāra and nirvāṇa. Śaṅkarācārya is known to have not lived beyond the age of thirty-two, yet he is unrivaled in making the Upaniṣadic school of tenets flourish by the three activities of explanation, debate, and composition. His works delineate how the world of mistaken illusion is established based on how ignorance creates superimpositions, and they extensively set forth reasonings that prove nonproduction for his own Upaniṣadic system.

Later, the eleventh-century master named Rāmānuja delineated a school of tenets called the view of Qualified Nonduality (Viśiṣṭādvaita), according to which individual ātmans have the ability to become one with the supreme Ātman despite the fact that the supreme Ātman, whom they call Viṣṇu and the Advaita assert to be Brahman, and particular ātmans of individuals remain different. After him, the thirteenth-century master Madhva abandoned the position of nonduality and set forth the view of Dualism (Dvaita), in which the supreme Ātman (Viṣṇu) and ātmans of particular individuals are similar in that they are permanent but in fact remain different. Vedānta gradually became three groups: the Nondualists (Advaita), the Qualified Nondualists (Viśiṣṭādvaita), and the Dualists (Dvaita).

This has been an explanation of the origin of Vedānta and a brief presentation of its philosophy based on what appears in the texts of Buddhist and non-Buddhist masters. [134]

8

The Jaina School

How This School of Tenets Arose

This system is similar to Buddhism in that it does not hold the Vedas to be a source of valid knowledge and does not accept the existence of a creator of the world. This summary of their tenets will have three parts: a history of this school's teachers and philosophy, its definition and etymology, and an explanation of its assertions.

According to the Jaina scriptures, the teacher who founded this school was Ṛṣabhadeva. He is also known as the First Conqueror (Ādijina). According to their tradition, among the six periods of declining lifespan, twenty-four teachers are said to appear during the fourth period called "more unhappy than happy," and he is the first. Each of the twenty-four teachers is asserted to be a conqueror (*jina*) and a great hero (*mahāvīra*).[252]

The last of these teachers has several names: in his youth, his name was Vardhamāna, but he is also known as Nirgrantha and Jñātṛputra. His birthplace was the city of Kuṇḍagrāma in the kingdom of Vaiśālī in India. He was born in the sixth century BCE as the son of a kṣatriya father of the Jñātṛ clan and a mother named Triśalā. After renouncing the householder life, he practiced asceticism for twelve years. Living in solitude on the bank of the Ṛjupālika River in the town of Jṛmbhikagrāma in Bihar, he attained perfect wisdom through cultivating the path. He is said to have passed away at the age of seventy-two.[253] Some assert that this teacher was born about sixteen years earlier than the Buddha Śākyamuni; others explain that he was born about thirty-five years earlier.

Turning to the Jaina scriptures, the Āgamas were initially transmitted orally to appropriate disciples. Later, two groups of scriptures branched off from that: treatises called *Aṅgapraviṣṭa* and *Aṅgabāhya*. After the First Conqueror extensively elucidated the Jaina tenets again, it appears that the Digambara ("sky clad") and the Śvetāmbara ("white clad") propagated many *Aṅga* ("limb") and *Upāṅga* ("subsidiary limb") texts. [135] The *Aṅgapraviṣṭa* is asserted to be the words spoken by the teacher Ṛṣabhadeva recorded in the form of a treatise by his followers. It is also called the "twelve limbed" or the *Enumerated Collection* (*Gaṇipiṭaka*). The contents of those Jaina scriptures and the history of their commentaries should be known from their texts. Here, because the philosophy of this school is primarily being presented, only the most important scriptures delineating its philosophy will be identified.

There are several well-known and extant scriptures of the Jaina tenets. The teacher named Kundakunda of the first or early second century CE composed a scripture called *Essence of the Five Existents* (*Pañcāstikāyasāra*). Shortly after that, the teacher Umāsvāti composed a famous treatise called *Sūtra on the Meaning of the Principles* (*Tattvārthasūtra*), which extensively delineates the seven principles of the Jaina system. The most important commentary on this is the *Proof of All Meanings* (*Sarvārthasiddhi*), composed by the master Pūjyapāda in the sixth century; it has ten chapters, and all the later Jaina hold it to be authoritative. Also, around the second century, a master named Samantabhadra composed a treatise on logic, the *Investigation of Authority* (*Āptamīmāṃsā*). During the fifth century, a logician named Akalaṅka composed the *Compendium of Valid Knowledge* (*Pramāṇasaṅgraha*) and the *Ascertainment of Reasoning* (*Nyāyaviniścaya*), and the master Siddhasena Divākara composed the *Introduction to Reasoning* (*Nyāyāvatāra*) and the *Sūtra of the Noble-Minded* (*Sanmatisūtra*) and spread them widely. After that, the most famous logician was Mallavādin (eighth century), who composed a treatise called *Wheel of Perspectives* (*Nayacakra*), known especially for its analysis of the Buddhist master Dharmottara's text on valid knowledge. In short, based on extensive historical documents, one can understand how for some two thousand years, a series of masters spread the tenets of this tradition and composed many treatises.

The Definition and Etymology of Jaina

The definition of the Jaina or Nirgrantha school is a philosophy that follows the teacher Ādijina and delineates the mode of being of objects of knowledge in terms of seven principles (*tattva*) and six substances (*dravya*). Names for Nirgrantha include [136] Nirgrantha (unbound), Acelaka (unclothed), Bhasmacchanna (ash covered), Jaina, Digambara (sky clad), Ārhata (followers of the Arhat), Anapatrapa (shameless), Kṣapaṇa (exhausters), Tapasvin (ascetics), Ājīvika (followers of the rules of livelihood) and Parivrājaka (mendicant).

They are Nirgrantha, "unbound," because the followers of this school assert that if one engages in the ascetic practice of being naked, one will be liberated. They are the Unclothed because they do not wear clothes. They are the Ash Covered because they follow the practice of smearing ashes on the body. They are the Jaina because they are the followers of Ādijina. They are the Digambara, the "sky clad," because they say that the cardinal directions are their clothes. They are the Ārhata because they hold the rishi Arhat [Mahāvīra] as their teacher. They are the Shameless because they are not ashamed of being naked. They are the Exhausters because they assert that liberation is attained by plucking out their hair and exhausting their karma each day. They are the Ascetics because they assert that liberation is attained by ascetic practices such as fasting and using the five fires. They are the Ājīvika because they do not have possessions other than the life (*jīva*) of their bodies. They are the Wanderers because they wander in all directions on their alms rounds.

Jaina Assertions

The Seven Categories of Objects of Knowledge

This system asserts that there are seven principles (*tattva*) with regard to objects to be known. The *Sūtra on the Meaning of the Principles*, composed by the master Umāsvāti (ca. third century CE), says:

> The principles are soul (*jīva*), nonsoul (*ajīva*), influx (*āsrava*), bondage (*bandha*), stoppage (*saṃvara*), extinction (*nirjarā*), and liberation (*mokṣa*).[254]

As this states, the seven principles are (1) soul, (2) nonsoul, (3) influx, (4) bondage, (5) stoppage, (6) extinction or decay, and (7) liberation. They are called *principles* because the person who seeks liberation from suffering must definitely understand those principles well and must know what to adopt and discard in order to achieve that liberation.

It can also be said that the assertions of the Nirgrantha are based on nine categories of objects of knowledge. For example, Bhāviveka's *Blaze of Reasoning*, when setting forth the assertions of this school, says, "Regarding 'soul and so forth,' the nine categories imputed by the Nirgrantha are: soul, influx, stoppage, [137] disassociation, bondage, karma, sin (*pāpa*), and merit (*puṇya*)."[255] Here, in addition to the previous seven categories, two are added: sin and merit. When they are taken to be seven, sin and merit are subsumed in either influx or bondage. Therefore the lists of nine or seven categories are merely different classifications; the meaning is similar. Based on Bhāviveka's *Blaze of Reasoning*, Chomden Rikpai Raldri says:

> Skilled in the treatises on the stars,
> they are naked ascetics who accept three forms of valid
> knowledge.
> They believe that the ātman is the size of a body
> and designate nine categories of objects of knowledge.[256]

1) Among the categories, they assert that the *soul* (*jīva*), also called the *self* (*ātman*), is the agent of actions and their effects. It has the quality of mind and has a nature of knowing and seeing. Furthermore, it is the exact size of a person's body. Because it is eternal by nature, it functions at all times. Because its aspects are impermanent, it is also said to have characteristics of the opposite nature. Udbhaṭasiddhasvāmin's *Praise of the Exalted* says:

> The Nirgrantha say that the soul shrinks and expands
> according to the size of a body.[257]

In this system terms such as *soul*, *living being*, *self*, and *sentient being* seem for the most part to be synonymous. However, there are contexts in which they take on different meanings. Thus Bhāviveka's *Blaze of Reasoning* says, "Among them, *soul* refers to the nine classes of living beings: earth, water, tree, fire, wind, worm, ant, bee, and human."[258]

2) *Nonsoul* (*ajīva*) is a substance that lacks the capacity to know, see, and view objects. When divided there are five: matter (*pudgala*), bondage (*bandha*), motion (*dharma*), rest (*adharma*), and time (*kāla*). These are

also called the five nonsoul substances. Together with soul, they constitute the six substances asserted by the Jaina; the definition of each is explained below in the section on the six substances. [138]

3) Regarding *influx* (*āsrava*), the *Blaze of Reasoning* says, "Influx is virtuous and nonvirtuous karma because they flow in."[259] Thus influx is the cause for the fruitional aggregates and bondage that arise from the coming together of soul and nonsoul, or it is an action that is the source of those. It is called *influx* because it causes faults and afflictions and descent into *saṃsāra*. When divided, there are ten virtuous deeds that are the causes of happiness and ten nonvirtuous deeds that are the causes of suffering.

4) *Bondage* (*bandha*) is a substance that causes the self and karma that has flowed in to remain mixed in one place. Again, the *Blaze of Reasoning* says, "Bondage is the wrong views imagined by the 363 schools."[260] In other words it is the wrong views imagined by the proponents of error. They assert that it is called *bondage* because the soul, which is the nature of consciousness, is surrounded by karma and cannot separate itself. There are four kinds: (1) *Bondage of nature* refers to the fact that because individual karmas have different natures, some karma obstructs the enjoyment of self and some karma obstructs the qualities. (2) *Bondage of duration* refers to the fact that karma obstructs the qualities and so forth as long as it remains. (3) *Bondage of differentiation* refers to the fact that different karma, depending on its strength, binds in different ways. (4) *Bondage by parts* refers to the size of the binding karma and the sequence of its fruition.

5) *Stoppage* (*saṃvara*) is something that blocks the influx of virtue and nonvirtue into the continuum of a sentient being. As the *Blaze of Reasoning* says, "Stoppage is the blockage of influx; no new karma is accumulated."[261] There are six ways in which it blocks inflows: (1) *Blocking by restraint* (*gupti*) is to guard against bad deeds of body and speech. (2) *Blocking by moderation* (*samiti*) is to act ethically in body and speech. (3) *Blocking by virtue* (*dharma*) is to practice the ten virtues such as forbearance, being peaceful and disciplined, and being truthful. (4) *Blocking by contemplation* (*anuprekṣā*) is to contemplate a body as impure and to examine one's intentions again and again. (5) *Blocking by endurance* (*parīṣahajaya*) is to rely on the twenty-two mortifications of the body, such as hunger and thirst, in order to exhaust influx. [139] (6) *Blocking by conduct* (*cāritra*) is to rely on the practice of such things as mindfulness and conscientiousness that are prerequisites of perfect wisdom so that the self can go to a pure realm.

6) Regarding *extinction* or *decay* (*nirjarā*), the *Blaze of Reasoning* says, "Decay is the definite decay of previously accumulated karma through ascetic practices such as stoppage, fasting, not drinking, meditation, and yoga; it is the cause for their exhaustion."[262] Thus it is the extinction of connections between the self and karma or of portions of previously accumulated karma through the power of ascetic practices such as fasting and not drinking. They also call it the cause of liberation and the root of virtue.

7) Regarding *liberation* (*mokṣa*), the *Blaze of Reasoning* says, "Liberation is going to the place called the Welfare of the World (*lokasaṅgraha*) located above all other realms through exhausting all karma."[263] Thus they assert that it is the complete exhaustion of karma and bondage through the power of stoppage, destruction, correct view, correct knowledge, and correct conduct.

The Six Substances

This system organizes the seven principles discussed above into six substances: (1) the substance of soul, (2) the substance of nonsoul—that is, matter (*pudgala*) or physical substance, (3) the substance of *dharma*, which is the basis of motion, (4) the substance of *adharma*, which is the basis of rest, (5) space, and (6) time. Among these, (1) the nature of *soul* was explained above. (2) The substance of *matter* is a substance that has form, smell, taste, and touch. Umāsvāti's *Sūtra on the Meaning of Principle* says, "That which has touch, taste, smell, and color is matter."[264] This is saying that it is the substance of form or matter. Regarding the etymology of *pudgala*, the Tibetan translation *gang zag* is composed of two terms, *gang ba* ("being full") and *zag pa* ("contamination"); in other words, that which has the quality of defilement is called *gang zag*. Therefore, in this school, *pudgala* (*gang zag*) does not mean "sentient being" [or "person" as it does in other schools]. (3)–(4) *Dharma* and *adharma* here must be understood as substances that are the bases for the activities of motion and rest. (5) The substance of *space* is a substance that opens a place for others and pervades all embodied beings. [140] As Umāsvāti's *Sūtra on the Meaning of the Principles* says, "Space is opening a place."[265] Because such space benefits souls and matter by means of offering them a place to exist, it is not considered unconditioned (*asaṃskṛta*) [as it is by the Buddhists] but is classified as something that performs a function. (6) The substance of *time* is asserted to be a substance that serves as the basis for many qualities, such as continuation, transformation, activity, temporal priority, and posteriority. The same sūtra says, "Continuation, transformation, activity, priority, and posteriority are of time."[266] Furthermore, they assert that due to the power of time, all internal and external things engage in the actions of production and cessation, and they change from one state to another. All actions rely on time. Things change from one size to another based on time.

They explain that the substance of matter is physical while the other five substances do not have form. Soul and matter are substances that are active; the others do not have movement. Therefore one can understand that this system, unlike the other tīrthika schools, does not assert that the self is something that lacks activity. Furthermore, the six substances other than time are also called the *pañcāstikāya*, or the five aggregate entities. Some scriptures of the Jaina lineage call them the *five substances* and specifically delineate them.[267]

The Identity and Difference of Substance and Its Aspects

The definition of *substance* is "that which possesses qualities (*guṇa*) and aspects (*paryāya*)." Umāsvāti's *Sūtra on the Meaning of the Principles* says, "That which possesses qualities and aspects is called *substance*."[268] In that work, it is said that the nature and aspects of a substance are subject to manifestation and, between those two, the former is permanent while the latter are impermanent. Like other tīrthika schools that emphasize the topic of substance and quality, such as Vaiśeṣika and Nyāya, Jaina does not assert that substance and quality are different entities but that they are the same entity. [141] On this school's assertions about the difference between substance and its aspects, as well as their relationship, Kamalaśīla's *Commentary on the Compendium of Principles* says:

> As long as their place, time, and nature are not different, substance and its aspects are asserted to be the same; they differ in detail, such as number. Number is one, many, and so forth. Thus substance has the number "one," whereas its aspects, such as happiness, are many. Their characteristics are also different; the characteristic of substance is to subsist while the characteristic of its aspects is to cease. The word *term* [in the root verse] means

> name, and the word *meaning* means effect. It is said, "Because their place, time, and nature are not different, the property and the property-possessor are not different. Because their number, name, characteristic, and effect are different, they are different, as in the case of a pot and its color." The color and so forth do not differ from a pot in terms of their location and so forth. That which is the location and nature of a pot is also the case for its color and so forth. They are different from the pot in terms of number and so forth. The pot is one whereas its color and so forth are many; thus they are different in number. The substance of the pot is characterized by its subsistence, whereas its aspects such as color are characterized by their cessation; thus they are different in characteristic. The pot has the function of holding water, whereas color and so forth have the function of dyeing cloth red and so forth; thus they are different in effect.[269]

Thus the Jaina assert that conditioned (*saṃskṛta*) phenomena are produced both from self and other from the perspective of their position that, in the division into substance and aspects, identity and difference are not mutually exclusive. Because effects and the causes from which they are produced are the same substance, effects are produced from self. Because cause and aspect are different in the way they manifest, they are also produced from other. Therefore, in this system, the tenet of production from both self and other is held to be the correct position. [142]

The Subject, Consciousness

This system explains that the seven or nine categories of objects of knowledge are ascertained through valid means of knowledge (*pramāṇa*) and viewpoints (*naya*).[270] There are five kinds of knowledge: sensory knowledge (*matijñāna*), scriptural knowledge (*śrutajñāna*), extrasensory knowledge (*avadhijñāna*), knowledge of others' minds (*manaḥparyāyajñāna*), and omniscience (*kevalajñāna*). These are subsumed under two forms of valid knowledge: the first two are valid knowledge that understand objects in an indirect or hidden way while the latter three are forms of direct perception (*pratyakṣa*) that understand their objects directly. Jaina positions on the knowing subject and valid comprehension have many unique elements that are unlike those of other Buddhist and non-Buddhist systems. In the case of valid knowledge, the Jaina system defines consciousness as the correct knowledge of such bases of knowledge as the six substances. Umāsvāti's *Sūtra on the Meaning of the Principles* says, "Valid knowledge causes complete understanding of the modes" and that "it determines the object for any consciousness."[271]

To further explain the five kinds of knowledge: (1) *Sensory knowledge* takes present things as its objects; it depends on the physical sense faculties and the mental faculty. (2) *Scriptural knowledge* [literally "knowledge arisen from hearing"] takes everything of the three times as its objects. (3) *Extrasensory knowledge* is asserted to be knowledge that arises from understanding the cause of existence and its conditions—namely, karma. (4) *Knowledge of others' minds* is asserted to be direct perception of the past, present, and future thoughts and activities of sentient beings. (5) *Omniscience* [literally "absolute knowledge"] is asserted to be the wisdom of an all-knowing being. Among these [as noted above], extrasensory knowledge, knowledge of others' minds, and omniscience are direct perception that directly comprehends their object, and sensory knowledge and scriptural knowledge are valid knowledge that comprehend objects indirectly.

They assert *direct perception* to be a consciousness that comprehends its object without depending on things such as the mind and sense faculties, which are other than the self. They assert two kinds of direct perception: partial direct perception and complete direct perception. They explain that extrasensory knowledge and knowledge of others' minds are direct perception that comprehends parts of objects; they are called *partial direct perception*. Omniscience takes all phenomena of the three times as its objects and is permanent in the sense of being unchanging; it is called *complete direct perception*. [143]

There are two other kinds of direct perception: nonconceptual direct perception that comprehends a generality and conceptual direct perception that comprehends a particularity. Valid knowledge that understands a hidden object depending on a single mode [of an inference] is called *inference*. Scriptural valid knowledge refers to authoritative words, such as the speech of the teacher Mahāvīra. Regarding *reasoning*, the basis of inference, they assert that the modes of a syllogism are mistaken because the three modes exist but are unreliable, as in the case of inferring that someone has a dark complexion by reason of being the son of someone named

Devadatta. Therefore there is only one mode, called *being otherwise impossible* (*anyathānupapannatva*). A reason that exists only in the property to be proved is considered valid.[272] For example, in the inference "all objects of knowledge exist because they are observed," there is no similar example or positive and negative concomitance. The mode of being a property of the position is also included in the single mode of being otherwise impossible. This is what Jaina master Pātrasvāmin says.

To briefly illustrate how the Jaina prove hidden things with reasoning, take for example their argument proving the sentience of plants. They say that plants have sentience because they are produced from similar things. For example, horses are born from horses, not from cows. They also say plants have sentience because they grow gradually. For example, just as a horse goes through the states of being a colt, a young horse, and an old horse, a plant grows gradually from the states of being a sprout, a stalk, and so forth. They say poisonous plants must have hostility toward others because they destroy others' lives. Also, plants must be sentient because they are born in a timely manner. Just as horses are born in spring and dogs are born in autumn, plants are born in spring and summer. Also, plants have sentience because they sleep in winter and go wild in summer, just as donkeys sleep at night and run wild during the day. This system asserts that such reasonings prove the sentience of plants. Bhāviveka's *Blaze of Reasoning* says:

> Thus barley sprouts arise from barley seeds, not rice sprouts. In this way, they are produced from what is similar. Just as horses grow through the stages of being a colt, young, and old, plants grow through the stages of sprout, tiny trunk, trunk, branch, leaf, flower, and fruit. This is *growth* [in the root verse]. Having the intention to harm is enmity; because a poisonous plant destroys lives, it is known to have enmity. Cows and horses are born in the spring. Dogs are born during autumn. In the same way, [144] plants are also born in the spring and summer. The division of time for plants is thus: It is said that plants sleep or go wild according to time. In the winter, they sleep. In the summer, they go wild, just as donkeys and so forth sleep [according to time].[273]

The Jaina also assert that plants are sentient because they have sense faculties. Bhāviveka's *Blaze of Reasoning* says:

> They say that plants have sentience because they have sense faculties just as humans do. This is asserted in the Threefold [Veda]. Thus creepers such as grapevines and wild gourds are seen to depend on others and grow in dependence of others. Also, the rat snake-headed flowers [perhaps *Fritillaria meleagris*] and sunflowers follow the movements of the sun. Therefore it can be inferred that they have the eye faculty. When thunder resounds from a thick cloud, plantain trees begin bearing fruit. Thus they have the ear faculty. When the rotten corpse of a dog is placed at the root of a citron tree, it bears many fruits. Thus it has the nose faculty. When one pours milk on gooseberry trees, they bear many fruits. Thus they have the tongue faculty. The milk plant contracts when touched. Thus it has the body faculty. A man feels pleasure and shame at the same time when he has sexual intercourse with a passionate woman of low caste. In the same way, an aśoka tree that does not blossom and bear fruit, upon being touched by the resin-smeared and ankleted foot of a young woman, flirtatious and intoxicated by desire, bursts into bloom and bears abundant fruit as if felt pleasure and shame. Also, when a young woman sprinkles liquor from her mouth onto an unflowering bakula tree and laughs, its flowers blossom and laugh. Trees also bloom and bear fruit in timely manner. Therefore they have the mental faculty.[274] [145]

This concludes a brief explanation of the Jaina system, which presents its tenets from the perspective of the nine categories of objects of knowledge, or seven principles, and the six substances. [146]

9

The Lokāyata School

When the various Indian tīrthika philosophies are gathered, there are two types: those that assert the existence of past and future lives—the eternalists—and those that do not—the annihilationists. The eternalists are those described earlier, from Sāṅkhya to Jaina. The Lokāyata school, described here, is annihilationist. Its assertions will be briefly summarized here in four sections: (1) the history of this school, (2) its definition and division, (3) an explanation of its assertions, and (4) how they justify their views.

How This School of Tenets Arose

According to what is stated in some ancient Buddhist and non-Buddhist texts, the school was founded by a rishi named Bṛhaspati, the guru of gods. Some early Buddhist texts say that a rishi named Lokākṣin founded this school. Further research is needed to determine if Lokākṣin is another name for Bṛhaspati or whether this is the name of his disciple. In any case, the rishi Avatārabalin was a disciple of the rishi Lokākṣin, and he spread the teachings of this school widely. Kambala and Aśvatara were his disciples. Much later, Jayarāśi Bhaṭṭa and others are known to have upheld this tradition. Kamalaśīla's *Commentary on the Ornament for the Middle Way* says, "The guru of the gods was Bṛhaspati. The followers of the views of Bṛhaspati are the Cārvāka."[275] Bodhibhadra's *Explanation of the Compendium of the Essence of Wisdom* says, "The great rishi Lokākṣin composed one hundred thousand texts on the annihilationist view. For his followers, actions do not exist; they deny causes. Liberation does not exist; they deny effects."[276] Avalokitavrata's *Commentary on the Lamp of Wisdom* says, "Regarding the Āvatārabalina, it is known that there was a disciple of the great rishi Lokākṣin named Avatārabalin. He introduced another view of Lokāyata, and those Lokāyata who accepted it are called the Āvatārabalina. Because they are a type and branch of Avatārabalin, they are called the Āvatārabalina."[277] Also, Śāntarakṣita's *Compendium of Principles* says: [147]

> "It is reasonable that consciousness
> originates from the body."
> So say Kambala and Aśvatara.[278]

This is saying that the teachers Kambala and Aśvatara together created the philosophy that asserts that consciousness is produced from the body and not from the continuation of a previous substance of the same type.

As to when this school arose, the general elements of the Lokāyata philosophy clearly predate Śākyamuni, such as the position that past and future lives do not exist and the view that actions and effects do not exist. The *Going Forth Sūtra* says, "Know this, bodhisattva. 'Now the world is covered by sin. All beings have malicious intent. Jambudvīpa is disturbed by the six logicians, the six proclaimers, and the six meditators.'"[279] Thus there were tīrthika teachers such as Pūraṇa Kāśyapa in India before Prince Siddhārtha was born. Ancient Buddhist and non-Buddhist scholars knew Pūraṇa Kāśyapa and so forth to be Lokāyata teachers. Modern researchers say that works such as the *Lokāyata Sūtra* were composed, and the views of this school spread through its reasoning, around the time of Śākyamuni in the sixth century BCE.

The primary text that sets forth the view of this school is the *Sūtra of Bṛhaspati* (*Bārhaspatyasūtra*) [also known as the *Lokāyata Sūtra*] by Bṛhaspati, the guru of gods, which teaches that past and future lives and virtue and sin do not exist. He composed it so that the gods in the Heaven of Thirty-Three could defeat the demigods in battle. How it gradually appeared in the human realm is clear from the Tibetan texts on tenets. The existence of such a treatise, no longer extant, can be inferred from the fact that Candrakīrti's *Autocommentary on Entering the Middle Way* along with Śāntarakṣita's *Compendium of Principles* and Kamalaśīla's commentary on it cite passages from that text. As stated above, Bodhibhadra's *Explanation of the Compendium of the Essence of Wisdom* also cites passages from that text. Avalokitavrata's *Commentary on the Lamp of Wisdom* also says, "Here, this is said because the great rishi named Lokākṣin, relying on one branch of Sāṅkhya, created the one hundred thousand tenets of Lokāyata."[280] Later, the rishi Avatārabalin, a disciple of Lokākṣin, composed a Lokāyata text, and then the Lokāyata [148] tenets spread widely. After that, the Lokāyata teacher named Śrī Jayarāśi Bhaṭṭa, a contemporary of Śāntarakṣita, composed the treatise called *Lion That Devours Principles* (*Tattvopaplavasiṃha*), which is still extant in Sanskrit.

The Definition and Divisions of Lokāyata

This school of tenets is defined as a tīrthika school whose fundamental philosophy is that actions have no karmic effects. This school accepts that if one does a good deed, it does not bring a good effect, and if one does a bad deed, it does not fructify as a bad effect. Karmic retribution and past and future lives do not exist. Because they thus "cast to a distance" the correct view of the world—that good and bad effects are the fruition of good and bad actions—they are called Those Who Cast Afar (Lokāyata); the Sanskrit word *loka* means "world" and *āyata* means "gone far." It is a philosophy that has strayed from the correct view of the world. Bodhibhadra's *Explanation of the Compendium on the Essence of Wisdom* says, "It is called Lokāyata because it is separate from the correct view of the world. *Āyata* means gone, separation, and going."[281]

Regarding the synonymous names for this school, the summary verses say:

> Daivaguru, Bārhaspatya,
> proponent of nature, proponent of annihilation,
> Lokāyata, annihilationist,
> Cārvāka: these are the synonyms.[282]

As it says, Daivaguru or Bārhaspatya, proponent of nature, Lokāyata, proponent of annihilation, Cārvāka, and nihilist are all synonyms. Because they are the followers of the guru of gods, or Bṛhaspati, they are the Bārhaspatya or the Daivaguru. Because they propound that things arise naturally without a cause, they are the proponents of nature. Because they have strayed far from the correct view of the world that good and bad effects arise from good and bad actions, they are the Lokāyata. Because they propound that the continuum of self ceases when one dies, they are proponents of annihilation. Because they propound that one is satisfied by whatever is good in this life, they are the Cārvāka [hedonists]. Because they propound that past and future lives, virtue and sin, and actions and effects do not exist, they are nihilists. [149]

Lokāyata is also called a proponent of no cause and a proponent of intrinsic nature because, unlike other schools of tenets, it propounds that a hidden cause, such as the creator of the world Īśvara and karma, does not exist and because it propounds that internal and external phenomena arise only from the four self-arisen elements.[283]

Regarding its divisions, on the terminological level, the *Explanation of the Compendium of the Essence of Wisdom* says, "Here, Lokāyata is of three kinds."[284] There are three in terms of misconception, secret speech, and the view of annihilation. The first are philosophers who do not understand the mode of being of phenomena. The second are those who take only common knowledge to be their fundamental principle, without connection to the four seals that mark a view as the word of the Buddha. The third are philosophers who propound the view of annihilation that actions and effects and past and future lives do not exist in any way. The first two are merely descriptions of Lokāyata views; the last one is the actual school. In the *Descent into Laṅkā Sūtra*, the Buddha says, "I, at that time, said that Lokāyata is of eleven kinds."[285] Here, although Lokāyata is said to be many, these are just features of their view; they are not the real divisions of Lokāyata.

Asaṅga provides a different classification in the *Yogācāra Levels*: "Who propounds that there is no causation? There are two: those who rely on concentration and those who rely on logic. This should be known in accordance with what appears in the sūtra itself."[286] Thus the *Lokāyata Sūtra* says that there are two classifications, meditators and logicians. It appears that each of these has two types: proponents of annihilation who assert past and future lives but do not assert karmic retribution, and proponents of annihilation who do not assert either past and future lives or karmic retribution.

LOKĀYATA ASSERTIONS

A General Explanation

Regarding the Lokāyata's tenets, the summary verses say:

> The Lokāyata, proponents of annihilation,
> followers of the guru of the gods, [150]
> say that everything—body, mind, and senses—
> is the four elements of earth and so forth.
> Because the only form of valid knowledge is direct perception,
> things that cannot be seen do not exist.[287]

Thus this system asserts that the body, the sense faculties, and the mind are included in the four elements—earth, water, fire, and wind—and that sentient beings, in whom body and mind are the same substance, arise from them. The body and mind that are the domain of the senses are the self. Because this world arises adventitiously and spontaneously, they do not assert that there is a creator of the world. Regarding valid means of knowledge, there is only direct perception; inference that engages with hidden objects does not apprehend the actual thing, and so it does not fulfill the criteria for valid knowledge. They refute inferential valid knowledge that comprehends hidden objects, saying that all reasoning, such as inferring that someone has a dark complexion because of being the son of someone named Devadatta, is mistaken.

To cite some famous assertions of this system that are set forth in the texts of the Tibetan Tengyur, Āryadeva's *Establishing Proofs That Refute Mistaken Views* sets forth the assertions of Lokāyata:

> All phenomena, the external and internal sources,
> are established from the entity itself, not from another.
> The roundness of peas, the length and sharpness of thorns,
> the multicolored tail and neck of a peacock,
> the rising of the sun and the falling of water
> are established from the entity itself; they are not caused.[288]

Similarly, Bhāviveka's *Blaze of Reasoning* says:

> Here, this is what Lokāyata propounds. It is true that things do not originate from self, other, or both. However, internal things are produced only from themselves without depending on causes and conditions. This is their thesis because various things produced for no obvious reason are seen to be well established, for example, lotuses whose anthers are fresh in color, slightly yellow and red, which are sweet-smelling and have beautiful filaments, soft leaves, and a coarse trunk; peacocks whose tails are of various distinct circular shapes, who have dark green wings, and who are timid; and thorns whose tips are sharp and rough without being chipped.[289] [151]

Thus the Lokāyata give examples of the soft leaves and the coarse trunks of lotus flowers, sharp thorns, and the multicolored eyes of a peacock's tail as things that arise naturally without being made by anyone. Internal sources of experience—that is, phenomena included in the continuum of a person—are asserted to be established naturally. Regarding the meaning of "established naturally," Avalokitavrata's *Commentary on the Lamp of Wisdom* says, "'Naturally' refers to all things being fully established by their own nature without depending on anything, spontaneous, and unfabricated. 'The proponents of nature' are those who propound that things are produced naturally. It refers to the great rishi Lokākṣin, the creator of Lokāyata tenets."[290] It should be understood in this way. The Lokāyata in general posit temporary cause and effect, like immediate conditions that are directly seen, such as a sprout arising from a seed. However, they do not accept the cause and effect of such things as the arising of pleasurable and painful effects from virtue and sin. It therefore must be concluded that they deny karmic retribution.

Candrakīrti's *Autocommentary on Entering the Middle Way* says that the rishi Lokākṣin's position that various living beings are produced from the nature of their own four elements is only slightly different from the Sāṅkhya position, which argues that the various transformations are produced from *prakṛti*, or primary nature. It says:

> Reality consists of only four things: earth, water, fire, and wind, which are the causes of all the various living beings. Various things like lotuses, pomegranate trees, peacocks, and chickens

> are nothing more than what they look like, the features of their maturation. Intelligence, which discerns the reality of those various things, is also produced from these things alone.[291]

The Lokāyata think that intelligence is contingent on the body and arises only from the elements; therefore they assert that there are no past and future lives. Kamalaśīla's *Commentary on the Compendium of Principles*, citing the *Lokāyata Sūtra*, says, "Since there is no world beyond this, there is no afterlife" and "'In the same way, reality consists of the four: earth, water, fire, and wind, [152] and from these, sentience emerges.' This is the meaning of that sūtra."[292] Furthermore, Bhāviveka's *Essence of the Middle Way* says:

> When a lump of clay is destroyed by another being,
> it is not produced [again] because it is destroyed
> or because it is an effect,
> just like a pot. If you argue thus . . .[293]

This is the example of a clay pot that is a result of its own cause, clay. Therefore, when it is destroyed, it becomes nonexistent. This is the opponent's assertion that persons established from the four elements become nonexistent after they die. Also, Bhāviveka's *Essence of the Middle Way* says:

> From the mindless elements,
> the existence of consciousness is produced
> because they have [capacity for] production,
> like drunkenness [from beer] and fire from a magnifying glass.[294]

This gives the examples of the power of drunkenness to arise from beer and fire to arise from a magnifying glass to assert that consciousness is produced from insentient elements, which are different in type from each other. Dharmakīrti's *Exposition of Valid Knowledge* and its commentaries say that the Lokāyata give three main reasons why the intellect arises from the body. For example, Prajñākaragupta's *Ornament of the Exposition of Valid Knowledge* states:

> Intellect is of the nature of body,
> an effect of body, a quality of body.

> Here, based on these three views,
> cultivation is impossible.[295]

As it says, intellect is of the nature of the body, like liquor's ability to inebriate; it is an effect of the body like a lamp and its light; it is a quality of the body like a wall and its mural. Therefore they assert that it depends only on the body. This accords with what the *Sūtra of Bṛhaspati* says:

> There is no afterlife
> because there is no world beyond.

It also says, "Actions and their bringing about of effects do not exist." And, "There is no fortunate rebirth, there is no liberation."[296] [153]

Turning to how the Lokāyata assert that karmic retribution does not exist, Kalyāṇamitra's *Commentary on the Chapters on the Vinaya* describes how logicians and meditators decide this matter in accordance with their own perspectives:

> First of all, seeing that some miserly people whose nature is not to give have great wealth and enjoyments and that some who believe in giving and whose nature is to give are poor and have few enjoyments, the logicians think, "If there were an effect of giving, the miserly people whose nature is not to give should be poor and have few enjoyments. Those who believe in giving and whose nature is to give should have great wealth and enjoyments. This would be reasonable, but it is not so; instead, it appears to be opposite. Thus there is no [effect of] giving. There is no sacrifice. There is no fire ritual. There is no good conduct. There is no bad conduct." They see it in this way and say that.
>
> Seeing that some miserly people whose nature is not to give are born into families that have great wealth and enjoyments and that some who believe in giving and whose nature is to give are born into poor families that are poor and have few enjoyments, the meditators think, "If there were an effect of giving, the miserly people whose nature is not to give should be born into poor families and have few enjoyments. And those who

> believe in giving and whose nature is to give should be born into families with great wealth and enjoyments. This would be reasonable, but it is not so; instead, it appears to be opposite. Thus there is no [effect of] giving. There is no sacrifice. There is no fire ritual. There is no good conduct. There is no bad conduct." They see it and say it in this way.[297]

Furthermore, in accordance with the fact that the Lokāyata do not accept past and future lives, they assert that there is no self or person who comes here from a previous life. The body of this life simply arises from the coming together of the four elements. The mind of a person is also caused by such a body. They also prove that past and future lives do not exist by saying the cognition of a present person is produced by just the body. Because the body is simply created by the coming together of the four great elements of the present, former births do not exist. At the moment of death, the body dissolves into the four great elements, and the sense faculties dissolve into space and are destroyed. [154] Thus nothing goes on to the next life. This way of refuting the existence of future lives is set forth in the *Basis of the Vinaya*.[298] Therefore they do not assert such things as complete liberation from suffering. The *Lokāyata Sūtra* says:

> Beautiful one, live well and eat.
> The supreme body, once gone, will not arise.
> This body is just a collection.
> Once destroyed and gone, it will not return.[299]

In this way, among the objects of valid knowledge, the Lokāyata only accept the specifically characterized and the manifest, not the generally characterized and the hidden. For the manifest, they set forth the two truths in which what is well known as being false, such as illusions and reflections, are conventional truths. Other than that, things that originate from adventitious conditions, such as pillars, pots, and consciousness, are imputedly existent ultimate truths. Self-arisen things that do not depend on adventitious conditions such as the four elements of earth, water, fire, and wind are substantially existent ultimate truths.

The Subject, Consciousness

Regarding how the nature of intellect is established, the *Sūtra of Bṛhaspati* says:

> Mind, the knower of objects,
> is an aggregation of the body and the sense faculties.[300]

They assert that what is called *consciousness that knows objects*, or the mind, is merely a collection of three: the internal body, which is the support of the senses; the object, the external body; and the physical sense faculties.

With regard to the subject consciousness, they assert that there are the sense consciousnesses and mental consciousness, as well as mistaken consciousnesses and nonmistaken consciousnesses. However, regarding valid means of knowledge, they assert only direct perception; they do not assert inferential valid knowledge that comprehends hidden objects. The *Sūtra of Bṛhaspati* says, "Only direct perception is a valid means of knowledge."[301] It also says:

> The person is limited
> to whatever is the domain of the senses.
> Noble lady, what is said by the learned
> is like the tracks of a wolf.[302] [155]

Thus they explain that only direct perception is a valid means of knowledge. Because inference that engages with hidden objects does not apprehend the actual object, it does not fulfill the definition of valid means of knowledge. They reject inferential valid knowledge, saying that all reasoning, such as inferring that someone has a dark complexion due to being the son of someone named Devadatta, is mistaken. As the *Sūtra of Bṛhaspati* says, "Inference is not a valid means of knowledge."[303]

It is clear that there are two kinds of direct valid knowledge for the Lokāyata: sense direct perception and mental direct perception. When the *Sūtra of Bṛhaspati* says "whatever is the domain of the senses,"[304] that is *sense direct perception*. Because meditators explain that they see past and future lives with their supersensory knowledge, it is clear that they assert *mental direct perception*. Furthermore, how they assert the six collections of consciousness appears clearly in Jñānavajra's commentary on the *Descent into Laṅkā Sūtra*, *Ornament for the Essence of the Tathāgata*: "Some, including the Lokāyata, do not accept anything other than the six consciousnesses. Because the six cease at the time of death, this is a view of annihilation. They say past and future worlds do not exist."[305]

How They Prove That Their Views Are Correct

The Lokāyata tenets are not only very different from all of the ancient Buddhist and non-Buddhist schools, they were also the object of vigorous refutation by the other schools, who called them annihilationists. However, those who upheld that view set forth reasoned proofs of their positions to justify them. If one understands just some examples of how they proved their assertions, this will help one understand the essential points of this school. They are set forth here briefly.

This system has what are known as the four proofs and the five refutations. Among the four proofs, (1) they assert that consciousness, although invisible, exists in the four elements, which are the cause of the body and the sense faculties. They argue that there are three stages in the development of a sentient being: a mere sentient being, when consciousness latently exists in the four elements that are its causes; a mostly sentient being, when a subtle consciousness resides in a state such as an embryo in a mother's womb; and a completely living sentient being, when the sense consciousnesses become manifest after the physical sense faculties, effects caused by the four elements, are fully developed. [156] Śākyabuddhi's *Commentary on the Exposition of Valid Knowledge* says, "'Consciousness existing in earth' means that earth has consciousness. This is the Lokāyata view."[306] That the assertion that there is consciousness in the four elements is the Lokāyata philosophy is also clearly stated in Prajñākaragupta's *Ornament of the Exposition of Valid Knowledge*, "According to the Lokāyata view, there are different stages in earth and so forth, called 'a sentient being,' 'a mostly sentient being,' and 'a complete sentient being.'"[307]

(2) They accept the existence of an evident self, the point when the effect that is consciousness becomes manifest in the body of the four elements, where the body and mind share the same substance.

(3) Some Lokāyata argue that there are only three kinds of beings: unmanifest beings of the four elements, manifest human beings, and

animals. Hence they assert that only three beings are directly perceived: the four elements in which consciousness is unmanifest and animals and human beings in which consciousness is manifest.

(4) They do not assert that there is inferential valid knowledge that understands what is beyond worldly perception and therefore do not assert reasonings that prove such things. They do, however, assert mere inferences or reasonings that are known in the world. The *Sūtra of Bṛhaspati* states:

> Inferences recognized by the world
> are asserted even by the Cārvāka.
> However, those who proclaim inferences
> about what is beyond the world
> are to be refuted.[308]

This clearly sets forth two kinds of inferences: those to be refuted and those to be accepted. Kamalaśīla's *Summary of the Opponents' Positions in the Drop of Reasoning* says, "One should know that although the Lokāyata do make inferences for others with respect to hidden objects that they wish to assert—reasoning 'If this does not exist, that does not occur'—they claim that inference is not a valid means of knowledge."[309]

An inference known to the world is, for example, the Lokāyata reasoning that refutes the assertion by other schools of tenets that a person's body and mind are different substances, arguing instead that body and mind are the same indivisible substance. [157] They argue that a pot can be partnered either with the body of a person whose mind and body are the same substance or with a pot, because a pot is a thing that is not a lotus, just as a wall is not a pot. When stated in this way, given that it is contradictory for a pot to be partnered with the pot itself, it is implicitly proven that it is partnered with the body of a person whose mind and body are the same substance. If that is proven, body and mind are established to be the same substance. Therefore, when the body is destroyed, the continuum of consciousness is severed. In that case, they think that it is proven that past and future lives do not exist. Thus the *Ornament of the Exposition of Valid Knowledge* says, "The Cārvāka say that the pot is an entity that is distinct either from a person characterized by a body with a manifest consciousness or from the pot, because it is not a lotus, like a wall."[310]

Turning to the five refutations, the first is that (1) past and future lives are refuted. There is no coming here from a former birth because consciousness is newly established in this life in a body that is a combination of the semen and blood of the father and mother. This is like the bodies and minds of the many worms that are newly produced on a heap of beef when the conditions are complete. Avalokitavrata's *Commentary on the Lamp of Wisdom* says:

> The creator of the hundred thousand tenets of the Lokāyata says, ". . . In the same way, internal sources are produced from a combination of semen and blood without karma and afflictions. Furthermore, when meat is piled as high as Mount Meru and rain falls there for seven days, a heap of worms the size of the heap of meat would be produced. Do that many sentient beings come from another world?" They think that production with no cause is proven with many such pseudo-examples.[311]

Also, the *Sūtra of Bṛhaspati* asserts that the virtuous deeds of this life do not benefit future lives:

> If beings who abide in heaven
> are gratified by offerings [from here],
> why don't you give [food] from here
> to those who abide on top of a palace?[312] [158]

This is explaining the erroneous belief that, if a person who has already gone to the next life were satisfied by offerings for the sake of their rebirth in heaven, then even a person far away would be able to benefit someone who lived on the top of a palace by giving them food. It also says:

> It is pointless to provide provisions
> to a person who is already traveling.
> They would be satisfied on the road
> by an offering made at home.[313]

As it says, when a traveler has set out on a journey, there would be no need to bring them provisions, because they would be gratified by being given an offering at home. They assert that just as it is observed by direct perception that it would not [benefit the traveler], so there is no benefit whatsoever in making offerings to the dead.

There is no going to the next life because when the coarse material body of this life is destroyed, the sense faculties and consciousness that depend on it become dormant and nonexistent and are not born again. For example, when a pot is destroyed, its smell, color, and shape are destroyed. Their refutations with many such reasonings are stated in the *Basis of the Vinaya*:

> A living being lives this life and later it ends. One is destroyed and after death does not rise again. The body of a person comes from the four great elements; when its time comes, the earth of the body dissolves into earth, the water of the body into water, the fire of the body into fire, and the wind of the body dissolves in wind. The sense faculties merge into space. A person's corpse is carried on a bier to the charnel ground by five men and burned. From that point, it is seen no more. What will burn becomes ashes. The bones become like the color of a pigeon.[314]

Thus it extensively sets forth how they assert that future lives do not exist. Thus Avalokitavrata's *Commentary on the Lamp of Wisdom* cites the *Sūtra of Bṛhaspati*:

> Live happily until death.
> After death there are no more objects to enjoy.
> Once the body has become ash,
> how could a life arise once more?[315]

The *Sūtra of Bṛhaspati* also gives the reasons why a mind separate from body and future lives does not exist: [159]

> If one leaves this body
> and goes to the next world,
> why do they not come back,
> tormented by love for their family?[316]

If a mind or self, separated from the body of this life, goes to the other world, then, tormented by love for their children and relatives from the former life, they would feel compelled to return from the other world to their former land. Why do they not return? With many reasonings like this, they prove that past and future lives do not exist.

(2) The Lokāyata also refute karmic retribution. Regarding the refutation of good and bad actions, they assert that the happiness and suffering of this life do not arise from previous good and bad actions because they arise adventitiously without depending on any cause or condition. This is like, for example, the sharpness of thorns and the roundness of peas, which arise naturally without depending on anything. The *Basis of the Vinaya* says:

> Then the two brahmins Upatiṣya and Kolita approached Pūraṇa Kāśyapa and asked him, "O wise one, what is your teaching? What is your instruction to your disciples? What is the effect of chastity? What is its benefit?"
>
> Pūraṇa answered, "O young brahmins, I see thus and speak thus: There is no [effect of] giving. There is no sacrifice. There is no fire ritual. There is no good conduct. There is no bad conduct."[317]

Kalyāṇamitra explains the meaning of this clearly in his *Commentary on the Basis of the Vinaya*: "There is no [effect of] giving. There is no sacrifice. There is no fire ritual. There is no good conduct. There is no bad conduct. These five statements refute causation."[318]

Turning to their refutation of karmic effects, they say future happiness and suffering are not the logically necessary effects of the good and bad actions of this life. The logicians see with their sense consciousnesses that, in this very life, some who are generous are poor and some who abandon killing live short lives. They also see that some who are miserly are wealthy [160] and some who kill live long lives. The meditators observe with their supersensory knowledge that some who are generous in this life become poor in the future and some who abandon killing have short lives in the future. On the other hand, they see that some who are miserly and like to kill have wealth and enjoyments and live long lives in the future. Based on these reasons, they assert that there are no effects of good and bad actions.

The *Basis of the Vinaya* says, "Good deeds and bad deeds have no effect or fruition."[319] The *Commentary on the Basis of the Vinaya* explains this line by saying, "This is the refutation of effects."[320]

Furthermore, Lokāyata's own scripture asserts that the tīrthikas' sacrifice of cattle has no effect whatsoever and is practiced by deceitful people simply as a means of livelihood. The *Sūtra of Bṛhaspati* states:

> If a cow, slain in the fire sacrifice,
> attains rebirth in heaven,
> why doesn't the sacrificer
> kill his own father here?[321]

If an animal attains rebirth in heaven by being slain in a sacrifice, it is reasonable for the sacrificer to kill his own father as well. Why isn't he killed? The same text says:

> Therefore these rituals for the dead
> performed by brahmins here
> are just their means of livelihood.
> They are nothing more than that.[322]

In brief, all actions that are causes and effects that are hidden from oneself are refuted because they are not seen by one's direct perception.

(3) Lokāyata refutes refuge and the [Three] Jewels. The existence of a person who has destroyed their faults through cultivation over many lifetimes cannot be proven because past and future lives do not exist and because mind, intellect, and thought rely only on the body; when the body has disintegrated, they also disintegrate, like the light of a lamp. Dharmakīrti's *Exposition of Valid Knowledge* says at the point of explaining the Lokāyata assertions:

> If you say that because intelligence depends on the body,
> it is not established through cultivation . . .[323] [161]

This is saying that the nonexistence of past and future lives is the reason why a person who cultivates such things as love and wisdom without limit and destroys all faults cannot be established. Passages such as this appear often in their texts. The *Sūtra of Bṛhaspati* states:

> There is no heaven, there is no liberation.
> There are also no beings of the next world.[324]

(4) Regarding the refutation of unseen things, a person is limited to the domain of only the senses of this lifetime. Therefore unseen things such as heavens and bad states in the next life do not exist. Because they are not seen by our direct perception, gods are also refuted. Avalokitavrata's *Commentary on the Lamp of Wisdom* says:

> The person is limited
> to whatever is the domain of the senses.[325]

(5) Regarding the refutation of other forms of valid knowledge, inference is not a valid means of knowledge because if the definition of valid knowledge is that which apprehends things, inference does not apprehend in that way; its object is always mistaken, like inferring that someone has a dark complexion due to being the son of someone named Devadatta. Therefore all reasoning is mistaken. They refute inferential valid knowledge in that way. Dharmottara's *Examination of Valid Knowledge* says, "Valid knowledge for Lokāyata is solely based on the reason of apprehending a thing."[326]

Thus they justify their philosophy with four assertions and five refutations. The four assertions are: (1) consciousness exists in the four elements, (2) an evident self is the same substance as body and mind, (3) only beings of the four elements, human beings, and animals exist, and (4) only inferences or syllogisms known to the world are asserted. The five refutations are: (1) past and future lives are refuted, (2) actions and effects are refuted, (3) refuge and the Three Jewels are refuted, (4) unseen things are refuted, and (5) other forms of valid knowledge are refuted. [162]

In sum, the *Sūtra of Bṛhaspati* says:

> A pigeon today
> is better than a peacock tomorrow.

A doubtless copper coin
is better than a doubtful gold coin.[327]

Thus they assert that just this life that is evident to oneself is much more important than various proofs for heaven and liberation that have a doubtful future. And with the proofs above, they delineate their philosophy with faultless debate.

This has been a brief explanation of the tenets of Lokāyata or Cārvāka based on ancient Indian texts. [163]

Part 2

Buddhist Schools of Tenets

10

Overview of the Buddhist Schools of Tenets

NEEDLESS TO SAY, the original source of Buddhist tenets is the teacher Śākyamuni, whose dates of birth, death, and so forth were provided in chapter 1. To the common sight of his disciples, after he came of age he became skilled in all the sciences of the land of India at that time, such as the manual arts (*śilpakarman*). When he was twenty-nine years old, moved by renunciation, he went forth from the home to the homeless life, and he then practiced asceticism for six years. Finally, he went to the foot of the Bodhi Tree and displayed the deed of achieving perfect and complete buddhahood. He turned the wheel of the Dharma for the first time in Vārāṇasī, beginning with the topic of the four truths, to his first audience, the good group of five. From that point until he displayed the deed of passing into final nirvāṇa in the town of Kuśīnagarī was a period of a little more than forty years. Placing his feet in many places in central India, he taught innumerable disciples numerous heaps of the Dharma in accordance with their individual capacities. The words that he spoke at various times, at various places, and to various audiences were later gathered by his followers and organized into three scriptural collections (*piṭaka*) based on their topic. Thus the scriptural collection of the Vinaya primarily teaches the topic of the training in ethics (*śīla*). The scriptural collection of the Sūtras primarily teaches the topic of the training in concentration (*samādhi*). The scriptural collection of the Abhidharma primarily teaches the topic of the training in wisdom (*prajñā*).

In early Buddhist texts there is another way to organize the statements of the Buddha, from the perspective of three different interests and capacities of his disciples. To disciples interested in the practice of freedom from attachment, he primarily taught practices free from attachment; this is the scriptural collection of the śrāvakas. To disciples interested in the vast, he taught such things as the ten levels (*bhūmi*) and the six perfections (*pāramitā*); this is the scriptural collection of the perfections or of the bodhisattvas. To those disciples especially interested in the profound, he primarily taught practices of desire; this is the scriptural collection of the Secret Vajra Vehicle.

Furthermore, in the Mahāyāna sūtras, according to what is said in such works as the *Explanation of the Intention Sūtra* (*Saṃdhinirmocanasūtra*), the Bhagavan turned the wheel of the Dharma three times in accordance with the different capacities and faculties of his disciples. In the first period after his enlightenment, in Vārāṇasī, he turned the first wheel, beginning with the four truths of the noble ones. After that, on Vulture Peak, he turned the Dharma wheel of signlessness, the middle wheel, primarily teaching the Perfection of Wisdom (*prajñāpāramitā*) sūtras. [164] In the final period, he taught the Dharma wheel of good differentiation at such places as Vaiśālī.

Among the four schools of Buddhist tenets, the two śrāvaka schools [Vaibhāṣika and Sautrāntika], which propound the tenets of the lower vehicle, take as their primary source the first teachings, the Dharma wheel of the four truths, using it to delineate the basis, path, and fruition of their own systems. As for the proponents of tenets of the higher vehicle, Madhyamaka takes as its primary source the pronouncements of the wheel of signlessness, and Cittamātra takes as its primary source the pronouncements of the wheel of good discrimination, using them to delineate the basis, path, and fruition of their own systems.[328]

Because the words of the Buddha were set forth in accordance with the various capacities and interests of his disciples, it was not possible for all the scriptures of the Bhagavan to be taken literally in their entirety. Just as one analyzes gold by burning it, cutting it, and rubbing it, they are to be analyzed using correct reasoning and divided into provisional sūtras and definitive sūtras in the manner set forth by the Buddha himself. This has already been discussed in the first volume of *Science and Philosophy in the Indian Buddhist Classics*.[329]

Thus the existence of so many different categorizations of the statements of the Bhagavan is due to the variety of different capacities, faculties, and interests of his disciples. When he preached the Dharma to his disciples, he did so in accordance with their different levels of acumen and different interests. The Bhagavan did not persistently teach the final view that was born in his own mind to those who were not suited to it because of their mental capacity. When the scriptures of the Buddha were organized in accordance with the faculties of his disciples, they were set forth in terms of the two vehicles from the perspective of practice: the Śrāvaka Vehicle (Śrāvakayāna) and the Bodhisattva or Great Vehicle (Mahāyāna). And from the perspective of the view, they were set forth in terms of the four schools of tenets—Vaibhāṣika, Sautrāntika, Cittamātra, and Madhyamaka.

The *Descent into Laṅkā Sūtra* explains how the Bhagavan set forth the Dharma in a way that was suitable for the mental capacity of his disciples:

> Just as a skilled physician
> analyzes each patient, [165]
> the Tathāgata teaches sentient beings
> in accordance with their interests.[330]

Nāgārjuna's *Precious Garland* says:

> Just as grammarians
> begin with reading the alphabet,
> so the Buddha teaches doctrines
> that disciples can bear.
>
> To some he teaches doctrines
> for the reversal of sins;
> to some for the sake of achieving merit.
> To some, doctrines based on duality;
> to some, doctrines based on nonduality.
> To some the profound, frightening to the fearful,
> having an essence of emptiness and compassion,
> the means of achieving enlightenment.[331]

As it says, just as, for example, those studying a text on grammar start by learning the alphabet, the Buddha initially taught his disciples as much of the doctrine as their minds could bear; he did not teach them doctrines that were not appropriate for their minds. He taught them in stages. To some disciples, he taught doctrines to turn them away from sins such as killing. To some he taught doctrines to bring about the fruition of virtue. To some he taught the doctrine that the self of the person is not real but that apprehended objects and apprehending subjects are distinct substantial entities. To some he taught that the consciousness that is not based on apprehended objects and apprehending subjects being different substantial entities—that is, the consciousness that is empty of apprehended and apprehender being different substantial entities—is the ultimate truth. To some with the sharpest faculties he taught the profound mode of being, that no phenomena are truly established, doctrines that have an essence of emptiness—creating fear in those who conceive things to be true—and of great compassion.

Furthermore, the Buddha did not teach his disciples the most profound topics from the start; he instead taught them progessively from the coarse level to the subtle. Āryadeva's *Four Hundred Verses* says:

> At the beginning, he turns them away from what is not
> meritorious.
> In the middle, he turns them away from self.
> Later, he turns them away from all views.
> One who knows this is wise.[332]

Thus, at the beginning, he turns them away from coarse misdeeds of body, speech, and mind that create nonmeritorious karma. Then, in the middle, he refutes the object of the twenty views of the perishable collection (*satkāyadṛṣṭi*) and turns them away from the coarse apprehension of self. [166] In the end, having taught them that no phenomena are truly established, he teaches the necessity of turning away from all views of permanence and annihilation.

The *Great Exegesis* (*Mahāvibhāṣā*) explains how long the Buddha stayed in various places when turning those various wheels of the Dharma:

> The Sage, the supreme being,
> lived for one year each
> at the place of the turning of the wheel of the Dharma and
> Vaiśālī,
> Makkolam and the abode of the gods,
> Śiśumāra Hill and Kauśāmbī,

Āṭavī and Caityagiri,
Veṇavana and Sāketu,
and in the city of Kapilavastu.
He spent two years in Jvālinī Cave,
four years in Bhaiṣajyavana,
five years in the city of Rājagṛha,
six years practicing austerities,
twenty-three years in Śrāvastī,
and twenty-nine years in the palace.[333]

Thus, regarding the places that the Bhagavan stayed, it is well known that he taught the excellent Dharma to many disciples, residing one year each at the place of the turning of the wheel of Dharma, Vaiśālī, Makkolam, the abode of the gods, Śiśumāra Hill, Kauśāmbī, Āṭavī, Caityagiri, Veṇavana, Sāketu, and in the city of Kapilavastu; two years in Jvālinī Cave; four years in Bhaiṣajyavana; five years in the city of Rājagṛha; six years practicing austerities; twenty-three years in Śrāvastī; and twenty-nine years in the palace.

When his body was about to pass into nirvāṇa, the Bhagavan entrusted the Dharma to the elder Mahākāśyapa. The noble Mahākāśyapa entrusted it to Ānanda, who entrusted it to Śāṇavāsin, who entrusted it to Upagupta, who entrusted it to Dhṛtaka, who entrusted it to Kṛṣṇa, who entrusted it to Mahāsudarśana. They are renowned as the seven generations of the teaching. As the *Chapters on the Fine Points of the Vinaya* says:

"The Bhagavan passed into nirvāṇa having entrusted the teaching to the venerable Mahākāśyapa. The venerable Mahākāśyapa entrusted it to the abbot. The abbot, having entrusted the teaching to me [Śāṇavāsin], passed into nirvāṇa. Son, I too will pass into nirvāṇa. [167] Now you are to protect the teaching and everything that was spoken by the Bhagavan carefully." Then, venerable Śāṇavāsin, having delighted both the patrons and the practitioners of celibacy by causing various miracles—igniting, burning, causing rain, and causing lightning—passed completely into the nirvāṇa with no remainder of the aggregates. The elder Upagupta [entrusted the teaching] to the venerable Dhṛtaka. The venerable Dhṛtaka, having fulfilled the needs of

> the teaching, [entrusted it to] the venerable Kṛṣṇa. The venerable Kṛṣṇa entrusted it to the venerable Mahāsudarśana. Thus the great elephants passed completely into nirvāṇa.[334]

After the Buddha had passed into nirvāṇa, followers of the Buddha such as Mahākāśyapa gathered to finalize the collections of doctrine that the Buddha had set forth to various disciples in the different places described above. In historical works, this is renowned as the first stage of the gathering of the word. It took place in the Cave of Great Bliss in Rājagṛha during the rains retreat of the year the Buddha passed into nirvāṇa, with King Ajātaśatru serving as the patron at the request of the great elder Mahākāśyapa. The elder Mahākāśyapa himself recited the Abhiharma Piṭaka, the arhat Upāli recited the Vinaya Piṭaka, and the arhat Ānanda recited the Sūtra Piṭaka. They added introductions at the beginning, such as "Thus did I hear at one time." In the middle, they provided transitions between sections, and at the end, they added a conclusion about how the audience had gathered and their praise of what the Bhagavan had spoken. They gathered all the words of the Buddha into three scriptural collections based on their topic and finalized their contents.

Then, 110 years after the Bhagavan had passed into nirvāṇa, with King Aśoka serving as the patron, seven hundred arhats such as the arhat Yaśas gathered in Vaiśālī and criticized ten inappropriate deeds of the monks of Vaiśālī. This is known as the second gathering of the word. Then, 116 years after the Bhagavan went to peace, in the city of Kusumapura four elders recited individual scriptures in Sanskrit, Apabhraṃśa, Prakrit, and Paiśācī. Because their students could not agree, they split into four main sects, then split further into eighteen smaller sects and debated with each other. When they discovered and read the *Dream Omen Sūtra* of King Kṛkin (*Svapnanirdeśasūtra*), they agreed that all eighteen sects were included in the single teaching of the Buddha. [168] This is known as the third gathering of the word. There are also other ways of explaining this third gathering of the word.

Those three stages of gathering the word are primarily from the perspective of the scriptural collections of the common vehicle [or Śrāvakayāna]. The primary gatherers of the Mahāyāna scriptures are the bodhisattvas Samantabhadra, Mañjuśrī, Guhyapati [Vajrapāṇi], and Maitreya. The gatherers of the tantras are Vajrapāṇi and the ḍākinīs. However, the manner and the time of the gathering of the tantras is set forth differently than that of the sūtras.

In the ancient accounts from the past, there are different descriptions of such things as how the divisions of the Buddhist systems of tenets came about; whether initially there were one, two, three, or four śrāvaka sects; and how the sects came to be subdivided into eighteen. From among these, a brief one will be provided below in the chapter explaining the tenets of Vaibhāṣika. In the system connected to the Mahāyāna scriptures, it is said that the Buddhist schools of tenets are definitely four: Vaibhāṣika, Sautrāntika, Cittamātra, and Madhyamaka. This does not appear explicitly in the scriptures of the sūtra category but appears clearly in the Buddhist tantras[335] and in the treatises (*śāstras*). For example, the bodhisattva Vajragarbha's *Commentary on the Condensation of the Hevajra Tantra* says:

> Then, understanding the system of Vaibhāṣika
> and then, that of Sautrāntika,
> from the doctrines of Vijñānavāda
> one then must understand Madhyamaka,
> the intention of the perfection of wisdom.

That same text also says:

> Śrāvakayāna, Pratyekabuddhayāna, and here
> the Mahāyāna is the third.
> For the Buddhists, a fourth [vehicle] and a fifth [school]
> was not the intention of the Sage.[336]

This is saying that among the proponents of Buddhist tenets, there are none that are not included among the four: Vaibhāṣika, Sautrāntika, Cittamātra, and Madhyamaka, and that among the Buddhist vehicles there is no vehicle outside of the Śrāvakayāna, the Pratyekabuddhayāna, and the Mahāyāna. [169] In the same way, Mañjughoṣa Narendrakīrti's *Brief Explication of the Assertions of Our Own View* says:

> They became Vaibhāṣika and Sautrāntika,
> Yogācāra and Madhyamaka.[337]

This is saying that schools of Buddhist tenets are counted as four.

The four schools of tenets are included in the schools of tenets of the greater and lesser vehicles; Vaibhāṣika and Sautrāntika are Śrāvakayāna schools and Cittamātra and Madhyamaka are Mahāyāna schools. Because Vaibhāṣika and Sautrāntika propound their tenets based on the śrāvaka scriptural collection, they are called the śrāvaka proponents of tenets or the śrāvaka schools. Because Madhyamaka and Cittamātra propound their tenets based on the vast sūtras of the Mahāyāna—that is, because they propound the modes of explanation unique to the Mahāyāna that are presented in these sūtras—they are called the proponents of Mahāyāna tenets. One might ask, "From what perspective are the vehicles divided into two—the vehicle of the śrāvakas and pratyekabuddhas and the vehicle of the bodhisattvas—and the schools of tenets into four—Vaibhāṣika, Sautrāntika, Cittamātra, and Madhyamaka?" Nāgārjuna's *Precious Garland* says:

> Because the bodhisattva's aspirations,
> deeds, and dedications are not explained
> in the śrāvaka vehicle,
> how could one become a bodhisattva through it?[338]

And Udbhaṭasiddhasvāmin's *Praise of the Exalted* says:

> Logicians assert that things
> are established independently.
> You, Lord of Language, have said well
> that nothing is independent.[339]

These say that the differences between the vehicles must be made on the basis of method. However, the differences between schools of tenets must be made primarily on the basis of view. Thus the differences between the schools of Vaibhāṣika, Sautrāntika, Cittamātra, and Madhyamaka are made based on their views, with their individual tenets related primarily to the basis, path, and fruition. They assert that all suffering is created by ignorance. Those who seek to eradicate it completely from the perspective of determining the selflessness of persons should be classified as Vaibhāṣika and Sautrāntika, the two śrāvaka schools. Those who seek to do so primarily from the perspective of determining the selflessness of phenomena should be classified as Cittamātra and Madhyamaka, the two Mahāyāna schools. [170] It is said that, compared to the lower schools of tenets, the way that the higher schools explain the meaning of selflessness is more profound. However, it is said that the difference between the great and small vehicles should be made primarily from the perspective of method, that is, whether they teach bodhicitta and great compassion. [171]

11

The Vaibhāṣika School

How This School of Tenets Arose

After the Buddha displayed the way to pass into nirvāṇa, the arhats gathered the discourses on the Abhidharma into seven books and finalized them. This school evolved from the compilation of the seven books of the Abhidharma and seems to have become widespread upon the compilation of the Abhidharma treatise called the *Great Exegesis* (*Mahāvibhāṣā*). After the Buddha had passed into nirvāṇa, his followers agreed to spread his teachings widely through dividing themselves into individual schools. There are several different descriptions of how they split into eighteen schools; among the works in the Tibetan Tengyur, the earliest and the clearest explanation of this topic appears to be Bhāviveka's *Blaze of Reasoning*, where three different descriptions of how the eighteen schools were divided are found. Because of its great importance, his description will be quoted here at some length. In the first way of dividing the schools, there are two main schools, the Mahāsāṅghika and the Sthāvira. The Mahāsāṅghika is further divided into eight subschools and the Sthāvira into ten. The *Blaze of Reasoning* says:

> One might ask, "What are the eighteen schools? How did their divisions arise?" This is what I have heard from the lineage of my teachers. When 116 years had passed after the Buddha, the Bhagavan, passed completely into nirvāṇa, in the city called Kusumapura during the reign of the king called Dharma Aśoka, there was a great schism in the saṅgha as the result of some disputed doctrines. Therefore, initially, they divided into two schools, the Mahāsāṅghika and the Sthāvira. The Mahāsāṅghika school gradually divided into eight: Mahāsāṅghika, Ekavyāvahārika,

> Lokottaravāda, Bahuśrutīya, Prajñaptivāda, Caitika, Pūrvaśaila, and Aparaśaila. The Sthāvira gradually divided into ten: Sthāvira, who are also called Haimavata; Sarvāstivāda who are called Vibhajyavāda and Hetuvāda, whom some call Muruṇṭaka; Vātsīputrīya; Dharmottarīya; Bhadrayānīya; Sāṃmitīya, whom some call Avantaka and others Kaurukullaka; [172] Mahīśāsaka; Dharmaguptaka; Suvarṣaka, whom some call Kāśyapīya; and Uttarīya, whom some call Saṅkrāntivāda. Those are the divisions of the eighteen schools.[340]

In the second description, there are three main schools: Sthāvira, Mahāsāṅghika, and Vibhajyavāda. There is a tradition of explanation in which the Sthāvira divided into Sarvāstivāda and Vātsīputrīya, and each of them then divided into subschools. Setting forth that system, the *Blaze of Reasoning* says:

> Others say that the basis [of the division] is like what was described before, but they say that the main division was into three: Sthāvira, Mahāsāṅghika, and Vibhajyavāda. The Sthāvira had two types, called Sarvāstivāda and Vātsīputrīya. The Sarvāstivāda also had two types, called Sarvāstivāda and Sautrāntika. The Vātsīputrīya had four types, called Sāṃmitīya, Dharmottarīya, Bhadrayānīya, and Ṣaṇṇagarika. Thus the Sthāvira had six types. The Mahāsāṅghika had eight types, called Mahāsāṅghika, Pūrvaśaila, Aparaśaila, Rājagirika, Haimavata, Caitika, Siddhārthika, and Gokulika. Those are called the divisions of Mahāsāṅghika. The Vibhajyavāda has four types, called Mahīśāsaka, Kāśyapīya, Dharmaguptaka, and Tāmraśāṭīya. Thus, having divided the schools of the noble ones, there came to be eighteen types.[341]

In the third description, as in the first system, the two main schools are Sthāvira and Mahāsāṅghika. However, this description differs in explaining how other subschools divided from those two. The section of the *Blaze of Reasoning* that sets forth this third system clearly identifies the main precepts or tenets of each of the eighteen schools. It is quoted here in its entirety.

Others say that when 137 years had passed after the Bhagavan had passed completely into nirvāṇa, in the city of Pāṭaliputra, kings named Nanda and Mahāpadma gathered a group of noble ones who had attained the state of tranquility and would not take rebirth again. [173] Residing in that community were arhats who had attained analytical knowledge, such as the ārya Mahākāśyapa, the ārya Mahāloma, Mahātyāga, Uttara, and Revata. At that time, the sinful Māra, opponent of all that is good, put on the robes of a monk and performed various miracles, creating a great schism in the saṅgha over five points. Learned elders named Nāga and Sthiramati praised the five points. They said that it is the teaching of the Buddha that [an arhat] teaches and gives answers to others, does not know, is of two minds, investigates, and [says] that caring for oneself is the path. Then the [community] divided into two schools, called Sthāvira and Mahāsāṅghika. Thus, for the next sixty-three years, the saṅgha was divided and remained in strife. Then, two hundred years after the passing of the Buddha, the elder Vātsīputra collected the teachings. When he had collected them, two types of Mahāsāṅghika arose, the Ekavyāvahārika and the Gokulika.

The primary precepts of the Ekavyāvahārika are that the bhagavan buddhas are supramundane; a tathāgata does not possess mundane qualities; no tathāgatas engage in speech; the statements of all the tathāgatas are concentrated in essence; tathāgatas do not take on the form in which they abide; when bodhisattvas [are in the womb], they do not go through the stages of the oblong shape, the oval shape, or the lump-like shape; becoming an elephant, bodhisattvas enter the body of their mother and emerge by themselves; thoughts of desire do not arise in bodhisattvas; they take rebirth in the evil realms through their own wish and bring sentient beings to spiritual maturity; the four truths are fully understood with a single wisdom consciousness; all six consciousnesses both have desire and are free from desire; the eye sees forms; even arhats achieve what is taught by others; they [arhats] do not know, are of two minds, they investigate, and they say "suffering" on the path of abandonment; in the state of meditative equipoise, one is able to speak; the impure is abandoned; by manifesting restraint (*saṃyama*), it is said that all fetters (*saṃyojana*) are abandoned; the tathāgatas do not possess worldly correct view; because the mind has a nature of clear light, one cannot say whether the predispositions (*anuśaya*) are similar to the mind or not; [174] the predispositions are one thing and their manifestations are another; past and future do not exist; and stream enterers attain the concentrations. These are the precepts of the Ekavyāvahārika.

The divisions of the Gokulika are called Bahuśrutīya and Prajñaptivāda. The primary precepts of the Bahuśrutīya are that there is no analysis on the path of emergence (*niḥsaraṇamārga*); the truth of suffering, conventional truths, and the truth of noble ones are the truths; by seeing the suffering of conditioning, one perfectly enters the faultless, not by seeing the suffering of suffering or the suffering of change; the saṅgha is supramundane; even arhats achieve what is taught by others; there is a correctly declared path; and even in the state of meditative equipoise, one is able to speak. These are the primary precepts of the Bahuśrutīya.

Regarding the Prajñaptivāda precepts, there is suffering without the aggregates; there are sources that are incomplete; conditioned phenomena are mutually imputed; suffering is ultimate; mental factors are not the path; there is no untimely death; the person is not an agent; and all suffering arises from karma. These are the primary precepts of the Prajñaptivāda.

Among the types of Gokulika are the elders called Caitika. A wanderer named Mahādeva became a monk and lived on a mountain that had a shrine (*caitya*). He asserted the points of the Mahāsāṅghika and established the school called Caitika. These are presented as the six schools of the Mahāsāṅghika.

The two types of Sthāvira are the earlier Sthāvira and the Haimavata. The primary precepts of the earlier Sthāvira are that arhats do not achieve what is taught by others; in the same way, the five points [of the Mahāsāṅghika] do not exist; the person exists; the intermediate state exists; the parinirvāṇa of arhats exists; the past and future exist; the goal of nirvāṇa exists. These are the primary precepts of the earlier Sthāvira. [175]

The primary precepts of the Haimavata are that bodhisattvas are not common beings (*pṛthagjana*); even non-Buddhists have the five supersensory knowledges; the person is said to be different from the aggregates because when passing into nirvāṇa, when the aggregates cease, the person remains; in the state of meditative equipoise, one is able to speak; and suffering is abandoned by the path. Those are the precepts of the Haimavata.

The first Sthāvira became two types: Sarvāstivāda and Vātsīputrīya. The primary precepts of the Sarvāstivāda are that everything is included in the two, the conditioned and the unconditioned. What follows from saying that? The person does not exist. As it is said:

> When this selfless body arises
> there is no agent and there is no knower.
> Listen, supreme śrāvaka,
> to how we enter the river of saṃsāra.

Those are primary precepts of Sarvāstivāda. Their other primary precepts are that everything is included in name and form; the past and future exist; the stream enterer is said to have the quality of not falling back [to the state of a common being]; conditioned phenomena have the three qualities of being conditioned; the four truths of the noble ones are realized in sequence; emptiness, wishlessness, and signlessness cause one to enter into the faultless state; one enters the fruition of stream enterer over fifteen moments; the stream enterer has achieved the concentrations; it is possible for even an arhat to fall back; there are common beings who have abandoned desire for the desire realm or harmful intent; even outsider non-Buddhists have the five forms of supersensory knowledge; even gods practice celibacy; all the sūtras are of provisional meaning; one enters into the faultless state from the desire realm; there is worldly correct view; and the five collections of consciousness neither have desire nor are free from desire. These are the primary precepts of the Sarvāstivāda.

It is also said that a division of Sarvāstivāda is the Vibhajyavāda. It is also divided; the types of Vibhajyavāda are Mahīśāsaka, Dharmaguptaka, Tāmraśāṭīya, and Kāśyapīya. The primary precepts of the Mahīśāsaka are: the past and the future do not exist; conditioned phenomena that arise in the present exist; by seeing suffering one sees all four of the truths; the predispositions (*anuśaya*) are one thing and conduct is another; the intermediate state does not exist; there is the practice of celibacy even in the abode of the gods; [176] even arhats accumulate merit; the five collections of consciousness both have desire and are free from desire; the person is equal in size to the body, including the head and so forth; the stream enterer achieves the concentrations; even common beings abandon desire for the desire realm or harmful intent; the Buddha is included in the saṅgha; [offerings] to the saṅgha bring about great effects, those to the Buddha do not; buddhas and śrāvakas have the same liberation; the person is invisible; minds and mental factors are merely phenomena of this lifetime and do not pass from this world to the next world; all conditioned phenomena are momentary; the action that increases conditioned phenomena is birth; conditioned phenomena do not remain; just as the mind exists, so does karma, but there is no physical or verbal karma; there is no phenomenon that does not deteriorate; making offerings to stūpas creates no effect; predispositions always arise in the present; and one enters into the faultless state by seeing conditioned phenomena. These are the primary precepts of the Mahīśāsaka.

The primary precepts of the Dharmaguptaka are that the Buddha is not a member of the saṅgha; [offerings] to the Buddha bring about great effects, those to the saṅgha do not; there is the practice of celibacy even in the abode of the gods; worldly qualities (*laukikadharma*) exist. Those are the precepts of the Dharmaguptaka.

The primary precepts of the Kāśyapīya are that the factor of the ripening [of karma] and the factor of ripening that will arise [in the future] exist, and that not understanding that one has achieved abandonment exists. Everything that is asserted by the Dharmaguptaka is also a precept of the Kāśyapīya.

The precept of the Tāmraśāṭīya is that the person does not exist. The Saṅkrāntika are a type of Sarvāstivāda who take the text of Uttara as their teacher. Their primary precepts are that the five aggregates pass from this world to the next world; the aggregates do not cease except on the path; there are aggregates that have the root downfalls; the person is not observed ultimately; and everything is impermanent. Those are the precepts of the Saṅkrāntika. The precepts of the Sarvāstivāda are found in those seven schools. [177]

The precepts of the Vātsīputrīya are: the appropriation of the appropriated is an imputation; no phenomenon passes from this world to the next world; the person, having appropriated the five aggregates, passes [to the next world]; there are both momentary and nonmomentary conditioned phenomena; the person cannot be said to be either the same as or not the same as the five appropriated aggregates; nirvāṇa cannot be said to be either the same as or different from all phenomena; it cannot be said that nirvāṇa exists or does not exist; and the five collections of consciousness neither have desire nor are free from desire. Those are the precepts of the Vātsīputrīya.

There are two types of Vātsīputrīya, the Mahāgirīya and the Sāṃmitīya. The primary precepts of the Sāṃmitīya are: that which will arise and that which arises, that which will cease and that which ceases, that which will be born and that which is born, that which will die and that which dies, that which will create and that which creates, that which will destroy and that which destroys, that which will go and that which goes, that which will become consciousness and that which is consciousness all exist. Such are the main precepts of the Sāṃmitīya.

There are two types of Mahāgirīya, the Dharmottarīya and the Bhadrayānīya. The primary precepts of the Dharmottarīya are: in birth there is ignorance, and in birth and cessation there is ignorance and cessation. The Bhadrayānīya say the same. Regarding the Ṣaṇṇagarika, some say that they are a type of Mahāgirīya. Others assert that they are a type of Sāṃmitīya. These are the four parts of the Vātsīputrīya school. By following the masters, they eventually became eighteen. Those are their main ideas.[342]

Vinītadeva's *Compendium Setting Forth the Different Sects* makes a division into four main schools: Sarvāstivāda, Mahāsāṅghika, Sthāvira, and

Sāṃmitīya. There is a famous statement about how those split into eighteen. That text says:

> Pūrvaśaila, Aparaśaila, Haimavata,
> the school of Lokottaravāda,
> and the school of Prajñaptivāda:
> those five groups are Mahāsāṅghika. [178]
> The schools of Mūlasarvāstivāda and Kāśyapīya,
> the school of Mahīśāsaka and the school Dharmaguptaka,
> Bahuśrutīya, Tāmraśāṭīya,
> and the school of Vibhajyavāda
> are Sarvāstivāda.
> Jetavanīya, Abhayagirika,
> and Mahāvihāravāsin are Sthāvira.
> Kurukulla, Āvantaka,
> and the school of Vātsīputrīya
> are the three types of Sāṃmitīya.
> They are called the eighteen different schools
> due to differences in locale, intent, and masters.[343]

Śākyaprabha's *Luminous Vinaya* explains that the eighteen schools split off from the single Mūlasarvāstivāda school. It says, "It is said that in the past there was only this Sarvāstivāda. Then the Bhagavan passed into nirvāṇa, and based on that, other schools arose. Because it served as their basis, it is taught that it is called the Mūlasarvāstivāda." And it says, "Then King Dharma Aśoka died, and in order to train those who were attached to reciting in Prakrit, Apabhraṃśa, and the central languages, arhats gradually began to compose other texts, such as those in the Sūtra Piṭaka, in the great language [Sanskrit]. There came to be up to eighteen types of the teaching. Therefore it is explained that it is called the basis."[344]

Thus, according to such a system, after the passing of the Dharma king [Aśoka], due to differences in the way that the arhats recited the scriptures, using languages such as Apabhraṃśa, eighteen schools split off from the single Mūlasarvāstivāda. Because the Mūlasarvāstivāda was the source from which those eighteen split off, it is asserted that it is called the "basis" (*mūla*). [179]

Among those schools, the etymologies of some of them appear in the statements of such masters as Bhāviveka. Thus, when they split into eighteen schools, because the majority were included in the Mahāsāṅghika, they are "the majority" (*mahāsāṅghika*). Because they propound that the three times, like the present, are substantially established, they are "those who propound that all bases exist" (*mūlasarvāstivāda*). Because they are the lineage of the noble elders, they are "the elders" (*sthāvira*). Because they uphold the system of masters who are esteemed by many people, they are "those esteemed by many" (*sāṃmitīya*). Because they propound that a supramundane buddha does not possess mundane qualities, they are "those who propound the supramundane" (*lokottaravāda*). Because they propound that conditioned phenomena are imputations, they are "those who propound imputation" (*prajñaptivāda*). Because they say they belong to the system of Kāśyapa, they are the Kāśyapīya. Because they protect the system of Dharmagupta, they are the Dharmaguptaka. Because they teach following the learned masters, they are "proponents of the learned" (*bahuśrutīya*). Because they copy the Tripiṭaka in copper-colored pages, they are the "red-robe school" (*tāmraśāṭīya*). Because they make distinctions such as that the past in which an effect has not arisen and the present substantially exist, and that the past in which the effect has already arisen and the future imputedly exist, they are "proponents of distinction" (*vibhajyavāda*). The daughter of the Vatsa clan is a Vatsī, and because they uphold the system of the master who was her son, they are those of the son of a Vatsī (*vātsīputrīya*). "Those of the eastern mountain" (*pūrvaśaila*), "those of the western mountain" (*aparaśaila*), "those of the snowy mountains" (*haimavata*), "those of Jetavana" (*jetavanīya*), "those of Mount Abhaya" (*abhayagirika*), and "those of the great monastery" (*mahāvihāravāsin*) are named based on locale. Furthermore, it is explained that the Kāśyapīya are also called the Suvarṣaka, the Mahīśāsaka are also called the Dārṣṭantika, the Dharmaguptika are also called the Dharmaguptaka, the Bahuśrutīya are also called the Mahīśāsaka, the Tāmraśāṭīya are also called the Uttarīya or the Saṅkrāntivāda, the Vibhajyavāda are also called the Hetuvāda and the Muruṇṭaka, and the Sāṃmitīya are also called the Avantaka and the Kaurukullaka. Because they say that the aggregates pass from this life to the next life, they are called "the proponents of passage" (*saṅkrāntivāda*). Because they assert that all conditioned phenomena of the elements or that are arisen from the elements have a cause, they are called "proponent of causes" (*hetuvāda*). Because they live on Mount Muruṇṭaka they are called Muruṇṭaka. Because they live in the city of Avantaka, they are called Avantaka. Because they live on Mount Kurukulla, they are called Kaurukullaka.[345]

Turning to Vaibhāṣika, a division found when the Buddhist schools of tenets are divided into four, the early texts do not clearly identify it with any of the eighteen schools cited above. However, in the texts of the Indian scholars of Nālandā that analyze the delineations of the Vaibhāṣika's system, Vaibhāṣika is identified with Sarvāstivāda.

According to the tradition of the noble Theravāda, at the time of King Aśoka, the elder Moggaliputtatissa was in charge and composed a text on the Abhidharma called the *Points of Controversy* (*Kathāvatthu*) which delineated their position. In that text the Sthāvira school specifically refuted its opponents, the Mahāsāṅghika and the Sarvāstivāda. [180] Therefore, regardless of whether all seven of the books of the Abhidharma of the Sarvāstivāda school existed prior to the outset of the Common Era, it appears that the school itself existed prior to the Common Era.

It appears that the Sarvāstivāda school was the most widespread in India during the early period of Buddhist history. From Pāṭaliputra in central India, this school of tenets began to spread to other places in India around the second century BCE. It initially spread to the region of Mathura; this school grew there due to the efforts of Upagupta.[346] Then, spreading gradually, it eventually reached the region of Kashmir; the Kashmiri Vaibhāṣika would later become known as the main Sarvāstivāda system.[347] In addition, according to what is stated in the travel journal of the Chinese monk Xuanzang of the Tang dynasty, along the Ganges River in northern and central India there were more than sixty thousand Sāṃmitīya monks among more than a thousand monasteries. In northwest India and Central Asia, among approximately six hundred monasteries, there were around sixteen thousand Sarvāstivāda monks. In southern India and Sri Lanka, among approximately two hundred monasteries, he mentioned that there were about twenty thousand Sthāvira monks. According to his travel journal, in Kashmir and Gandhāra there were around a thousand monks in approximately twenty Mahāsāṅghika monasteries. Mahāyāna monks spread to many regions of India; in Afghanistan and Khotan together, there seem to have been around seventy thousand monks.[348] Some say that Sautrāntika also emerged later as an offshoot of Sarvāstivāda.[349]

The Texts on Which This System Primarily Depends

One might ask, "What sūtras and treatises are the sources of this Vaibhāṣika school?" Among the sūtras, it said that this system is based on the first teachings, the wheel of Dharma of the four truths, and such sūtras as the *Hundred Instructions* (*Upadeśaśataka*), the *Three Interwined Garlands*, the *Kātyāyana Sūtra*, and the *Brahmā's Net Sūtra* (*Brahmajālasūtra*).[350] [181] The treatises it depends on are the seven works on the Abhidharma and the *Great Exegesis*, which summarizes their meaning, renowned for having been composed by the ārya Upagupta and others after the Buddha passed into nirvāṇa. In this system, the seven works on the Abhidharma are accepted as the word of the Buddha, and they assert that the noble Śāriputra and others gathered the statements of the Bhagavan and arranged them [into the seven works]. Regarding who arranged the seven works, *Clarifying the Meaning: A Commentary on the Treasury of Abhidharma* by the master Yaśomitra, an Indian prince, says:

> Thus it is said that the *Establishment of Knowledge* (*Jñānaprasthāna*) was composed by the noble Kātyāyanīputra, the *Exposition* (*Prakaraṇapāda*) was composed by the elder Vasumitra, *Groups of Consciousnesses* (*Vijñānakāya*) was composed by the monk Devaśarman, the *Collection of Dharmas* (*Dharmaskandha*) was composed by the noble Śāriputra, the *Treatise on Designations* (*Prajñaptiśāstra*) was composed by the noble Maudgalyāyana, the *Groups of Elements* (*Dhātukāya*) was composed by Pūrṇa, and the *Recitation Together* (*Saṅgītiparyāya*) was composed by Mahākauṣṭhila."[351]

Some Vaibhāṣika assert that among the seven works on the Abhidharma, the treatise *Establishment of Knowledge* is primary and the other six, *Collection of Dharmas* and so on, are like branches around it. *Clarifying the Meaning* says, "According to others, what is called the *treatise* is the *Establishment of Knowledge*. It is a body that has six limbs: the *Exposition*, *Groups of Consciousnesses*, *Collection of Dharmas*, *Treatise on Designations*, *Groups of Elements*, and *Recitation Together*."[352] At the time that Kātyāyanīputra composed the *Establishment of Knowledge*, he compiled all of the assertions of the Sarvāstivāda system and then commented on the actual meaning of the text itself. In his treatise, not only did he compile well in one place the assertions of the early Abhidharma, he adopted many new assertions of other schools of the tenets that had arisen at that time. Before long his invention of a unique mode of explanation became renowned as the primary treatise for explaining Sarvāstivāda.

Modern scholars have analyzed the sequence of the seven works on the Abhidharma in detail. According to what they have established, *Recitation Together* and *Collection of Dharmas* were the earliest treatises. After that, in the second period, the *Treatise on Designations*, *Groups of Elements*, *Groups of Consciousnesses*, and the *Exposition* were composed. [182] It is explained that the *Establishment of Knowledge* appeared last.[353] All of the seven works of the Sarvāstivāda Abhidharma are available today in Chinese translation. As for Tibetan translations, apart from what are known as the "three designations" in the *Treatises on Designations*—the *Designation of the World* (*Lokaprajñapti*), the *Designation of Causes* (*Kāraṇaprajñapti*), and the *Designation of Actions* (*Karmaprajñapti*)—the others were not translated in the past and thus are not found in the Kangyur and Tengyur. In the early twentieth century, the *Establishment of Knowledge* together with the *Great Exegesis* was translated in their entirety from Chinese by the Chinese translator Fazun (Losang Chöpak). Therefore they are available today in Tibetan translation.[354] When the Tibetan translation is analyzed, the text of the *Establishment of Knowledge* seems to be the primary basis for the explanations found in the *Great Exegesis*. It is a vast work, having twenty fascicles (*bam po*), eight chapters, and forty-four subsections.

Turning to the many Abhidharma topics in the *Great Exegesis*, the positions of the masters of the past are set forth, especially those of the four famous Sarvāstivāda masters: Dharmatrāta, Ghoṣaka, Vasumitra, and Buddhadeva. Many difficult points are analyzed and settled with an emphasis on the Sarvāstivāda position. Furthermore, in that text, what is called the *earlier Abhidharma*—the Vātsīputrīya school following the Abhidharma texts of Śāriputra—is explained and their systems refuted. It also refutes the views of the Vibhajyavāda and the Mahāsāṅghika. Two early treatises on Sarvāstivāda are extant: *Heart of the Abhidharma* (*Abhidharmahṛdaya*) by Dharmaśreṣṭhin, with ten chapters, and *Ambrosia of the Abhidharma* (*Abhidharmāmṛta*) by Ghoṣaka, with sixteen chapters. Today, those two ancient texts are not available in any language other than Chinese.

Around the fourth century, Vasubandhu composed the *Treasury of Abhidharma* (*Abhidharmakośa*) and its commentary. This became the most famous Sarvāstivāda text; in the great Tibetan monasteries, among the Abhidharma texts of the Sarvāstivāda system, it alone is held to be primary. The tradition of its study spread widely, as is clear from the existence of so many commentaries, general explanations, and analyses of the *Treasury of the Abhidharma* by Tibetan scholars. [183]

Among the noble Theravāda, in general there are seven famous treatises on Abhidharma, but when one analyses the collection called the Abhidhamma Piṭaka among their scriptures, which today are in the Pāli language, their way of enumerating the seven treatises is different from that of the Sarvāstivāda. According to the Theravāda, the seven treatises on the Abhidharma include the *Enumeration of Dharmas* (*Dhammasaṅganī*), the *Analysis* (*Vibhaṅga*), and the *Discourse on the Elements* (*Dhātukathā*); the enumeration of those three is similar to that of the Sarvāstivada. In addition, there is the *Description of the Person* (*Puggalapaññatti*), the *Points of Controversy* (*Kathāvatthu*), the *Pairs* (*Yamaka*), and the *Conditions* (*Paṭṭhāna*). Among those, *Points of Controversy* is a treatise (*śāstra*), and the others are accepted as the word of the Buddha. Today the most famous and widespread Theravāda treatises on the Abhidharma are Anuruddha's *Compendium of Abhidhamma* (*Abhidhammatthasaṅgaha*)[355] and Buddhaghoṣa's *Path of Purification* (*Visuddhimagga*). There are many commentaries on these two.

The Definition and Divisions of Vaibhāṣika

The Vaibhāṣika school is a Buddhist school of tenets whose foundational tenets are the assertion that an aspect (*ākāra*) of sense objects and reflexive awareness (*svasaṃvedana*) do not exist and the assertion that external objects are truly established.

They are called Vaibhāṣika because they hold that the three times [past, present, and future] are substances or because they set forth their tenets in accordance with the *Great Exegesis*. Bodhibhadra's *Explanation of the Compendium of the Essence of Wisdom* says, "This is explained as the text of the Vaibhāṣika who live in Kashmir in western India. They are so called because they accept that the past and future are causes and propound that the three times are instances of substances or because they propound tenets in accordance with the system of the *Great Exegesis*."[356]

Their position that the three times are instances of substances means that they hold that the three times are the instances of the substance on which they are posited as substantially established things. For example, a sprout exists in the three times; the sprout itself is the generality, and the three times in which it exists are asserted to be instances of the sprout. In accordance with the assertion that Sarvāstivāda and Vaibhāṣika are the same, as the text called *Treatise on Conforming to Reasoning in the Abhidharma* (*Abhidharmanyāyānusāra*) by the Kashmiri monk Saṅghabhadra explains, not only do the Vaibhāṣika assert that the three times are truly established, they also have to assert that the three unconditioned phenomena [space, analytical cessations, and nonanalytical cessations] are truly established. [184] If they did not assert that, they would not be Sarvāstivāda. According to the text called *Wheel Setting Forth the Differences of the Systems* (*Samayabhedoparacanacakra*) by the monk Vasumitra, this school propounds that all phenomena, both the conditioned and the unconditioned, are truly established; he says that they are known as Proponents of Causes (Hetuvāda).

Turning to their divisions, Yaśomitra's *Clarifying the Meaning* says, "There are also Vaibhāṣika who are not Kashmiri; those are Aparāntaka Vaibhāṣika."[357] He is referring to the actual names of two, the Kashmiri Vaibhāṣika and the Aparāntaka. Others divide them into three: Kashmiri Vaibhāṣika, Aparāntaka, and Magadha Vaibhāṣika. There also seems to be another division into three: Kashmiri Vaibhāṣika, Aparāntaka, and Aparaśaila.

A General Explanation of Vaibhāṣika Assertions

The main points of this system's tenets are just as they are delineated in the seven treatises on Abhidharma mentioned above. Its comprehensive and unique assertions and their supporting proofs are found in detail in the *Great Exegesis* and Vasubandhu's *Treasury of Abhidharma* and its autocommentary. Based on those sources, just a rough explanation of what Vaibhāṣika asserts will be provided here. Some of the foundations of its tenets have already been explained briefly in the other volumes of *Science and Philosophy in the Indian Buddhist Classics*. One can understand that a complete presentation of the Vaibhāṣika tenets, fully setting forth the foundations and the main philosophical points of their system, would require an entire volume. For the sake of convenience, in this volume, the points that have already been explained elsewhere will be summarized and what has not been explained will be set forth somewhat more extensively. This approach will be followed in explaining the other Buddhist schools of tenets as well.

In this Vaibhāṣika system, all objects of knowledge are included and delineated under five categories: (1) the foundation of appearing forms (*rūpa*), (2) the foundation of main minds (*citta*), (3) the foundation of accompanying mental factors (*caitta*), (4) the foundation of nonassociated compositional factors (*viprayuktasaṃskāra*), and (5) the foundation of the unconditioned (*asamskṛta*). They assert that all five categories of objects of knowledge are able to perform a function and are substantially established things. [185] Thus, regarding conditioned phenomena, there are three: form, associated compositional factors, and nonassociated compositional factors. Associated compositional factors have two divisions: minds and mental factors. Regarding unconditioned phenomena, the Kashmiri Vaibhāṣika assert that there are three: space (*ākaśa*), analytical cessations (*pratisaṅkhyānirodha*), and nonanalytical cessations (*apratisaṅkhyānirodha*). To that, the Magadha Vaibhāṣika add a fourth: reality (*tathatā*).

The four characteristics of conditioned phenomena—production, abiding, aging, and disintegration—are not asserted to be that which arises and so forth; they are asserted to be what causes the production and so forth of this and that conditioned phenomenon. For things that are instances of form and so forth, the four characteristics exist simultaneously but are asserted to operate sequentially: first something is produced, then it abides, then it ages, then it ceases. Although in this Vaibhāṣika system, it is asserted that conditioned phenomena are necessarily momentary, they accept that there is a state of abiding between production and disintegration that is different from them. The way that they posit momentariness is quite coarse compared to Sautrāntika and above [i.e., Cittamātra and Madhyamaka]. Regarding their assertion of permanence, they assert that something that is permanent retains at a later time everything that it has at an earlier time. Sautrāntika and above do not assert the meaning of permanence in that way.

In addition to their unique way of asserting the six causes, the five effects, and the four conditions, they also explain that cause and effect are simultaneous. When a seed is planted in a field, the state of the sprout not yet produced is the future sprout. The sprout that has been produced but has not been destroyed is the present sprout. When it is destroyed, that is the past sprout. Thus they posit the three times from the perspective of the action.[358] Because the times are endowed with the four characteristics of production and so forth, they do not assert that they are permanent. The present consciousness that observes the past and the future has an object; it is produced in dependence on the object and the sense faculty. The effect of a past deed can ripen in the present. At the time of the sprout's future and the sprout's past, the sprout exists. Their assertion that the three times substantially exist is different from that of the Vibhajyavāda, one of the seven schools of the Sarvāstivāda. The Vibhajyavāda make the distinction that the present and the past that has not produced an effect are substantially established and that the future and the past that has already produced an effect are not substantially established.[359] [186]

To take a pot as an example, with regard to how the pot exists at the time of its past and future and how the past and future of the pot are posited as a pot: when someone begins to look at a pot, because both the eye sense faculty in the continuum of the person that sees the pot and the pot that is its object are being produced, they are the future. At the time that the pot is being seen, both the eye sense faculty in the continuum of the person seeing the pot and the pot that is its object are the present. Having seen it, as soon as the person has turned away, both the eye sense faculty in the continuum of the person seeing the pot and the pot that is its object are posited as being the past. Thus they assert that a pot exists at the time of the pot's past and the pot's future. And because the past pot and the future pot are, respectively, what has already existed as a pot and what will exist as a pot, and because they are similar in type to the present pot, they posit them as a pot. For example, although some wood in a forest has not been used for firewood, because it is a type of wood that is used to make fire, it is called *firewood*. This is similar in type to milk that has already been milked from an udder; what is in the body of a milk cow is called *milk*. They assert that it is like this.

A conventional truth is posited as that which, after being destroyed or after its parts have been eliminated, the mind that apprehends it is destroyed and completely ceases to exist. For example, when the parts of a pot are destroyed by a hammer, the mind apprehending the pot is lost, and when the qualities of the water inside the pot, such as its taste, are individually eliminated by the mind, the mind apprehending water is destroyed. They assert that *conventional truth* and *imputed existent* are synonyms. Ultimate truths are posited as things like forms and partless particles, for which the mind apprehending them is not lost when they are destroyed or when their parts are individually eliminated by the mind. They assert that *ultimate truth* and *substantial existent* are synonyms. For them, any phenomenon must be something whose entity is apprehended separately. They do not understand what it means to be merely imputed to the parts of another phenomenon. Therefore they assert that all phenomena are substantially established. However, being substantially established does not make something substantially existent.

In this system, that which bears its own entity is asserted to be the meaning of the term *phenomenon* (*dharma*). Because any phenomenon included in the two truths bears its own nature or its own entity, they are all phenomena. Regarding this, the *Treasury of Abhidharma* says, "Because of its own entity."[360] Pūrṇavardhana's *Investigating Characteristics* says, "Because it bears its own entity, it is a phenomenon. If someone says that this is absurd, because this is what they assert, there is no fault. According to us, because everything bears its own character, it does not pass beyond the nature of a phenomenon."[361] [187] Regarding "entity" in the line "that which bears its own entity," there are two—the unshared entity and the shared entity. Although the shared and the unshared entity of something are two, they depend on different bases and do not contradict each other. That they are gathered in the manner of attributes on a single basis is also not contradictory. For example, the attribute of being momentary is an unshared entity from the perspective of the basis of impermanence. However, being momentary is a shared entity from the perspective of a basis of such things as pots and pillars. The attributes of solidity, moisture, heat, and motility are respectively the unshared entities of earth, water, fire, and wind. The qualities of impermanence, emptiness, and so forth are the shared entities of the foundations earth, water, and so forth. Thus, the *Great Exegesis of the Abhidharma* says, "According to others, there are two kinds of characteristics: specific characteristics and general characteristics. The characteristics of solidity, moisture, heat, and motility are specific characteristics. The characteristic of form is a general characteristic. Thus the two characteristics are not contradictory; although they are posited for a single phenomenon, there is no fault."[362] *Clarifying the Meaning* says:

> Mental engagement with specific characteristics is to bring into one's attention the specific characteristics. It is like thinking, for example, that such things as form have the characteristic of being capable of being damaged. The expression "such things" includes such things as saying that feeling has the characteristic of experience. Regarding mental application to general characteristics, this refers to mental application to impermanence and so forth. It is endowed with the sixteen aspects [of the four truths], from impermanence to release.[363]

A general characteristic (*sāmānyalakṣaṇa*) must be posited as a shared nature. Its opposite, a specific characteristic (*svalakṣaṇa*), must be posited as an unshared nature. *Investigating Characteristics* says, "The specific characteristic of a substance is the unshared entity of blue and so forth. It is known by the eye consciousness and so forth."[364] [188]

Also, this system holds that at the conclusion of analyzing such things as form and consciousness, they must be found. In the end, seeing that partless particles and partless moments of time must exist, they accept partless particles as the basic components of coarse objects and partless moments as the basic components of a sequence of time. Because various coarse phenomena are established through the accumulation of subtle partless particles, they assert that external objects are truly established. Because there is no difference between earth and the earth element, water and the water element, fire and the fire element, and wind and the wind element, and because the functions of all four elements are fully present in all composite forms, they assert that the actual four elements are present in all composite forms.

The Vaibhāṣika divide action (*karman*) into motivating and motivated action. *Motivating action* is a motivation associated with the mental consciousness and is the motivations that are the mental factors that produce physical and verbal actions. It is also called *mental action*. *Motivated action* is the physical action and the verbal action produced by that motivating action. Both [physical and verbal action] have both revelatory (*vijñapti*) and nonrevelatory (*avijñapti*) forms. Sautrāntika, Cittamātra, and Svātantrika do not assert that action has form. Vaibhāṣika and Prāsaṅgika Madhyamaka assert that physical and verbal action have form.

Although a long period of time may elapse between an action and its effect, the specific effects of happiness resulting from virtue and of suffering resulting from nonvirtue do not become confused. According to some Vaibhāṣika, once an action has been performed, as long as its effect has not ripened, there is an entity of noncompositional factors called *not wasted* (*avipraṇāśa*). It becomes a different entity from the action, and it connects the action and effect. For example, if someone else has a certificate of a loan, that loan, together with its interest, is not wasted. Because it is like this, they say that there is no fault. A division of Vaibhāṣika asserts that, through what is called the *acquisition* (*prāpti*) of virtuous and nonvirtuous actions, a nonassociated compositional factor that is a different entity than those two actions connects the action and effect.

Regarding how they identify the self that is the basis of actions and effects, some members of the Sāṃmitīya subschool of Vaibhāṣika assert that it is the aggregates that do this. The Kaurukullaka school, a subschool of Sāṃmitīya, asserts that it is all five aggregates. The Avantaka, another Sāṃmitīya subschool, asserts that it is the mind alone. The Vātsīputrīya, also a Sāṃmitīya subschool, asserts that it is the inexpressible self.[365] The Kashmiri Vaibhāṣika and some Sautrāntika assert that the continuum of the aggregates is the referent of the self that serves as the basis of actions and effects. [189] Those who assert that all five aggregates are the referent of the person do not say that each of the five aggregates is the person; they assert that the collection of the five aggregates is the person. Those who assert that consciousness is the referent of the person posit as the person the mental consciousness that is the accumulator of actions and the experiencer of effects and that travels without interruption in all past and future lifetimes.

In this Vaibhāṣika system, they assert that whatever is an established base is necessarily a self of phenomena. Therefore they do not accept a coarse and subtle selflessness of phenomena. They posit the person being empty of being permanent, partless, and independent to be the coarse selflessness of persons and the person being empty of being self-sufficient and substantially existent to be the subtle selflessness of persons. They assert that *subtle selflessness* and *subtle selflessness of persons* are synonyms.

The Vātsīputrīya subschool of Sāṃmitīya Vaibhāṣika assert a self that is self-sufficient and substantially existent. Therefore they do not assert that being empty of that is the subtle selflessness of persons. If the self were something other than the aggregates, there would be the fault that it would be permanent, as in the tīrthika systems, and there would be fault that the self would be something that could be conceived of separately without conceiving of the aggregates. Yet if one asserts that the self is the aggregates, it would absurdly follow that there would be many persons. It would also absurdly follow that when the aggregates disintegrated, the self would disintegrate such that, like the aggregates, at the time of death the continuum would cease. And it would absurdly follow that actions performed would be lost without producing an effect. Therefore they assert a self-sufficient person that cannot be described as either permanent or impermanent. Thus, in their system, subtle selflessness is just the selflessness of being empty of being permanent, partless, and independent.

Turning to the topic of valid means of knowledge (*pramāṇa*), there are two: direct perception and inference. There are three types of direct perception: sense direct perception, mental direct perception, and yogic direct perception; they do not assert reflexive-awareness direct perception. They assert that the physical sense faculties are valid means of knowledge and that when a sense consciousness apprehends its object, it apprehends it nakedly, without the aspect (*ākāra*) of the object appearing. They distinguish between seeing and knowing, saying that the eye sense faculty sees form and that the eye consciousness apprehends or knows form. There are many such assertions.

The general explanation presented above of what Vaibhāṣika asserts for the most part belongs to the system of the Kashmiri Vaibhāṣika. The essence of their assertions is summarized in the *Compendium on the Essence of Wisdom* in this way:

> Space and the two cessations,
> the three unconditioned, are permanent.
> The conditioned completely lack self;
> they have no creator and are momentary.
> Awareness is produced from the eye and is without aspect;
> what is directly perceived are collections of particles.
> This is explained in the texts of the Kashmiri Vaibhāṣika

who are called the intelligent ones.[366] [190]

Very similar to that, Jetāri's *Verses on Distinguishing the Sugata's Texts* says:

The three unconditioned are permanent:
space and the two cessations.
All conditioned phenomena are momentary;
there is no self and no creator.

Regarding consciousness, an awareness produced by a sense
faculty
directly perceives aggregations of subtle particles.
Scholars explain that this is the system
of the Kashmiri Vaibhāṣika.[367]

The Five Categories of Objects of Knowledge

A general explanation of the Vaibhāṣika assertions was summarized above. Some of the most important tenets that are unique to them are explained somewhat more extensively in what follows.

When the basis in this system is delineated in Abhidharma texts such as the *Treasury of Abhidharma* and its autocommentary, all phenomena are included in the aggregates (*skandha*), constituents (*dhātu*), and sources (*āyatana*). All conditioned phenomena are included in the five aggregates: (1) the form (*rūpa*) aggregate, (2) the feeling (*vedanā*) aggregate, (3) the discrimination (*saṃjñā*) aggregate, (4) the compositional factors (*saṃskāra*) aggregate, and (5) the consciousness (*vijñāna*) aggregate. When the term *sources* is used, it refers to the division into twelve sources: the six external sources, from the form source to the phenomena (*dharma*) source, and the six internal sources, from the eye source to the mind (*manas*) source. When these are divided extensively they present the eighteen constituents. The eighteen constituents are the six elements that are objects of observation—forms, sounds, odors, tastes, objects of touch, and phenomena; the six sources that are the supporting sense faculties, from the eye sense faculty to the mind sense faculty (*manendriya*); and the six sources that are the supported consciousnesses, from the eye consciousness to the mental consciousness. All phenomena are included in the sources and constituents.

Unconditioned phenomena are included in the phenomena constituent among the eighteen constituents and the phenomena source among the twelve sources.

Also, all phenomena are included in the form aggregate, the mind source, and the phenomena constituent. Included in the form aggregate is the form aggregate from among the five aggregates; the ten physical constituents, such as the eye constituents from among the eighteen constituents; the ten sources, such as the form source from among the twelve sources; and nonrevelatory form (*avijñaptirūpa*), which is one part of the phenomena source and the phenomena constituent. [191] Included in the mind source is the consciousness aggregate from among the five aggregates, the mind source from among the twelve sources, and the seven mental elements from among the eighteen constituents. Included in the phenomena constituent is nonrevelatory form, which is one part of the form aggregate, the feeling aggregate, the discrimination aggregate, and the compositional factors aggregate from among the five aggregates; the phenomena source from among the twelve sources; and the phenomena constituent from among the eighteen constituents. The Abhidharma treatise *Establishment of Knowledge* says, "If someone asks, 'Are all phenomena included in one constituent, one source, and one aggregate?' The answer is they are. The one constituent is the phenomena constituent. The one source is the mind source. The one aggregate is the form aggregate."[368] Summarizing its meaning, the *Treasury of Abhidharma* says, "Everything is included in one aggregate, one source, and one constituent."[369]

As was already discussed roughly above, Vaibhāṣika's own system seems to delineate the nature of reality from the perspective of the five categories of objects of knowledge. For example, this can be known from what appears in Vasubandhu's *Commentary on the Treasury of Abhidharma*: "All these phenomena are included in the five: forms, minds, mental factors, what is not associated with mind, and the unconditioned."[370] And Yaśomitra's *Elucidation of the Compendium of the Abhidharma* says, "Regarding objects of knowledge, there are five types: forms, minds, phenomena arisen from minds, compositional factors that are not associated with minds, and the unconditioned."[371]

All internal and external physical phenomena, such as the five objects, such as form, and the five senses, such as the eye, are included in the foundation of appearing forms. The phenomena that are internal consciousnesses are included in the two categories of main minds and mental factors. Such things as production, abiding, and disintegration, which are features of conditioned phenomena, and conditioned phenomena such as the three times that are not classified as either form or consciousness are included in the foundation of nonassociated compositional factors. Those phenomena that are not produced by causes and conditions are included in the foundation of the unconditioned. Thus they introduced a way of delineating all objects of knowledge by dividing them into five categories. [192]

The Category of Appearing Forms

Regarding the foundation of appearing forms, they assert that there are eleven: the five external forms, from the form source to the object of touch source; the five internal forms, from the eye source to the body source; and nonrevelatory form. Regarding what is called *nonrevelatory form* (*avijñaptirūpa*), the *Treasury of Abhidharma* says it is "also in the distracted and those without mind."[372] As this indicates, it is a special type of form that does not reveal itself and that is unobstructed, and it has five qualities: (1) it occurs even in states of distraction and mindless states, (2) it is either virtuous or nonvirtuous, (3) it is continuous in both past and future, (4) it is caused by the four great internal elements, and (5) it is not revelatory.

Regarding the five external objects such as form and the five internal forms—the sense faculties—this system asserts that the four great elements serve as their cause and that they are external objects that are established through the accumulation of subtle particles. Because the way in which external objects are established from the accumulation of partless particles is a fundamental tenet of Vaibhāṣika, it will be discussed briefly. In general, it is explained that things begin from particles that are the smallest forms, syllables that are the shortest words, and moments that are the shortest times. The *Great Exegesis* says, "Conditioned phenomena have three measures: time, form, and word. The shortest time is called a single moment, the smallest form is called a single particle, and the shortest word is based on a single syllable."[373]

They assert that a subtle particle is not only the smallest of particles and that it is the original basic component of anything that has form; a subtle particle is also partless, is one surrounded by many, and abides without touching another subtle particle. They also assert that they have the quality of retaining their nature, that they cannot be divided into parts, and that when a single subtle particle at the center is surrounded by other subtle particles, if they were to touch on all sides they would become mixed, and if they were to touch on one side they would have parts. The *Great Exegesis* says:

> If someone asks, "How is the size of a subtle particle to be understood?" this is said: A subtle particle is understood to be the most subtle form; it cannot be cut, destroyed, or pierced. It cannot be grasped, thrown, ridden, pushed, held, or pulled. It is not long or short, square or round, proportional or not proportional, high or low. [193] It is partless, cannot be destroyed, cannot be seen, cannot be heard, cannot be smelled, cannot be tasted, cannot be touched. Therefore the subtle particle is called the most subtle form.[374]

That same text states, "Vasumitra says, if someone asks, 'Do subtle particles touch each other?' this is to be said: 'They do not touch each other. If they did touch each other, they would remain until the second moment.'"[375]

In accord with this, Śubhagupta's *Proof of External Objects* says:

> They do not touch each other;
> they abide without having parts.
> Therefore the circle of the earth
> arises from their accumulation.[376]

Between the two, substantial subtle particles and composite subtle particles, substantial partless particles are, for example, each of the eight substantial partless particles: the four partless particles of the four elements—earth, water, fire, and wind—and the four partless particles of the four elemental evolutes—form, smell, taste, and object of touch. Composite subtle particles are, for example, the smallest particles that are accumulations of those eight. They assert that substantial subtle particles are partless and composite subtle particles have parts, and they assert that an accumulation of seven subtle particles is the size of one particle. The initial basic component of a material external object is a single partless subtle particle that cannot be broken down into parts. Because various coarse phenomena are established through the accumulation of those, they assert that external objects are truly established. To illustrate this with something that is blue, they assert that it is not just an appearance to the mind as blue; instead, it is an external object that arises from an object made up of basic components that are partless subtle particles.

In general, the existence of external objects is established by valid [sense] experience. They assert that if one were to analyze how they exist using reasoning, coarse phenomena must be established through the accumulation of the subtle parts that compose them. Removing the parts of coarse forms, they become gradually smaller, until finally one must posit a final substance that cannot be divided into parts at all. If such a final phenomenon did not exist, one could not explain how the coarse is established through the accumulation of the subtle. Breaking a coarse form like a rock into chunks—that is, dividing it into individual parts—one must come to a final particle of which there is nothing smaller. If such a particle had parts, there would still have to be something that could be divided into parts. [194] Thus there would be the fault of there not being that which is the smallest. Therefore it must be the case that one either accepts that it is partless or one accepts that parts are endless. If they accepted that parts are endless, then if one [continues to] divide a single subtle drop of water, it would never come to an end. Thinking in this way, they accept that [particles] are partless.

Just as they assert that the subtle particles that serve as the fundamental basic components of physical phenomena are partless, so they say that consciousnesses, which are conditioned phenomena that are not physical, are divided into final units of the earlier and later moments of time, which themselves cannot be broken down into smaller earlier and later parts. They therefore say that moments of time are partless.

Vaibhāṣika and Sautrāntika are similar in asserting that subtle particles are partless and that they do not touch each other. However, they differ in how they assert this, with Vaibhāṣika saying there is space in between the particles and Sautrāntika saying there is no space in between them. Also, Vaibhāṣika asserts that there is no difference between the four elements and the constituents that are the four elements and that, because the functions of the four elements are fully present in all composite forms, they have the four actual elements. Sautrāntika and above make a distinction between the four elements and the constituents that are the four elements and assert that the constituents that are the four elements are fully present in all composite forms but that the actual four elements do not need to be present; something like the water substance in a collection of subtle particles is the element or capacity of water, it does not have to be actual water. Such modes of assertion together with their textual sources have already been explained in detail in the first volume of *Science and Philosophy in the Indian Buddhist Classics*.[377]

The Categories of Main Minds and Accompanying Mental Factors

Regarding the foundation of main minds, there are six collections of consciousness, from the eye consciousness to the mental consciousness.

Regarding the accompanying mental factors, according to Vasubandhu's *Treasury of Abhidharma* there are five categories of the definite: the extensive foundation (*mahābhūmika*) of mind, the extensive foundation of the virtues, the extensive foundation of the great afflictions, the extensive foundation of the nonvirtues, and the extensive foundation of the small afflictions. Adding the category of the indefinite, they divide them into six and explain that there are forty-six mental factors. According to Asaṅga's *Compendium of Abhidharma*, his autocommentary, and Vasubandhu's *Investigation of the Five Aggregates*, aspiration, wisdom, memory, interest, and samādhi are explained to be determining factors; they are not asserted to be extensive foundations. In this system, it is asserted that those accompany all minds. [195]

Even a mind associated with doubt has some wisdom; it may be a small amount of wisdom and much doubt, like a stream that mixes with the salty sea. In the same way, there are ways in which there is aspiration in a mind of anger, samādhi in a mind of distraction, memory in a forgetful mind, and belief in a mind without faith; they explain that they must be posited based on the amount.

The root virtue of nonobscuration, the root affliction of wrong view, nonintrospection, forgetfulness, and distraction explained in Asaṅga's *Compendium of Abhidharma* are not enumerated in the *Treasury of Abhidharma*. In the *Treasury of Abhidharma*, the description of the forty-six mental factors is primarily in terms of the different natures of the individual mental factors. The root virtue of nonobscuration, the root affliction of wrong view, and nonintrospection have a nature of wisdom. Forgetfulness and distraction have a nature of memory and samādhi respectively. Therefore it appears that the intention is that they do not have a nature different from that of the forty-six mental factors. The way in which they divide mental factors into the substantial and the imputed has already been set forth in some detail in the second volume of the *Science and Philosophy in the Indian Buddhist Classics*. One can learn about it there.[378]

The Category of Nonassociated Compositional Factors

Regarding the foundation of nonassociated compositional factors, they are posited as fourteen: (1) acquisition (*prāpti*), (2) nonacquisition (*aprāpti*), (3) similarity (*sabhāgatā*), (4) nondiscrimination (*āsaṃjñika*), (5) absorption of nondiscrimination (*asaṃjñisamāpatti*), (6) absorption of cessation (*nirodhasamāpatti*), (7) life force (*jīvita*), (8–11) the four qualities of conditioned phenomena: production (*jāti*), abiding (*sthiti*), aging (*jarā*), and disintegration (*anityatā*), (12) groups of words (*nāmakāya*), (13) groups of sentences (*padakāya*), and (14) groups of letters (*vyañjanakāya*). The *Treasury of Abhidharma* says:

> Nonassociated compositional factors are
> attainment, nonattainment, and similarity,
> absorption of nondiscrimination,
> life force, the [four] qualities,
> groups of words, and so forth.[379]

Those fourteen are conditioned phenomena that are not form, nor are they associated with minds and mental factors. Therefore they are called *nonassociated compositional factors* (*viprayuktasaṃskāra*). Vaibhāṣika asserts that they are things that are different substantial entities from forms, minds, and mental factors. Sautrāntika and above assert that they are simply imputations to instances of those three. Therefore they assert that they are not separate substantial entities from them. [196]

Among these, *acquisition* (*prāpti*) is explained to be a substance that causes an acquired phenomenon to be possessed in the continuum of a person. Just as a rope that binds a load is separate from the load, it is an existent that is held to be a separate entity from the acquired phenomenon. *Nonacquisition* (*aprāpti*) is asserted to be a substance that causes a phenomenon that is not acquired not to be possessed. *Similarity* (*sabhāgatā*) is a substance that causes the deeds, thoughts, and natures of sentient beings to be similar. *Nondiscrimination* (*āsaṃjñika*) is a substance that temporarily causes the cessation of minds and mental factors in the continuum of gods born in the state of nondiscrimination. The *absorption of nondiscrimination* (*asaṃjñisamāpatti*) is a substance that serves as the cause of its effect, nondiscrimination; when one has entered into that absorption, it causes minds and mental factors to cease until one rises from it. The *absorption of cessation* (*nirodhasamāpatti*) is posited as a substance in the continuum of noble ones that temporarily causes the cessation of minds and mental factors in dependence on a mind of the Peak of Existence (*bhavāgra*), the most subtle mind in the three realms.

Life force (*jīvita*) is asserted to be a substantially established nonassociated compositional factor that serves as the basis for the body and for consciousness. Śamathadeva's *Salient Points* cites the *Sūtra of the Nun Dharmadinnā*:

> When the life force, heat, and consciousness
> have abandoned the body,
> it is left behind,
> mindless, like a log.[380]

This is what the Vaibhāṣika say. In response the Sautrāntika say, "If you assert that the body and consciousness depend on the life force, on what does the life force depend? It also cannot remain without depending on something, just as the body and consciousness cannot do so. You might say that the life force depends on the body and consciousness. In that case, because they would be mutually dependent, neither would be established, or even if they were established, the life force would never cease because it would not be possible for its cause, consciousness, to be incomplete. Therefore you are designating the mental consciousness together with its seeds of a similar type to be the life force."[381] The Yogācārin find fault with both of these positions and assert that, through the power of karma, the foundation consciousness (*ālayavijñāna*) endures by retaining its same status and that this is designated as the life faculty (*jīvitendriya*).

Regarding the four qualities of conditioned phenomena, production and so forth, because they are phenomena that qualify conditioned phenomena, they are called the *qualities of conditioned phenomena*. *Production* (*jāti*) is the agent of production, *abiding* (*sthiti*) is the agent of abiding, *aging* (*jarā*) is the agent of growing old, and *impermanence* (*anityatā*) is the agent of disintegration. The Vaibhāṣika assert that they are produced simultaneously with the conditioned phenomena that they qualify and that their own nature is held to be a different substance from that of conditioned phenomena. [197] The Abhidharma treatise the *Establishment of Knowledge* says, "Someone might ask, 'Should the production, abiding, aging, and impermanence of conditioned phenomena be called *conditioned* or *unconditioned*?' This is to be said: 'They are to be called *conditioned*.'"[382] And the *Great Exegesis* says, "A phenomenon that comes forth due to production, weakens due to aging, and disintegrates due to impermanence is the meaning of *conditioned*. That which is the opposite of that is the meaning of *unconditioned*."[383]

Someone might ask, "Why is it that in the sūtras, the qualities of conditioned phenomena are said to be production, abiding, and disintegration?" It is explained that aging is included in abiding; they are said to be the same quality. The purpose for this is said to be that abiding is the source of attachment. Therefore, in order to stop attachment to it, abiding and aging are combined into one characteristic. The *Commentary on the Treasury of Abhidharma* says:

> Someone might say, "The sūtra says, 'For conditioned phenomena, production is evident, disintegration is evident, abiding and changing into another state are evident.'" . . . Foolish beings who are blinded by ignorance become attached through believing that the continuum of compounded things is the self and mine. In order to overcome that belief, the Bhagavan taught that the continuum of compounded things is conditioned and dependently arisen. He only said that these three are the qualities of conditioned phenomena; he did not say that they occur in each moment.[384]

Someone might say, "If it must be the case that there are four qualities that qualify even these four qualities as conditioned phenomena, it would be an infinite regress. If this does not need to be the case, then the four qualities would become unconditioned." To respond one may say, if one takes a single thing such as a pot as an instance of something qualified as conditioned, then when it is produced there is the pot itself and the four primary qualities: that which causes it to be produced, that which causes it to abide, that which causes it to age, and that which causes it to disintegrate. The four secondary qualities are: the production of the production that causes the primary production to be produced, the abiding of the abiding that causes the primary abiding to abide, the aging of the aging that causes the primary aging to age, and the disintegration of the disintegration that causes the primary disintegration to disintegrate. Those nine—the instance, which is the conditioned phenomenon itself; the four primary qualities; and the four secondary qualities—are produced simultaneously. [198] Primary production causes eight things: the instance, which is the conditioned phenomenon itself; the three other primary qualities, such as abiding; and the four secondary qualities. Because it is not suitable for production itself to be produced by itself, it is produced by the production of production.

Thus the production of production produces only the primary production; this applies in the same way to the other three qualities. Therefore all four of the qualities of conditioned phenomena are instances of conditioned phenomena, with each having the three other qualities, excluding itself, and having all four qualities by adding each of the secondary qualities, such as the production of production. In summary, Vaibhāṣika asserts that because those are mutually dependent, there is no fault of infinite regress. Thus the *Commentary on the Treasury of Abhidharma* says:

> Including the phenomenon itself, together with the eight qualities and secondary qualities, nine are produced together. Production causes the production of eight factors that are other than itself. The production of production produces only production. For example, some chickens have many chicks, others have a few chicks. Abiding causes the abiding of eight factors other than itself. The abiding of abiding causes the abiding of only abiding. This is to be applied accordingly to aging and impermanence as well. Therefore it is well known that they say the consequence of infinite regress does not arise.[385]

This system asserts that when a conditioned phenomenon such as the form aggregate is qualified by the qualities of conditioned phenomena—production, disintegration, and abiding—it is not qualified by its being produced and so forth; it is qualified as conditioned by a different existing object, such as its producer. Therefore Vaibhāṣika does not assert that the qualities are the action of production and so on; it asserts that these qualities are the agent of production, the agent of abiding, and the agent of disintegration, which are different substantial objects. The *Commentary on the Treasury of Abhidharma* says, "Production produces that phenomenon, abiding makes it abide, aging makes it age, and impermanence makes it disintegrate."[386] And *Clarifying the Meaning* says, "Here, because they assert that the qualities of conditioned phenomena are entities that are different substances, it is not suitable to find fault."[387]

Therefore, in the Vaibhāṣika system, for things such as form, the four qualities are simultaneous. However, they assert that when those four operate on that [form], they do so sequentially: first there is the act of production, then the act of abiding, then the act of aging, and then the act of disintegration. [199] In the Buddhist tenet systems of Sautrāntika and above, the qualities of conditioned phenomena—production and so forth—are asserted to be the production, the disintegration, and the abiding of those phenomena such as form. Because production and so forth are not different substances from form and so forth, they are imputedly existent. Taking the example of a sprout, they assert that the new arising of what did not exist in the past is production, the abiding of what is similar in type to what existed before is abiding, the inability to remain for a second moment after the moment of its production is disintegration, and having a different quality from the previous moment is aging. They assert that those qualities are simultaneous.

The Mahīśāsaka, Kashmiri Vaibhāṣika, and the Vaibhāṣika in general assert that conditioned phenomena are necessarily momentary. They accept a period of abiding between production and disintegration that is different from those two. This way of positing momentariness is different from that of Sautrāntika and above. The Sautrāntika find fault with the Vaibhāṣika assertion, saying that in such a case, conditioned phenomena would not be momentary. The Vaibhāṣika reply that momentariness refers to however long it takes for the four activities to be completed. [Referring to the Vaibhāṣika] the *Commentary on the Treasury of Abhidharma* says, "They say, 'Momentariness for us is how long it takes for all of this to be completed.'"[388] Thus it states that the completion of all four of the four activities of qualities, such as production, must be posited as a moment. Regarding their assertion that all conditioned phenomena are momentary,

Bhāviveka's *Blaze of Reasoning* says, "All conditioned phenomena are momentary . . . This is a root precept of the Mahīśāsaka."[389] Jetāri's *Commentary on Distinguishing the Sugata's Texts* says, "All conditioned phenomena that are the nature of the five aggregates are momentary. All the aspects of things that are made through the assembly and gathering of causes and conditions are momentary because they exist only for the moment of their production."[390]

The Vātsīputrīya assert that among conditioned phenomena there is the momentary and the nonmomentary. The momentary are minds and mental factors and such things as sounds, tongues of fire, lightning, and rivers. The four elements and so forth are not momentary. They assert that disintegration depends on other causes that arise later and that once they encounter the cause of disintegration, they become impermanent. The *Commentary on the Treasury of Abhidharma* says, "If someone asks, 'What is this *momentariness*?' Things such as wood are seen to be destroyed by encountering fire; because there is no reliable valid means of knowledge apart from seeing, it is not the case that the disintegration of everything arises without a cause."[391] [200] Also, Pūrṇavardhana's *Investigating Characteristics* says, "They do not accept that all conditioned phenomena are momentary. Why? They think that minds, mental factors, some forms, and some nonassociated compositional factors are momentary, but that some forms and some nonassociated compositional factors are not momentary. They think that because the body is not momentary, it is not nonexistent after changing its form. Therefore it is not contradictory for the body to move to another place."[392] And Bhāviveka's *Blaze of Reasoning* says, "There are momentary and nonmomentary conditioned phenomena . . . This is a precept of the Vātsīputrīya."[393]

Other Vaibhāṣika find fault with this assertion of the Vātsīputrīya, saying that if disintegration depends on other causes that arise later, then in some cases disintegration would not occur for things that do not have other causes of disintegration—things such as minds, sounds, tongues of fire, and lightning—because they have no causes [for their disintegration] that arise later. If you assert that they disintegrate naturally, your assertion that in general disintegration depends on other causes that arise later is undermined. Pūrṇavardhana's *Investigating Characteristics* says:

> [They assert that] production is becoming itself and that both the momentary and the nonmomentary have causes. Accord-

> ing to that assertion, there would also need to be causes for the disintegration of everything. If they do not assert that, it would absurdly follow that because the time of the cause of disintegration is uncertain, the time of the disintegration of momentary things like minds and tongues of flame would also be uncertain. Therefore they must accept that everything [disintegrates] without a cause, as minds and so forth do.[394]

Furthermore, the Vātsīputrīya might say, "We accept that conditioned phenomena definitely disintegrate, but we do not accept that they disintegrate as soon as they are produced from a cause." That is untenable. If you accept that conditioned phenomena disintegrate because the disintegration of conditioned phenomena does not depend on causes that arise later, then you must accept that disintegration is established at the same time that those pheneomena are produced. If the disintegration of conditioned phenomena depends on causes that arise later, you do not have to accept that disintegration is established as soon as the conditioned phenomena are produced. However, because that is not tenable, you would have to accept that disintegration is established as soon as conditioned phenomena are produced. If you do not accept that disintegration is established as soon as conditioned phenomena are produced, then disintegration would also not take place later. Regarding how such faults are expressed, Pūrṇavardhana's *Investigating Characteristics* says: [201]

> They say that conditioned phenomena definitely disintegrate but do not do so as soon as they are produced. If you assert that there is disintegration, you must definitely accept that conditioned phenomena disintegrate as soon as they are produced. Why? Because the disintegration of things is causeless. If it had a cause, because it would rely on that cause, it would not undergo change the instant that it arose; in that case it would also be causeless. If you do not assert that [disintegration occurs] as soon as something is produced, it would also not change later. Therefore conditioned phenomena would not disintegrate. Because that is not the case, one must accept that conditioned phenomena disintegrate as soon as they are produced.[395]

In general, the meaning of *momentary* does not need to be explained only as disintegration. Saying that a vessel is momentary refers to its being empty. Saying that someone named Devadatta is momentary refers to Devadatta being inactive. Saying that a period of time is momentary means that it has ended. As Pūrṇavardhana's *Investigating Characteristics* says:

> The term *momentary* expresses many meanings. Thus, one might ask, "What does *momentary* mean?" The term *momentary* refers to being empty; the statement that a vessel is momentary is understood to mean that it is empty. It means being inactive; the statement that Devadatta is momentary is understood to mean that he lacks activity. The end of a period of time is called *momentary*.[396]

Among groups of words (*nāmakāya*), groups of sentences (*padakāya*), and groups of letters (*vyañjanakāya*), *word* indicates that which sets forth just the entity of the object—for example, the term *form*. A *sentence* is that which attaches a quality to the nature of the object—for example, "Form is impermanent." A *letter* serves as the basis for both words and sentences, like the Tibetan letter *ka*. A *group of words* refers to a gathering of them. Regarding how the Vaibhāṣika assert that the three—groups of words, sentences, and syllables—are nonassociated compositional factors, they say that when the word "pot" is spoken aloud, the meaning of "pot" that appears to the mind is posited as something having that name that makes one understand the meaning; the meaning cannot be understood through speech alone. For example, it is like not being able to understand the meaning of the speech of an ox. Thus Vasubandhu's *Commentary on the Treasury of Abhidharma* says, "Those are not the nature of speech. If speech were sound, one could not understand any meaning through sound alone. Why? Speech engages with words and words express meaning."[397] Therefore the Kashmiri Vaibhāṣika assert that the three—word, sentence, and syllable—as well as that which is a collection of all three, are strings of sound generalities that appear to thought. [202] The Sautrāntika assert that they are form because articulate vocal sound is specifically characterized.

The Foundation of the Unconditioned

Regarding the foundation of the unconditioned, the Kashmiri Vaibhāṣika assert that there are three: space (*ākāśa*), analytical cessations (*pratisaṅkhyānirodha*), and nonanalytical cessations (*apratisaṅkhyānirodha*). However, it is said that the Magadha Vaibhāṣika assert that there are four, adding reality (*tathatā*). *Space* is asserted to be a permanent substance that provides place and serves as the basis of wind; not only does it not obstruct other forms, it is not obstructed by other forms. The element of space is different; it is one of the six elements and is asserted to be a form source that becomes the nature of either light or darkness.

Analytical cessations stop their object of negation, the contaminated; *nonanalytical cessations* stop the production of their object of negation. Therefore the Vaibhāṣika assert that all three of the unconditioned have the quality of being substantially established unconditioned phenomena. The Magadha Vaibhāṣika who assert that reality is a foundation of the unconditioned assert that it is also substantially established. They do not understand how to posit reality as the unconditioned that is a nonimplicative negation (*prasajyapratiṣedha*). Bodhibhadra's *Explanation of the Compendium of the Essence of Wisdom* says:

> The Kashmiri Vaibhāṣika say that the unconditioned are three and assert that they are permanent. The Magadha Vaibhāṣika assert that the unconditioned are four . . . They argue, 'Thus, regarding the four unconditioned, our position is that they are asserted to be substantially existent. What are the four? They are space, nonanalytical cessations, analytical cessations, and reality.'"[398]

Thus, in the Abhidharma texts, there are eleven forms, six minds, forty-six mental factors, fourteen nonassociated compositional factors, and three unconditioned phenomena. Taking objects of knowledge as the basis of division into the five categories, they explain there are eighty phenomena. The foundations of form, nonassociated compositional factors, and the unconditioned have already been explained extensively in the first volume of *Science and Philosophy in the Indian Buddhist Classics*. The foundations of minds and mental factors have already been extensively explained in the second volume of *Science and Philosophy in the Indian Buddhist Classics*. [203]

Cause and Effect

The Six Causes

Among the five categories of objects of knowledge explained above, the first four are conditioned and the last is unconditioned. For something to be conditioned, it must arise in dependence on its causes and conditions. Therefore one might ask how cause and effect are posited in this system. A presentation of six causes appears in such works as the *Treasury of Abhidharma*. Because the Sautrāntika and others do not assert that cause and effect are simultaneous, they assert that a phenomenon's simultaneously arising cause and a phenomenon's concomitant cause are merely imputed to be causes of that phenomenon; they do not assert that they are actual causes of that phenomenon. The Vaibhāṣika assert that those two are actual causes of that phenomenon. Therefore they assert that there are cases when the causes and effects of things are simultaneous.

When causes are divided, there are six: activity cause (*kāraṇahetu*), simultaneously arising cause (*sahabhūhetu*), cause of similar type (*saṃprayuktahetu*), concomitant cause (*sabhāgahetu*), omnipresent cause (*sarvatragahetu*), and fruitional cause (*vipākahetu*). As the *Treasury of Abhidharma* says:

> Activity cause, simultaneously arising cause,
> cause of similar type, concomitant cause,
> omnipresent cause, and fruitional cause:
> six types of causes are asserted.[399]

When those six causes are explained according to the system set forth in the *Treasury of Abhidharma*, the first is the activity cause (*kāraṇahetu*). The definition of *activity cause* is a phenomenon that does not impede the production of a phenomenon that is other than itself. For example, because a pot does not impede the production of a pillar, that pot is posited as an activity cause of a pillar. Thus the *Commentary on the Treasury of Abhidharma* says, "All phenomena except for itself are causes that are activity causes of a conditioned phenomenon because they remain in the state of not impeding its production."[400]

Furthermore, there are two ways in which an effect is not produced: it is not produced because the collection of causes is not complete, or it is not produced because, although the substantial cause and cooperative conditions are complete, there is some impediment. An example of the latter would be planting a seed in a field where water, manure, heat, moisture, and so on are present, yet although these other causes are complete, the seed is eaten by a bird; in this case, [the effect] is not produced due to an impediment.

For an effect to be produced, two causes are necessary: the complete causes and conditions and the absence of an impediment. For those reasons other phenomena that do not impede the production of that effect are posited as its cause. Regarding that, as Pūrṇavardhana's *Investigating Characteristics* says:

> One might ask how it is that all phenomena are activity causes; it is because they remain in the state of not impeding production. There would be two cases in which an effect is not produced: because the cause does not exist or because there is an impediment. [204] Otherwise, when the cause exists and there is no impediment, there is production. Therefore that which remains in a state of not impeding that which is other than itself establishes a cause that is an activity cause.[401]

The second, *simultaneously arising cause* (*sahabhūhetu*), is defined as the common locus of (1) that which is simultaneous and a different substance and (2) that which is beneficial to mutual production. Examples are the four great elements, such as earth, in a single composite and a mind and its accompanying mental factors, such as feeling. The *Commentary on the Treasury of Abhidharma* says, "The four great elements are simultaneously arising causes of each other. Mind is [the simultaneously arising cause] for the factors that accompany mind, and they are for mind."[402]

The third, *cause of similar type* (*saṃprayuktahetu*), is defined as that which produces a subsequent type that is similar to itself. For example, the first moment of a pot is a cause of similar type of the second moment of that pot. The *Treasury of Abhidharma* says, "The similar are causes of similar type."[403] The majority of conditioned phenomena are asserted to have a cause of similar type.

The fourth, *concomitant cause* (*sabhāgahetu*), is defined as the common locus of (1) that which is concomitant in the sense of having the five types of mutual concomitance and (2) that which does not impede each other's production. For example, because an eye consciousness and the feeling that accompanies it are concomitant from the perspective of the five types of concomitance, they are posited as concomitant causes of each other. The *Commentary on the Treasury of Abhidharma* says:

> Those minds and mental factors that have a concomitant basis are mutually concomitant causes. *Concomitant* means not different. For example, a moment of the eye sense faculty that is the basis of the eye sense consciousness is also [the concomitant cause of] the feeling and so forth that are concomitant with it. One should know that this is also the case up to a mental consciousness and a moment of mind that is concomitant with it. That which is a concomitant cause is also a simultaneously arising cause.[404]

Minds and mental factors are concomitant in five ways: (1) a concomitance of basis, (2) a concomitance of object, (3) a concomitance of aspect, (4) a concomitance of time, and (5) a concomitance of substance. [205] Regarding *concomitance of basis*, both a main mind and its accompanying mental factors depend on the same sense faculty. The accompanying mental factors depend on the sense faculty that is the dominant condition upon which the main mind depends. *Concomitance of object* is observation of a single object; the object that is observed by the mind is also observed by the mental factors that accompany it. *Concomitance of aspect* is the same object of apprehension. The mind that is produced having the aspect of the object and the accompanying mental factors produced having the aspect of that same object have a concomitant aspect or mode of apprehension. Regarding *concomitance of time*, they arise simultaneously; the mind and its accompanying mental factors have the same production, abiding, and disintegration. Regarding *concomitance of substance*, each mind and its accompanying mental factors are not produced from separate substances. This is called *concomitance of substance* in that accompanying each main mind is one factor of feeling, one factor of discrimination, and so forth, such that both the main mind and the accompanying mental factors are uniform in each having a single substance.

The fifth, *omnipresent cause* (*sarvatragahetu*), is defined as the afflicted state that produces a subsequent afflicted state of the same level, which becomes its effect. It is called *omnipresent cause* because this cause is necessary for all afflicted states of the same level as itself. The view of the perishable collection and extreme views are examples of omnipresent causes. The *Commentary on the Treasury of Abhidharma* says, "The omnipresent qualities of the same level that were produced earlier are the omnipresent causes of later afflicted qualities." It goes on to say, "Because this is a cause that it is shared by afflicted qualities, it is presented separately from cause of similar type."[405]

The sixth, *fruitional cause* (*vipākahetu*), is defined as that which is included in either nonvirtue or contaminated virtue. It is called *fruitional cause* because it brings about fruition. Examples of fruitional causes are nonvirtuous actions and contaminated virtuous actions. Because neutral actions do not have the power to produce fruitional effects, like a rotten seed that cannot produce a sprout, they are not fruitional causes. The *Commentary on the Treasury of Abhidharma* says, "Nonvirtues and contaminated virtues are fruitional causes because they have the quality of fruition. One might ask why neutral phenomena do not establish fruitions. It is because their power is weak, like a rotten seed."[406] [206]

The Four Conditions

The Vaibhaṣika system's way of positing the four conditions is unique. As Yaśomitra's *Clarifying the Meaning* says, "One might ask, what is the difference between causes and conditions? There is none whatsoever."[407] In general, because *cause* and *condition* are synonyms, there is no difference between them. However, there are cases in which the phrase "the cause of that phenomenon" should be understood to mean the main thing that produces that phenomenon—that is, its substantial cause—and there are cases in which "condition" should be understood to mean the cooperative condition that assists the cause in producing its effect.

Dignāga's *Commentary on the Treasury of Abhidharma: Lamp for the Essential Points* says of the four conditions, "What are the conditions? The conditions are said to be four. Where is that said? The sūtra says that the conditions are four."[408] The four are the causal condition (*hetupratyaya*), the immediately preceding condition (*samanantarapratyaya*), the object of observation condition (*ālambanapratyaya*), and the dominant condition (*adhipatipratyaya*).

Regarding the definition of *causal condition*, it includes any of the five causes outlined above, with the exception of the activity cause, and aids in the production of its own effect. All five causes, with the exception of the activity cause, are causal conditions. The definition of *immediately preceding condition of the similar* is that which is similar and produces a subsequent consciousness, which is its effect. Similar minds and mental factors, with the exception of the minds and mental factors of a person whose continuum is about to cease [upon the achievement of nirvāṇa], are asserted to be immediately preceding conditions of the similar. The definition of *object of observation condition* is that which is suitable to be the object of the consciousness that observes it. In this system, all phenomena are posited as object of observation conditions. The definition of *dominant condition* is that which is suitable as a condition from the perspective of not impeding production. Because they assert that whatever is an activity cause is a dominant condition, all phenomena are dominant conditions. Thus the *Great Exegesis* says, "Causal condition includes all conditioned phenomena, and immediately preceding condition of the similar includes all minds and mentally arisen phenomena of the past and present, with the exception of the final collection of consciousness of an arhat. The object of observation condition and the dominant condition include all phenomena."[409] And the *Treasury of Abhidharma* says:

> *Cause* is the five causes.
> Minds and mental factors that are produced,
> with the exception of the last, are immediately preceding of
> the similar.
> Observation is all phenomena.
> Activity causes are explained to be dominant.[410] [207]

If someone were to ask, "From how many conditions are conditioned phenomena produced?" minds and mental factors are produced from all four conditions. The absorption of nondiscrimination and the absorption of cessation are produced from three conditions, excepting the object of observation condition. Nonassociated compositional factors other than the two absorptions and those which have form are produced by causal conditions and dominant conditions. The *Treasury of Abhidharma* says:

> By four, minds and mental factors.
> By three, the two absorptions.
> The rest are produced by the two.[411]

In summary, all conditioned phenomena have both a dominant condition and a causal condition, and all things having similarity are asserted to have all four conditions. All phenomena are asserted to be both object of observation conditions and dominant conditions.

The Five Effects

When effects are divided terminologically, there are five: (1) fruitional effect (*vipākaphala*), (2) dominant effect (*adhipatiphala*), (3) effect that accords with its cause (*niṣyandaphala*), (4) effect made by a person (*puruṣakāraphala*), and (5) separation effect (*visaṃyogaphala*). Conditioned phenomena have four effects: fruitional, that which accords with its cause, dominant, and effect made by a person. Unconditioned phenomena have two effects: effect made by a person, which is an attainment, and separation effect, which is separation from any contaminant through the power of an antidote. The *Commentary on the Treasury of Abhidharma* states, "The treatise says: What phenomena are effects? It is all conditioned phenomena and analytical cessations."[412]

A *fruitional effect* is the effect of a fruitional cause, the last of the six causes. A *dominant effect* is the effect of an activity cause, the first of the six causes. An *effect in accordance with its cause* is the effect of two causes: a cause of similar type and an omnipresent cause. An *effect made by a person* is the effect of two causes: a simultaneously arising cause and a concomitant cause. As the *Treasury of Abhidharma* says:

> Fruitional effect is the effect of the last cause.
> Dominant effect is the effect of the first cause.
> Effect in accordance with its cause is the effect of the similar
> effect and the omnipresent effect,
> and effect by a person is the effect of two causes.[413] [208]

The definition of the first, *fruitional effect* (*vipākaphala*), is posited as that whose nature is unobstructive and neutral, is included in the continuum of a sentient being, and is the effect of either the nonvirtue or the contaminated virtue that is its cause. An example is a feeling of suffering. The *Commentary on the Treasury of Abhidharma* says:

> The fruitional effect is an unobstructed and neutral phenomenon. Some are indicative of sentient beings [that is, exist in sentient beings], others are not. Therefore it says, 'indicative of sentient beings.' Because some arise through increasing and some arise in accordance with their cause, it says, 'They arise later than a non-neutral action.' Because it brings about the fructification of virtue and nonvirtue, they are called *determinate*.[414]

The definition of the second, the *dominant effect* (*adhipatiphala*), is a conditioned phenomenon that does not arise prior to its cause. For example, a dominant effect is the worldly environment of shared resources, which is created later in dependence on its cause, the shared actions of sentient beings. The *Commentary on the Treasury of Abhidharma* says, "Conditioned phenomena that are other than what arose earlier are the dominant effects of all conditioned phenomena."[415]

That which is produced that is similar in type to its cause is the definition of the third, *effect that accords with its cause* (*niṣyandaphala*). For example, the second moment of a pot is an effect that accords with its cause because it is similar in type to its cause, the first moment of the pot. The *Commentary on the Treasury of Abhidharma* says, "That phenomenon which is similar to its cause is an effect that accords with its cause. This is the effect of a cause of similar type and an omnipresent cause."[416] Between the two types of effects that accord with their cause, the first is the effect that accords with its cause that is an experience; for example, by killing another in a past [life], in the present [life] one's lifespan will be short. The second is the effect that accords with its cause that is an activity; for example, by becoming accustomed to killing others in a past [life], one enjoys killing in the present [life].

If this is illustrated with an act of killing, it is asserted that the fruitional effect is that due to killing another, one will be reborn as an animal, and so forth. The effect that accords with its cause is that, after having been born in an evil realm, although one is later born as a human, one's lifespan will be short and one will enjoy killing. The dominant effect is that the food, drink, medicine, and harvests in the next world will be of poor quality. [209]

The fourth, *effect made by a person* (*puruṣakāraphala*), is defined as that which has been produced by or obtained through the power of a specific cause. For example, a clay pot made by a potter is an effect created through the power of the person who is its cause. The *Treasury of Abhidharma* says:

> The effect created by whoever is its cause
> is an effect created by a person.[417]

The definition of the fifth, *separation effect* (*visaṃyogaphala*), is a separation that is the abandonment of an object of abandonment through the power of analysis with regard to its object, the truths. For example, it is the separation that is the abandonment of the conception of permanence, its corresponding object of abandonment, through the power of the wisdom that realizes impermanence. The *Commentary on the Treasury of Abhidharma* says, "Separation is extinguishing by the mind. Extinguishing is ceasing. The mind is wisdom. Therefore an analytical cessation is a separation effect.[418]

Consciousness, the Knowing Subject

If this is how this system presents objects, how do they present the consciousnesses that know those objects? In general, like Sautrāntika, Vaibhāṣika posits *consciousness* as that which knows an object or that which apprehends an object. The *Great Exegesis* says:

> Why is it called a *knower*? It is called a *knower* because it makes an object of knowledge known. Why is it called *object of knowledge*? It is called *object of knowledge* because it is the object that is known by a knower. According to the venerable Ghoṣaka, "Because it comprehends, it is called a *knower*. Because it is the object that is comprehended, it is called an *object of knowledge*. Comprehender and comprehended and inference and inferred are to be understood in the same way." According to

> the venerable Pārśva, "Because it knows it is called a *knower*. Because a phenomenon is known, it is an object that is engaged, observed, and apprehended. Therefore it is an *object of knowledge*." Knower and object of knowledge are posited in dependence on each other. Therefore there is no knower that does not know an object of knowledge; there is no object of knowledge that is not known by a knower. If there is a knower, there is an object of knowledge; [210] if there is no object of knowledge, there is no knower.[419]

However, in some contexts, the terms *knower* and *awareness* also refer to wisdom.

With regard to comprehending consciousnesses, they assert that there is sense consciousness and mental consciousness, minds and mental factors, valid knowledge and invalid knowledge, and so on; that with regard to valid knowledge, there is direct perception and inference; that with regard to direct perception, there are three: sense direct perception, mental direct perception, and yogic direct perception; and that the supporting physical sense faculty is a valid means of knowledge. It appears that some Vaibhāṣika, such as the Vātsīputrīya, assert that there is no mental direct perception that is different in entity from sense direct perception.

They do not assert reflexive awareness (*svasaṃvedana*). Although they accept that the experience of consciousness is like a factor that is clear and knowing, they in no way assert that between the object, such as form, and the eye consciousness that perceives it there is something else that is neither of them, called "the aspect of the object that appears to the awareness and the aspect that apprehends that." Furthermore, consciousnesses determine other objects; they do not determine themselves. Because consciousness itself cannot be both the determined and what determines, they in no way assert reflexive awareness. Thus the *Great Exegesis* says, "If it observed its own entity, it would contradict reason because something does not apprehend itself."[420] As Kamalaśīla's *Summary of the Opponents' Positions in the Drop of Reasoning* says, "The Vaibhāṣika say that reflexive awareness direct perception is also not reasonable because it is contradictory for it to act on itself.[421]

Regarding how consciousness comprehends its object, Sautrāntika and so forth assert that a blue object casts an aspect that is similar to it to the eye consciousness apprehending blue. The eye consciousness continues to see the aspect that is like the blue object, which has ceased at that time and no longer exists. However, in this [Vaibhāṣika] system, objects such as form appear to the sense faculty; because the sense consciousnesses are not physical, it is impossible for an aspect of form to appear to it in the manner of a reflection. Therefore they do not assert the appearance of aspects of objects such as blue and yellow to the sense consciousnesses. When an object is apprehended by a sense consciousness, it is apprehended nakedly, without an aspect of the object appearing. [211] To prove that, they assert that if what appears directly to the consciousness were not the actual object, then there would have to be objects that do not appear directly, and this cannot be proven. They assert that even if one says that this coarse appearance is a consciousness, it would absurdly follow that the coarse object is not a collection of particles.

They make a difference between seeing and knowing, saying that the eye sense faculty sees form but that the sense consciousness does not see form. When a form is seen by a supporting eye sense faculty, form is apprehended or cognized by the eye consciousness. The *Great Exegesis* says that "the activity of the eye element is seeing form"[422] and that "Forms are only objects of knowledge by the eye consciousness; the eye sense faculty does not cognize forms."[423]

Sautrāntika does not distinguish between seeing and knowing. They assert that that which cognizes form sees form, and so there is no difference between seeing and knowing. Vaibhāṣika states the fault that if only the eye consciousness sees form, as Sautrāntika explains, then because consciousness would be unimpeded, it would have to see through obstructing forms such as walls. As the *Treasury of Abhidharma* says:

> The eye, which is the support, sees forms;
> the consciousness, the supported, does not,
> because it does not see through
> forms that are obstructing.[424]

Vaibhāṣika asserts that subtle particles or accumulations [of them] do not appear to the eye consciousness, and the eye consciousness does not comprehend subtle particles individually; a coarse mass of accumulated subtle particles is directly comprehended. For example, they say that from a distance one cannot see an individual, an isolated hair, or a grain of sand, but a mass that is an accumulation of many of them is directly seen. Setting forth the way in which objects are known by sense consciousnesses in the Vaibhāṣika system, Jetāri's previously cited *Commentary on Distinguishing the Sugata's Texts* says it occurs "by an awareness [that is] a consciousness produced by a sense faculty."[425] He comments on this by saying:

> Awareness, which is called *directly perceiving awareness*, produced from the sense faculties that empower it, does not have an aspect of the object. Therefore, without there being an intervening aspect similar to them as imagined [by the Sautrāntika], the awareness directly knows, that is, cognizes an aggregation of accumulated particles, that is, subtle particles. [212] It does not have parts, as posited by others. If subtle particles are beyond the ken of the sense faculties, how can they be perceived? Although individually they are beyond the ken of the sense faculties, other things of similar type are simultaneously gathered with it and become the object of the sense faculties. It is not certain that that which cannot be perceived individually cannot be perceived when they are collected. Scattered things like hairs cannot be seen from a great distance but they are observed when placed together.[426]

Among the four Buddhist schools of tenets of India, this has been a brief explanation of the tenets of the Vaibhāṣika, who assert that external objects are truly established and do not assert reflexive awareness, the famed philosophical tradition that emphasizes the treatise called the *Great Exegesis*. [213]

12

The Sautrāntika School

How This School of Tenets Arose

A DEFINITIVE and detailed explanation of how the tenets of Sautrāntika arose does not appear in the ancient texts. However, it is clear that they developed more than one hundred years after the Buddha passed into nirvāṇa. Some scholars explain that, because the Sarvāstivāda was the root of all the śrāvaka schools, this system of tenets must have split off from the Sarvāstivāda.[427] Others explain that Kashmiri elders such as Bhadanta Śrīlāta refuted untenable elements of the Sarvāstivāda system within Vaibhāṣika and clarified this Sautrāntika system, and that this system therefore split off from the Sarvāstivāda.[428]

According to what is found in historical texts, the person who first disseminated the Sautrāntika philosophy was an Indian master named Kumāralāta. It must be noted that he is identified as such on the assumption that Sautrāntika and Dārṣṭāntika are the same school. Not only is this master renowned as the founder of Dārṣṭāntika, some modern researchers say that references to the works of this master can be found in the writings of both Asaṅga and Vasubandhu. That Sautrāntika and Dārṣṭāntika are synonyms is clear in Bodhibhadra's *Explanation of the Compendium on the Essence of Wisdom*.[429] The story of the Sautrāntika master Kumāralāta is not clear in other historical texts; a brief account appears in the travel journal of the Tang dynasty Chinese monk Xuanzang:

> The master was born in the land of Takṣaśilā. His analytical understanding was awakened when he was small. When he was a young man, he was ordained, and having listened carefully to the great texts, he delighted in their profound meaning. Each

> day he recited thirty-two thousand stanzas from memory and was able to read and write thirty-two thousand stanzas. Then, when he had become the crown ornament of the scholars of that time, he was renowned throughout the world. He established the correct view, and he destroyed the collection of wrong views. Setting forth the correct explanation well, there was no question that he was unable to answer. [214] He was respected in all the kingdoms of the five regions of India. The dozens of treatises that he composed were disseminated extensively, and there was no one who did not study them. He is the founder of Sautrāntika. In his era, Aśvaghoṣa in eastern India, Āryadeva in the south, Nāgārjuna in the west, and Kumāralāta in the north were known as "the four suns that illuminate the world." Hearing of the greatness of the master, a king together with his army frightened and intimidated the land of Takṣaśilā and captured the venerable master. This temple was built [for him] and the faithful believed in him.[430]

Regarding the treatises that Kumāralāta composed, it is explained that they are the *Garland of Examples*, the *Garland of Obscuration*, the *Clarifier*, the *Rising of the Sun*, and the *Nine Hundred*. However, they are no longer extant.[431]

The most famous disciples of this master are Śrīlāta (ca. 300 CE) and Harivarman. Śrīlāta composed the *Explanation of Sautrāntika* (*Sautrāntikavibhāṣa*). In his *Treatise on Conforming to Reasoning in the Abhidharma* (*Abhidharmanyāyānusāra*), Saṅghabhadra calls this master "the elder" (*sthāvira*) and refutes him. Harivarman composed the *Treatise Establishing the Truths* (*Satyasiddhiśāstra*). He studied the views of both the great and the small vehicles, and in that work he even cites a passage from Āryadeva's *Four Hundred Verses*. From what appears in the Chinese travel journals, it seems that Sautrāntika and the Mahāyāna tenet systems had many shared assertions. It is explained that the masters who clarified the tenets of Sautrāntika were the Kashmiri elder Bhadanta, the monk Kumāralāta, the monk Śrīlāta, the monk Upāma, the monk Adhigamadeva, and so forth.[432] [215]

The Texts upon Which This System Primarily Relies

Because they base themselves only on sūtras that are scriptures of the Buddha, they are designated with the name Sautrāntika ["followers of the sūtras"]. The sūtras upon which the Sautrāntika primarily base themselves are from the first teaching, the wheel of the four truths. The Vaibhāṣika assert that the seven books of the Abhidharma are the word of the Buddha. However, the Sautrāntika assert that the seven books of the Abhidharma are not the word of the Buddha and that they were composed by arhats. Indeed, the majority of the Sautrāntika say that because there are many mistakes in those [books], such as the explanation that space is a permanent substance, they were not made by arhats but by common beings who had the same names as the arhats. Therefore they say that they are not treatises that have the validity of sūtras. To that, the Vaibhāṣika say, "In the sūtras, a monk who is skilled in the Tripiṭaka is called a *trepiṭaka*. If what you say is correct, the Tripiṭaka would not be complete because, apart from these seven books of the Abhidharma, an Abhidharma Piṭaka is not to be seen." The Sautrāntika respond by saying that those faults are not incurred because among the sūtras, those parts that delineate the ultimate and describe the characteristics of phenomena constitute the Abhidharma Piṭaka.[433]

Among the treatises that are extant today, at many points in Vasubandhu's autocommentary to the *Treasury of Abhidharma* the unshared assertions of the Kashmiri Vaibhāṣika are refuted one by one; it is well known that Vasubandhu himself held the Sautrāntika position. Furthermore, it seems that such works as the Kashmiri master Śubhagupta's *Proof of External Objects*, *Analysis of Exclusion of Others*, *Examination of the Veda*, and *Proof of Omniscience* are suitable to be taken as the Sautrāntika's own texts. Atiśa seems to have asserted that Dharmottara's works on valid knowledge are treatises that principally present the standpoint of the Sautrāntika system. In his *Open Casket of Jewels*, Atiśa says, "Such masters as Śubhagupta, Dharmottara, and the early Vasubandhu composed extensive treatises of the śrāvaka Sautrāntika."[434] In addition, the works of Dharmakīrti where he delineated his system based on the position that external objects exist—such as his large treatise on valid knowledge called the *Exposition of Valid Knowledge*, his middle-length treatise the *Ascertainment of Valid*

Knowledge, and his autocommentary on the first chapter of the *Exposition of Valid Knowledge*—must be taken as texts that set forth the tenets of Sautrāntika. As Dharmakīrti himself famously said: [216]

> When entering into the analysis of external objects,
> we rely on the steps of the sūtras.[435]

The Definition and Divisions of Sautrāntika

The Sautrāntika school of tenets is defined as a Buddhist school whose primary tenets include the assertion that both reflexive awareness (*svasaṃvedana*) and external objects are truly established. As already noted, Sautrāntika and Dārṣṭāntika are synonyms.

Because they assert their tenets primarily following the sūtras of the Buddha, without following the *Great Exegesis*, they are called Sautrāntika. Because they are skilled in setting forth all phenomena through examples, they are also called Dārṣṭāntika [Exemplifiers]. As Bodhibhadra's *Explanation of the Compendium on the Essence of Wisdom* says,[436] "They accept literally such sūtras as the *Six Doors* and the *Good Conduct*. Because they follow those sūtras, they are Sautrāntika. Because they are skilled in setting forth phenomena with examples, their other name is Dārṣṭāntika."[437] However, it is difficult to discern whether the unshared assertions of Sautrāntika derive directly from the *Extensive Sport* and the *Ten Levels Sūtra* as well as the *Six Door Dhāraṇī* and the *Prayer of Good Conduct* found in the Kangyur. Therefore whether the Sautrāntika accept those sūtras as the scriptures of the Buddha that are the source of their tenets appears to require more investigation.

If the Sautrāntika are divided, they must, according to what appears in Tibetan tenets texts, be posited as two: the Sautrāntika Following Scripture and the Sautrāntika Following Reasoning. The first are those who propound tenets from the perspective of merely asserting literally what appears in the sūtras. They are, for example, the Sautrāntika who follow the autocommentary of the *Treasury of Abhidharma*. The second, the Sautrāntika Following Reasoning, propound tenets following reasoning in accordance with what is explained in Dharmakīrti's seven treatises on valid knowledge. [217] They are, for example, the Sautrāntika who accept the shared reasonings presented in the *Exposition of Valid Knowledge*.

A General Explanation of Sautrāntika Assertions of Its Tenets

The most important assertions of this system are easy to identify. If one cites the verses that set forth the assertions of this school in Āryadeva's *Compendium on the Essence of Wisdom* and Jetāri's *Verses on Distinguishing the Sugata's Texts*, it brings about an understanding of the most important general precepts of the Sautrāntika system. Thus Āryadeva's *Compendium on the Essence of Wisdom* says:

> What is seen is not an object of the sense faculties.
> Consciousness is produced having an aspect.
> Space is like the child of a barren woman.
> Cessation is like space.
> Material compositional factors do not exist.
> The three times are not accepted.
> There are no formless composites.
> The Sautrāntika are wise.[438]

Jetāri's *Verses on Distinguishing the Sugata's Texts* says:

> Consciousness knows by way of perceiving aspects
> of objects that appear to the sense faculty.
> Space is like the child of a barren woman.
> The two cessations are like space.
> Compositional factors not associated with mind do not exist.
> Things do not exist across the three times.
> The obstructive formless does not exist.
> Those who are Sautrāntika are called wise.[439]

Both of these passages identify the five most important assertions unique to Sautrāntika. (1) The Vaibhāṣika explanation that the physical sense faculties understand an object without an aspect (*ākāra*) is incorrect. In the Sautrāntika system, they assert that the aspect of the object appears to the consciousness in dependence on the sense faculty; the object is known from a sense consciousness having the aspect of the object. (2) What is called *space* is posited as a nonimplicative negation—the mere negation of obstructive contact. Like the child of a barren woman, it is not a functioning thing. Both analytical and nonanalytical cessations, like space, are posited as nonimplicative negations. (3) Compositional factors not associated with minds (*viprayuktasaṃskāra*) do not exist as material substances and are imputedly existent. [218] (4) Things are merely momentary conditioned phenomena and do not extend across the three times. (5) Nonrevelatory form (*avijñaptirūpa*) is not actual form, and because of that, physical, verbal, and mental actions must be the mental factor of intention (*cetanā*).

In general, the way proponents of this system delineate the aggregates, constituents, and sources for the most part agrees with what appears in such works as Asaṅga's *Compendium of Abhidharma* and Vasubandhu's *Treasury of Abhidharma* and *Explanation of the Five Aggregates*. They differ from the Vaibhāṣika in that they do not accept that all phenomena are substantially established and that nonrevelatory form is actual form.[440] They do not accept the foundation consciousness (*ālayavijñāna*) and the afflicted mental consciousness (*kliṣṭamanas*) asserted by Cittamātra, and they also differ from them in asserting that the mental consciousness is the referent of the self that serves as the foundation of actions and effects. In addition, this system agrees with Vaibhāṣika that external objects are established from the accumulation of partless particles, that subtle particles are partless, and that they do not touch each other. However, Vaibhāṣika asserts that there is a space between subtle particles, and Sautrāntika asserts that there is no space between them. Also, Vaibhāṣika does not make a distinction between the four elements and the constituents of the four elements, whereas Sautrāntika and the higher schools do make that distinction; it appears that they assert that although the constituents of the four elements are all present in all composite forms, the actual four elements are not necessarily present.

The Specifically Characterized and the Generally Characterized

Some essential assertions of this school of tenets were set forth in summary form above. Now the assertions of this school of tenets will be explained in somewhat more detail. These tenets will be explained: (1) the specifically characterized and the generally characterized, (2) the proof that conditioned phenomena are momentary, (3) the proof that cause and effect are necessarily sequential, (4) the way external objects are posited, and (5) the division into the five objects and the minds that comprehend them.

First is the explanation of the specifically characterized and the generally characterized. When the system of Sautrāntika Following Reasoning is emphasized, the ultimate and the conventional should be posited from the perspective of the specifically characterized and the generally characterized. [219] Thus, in his *Exposition of Valid Knowledge* at the point of distinguishing these, Dharmakīrti says:

> That which is ultimately able to perform a function:
> that is what exists ultimately here.
> The others exist conventionally.
> Those are explained to be the specifically and the generally characterized.[441]

He is saying that all those phenomena that are able to perform the function of producing their own effect as witnessed by direct perception—an ultimate awareness—ultimately exist in this system. On the other hand, all those phenomena that are not able to perform a function exist conventionally. That which ultimately exists and that which conventionally exists are called, respectively, the *specifically characterized* (*svalakṣaṇa*) and the *generally characterized* (*sāmānyalakṣaṇa*) Thus, because it is true as an entity for an ultimate awareness—that is, direct perception that is unmistaken with respect to its appearing object—it is called an *ultimate truth*. Because it is true as an entity for a conventional awareness—that is, thought—it is called a *conventional truth*. The ways of positing the two truths from the perspective of how they appear to awareness and whether they are ultimately able to perform a function is explained in the fourth volume of *Science and Philosophy in the Indian Buddhist Classics*.

That which is not merely imputed by thought but is established from its own side is the meaning of *specifically characterized*. *Specifically characterized*, *thing*, *impermanent*, *ultimate truth*, *conditioned phenomenon*, *product*, and *actual object of comprehension of direct valid knowledge* are synonyms. Examples are a pot, a pillar, and a consciousness. Because they provide an appearance, which is not imputed by thought, for the direct perception that apprehends them from the side of their own mode of subsistence, they are said to be established by their own characteristics without being mere imputations by thought.

When the specifically characterized is divided, there are three: forms, consciousnesses, and nonassociated compositional factors. These have already been explained extensively in part 2 of *Science and Philosophy in the Indian Buddhist Classics,* volume 1. If something is specifically characterized it must be a thing whose place, time, and nature are not mixed with anything else. To illustrate how the place, time, and nature are unmixed, take a pillar as an example. In general, pillars exist both to the east and to the west; however, the pillar that exists in the east does not exist in the west. This is "unmixed place." A pillar can be posited as existing at both an earlier time and a later time; however, the pillar that exists at an earlier time does not exist at a later time. This is "unmixed time." It is possible to assert that being a pillar in general encompasses both wooden pillars and iron pillars. However, the factor that pervades a wooden pillar does not pervade an iron pillar; this is "unmixed nature." It is explained that because the specifically characterized are true in the face of an ultimate awareness, direct perception, they are called *ultimate truths.* [220]

A phenomenon that is a mere imputation by thought is the meaning of *generally characterized. Generally characterized, conventional truth, permanent*, and *unconditioned phenomenon* are synonyms. An example is space [which is a mere absence]. Apart from being mere appearances to thought, they are phenomena that do not appear to direct perception. Therefore they are asserted to be mere imputations by thought. Thus, not only must the three unconditioned phenomena—space and the two cessations—be posited as generally characterized unconditioned phenomena, but also conceptual constructs, such as the categories of quality and qualified and generality and particular. Dharmakīrti's *Exposition of Valid Knowledge* says:

> Positing quality and qualified
> and how things are different and not different
> does not analyze the meaning of reality.
> Yet by relying on these,
> just as they are known in the world,
> the wise make use

> of all forms of proven and proof
> in order to enter the ultimate reality.[442]

As was explained above, things like generality, common locus, particularity, sameness and difference, relation and contradiction, and what is to be proven and proof, which are concepts imputed by thought, are in themselves generally characterized categories. However, whatever is one of those is not necessarily generally characterized. For example, a golden pot is a generality, a common locus of a thing and a pot, a particularity, and is one; being a product is a proof; sound being impermanent is something proven; fire and smoke is a relation; hot and cold are a contradiction. In addition, these are also all specifically characterized.

Two things, such as being a product and being impermanent, are differentiated by thought as different in the sense of excluding what is not itself. If such differentiating factors were established from the object's own side without being merely appearances to thought, being a product and being impermanent would have to become different entities. In that case, one would have to assert that those two were different entities that were not the result of cause and effect, and that would entail the absurd consequence that they were unrelated different objects. Therefore Sautrāntika accepts that [functioning] things are established from their own side without being mere imputations by thought and that unconditioned phenomena are mere imputations by thought.

When the generally characterized are divided, there are three: the generally characterized that depend on things, the generally characterized that depend on nonthings, and the generally characterized that depend on phenomena that are common to both things and nonthings. Examples are, respectively, the appearance of a pot to a thought consciousness apprehending a pot, the appearance of space to a thought consciousness apprehending space, and the appearing object of the thought that apprehends a place where there is no pot. Dharmakīrti's *Exposition of Valid Knowledge* says:

> Because they depend on things, nonthings, and both,
> there are three types of the generally characterized.[443] [221]

He is saying that although the generally characterized is not divided from the perspective of an independently established nature, it is divided from the perspective of its support—such as things, nonthings, and phenomena common to both. Depending on these three, it exists as the objects apprehended by thought.

In brief, the specifically characterized have four features: (1) the feature of their nature is that they are able to perform functions, (2) the feature of their mode of appearance is that they appear uniquely, (3) the feature of the subject is that they are not objects that appear merely through the dominant condition of the words that express them, and (4) the feature of their function is that they produce the consciousness that apprehends them. The features of the generally characterized are the opposite of those: (1) they are not able to perform a function, (2) they are similar in the sense that they appear commonly to the consciousness that takes them as its appearing objects, (3) they become appearing objects merely through the dominant condition of the words that express them, and (4) they do not produce the awareness that apprehends them. Regarding these points, Dharmakīrti's *Exposition of Valid Knowledge* says:

> Because they are able and unable to perform functions . . .
> Because of being similar and not similar
> and because of being and not being the objects of terms,
> and because, when the other causes are present,
> awareness exists or does not exist.[444]

He delineates this extensively at this point [of his text].

In the chapter on inference for oneself and especially in the chapter on direct perception in Dharmakīrti's *Exposition of Valid Knowledge*, he extensively sets forth reasonings to prove that the generally characterized are not [functioning] things. For example, something like the appearance of the pot in the manner of being the opposite of non-pot to the thought consciousness apprehending pot [that is, the mental image of the pot] is the meaning of the term that serves as the explicit object of expression of the term *pot*; it not the functioning pot itself. If the pot itself were the meaning of the term, then by merely using the term *pot*, the pot itself would have to become the appearing object of the thought consciousness apprehending pot. In that case, even the thought consciousness apprehending pot would have to clearly perceive the pot, as does an eye consciousness apprehending pot. Just as the eye consciousness still exists even in those whose eyes, its dominant condition, are impaired, the pot would have to appear clearly [to their thoughts], but it does not appear in that way. Such things as an eye sense faculty are needed to produce the consciousness that clearly perceives the pot. Therefore a consciousness that clearly perceives a pot is not produced in dependence on just the term *pot*. Thus Dharmakīrti's *Exposition of Valid Knowledge* says:

> This is not a functioning thing because it is expressed [by
> a word]
> and because the sense faculties have effects.[445] [222]

Also, the same text says:

> Words indicate what terms designate;
> they are for the purpose of conventions.
> At that time, the specifically characterized is absent.
> Therefore terminology does not designate it.[446]

He is saying that the specifically characterized are not the explicit objects of terms. If they were, it would absurdly follow that the specifically characterized thing to which a term is applied earlier would have to exist later when the term is used. So what then is the actual object of a term? The appearing object of the thought consciousness is the actual object of the use of the term. For example, in the case of a thought consciousness that apprehends a golden pot to be a pot, the golden pot appears as a pot, and its actual object of apprehension also appears as a pot. Those two things that appear [the golden pot and the mental image of a pot] become mixed into one in how they appear [to thought] and remain that way. This mode is what is called *mixing its appearance and its designation into one*. Dharmakīrti's *Exposition of Valid Knowledge* says:

> The awareness that understands that [term] mistakenly
> sees them as if they were one.[447]

He is saying that, based on the use of the word *tree*, there is an appearance to a thought consciousness that apprehends a tree, which comes to understand it to be that which has branches and leaves. Although that appearance is not a specifically characterized tree, due to the appearance and the designation being mistaken as the same, its appearance [to thought] and the specifically characterized external object appear to be the same. This *appearance* in the phrase "the appearance and the designation being mistaken as the same" refers to the basis of appearance, which is the specifically characterized external thing; the *designation* is the meaning of the word, a nonfunctioning phenomenon; it must be taken as the explicit object of thought.

The topic of the meaning of words is of the utmost importance in the Buddhist understanding of the valid means of knowledge. Because there is much to discuss, such as how it was first delineated by Dignāga and later expanded upon by Dharmakīrti, it will be considered in the fourth volume of *Science and Philosophy in the Indian Buddhist Classics*.

Thus, just as it is incorrect that specifically characterized things are the referents of terms, it is similarly incorrect that they are the objects apprehended by thought. If what is perceived by the cognition that apprehends the generality *tree* were a real entity, the conceptual cognition apprehending tree would be unmistaken. In that case, there would inevitably be two faults: it would mean that the generality that is substantially distinct from the individual instances of tree that it pervades could appear to an unmistaken awareness, and the individual instances of tree would become conflated. Also, if the awareness of the generality of tree were unmistaken, not only would the appearance to awareness of the generality of *tree* have to be specifically characterized, it would also have to be a tree. Thus wherever there were a thought consciousness apprehending tree, there would be a tree; it would be impossible for anyone to be deprived of wood. [223] In the same way, that the tree itself, which appears as an external object, is a functioning thing would have to be refuted. There would also be such faults as that tree and instances of tree would be different substances and unrelated. Thus Dharmakīrti's *Exposition of Valid Knowledge* says:

> The nature that appears as external,
> as one, and as something differentiated from others
> has no elements to investigate.
> Therefore it is not real.[448]

He is saying that if such nonfunctioning phenomena were not mere designations by thought, one would improperly have to assert that they would be able to perform functions. Therefore one would have to assert that any appearance to the thought apprehending tree—that it appears as the nature of a tree, that it appears to be the same as an external tree, that it appears as differentiated from what is non-tree—is a tree. However, those appearances to thought are not able to fulfill what is needed for a tree according to the wishes of a person seeking a tree. Therefore the appearance to awareness of the generality of tree is not a tree.

In summary, the essential point of these reasonings is that if those phenomena for thought were established as functioning things themselves, those subjective thought consciousnesses would not be mistaken with respect to their appearing objects. In that case, they would have to be established in the way that they appear to those thought consciousnesses. The fault would absurdly follow that the mode of being of things would be confused because they would have to be established in the confused way that they appear to thought.

Proof That Conditioned Phenomena Are Momentary

Sautrāntika does not assert, as Vaibhāṣika does, that the characteristics of conditioned phenomena—being produced and so forth—are sequential. They assert instead that at the very time that a conditioned phenomenon is produced, it also abides and ceases. Therefore they prove that conditioned phenomena are momentary in the sense of disintegrating each moment. In general, the meaning of *impermanence* can be posited as of two types: continuous impermanence and momentary impermanence; the first is also called *coarse impermanence* and the second is called *subtle impermanence*. If these are illustrated with a person named Devadatta, the fact that Devadatta does not remain after his death is something that can be directly ascertained by an uneducated cowherd. Therefore it is very coarse. The fact that the Devadatta of the first moment does not remain in the second moment is subtler that that. The fact that he disintegrates from his very first moment is subtler than that. Therefore, to understand subtle impermanence, generally one must first develop an understanding of coarse impermanence. [224]

Here, *momentary* in the phrase "conditioned phenomena are proven to be momentary" must be taken to mean that all conditioned phenomena have a nature of disintegration due to the cause that produces them and that they do not remain for a second moment from the time they are established. For that reason, when conditioned phenomena are proven to be momentary, the main point that must be proven is that their disintegration does not depend on a cause that arises later. This is extremely important. In his *Exposition of Valid Knowledge*, Dharmakīrti says:

> Without a cause, they disintegrate.
> This follows from their own nature.[449]

This is saying that as soon as a product is established, its disintegration follows naturally due to its own nature. Its own destruction is produced by the very cause that brought about its creation, without relying on any cause beyond the cause that brought it into existence. Dharmakīrti's *Ascertainment of Valid Knowledge* says, "Products that have the nature of the aggregates, constituents, and sources are established as impermanent. Therefore there is no fault."[450] This passage removes objections about the identification of conditioned phenomena, about the proof that they are impermanent, and about the fact that their disintegration does not depend on a cause that arises later. One should know that such statements as "it does not follow that disintegration is causeless" and "disintegration is the nature of things" are delineated extensively there [in that text].

Furthermore, in such texts as the thirteenth chapter of Śāntarakṣita's *Compendium of Principles* on the analysis of stable things, its commentary by Kamalaśīla, and the *Proof of Momentariness* by Dharmottara and its explanation by the brahmin Muktākumbha, subtle and profound points of reasoning are delineated that prove that conditioned phenomena are momentary. Among these texts, let us set forth some crucial points from Dharmottara's *Proof of Momentariness*:

> Furthermore, what is the thing that will disintegrate? Is it produced having a quality of extinction from a natural cause? Or is it produced having the quality of abiding? Regarding the first idea, a thing will disintegrate by itself through its quality of extinction. Therefore a cause of disintegration does not act in any way whatsoever. If it were something whose nature is not to cease, then even if there were a hundred causes of disintegration, it would not deviate from its nature. Because it would not

> be able to disintegrate, a cause of disintegration would have no effect on it whatsoever.[451] [225]

Here, someone asserts that the disintegration of a thing depends on its being disintegrated by another cause that arises later. This is investigated from two perspectives: things are produced from their own cause with the nature to naturally disintegrate, or they are produced with a nature to abide without disintegrating. According to the first position, disintegration is established without depending on a cause that arises later. According to the second position, even if there came to be a hundred causes of disintegration that arose later, the nature of something to abide would not change. Therefore [the passage] presents an absurd consequence concerning the impossibility of disintegration of conditioned phenomena taking place due to a cause of disintegration that arises later.

The same text says, "Therefore whoever imagines that a thing, through its own cause, abides briefly and then disintegrates but does not disintegrate as soon as it is produced is incorrect."[452] If one says that conditioned phenomena are produced in the first moment and then abide in the second moment, then there would have to be both production and abiding in the second moment, just as there was in the first moment. Because there would have to be both production and abiding in its second moment as well, it would never disintegrate. [The passage] presents this fault and refutes [the objection].

Also, someone might say, "A pot is not established as having a nature of disintegration based merely on its own entity; it must be established as impermanent in dependence on a cause of disintegration that arises later." [To respond:] The fault with this is that it is certain, for example, that a white piece of wool cloth becomes red in dependence on the red dye that arises later; there is no certainty that it will become red [without the dye]. In the same way, because it would be certain that the disintegration of a pot would depend on a cause that arose later, there would be no certainty that it will disintegrate. Furthermore, there is the fault that because things are limitless, although there would be some things that disintegrated due to a cause of disintegration that arose later, there would also be some things that did not encounter a cause of disintegration that arose later, thereby making them permanent.

Someone might ask, "In that case, if things are impermanent, how does one identify something by saying, 'This is the pillar that I saw yesterday'?" [To respond:] There is no fault because we see things as being the same [over time] because they occur in an unbroken continuum of similar type and because we are conditioned by the conception of permanence that apprehends earlier and later moments as the same.

Prajñākaragupta's *Ornament of the Exposition of Valid Knowledge* says, "If disintegration meant that a thing exists at one time and disintegrates at another time, it would not be correct. Whenever a thing exists, its disintegration exists. Therefore it is correct to say that it is endowed with disintegration."[453] Thus it must be accepted that whatever is a thing is established simultaneously with its own disintegration. If this is not accepted, it would not be correct that conditioned phenomena are momentary. This is what Sautrāntika asserts. [226]

Someone might say, "Conditioned phenomena are seen to remain for many moments without disintegrating. Therefore it is not certain that they disintegrate in each moment." [To respond:] Consider a conditioned phenomenon that remains without disintegrating for a period of five moments. In the second moment, is the substance that remains for five moments lost or not lost? If you say that it is lost, then at the time of the second moment of a thing that remains for five moments, due to the substance that remains for five moments having been lost, it would not remain for more than a single moment, thereby proving that it is momentary. If you say that in the second moment the substance that remains for five moments is still not lost, then the substance that remained from the previous first moment and the substance that remains for five moments would still not be lost in the second moment, entailing the fault that that thing would have a period of six moments. That conditioned phenomena are momentary is proven with many such arguments.

Thus the way that Sautrāntika posits that conditioned phenomena are momentary is different from that of Vaibhāṣika. Because of this important point, the way that they posit the three times is also very different from Vaibhāṣika. In the Sautrāntika system, conditioned phenomena are necessarily in the present. Among the three times, only the present is a functioning thing; the other two—the past and the future—are posited as nonfunctioning things. For example, when a single thing such as a sprout disintegrates, all the entities of the parts of the sprout cease, and nothing else is obtained. Therefore they assert that the past is a nonfunctioning thing, a nonimplicative negation that is the mere cessation of the impermanent thing that has disintegrated. The future is posited as the factor of not being produced due to the fact that the cause for the production of a phenomenon exists but the conditions are not complete. Therefore, like the past, the future has no entity at all; it is the mere elimination of its object of negation. Thus they assert that it must be posited as a nonfunctioning thing.

Thus, regarding the way that the permanent is posited—that is, as the opposite of momentary and as nondisintegrating—the *Exposition of Valid Knowledge* says:

> That whose nature does not disintegrate
> the wise call *permanent*.[454]

Permanent is asserted to be a phenomenon whose nature does not disintegrate. Someone might say, "Something like the disintegration of a pot does not exist when the pot has not disintegrated but does exist when the pot has disintegrated. Therefore its disintegration would be impermanent." [To respond:] The nature of disintegration is the mere elimination of the object of negation; it is not a case of it turning into something that is different from that nature. Therefore there is no fault in the statement. In the same way, with regard to something like the isolate of pot, when the pot ceases, it too is no more. However, such a cessation of existence is due to the cessation of the existence of its basis; it is not because it had turned into some other entity. Therefore it does not become impermanent.

Someone might say, "Isn't the disintegration of a golden pot something that did not exist earlier but is newly produced later?" [To respond:] If it is newly produced later, it must be posited in dependence on causes and conditions. The disintegration of a pot is not posited in dependence on causes and conditions. That the previous pot becomes nonexistent is merely designated by the mind as "the disintegration of the pot." Therefore there is no fault. [227]

Furthermore, an essential point relating to the momentary disintegration of conditioned phenomena and the fact that the opposite of that is posited as permanence is the topic of negation and elimination. In the texts on the valid means of knowledge, *elimination*, *negation*, *isolate*, and *elimination of the other* are synonyms; they are different ways of saying the same thing depending on the context. This is because when things are stated verbally or when they appear to thought, they do so through the elimination of what is not them; they do not appear through their aspect being revealed to the mind by a specifically characterized object. Because negation has already been discussed in detail in the first volume of *Science and Philosophy in the Indian Buddhist Classics*, one should look there.[455]

Proof That Cause and Effect Are Sequential

Derived from the proof that conditioned phenomena are momentary, this system asserts that cause and effect are necessarily sequential. As was discussed at length in previous volumes of *Science and Philosophy in the Indian Buddhist Classics*, the Buddhist schools all reject the notion that there can be production without a cause, that the world was established by the prior movement of the mind of a creator, and that an effect arises from a permanent cause. There is also no disagreement among Buddhist schools in asserting that cause and effect must share a similar type and that the various qualities of an effect arise from the various qualities of a cause.

In the case of causation, from the perspective of time, there is the division into direct cause and indirect cause. On how effects arise, Sautrāntika makes a division into substantial causes and cooperative conditions. The *direct cause* is posited as the nearby cause of its effect, whereas the *indirect cause* is the distant cause. They assert that the *substantial cause* acts as the unique cause and the *cooperative conditions* act as the common cause. For example, a barley seed acts as the cause of a barley sprout; it does not act as the cause of a rice sprout. In the same way, a rice seed acts as the cause of a rice sprout; it does not act as the cause of a barley sprout. Therefore those seeds are unique causes. Water and manure act as causes of both; they are posited as common causes. The production of a sprout, such as a barley sprout or a rice sprout, takes place primarily due to the substantial cause. Its many qualities, such as whether that sprout is large or small or good or bad arise primarily by the power of the cooperative conditions. For effects, from the perspective of time, one can posit direct effects and indirect effects, and from the perspective of continuity, one can posit substantial effects and cooperative effects. [228]

In this system it is asserted that cause and effect are necessarily sequential and that as soon as the cause ceases, its effect arises without interruption; the two actions—the cessation of the cause and the arising of the effect—are simultaneous. It is like the two sides of a scale: one side goes up and the other goes down simultaneously. If cause and effect were simultaneous, both would have to be similar in having already been established. There is no need for something that has already been established to be produced by a cause again; they assert that it is infeasible for cause and effect to be simultaneous. The *Exposition of Valid Knowledge* says, "That which benefits is a producer."[456] As this says, for something to be posited as a cause, it must aid in the production of its effect. For things that are simultaneous, it is not tenable for one to produce or benefit the other.

The Vaibhāṣika assert that the activity cause of a phenomenon, the simultaneously arising cause of a phenomenon, and the cause of similar type of a phenomenon are actual causes of a phenomenon and that cause and effect are therefore simultaneous. This derives from the presentation of [the twelve links of] dependent origination in the Vaibhāṣika's own system. The *Treasury of Abhidharma* says, "Sixfold contact arises from the combination [of the sense faculty, the object, and the consciousness]" and "There are three [types of contact], such as leading to pleasure."[457] They identify the sequence of contact and feeling in that way. The Sautrāntika asks, "In general, does feeling arise after contact or do the two arise simultaneously?" And as Vasubandhu's autocommentary on the *Treasury of Abhidharma* asks, "Do you say that feeling arises after contact or that they arise simultaneously?"[458] To that, the Vaibhāṣika replies, "In general, contact and feeling are mutual and simultaneous causes of each other. Therefore they arise simultaneously without one arising earlier and the other later." As Vasubandhu's autocommentary on the *Treasury of Abhidharma* says, "The Vaibhāṣika says that because they mutually arise together, they are simultaneous."[459]

Also, the Sautrāntika says, "How can two phenomena that arise together be established as both a phenomenon that causes production and a phenomenon that is produced? They cannot, because they do not have the power to produce each other. No phenomenon has the power to reproduce a phenomenon whose entity has already been produced." As Vasubandhu's autocommentary on the *Treasury of Abhidharma* says, [229] "How can two things that arise together be established as things that are the producer and the produced? Why are they not established? Because they do not have the power to do so. For something that has already been produced, other things have no power [to reproduce it]."[460]

The Vaibhāṣika says, "You Sautrāntika say that two phenomena that arise together are not established as phenomena that are the producer and the produced. This is similar to your statement that for a phenomenon whose entity has already been produced, there is no phenomenon whatsoever that has the power to produce it again. Therefore there is no difference in what you have stated as the probandum and the proof." As Vasubandhu's autocommentary on the *Treasury of Abhidharma* says, "To say that for what arises together, there is neither the producer nor the produced is to say that for a phenomenon that has already been produced, there is no phenomenon that has the power [to produce it again]. Therefore this is no different than your thesis."[461]

The Sautrāntika says, "There would be the fault that it would absurdly follow that two phenomena that are simultaneous would produce each other." Thus Vasubandhu's autocommentary on the *Treasury of Abhidharma* says, "It would absurdly follow that they produce each other."[462]

The Vaibhāṣika replies, "We Vaibhāṣika do assert that two phenomena that arise together produce each other. Therefore we do not incur the fault of an absurd consequence. What are simultaneously arisen causes for each other are simultaneously arisen effects of each other. There are many such things—for example, the contact and feeling that we are debating about. This is what we assert." As Vasubandhu's autocommentary on the *Treasury of Abhidharma* says, "Because we assert this, there is no fault. We are only asserting that there are many cases of simultaneously arisen causes being effects of each other."[463]

The Sautrāntika says, "Even if you Vaibhāṣika do assert that contact and feeling are examples of causes that arise together, this assertion of yours that contact and feeling are causes or effects that arise together is not the intention of the authoritative scriptures of the Buddha. A sūtra says, 'In dependence on contact of the eye, feeling is produced that arises from contact of the eye. It is not the case that contact of the eye is produced in dependence on feeling that arises from contact of the eye.'" [230] Even from the perspective of the example and the reason, it is contradictory for a phenomenon [that is produced] to be simultaneous with the phenomenon that produces it. Therefore Sautrāntika holds that this simultaneity of cause and effect is untenable. Any phenomenon that is a producer is earlier, and the phenomenon that it produces is later. This is accepted by the world and known to be valid. For example, the world accepts that a seed, the cause, is earlier and its effect, a sprout, is later. Similarly, milk is earlier, and its effect, yogurt, is later; striking a drum is earlier, and its effect, sound, is later; the mental sense faculty is earlier, and its effect, the mental consciousness, is later.

[The Vaibhāṣika might say,] "Even though the cause, the eye and so forth, and the effect, the eye consciousness, are established as things that are earlier and later, the dominant condition, the eye sense faculty, and the observed object condition, the form, are established as things that are simultaneous. For example, the effect, the eye sense consciousness, and the accompanying feeling and contact are simultaneous; the causes, the eye and the form, are simultaneous; the four elements are simultaneous; and the seven elemental evolutes are simultaneous."

[The Sautrāntika says:] "The causes, the sense faculty and the object, are earlier, and the effect, the consciousness, is later. The causes, the collection of elements, are earlier, and the effects, the collection of elemental evolutes, are later. If this is what you assert, there is nothing to refute." Vasubandhu's autocommentary on the *Treasury of Abhidharma* says:

> This is what you [Vaibhāṣika] assert, but this assertion that contact and feeling are effects of each other is not asserted in the sūtras, which say, "In dependence on contact of the eye, feeling is produced that arises from contact of the eye. It is not the case that contact of the eye is produced in dependence on the feeling that arises from contact of the eye." Because [your assertion] is contrary to the factor of being a producer, it is not correct. It is well known that any factor that is the producer of any phenomenon exists at a different time. For example, a seed is earlier and a fruit is later; milk is earlier and yogurt is later; striking is earlier and sound is later; and mind is earlier and mental consciousness is later.
>
> [The Vaibhāṣika says:] "We are not saying that cause and effect are not established as earlier and later. However, they can also be established as simultaneous—for example, the eye consciousness and so forth, the eye and form, and the elements and elemental evolutes.

> [The Sautrāntika says:] "The sense faculties and the objects are earlier, and that consciousness is later; and the elements and the elemental evolutes arise later from an earlier collection of causes. If this is what you assert, what is there to refute?"[464] [231]

The Vaibhāṣika says, "It is the case that the two causes, the sense faculty and the object, are earlier and that the effect, the consciousness, is later. However, just as in the world a barley sprout and its shadow are simultaneous, the cause 'contact' and the effect 'feeling' are simultaneous in that way." As Vasubandhu's autocommentary on the *Treasury of Abhidharma* states, "The Vaibhāṣika says, 'Just as a sprout and its shadow [are simultaneous], contact and feeling are like that.'"[465]

The Sautrāntika says, "The cause 'contact' and the effect 'feeling' do not arise simultaneously, like the simultaneity of a barley sprout and its shadow; the effect feeling arises after the establishment of the cause contact. The dominant condition, the sense faculty, and the observed object condition, the object, are earlier; after that arises the effect, consciousness. In the first moment, three things gather: the dominant condition, the sense faculty; the observed object condition, the object; and the consciousness. In the second moment after they have gathered, contact is the mental factor that, through its own power, engages its object in accordance with the feeling that will be experienced. Due to the condition of the mental factor contact, its effect, feeling, arises in the third moment. As Vasubandhu's autocommentary on the *Treasury of Abhidharma* says, "Others say, 'Feeling arises after contact. The sense faculty and the object are earlier; consciousness is after that. The gathering of those three is contact. Due to the condition of contact, feeling arises in the third moment.'"[466]

The Vaibhāṣika disputes this, saying, "In that case, feeling would not accompany all main minds, and contact would also not accompany all of those main minds." As Vasubandhu's autocommentary on the *Treasury of Abhidharma* says, "In that case, there would not be feeling for all consciousnesses; there would also not be contact for all consciousnesses."[467]

The Sautrāntika answers, "There is no fault in there not being feeling that accompanies all main minds and there not being contact that accompanies all of them. For example, the feeling that exists simultaneously with the later contact that observes sound, which is induced by the earlier contact that observes form, arises from being caused by the earlier contact that observes form. Therefore every contact has a feeling that is simultaneous with it, and each consciousness has the contact that accompanies it." [232] As Vasubandhu's autocommentary on the *Treasury of Abhidharma* says, "There is no fault. The feeling that the later contact has arises from the cause of the earlier contact. Therefore all contact has feeling; all consciousness has contact."[468]

The Vaibhāṣika says, "This explanation by you Sautrāntika of the way in which all minds have feeling and all minds have contact is contradicted by scripture and reasoning, and so is incorrect. For example, you Sautrāntika say things like, 'In dependence on earlier contact observing a different object such as form, feeling arises at the same time as a later contact that observes sound. In what way is this mode of explanation untenable?' It would absurdly follow that the feeling that arises from earlier contact observing a material form would also observe sound, which is a different type of object than the object of the earlier contact that induced it. Also, it would absurdly follow that the feeling that exists at the same time as a later contact that is concomitant with any mind observing sound would also observe form, which is different from the sound that the main mind is observing. If you assert that the objects of observation of the earlier and later contact and feeling are different, then when the earlier object of observation shifts and sound is observed, it would absurdly follow that there would be no feeling whatsoever observing the sound that was induced by the previous contact observing form. Or, while observing form prior to observing sound, there would have to be contact observing sound that was simultaneous with the feeling that accompanied the consciousness observing form. However, that does not exist because, due to the conditions not being complete while observing form prior to observing sound, there is no contact observing sound that is simultaneous with the feeling that accompanies the consciousness observing form.' This is what you say." As Vasubandhu's autocommentary on the *Treasury of Abhidharma* says:

> This is not correct. Why is it not correct? Among contacts that have different objects of observation, a feeling that exists with a later contact would arise from the cause of an earlier contact. Why? The feeling that arises from the contact that observes a different type of object would observe another object. Or, it would observe something other than the mind with which it

> was concomitant. In that case, at that time, the consciousness that becomes contact would have no feeling. Whatever has the feeling of the previous consciousness would have no contact because the conditions were not complete.[469] [233]

The Sautrāntika says, "While form is observed prior to the observation of sound, although the contact observing sound that is simultaneous with the feeling accompanying the consciousness observing form is absent due to the conditions not being complete, there is no fault." Vasubandhu's autocommentary on the *Treasury of Abhidharma* says, "If that is the cause, what fault is there?"[470]

The Vaibhāṣika says, "If it is the case in your Sautrāntika system that while form is observed prior to the observation of sound, the contact observing sound that is simultaneous with the feeling accompanying the consciousness observing form does not exist because the conditions are not complete, then it would absurdly follow that there is no certainty of the universal mental factors (*mahābhūmika*) of the mind [despite the statement] 'All the minds of sentient beings have ten universal mental factors.' If you ask on the basis of what valid scripture this is conclusively proven to be valid, it is proven to be valid on the basis of the treatise of the Abhidharma." As Vasubandhu's autocommentary on the *Treasury of Abhidharma* says, "This undermines the certainty of the universal mental factors [despite the statement] 'All the minds of sentient beings have ten universal mental factors.' Where is this conclusively proven? In the treatise."[471]

The Sautrāntika says, "We take the sūtras to be valid; we do not take the treatises of the Abhidharma to be valid because the Bhagavan himself said that one should base oneself on the sūtras. Furthermore, according to what is explained in the treatises of the Abhidharma concerning the statement 'All the minds of sentient beings have ten universal mental factors,' this does not mean that a single mind has all ten universal mental factors, such as feeling."

Regarding the meaning of the universal mental factors, [there are]: the factor accompanied by both investigation (*vitarka*) and analysis (*vicāra*); the factor without investigation but just analysis; the factor without investigation or analysis; the factor of virtue; the factor of nonvirtue; the factor of neutrality; the factor of training; the factor of nontraining; and the factor of neither training nor nontraining. Whichever of those that exist for any mind is the meaning of *universal mental factors*. Those that exist only in virtuous minds, such as faith, is the meaning of *virtuous universal mental factors*. Those that exist only for afflicted mental consciousnesses, such as obscuration, is the meaning of *afflicted universal mental factors*. Vasubandhu's autocommentary on the *Treasury of Abhidharma* says:

> We take the sūtras to be valid; we do not take the treatises to be valid because the Buddha said that one should base oneself on the sūtras. Furthermore, "All minds have these" is not the meaning of the universal mental factors. What is the meaning of the universal mental factors? [234] Three states are: the state accompanied by investigation and accompanied by analysis, the state without investigation but with just analysis, and the state without investigation or analysis. Another three are the state of virtue, the state of nonvirtue, and the state of neutrality. Another three are the state of training, the state of nontraining, and the state of neither training nor nontraining. The mental factors that exist in all these states are the universal mental factors. Those that exist only in virtuous states are the virtuous universal mental factors. Those that only exist in afflicted states are the afflicted universal mental factors.[472]

The Vaibhāṣika says, "If you Sautrāntika say that contact and feeling do not arise simultaneously and that feeling arises after contact, you must provide a factual response to the sūtra that says, 'In dependence on the eye and a form, the eye consciousness [is produced]; the assembly of those three is contact. Feeling, discrimination, and intention are produced at the same time.'" Expressing the fault of contradicting the sūtra, Vasubandhu's autocommentary on the *Treasury of Abhidharma* says, "If you say that feeling arises after contact, you must provide a response to the sūtra that says, 'In dependence on the eye and a form, the eye consciousness [is produced]; the assembly of those three is contact. Feeling, discrimination, and intention are produced at the same time.'"[473]

The Sautrāntika says, "The sūtra says, 'feeling is produced at the same time.' It does not say, 'the feeling is produced at the same time as contact.'" Therefore there is no fault. Vasubandhu's autocommentary on the *Treasury of Abhidharma* says, "It says, 'produced at the same time.' It does not say, 'produced at the same time as contact.' In that case, what is there to respond to?"[474]

A śrāvaka scholar, citing the sūtra that says, "That which is the connection and the assembled collection of these three phenomena is contact," says that this means that although the six feelings and the six attachments are set forth as separate from the phenomena source, they are not separate from it in nature. In the same way, although contact is set forth as separate from the object, the sense faculty, and the consciousness, it is not separate from them in nature. By this reasoning, only the assembly of the three—the object, the sense faculty, and the consciousness—is contact. [235]

Another śrāvaka scholar cites a sūtra, "What are the six groups of six types of phenomena? They are the six inner sources, the six outer objects, the six collections of consciousness, the six collections of contact, the six collections of feeling, and the six collections of attachment." He reasons that the effect "contact" is designated to the assembly of the three causes: the object, the sense faculty, and the consciousness. He therefore says that because contact is set forth separately from the three—the sense faculty, the object, and the consciousness—contact is a separate mental factor.

Also, Vasubandhu's autocommentary on the *Treasury of Abhidharma* says, "If it is correct that 'Because of being produced at the same time' means that the five sense faculties are assembled with the object and the consciousnesses . . ."[475] On this point in the text, Pūrṇavardhana's *Investigating Characteristics* says, "Thinking that *assembly* means arising simultaneously, the statement 'Because of being produced at the same time' appears widely.'"[476] If one considers the statement of the opponent, one who accepts that the meaning of "the assembly of the object, the sense faculty, and the consciousness" is that those three arise at the same time, then it is clear that there is someone who says that the meaning of "the assembly of the object, the sense faculty, and the consciousness" is that the three are assembled together.

In brief, with regard to the meaning of the assembly of the three—the object, the sense faculty, and the consciousness—in the systems of both the Vaibhāṣika and Sautrāntika, Vasubandhu's autocommentary on the *Treasury of Abhidharma* says, "Whatever is a cause or an effect is their assembly. Also, all three of those come together to produce contact. Therefore they assert that having a single effect is the meaning of *assembly*."[477] As it says, both Vaibhāṣika and Sautrāntika assert that the presence of the two causes—the object and the sense faculty—and their effect, the consciousness, is the meaning of "the assembly of the three—the object, the sense faculty, and the consciousness." Or they assert that the meaning of this is that those three causes are concordant in producing the effect, contact. This is very clear. However, the Vaibhāṣika description of the way that the three causes accord with production of the effect contact is based on their position that the assembly of the three causes is simultaneous with contact. The Sautrāntika base this on the fact that contact arises after the assembly of the three causes and therefore they are not simultaneous. That is the difference.

Let us turn now to a brief illustration of the reasonings that appear in the texts on valid knowledge used by the Sautrāntika system to prove that cause must be earlier and effect must be later. Dharmakīrti's *Exposition of Valid Knowledge* says:

> What did not exist earlier has no power;
> what exists later no connection.
> Therefore all causes are earlier.[478] [236]

If cause and effect were simultaneous, the cause would not exist prior to the effect and therefore would have no power to aid in the production of the effect. And because the effect would have already been established later, there would be no need for the cause to aid in the production of the effect. These faults would arise. Therefore all causes must exist prior to their effects. Vinītadeva's *Extensive Commentary on Analysis of Relations* says, "Regarding the statement 'Because at that time, cause and effect are not assembled together. Because when the effect has been produced, the cause ceases,' when the effect has been produced, the cause ceases. Therefore the two are not assembled together."[479] This school asserts that when the effect has been produced, the cause on which it relied ceases. Therefore they assert that it is impossible for the two, cause and effect, to be assembled at the same time. Thus one should understand that, unlike Vaibhāṣika, Sautrāntika does not assert that a simultaneously arising cause of a phenomenon and a cause of similar type of a phenomenon are actual causes of that phenomenon. Because they speak of an effect sign (*phalaliṅga*) that proves a preceding cause, they prove that cause must be earlier and effect must be later.

How Sautrāntika Posits External Objects

This system asserts that external objects—form, sound, and so forth—arise from their causes, the four great elements. They are established from the accumulation of external subtle particles; the subtle particles that are the basis of composition of such physical things are partless and do not touch each other. Such assertions are shared by Vaibhāṣika and Sautrāntika. However, Vaibhāṣika asserts that there is space between [the particles], and Sautrāntika asserts that there is no space. This system's position on partless particles and how coarse forms are established from their accumulation has already been explained in detail in the first volume of *Science and Philosophy in the Indian Buddhist Classics*, taking this passage from Śubhagupta's *Proof of External Objects* as its source:

> Not touching one another,
> they exist devoid of parts;
> therefore the earth and so on
> come into being from accumulation.[480]

Its meaning can be understood there.

As this shows, Sautrāntika asserts that external objects are truly established. This is refuted by Cittamātra, who explain that such things as forms are merely appearances to internal consciousnesses, that their appearance as external is merely mistaken appearance, and that sense consciousnesses such as the eye consciousness—which perceives things such as forms as external, distant, and cut off—are mistaken consciousnesses. In order to demonstrate how that is refuted by Sautrāntika, Śubhagupta's *Proof of External Objects* says: [237]

> The object of the consciousness of a healthy eye
> is not an external object.
> It is because it is consciousness and because it appears as an
> external object,
> like a dream or seeing a double moon.

And:

If you think that this is because the consciousness is mistaken
or things such as form are unsuitable to be objects,
there would be no objects of observation.
Both would be unpleasing.[481]

Cittamātra asserts that forms, the objects of valid consciousnesses that rely on sense faculties such as the eye, are not external objects but instead have the nature of internal consciousness. Therefore their appearance as external objects is simply mistaken, like a mind that perceives various objects in a dream and a mind that perceives one moon as two moons. [Sautrāntika] says that that is untenable: "You Cittamātra assert that forms are not perceived as they appear to the eye consciousness, as if they were external, distant, and cut off. Are you saying that this is because the consciousness that perceives them in that way is mistaken with respect to its own object? Or are you saying that such forms are not suitable as objects of valid consciousnesses that rely on the sense faculties? Regardless, it is untenable because such a consciousness would have no object of observation." These are the faults [of the Cittamātra position] that they express.

Furthermore, in dreams, things happen like having a limb cut off, but the events in those dreams do not exist in reality. If external objects did not exist at all and were like being beheaded in a dream, then at the time of an actual execution, the beheading would not take place at all. If you accept that being beheaded at the time of execution and the growth of the body are like things in a dream, then there would be no need to try to stop one's enemy from cutting off one's head or to try to bring about the growth of the body. These are the faults [of the Cittamātra position] that they express. Śubhagupta's *Proof of External Objects* says:

Things seen in dreams,
like the loss of a limb, do not exist.
If nothing at all exists,
then even when awake, would it never happen?

If, as you assert, being beheaded
and the body's growth while awake are like a dream,
then why avoid death
or try to grow?[482]

Thus a consciousness that is deceived with regard to such things as its object or its time is mistaken. A consciousness that is not deceived with regard to its object is not mistaken. Apart from that, there is no definition of an unmistaken consciousness. Therefore it is not tenable to assert that such things as an eye consciousness that realizes forms is a mistaken consciousness. It is true that consciousnesses whose dominant condition, the sense faculty, is damaged through such things as disease are mistaken. [238] However, in the absence of those causes of error, the Cittamātra statement that all sense consciousnesses are mistaken is sheer fancy. Expressing the faults of not accepting external objects, Śubhagupta's *Proof of External Objects* says:

> An undeceived consciousness is unmistaken.
> Those that are deceived are mistaken.
> A consciousness that is undeceived
> with regard to object, time, and another person,
> is known to be unmistaken.
> There is no other definition of unmistaken.[483]

And the same text says:

> Sometimes due to a sense faculty being damaged,
> a consciousness produced from the sense faculty is mistaken.
> Beyond that, to say that all are mistaken
> is foolish talk.[484]

Cittamātra expresses the fault that, if external objects existed, then it would absurdly follow that when the form of a single person was seen by a friend and by an enemy, that single form would have the nature of being both desirable and undesirable. To dispel that fault, they say that it is not tenable that a single external form would appear as desirable to a friend and undesirable to an enemy. Therefore that form is merely the nature of an internal mind. [The Sautrāntika] says that this is untenable. Such things as beauty and ugliness arise in dependence on the cause of growing accustomed to the faults and good qualities of a single form. Through growing accustomed in that way, such differences arise, leading to the production of an awareness of what is desirable and undesirable. To say that differences arise in that way merely through the power of the nature of internal consciousness is nonsense. To prove that the position that external objects exist is correct, Śubhagupta's *Proof of External Objects* says:

> "A real form that is both desirable and undesirable
> cannot be a single external [object].
> In the same way, this is merely a mind."
> To say that is nonsense.
> The beauty of something
> is caused by growing accustomed to its qualities.
> A division in causes creates a division in effects,
> the instances of what is beneficial.[485] [239]

This text also discusses at length how the Cittamātra argument for the certainty of simultaneous observation, which they use to refute external objects, is untenable.

Comprehending Awareness

In accordance with what appears in such works as Dignāga's *Compendium of Valid Knowledge* and Dharmakīrti's *Exposition of Valid Knowledge*, Sautrāntika asserts that there are two valid means of knowledge: direct perception and inference; that there are two types of direct valid knowledge: reflexive awareness and awareness of what is other; and that there are three types of awareness of what is other: sense direct perception that relies on the physical sense faculty as its unique dominant condition, mental direct perception that relies on just the mind as its dominant condition, and yogic direct perception that relies on the union of serenity (*śamatha*) and insight (*vipaśyanā*) as its dominant condition. The divisions of direct perception have already been explained in the second volume of *Science and Philosophy in the Indian Buddhist Classics*. Valid knowledge and its effects, an essential point related to how direct perception is posited, as well as proofs for the two types of awareness that establish [valid knowledge] will be discussed extensively in volume 4.

This system asserts that there are three conditions for sense direct perception: the *observed object condition* (*ālambanapratyaya*), which is the external object that is apprehended; the *dominant condition* (*adhipatipratyaya*), which is the sense faculty that is its foundation; and the *immediately preceding condition* (*samanantarapratyaya*), which is the minds that arise earlier or immediately before. Many important points, such as how these arise, how they assert the collections of consciousness to be six, the fifty-one mental factors as they appear in Dignāga's *Compendium of Valid Knowledge*, as well as how they assert that minds and mental factors are the same entity have already been explained in the second volume of *Science and Philosophy in the Indian Buddhist Classics*.

Vaibhāṣika does not assert self-experiencing consciousness or reflexive awareness. However, for Sautrāntika, Śubhagupta's *Proof of External Objects* says:

> Just as a butter lamp
> illuminates itself and other,
> so consciousness also
> has objects of two natures.[486]

Just as a butter lamp illuminates both itself and other phenomena, an internal consciousness or awareness not only illuminates its object, it also illuminates itself. Therefore they assert, in accordance with this passage, that a single consciousness has two natures or modes: the aspect of apprehending the internal object and the aspect of apprehending the external object. In accordance with this, Jetāri's *Verses on Distinguishing the Sugata's Texts* explains:

> One understanding illuminates the internal.
> The other illuminates the external. [240]
> They are like two butter lamps;
> they are not the illuminated and the illuminating.[487]

Turning to the reasonings that prove reflexive awareness, the primary one is found in Dignāga's *Compendium of Valid Knowledge*, which says it is proved "through being recalled at a later time"[488]—that is, it is proved by the fact of memory. In addition, in his *Exposition of Valid Knowledge*, Dharmakīrti says, "Pleasure and so forth do not depend on something different."[489] That is, at the same time that a sense consciousness that cognizes an external object becomes manifest, an awareness of its own feelings, such as pleasure, must be posited. If reflexive awareness did not exist, it would lead to the most absurd consequences, such as that a mind that apprehends a long string of letters would not be possible. These points, set forth extensively in the direct perception (*pratyakṣa*) chapter of the *Exposition of Valid Knowledge*, must be accepted as the Sautrāntika system as well. The arguments that the two masters of valid knowledge use to prove reflexive awareness are closely related to their arguments for the two modes of awareness. They will be analyzed and set forth in some detail in the fourth volume of *Science and Philosophy in the Indian Buddhist Classics*.

Another position unique to Sautrāntika and not shared with Vaibhāṣika is that this system asserts that there is nonconceptual mental direct perception in which a sense consciousness serves as the immediately preceding condition and for which, like a sense consciousness, its object of apprehension is things such as external forms. They assert that this is set forth in a sūtra that says, "Monks, knowledge of form has two aspects; it relies on the eye and the mind."[490]

The existence of such mental direct valid knowledge is disputed by the tīrthika Aviddhakarṇa, the Buddhist śrāvaka Vātsīputrīya school, and others. They assert that if there were mental direct valid knowledge, either it would apprehend exactly what the earlier sense direct perception had already apprehended or it would apprehend something that the sense direct perception had not apprehended. In the first case, if it apprehended something previously apprehended by sense direct perception, it would not be a valid means of knowledge [because it can only be valid if it is an initial perception]. In the second case, if mental direct perception apprehended an object that was not apprehended by sense direct perception, then even a blind person would be able to see such things as forms because, even without the eyes, mental direct perception would directly apprehend form. Regarding their assertions, the *Exposition of Valid Knowledge* says:

> If it apprehended what was experienced before,
> the mind would not be a valid means of knowledge. [241]
> If it apprehended what was not seen,
> even the blind would see objects.[491]

In the system of the proponents of valid knowledge, the mental direct perception that apprehends form apprehends its own object, which is different from the object apprehended by the sense direct perception apprehending form that precedes it. Therefore it is not a subsequent cognition. That mental direct perception is produced from the earlier sense direct perception apprehending form, its immediately preceding condition. Therefore a blind person cannot see forms. Rejecting these objections, the *Exposition of Valid Knowledge* says:

> Therefore it arises from the sense consciousness,
> its immediately preceding condition,
> but the object the mind apprehends is different.
> Therefore the blind cannot see.[492]

Even though mental direct perception apprehends an object that is different from the object of sense direct perception, that apprehension of an object is not separated by place or time. Because the earlier sense direct perception is its immediately preceding condition, the mental direct perception does not apprehend something that is different in *type* from the object of sense direct perception; it apprehends something that is different in *entity*. Therefore, even if that mental direct perception apprehends an object that is different from the object of the sense direct perception that is its immediately preceding condition, it is asserted that it apprehends only a specific and manifest object; it does not apprehend things that are physically and temporarily remote from each other. The *Exposition of Valid Knowledge* says:

> The sense consciousness, which is its cause,
> depends on an object related to its own object.
> Therefore, although it apprehends something different,
> it is asserted that it apprehends a specific thing.[493]

On the question of how such mental direct perception is produced, there are three different and famous assertions among the Buddhist scholars of valid knowledge: (1) the assertion that sense direct perception and mental direct perception alternate, (2) the assertion that three progressions are produced, and (3) the assertion that it is produced at the end of the sequence of sense direct perception.[494]

The first, the assertion that they alternate, is the system of Prajñākaragupta,[495] author of *Ornament of the Exposition of Valid Knowledge.* According to this system, first a moment of sense direct perception is produced, then a moment of mental direction perception is produced, and then a moment of sense direct perception is produced. [242] In brief, sense direct perception leads and mental direct perception concludes. He asserts that sense direct perception and mental direct perception alternate.

The second, the assertion that three progressions are produced, is the system of the great brahmin Śaṅkarānanda,[496] according to which initially a single moment of sense direct perception apprehending form is produced, and then, directly induced by that, the three—the first moment of mental direct perception apprehending form, the second moment of sense direct perception apprehending form, and the reflexive awareness that experiences those two—are produced simultaneously. Śaṅkarānanda says that three types of awareness are produced: two types of awareness of the object, facing outward, and a reflexive awareness, facing inward.

The third, the assertion that mental direct perception is produced at the end of the sequence, is the assertion of Dharmottara. According to this system, as soon as the last moment of sense direct perception ceases, it serves as the dominant condition to produce a moment of the mental direct perception. For example, in his *Vast Commentary on the Drop of Reasoning,* Dharmottara says, "The mental consciousness is asserted to be direct perception at the time when the activity of the eye has passed. When the eye is functioning, everything that knows form only depends on the eye. Otherwise, it would be untenable for any consciousness to depend on the eye."[497]

Dharmottara's essential point is this: The mental direct perception that is produced at the end of a sequence of sense direct perception is *mental direct perception that knows an object.* Thus, when each sense direct perception apprehending form is produced in the continuum of a common being, as long as it has the unique function of its dominant condition, the eye sense faculty, it remains connected to the sequence of that sense direct perception apprehending form. Thus the sense direct perception apprehending form that depends on its dominant condition, the eye, is still produced. However, when each sense direct perception apprehending form is being produced, if it does not have the unique function of its dominant condition, the eye sense faculty, then mental direct perception apprehending form is produced, which is appended to the sequence of that sense direct perception apprehending form. [243]

According to the position of Dharmottara, the reason why the first assertion is untenable is because the *Exposition of Valid Knowledge* says:

> If things were apprehended sequentially,
> the experience of them would not be uninterrupted.[498]

If sense direct perception and mental direct perception were produced alternately each moment, the earlier and later moments of sense direct perception would be interrupted by mental direct perception. Therefore there would be the fault that sense direct perception would not be able to apprehend its object without interruption. According to the second assertion of the three types, if sense direct perception is not produced continuously, it is not able to comprehend its object. If you accept that it is produced continuously, there is no opportunity for mental direct perception to be produced simultaneously with it. Because of this fault, it is proven to be untenable. Therefore, because this third system has arguments proving [that the other two] are unsuitable, many later Indian and Tibetan scholars of valid knowledge said that its assertion, that [mental direct perception] is produced at the end of the sequence of sense direct perception, is correct.[499]

The Aspects That Appear to Consciousness

Turning to the way in which a consciousness comprehends an object, in general, Sautrāntika and the higher schools assert that when a consciousness comprehends an object, it does so through the appearance of the *aspect* (*ākāra*) of the object. There are three different assertions about how an aspect appears to a sense consciousness: (1) the nonpluralist, which is the assertion that many aspects appear to a single consciousness, (2) the half-eggist, which is the assertion that only one aspect appears to a single consciousness, and (3) the equal number of subjects and objects, which is the assertion that when many aspects appear, there are many consciousnesses. How these arose has already been explained briefly in chapter 17 of the second volume of the *Science and Philosophy in the Indian Buddhist Classics*. How these assertions are debated by their proponents will be explained in some detail below in the chapter on Cittamātra. In brief, for Sautrāntika, using color as an example, blue and the eye consciousness apprehending blue are two different entities. However, blue and the reflection or aspect of blue, which is the nature of the consciousness that is established by that blue, are similar and are cause and effect. They use the phrase "blue appears" to refer to the mind apprehending blue being produced in an aspect that is blue-like. Therefore this system asserts that consciousness has aspects. To set this forth, Bodhibhadra's *Explanation of the Compendium of the Essence of Wisdom* says [244]:

> Now, explaining what is set forth in the tenets of Sautrāntika, they say, "What is seen is not an object of the senses." Forms and so forth that are directly seen by the eye and so forth are apprehended by consciousness; they are not objects of the sense faculties such as the eye sense faculty [which are matter]. Why? Because those consciousnesses of the eye and so forth are produced having the aspect of the object. This is because it is not suitable for matter to appear [to immaterial consciousness]. Consciousness is produced having its aspect.[500]

This means that Sautrāntika asserts that consciousness has an aspect. That same *Explanation* says:

> Thus these Sautrāntika say that when a person looks at a clear crystal that has turned the color of the hue it has been placed next to, both the crystal and whatever the hue is are apprehended by their eye. At that time, the crystal itself is apprehended directly; the hue is apprehended through its reflection. Just as the person apprehends both objects, what appears to direct perception is the aspect of the consciousness alone. The basis that appears to consciousness as color and shape is asserted to be a distinct entity that is a collection of minute particles that do not have space between them and do not touch each other. Therefore they say that there are two objects.[501]

This is like saying that although both the crystal and the hue are similar in that they are seen by the sense consciousness, the crystal is understood from its own side and the hue is understood in the manner of a reflection.

The final point proving that consciousness has an aspect is this: If the mind [which is by nature luminous] were to perceive an external object vividly without an aspect, the object would become the nature of luminosity, and if one asserts that it is the nature of luminosity, there would be the fault that blue and so forth would be luminous independently of the consciousness apprehending it. Therefore the clear *appearing* of objects, such as blue color, is consciousness; the *basis* that appears as blue is a phenomenon made of subtle particles. This means that Sautrāntika accepts that phenomena exist externally.

In any case, regarding the way a sense consciousness apprehends its object, Vaibhāṣika explains that a sense consciousness apprehends an object that is simultaneous with itself. However, Sautrāntika asserts that the object of apprehension of a sense consciousness and the sense consciousness are cause and effect and therefore are not simultaneous. If they are not simultaneous, how does the sense consciousness apprehend it? Although the object of apprehension of the sense consciousness has ceased, by experiencing the aspect of the consciousness projected by the object, [they assert] that the object of apprehension is experienced. Thus Dharmakīrti's *Exposition of Valid Knowledge* says [245]:

> Because they are at different times, how is [the object]
> apprehended?
> Masters of reasoning know that
> the cause that has the capacity to establish the aspect of
> consciousness
> is the object that is to be perceived.[502]

Also:

> Apart from the thing that is the cause,
> there is nothing else to be called the object.
> That which appears to the mind
> is said to be its object.[503]

This is saying that the object of apprehension of a sense consciousness must be one of its causes; there is no object of apprehension other than the observed object condition of that sense consciousness. Given that such an object appears directly to that sense consciousness, it must be said that it is the object of apprehension.

In summary, both Sautrāntika and Cittamātra, which arose from the texts on valid knowledge by Dignāga and his heir Dharmakīrti, are similar in their presentation of inference for oneself and inference for others, in the proof that the meaning of words arises through excluding what is other, in the general presentation of minds that apprehend, and in the proof that awareness has two modes [of objects and of itself]. In addition, the Sautrāntikas' own system is based on the position that asserts the existence of external objects. For example, they assert that other-knowing direct perception, like an eye consciousness apprehending form, is produced by taking an external object as the object of apprehension, and based on that they take the first delineation of the presentation of valid knowledge and its effect to be the correct position.

Thus, from among the four Buddhist schools of tenets of India, this completes the rough presentation of the tenets of Sautrāntika, which asserts reflexive awareness and that external objects are truly established. [246]

13

The Cittamātra School

How This School of Tenets Arose

It is well known that the founder of this school is Ārya Asaṅga, a great master—prophesied in the scriptures of the Buddha—who appeared in India in the fourth century.[504] This master explained that the intended meaning of the Mahāyāna sūtras in general and of the Perfection of Wisdom sūtras in particular was consciousness only (*vijñaptimātra*), and through delineating this he founded and spread widely this Vijñaptika school, which is included among the Mahāyāna schools of tenets. Nāgārjuna introduced the Madhyamaka school, which asserts that the emptiness of intrinsic existence of all phenomena is the intention of the Perfection of Wisdom sūtras. Asaṅga, emphasizing the three wheels of the Dharma set forth in the *Explanation of the Intention Sūtra*, explained that the statements in the Perfection of Wisdom sūtras regarding how phenomena lack entityness were set forth intending the three types of entitylessness (*niḥsvabhāvatā*), and he explained that those statements were not to be understood literally. He introduced the proof that the *Explanation of the Intention Sūtra*, the final words of the Buddha known as the wheel of the Dharma of good discrimination, is the definitive meaning. By doing so, he founded and widely disseminated the school renowned as Cittamātra. In general, for Nāgārjuna and Asaṅga—these two great founders of Madhyamaka and Cittamātra, respectively—there are not great differences in the domain of practice, whether it be in the practice of the stages of the path that is common to all vehicles—the four truths, the twelve links of dependent origination, or the four establishments of mindfulness—or that which is specific to the Mahāyāna stages of the path—the aspiration to enlightenment (*bodhicitta*) rooted in compassion and how to practice the six perfections. However, there is a great difference in the domain of the view, such as how to delineate the two selflessnesses [of persons and phenomena].

Because the śrāvaka schools in general do not accept the Mahāyāna sūtras as the word of the Buddha, they do not present the three stages of the wheels of the Dharma. However, the followers of the Mahāyāna explain that from the year that the Buddha displayed the mode of complete and perfect buddhahood, the śrāvaka scriptural collection, such as the wheel of the Dharma of the four truths, and the Mahāyāna scriptural collection appeared at the same time.[505] [247] The middle wheel, called the wheel of the Dharma of signlessness, and the final wheel, called the wheel of the Dharma of good discrimination, are accepted as part of the Mahāyāna scriptural collection. There are differences in the presentations of the three wheels. Since the śrāvaka schools contest the claim that the Mahāyāna sūtras are the word of the Buddha, works of the early Mahāyāna masters—such as Nāgārjuna's *Precious Garland*, Maitreya's *Ornament of the Mahāyāna Sūtras*, Bhāviveka's *Blaze of Reasoning*, and Śāntideva's *Entering the Bodhisattva Way*—supply proofs that the Mahāyāna sūtras are indeed the word of the Buddha.

The Texts on Which This System Primarily Depends

This Cittamātra school relies mainly on the *Explanation of the Intention*, the Buddha's teachings in the final turning of the wheel of the Dharma. In addition, it relies on such texts as the Perfection of Wisdom sūtras, the *Flower Garland Sūtra*, the *Descent into Laṅkā Sūtra*, the *Ten Levels Sūtra*, and the *Dense Array Sūtra*. For example, Kamalaśīla says in his *Illumination of the Middle Way*:

> Because the noble *Ten Levels Sūtra* says, "It is thus: these three realms are mind only," and in the same way, such sūtras as the noble *Explanation of the Intention*, the *Descent into Laṅkā*, and the *Dense Array* teach that all phenomena have a nature of mind only, they teach that only the mind exists ultimately; nothing else does. Therefore it is not the case that all phenomena are established as without entityness.[506]

He is saying that based on those sūtras, Cittamātra asserts that external objects do not exist and that mind alone is truly established.

The texts by Ārya Asaṅga that establish the tenets of Cittamātra are the five treatises that together are called the *Yogācāra Levels*: (1) the *Chapters on the Levels* (*Bhūmivastu*), which includes the well-known *Śrāvaka Levels* and *Bodhisattva Levels*, (2) the *Compendium of Ascertainments* (*Viniścayasaṅgraha*), (3) the *Compendium of Bases* (*Vastusaṅgraha*), (4) the *Compendium of Enumerations* (*Paryāyasaṅgraha*), and (5) the *Compendium of Explanation* (*Vivaraṇasaṅgraha*). He also composed two summaries: the *Compendium of Abhidharma*, which is a summary of what is common to the vehicles, and the *Compendium of the Mahāyāna*, which is a summary of what is unique to the Mahāyāna. Among the texts of this system, the *Compendium of the Mahāyāna* seems to be the most important; it is said that if one does not understand it, one does not understand the meaning of mind only, and one does not understand how to explain the intention of many sūtras, such as the Perfection of Wisdom sūtras.[507] This is also the reason that the *Compendium of the Mahāyāna* is greatly valued by the followers of Asaṅga. There is a commentary on the *Compendium of the Mahāyāna* composed by Vasubandhu. [248] The explanation of the first chapter of the *Compendium of the Mahāyāna* called *Condensed Explanation Revealing the Secret Meaning* appears to be a treatise that delineates its intended meaning, emphasizing the most important points.[508] There is also an extensive commentary composed by Asvabhāva, the *Explanation of the Compendium of the Mahāyāna*. These are found today in the Tengyur.

Turning to the Vijñaptika treatises composed by Vasubandhu, the great upholder of the tradition, there are those renowned as the Eight Treatises: the *Commentary on the Ornament of the Sūtras*, the *Commentary on Distinguishing the Middle from the Extremes*, the *Commentary on Distinguishing Phenomena and Suchness*, *Principles of Exegesis*, *Treatise Proving Actions*, *Treatise on the Five Aggregates*, *Twenty Verses*, and *Thirty Verses*. There are also many commentaries on sūtras and treatises composed by this master, such as the *Explanation of the First Dependent Origination and Its Divisions*, his commentary on the *Sūtra Set Forth by Akṣayamati*, the *Commentary on the Ten Levels Sūtra*, the *Commentary on the Compendium of the Mahāyāna*, and his commentary on the three recollections (*anusmṛti*) [of the Buddha, Dharma, and Saṅgha]. In addition, there are the Five Books of Maitreya: the two ornaments—the *Ornament of Realizations* and the

Ornament of the Mahāyāna Sūtras—the two distinguishings—*Distinguishing the Middle from the Extremes* and *Distinguishing Phenomena and Suchness*, and also the *Sublime Continuum*.[509] These, together with Asaṅga's Five Treatises on the Levels, the two compendia, and Vasubandhu's Eight Treatises, are renowned among the scholars of Tibet as the twenty teachings connected to Maitreya.

After Asaṅga began the tradition of explaining the tenets of Cittamātra, there were many masters who upheld the tenets of this system, such as Vasubandhu, who has already been described, Dignāga, the elder Dharmapāla, Sthiramati, Dharmakīrti, Devendrabuddhi, Śākyabuddhi, the great paṇḍita Dharmottara, Prajñākaragupta, the brahmin Śaṅkarānanda, Dharmakīrti of Suvarṇadvīpa, and Śāntipa. Among these, there seem to be some who were Cittamātra in the first part of their life and became proponents of Madhyamaka later in life. According to Tibetan scholars, Asaṅga in his commentary on the *Sublime Continuum* delineates the meaning of that text from the perspective of the emptiness of intrinsic nature of the proponents of *niḥsvabhāva*. [249] Therefore they assert that although Asaṅga founded the tenets of Cittamātra, the view of the master himself remained that of Madhyamaka.[510]

Thus Asaṅga and his brother expanded the tradition of Cittamātra Following Scripture, both in general and specific ways. After that, Dignāga, who appeared in the sixth century, composed the *Compendium of Valid Knowledge* and its commentary and *Investigation of the Support* and its commentary. Dharmakīrti, who appeared in the seventh century, composed the Seven Books on Valid Knowledge: the *Exposition of Valid Knowledge*, the *Ascertainment of Valid Knowledge*, the *Drop of Reasoning*, the *Drop of Reasons*, the *Proof of Other Minds*, the *Analysis of Relations*, and the *Principles of Debate*. They expanded the tradition of Cittamātra Following Reasoning.

THE DEFINITION AND DIVISIONS OF CITTAMĀTRA

The Cittamātra school of tenets is a Buddhist school that has as its root tenet that external objects do not exist and accepts that consciousness is truly established. Cittamātra, Vijñaptika, and Yogācāra are synonyms.

Because they propound that all phenomena are only the nature of consciousness, they are called Cittamātra ("mind only"). Because they propound that phenomena that appear to awareness as if they were external are only internal awareness, they are called Vijñaptika ("proponents of awareness"). Because they propound that although external objects do not exist, they appear to the internal mind as if they do, like earth turning into gold through the power of the imagination of a yogin, they are called Yogācārin ("practitioners of yoga"). The name Cittamātra became the name of this school based on what appears in the Mahāyāna sūtras. For example, the *Ten Levels Sūtra* says, "Thus these three realms are mind only."[511] The *Descent into Laṅkā* also says:

> Through abiding in mind only,
> external objects are not discerned.[512]

There is an important point that should be understood about the phrase "mind only" in the passage from the *Ten Levels Sūtra.* Madhyamaka says that the term "only" in that sūtra does not refute external objects but instead refutes a creator of the world that is other than mind; one finds differences like this in how Madhyamaka and Cittamātra comment on such passages. [250] In the same way, not every instance of the term *yogācāra* ("practitioner of yoga") in a Buddhist text refers to Cittamātra. For example, there is the the title of Āryadeva's *Four Hundred Verses on the Yogic Practice of Bodhisattvas.*[513]

When Cittamātra is divided, there are two: (1) Cittamātra Following Scripture and (2) Cittamātra Following Reasoning. The first are those who follow Asaṅga's five treatises in the *Yogācāra Levels*, and the second are those who follow Dharmakīrti's Seven Works on Valid Knowledge. Cittamātra is also divided from the perspective of the aspect into the Cittamātra who are called (1) True Aspectarians and (2) False Aspectarians. In general, both the True and False Aspectarians accept that to an eye consciousness, form appears to be distant and cut off, to be a coarse object, and to be form. However, the False Aspectarians assert that these three—form appearing to be distant and cut off, form appearing to be a coarse object, and form appearing to be form—are mixed, and the True Aspectarians assert that they are not mixed. The False Aspectarians assert that all three of those appearances are polluted by the predispositions of ignorance, and the True Aspectarians assert that they are not. Cittamātra appears to be divided into these two groups, True and False Aspectarians, based on these points of disagreement.

It is explained that it is suitable to further divide True Aspectarian Cittamātra into the Nonpluralists, Half-Eggists, and Proponents of an Equal Number of Subjects and Objects. It is also suitable to further divide False Aspectarian Cittamātra into the Stained False Aspectarian and the Stainless False Aspectarian. The *Detailed Explanation Illuminating All the Vehicles* composed by the brahmin monk Subhūtighoṣa says:

> For the Nonpluralist True Aspectarians
> the entity of a single consciousness is true.[514]

And:

> Those who do and do not assert cause and effect
> are called the Cittamātra with Elaboration
> and the Cittamātra without Elaboration.
> The False Aspectarians are also asserted to be two:
> the Pure and the Stained.[515] [251]

As he explains, there is the division into True and False Aspectarians, and those two are also referred to as Cittamātra with Elaboration and without Elaboration. The False Aspectarians are further subdivided into the Pure or Stainless and the Stained. Bodhibhadra's *Explanation of the Compendium on the Essence of Wisdom* says:

> Here, there are two types of Yogācāra: those with aspect and those without aspect. Having an aspect is the assertion of those such as the master Dignāga, who teaches from the perspective of there being another aspect. Therefore, as he says,
>
> > The nature of an internal object
> > that appears to be external
> > is not real.
>
> They say that there are six collections of consciousness. Those without aspect are the master Ārya Asaṅga and so forth. They say that the imagined aspect is like the floating hairs seen by someone with myodesopsia. Therefore they say,

If objects were established as objects
there would be no nonconceptual wisdom.
Without that, the attainment of buddhahood
would not be possible.

And, similarly,

When nonconceptual wisdom comes into being
no objects appear.
Therefore one should realize that there are no objects.
Because they do not exist, there is no consciousness of them.

There are those who say there are eight collections of consciousness and those who say that there is one. Some [True and some False] Aspectarians also assert that there is only one.[516]

A General Explanation of Cittamātra Assertions

At the outset, to establish the best approach for summarizing the key assertions unique to this system, we will look at verses from Āryadeva's *Compendium on the Essence of Wisdom* and Jetāri's *Verses on Distinguishing the Sugata's Texts*. The *Compendium on the Essence of Wisdom* says:

"Having parts" does not exist,
and minute particles do not exist.
Individual appearances do not exist as they are observed.
Experience is like a dream. [252]

Consciousness free from apprehended and apprehender
exists ultimately.
This is known in the texts of the Yogācāra,
who have crossed the ocean of awareness.[517]

Very similar is this passage from *Verses on Distinguishing the Sugata's Texts*:

"Having parts" does not exist,
and minute particles do not exist.

Appearances do not exist as they are observed.
Experience is like a dream.

Consciousness free from apprehended and apprehender
exists ultimately.
This is what is said by those who have crossed
the ocean of the texts of Yogācāra.[518]

These two nearly identical summaries of the tenets of Cittamātra identify the three primary doctrines unique to this system. These are as follows: (1) External objects that have coarse elements or phenomena that have parts do not exist, nor do the partless particles from which [others] explain that they are made. (2) Therefore phenomena that appear to a mistaken sense consciousness to be external are like a dream; in reality, they do not exist as they are observed. (3) Thus the nondual consciousness that has passed beyond apprehended and apprehender being different substantial entities is asserted to exist ultimately. All Cittamātra are in agreement on those three primary tenets.

The Characteristics of Objects of Knowledge: The Three Natures

In general, when this system delineates its views on the nature of reality, it does so in terms of the two truths as they appear in the Mahāyāna sūtras and in such works as Nāgārjuna's *Root Verses on the Middle Way*. However, it also does so uniquely from the perspective of the three natures set forth in the *Explanation of the Intention Sūtra*. Thus, they describe three natures or entities of objects of knowledge: (1) the *dependent nature* (*paratantra*), which is composed by causes and conditions, (2) the *imaginary nature* (*parikalpita*), which is established as mere superimpositions by thought, and (3) the *consummate ultimate nature* (*pariniṣpanna*), which, taking the dependent to be the basis that is empty, is empty of the imaginary, the object of negation. [253] This system posits consummate ultimate nature to be the final mode of being of phenomena and the subtle selflessness. Among the three natures, they assert that the imaginary does not exist ultimately and that both the dependent and the consummate do exist ultimately. When the natures are set forth in Asaṅga's *Compendium of the*

Mahāyāna, it says, "If one asks how the natures of objects of knowledge are to be viewed, in brief, it is this. There are three types: the dependent nature, the imaginary nature, and the consummate nature."[519] In his *Exposition of the Three Natures*, Vasubandhu says:

> Things that operate through the power of conditions
> and that are mere imputations;
> that which appears is the dependent;
> how it appears is the imaginary.
>
> How it appears in that which appears
> is something that never exists.
> Because it is called the *unchanging*,
> it is the consummate nature.[520]

This passage clearly states that a thing's own nature arises from causes and conditions. It appears as if it is external, distant, and cut off from the mind, yet it is merely imagined to exist in that way; it is not established as an external object. The basis upon which what is being negated is perceived is the *dependent*. External reality, which is perceived in the dependent although it does not exist there, is the object of negation, the *imaginary*. The nonexistence of the dependent as an external object, as it falsely appears to be, is the unchanging *consummate nature*. When examples are provided for those three natures, that same text says:

> By creating an illusion through the power of mantra,
> an elephant, for example, appears.
> It is just an aspect that appears;
> the elephant does not exist.
>
> The elephant is like the imaginary nature.
> The dependent is like its aspect.
> The consummate is asserted to be
> like the nonexistence of the elephant there.[521]

The passage is saying that in dependence on substances and the mantras of a magician, a pebble or a stick is made to appear as an elephant. At that time, apart from the mere appearance of the aspect on the basis of the pebble or stick, an elephant is completely nonexistent there. In accordance with this example, the imaginary nature, which is established as being external, distant, and cut off, is superimposed onto the dependent, although it does not exist there—like the elephant appearing on the basis of the pebble or stick, although it does not exist there. [254] The dependent nature appearing to consciousness as external, distant, and cut off is like the aspect of the pebble or stick appearing as an elephant. The consummate nature, which is the mere negation of the imaginary, its object of negation, in the dependent is like the absence of the elephant in the stick or pebble.

In his *Exposition of the Three Natures*, Vasubandhu sets forth the natures in relation to verbal conventions, the sequence of the divisions, and the sequence of understanding them in terms of engagement. Thus the *dependent* is the nature that designates verbal conventions, the *imaginary* is the nature that is a mere designation by verbal conventions, and the *consummate* is the nature that is complete elimination of the nature that is a mere designation by verbal conventions. Regarding the sequence of engagement, first one engages with the dependent, which has the nature of nonduality of apprehended and apprehender. Then one engages with the imaginary, because the duality of apprehended and apprehender is imputed to exist in the dependent even though it does not. Then one engages with the consummate, which is the nature or reality that is ascertained to be the absence of the duality of apprehended and apprehender in the dependent.[522]

Thus the consummate is the reality that is the emptiness of the object of negation—the imaginary—in the basis that is empty—the dependent. Just as impermanence is the nature of the conditioned, so the consummate is the nature of the dependent. Therefore, regarding the way that the consummate is in no way a different entity from the dependent but has a different isolate, Vasubandhu's *Thirty Verses* says:

> Thus it is said not to be different from the dependent
> and also not nondifferent,
> like impermanence and so forth.[523]

Cittamātra also asserts that such a consummate nature is their system's middle path free from the two extremes of existence and nonexistence. For example, Maitreya's *Distinguishing the Middle from the Extremes* says:

> The imagination of what is unreal exists;
> duality does not exist.
> Emptiness exists in that;
> that also exists in it.
>
> Neither empty, nor not empty;
> therefore all is explained.
> Because it is existent, nonexistent, and existent,
> that is the middle path.[524] [255]

This is saying that the dependent, as the imagination of what is unreal, exists ultimately. The dependent, which is the basis that is empty, is empty of apprehended and apprehender being established as different substantial entities. Such an emptiness ultimately exists as the final mode of being of the dependent. That consummate emptiness has always been the final mode of being of the dependent, the basis that is empty. However, the imagination that apprehended and apprehender are different substantial entities does not see the consummate due to its being obstructed. In this way, the dependent and the consummate are not empty of being truly established, and all phenomena are not nonempty of apprehended and apprehender being different substantial entities. Therefore the Perfection of Wisdom sūtras explain that everything is utterly not empty and not nonempty. The dependent truly exists, and the apprehended and apprehender do not exist as different substantial entities; the dependent and the consummate exist in each other in the manner of the quality and the qualified. Therefore the dependent and the consummate are truly established, and all phenomena are not established as apprehended and apprehender being different substantial entities. For that reason, the dependent's emptiness of apprehended and apprehender being different substantial entities is said to be the middle path, free from the two extremes. The three natures are included in the two truths in this way: the imaginary and the dependent are conventional truths, and the consummate is the ultimate truth.

Thus, among the three natures, the first to be explained is the imaginary. The definition of the *imaginary* is that which is a mere designation by the thought that apprehends it. Examples are the factor of difference between pot and pillar and phenomena being established as external objects. Because it is merely a factor designated completely by thought, it is called *imaginary*. The *Compendium of the Mahāyāna* says, "Because it is observed to be merely a conception, without its own nature, it is called *imaginary*."[525]

When the imaginary is divided, there is the *nominal* imaginary and the *eliminated* imaginary. The first are imaginaries that exist among objects of knowledge; they are also called *existent imaginaries*. That [category] and the permanent that are not emptiness are synonyms. An example is space. The second are imaginaries that do not exist among objects of knowledge; they are also called *nonexistent imaginaries*. An example is apprehended and apprehender being different substantial entities.

When the imaginary is divided from the perspective of how they superimpose, there is the imaginary that is the imagination of an entity and the imaginary that is the imagination of a quality. The first would be like form being naturally established as the basis of the operation of the name and the thought "form." [256] The second would be like the production of form being naturally established as the basis of the operation of the name and the thought "production of form." Thus the *Explanation of the Intention Sūtra* says:

> That which is affixed by names and terms to natures or particulars such as "the form aggregate," objects of thought, the base of the imaginary nature that has the character of the conditioned, and that which is affixed by names and terms to natures or particulars, such as "the form aggregate is produced," "it ceases," "the form aggregate is abandoned," and "it is known," are *imaginary natures*.[526]

Above, "objects of thought, the base of the imaginary nature that has the character of the conditioned" indicates that the basis of the imaginary is the dependent. "The form aggregate" and so forth indicate the nature of form, and "the form aggregate is produced" and so forth indicate the particulars or qualities of the form aggregate, such as the production of form. "Affixed by names and terms" indicates that those are imagined to be naturally established as the bases of designation by words and thoughts. In brief, this passage is indicating that the imaginary designates natures and qualities to the dependent.

The definition of the *dependent* is that which is produced in dependence on its causes. *Dependent*, *conditioned*, and *dependently arisen* are synonyms.

The *Explanation of the Intention Sūtra* says, "The dependent nature is that which is the object of thought, the base of the imaginary nature that has the character of the conditioned."[527] This passage is indicating that the dependent has three qualities. First, "that which is the object of thought" indicates that the dependent is the object of a subject. Second, "the base of the imaginary nature" indicates that that dependent is the basis of designation onto which the imaginary designates natures and qualities. Third, "which has the nature of the conditioned" indicates the nature of the dependent, that is, that it is something that has unique characteristics that appear to the mind that takes it as its object. [257]

It is also explained that the dependent has three qualities: (1) Its *causal quality* is that it arises from internal predispositions without being established by the power of the accumulation of external subtle particles. (2) Its *natural quality* is that it intrinsically exists. (3) Its *objective quality* is that ultimately it is not the object of any words or thoughts.[528]

It is called *dependent* [literally "other-powered"] because it comes to be under the power of other causes and conditions, or it is called *dependent* because having been produced, it is not able to remain for more than a moment. The *Compendium of the Mahāyāna* says, "Why is it called *dependent*? Because it is produced from the seeds of one's own predispositions, it is dependent on conditions. Having been produced, its nature is not to be able to remain for more than a moment. Therefore it is called *dependent*."[529]

The *consummate* is defined as the mode of being that is empty of being established in the way that is superimposed by the conception of self. *Consummate*, *emptiness*, *suchness*, *limit of reality*, *signless*, *ultimate truth*, and *sphere of reality* are synonyms. Thus *Distinguishing the Middle from the Extremes* says:

> The synonyms of *emptiness*, in brief,
> are *suchness* and the *limit of reality*,
> the *signless*, the *ultimate*,
> and the *sphere of reality*.[530]

Regarding the consummate, the *Explanation of the Intention Sūtra* says, "That which is an object of thought, the basis of the imaginary nature, and has the character of being conditioned is not established as the imaginary nature; that which is devoid of such [an imagined] nature, the entitylessness, the absence of selfhood of phenomena, which is suchness, and is the pure object, this is the consummate nature."[531] Here, "object of thought, the basis of the imaginary nature, and has the character of the conditioned" identifies the basis that is empty, the dependent. "Is not established as the imaginary nature" indicates that the imaginary nature, the object of negation, is not established in the dependent, the basis that is empty. "That which is devoid of such [an imagined] nature, the entitylessness, the absence of selfhood of phenomena" indicates that the subject, the dependent not being established as the imaginary nature, the object of negation, is the selflessness of phenomena. [258] "Which is suchness, and is the pure object, this is the consummate nature" indicates that the suchness that is the ultimate object on the path of purification is the consummate nature.

It is called the *consummate* because its nature does not change into something else due to causes and conditions and because it is established as the ultimate object on the path of purification. The *Compendium of the Mahāyāna* says, "Why is it called the *consummate*? It is consummate because it does not change into something else. It is the supreme object because it is the pure object and is supreme among all virtuous objects. Therefore it is called the *consummate*."[532]

Because this system divides the nature, or character, of objects of knowledge into three, the intended meaning for Cittamātra of the statements in the Perfection of Wisdom sūtras that say phenomena lack entityness is different from that for Madhyamaka. Accepting what is set forth in the *Explanation of the Intention Sūtra*, they connect the entityness that does not exist to each of the three natures: the imaginary lacks the entityness of character, the dependent lacks the entityness of production, and the consummate is the ultimate and without entityness. The *Explanation of the Intention Sūtra* says, "Paramārthasamudgata, what is the entitylessness of character of phenomena? It is the character of the imaginary. Why? It is thus. It is the characteristic defined by way of names and terms; it is not a characteristic that exists by its own intrinsic nature. Thus it is called the *entitylessness of character*." It continues, "Paramārthasamudgata, it is thus. One should view the entitylessness of character as like, for example, a flower in the sky."[533] This is saying that from the positive side, the imaginary is merely that which is affixed by names and terms, and from the negative side, because it is not established by way of its own character, it lacks the entityness of character. They posit two types of the imaginary: the imaginary that exists and the imaginary that does not exist. Therefore the explanation that the imaginary is like a flower in the sky is an example of what is not established by way of its own character but is merely imputed by thought; it is not an example of what does not exist at all.

Turning to how this school posits that the dependent lacks the entityness of production, when a magician, for example, conjures a pebble or stick as a horse or an elephant, the pebble or stick appears to the audience as a horse or an elephant, but they are not a real horse or elephant. In the same way, the dependent appears to be established as an external object but is not established as an external object. Because it lacks the entityness of being produced by its own power, it is called the *entitylessness of production*. The *Explanation of the Intention Sūtra* says, [259] "Paramārthasamudgata, it is thus. The entitylessness of production should be viewed as like an illusion." And it goes on to say, "Paramārthasamudgata, what is the entitylessness of production of phenomena? It is the dependent nature of phenomena. Why? It is thus. It arises through the power of other conditions, not by itself. Therefore is called the *entitylessness of production*."[534]

Regarding how this school posits that the consummate is the ultimate and the lack of entityness, just as space, for example, is the mere absence of obstructive contact, its object of negation, and pervades all directions, the consummate is the mere absence of the self of phenomena, its object of negation, and pervades all objects of knowledge. Because the nature of the self of phenomena, the object of negation, is not established, it is called the *ultimate* and the *lack of entityness*. The *Explanation of the Intention Sūtra* says, "Paramārthasamudgata, that which is the selflessness of phenomena is called their *entitylessness*. That is the ultimate. Because the ultimate is distinguished by being the entitylessness of all phenomena, it is called the *ultimate* and the *lack of entityness*." And, "Paramārthasamudgata, it is thus. Space is distinguished by being the mere absence of the entityness of form, and it goes everywhere. In the same way, that which is the ultimate and the lack of entityness should be seen as distinguished by being the lack of a self of phenomena and as something that goes everywhere."[535]

In brief, Cittamātra asserts that that which is established from its own side, without being merely designated by thought, is specifically characterized, established by way of its own character, and truly established. Phenomena that are established as merely designated by thought are the opposite of that. They assert that both the dependent and the consummate are the former and the imaginary is the latter. In this system, unlike the other Mahāyāna proponents of tenets, in the context of delineating the view of the basis, there are two modes of refuting the object of negation based on what appears, respectively, to the conceptual and the nonconceptual. Describing those two objects of negation in terms of what is to be negated, later commentators coined the phrases "the object of negation based on the conceptual mental consciousness" and "the object of negation based on the nonconceptual sense consciousnesses," respectively. This or that phenomenon being established by the object's own reality as a basis to be engaged by words and thoughts that apply names for entities and attributes, as if they did not depend on the application of those names, is the measure of being established as a self of phenomena based on the conceptual mental consciousness. [260] On the other hand, phenomena such as form being established as entities distinct from the sense consciousnesses that apprehend them, and established as distant and cut off from them without being mere natures or factors of appearance to those sense consciousnesses, is the measure of being established as the self of phenomena based on the nonconceptual sense consciousnesses. These will be explained extensively in the fourth volume of *Science and Philosophy in the Indian Buddhist Classics*.

The Cittamātra Assertions on the Number of Consciousnesses

To explain the foundation consciousness, the abode of objects of knowledge, we first turn to the Cittamātra assertions on the number of consciousnesses. Among the various proponents of Buddhist tenets, there are those who assert one consciousness, two consciousnesses, six consciousnesses, seven consciousnesses, eight consciousnesses, and nine consciousnesses. To begin with the assertion of one consciousness: when a single consciousness, in dependence upon the individual sense faculties, moves to individual objects, it receives the name *individual consciousness*. This is like a single monkey looking out from the individual windows of a house. One might say: In that case, because one can hear a sound with the ear while seeing a form with the eye, one would have to posit a separate eye consciousness that apprehends form and an ear consciousness that apprehends sound. The proponent of the one consciousness would respond that when a single fire blazes in a house with many windows, light appears in each of the windows; in the same way, while a portion of that [single] consciousness is apprehending form, another part is apprehending sound. Thus the *Collection of Aphorisms* says:

> The formless one abides in the hollow place
> and travels alone and afar.
> The mind is to be tamed.[536]

This is saying that it is without a body or form, that it has the quality of being supported in the hollow or abode of the sense faculty, which is its support. It is asserted [that there is one mind] based on many such passages.

The primary proponent of a single consciousness was a sect of the śrāvaka school called the "bodhisattvas who say there is one consciousness." Vasubandhu's commentary on the *Compendium of the Mahāyāna* sets this forth, giving an example:

> Some bodhisattvas assert that there is only one consciousness. Their sequence will be set forth. They say that it is like referring to intention as physical and verbal actions. When intention enters through the door of the body, it is called *physical action*; through the door of speech, it is called *verbal action*; action of the mind is called *mental action*. [261] In the same way, when there is a single mental consciousness that acts in dependence on the eye, it receives the name *eye consciousness*. In the same way, it receives names up to *body consciousness*.[537]

Regarding this assertion of one consciousness, there are two positions: those who say that there is a single foundation consciousness and those who say that there is a single mental consciousness. Those who say that there is a single foundation consciousness are a subschool of Cittamātra. This is made clear in the Kashmiri scholar Lakṣmī's *Commentary on the Five Stages*, which says when setting forth the four assertions of the Yogācāra Cittamātra position, "Some assert only the foundation consciousness exists."[538]

When explaining the difference between True Aspectarians and False Aspectarians in his *Explanation of the Compendium on the Essence of Wisdom*, Bodhibhadra explains that among those who say that there is a single consciousness, there are both True Aspectarians and False Aspectarians, "Here, for Yogācāra, there are two types: those with aspect and those without aspect. That [consciousness] has an aspect is the assertion of such masters as Dignāga." He also says, "That it has no aspect [is the assertion of] such masters as Asaṅga." And, "Some say that there is a single [consciousness], and some of those say that the single [consciousness] has an aspect."[539] In the context of explaining the difference between True Aspectarians and False Aspectarians, this explains that among those who say there is one consciousness, there are also True Aspectarians and False Aspectarians.

Based on the treatise *Proof of Consciousness Only*,[540] the Indian master Bodhiruci posits two types of consciousness: the mind of reality and the associated mind. The first, the mind of reality (*dharmatā*), is asserted to be the nature of suchness, and although it is called *mind*, it has no object. The second, the associated mind, is asserted to be the mind associated with mental factors such as faith and desire. Furthermore, the *Extensive Commentary on the Explanation of the Intention* composed by the Korean master Wŏnch'ŭk says, "Based on the treatise *Proof of Consciousness Only*, the Indian master Bodhiruci posits two types of consciousness."[541]

Vaibhāṣika, Sautrāntika, Cittamātra Following Reasoning, Svātantrika Madhyamaka, and Prāsaṅgika Madhyamaka explain that there are six collections of consciousness. [262] The six collections are the eye consciousness, ear consciousness, nose consciousness, tongue consciousness, body consciousness, and mental consciousness. The *Meeting of Father and Son Sūtra* says:

> Great king, if you ask what are the constituents of consciousness, the eye sense faculty is the dominant [condition], form is the object of observation, and the cognition of individual forms [is the eye consciousness] . . . the cognition of sounds, the cognition of smells, the cognition of tastes, the cognition of objects of touch, or the cognition of phenomena, this is the ear consciousness constituent through to the mental consciousness constituent. Thus the six sense faculties are the dominant [condition] constituents, the six objects are the objects of observation constituents, and the cognitions of the objects are the consciousness constituents.[542]

The *Commentary on the Treasury of Abhidharma* says, "There are six collections of consciousness, from the eye consciousness to the mental consciousness."[543] Furthermore, in the Perfection of Wisdom sūtras, reality is delineated having divided consciousness into only six collections of consciousness. In the Hīnayāna sūtras, when the aggregates, constituents, and sources are delineated, they present only six consciousnesses as the consciousness aggregate, the mental source, and the mental constituent.

Turning to the reasoning behind the assertion that there are six collections of consciousness, Candrakīrti's *Extensive Commentary on the Four Hundred Verses* says, "The eye and so forth are the six sense faculties; form and so forth are the six objects in accordance with their nature. Due to [the number] of sense faculties and objects, there come to be six collections of consciousness."[544] He is saying that the uncommon dominant conditions of consciousness are determined to be six, from the eye sense faculty to the mental sense faculty. Their objects, from the form source to the phenomena source, are limited to six. Therefore the six collections of consciousness are determined to be six. From among those, the first five rely on an uncommon dominant condition of a physical sense faculty. The mental consciousness is produced in dependence on the uncommon dominant condition of the mental sense faculty.

As for the assertion of seven consciousnesses, the Kashmiri scholar Lakṣmī's *Commentary on the Five Stages* says, "Some assert that there is only the afflicted mental consciousness and the operative consciousnesses."[545] He explains here that they assert seven consciousnesses, adding the afflicted mental consciousness to the six operative consciousnesses. [263]

When Asaṅga and Vasubandhu distinguished between interpretable and definitive scriptures following the *Explanation of the Intention*, they presented eight collections of consciousness, adding the foundation consciousness and the afflicted mental consciousness to the six collections of consciousness. In Wŏnch'ŭk's *Extensive Commentary on the Explanation of the Intention* it is said that the Chinese monk Xuanzang asserted that there are eight collections of consciousness based on such sūtras as the *Descent into Laṅkā* and the works of Dharmapāla. Wŏnch'ŭk himself, following Xuanzang, asserted that there are eight collections of consciousness. Cittamātra Following Scripture asserts that when one searches for the object designated among the aggregates, which are the basis of designation, it must be posited that a person is found. Therefore they posit that the fruitional foundation consciousness is the support and explain that the predispositions on it are the foundation consciousness of the supported, the seeds. This will be explained in more detail below.

The Indian master Paramārtha asserted nine collections of consciousness. In addition to the six collections of consciousness, the seventh is the appropriating consciousness or afflicted mental consciousness, the eighth is the foundation consciousness, and the ninth is the stainless consciousness. Wŏnch'ŭk's *Extensive Commentary on the Explanation of the Intention* says, "Based on the treatise called the *Treasury of Ascertainment*, Paramārtha posited the meaning of nine consciousnesses."[546] The *Treasury of Ascertainment* (*Juedingzang lun*) appears to be [the *Viniścayasaṅgraha* from] Asaṅga's *Yogācāra Levels* translated into Chinese by Paramārtha. Wŏnch'ŭk's *Extensive Commentary on the Explanation of the Intention* says that because there is nothing in the *Yogācāra Levels* called the "Chapter on the Nine Consciousnesses," Paramārtha's explanation is not correct.

Regarding what this master calls the seventh, the *appropriating consciousness*, he asserts that someone who will not become a buddha is endowed with obstructions that are only afflicted, observing the foundation consciousness and apprehending it as "I" and "mine." The eighth, the foundation consciousness, is threefold. The first is the *foundation consciousness of nature*, which is asserted to be a consciousness endowed with the goal of achieving buddhahood. The second is the *fruitional foundation consciousness*, which observes the eighteen constituents. The third is the *thoroughly afflicted foundation consciousness*, which is described as a consciousness that, having observed the reality of its object, apprehends it as a self of phenomena. The ninth is the *stainless consciousness*, which is endowed with one nature of reality and two meanings. The first meaning is the reality that is the object to be observed, and the second meaning is the observer, called the *stainless consciousness*. [264] Wŏnch'ŭk's *Extensive Commentary* says that is also called the *primordial knower*.

The Support, the Fruitional Foundation Consciousness

Having briefly explained the different assertions about the number of consciousnesses that appear in Buddhist texts, the eight collections of consciousness asserted by Cittamātra will be explained in some detail. A crucial assumption behind the statement by Asaṅga and Vasubandhu that all phenomena are mind only is their acceptance of the foundation consciousness. When, for example, Asaṅga delineates the ten phenomena in his *Compendium of the Mahāyāna*, the first thing he sets forth is the abode of objects of knowledge, the causal foundation consciousness. Thus what is called the *foundation consciousness* is continuous and very stable; its nature is neutral, neither virtuous nor nonvirtuous; it is the basis from which the various external and internal experiences arise; it has existed from beginningless time and so is the fundamental consciousness that takes rebirth. The acceptance of such a foundation consciousness by Asaṅga, his brother Vasubandhu, and their followers is based primarily on some Mahāyāna sūtras. For example, the *Explanation of the Intention* says:

> The appropriating consciousness is profound and subtle.
> All the seeds flow like the current of a river.
> If one regards it as a self, that is wrong.
> I do not teach it to the childish.[547]

And the *Dense Array Sūtra* says:

> Just as the moon and collection of stars
> abide together in the sky,
> the consciousnesses and the foundation
> abide together in the body.[548]

This is saying that, for example, just as the moon and the collection of stars abide together in the sky, so the seven collections of consciousness—the six such as the eye consciousness as well as the afflicted mental consciousness—abide in the body together with the foundation consciousness.

In addition, the *Descent into Laṅkā Sūtra* says, "Because it infuses the many types of predispositions for taking on bad states, proliferating from beginningless time, it is known as the *foundation consciousness*."[549] [265] And the *Abhidharma Sūtra* cited in the *Compendium of the Mahāyāna* says:

> The sphere from beginningless time
> is the abode of all phenomena.[550]

The sphere (*dhātu*) or causal foundation consciousness, which has existed naturally in sentient beings from beginningless time, is the abode or foundation that infuses the seeds that establish all phenomena—virtuous, nonvirtuous, and neutral. They use such statements from the Mahāyāna sūtras as their sources.

One might ask what the object of observation is for the foundation consciousness. Vasubandhu's *Thirty Verses* says:

> That is the one whose appropriation and perception of abodes
> are not cognized.
> It always has contact, mental engagement,
> feeling, discrimination, and intention . . .
> It is unobstructed and neutral.[551]

This is setting forth four qualities of the foundation of consciousness: (1) the object of observation, (2) the aspect, (3) what accompanies it, and (4) its nature. It explains that there are three objects of observation of the foundation consciousness: the sense faculty, the object, and the predispositions (*vāsanā*). Its aspect is that, although the object appears to it, it does not understand it. The entity is unobstructed and neutral, and it is accompanied by the five omnipresent factors.

1) Regarding the objects of the foundation consciousness, it says, "That is the one whose appropriation and perception of abodes." This is saying that the predispositions for attachment to self and phenomena and the abodes—the five objects such as form and the worlds of the external environment—are the objects of observation of the foundation consciousness. The predispositions for verbalization appear to the foundation consciousness but do not become its object. However, through the power of those predispositions, the environments and inhabitants of the five sense faculties and the five objects appear to the foundation consciousness. Therefore it is explained that they are objects of observation of the foundation consciousness. Unconditioned phenomena merely come to be objects through being superimposed by the sixth, the mental consciousness. The foundation consciousness lacks the discrimination to discern objects in such a way as to designate various verbal conventions. Therefore unconditioned phenomena are not posited as objects of observation of the foundation consciousness.

2) Regarding the aspects, it says, "perception of abodes are not cognized." This is saying that although those environments and inhabitants are perceived—that is, appear clearly—they are not cognized, meaning the foundation consciousness itself is not able to ascertain them and is not able to remember them later.

3) Regarding what accompanies the foundation consciousness, it says, "It always has contact, mental engagement, feeling, discrimination, and intention." [266] The foundation consciousness always—as long as the force of fruition is not complete—arises concomitantly only with the five omnipresent factors that accompany it: contact, mental engagement, feeling, discrimination, and intention. "Feeling" in this case is only equanimity. Except for the five omnipresent factors that accompany the foundation consciousness, no other mental factors arise. Because the foundation consciousness is unobstructed and neutral, neither the virtues nor the root and secondary afflictions arise with it. Because it does not clearly distinguish the features of the object, the five determining factors [aspiration, belief, mindfulness, samādhi, and wisdom] also do not arise. Because what accompanies it must be something of a similar type and be something that arises uninterruptedly, the four changeable mental factors [investigation, analysis, regret, and sleep] also do not arise with it.

4) Regarding the nature of the foundation consciousness, it says, "It is unobstructed and neutral." The foundation consciousness is the basis for the infusing of virtuous and afflicted predispositions, and it arises simultaneously with manifest virtuous and nonvirtuous minds in the same continuum. Therefore they assert that it is unobstructed and neutral. Thus the definition of the *foundation consciousness* is the primary mental consciousness, which is very stable, serves as the basis for infusing the predispositions, and observes any of the three: the sense faculty, object, or predisposition; its aspect is unobstructed and neutral; and although both the sense faculty and the object appear to it, it does not ascertain them.

In general, *mind* (*citta*), *mental consciousness* (*manas*), and *consciousness* (*vijñāna*) are synonyms. However, if explained in terms of their etymology, the foundation consciousness is *mind* because it is the foundation of the accumulated predispostions; it is *fruitional consciousness* because it is the fruition of contaminated actions. The afflicted mental consciousness is *mind* because it constantly thinks "I" due to the power of beginningless habituation. The six operative consciousnesses are *consciousness* because they individually know the six objects, such as form. Thus each of the terms can be applied based on its respective context. Sthiramati's *Commentary on the Thirty Verses* says, "*Fructification* is the establishment of effects that are impelled by the power of the complete fruition of the predispositions of virtuous and nonvirtuous actions. Because the afflicted mental consciousness has a nature of constantly thinking 'I,' it is a mind thinking 'I.' Because objects such as form appear individually, the six consciousnesses such as the eye consciousness cognize objects."[552]

Because it is the foundation for infusing all the seeds of phenomena, it is the *foundation consciousness*. Because it holds on to the body, from the time one takes on a body in the place of rebirth until death, it is the *appropriating consciousness*. Vasubandhu's *Explanation of the First Dependent Origination and Its Divisions* says, "Why is this called the *foundation consciousness*? It is the foundation of the seeds of all phenomena. [267] It is also the *appropriating consciousness* because beginning from the moment of conception into a different body until death, it holds onto the body."[553]

Foundation consciousness is synonymous with *abode of objects of knowledge, keeper of all seeds, appropriating consciousness, root consciousness, aggregate that lasts as long as saṃsāra*, and *consciousness of the branches of existence*. The *Compendium of the Mahāyāna* says, "Therefore that which is the abode of objects of knowledge is described as the appropriating consciousness itself, mind itself, the foundation consciousness itself, the root consciousness itself, the aggregate that lasts as long as saṃsāra, and the consciousness of the branches of [cyclic] existence. That is the *foundation consciousness*. This establishes the great path of the foundation consciousness."[554] Because it is the abode of the three natures of objects of knowledge, it is the *abode of objects of knowledge*. Because it serves as the basis of all seeds, it is the *keeper of all seeds*. Because it appropriates the fruitional body, it is the *appropriating consciousness*. These are stated in the Mahāyāna scriptural collection. In the Mahāsāṅghika scriptures of the śrāvaka scriptural collection, it is stated that because it is the root of all afflicted phenomena, it is the *root consciousness*. In the Mahīśāsaka scriptures it is stated that because it operates as long as one is not liberated from saṃsāra, it is the *aggregate that lasts as long as saṃsāra*. In the Sthāvira scriptures, it is stated that because it serves as the cause of [cyclic] existence, it is the *consciousness of the branches of [cyclic] existence*. In the scriptures of the Sāṃmitīya, it is stated that because it is the fruition of contaminated actions, it is the *fruitional consciousness*. In the scriptures that are common to all the vehicles, it is stated that because it serves as the foundation of all of saṃsāra and nirvāṇa, it is the *foundation consciousness*. These are the synonyms.

Eight Reasonings That Prove the Existence of the Foundation Consciousness

In general, many reasonings that prove the existence of the foundation consciousness appear in the Cittamātra texts. When the most important reasonings are collected, there are eight. They say that if the foundation consciousness did not exist, there would be eight consequences: (1) it would be impossible to take on a body, (2) it would be impossible for [one consciousness] to exist primordially, or initially, (3) clarity [of consciousness] would be impossible, (4) seeds would be impossible, (5) actions would be impossible, (6) the experience of bodily feelings would be impossible, (7) the mindless absorptions would be impossible, and (8) transmigrating from one life to another would be impossible. The *Compendium of Ascertainments* says:

> Taking, beginning, clarity,
> seeds, action, bodily feeling,
> the mindless absorptions,
> and death and rebirth would be illogical.
> The existence of the foundation consciousness
> is understood for these eight reasons.[555] [268]

Yaśomitra's *Elucidation of the Compendium of Abhidharma* similarly says, "The existence of a consciousness that appropriates thoroughly should be understood through eight points. Without a consciousness that appropriates everything, taking on a body would be impossible; arising primordially would be impossible; clarity would be impossible; seeds would be impossible; action would be impossible; bodily experience would be impossible; the mindless absorptions would be impossible; and if [such] consciousness did not exist, death and rebirth would be impossible."[556]

First, if the foundation consciousness did not exist, taking on a body would be impossible. In general, if a consciousness is the kind that takes rebirth, it cannot be the kind that sometimes exists in one's continuum and sometimes does not exist; it must have all the qualities, such as operating uninterruptedly from the moment of conception until death. Because the six collections of consciousness do not have all those qualities, they are not suitable to take rebirth; the foundation consciousness has all those qualities. If the foundation consciousness did not exist, it would not be tenable to posit the existence of the afflicted mental consciousness, which has the aspect of observing it and then thinking "I." The ability to newly take on a body would not exist.

Second, someone might object, "If you accept the existence of a foundation consciousness, because the foundation consciousness operates in one's continuum continually and any of the six consciousnesses can arise in one's continuum occasionally, there would be the fault that two consciousnesses would be manifest in the continuum of a single person simultaneously." If it were impossible for two streams of consciousness to arise simultaneously in a single person, there would be this fault. However, consider this example: the six sense faculties exist together in the continuum of a single person, and the six objects, such as form, also exist together. When it is feasible for intentions such as "I want to see that" and "I want to hear that" to operate equally, it would not be feasible for one among the six collections of consciousness to be produced before another. To that, [the opponent] might object because a sūtra says, "The arising of two consciousnesses at once is not possible and does not occur." However, there is no fault because this means that two consciousnesses of the same type are not explicitly produced simultaneously.

Third, if two consciousnesses do not arise simultaneously, then there would be the fault that, for example, when an eye consciousness that directly sees shapes and colors becomes manifest, a clear mental consciousness in the continuum of the person who recognizes those shapes and colors would not arise. [269] Furthermore, for such a mental consciousness the aspect of the object would be clear, but for the mental consciousness that remembers the past object that has been experienced earlier by the eye consciousness apprehending form, the aspect of the object would not be clear.

Fourth, for the six collections of consciousness, nonvirtue arises after virtue, and virtue arises after nonvirtue. One wanes, even for a long time, and then arises at some other time, and its continuity is unsteady. Therefore only the foundation consciousness is the foundation for infusing the predispositions. If there were no foundation consciousness, there would be no foundation for infusing the seeds of such things as virtue and nonvirtue, and so even the seeds would not exist.

Fifth, if such things as where one is going, the goer, and the act of going did not appear as objects of the mind, there would be no way to perform actions such as going to another place. If two consciousnesses did not exist simultaneously, when going to another place the various awarenesses of the route to follow, moving one's feet, thinking "I," and seeing earth and rocks would not exist simultaneously. Therefore there would be the fault that actions such as going and staying would be impossible. It is proven by experience that these perceptions arise simultaneously in each moment, and it is not feasible to perceive those phenomena that are different entities in a single moment of consciousness.

Sixth, if the foundation consciousness did not exist, then at the time of such things as focusing the mind one-pointedly on another object or falling into deep sleep, there would be no foundation that holds the seeds that produce physical feelings of pleasure and pain. Therefore, when the body is benefited or harmed at those times, it would not be tenable to experience feelings of physical pleasure or pain.

Seventh, if the foundation consciousness is not accepted, it would follow that the body of a person abiding in either of the two highest of the four absorptions of the formless realm in which all six operative consciousnesses have ceased would be a corpse, because the six collections of consciousness are absent and the foundation consciousness does not exist. There would be the fault that this contradicts the statement by the Bhagavan: "Their consciousness is not separated from the body."

Someone might say, "Because an unmanifest form of the sixth mental consciousness exists in the continuum of those in the two absorptions, there is no fault that their bodies lack all consciousness and no fault of contradicting that sūtra." That is infeasible because if there were an unmanifest form of the sixth mental consciousness, there would have to be contact from the coming together of the three: the object, the sense faculty, and the consciousness. If that existed, feeling and discrimination would also exist, meaning that it would be untenable for those two absorptions to be absorptions in which discrimination and feeling have ceased. One might wonder, "Even if one accepts the foundation consciousness at that time, because the accompanying feeling and discrimination exist, it would be untenable for those two absorptions to be absorptions in which discrimination and feeling have ceased." [270] However, because the feeling and discrimination that accompany the six collections of consciousness are coarse, they cease in absorption. The two that accompany the foundation consciousness are much subtler than that and therefore do not cease in absorption.

Eighth, when we die, a single consciousness gradually gathers warmth and feeling from the individual parts of the body. From that point, one must die, and the consciousnesses of the five sense doors are not able to gather warmth and feeling. If they were, because those consciousnesses abide in various parts of the body, it would absurdly follow that warmth and feeling would gather where they are not present, just as it would absurdly follow that even fainting would be death. The mental consciousness does not abide in just a particular part of the body, as the sense consciousnesses do. However, it also does not remain steady in the sense of pervading the body the way that the foundation consciousness does. Therefore the act of gradually gathering the warmth of the body at the time of death is also not performed by the mental consciousness. If it were, the mere presence of the mental consciousness would prevent the gathering of the warmth of the body, which would mean that no gathering of warmth would take place until the severing of the life force itself. However, prior to the point of death, while the mental consciousness clearly exists, the gathering of warmth is established by direct perception. Therefore, through the force of the reasoning that refutes other possibilities, if the foundation consciousness did not exist, death and rebirth from the perspective of the gradual gathering of the warmth and feeling of the body would be infeasible.

Thus, among the eight main reasonings proving the existence of the foundation consciousness that have been summarized and set forth here, the three consequences of the infeasibility of being first, the infeasibility of clarity, and the infeasibility of action are reasonings that dispel the main refutation of the foundation consciousness by its opponents, which is that it contradicts the scripture that says, "For sentient beings, the continuums of their consciousness are singular." The other five are the actual reasonings that prove the existence of the foundation consciousness.

In summary, the most important reason why Cittamātra Following Scripture, such as Asaṅga and his brother, accept the foundation consciousness is this: one must posit a foundation for actions and effects, a referent of the person that continues from one lifetime to the next. The six collections of consciousness, such as the eye consciousness, are coarse, and their continuity is unstable. Because they do not exist at conception, it is not tenable that they can take rebirth and serve as the basis for the infusing of predispositions. Without another basis for seeds, if one did not assert a foundation consciousness, all the seeds of virtue and nonvirtue would become spoiled. Considering this, they accept the existence of a consciousness, separate from the six collections of consciousness, that makes the connection between lifetimes and serves as the basis of virtue and sin, called the foundation consciousness. [271]

The Foundation Consciousness of the Supported Seeds

We now turn to the definition of the seeds, or predispositions. As was discussed above, there is the *fruitional foundation consciousness*, which is the support, and the *foundation consciousness of the seeds*, which are supported on it. What is called the *foundation consciousness of the supported seeds* is seeds or predispositions deposited there that arise from any of the fifteen cognizances (*vijñapti*), among which are the cognizances of the body, the embodied, and the consumer; the cognizance of the enjoyer; and the cognizances of time, number, place, and verbal conventions.[557] What is called a *predisposition* in this context is a potency that is deposited by a consciousness; the place where predispositions are deposited is the foundation consciousness. Like pouring oil onto sand or stamping a seal on paper, predispositions are infused or deposited onto the foundation consciousness, the basis of infusing. The phrases "predispositions deposited by consciousness," "internal seeds deposited by consciousness," "potencies deposited by consciousness," and "foundation consciousness of the supported seeds" have a similar meaning. Among form, consciousness, and nonassociated compositional factors, predispositions are nonassociated compositional factors. Among virtuous, nonvirtuous, and neutral, they are neutral. Between substantially existent and imputedly existent, they are imputedly existent.

Asvabhāva's *Explanation of the Compendium of the Mahāyāna* says, "What is called a *predisposition* is a type of potency. A potency and that which possesses the potency are not said to be the same or different. To ask whether they are different or not different from each other is not appropriate because [potency] is imputed on the basis of serving as the cause of what it empowers."[558] That which possesses the potency, the foundation consciousness, is substantially existent, and the potency is something imputedly existent that is imputed to it. Therefore it is said that the potency and that which possesses the potency are neither the same nor different substantial entities. Thus this statement that the two—the predispositions and the foundation consciousness that is their support—are neither the same nor different substances appears to be a mode of analysis that is not the usual case of *merely* not being the same or different substances; rather it is not being the same or different substances in the sense of substantial existence.

Regarding how to understand the meaning of *predisposition*, Vasubandhu's *Condensed Explanation Revealing the Secret Meaning* says:

> Concerning predispositions, it is asked, "What is it that is called *predispositions*?" There are two questions to consider: "What do predispositions conform with?" and "What are predispositions?" The foundation consciousness, that is, the infused, is produced and ceases at the same time as the phenomena that infuse it. Those phenomena that infuse serve as causes that produce the future. They are the predispositions. For example, in the world, when sesame seeds are touched by a flower, the seeds smell like that [flower] because they are produced and cease at the same time. Or, for example, in the treatise, predisposition is a reason for producing similar minds that are produced and cease at the same time, such as a desire that is concordant with the afflicted class and learning, [272] which includes mindfulness, wisdom, and so forth that are concordant with the pure class.[559]

If the nature and function of predispositions are explained in terms of how they give rise to effects from the accumulation of actions, they are easy to understand. *Action* (*karma*) is posited as an act of an agent engaging with an object. The performance of any good or evil movement of our body, speech, or mind accumulates an action. That action places various good and evil predispositions on our mind, which will manifest as various effects of happiness and suffering in the future. If this is illustrated with an action like murder, when that action is accumulated, that action has two potencies: a potency that is the cause for the fruition of a negative effect in the future, and a potency that becomes the substantial continuum of that action, even though the action itself has ceased. Regardless of the action, whether benefit or harm are induced immediately, a potential is definitely transferred to the mind. Therefore the potency that is placed by the mind has a power to subsequently produce a mind that is similar in type to that mind that produced it as well as a power to produce an effect that is different from that mind. For example, the fragrance of incense remains in an incense vase even when there is no incense in it.

What is called the *foundation consciousness of the supported seeds* is a potency that is deposited in the foundation consciousness, the basis of infusing, by the seven collections of consciousness that infuse, together with what accompanies them, to subsequently produce similar versions of themselves when they are beginning to cease. It also refers to any capacity that will produce such things as fruitional effects. Infusing takes place due to the basis and the infusers themselves being produced and ceasing at the same time.

How the Predispositions Are Infused

When sesame seeds and a fragrant flower are placed next to each other, the fragrance of the flower remains on the sesame seeds even after the flower is gone. In the same way, when the infused and the infuser are brought together in a single continuum, later, even though the infuser has ceased, its predispositions remain on the basis of infusing. The *Compendium of the Mahāyāna* says, "When one speaks of *predispositions*, it refers to the cause for something to arise in dependence on having arisen and ceased at the same time as that phenomenon. [273] For example, when sesame seeds are infused by a flower, the sesame seeds and the flower arise at the same time; although [the flower] has ceased, it serves as a cause of the sesame seeds having a different fragrance."[560]

It is asserted that the foundation consciousness that is the basis of infusing must have five qualities: (1) stability, (2) neutrality, (3) suitability to be infused, (4) connection to infusing, and (5) being the absolute support.

1) Regarding *stability*, it must be constantly stable, like a stone that is the basis of infusing by the fragrance of a flower; even though it is infused,

the fragrance will not form on something unstable, like the sound of the last clap of thunder. Even if it were to form, it would spoil. The seven collections of consciousness are not suitable as the basis for infusing virtuous, nonvirtuous, or neutral predispositions. As for the six operative consciousnesses, when coarse forms of consciousness have ceased, they no longer exist, such as when one falls into deep sleep or faints. Because the afflicted mental consciousness does not exist when one enters the absorption of cessation (*nirodhasamāpatti*), it is not constantly stable.

2) Regarding *neutrality*, for example, the fragrance of a flower can infuse something that has a neutral fragrance, like sesame seeds; it cannot infuse something with a distinctive fragrance, like garlic or sandalwood. In the same way, like something with a neutral fragrance, [the foundation consciousness] can be infused with predispositions because it is neutral. Like something with a distinctive fragrance, a virtuous or nonvirtuous [foundation consciousness] could not be infused with predispositions.

3) Regarding the *suitability* to be infused, if the basis for infusing predispositions must be stable and neutral, does what is infused need to be an unconditioned phenomenon? For example, something that is impermanent that can hold the fragrance of a flower can be infused. Something that is permanent, which can perform no action at all, such as holding a fragrance, is not able to be infused. In the same way, the [consciousness] must be impermanent to be suitable for predispositions to be infused; if it were permanent, it would not be suitable for them to be infused.

4) Regarding *connection to infusing*, it is not enough for the basis of infusing simply to be impermanent. For example, the fragrance of flowers can infuse sesame seeds in a single vessel when they have the connection of being produced and ceasing at the same time; the fragrance of a flower in the east that is not connected in that way cannot infuse sesame seeds far away in the south. In the same way, the seven collections that infuse that have the connection of being produced and ceasing at the same time in the same mental continuum can infuse predispositions on the foundation consciousness that is the basis of infusing. The seven collections of a person named Devadatta are not able to infuse predispositions on the foundation consciousness of Yajñadatta. Also, even in the same mental continuum, the consciousness of yesterday is not capable of infusing predispositions on the consciousness of today, given that it lacks the connection of being produced and ceasing at the same time. [274]

5) Regarding *being the absolute support,* for example, a minister who is appointed by the king as the ruler of a particular region of the country is not the absolute ruler of the country. In the same way, the feeling and so forth that accompany the foundation consciousness must rely on the foundation consciousness. Therefore they are not suitable to be the basis of infusing. The foundation consciousness is the basis for the infusing of predispositions through its own power. Therefore it is asserted to be the absolute support of the predispositions.

Yogācāra masters make three assertions regarding how predispositions are deposited in general. (1) There are those who assert that they are merely sustained due to the ancient naturally abiding predispositions themselves, without relying on being deposited through infusing. (2) There are those who assert that predispositions are only newly deposited through infusing. (3) There are those who accept that there are both predispositions sustained by the naturally abiding predispositions and newly deposited predispositions that did not exist before. To consider these in sequence, Vasubandhu's commentary on the *Compendium of the Mahāyāna,* called *Condensed Explanation Revealing the Secret Meaning,* says, "Regarding this, there are three ideas. Some say that predispositions do not rely on infusing but abide naturally. Because desire and so forth are produced and cease at the same time, [prediposition] are simply sustained; they are not produced." He goes on to say, "Others, seeing that predispositions rely on infusing, like sesame seeds [by a flower], assert that predispositions that did not exist before are produced through infusing and that those produced earlier are sustained through infusing." And, "Yet others assert that there are predispositions that abide naturally and are sustained and that there are also newly produced [predispositions] that did not exist before."[561]

Among these assertions, if one accepts that there are only predispositions that abide naturally, then in this lifetime there would be no way to deposit predispositions through such things as maintaining ethics and giving gifts, rendering them pointless. Therefore such a position is untenable. If one accepts that predispositions are newly deposited through infusing, then there would be no seeds in the naturally abiding mind that do not depend on infusing. Thus, in this system, it is asserted that one must accept both predispositions that are newly deposited and predispositions that abide naturally.

Divisions of Predispositions

Among the many ways of dividing the foundation consciousness of what are called the seeds, the supported, or the predispositions on the foundation consciousness, there is a division into six, a division into three, and two different divisions into four. [275]

The division into six is a division that does not differentiate between the actual predispositions and what are designated as predispositions: (1) *external seeds*, such as wheat and barley, and (2) *internal seeds*, the predispositions on the foundation consciousness. Because it is not evident whether those two are virtuous or nonvirtuous, they are called, respectively, (3) *external seeds that are not evident* and (4) *internal seeds that are not evident*. Also, those two are respectively called (5) *conventional seeds* because they merely appear and (6) *ultimate seeds* because they are final seeds. External and internal seeds that are not evident and ultimate and conventional seeds are not categories separate from external and internal seeds. With respect to their nature, in the context of external and internal seeds that are not evident and what is merely seen and renowned without being examined or analyzed, such things as barley and rice are called *seeds*. However, in reality, external and internal phenomena such as sprouts of barley and rice are established through the power of the fruition of predispositions on the foundation consciousness; without depending on the fruition of internal predispositions, the arising of such things as sprouts would be impossible. Therefore, if this is analyzed well, the final seeds of effects must be taken to be the seeds on the foundation consciousness. In that case, both conventional and ultimate seeds are posited in relation to the mind. Regarding the division of predispositions into six, the *Compendium of the Mahāyāna* says:

> External and internal, the two that are nonevident,
> and conventional and ultimate:
> together those are asserted to be
> the six types of seeds.[562]

These are discussed extensively in this text and its commentaries.

The division into three occurs from the perspective of the effects of predispositions; there are: (1) predispositions of verbal expressions, (2) predispositions of the view of self, and (3) predispositions of the branches of existence. The *Compendium of the Mahāyāna* says, "Since there are three types of predispositions, these are the three: the type of predisposition of verbal expression, the type of predisposition of the view of self, and the type of predisposition of the branches of existence."[563] The first are predispositions deposited by thought. The second are predispositions deposited by the conception of the self of persons, such as the afflicted mental consciousness. The third are predispositions deposited by virtuous and nonvirtuous actions.

Turning to the differences among those three types of predispositions, (1) what are called *predispositions of verbal expressions* are predispositions that serve as the cause for applying verbal conventions, such as "This is this" for phenomena. [276] It is also called *predispositions of elaboration in terms of being the seeds* because it causes the mental consciousness to engage with various objects. For example, it is the predispositions that serve as the cause of designating various verbal conventions such as "This is yellow" and "This is blue."

(2) What are called the *predispositions of the view of self* are predispositions that constantly produce the thought "I." Because they are the predispositions that produce the view of the perishable collection, they are also called *predispositions of the view of the perishable collection*. For example, due to the power of predispositions of the view of self, phenomena appear to be external objects separate from one's own mind, appearing from the object's own side, whereas in fact such appearances do not arise from an external object but arise in dependence on predispositions in one's own mind. Without those predispositions, although an object might exist in front of oneself, one would not be able to induce such an appearance.

(3) The predisposition that serves as the cause of the birth and death of transmigrating beings is called the *predisposition of the branches of existence*. Because fruitions arise through the power of the ripening of this predisposition, it is also called the *predisposition of fruition*. Through the power of that predisposition, these various forms of good and bad rebirth and of happiness and suffering arise.

If one were to clearly explain those three predispositions using examples, by labeling, such as "This is wood" and "This is water," they come to appear in such a way that one thinks that they are wood and water. This arises in dependence on predispositions of verbal expressions. After that appearance has arisen, one's mind comes to perceive that name not as imputed to an external object by one's mind but as established from the object's own side. This perception arises through the power of the predispositions of the view of self. Based on that appearance, one engages with various objects and accumulates a variety of good and evil actions, and based on the predispositions of those actions, the rebirths and the happiness and suffering of transmigrating beings are established. That arises through the power of the predispositions of the branches of existence.

The fifteen cognizances are established from those three predispositions. Nine cognizances—of the body, the embodied, the consumer, the enjoyed, the enjoyer, time, number, place, and verbal convention—arise from the predispositions of verbal expressions. Two cognizances—of self and of other—arise from the predispositions of the view of self. Four cognizances—of good rebirth, bad rebirth, death, and birth—arise from the predispositions of the branches of existence. The *Compendium of the Mahāyāna* says:

> The cognizances of the body, the embodied, and the consumer, the cognizance of what is enjoyed, the cognizance of the enjoyer, and the cognizances of time, number, place, and verbal convention arise from the seeds of predispositions of verbal expressions. The cognizances of the distinction between self and other arise from the seeds of the predispositions of the view of self. The cognizances of good rebirth, bad rebirth, death, and birth arise from the seeds of the predispositions of the branches of existence.[564] [277]

Regarding these fifteen cognizances, cognizance of the body consists of the five constituents (*dhātu*) such as the eye sense faculty; cognizance of the embodied is the afflicted mental consciousness; cognizance of the consumer consists of the mind; the cognizance of what is enjoyed by the mind consists of the six such as external form; the cognizance of the enjoyer consists of the six consciousnesses. The cognizance of time is the uninterrupted continuity of saṃsāra; one, ten, and so forth is the cognizance of number; the worldly environment is the cognizance of place; cognizance of the verbal conventions is the four of seeing, hearing, making distinctions, and consciousness. The perception of self and what belongs to self is the cognizance of what appears as self. The perception of other and what belongs to other is the cognizance of what appears as other. The cognizance of a good rebirth is, for example, being a human, and the cognizance of a bad rebirth is, for example, being an animal. The dependent arising of death is the cognizance of death. The dependent arising of birth is the cognizance of birth. Thus Vasubandhu's *Commentary on the Compendium of the Mahāyāna* says:

> Regarding what are called the *cognizances of the body, the embodied*, and *the consumer*, that of the body is the five such as the eye; that of the embodied is the afflicted mental consciousness; and that of the consumer is the mind. The *cognizance of what is enjoyed by them* is the six such as external form. The *cognizance of the enjoyer* is the six consciousnesses. The *cognizance of time* is the uninterrupted continuity of saṃsāra. The *cognizance of number* is enumeration. The *cognizance of place* is the worldly environment. The *cognizance of verbal convention* is the four conventions: what is seen, what is heard, what is known, and what is conceived. Here, these [nine] cognizances, which are taught to be the abodes of objects of knowledge, have as their cause the predispositions for verbal expression. The cause of the specific basis of the *cognizance that distinguishes between self and other* is the predispositions for the view of self. The *cognizances of good rebirth*, of *bad rebirth*, of *death*, and of *rebirth* are the various realms in saṃsāra; they arise from appropriating the seeds that are the predispositions of the branches of existence.[565] [278]

The phrase "what is known" above, discussing the four verbal conventions, has a meaning similar to "making distinctions" among the four verbal conventions set forth in the *Explanation of the Intention*. What is called the *cognizance* of these phenomena means that they are merely appearances to the mind.

Third, there are two ways to divide seeds into groups of four. The first group of four is a division from the perspective of how the world of environments and inhabitants is established, and includes: (1) shared seeds, (2) unshared seeds, (3) seeds with feeling, and (4) seeds without feeling. The *Compendium of the Mahāyāna* says:

> Regarding the division [of seeds] in terms of their characteristics, there are those that have the shared characteristics, those that have the unshared characteristics, those that have the characteristic of arising without feelings, and those that have the characteristic of arising with feelings. The *shared* are the seeds of the worldly environment. The *unshared* are the seeds of the sources (*āyatana*) of individuals. That which is *shared* are seeds of what arises without feelings. When the antidotes arise, they oppose the unshared only.[566]

The seeds on the foundation consciousness that establish the worldly environment that is used commonly by living beings are *shared seeds*. These are the seeds that produce the insentient external world. The seeds on the foundation consciousness that establish the six sources such as the eye source, which are used in an unshared way by individuals, are *unshared seeds*. These are the seeds that produce the sentient internal world. Therefore, the former two types of seeds [the shared and unshared] are not different from the latter two [those without feeling and those with feeling].

The second group of four are: (1) the seeds for perpetuating bad states, (2) the seeds of purification, (3) the seeds of what has already been experienced, and (4) the seeds of what has not already been experienced. The *Compendium of the Mahāyāna* says, "There is the characteristic of perpetuating bad states and the characteristic of purification. The characteristic of perpetuating bad states are the seeds of the afflictions and the secondary afflictions. The characteristic of purification are the seeds of contaminated virtuous phenomena." It goes on, "There are characteristics of what has already been done and not done. The characteristic of what has already been done are virtuous and nonvirtuous seeds that have already borne fruit. The characteristic of what has not been done are the seeds of the predispositions for verbal expression—that is, the seeds that have produced elaborations since beginningless time."[567]

1) The seeds for perpetuating bad states are, for example, the seeds of the primary afflictions and secondary afflictions. [279] Because those seeds are the seeds that cause the perpetuation of bad states of rebirth or because they are seeds that cause the mind to be unserviceable, they are called *seeds for perpetuating bad states*.

2) Seeds of purification are seeds of the ten virtues, such as faith and conscientiousness, in the continuum of ordinary worldly beings. Because these are seeds for the pliancy or cultivation of the mind or because they are seeds that cause the mind to be serviceable, they are called *seeds of purification.*

3) Seeds of what have already been experienced are the seeds of virtuous and nonvirtuous actions that have already essentially borne the fruit of their respective effects. Because they will not fructify again, they are called *seeds of what has already been done.*

4) *Seeds of what has not already been experienced* refers to predispositions for verbal expressions that designate mental conventions to phenomena, such as thinking "this" and "that." These are not the opposite of the seeds of what has already been experienced. These seeds cannot become exhuasted simply through being experienced until the error of the dualistic appearance of apprehended and apprehender has ceased, and so they are called *seeds of what has not already been experienced.*

The Afflicted Mental Consciousness

This system asserts that there are eight collections of consciousness, adding the afflicted mental consciousness to the foundation consciousness and the six operative consciousnesses. What is called the *afflicted mental consciousness* (*kliṣṭamanas*) is posited to be a mind that views the foundation consciousness abiding in the same continuum, constantly apprehending it and thinking "I" and "mine." The *Thirty Verses* says:

> That which observes it is called *mind.*
> It is the consciousness that has the nature of thinking "I."
> It is always accompanied by
> four obstructed but neutral afflictions:
> view of self, delusion of self,
> pride in self, and attachment to self.
> . . . and contact and so forth.[568]

This is explaining four qualities of the afflicted mental consciousness: its object of observation, aspect, entity, and accompaniers. (1) The *object of observation* of the afflicted mental consciousness is the foundation consciousness. (2) Its *aspect* is observing the foundation consciousness and constantly thinking "I" and "mine." (3) Its *entity* has the nature of being obstructed but neutral. (4) Its *accompaniers* are the four root afflictions—view of self, ignorance, pride, and desire that is obstructed and neutral—and the five omnipresent factors are said to be concurrent with it. [280] In addition, it is always accompanied by—in the sense of being concurrent with—the five concurrences with the six secondary afflictions: the distraction that is imputed to wrong view; the lack of faith, the laziness, and the lethargy that are imputed to obscuration; the excitement that is imputed to desire; and the nonconscientiousness that is imputed to desire and obscuration. These are clearly set forth in the *Explanation of the Thirty Verses* composed by Sthiramati, which says, "'That which observes it' means that it has just the foundation consciousness as its object of observation. Because it is concurrent with the view of the perishable collection and so forth, it observes the foundation consciousness as 'I' and 'mine.'"[569] That same text says:

> To the question of its nature, the verse says, "It has the nature to think [of the foundation consciousness] as I." Because of its nature thinking "I," etymologically it is called *mind*. Because it is of the nature of consciousness, it must be concurrent with mental factors, but for which mental factors, how many, and for how long is difficult to understand. Therefore the verse says, "It is always accompanied by four obstructed but neutral afflictions." The mental factors are of two types: the afflicted and what is other than that. In order to differentiate them from what is other than that, the verse says "afflictions." Although there are six afflictions, because it is not concurrent with all of them, the verse says "four." "Accompanied" means concurrent. Afflictions are of two types: the nonvirtuous and the obstructed but neutral. To differentiate them from the nonvirtuous, the verse says "obstructed but neutral." An obstructed consciousness is not concurrent with the nonvirtues because the obstructed is afflicted. "Neutral" means not set forth in the scriptures as virtuous or non-virtuous. "Always" means at all times. As long as it exists, it will be concurrent with them.[570] [281]

The Scriptures and Reasonings That Prove the Existence of the Afflicted Mental Consciousness

Several sūtras mention the afflicated mental consciousness. For example, the *Dense Array Sūtra* says:

> The mind is the foundation consciousness.
> It has the nature of thinking of it as "I."[571]

Because it is the foundation for the accumulation of predispositions, the foundation consciousness is called *mind*. Because it constantly thinks of it as "I," the afflicted mental consciousness is called *mental consciousness*. The *Descent into Laṅkā* says:

> The nature of mind is pure;
> it is the mental consciousness that sullies.[572]

The pure nature of the mind is not penetrated by defilements. However, it is sullied temporarily by the afflicted mental consciousness. The sūtras cited above that set forth the foundation consciousness also set forth the afflicted mental consciousness.

Turning to the reasonings that prove the existence of the afflicted mental consciousness, the *Compendium of the Mahāyāna* provides six reasonings. The first reasoning is that if the afflicted mental consciousness did not exist, unadulterated ignorance would not exist. If the afflicted mental consciousness did not exist, there would be no ignorance that is the unadulterated basis that is constantly manifest in ordinary beings, because the foundation consciousness is not suitable to be afflicted and because the continuity of six operative consciousnesses is unstable. Because this ignorance only accompanies its basis, the afflicted mental consciousness, it is called the *unadulterated basis*. Furthermore, because this unadulterated ignorance is a mental factor, it must be concurrent with a main mind. Because it is an affliction, it is not concurrent with the foundation consciousness. Because it is continuous, without interruption, as long as the pure object is not directly perceived, it is not concurrent with the six collections of consciousness. Therefore, among the eight collections of consciousness, it is proved by reasoning that it must be concurrent only with the afflicted mental consciousness. The consequence is thus inescapable: if the main afflicted mental consciousness did not exist, the unadulterated ignorance that accompanies it would not exist. The *Compendium of the Mahāyāna* says, "What is the evidence of the existence of that afflicted mental consciousness? There is the fault that, if it did not already exist, unadulterated ignorance would not exist."[573]

The second reasoning that proves the existence of the afflicted mental consciousness is that if the afflicted mental consciousness did not exist, there would be the fault that [the mental consciousness] would not be similar to the five other consciousnesses. If the afflicted mental consciousness did not exist, although the five sense consciousnesses each have an individual sense faculty, the mental consciousness would lack a basis that is unique and is simultaneously arisen. The *Compendium of the Mahāyāna* says, "There would be the fault that [the mental consciousness] would not be similar to the five, in the way that the eye and so forth are the abodes for the simultaneous arising of the five collections of consciousness."[574]

The third reasoning is that if the afflicted mental consciousness did not exist, there would be the fault that there would be no difference in pacification in the two highest absorptions of the formless realm. At the time of the absorption of cessation (*nirodhasamāpatti*), one is concordant with peace due to the absence of the afflicted mental consciousness. [282] At the time of the absorption of no discrimination (*asaṃjñisamāpatti*) in which the six operative consciousnesses have ceased, one is not concordant with peace due to the presence of the afflicted mental consciousness. If the afflicted mental consciousness did not exist, it would not be possible to distinguish these states based on whether they are peaceful. The *Compendium of the Mahāyāna* says, "There would be the fault that there would be no difference between the absorption of no discrimination and the absorption of cessation. The absorption of no discrimination is distinguished by having the afflicted mental consciousness; the absorption of cessation is not. Otherwise these two could not be distinguished from each other."[575]

The fourth reasoning is that if the afflicted mental consciousness did not exist, there would be the fault that the contextual etymology—because it constantly thinks of it as "I," it is called *mind*—would not apply to any consciousness. If the afflicted mental consciousness did not exist, there would be no thought of "I" with respect to the foundation consciousness and the sense consciousnesses. Although the thought "I" would accompany the mental consciousness, it would not be constant. Therefore there would be the fault that the contextual etymology (*nirukti*)—because it constantly thinks of it as "I," it is called *mind*—would not apply to any consciousness. The *Compendium of the Mahāyāna* says, "There would be the fault of no contextual etymology."[576]

The fifth reasoning is that if the afflicted mental consciousness did not exist, there would be the fault that those reborn in the absorption of no discrimination would not have the conception of "I." If the afflicted mental consciousness did not exist, there would be the fault that there would be no conception of "I" or pride thinking "I" in the minds of persons born in the absorption of no discrimination, whose minds lack coarse feeling and discrimination. The *Compendium of the Mahāyāna* says, "If the conception of 'I' and pride thinking 'I' did not exist in those in the absorption of no discrimination, there would be the fault that as long as they are reborn in the absorption of no discrimination, they would not have the afflictions."[577]

The sixth reasoning is that if the afflicted mental consciousness did not exist, there would be the fault of not being able to account for the constant arising of thought, "I am." If the afflicted mental consciousness did not exist, the conception of "I" would never arise in the motivations of ordinary beings to perform virtuous and neutral deeds. For example, in all virtuous thoughts such as "I will cultivate loving kindness," nonvirtuous thoughts such as "I will commit murder," and neutral thoughts such as "I will eat food," it is known through experience that the conception of "I" is present. If the afflicted mental consciousness did not exist, the conception of "I" would be concurrent only with nonvirtuous thoughts. Therefore it would not be tenable for it to occur simultaneously with virtuous and neutral thoughts. Considering that the afflicted mental consciousness does exist, it is fitting for the conception of "I" to accompany the afflicted mental consciousness. Because the afflicted mental consciousness is itself neutral, it is not contradictory for it to operate simultaneously with all virtuous and nonvirtuous thoughts and their concomitant mental factors. [283] The *Compendium of the Mahāyāna* says, "In all virtuous, nonvirtuous, and neutral thoughts, the conception of 'I' is always observed to arise. Otherwise, because it would be concurrent with only nonvirtuous thoughts, the afflicted thought of 'I' would not be [concurrent] with virtuous and neutral thoughts that arise."[578]

How They Prove Mind Only

The general explanation above of the assertions of this school were drawn from a rough summary in Bodhibhadra's *Explanation of the Compendium on the Essence of Wisdom*. As stated there, the ultimate existence of consciousness, empty of object and subject, must be posited as the foundational tenet of this system. Based on this, Cittamātra is widely renowned as those who declare that external objects do not exist and that all phenomena are established as mind only or cognition only (*vijñaptimātra*). There are two traditions regarding how all phenomena are established as cognition only: Cittamātra Following Scripture, whose proponents include Asaṅga and his brother Vasubandhu, and Cittamātra Following Reasoning, whose proponents include Dignāga and his heir Dharmakīrti. Cittamātra Following Scripture—as was detailed above in the context of the explanation of the foundation consciousness—state that the various appearances of environments and beings, such as what appear to be external objects, arise from the fruition of seeds, the supported, on fruitional foundation consciousness, the support. Therefore they say that all of those are cognition only. For example, after identifying each of the fifteen cognizances and explaining how they arise from the three predispositions, the *Compendium of the Mahāyāna* says:

> Because those cognizances lack objects, they are called *cognitions only*. What would an example be? They should be viewed using the example of dreams. In dreams, without there being an object, the aspects of various objects—forms, sounds, smells, tastes, and objects of touch—appear to consciousness, yet those objects do not exist at all. With this example, one can come to understand that everything is cognition only.[579]

This clearly sets forth the meaning of *cognition only* in their system. Scriptural sources include the line in the *Ten Levels Sūtra*, "These three realms are mind only,"[580] as well as the following statement in the *Explanation of the Intention*: [284]

> "Bhagavan, is the image that is the object of samādhi said to be different from that mind or not different?"

> The Bhagavan said, "Maitreya, it is said to be not different. Why? Because I have explained that consciousness is distinguished by cognizing only the object of observation."
>
> "Bhagavan, if the reflection that is the object of samādhi is not different from the mind, how does that mind apprehend that mind?"
>
> "Maitreya, no phenomenon apprehends any phenomenon. However, whatever mind that is produced in that way appears in that way. For example, through form serving as a condition, the form itself is seen [in a mirror], yet one thinks, 'I see an image.' For such a person, the form and the appearance of the image appear to be different objects. In the same way, the mind that is produced in that way appears to be a different object from that."[581]

After citing this passage, the *Compendium of the Mahāyāna* explains, "This scripture also sets forth that reasoning,"[582] that is, the reasoning that proves that appearances such as form are cognition only. Thus that very passage from *Explanation of the Intention* delineates how phenomena are established to be cognition only.

In accordance with the *Compendium of the Mahāyāna*, Vasubandhu's *Thirty Verses* says:

> Designated as *self* and as *phenomena*,
> whatever various things appear
> are transformations of consciousness.[583]

This is saying that the various aspects that are designated as *self* and *phenomena*—that is, what is designated as *self, living being, person*, and so forth and what is designated as *phenomenon, aggregate, constituent, source*, and so forth—in fact are merely the appearance factor of consciousness. The *Twenty Verses* says:

> These are cognition only
> because nonexistent things appear.
> For example, someone with myodesopsia

> sees what does not exist, such as floating hairs and [double]
> moons.[584]

This is stating that, as in the example of someone with myodesopsia seeing floating hairs, various aspects of external objects appear to the operative consciousnesses even though they do not exist. [285] Someone might raise the objection: If external objects such as form do not exist as external objects, why is it that appearances such as form appear in some places and do not appear in others, and that in a specific place, they appear at some times and do not appear at other times? [If external objects did not exist,] establishing such things as place and time would be untenable. Providing a detailed response to refute that objection, [a Cittamātra proponent] says that although they are cognition only, such verbal conventions are tenable. Someone might ask: If external objects do not exist, does this not contradict the statements in the sūtras setting forth the sources such as form? [In response,] that same text says:

> The existence of sources such as form
> was set forth with the intention to benefit
> beings who will be tamed by that,
> such as sentient beings who are born spontaneously [for example, in the heavens].[585]

The statements by the Buddha that set forth the existence of external objects were merely set forth for disciples who need to be taught in that way. They are therefore provisional and intended for a specific audience. Regarding their intention, the same text says:

> A cognition, having that appearance,
> arises from its own seed.
> The Sage spoke of those two
> as the [internal and external] sources.[586]

The autocommentary on this passage says, "Regarding the seeds from which specific transformations arise, the seed itself and what appears to it were described by the Bhagavan as the *eye source* and *form source* respectively."[587]

Turning to the explanation of the intended purpose of the sūtra, the benefit of the Buddha setting forth an external world was so that his disciples would come to understand the meaning of the two types of selflessness. Furthermore, no external objects that are composed of subtle particles—individual, multiple, or composites—come to be objects of cognition. Therefore external forms do not become individual objects of cognition. Regarding the partless subtle particles that constitute external objects, which are asserted by Vaibhāṣika and Sautrāntika, the *Twenty Verses* says:

> When six [subtle particles] are conjoined simultaneously,
> the subtle particle would have six parts.[588]

Using such reasoning, Cittamātra delineates the tenability of their own system, in which external objects do not exist and consciousness is truly established. Therefore the two brothers are of one mind on the meaning of cognition only. [286]

It seems that the Cittamātra Following Reasoning, such as Dignāga and his philosophical heirs, composed commentaries on the meaning of cognition only without positing it from the perspective of mere appearances through the power of the activation of seeds on the foundation consciousness. Instead, they posited it primarily from the perspective of investigating the nature of consciousness and its objects.[589] For example, Dignāga's *Investigation of the Support* commentary says:

> Some assert that the object of observation of consciousnesses, such as that of the eye, are external objects. They suppose that it consists of subtle particles because it is the cause [of the consciousness], or that it is a composite because it produces the consciousness that perceives it. Regarding the first:
>
> > Subtle particles might be the cause
> > of sense cognition.
> > Yet because they do not appear to it,
> > subtle particles are not its object, nor are the sense faculties.
>
> An *object* is that whose identity is apprehended by consciousness because it is produced in its aspect. Subtle particles may be its cause, but it does not perceive them, just as it does not

perceive the sense faculty. In that case, subtle particles are not the object of observation.

> A composite may appear to that [sense consciousness],
> but what appears does not come from it.

It is reasonable that an object that produces the cognition that perceives it is the object of observation because it is explained to be the condition that produces the cognition. A composite does not do so because it does not substantially exist, like a double moon. A person whose sense faculties are incomplete may see a double moon, but that false appearance is not its object. In the same way, because it does not substantially exist, a composite is not a cause and therefore is not an object of observation.[590]

This passage proves that it is untenable for what is called an *external object*—whether it is considered to be individual subtle particles or a collection of them—to be the object of the sense consciousness that apprehends it and the observed object condition that produces it. [287] That same text says:

> Both of those kinds of external objects
> are unsuitable as objects of the mind.

Because one factor is incomplete, an object that is called an external subtle particle or a composite is not an object of observation.[591]

This refutes external objects, and yet, even though external objects do not exist, there is a way to posit the observed object condition of sense consciousnesses. The *Investigation of the Support* says:

> An internal object of knowledge
> that appears as if it were external
> is the object because its nature is consciousness
> and because it is the condition.
> Although they are simultaneous, because it is unmistaken, it is
> the condition.[592]

Although the object of knowledge that becomes the nature of an internal consciousness is not established as an external object, that which appears to be so established, such as blue, is asserted to be the observed object condition of the eye consciousness apprehending blue. The reason that this is the case is that the eye consciousness apprehending blue comes to be the nature of blue. Therefore the appearance as blue to the eye consciousness is not only the appearing object of that eye consciousness, it is also its condition. One might ask how it can be the condition, since the two are simultaneous and of the same entity. [To respond:] It is neccesarily the case that if it exists, the sense consciousness is produced; and if it does not exist, it is not produced. Therefore it is explained that it is a "condition." In summary, the form, sound, and so forth that come to be the nature of a sense consciousness are both the object of observation of the sense consciousness and the condition of that consciousness. Therefore they are described as that which is the quality of both the object and the condition, or simply the object and condition that appear. This is in terms of its being the so-called observed object condition (*ālambanapratyaya*).

With regard to the actual observed object condition in the system of Dignāga, *Investigation of the Support* says, "Because it provides potency, it is sequential."[593] This is illustrated by the way the potency residing on an earlier sense consciousness apprehending blue, for example, provides a later sense consciousness apprehending blue; the aspect of blue is asserted to be the observed object condition of the next sense consciousnesses in sequence. That same text says:

> That which has the nature of a cooperative sense potency
> is a sense faculty.[594]

This is saying that in the case of blue and an eye consciousness apprehending blue, which arise together, the potency that empowers that consciousness is not only the observed object condition of the subsequent sense consciousness apprehending blue, it is also called the *sense faculty*. Furthermore, the *Commentary on Investigation of the Support* says: [288]

> In dependence on a potency called *the eye* and on an internal form, a consciousness that perceives an object is produced without their being differentiated. These two serve as the cause of

> one another and have existed since beginningless time. Sometimes, from the fruition of the potency, the aspect of the object of the consciousness arises; sometimes the potency [arises] from the aspect. Whether one says that those two are different or not different from consciousness is a matter of preference. Thus, because the internal object of observation has two natures, it is tenable that it be the object.[595]

From these statements, one can infer how Dignāga comments on the meaning of being established as cognition only and the primary reasonings he relies upon to prove it.

Regarding Dharmakīrti, in his *Exposition of Valid Knowledge* he extensively refutes the Sautrāntika proofs that the apprehended and apprehender are different substantial entities, explaining that the natures of object and subject are produced similarly and setting forth extensive reasonings that undermine the position of those who assert external objects. Among those, the most famous of the reasonings that refutes that apprehended and apprehender are different substantial entities is called "certainty of simultaneous observation." In the *Exposition of Valid Knowledge*, that reason is stated in order to directly prove the two modes of awareness. In the *Ascertainment of Valid Knowledge*, that reasoning is used to refute that the apprehended and apprehender are different substantial entities. It says:

> Because of the certainty of simultaneous observation,
> blue and the awareness of it are not different.

> Although it appears to be different, blue is not a different entity from the experience of it because they are certain to be observed simultaneously, like a double moon. For these, if one is not observed, the other is not observed. It is not tenable that they have different natures because there is no reason for them to be connected. Form and light either have a nature that is suitable to produce consciousness of them, or they have a connection with a nature that produces a suitable sense faculty. Therefore, without light, form is not observed because the effect is not mistaken for the cause. Form is apprehended because it has the nature of being apprehended together with uninterrupted light. Furthermore, some lights can be seen, and some types of beings

> see forms without light. In those cases [of form and light], there is no certainty of simultaneous observation; there is a certainty [of simultaneity] of the aspect of blue and the knowledge of it. However, this is not the case for the knowledge of different things, as in the case of distinguishing blue and yellow.[596] [289]

Addressing the meaning of this passage, Dharmottara's *Commentary on the Ascertainment of Valid Knowledge* says, "Those things that have certainty of simultaneous observation are not different from each other, like [seeing] a second moon from a first moon. The aspect of the apprehended, such as blue, has certainty of simultaneous observation with consciousness."[597] The statement of this reasoning is that objects of the sense consciousnesses, like those that apprehend blue, are proven to be only appearances of the mind. This is seen to be the same point of the reasonings set forth by Dignāga in his *Investigation of the Support*.

Regarding the meaning of "certainty of simultaneous observation," "simultaneous" means at the same time, and "observation" means realization. "Certainty" means necessity and must be taken to mean the necessity of being understood at the same time. The property of the position of that reason is that the two—blue and the mind apprehending it—are established by reflexive-awareness direct perception as certain to be observed simultaneously. The necessity is established by reasoning that it is impossible for two phenomena that are necessarily observed simultaneously to be different substantial entities. It appears that at a later time this way of proving cognition only, from the perspective of the certainty of simultaneous observation, became widespread. One can infer this generally from how this reasoning is emphasized in such treatises as Prajñākaragupta's *Proof of the Certainty of Simultaneous Observation* and Ratnākaraśānti's *Proof of Cognition Only*. Because there is much more to say about this reasoning for the certainty of simultaneous observation, it will be explained extensively in the fourth volume of *Science and Philosophy in the Indian Buddhist Classics*.

Debates about True and False Aspects

As explained above, the division of those who propound the tenets of Cittamātra into True Aspectarians and False Aspectarians is well known. Because there are differing statements among later scholars on the question of who among the great Vijñaptimātra masters of the past were True Aspectarians and who were False Aspectarians, it is difficult to make a conclusive statement. In Bodhibhadra's *Explanation of the Compendium on the Essence of Wisdom*, Asaṅga and Vasubandhu are identified as False Aspectarians and Dignāga and his philosophical heirs are identified as True Aspectarians. However, Devendrabuddhi and Śākyabuddhi explain the intended meaning of Dharmakīrti's Seven Treatises on Valid Knowledge as well as Dignāga's *Compendium of Valid Knowledge* to be True Aspectarian, while Prajñākaragupta and Dharmottara explain it be False Aspectarian. Furthermore, Bhāviveka's refutation of the system of Asaṅga and his brother in the *Blaze of Reasoning* explains that they are True Aspectarians. Therefore the statement by some Tibetan scholars that both the True and False Aspectarian positions appear without preference in the texts of Asaṅga and Vasubandhu, as well as those of Dignāga and his heirs, appears to be accurate.[598] [290]

The differing views of the True Aspectarian and False Aspectarian must be posited in terms of their explanation of the aspect of the apprehended—the object that appears as blue and so forth to a sense consciousness. If this is illustrated with the example of an eye consciousness apprehending blue, then the appearance of blue as blue to that sense consciousness is the aspect that is the point of contention between the True Aspectarians and False Aspectarians. They are similar in asserting that to the eye consciousness apprehending blue, that blue appears as blue, as coarse, and as an external object. However, the True Aspectarians assert that the appearance of blue as an external object to the eye consciousness apprehending blue is polluted by ignorance but that the appearance of blue as blue and as coarse is not polluted by ignorance. The False Aspectarians are different, asserting not only that the appearance of blue as an external object is polluted by ignorance but that the appearance of blue as blue and the appearance of blue as coarse are polluted as well; they say therefore that it is a mistaken appearance.

In brief, the True Aspectarians accept that because the appearance of blue as blue is established in the way that it appears to the eye consciousness apprehending blue, it is true. The False Aspectarians accept that because the appearance of blue as blue is not established in the way that it appears to the eye consciousness apprehending blue, it is false or mistaken. Furthermore, they are not asserting that it is a mistaken appearance in the sense that blue appears as coarse when it is not coarse; they are asserting that it is a mistaken appearance in the sense of being a coarse thing that is established as a different substantial entity from that sense consciousness.

In a debate, the False Aspectarians would say, "When an eye consciousness is produced in the aspect of blue, if the blue is established in the way that it appears, it is either produced in the aspect of something coarse or it is produced in the aspect of the assembly of many subtle particles. In either case, because it is undermined by the reasoning that refutes external objects, it is untenable." The True Aspectarians would respond, "That fault arises in the case of the assertion of something embodied or physical that is composed of external particles that is a different substantial entity from consciousness. We do not accept an embodied external object, and so that fault does not arise." Dharmottara's *Commentary on the Ascertainment of Valid Knowledge* says, "This fault is for the embodied. It is not for what is not embodied, correct?"[599] To that, the False Aspectarian would reply, "Something embodied or physical that is an external object is not different from a newly protruding horn. When many small particles of the horn block each other's place and their growth in size is established in a way that they begin to appear to a sense consciousness, these particles are established as an embodied external object—a horn. This is undermined by the reasoning that refutes external objects." [291] Refuting the assertion of the True Aspectarians, Dharmottara's text also says, "What is called *embodied* is not a protruding horn. However, because it is produced through many small things losing their own place, it becomes a larger object. That is the embodied."[600] Such debates have occurred.

Therefore, in the debates about the true and the false between the True Aspectarians and False Aspectarians, the meaning of *true* is: the apprehended object of a consciousness that is not posited by the power of being polluted by ignorance. The meaning of *false* is: the appearing object of a consciousness that is posited by the power of being polluted by ignorance. Dharmottara asserts the meaning of *false* in that way. Therefore the true and false that are explained here do not refer to such things as being able to perform a function or not, or the true and false that Madhyamaka and Cittamātra debate about.

Within True Aspectarian Cittamātra, there are various subdivisions based on such assertions as how an object is realized through its aspects when it is realized by a sense consciousness. Suppose someone raises the objection, "When one sees a painting with a variety of colors, there must be the same number of aspects as there are different colors in the painting. Otherwise, because the aspects would not appear in accordance with the object, it would not be possible to realize the object just as it is. And because it is not suitable for consciousness to be a different entity from the aspect, if there are a certain number of aspects, there must be that same number of consciousnesses." In response to that, three different systems appear. (1) The assertion that if many aspects of the object appear to consciousness, there are many consciousnesses is called *equal number of subjects and objects*. (2) The assertion that only one aspect appears to a single consciousness is called *half-eggist*. (3) The assertion that many aspects appear to a single consciousness is called *nonpluralist*. Debating with each other and dispelling each other's objections, they delineate their own positions.

Among those, this is how a Proponent of an Equal Number of Subjects and Objects responds to the objection above. When a painting with a variety of colors is seen, the same number of eye consciousnesses of similar type as there are different colors arise simultaneously. It is like, for example, an ear consciousness apprehending sound at the same time as an eye consciousness is apprehending form. It is like many consciousnesses dissimilar in type, such as of the eye and the ear, arising at the same time. This assertion is set forth clearly in Śāntarakṣita's commentary on his *Ornament of the Middle Way*. That texts says, "Some set forth a system in which they think that many consciousnesses of similar type arise simultaneously in accordance with the number as the aspects, like in a painting, as would be the case with consciousnesses that are not similar in type, like those of form and sound."[601] [292] On this point, in his *Commentary on the Ornament of the Middle Way*, Kamalaśīla says, "The word 'some' refers only to some proponents of external objects. In their system, although consciousness has an aspect, it is not contradictory for such things as [the various colors of] a large painting to appear simultaneously."[602]

Someone might object, saying that in such a case, if many eye consciousnesses of a similar type are produced simultaneously upon seeing a multicolored painting, then when seeing the part that is one color, like white, many eye consciousnesses of a similar type would be produced simultaneously in accordance with the many parts [that are white]—such as its edges and center. How the Proponent of an Equal Number of Subjects and Objects responds to the assertion that many consciousnesses would arise simultaneously in that way is treated in sequence in the *Ornament for the Middle Way*:

> In that case, even to know a single aspect
> such as white,
> there would be a variety of objects
> such as top, center, and edges.[603]

The autocommentary to *Ornament of the Middle Way* adds: "If someone says, 'I assert that there are many.'"[604] To that, someone might object by saying that the occurrence of only a single consciousness would not exist. In response, a Proponent of an Equal Number of Subjects and Objects would argue that when a partless subtle particle is apprehended, only a single consciousness occurs. In order to set forth in sequence [that position] and its refutation, saying that that assertion is untenable because partless subtle particles are not established by a valid means of knowledge, the autocommentary to the *Ornament of the Middle Way* says, "What is single? It is the apprehension of an object that is a partless particle." And it goes on to say, "A particle that lacks all parts is not seen."[605]

As indicated above, Proponents of an Equal Number of Subjects and Objects are so called because when a single person, for example, looks at a painting with a variety of colors, they assert that, for as many colors that there are, such as blue and yellow, the subject, the eye consciousness having the aspect of those, is produced in equal number. Śāntarakṣita's *Ornament of the Middle Way* says:

> When an unrolled painting is seen,
> there are many minds in accordance with it.[606] [293]

For the Half-Eggist, or Split-Eggist, the aspect of the object or the mind that realizes the object and the aspect of the subject or the mind that realizes the subject are asserted to be produced sequentially and to be different substantial entities, like splitting an egg in two. Candrahari's *Jewel Garland* says:

> The True Aspectarian Cittamātra
> called Split-Eggist

agree with Vaibhāṣika
that the aspect of the apprehended
and the aspect of the apprehender are different.[607]

However, in this system of the Half-Eggists, the eye consciousness apprehending blue and the mind realizing the apprehension of blue are produced sequentially and therefore are different substantial entities. In general, both are accepted to be of the nature of consciousness.

According to the Nonpluralists, although there are many objects, consciousness does not become many. Because many objects appear clearly to a single consciousness, it is not contradictory for many aspects to be reflected in even a single consciousness. They assert that if one does not accept the Nonpluralist assertion, a single consciousness of a similar type would never be produced. Jetāri's *Commentary on Distinguishing the Sugata's Texts* says, "Thus to say that consciousness is without aspect is vile. It has aspect, but if one is averse to the Nonpluralists, there is no unity anywhere."[608]

They are called Nonpluralists because, for example, when one person sees something multicolored, they focus on each of as many aspects as there are in the object, such as the blue and yellow of the multicolored object. However, they assert that the subject, the consciousness, is produced having the aspect of only the multicolored object. Therefore they are called Nonpluralists.

The Nonpluralists and Śāntarakṣita find fault with the assertion of the Proponents of an Equal Number of Subjects and Objects set forth above. The autocommentary to *Ornament of the Middle Way* says, "Regarding them, without being earlier and later, two minds would occur, and that is said to be inappropriate and impossible. In the same way, it is difficult to avoid contradicting the scripture that says, 'For sentients beings, the continuums of their consciousness are singular.' If you assert that that was stated in terms of the fruitional consciousness . . ."[609] [294] This passage is disputing and refuting [their position], saying that if many consciousnesses of similar type arose simultaneously, one person would become many different continuums, and furthermore it would contradict the statement in the sūtra that, "For sentients beings, the continuums of their consciousness are singular." The Proponents of an Equal number of Subjects and Objects counter this objection, saying that the statement in the sūtra that many consciousnesses do not occur is made in terms of many foundation consciousnesses not arising and that, although there are many operative consciousnesses, this does not mean that there are many persons.

The Nonpluralists find fault with the assertions of the Half-Eggists, saying that if the mind realizing the object and the mind realizing the subject are different substantial entities, then they would be hidden from each other, like the minds of different persons. If you accept that, then because the apprehension of blue would be hidden from the mind realizing it, it would be untenable that one could later remember, saying, "I have seen this blue before." If you accept that the apprehension of blue and the mind realizing it are hidden from each other but nonetheless produce such memory, then another person who saw blue earlier and whose mental continuum is different from one's own could produce the memory in oneself of seeing blue, saying, "I have seen that blue before." The Half-Eggists have many ways of disputing this, such as saying, "Because they are produced from a single foundation consciousness, there is no potency to produce such a memory in another person; it is tenable for such a memory to be produced in a single person. Jetāri's *Commentary on Distinguishing the Sugata's Texts* says, "If the consciousnesses that are asserted to be object and subject are different, then at that time they would be hidden from each other, like those of separate persons." It also says:

> What is the fault in their being hidden from each other? If you say that it would not be tenable to think "I have seen this," then how is it contradictory for such a thought to arise from the potency of both object and subject? If you say that it would absurdly follow that it would exist in separate persons, that is not the case because it does not have the potency for that and because, if the potency exists, its production of the effect is inevitable. One might ask how this has a single cause. If you say that it does because it is produced in the single foundation consciousness . . .[610]

From among those assertions above, the majority of Madhyamaka and Cittamātra masters accept that the Nonpluralist system of many aspects appearing to a single consciousness is the correct position. In that case, in the apprehension of the variety of colors of a multicolored object, they assert that a single eye consciousness apprehending the many colors apprehends them simultaneously, without needing two or more eye consciousnesses to apprehend them. [295] They assert that if they are not apprehended in this way, it would be impossible for the many colors—blue, yellow, and so forth—on the wings of a butterfly to appear to a single eye consciousness. The *Exposition of Valid Knowledge* says:

> How could many forms,
> like the colors of a butterfly, appear?[611]

These are merely the three most important assertions about how the aspect of an apprehended object appears to a sense consciousness. How the proponents of these assertions debate with each other is set forth here in just a rough form; to understand them in detail, one needs to study the great treatises. There are many other positions, such as that between the True Aspectarians and the False Aspectarians, the tenets of the False Aspectarians are asserted to be more reliable, and that the tenets of the True Aspectarian Nonpluralists are more reliable. As noted, most Buddhist schools hold the assertions of the True Aspectarian Nonpluralists to be their own position.

Valid Means of Knowledge

Turning to this system's assertions about the valid means of knowledge, statements by Asaṅga and Vasubandhu appear to posit three: direct perception (*pratyakṣa*), inference (*anumāna*), and scriptural (*āgama*) valid knowledge. Later, beginning with the tradition of Buddhist logic and epistemology broadly delineated by Dignāga, the Vijñaptika would come to uphold with a single voice the system in which valid means of knowledge are certain as two: direct perception and inference. In asserting that there are four subdivisions of direct perception—sense direct perception (*indriyapratyakṣa*), mental direct perception (*mānasapratyakṣa*), reflexive awareness (*svasaṃvedana*), and yogic direct perception (*yogipratyakṣa*)—they are similar to the Sautrāntika. One important difference surrounds the question of whether direct perception is necessarily nonmistaken. The Sautrāntika define *direct perception* as "free from thought and unmistaken." For Vijñaptika it is mistaken in the sense that an apprehended object appears to a sense consciousness to be established as an external object.

They assert that this occurs by the power of pollution from the predispositions of the view of self that occur beginninglessly and continuously. Therefore they accept that even a valid sense direct perception apprehending blue is mistaken with respect to how the object appears to it. Because of this important point, in Dharmakīrti's *Ascertainment of Valid Knowledge*, the definition of *direct perception* is posited as awareness that is free from thought and that arises based on predispositions. That text says:

> Someone might say, "If all objects of consciousness were rejected, how could could one speak of distorted cognition and its opposite?" Due to the fault of polluting predispositions, the unwise see without having confidence in conventions. Therefore one is called *invalid*. The other, because it based on firm predispositions, is followed as long as one is not free from saṃsāra. And based on it not being mistaken about conventions, here it is a valid means of knowledge.[612] [296]

This is saying that someone might raise the objection "In this Vijñaptika system, the apprehended objects of all sense consciousnesses are refuted. In that case, because it is not tenable to differentiate between what is polluted and what is not polluted by causes of error, one cannot divide sense consciousnesses into the valid and not valid." In response, Dharmakīrti sets forth how it is tenable to divide sense consciousnesses into the valid and the invalid from the perspective of whether they are polluted or not polluted by adventitious causes of error. A mind that is a sense consciousness that is free from thought and arises based on stable predispositions and that, although affected by error, is not mistaken about conventions is from that perspective suitable to be posited as a valid means of knowledge. Presenting [valid knowledge in that way] is a key point in this system.

Furthermore, because this system does not assert external objects, in the context of the observed object condition of a sense consciousness, they identify two: the observed object condition that appears and the observed object condition that exercises potency. The former is posited as the imputed observed object condition and the latter is posited as the actual observed object condition. Such assertions are their unique way of presenting the three conditions. From a general perspective, their presentation of inference for oneself is similar to that of the Sautrāntika Following

Reasoning. Because they assert that external objects do not exist, the *Exposition of Valid Knowledge* says:

> A sprout is produced from a seed,
> and fire is inferred from smoke.
> What is their creator or the proof
> that they are based on external objects?[613]

Someone might raise the objection, "In the Vijñaptika's own system, how is it tenable that a sprout is produced by a seed and the existence of fire on a mountain pass is proved by the sign of smoke?" In response, Dharmakīrti says that there is a unique way of positing those objects and agents in terms of the explanation of cognition only. Furthermore, in Dharmakīrti's *Proof of Other Minds*, the objection is raised that if one refutes that the object and subject are different substantial entities, then the mind that understood the mind of another person would be the same substantial entity as the consciousness it was apprehending, in which case it would be untenable that they were different persons. The way that he refutes such an objection in terms of the explanation of cognition only is one of many difficult points of this system. One should understand them from the Seven Treatises on Valid Knowledge together with Dignāga's *Compendium*.

Another difficult point related to this system's assertions about valid knowledge is their unique way of presenting valid knowledge, its effect, and its object. The meaning of these is set forth first in the *Compendium on Valid Knowledge*. Based on that, Dharmakīrti delineated them very extensively in his *Exposition of Valid Knowledge* and his *Ascertainment of Valid Knowledge*. This will be discussed as part of the detailed explanation of valid means of knowledge in the fourth volume of *Science and Philosophy in the Indian Buddhist Classics*. [297]

In addition, Cittamātra Following Scripture, who assert the foundation consciousness, have a unique way of presenting the path and fruition based on the various ways of entering into the understanding that there is cognition only. They do so from the perspective of their explanation of the transformation of the foundation consciousness, the four thorough investigations—of names, meanings, entities, and qualities—and in dependence on that, the four thorough knowledges (*parijñāna*). In accordance with what is set forth in the context of lineage (*gotra*) in such texts as the

Asaṅga's *Bodhisattva Levels* and *Compendium of the Mahāyāna* and Maitreya's *Ornament of the Mahāyāna Sūtras*, they assert that the naturally abiding lineage [which determines whether one will become an arhat or a buddha] has three qualities: of natural attainment, of coming into being in succession without beginning, and of the six sources. They have many unique positions, such as the explanation that there are persons whose lineage is completely severed [and thus will never achieve liberation]. Here, we have been focused only on the philosophical positions related to the basis in this school; its positions concerning the path and fruition can be found elsewhere.

This concludes the chapter on Cittamātra, a unique Mahāyāna school founded by the great master Asaṅga and then delineated extensively using scripture and reasoning by the great masters of India—Vasubandhu and his followers, the great scholar of valid knowledge Dignāga and his followers such as Dharmakīrti. The important tenets of this system have thus been gathered and explained here in one place. [298]

14

The Madhyamaka School

How This School of Tenets Arose

THE EXPLANATION of the tenets of Madhyamaka, the Proponents of No Entityness, begins with how this school of tenets arose. As explained above, the founder of the Mahāyāna school of tenets in general, and the school of tenets that propounds no entityness specifically, is renowned to be the master called Ārya Nāgārjuna, who is praised as if he were the second Buddha. This master assiduously proved that the meaning of the Buddha's scriptures in general, and especially the Mahāyāna Perfection of Wisdom sūtras, is that phenomena exist in the mode of nonentityness (*niḥsvabhāva*). In order to delineate that, he composed treatises that are collections of reasoning: (1) *Root Verses on the Middle Way* [*called Wisdom*], (2) *Sixty Stanzas on Reasoning*, (3) *Seventy Stanzas on Emptiness*, (4) *Refutation of Objections*, and (5) the *Finely Woven*. When one adds to those (6) the *Precious Garland*, these are his famous Six Collections of Reasoning. Among those, he composed autocommentaries on *Seventy Stanzas on Emptiness*, *Refutation of Objections*, and the *Finely Woven*,[614] and based on such works he firmly established the tradition of the tenets of nonentityness. Nāgārjuna's followers, such as Āryadeva, commented on the intended meaning of his works, and from there the Madhyamaka tradition of tenets spread widely. Because this school of tenets asserts that all phenomena lack entityness, its proponents are also known as the Niḥsvabhāvavādin, or Proponents of No Entityness. Because they assert that the statements in the Perfection of Wisdom sūtras that all phenomena are empty (*śūnya*) of intrinsic nature are to be taken literally, they are also known as the Śūnyavādin, or Proponents of Emptiness.

The followers of Nāgārjuna, Madhyamaka scholars, assert that it was prophesied in the scriptures of the Buddha that this master would illuminate the meaning of the Mahāyāna sūtras without error. Thus the *Descent into Laṅkā Sūtra* says:

> In the south, in the land of Vedalī,
> an illustrious and distinguished monk
> called by the name of Nāga
> will destroy the positions of existence and nonexistence.
>
> He will fully explain to the world
> my vehicle, the unsurpassed Mahāyāna.
> He will then achieve the Joyful [level]
> and go to the Land of Bliss.[615] [299]

This passage clearly makes the prophecy that Nāgārjuna himself would correctly explain the vehicle of definitive meaning, free from the extremes of existence and nonexistence. Similar words prophesying the master appear in such texts as the *Great Cloud Sūtra in Twelve Thousand Verses* and the *Great Drum Sūtra*. After the Buddha had passed into nirvāṇa, Nāgārjuna composed many treatises that extensively illuminated how there are no phenomena whatsoever that are truly established and yet actions and effects are tenable conventionally. Also, based on such sūtras as the *Teaching of Akṣayamati Sūtra* and the *King of Samādhis Sūtra*, he extensively explained how the sūtras of the middle wheel that set forth the final definitive meaning—the wheel of the Dharma of no characteristics, or the Perfection of Wisdom sūtras and the scriptures that accord with them—are definitive in the sense that their meaning cannot be suitably interpreted otherwise. He also explained how the meaning of sūtras that do not accord with that must be interpreted otherwise. From those perspectives, he is the founder of the Madhyamaka tradition.

The sūtra source in dependence upon which the protector Nāgārjuna divided scriptures into the provisional and definitive does not appear explicitly in the works of the master himself, such as the Six Collections of Reasoning and the *Compendium of Sūtras*. However, the source can be determined implicitly based on how he explains the meaning of sūtras. Furthermore, in his *Clear Words*, Candrakīrti says, "This should be understood extensively from such works as the *Teaching of Akṣayamati*." That is to say that the Madhyamaka's own system of dividing scriptures into the provisional and the definitive is established in dependence on the *Teaching of Akṣayamati Sūtra*. Avalokitavrata's explanation in his *Commentary on the Lamp of Wisdom* accords with that.[616] In his *Illumination of the Middle Way*, Kamalaśīla names that same sūtra as his system's source for the division into provisional and definitive.[617] Therefore the *Teaching of Akṣayamati* is known to be the source of the division into the provisional and definitive. The sūtra itself says, "Those sūtras that set forth what is established as conventional are called 'of provisional meaning.' Those sūtras that set forth what is established as ultimate are called 'of definitive meaning.'"[618] [300] In this way, the differentiation of sūtras into the provisional and the definitive is not posited from the perspective of such things as place and time; the division is made from the perspective of the subject matter. This is saying that sūtras that explicitly set forth conventional truths primarily are posited as sūtras of provisional meaning and sūtras that explicitly set forth ultimate truths primarily are posited as sūtras of definitive meaning.

The need to divide the scriptures of the Buddha into the provisional and the definitive can be clearly understood from what is said in Candrakīrti's *Clear Words* about the need for Nāgārjuna to compose *Root Verses on the Middle Way*. Candrakīrti cites statements about how all conditioned phenomena are said to have the quality of falsity and that, in dependence on the analytical wisdom of phenomena, one will attain the rank of the pacification of all composed things—that is, one will realize selflessness. At the conclusion, he says:

> Because of not understanding the intention of the teaching, some will come to have doubts about which teaching has the meaning of reality here and which is intended [for a specific audience] here. Some who are dull-witted will think that teachings of provisional meaning have definitive meaning. In order to clear away the doubt and misunderstanding of both through reasoning and scripture, the master composed this work.[619]

The primary scriptures that are the sources of the Madhyamaka tenets are undeniably the Perfection of Wisdom sūtras of the middle wheel. According to the great Madhyamaka masters who commented on the thought of Nāgārjuna, such as Bhāviveka and Candrakīrti, Nāgārjuna himself is described as disseminating the primary Perfection of Wisdom sūtras on earth and reviving the teachings of the Mahāyāna. Other sūtras that are sources of Madhyamaka tenets include the *Meeting of Father and Son Sūtra*, the *King of Samādhis Sūtra*, the *Teaching of Akṣayamati Sūtra*, the *Ten Levels Sūtra*, the *Kāśyapa Chapter Sūtra* of the *Pile of Jewels* (*Ratnakuṭa*) collection, the *Entering into the Two Truths Sūtra*, and the *Questions of King Dhāraṇīśvara*.

How Nāgārjuna Delineated the Profound Madhyamaka View

In order to delineate the meaning of the profound emptiness, citing the supporting scriptural sources, Nāgārjuna composed the *Compendium of Sūtras*. In order to prove with many types of reasoning the profound emptiness that refutes intrinsic existence in both persons and phenomena, he composed collections of reasoning such as *Root Verses on the Middle Way*, *Seventy Stanzas on Emptiness*, *Refutation of Objections*, *Sixty Stanzas on Reasoning*, and the *Finely Woven*. [301] The subject matter of such wondrous treatises brings together the profound emptiness—the center or *middle* that is free from the two extremes of permanence and annihilation—and the *way* to free oneself from saṃsāra by the path of realizing the meaning of such a middle. The first is primarily set forth in *Root Verses on the Middle Way* and the treatises derived from that: the *Finely Woven*, *Refutation of Objections*, and *Seventy Stanzas on Emptiness*. The second is primarily set forth in the *Sixty Stanzas on Reasoning* and the *Precious Garland*.[620]

Among the works of this master, *Root Verses on the Middle Way* is like the king of all his treatises. How Nāgārjuna delineates the profound view of the middle way will be briefly explained based on it. According to what is stated in Candrakīrti's *Clear Words* commentary, the two verses of the expression of worship that open this text summarize and delineate the essence of the subject matter of the treatise.[621] The essence of the subject matter of *Root Verses on the Middle Way* is to emphasize that phenomena are not intrinsically produced and to explain that such an emptiness is the meaning of dependent arising—allowing one to realize that *emptiness*, *dependent arising*, and the *middle path* are synonyms.

The first chapter of *Root Verses on the Middle Way* refutes the production of dependently arisen phenomena from the perspective of the four extremes. Specifically, he refutes the assertion by the proponents of true existence among Buddhist schools who, taking as their basis the four conditions set forth in the sūtras, accept that things are intrinsically produced. In the chapter's conclusion, he proves that it is utterly untenable for a nature that is established by its own entity to arise from conditions, concluding that since its own nature is not tenable, then other things that are its counterparts are also untenable. Therefore he emphatically proves that presentations of cause and effect that take things that are true as their foundation are untenable. The clear and extensive proof that production from any of the four extremes is not tenable can be regarded as the thread that runs through every chapter of *Root Verses on the Middle Way*.

When one analyzes how, in the first chapter, he refutes that conditions are established by way of their own entity, one can understand the progression of the unique reasoning in his system. Because production is untenable from any of the four extremes, it is proved that intrinsic production does not exist, and for that reason, a condition that is established by its own entity cannot be posited. If there is no production, there is no activity of the condition, and a condition that has no activity is never tenable; as long as an effect is not produced, a compounded phenomenon cannot become a condition. Furthermore, if one says, "That is produced by this," what is produced must be either something that exists or something that does not exist. But if something that exists is produced, then the condition has no purpose, because if something exists, it has already been produced, and because that which exists by its own entity has no need for a condition. Likewise, something that does not exist also cannot be produced, because if the thing in relation to which one speaks of a condition does not exist, the statement "This is a condition of that" becomes untenable. If it were reasonable to produce something that does not exist, then it would absurdly follow that the horns of a rabbit could be produced. [302] In the same way, a condition does not produce something that both does and does not exist because it is contradictory for what exists and does not exist to occur together. Thus [the chapter] establishes how, when analyzed with reasoning, if one asserts that a condition is established by way of its own entity, then it is untenable for it to be a cause that produces any compounded phenomenon. Beginning with the extremes of existence, nonexistence, and both existence and nonexistence, using a process of elimination, the chapter delineates the utter impossibility of something established by its own entity to be called "a condition."[622]

Progressing in order from the second chapter, which is an analysis of going and coming, Nāgārjuna then refutes the intrinsic existence of each of the categories that are typically used to prove that phenomena such as the aggregates intrinsically exist: the activity of movement; the sense faculties such as seeing form; the foundational aggregates, constituents, and sources; mental phenomena such as desire; and the production, abiding, and disintegration of the conditioned. In addition, he individually refutes the objects and agents on the basis of which the proponents of true existence posit that phenomena intrinsically exist: the composite, conjunction, bondage and liberation, actions and their effects, self and phenomena, time, collection, arising and disintegration, and so forth. In the same way, he proves that even the objects that Buddhists greatly esteem do not intrinsically exist: the tathāgata; the four inverted views—the conceptions of purity, pleasure, permanence, and self—that are to be abandoned; the four truths that are the focus of the path; the goal of nirvāṇa; and the twelve links of dependent arising. He concludes the text with an analysis of extreme views.

In summary, according to the reliable commentators on *Root Verses on the Middle Way*, the second chapter, the ninth through the twelfth chapters, and the eighteenth chapter of the *Root Verses* primarily refute the self of persons. The first chapter and the third through the eighth chapters primarily refute the self of phenomena. The eighth combines refutations of the intrinsic existence of persons and phenomena. The thirteenth chapter refutes the intrinsic existence of things, without dividing them into persons and phenomena. In order to refute the intrinsic nature of things, sometimes dividing them into persons and phenomena and other times not, the other chapters refute the proofs of their intrinsic existence.[623]

Among the master's texts, the way to refute partless moments of time that constitute truly existent consciousness appears clearly in the *Precious Garland*. Regarding the refutation of the constituents of truly existent physical phenomena—apart from the analysis of the four elements, individually and collectively—an analysis of partless particles does not appear clearly in either the *Precious Garland* or *Root Verses on the Middle Way*. However, in a text by Nāgārjuna called the *Chapter on Understanding What Is Not Understood*, it does appear clearly: [303]

Even subtle particles do not exist:

> When parts, in terms of spatial directions, can be seen,
> even for subtle particles, divisibility can be observed.
> When analyzed in terms of such parts,
> how can their subtle particles exist?

If you concede that they do not exist:

> If things do not exist,
> how can nonthings exist in any way?
> And who can know existence and nonexistence?

This refers to the selflessness of phenomena.[624]

How partless particles are refuted is set forth extensively in the ninth chapter of Āryadeva's *Four Hundred Verses*.

In the *Finely Woven*, Nāgārjuna refutes the sixteen categories of the Nyāya school, such as valid means of knowledge and the object of comprehension, which are used by the proponents of tīrthika tenets to prove that persons and phenomena intrinsically exist. Also, *Root Verses on the Middle Way* says:

> The nature of a thing
> does not exist in conditions.[625]

This is saying that if, prior to their production, the effects—namely, external and internal things—were to exist in individual causes and conditions, in their collections, or in something else, then [the effects] would have to be produced by their own nature, but they are not produced by their own nature. *Refutation of Objections* says:

> If all things
> lacked intrinsic nature,
> then your words would lack intrinsic nature
> and so could not refute intrinsic nature.[626]

Nāgārjuna composed *Refutation of Objections* in response to this objection raised by the proponents of true existence among Buddhist schools, who say that if all objects of knowledge lack an intrinsically established nature, then texts that refute intrinsic establishment would also have to lack an intrinsically established nature and therefore would not be able to refute intrinsic establishment.

. In *Refutation of Objections* he says that the emptiness of intrinsic establishment is the meaning of dependent arising, and although words lack an intrinsically established nature, words are able to prove what is to be proved and negate what is to be negated. Therefore he shows how, for a system that does not accept a nature that is established from its own side, it is possible to accurately posit refutations and to prove valid means of knowledge and objects of comprehension. He also shows how, for a system that accepts a nature that is established from its own side, it is not possible to accurately posit valid means of knowledge and objects of comprehension. [304] *Root Verses on the Middle Way* says:

> Like a dream, like an illusion,
> like a city of the gandharvas—
> this is how production, abiding,
> and disintegration are described.[627]

This is saying that just as such things as a dream, an illusion, and a city of celestial beings lack an intrinsic nature that is established from its own side, in the same way, production, abiding, and disintegration lack an entity that is intrinsically established. The proponents of true existence among the Buddhist schools object to this. Thinking that if those do not intrinsically exist, they cannot exist even conventionally, they say that it contradicts what the Buddha said about production, abiding, and disintegration—for example, "O monks, these three are the characteristics of conditioned phenomena. It is clear that conditioned phenomena are produced. It is clear that they disintegrate. It is clear that they change into other states."[628] In response to the statement, Nāgārjuna composed *Seventy Stanzas on Emptiness*. It says:

> The Buddha has spoken of abiding, production, disintegration,
> existence, nonexistence, low, middling, and special
> from the perspective of worldly conventions,
> not from the perspective of the real.[629]

This is indicating that those things such as production and abiding were spoken of by the Buddha merely from the perspective of worldly conventions; he did not set them forth from the perspective of being established from their own side.

Two texts primarily set forth that one is liberated from saṃsāra by a path that does not hold the extreme views of either permanence or annihilation. *Sixty Stanzas on Reasoning* says:

> One is not liberated by existence;
> one does not pass beyond this world by nonexistence.[630]

This is saying that by falling to the extreme view that all phenomena are intrinsically established or the extreme view that everything is utterly nonexistent, one is not able to free oneself from the bonds of the world. That same text says:

> By understanding both existence and nonexistence,
> a great being is freed.[631] [305]

This is indicating that through relying on a path that understands unmistakenly that both the existence that is saṃsāra and the nonexistence that is nirvāṇa exist merely conventionally and do not exist intrinsically, great beings who are noble ones are able to free themselves from the world.

In the *Precious Garland*, Nāgārjuna says that the cause that brings about high rebirth is faith in actions and their effects and that, based on that faith, one becomes a suitable vessel for the wisdom that analyzes phenomena, which is the cause for achieving the auspicious state [of liberation]. The wisdom that analyzes phenomena is the realization that "I" and "mine" do not intrinsically exist. Based on such wisdom, one understands that the aggregates do not truly exist, and based on meditating on that again and again, the conception of "I" is extinguished. As long as the conception of the true existence of the aggregates is not extinguished, one is not liberated from saṃsāra; when it is extinguished, one is liberated from saṃsāra. One falls into the abyss of error by viewing all phenomena as utterly nonexistent. Yet by viewing everything as intrinsically existent, one only wanders in the happy realms of saṃsāra. Therefore, in order to be free from both of those, one needs a path to realize the profound emptiness, the true meaning which does not rely on the two extremes: that all phenomena are intrinsically existent and that they are utterly nonexistent.

Therefore, although both *Sixty Stanzas on Reasoning* and the *Precious Garland* repeatedly set forth the profound reality of dependent arising that refutes that persons and phenomena are intrinsically established, they primarily set forth the definite necessity of being liberated from saṃsāra by a path that realizes emptiness, the perfect object, which does not abide in either of the two extremes of permanence or annihilation. Although overcoming the ignorance that is the root of saṃsāra by a path that realizes the profound reality is set forth in *Root Verses on the Middle Way*, the *Finely Woven*, *Refutation of Objections*, and *Seventy Stanzas on Emptiness*, in these texts the object that is primarily delineated is the reality of dependent arising.

Three texts—*Root Verses on the Middle Way*, *Sixty Stanzas on Reasoning*, and the *Precious Garland*—each independently and extensively set forth the emptiness of intrinsic existence of all phenomena with many different types of reasoning. They are classified as the trunk treatises. Three more—*Refutation of Objections*, *Seventy Stanzas on Emptiness*, and the *Finely Woven*—set forth the emptiness of intrinsic existence of all phenomena with many different types of reasoning in a way that branches out from those in the *Root Verses on the Middle Way*. Therefore they are classified as the treatises that spread out from the trunk of a tree like branches.

Candrakīrti's *Commentary on the Sixty Stanzas on Reasoning* says, "This *Sixty Stanzas on Reasoning*, like the *Middle Way* [*Verses*], was primarily composed as an analysis of dependent arising. Therefore it is not as if it branched out from the *Middle Way* [*Verses*]."[632] [306] This is saying that just as the profound emptiness is independently and extensively set forth with limitless reasonings in *Root Verses on the Middle Way*, the profound emptiness is also independently and extensively set forth with limitless reasonings in *Sixty Stanzas on Reasoning*. For this reason, it is called a "treatise that is like the trunk." For that same reason, it is easy to prove that the *Precious Garland* is a treatise that is like the trunk.

Turning to how the three treatises that are like spreading branches extend out from the chapters of *Root Verses on the Middle Way*, *Refutation of Objections* branches out from the negation of production from something that is other found in the first chapter, "Analysis of Conditions," from the perspective of removing contradictions from one's own words. *Seventy*

Stanzas on Emptiness branches out from the refutation of the inherent establishment of the three characteristics of conditioned phenomena—production, abiding, and disintegration—found in the seventh chapter, "Analysis of Production, Abiding, and Disintegration," from the perspective of removing contradictions raised by the proponents of true existence regarding what is said about production, abiding, and disintegration in the sūtras. The *Finely Woven* branches out from the refutation of the intrinsic establishment of persons and phenomena in the chapters of *Root Verses on the Middle Way* from the perspective of refuting the sixteen categories of the Nyāya school, such as valid means of knowledge (*pramāṇa*) and object of comprehension (*prameya*). According to the tīrthikas those categories represent proofs for true existence.

The *Commentary on the Sixty Stanzas on Reasoning* says, "Why does the master not provide an opening expression of worship in *Seventy Stanzas on Emptiness* and *Refutation of Objections*, yet he does so in *Root Verses on the Middle Way*? It is because *Seventy Stanzas on Emptiness* and *Refutation of Objections* are branches extending out from *Root Verses on the Middle Way*; since they do not have an independent continuity, they do not have a separate expression of worship."[633] Neither *Seventy Stanzas on Emptiness* nor *Refutation of Objections* express worship to the Bhagavan at the beginning of the text, whereas there is an expression of worship in *Root Verses on the Middle Way*. The reason is that the continuity or stream of the words that are expressed in those two treatises is not independent and separate from the *Root Verses*. Therefore those two are explained as branches extending out from the *Root Verses*. Because the *Finely Woven* fulfills this quality as well, it is also a treatise that extends out from *Root Verses on the Middle Way*.

Other Madhyamaka treatises attributed to Nāgārjuna in the Tibetan Tengyur are: the *Hundred Letters on the Middle Way* and its commentary, the *Chapter Called Understanding What Is Not Understood*, *Transferring into Another Existence*, the *Chapter on the Essence of Dependent Arising* and its commentary, the *Twenty Verses on the Mahāyāna*, and the *Proof for Entering into the Three Natures*.[634] In addition, there is the *Compendium of Sūtras*, *Letter to a Friend*, *Discourse on the Dream*, and praises such as *Praise of the Inconceivable*.[635] [307]

Many commentaries on Nāgārjuna's *Root Verses on the Middle Way* were composed by scholars in India. Among the most famous are eight commentaries: the *Fearless*, understood as an autocommentary; the commentary by

Devaśarman, *Creating Purity*; the commentary by Bhāviveka, the *Lamp of Wisdom*; the commentary by Candrakīrti, *Clear Words*; and the commentaries by Guṇamati, Guṇaśrī, Sthiramati, and Buddhapālita. Among these, the *Fearless*, the commentary by Buddhapālita, the *Lamp of Wisdom*, and the *Clear Words* were translated into Tibetan and thus are found in the Tibetan Tengyur.

In his treatises such as *Root Verses on the Middle Way*, Nāgārjuna emphatically refutes the intrinsic existence of all phenomena. What is this inherent establishment that is refuted? The fifteenth chapter of *Root Verses* says:

> It is not correct that intrinsic nature
> arises from causes and conditions.
> An intrinsic nature that arose from causes and conditions
> would be a product.[636]

This is indicating that arising from causes and conditions and existing intrinsically are mutually exclusive, and if one asserts that intrinsic nature arises from causes and conditions, it would have, as a product, a fabricated nature. In brief, that which is established independently, without relying on imputation by thought, is asserted to be *intrinsic establishment* or *establishment from its own side*. This is the object of negation for phenomena. [308]

Phenomena lack such an intrinsic nature; to hold that they do constitutes the view of permanence. To hold that intrinsically real things that once existed before are now no more constitutes the view of annihilation. Therefore it is said that in the Madhyamaka system, one does not abide in the view of either existence or nonexistence. The emptiness that is a lack of intrinsic nature is referred to with the terms *nonabiding* and *nonobservation* in the *Sixty Stanzas on Reasoning*[637] and the *Precious Garland*.[638] The great beings who abide in nonabiding or nonobservation are said to have crossed the ocean of existence without being influenced by the great poisons that are the afflictions.[639] The *Questions of the Nāga King Anavatapta* says, "Whoever understands emptiness is vigilant."[640] This means that whoever understands the emptiness that is the lack of intrinsic nature will be endowed with vigilance. That emptiness is the ultimate mode of being of phenomena. Regarding its nature, the eighteenth chapter says:

> Not known from what is other, peaceful,
> not proliferated through elaboration,
> without conceptions, without different meanings;
> that is the nature of reality.[641]

If it is explained from the perspective of its synonyms, this verse says that there are five qualities of emptiness: it is (1) not known from what is other, (2) peace, (3) free from elaboration, (4) an object without conceptions, and (5) not different. Thus it is saying that in the final analysis, the very fact that phenomena are dependently arisen proves that they do not intrinsically exist; *emptiness* must be understood as the meaning of dependent arising. For example, in the twenty-fourth chapter of *Root Verses on the Middle Way*, Nāgārjuna undermines the proponents of true existence among the Buddhist schools who say that the Madhyamaka proponents of emptiness deprecate such things as the four truths and the Three Jewels. He says that the proponents of true existence do not understand the purpose of teaching emptiness, the nature of emptiness, and the meaning of emptiness, and do not understand well the distinction between conventional truth and ultimate truth. The purpose of teaching emptiness is to completely pacify all elaborations of the conception of true existence, the delusion that is the root of desire and so forth. The nature of emptiness must be taken to be that which is endowed with the five qualities, as set forth in the passage from *Root Verses on the Middle Way* cited above, "Not known from what is other . . ." The meaning of emptiness is said to be the meaning of dependent arising.[642] [309] Any phenomenon that arises in dependence on another phenomenon is not inherently the same as or different from the phenomenon on which it depends. Therefore it is free of the two extremes of permanence and annihilation.[643] The mode of being of things is said to abide as just the dependent arising of mere conditionality. Setting forth such an emptiness as the meaning of dependent arising, *Root Verses on the Middle Way* says:

> That which dependently arises
> is explained to be emptiness;
> it is dependently designated.
> Just that is the middle path.

> There are no phenomena
> that are not dependently arisen.
> Therefore there are no phenomena
> that are not empty.[644]

These statements are a great summary of the central message of the text. They are of crucial importance.

Thus the meaning of the emptiness of intrinsic existence of phenomena is the meaning of dependent arising. Seeing that the Buddha was a valid teacher who set forth the reality of dependent arising in that way, he was therefore praised and extolled in the expressions of worship found in *Root Verses on the Middle Way, Sixty Stanzas on Reasoning, Refutation of Objections,* and such works as *Praise of the Inconceivable.*

How the Commentaries on Nāgārjuna's Works Arose

Nāgārjuna's primary direct disciple was Āryadeva. He composed *Reasonings for Destroying Error*, the *Measure of What Is at Hand* and its commentary, *Destruction of Errors about Madhyamaka*, and the *Parts of the Constituents*. According to what appears in the Tengyur, he also composed a number of miscellaneous works such as the *Compendium on the Essence of Wisdom.*[645] However, his primary Madhyamaka work is his famous treatise in sixteen chapters called the *Four Hundred Verses*. [310] In that work, he comments extensively on Nāgārjuna's propositions, clearly and extensively refuting the misconceptions of others about the two truths in Nāgārjuna's *Root Verses on the Middle Way* and delineating the yogic practice for properly meditating on the nature of the two truths. In accordance with the statement from *Root Verses* "Without relying on the conventional, one cannot realize the ultimate," the first eight chapters of the *Four Hundred Verses* set forth the yogic practice of relying on conventional truths as a method for realizing the ultimate truth, and the next eight chapters delineate the yogic practice for meditating on the ultimate truth. When this text is read in conjunction with the *Root Verses*, each text enables one to clarify the meaning of the other. Āryadeva was held by subsequent great Mādhyamika such as Buddhapālita, *Śūra, Bhāviveka, Candrakīrti, and Śāntarakṣita to be a valid source in the way that Nāgārjuna is. The early scholars of Tibet called them the "noble father and son" and the "Mādhyamika of the original texts."

After Āryadeva, Buddhapālita composed a commentary on *Root Verses of the Middle Way* referred to simply as the *Buddhapālita*, and in it he clarifies the meaning of the reasonings explained in the *Root Verses* primarily using consequences (*prasaṅga*) and, having commented on the thought of Nāgārjuna and Āryadeva, does not supply autonomous (*svatantra*) reasons. He is known to have composed other treatises, but they were not translated into Tibetan. After that, Bhāviveka composed his commentary on the *Root Verses on the Middle Way* called the *Lamp of Wisdom*. He found fault with each of the consequences in the refutation of production from the four extremes in Buddhapālita's commentary and refuted them extensively. He explained many reasons why it is necessary to state autonomous reasons even in the Madhyamaka system and founded the Svātantrika subschool. In his independent works—the *Essence of the Middle Way* and its autocommentary, the *Blaze of Reasoning*—he clearly sets forth many features of non-Buddhist and Buddhist schools of tenets. Because essential points of the Madhyamaka view, meditation, and practice appear extensively there, Atiśa is known to have explained the *Blaze of Reasoning* many times in India and Tibet. Atiśa himself translated both the *Essence of the Middle Way* and its commentary into Tibetan together with his direct disciple, Naktso Tsultrim Gyalwa.

After that came Candrakīrti's commentary, the *Clear Words*. Here he says, "If one is a Mādhyamika, it is not suitable to use autonomous inferences because one does not accept any other position." He continues, "When the master [Nāgārjuna] composed his commentary on *Refutation of Objections*, he did not use syllogisms."[646] [311] In this way he rejects the faults that Bhāviveka expressed about Buddhapālita. Having made an extensive and distinctive refutation of the position that accepts autonomous reasons, he founded the Prāsaṅgika subschool of Madhyamaka. He showed that Buddhapālita did not accept autonomous reasons and set forth many proofs that what is autonomous is not suitable for a Mādhyamika. Having provided many refutations of autonomous syllogisms and of own-character (*svalakṣaṇa*) in his own system, he established a way of commenting on the intention of *Root Verses of the Middle Way* that is unshared with Svātantrika. The most famous works composed by this master are his commentary on the *Root Verses*, the *Clear Words*; his *Commentary on*

Sixty Stanzas on Reasoning; his *Commentary on Seventy Stanzas on Emptiness*; his *Extensive Commentary on the Four Hundred Verses* based on Āryadeva's text; and his independent work *Entering the Middle Way* and its autocommentary.

Jñānagarbha composed the Svātantrika text *Distinguishing the Two Truths* and its commentary. He and Bhāviveka belong to a system that accepts external objects conventionally and does not accept the foundation consciousness and reflexive awareness. Śāntarakṣita composed the Madhyamaka text *Ornament of the Middle Way* and its commentary and was the first to introduce the Yogācāra Madhyamaka tradition, which holds that external objects do not exist conventionally, reflexive awareness exists, and consciousness is not truly established. Kamalaśīla composed the *Illumination of the Middle Way* and the three texts with the title *Stages of Meditation*. In *Illumination of the Middle Way*, he clearly distinguishes what is unique to the systems of the founders of Madhyamaka and Cittamātra. In Tibet, *Distinguishing the Two Truths*, *Ornament of the Middle Way*, and *Illumination of the Middle Way* are known as the three texts of the eastern Svātantrika. The works of Haribhadra, Buddhajñāna, and Abhayākara follow the system of Yogācāra-Svātantrika in delineating the view. Prior to Śāntarakṣita and Kamalaśīla, there were a few, such as Ārya Vimuktisena, who asserted a Madhyamaka system in which external objects do not exist. However, it is well known that the person who widely introduced the tradition of Madhyamaka tenets in which external objects do not exist was Śāntarakṣita.

Śāntideva composed many excellent works that commented on the intention of Nāgārjuna as Prāsaṅgika, such as *Entering the Bodhisattva Way* and the *Compendium of Practice*. Prajñākaramati composed the *Commentary on Entering the Bodhisattva Way*. Atiśa composed the *Entry to the Two Truths*, *Instructions on the Middle Way*, and *Lamp for the Path to Enlightenment*. *Lamp for the Path to Enlightenment* is a treatise that summarizes the essential points of the complete teachings of the Buddha. [312] The way that the view is delineated in the works of such scholars as Śūra and Nāgasena belongs to the Prāsaṅgika Madhyamaka system. Thus the masters who commented upon the intention behind Nāgārjuna's texts that propound nonentityness as belonging to either the Prāsaṅgika Madhyamaka or Svātantrika Madhyamaka system were given the name Partisan Mādhyamika by early Tibetan scholars.

The Definition and Divisions of Madhyamaka

The Madhyamaka school is defined as a Buddhist philosophical school whose fundamental tenet is that all phenomena lack true existence. As was already explained above, Madhyamaka and Proponent of No Entityness are synonyms.

Because they accept a middle free from the two extremes of permanence and annihilation, that are called Mādhyamika ("middle-ists"), and because they propound that phenomena lack truly existent entityness, they are called Proponents of No Entityness. Also, because they avoid the two extremes of existence and nonexistence, it is *middle* (*madhya*), and due to fact that they express that middle, treatises on the middle, tenets about the middle, and persons who propound tenets about the middle are called Mādhyamika. At the point of explaining the etymology of the term *madhyamaka*, Bhāviveka's *Blaze of Reasoning* says:

> It is *madhyama* because it is similar to *madhya* ["middle"] in that it avoids two extremes. *Madhyama* means "being in the middle"; [*-ma*] is a *taddhita* suffix that means [the original word] itself. Because it teaches and proclaims the middle path, *-ka* is added. Based on the verbal root [*-ka*], [the word *madhyamaka*] refers to [Nāgārjuna's] *Verses on the Middle Way* or something that bears the name *madhyamaka*. Or again, *-ka* is added as a nominal [suffix], referring to Madhyamaka—that is, Madhyamaka philosophy.[647]

Regarding the two extremes of permanence and annihilation, that all phenomena are ultimately established is the extreme of existence, and that they do not exist even conventionally is the extreme of annihilation. Thus *Root Verses on the Middle Way* says:

> *Existence* is conceiving of permanence.
> *Nonexistence* is the view of annihilation.
> Therefore the wise should not abide
> in existence or nonexistence.[648]

Extreme of existence, *extreme of permanence*, and *extreme of superimposition* are synonyms. *Extreme of nonexistence*, *extreme of annihilation*, and *extreme of denial* are synonyms. Therefore an extreme is a place that one falls into; in the world, a cliff is an example of an extreme, and falling off a cliff is called "falling into an extreme." [313] Furthermore, all Buddhist schools from Vaibhāṣika to Cittamātra assert that things have a true nature. Therefore, although they do not speak of things being permanent, when pushed by logical reasoning, they do become those who view things as permanent. If one asserts that something that truly existed at a previous time is destroyed in the next moment, although one does not accept the annihilation of its continuum, it becomes a view of annihilation. Whenever one asserts that things have a true nature, one cannot avoid falling into the extreme views of permanence and annihilation.

As discussed above, Madhyamaka asserts that being dependently arisen means being empty of true existence and that being empty of true existence means being dependently arisen. However, this does not mean that phenomena are nonthings that lack the ability to perform a function. Therefore Madhyamaka does not need two separate reasons to refute the two extremes, and all presentations of such things as actions and effects are tenable for that very basis where a nature of true existence is refuted. Thus both extremes, of permanence and annihilation, are refuted just by the reason that they are dependently arisen.

If Madhyamaka is divided in terms of how it presents the conventional, there are two: (1) Madhyamaka that asserts external objects and (2) Madhyamaka that does not assert external objects. The first includes Bhāviveka, Candrakīrti, and their followers, and the second includes such scholars as Śāntarakṣita and his heir Kamalaśīla. The school can also be divided from the perspective of how to produce in the mind the view that ascertains the ultimate emptiness: (1) Svātantrika Madhyamaka and (2) Prāsaṅgika Madhyamaka. Those two are also called, respectively, Madhyamaka that propounds intrinsic existence and Madhyamaka that propounds the lack of intrinsic existence.[649] Based on some works by scholars from India, some Tibetan scholars referred to Svātantrika Madhyamaka and Prāsaṅgika Madhyamaka with the terms, respectively: (1) Madhyamaka establishing illusion with reasoning and (2) thoroughly nonabiding Madhyamaka.[650] [314]

Turning to the difference between Prāsaṅgika and Svātantrika Madhyamaka,[651] in the context of the basis, the Madhyamaka followers of Nāgārjuna are in agreement that there is not even a subtle particle that is truly established in persons or phenomena and that conventionally all topics can be posited without even one of them becoming confused. They agree in extensively refuting the two extremes—the extreme of nonexistence in which nothing exists even conventionally and the extreme of existence in which things or substances are ultimately or truly established—and having done so, they present dependent arising, which is like an illusion and a dream. Thus, in general, it is asserted that there is no difference in the view for Prāsaṅgika Madhyamaka and Svātantrika Madhyamaka. However, as will be explained below, Bhāviveka in the section refuting Cittamātra in his *Lamp of Wisdom* commentary on *Root Verses on the Middle Way* says that to view the imaginary—names and terms that designate and the phenomena they designate—as not established by way of their own character is a deprecation. Specifically, the *mahāsiddha* Maitrīpāda's *Ten Verses on Reality* says:

> For those who wish to understand reality,
> there is neither Aspectarian or Nonaspectarian.
> Even Madhyamaka that is not adorned
> with the guru's speech is only mediocre.[652]

The commentary on this verse by the paṇḍita Sahajavajra says, "The exalted Śāntarakṣita and so forth are asserted to be Aspectarian Madhyamaka . . . Therefore, 'Even Madhyamaka that is not adorned / with the guru's speech is only mediocre.'"[653] Because it says that "middling Madhyamaka" refers to the system of Śāntarakṣita, if it is therefore calling those who assert the Prāsaṅgika system to be "great Madhyamaka," then it is clear that there is a difference in view between Prāsaṅgika and Svātantrika. For example, something being established by its own entity or its own nature, which is asserted as the object of negation of the reasoning that analyzes the ultimate in Prāsaṅgika, is asserted to conventionally exist by Svātantrika. This will be discussed in detail below. [315]

In such systems as Svātantrika, it is asserted that when seeking the designated object, if it is not found, then it is not possible to posit the existence of that phenomenon. For example, when searching for a designated object such as the person, it is asserted that among the aggregates that are its basis of designation, the mental consciousness is found, and therefore that is posited as the referent of the person. In the Prāsaṅgika system, however, when searching for the designated object, it is asserted that no phenomenon whatsoever is found. When searching for the designated object of the person, one is not searching to simply determine whether that person exists; one is searching to determine how that person is established, not being satisfied that it is a mere projection by the mind. A reasoning consciousness that searches in that way does not find the aggregates, individually or collectively, to be the person, and it also does not find the person anywhere else. That not finding is the meaning of the person being not intrinsically established; it does not mean that the person is utterly nonexistent. The important point is that if something exists intrinsically, it must be found when searched for in that way, but its mere existence does not need to be found.

Both Prāsaṅgika and Svātantrika agree in asserting that the person cannot withstand analysis by reasoning. However, they do not agree on the point at which it can or cannot withstand analysis by reasoning, nor do they agree on the threshold for ultimate analysis. In Prāsaṅgika, not being satisfied by mere conventional designations such as "I accumulated this karma" and "I experienced this effect," one searches to determine where that designated object is established—in the aggregates individually, collectively, or as something else. It is at this point that it becomes ultimate analysis. Having searched in that way, if something is found in what is being analyzed, then it is asserted that it can bear analysis by reasoning. Svātantrika asserts that such reasoning is conventional valid knowledge, that it is not reasoning that analyzes the ultimate. If something is found when sought by it, it is not established as something that can withstand analysis by reasoning. For them, the threshold of ultimate analysis is analyzing whether phenomena are established from the side of the objects' own mode of being, without being posited through the power of appearing to a nondefective awareness. When sought by that, if what is being analyzed is found, they assert that it can withstand analysis by reasoning. Thus, for any of the schools of tenets, when the mode of being of any phenomenon is analyzed, the threshold for ultimate analysis is a crucial point.

The actual threshold for analysis of reality in the Prāsaṅgika Madhyamaka system is the point from which one begins to search for how this "I" or self in one's continuum is established, not being satisfied that the "I" is something that is merely posited by the power of conventional designation. It must be satisfactory to use conventions like "I am staying here," "I see," "I feel," and "I remember." Yet when one is not satisfied with just those conventions, one searches and finds that the "I" is not the individual aggregates, such as the eye and ear, and is not their collection, and that the "I" does not exist someplace else. They assert that this is the way in which the "I" does not intrinsically exist. [316] Svātantrika and below [Cittamātra, Sautrāntika, and Vaibhāṣika] hold that an object that lacks such intrinsic existence is utterly nonexistent; they assert that to conceive an object in this way is the view of annihilation. In contrast, Prāsaṅgika holds that the fact that things do not intrinsically exist is not enough for them to be nonexistent and the fact that they conventionally exist is enough for them to be existent. They assert that the two extremes are eliminated because of dependent arising, in which all phenomena lack intrinsic existence, yet all categories of phenomena are conventionally tenable. That is a unique feature of this system. Therefore Prāsaṅgika and Svātantrika differ in their identification of the object of negation, and because of that, they differ on the threshold for analysis of suchness. If one does not ascertain this dividing line well, it is difficult to see the subtle difference between Prāsaṅgika and Svātantrika.

In brief, the primary factor that distinguishes Prāsaṅgika and Svātantrika is whether they accept that phenomena are established by way of their own nature. Those who they refute true existence in dependence on correct reasons whose three modes are established from their own side are called Svātantrika. Those who primarily refute true existence with consequences are called Prāsaṅgika.

The Svātantrika Madhyamaka School of Tenets

The founder of the Svātantrika Madhyamaka tenet system is Bhāviveka. He is said to have been born into the royal caste in Malaya in southern India in the sixth century. It is explained that he was known as Bhavya, Bhāviveka, and Bhāvaviveka. This scholar composed the *Lamp of Wisdom*, an extensive work commenting on the intention of *Root Verses on the Middle Way* from the Svātantrika perspective, as well as his independent work *Essence of the Middle Way* and its autocommentary the *Blaze of Reasoning*, mentioned frequently above. He is the founder of Svātantrika Madhyamaka in general, which explains that all phenomena are established by way of their own character but do not truly exist, and he is the founder of Sautrāntika-Svātantrika Madhyamaka in particular.

A unique feature of Bhāviveka's Madhyamaka treatises is that he saw that in the system of Nāgārjuna, the view of reality, or the profound middle way, is to be delineated through the use of reasons in which the three modes are complete that appear in the works of Dignāga. Based on this fact, he proved that in the context of delineating the view, one needs autonomous reasons in which the three modes are complete. In addition, when determining the limits of what is to be refuted and proved by reasoning in general, and the limits of what is refuted by reasonings that analyze the ultimate in particular, it is critical to understand how negation is divided into implicative negation and nonimplicative negation. [317] Therefore, at many points in his own works, he emphasizes and explains the two types of negation. This appears clearly in his *Blaze of Reasoning*:

> Here, the negation "is not" is taken to be a nonimplicative negation; it is not taken to be an implicative negation. One might ask how nonimplicative negation and implicative negation are distinguished. In an implicative negation, negating the nature of a thing implies a different nature of that thing. For example, the negation "He is not a brahmin" conveys that he is not a brahmin but, for example, a *śūdra*, inferior in austerities and learning. A nonimplicative negation simply refutes the nature of a thing; it does not convey a thing that is other than the object negated. For example, "Brahmins do not drink beer" is simply refuting that. It is not saying, "They drink something else" or "They drink nothing." Therefore here, this is simply making the refutation that the earth and so forth that are designated by the world are not the nature of the elements ultimately. It is not proving that they are the nature of something else or that they are the nature of nonthings.[654]

Also, Bhāviveka says that someone might raise the qualm "If one is able to prove the ultimate truth in dependence on a reason with the three modes, why does it say in a sūtra that the ultimate truth transcends the spheres of all forms of awareness?" To dispel that contradiction, he responds that in the term *ultimate truth*, the consciousness based on which the ultimate is posited as the ultimate object is of two types: *uncontaminated wisdom*, which is free from elaborations, and *mundane wisdom*, which has elaborations.[655] In general, in the *Blaze of Reasoning*, he sets forth three ways of positing the ultimate in the context of the term *ultimate truth*. This will be explained in the fourth volume of *Science and Philosophy in the Indian Buddhist Classics* in the context of the two truths in Madhyamaka. In the *Blaze of Reasoning*, he also sets forth how a Mādhyamika engages in refutation using the qualification "ultimate" in the context of arguing that the elements such as earth are not ultimately established. [318]

> [In the statement "earth and so forth are not the natures of the elements] ultimately," "ultimately" means that which exists ultimately. "Elements" are elements because they arise as themselves or give rise to something else. "Natures" means the natures of the elements because they are the nature of the elements such as earth. "Are not" is a term indicating negation; it means that they "are not." What is it that "are not"? It refers to "Earth and so forth are not the natures of the elements ultimately."[656]

To summarize, Bhāviveka argued that even in the Madhyamaka's own system, it is correct to employ the three modes of autonomous syllogisms. In dependence on that, a new Madhyamaka tradition arose that disagreed with Buddhapālita on many important points in commenting on the intention of Nāgārjuna. Later scholars would coin the term Svātantrika Madhyamaka for this tradition.

The Svātantrika school is defined as a subschool of Madhyamaka philosophy that accepts that the three modes of reasons proving that phenomena do not truly exist are established from their own side. *Svatantra* ("autonomous") refers to the subject [of a debate] that is established as appearing commonly to the unmistaken valid consciousnesses of the two parties in a debate through the power of the mode of subsistence of the object from the side of the basis of designation, without being led merely by the assertions of the opponent; and that, based on that subject, an inference is generated that comprehends the thesis, having ascertained how the modes of that reasoning are established. A Mādhyamika who accepts such viability is called a Svātantrika Mādhyamika. The *Lamp of Wisdom* says, "The thirteenth chapter was composed with the purpose of setting forth the way in which conditioned phenomena lack entityness in terms of another aspect, through the power of answers to refutations and independent inferences."[657] *Autonomous*, *independent*, and *sovereign* are synonyms. As Amarasiṃha's glossary, *Treasury of Amara*, says, "Autonomous, independent, sovereign."[658] Those terms as well as *established from its own side*, *intrinsically established*, and *established by way of its own character* make the same point. [319]

In the Svātantrika system, nondefective consciousnesses are not mistaken about their object of engagement appearing to exist by way of its own character conventionally. The reason that they are nonmistaken in that way rests on the fact that forms and so forth appear to nondefective consciousnesses to be established by way of their own entity, and they assert that forms and so forth are in fact established by way of their own entity. Therefore the reason that they assert autonomous syllogisms in their system rests on this assertion that establishment by way of the object's own entity exists conventionally.

There are two divisions: Sautrāntika-Svātantrika Madhyamaka and Yogācāra-Svātantrika Madhyamaka. A Mādhyamika who does not accept reflexive awareness and who accepts that external objects are established by way of their own character is called a Sautrāntika-Svātantrika Mādhyamika. A Mādhyamika who does not accept external objects and who accepts reflexive awareness is called a Yogācāra-Svātantrika Mādhyamika. Sautrāntika-Svātantrika accepts, in conformity with Sautrāntika, that external objects are composites of minute particles. Yogācāra-Svātantrika accepts, in accordance with Yogācāra, the lack of external objects conventionally. These two subschools of Svātantrika Madhyamaka are explained more fully in their respective sections below.

Both types of Svātantrika Madhyamaka assert that true establishment, ultimate establishment, and real establishment do not exist in objects of knowledge but assert that establishment by way its own entity, establishment by way of its own character, and intrinsic establishment exist conventionally. Bhāviveka's *Lamp of Wisdom* says, "Regarding that, if you say here that that which is the entity of imaginary natures that express 'form' to the mind and that express 'form' in words does not exist, then this is a deprecation of things because it deprecates what is expressed to the mind and expressed in words."[659] This is saying that when Cittamātra says that imaginary natures are not established by way of their own character, that imaginary nature refers to either expressions to the mind (that is, thoughts) or expressions in words (that is, names), which impute an entity ("this is form") or a quality ("production of form"). If that is the case, because both thoughts and names are functioning things, it becomes a deprecation of things for Cittamātra to call them imaginary natures. This statement is the clearest source for the assertion by this master that things are established by way of their own character conventionally.[660] [320]

Similarly, Candrakīrti explains in his autocommentary to *Entering the Middle Way*, "Here, they say that given that production does not exist ultimately, it is indeed the case that production from self and other can be refuted. However, the nature of things such as form and feeling that are the objects of direct perception and inference are unquestionably produced from other."[661] Candrakīrti is stating here the assertion of the opponent who, when refuting inherently established production, does not accept ultimately established production but does accept production from other. This makes it clear that Svātantrika Madhyamaka accepts establishment by way of its own character. Furthermore, because they assert that when the designated objects of phenomena are searched for, they are found from the side of their own basis of designation, they assert establishment from the object's own side. For example, Śāntarakṣita's *Compendium of Principles* says:

> Being the basis of pride,
> the mind is called "I."
> It exists conventionally;
> its object does not exist ultimately.[662]

The way that consciousness is described in Bhāviveka's *Blaze of Reasoning* as conventionally designated as the self will be discussed below in the section on the tenets of Sautrāntika-Svātantrika Madhyamaka. Similar to that, Śāntarakṣita says that when one searches for the designated object of the person, because it is the basis of producing the pride that thinks, "I am," the mind is conventionally called *self*. His autocommentary to the *Ornament of the Middle Way* says, "In cases when nothing is analyzed, we do not refute the pleasant nature of any experience, from the state of a foolish being to the state of omniscient wisdom."[663] This is saying that in a situation that is not analyzed by reasoning, objects that are established by the experience of everyone from an ordinary being to someone with omniscient wisdom are intrinsically established. Kamalaśīla's *Illumination of the Middle Way* says, "That which abides as only the lack of entityness of all phenomena, ultimately, always, and intrinsically, is the consummate nature because it is established as always being free of superimposition."[664] This is also proven by the fact that he adds the qualification "ultimately" to the lack of intrinsic existence.

Therefore, although nothing is established from its own side without being posited by the power of appearing to a nondefective awareness, this does not contradict that there is establishment from the side of the object in this system in general. Thus they assert a combination of all phenomena being established from the side of the object and being posited by the power of appearing to awareness. [321] Furthermore, because Svātantrika does not identify which awareness posits everything as conventionally existent, phenomena must be posited as conventionally existent by the power of an awareness that is not undermined by valid means of knowledge. In that case, it must be a combination of the two: (1) from the appearance side, phenomena such as form are established in a mode of subsistence that is merely posited by the power of appearing to a nondefective awareness, and (2) from the emptiness side, they are empty of being established from the side of the object's own mode of subsistence that does not rely on being posited by an awareness.

The word "merely" in the phrase "merely posited by the power of appearing to an awareness" eliminates an object being established by its own mode of subsistence, which is not posited by the power of an awareness; it does not eliminate mere existence as a mode of subsistence. If these points are understood well, one is able to distinguish how the way that the two truths are posited by Svātantrika is more subtle than that of the proponents of true existence and is more coarse than that of Prāsaṅgika Madhyamaka.

In this system there are two objects of negation for reasonings that analyze the ultimate. The first takes *the ultimate* to be the reasoning consciousness that analyzes the ultimate in a specific subject, and then posits the subject itself existing in the face of that analysis to be the object of negation of the reasoning analyzing the ultimate. The second takes *the ultimate* to be establishment from the side of the object's unique mode of subsistence, which is not posited by the power of appearing to a nondefective awareness, to be the object of negation of the reasoning analyzing the ultimate.

The first of these is taken to exist from the perspective of reality, being in the field of vision of the inferential reasoning consciousness and the uncontaminated meditative equipoise that realize the emptiness of conventional phenomena. This is called the "object of negation in the face of reasoning." The unfindability of that subject at the conclusion of analyzing it with the reasoning consciousness that analyzes the ultimate is called "realizing emptiness in terms of that subject." Apart from the difference in subtlety of the object of negation, Prāsaṅgika and Svātantrika are similar on this. Thus the *Questions of Brahmaviśeṣacinti* says, "Not to see is to see the truth."[665] And the *Condensed Perfection of Wisdom* says:

> Not seeing form and not seeing feeling.
> Not seeing discrimination and not seeing the mind.
> Not seeing consciousness, mind, and mental consciousness.
> The Tathāgata taught that this is seeing the Dharma.
>
> Sentient beings say, "I see space." [322]
> Analyze this in the way we see space.
> The Tathāgata taught us to see phenomena in that way.
> Seeing cannot be explained with other examples.[666]

This passage is teaching that emptiness is a nonimplicative negation. Space is simply the elimination of obstructive contact. When it is seen or realized, if there were something visually obstructive to be seen, it would be suitable for it to appear. However, apart from a mere lack of obstructive contact, nothing whatsoever is seen. In the same way, if conventional phenomena existed ultimately, they would have to exist in the field of vision of the ultimate perceived by the meditative equipoise realizing emptiness. However, because they do not, they are not seen in such a field of vision. In the case of space, what is seen is space and what is not seen is obstructive contact. That valid consciousness does not see any obstructive contact; it sees its mere absence. This is called "seeing space." In the same way, the uncontaminated reasoning consciousness of meditative equipoise does not see any conventional phenomenon in its field of vision; it sees its mere absence in its field of vision. Therefore what is not seen is the basis of the attribute, all conventional phenomena, and where it is not seen is in the field of vision of the ultimate. What is seen is the mere absence and the mere nonexistence of that. These verses from the *Condensed Perfection of Wisdom* are clearly referring to that.

Regarding how the uncontaminated meditative equipoise eliminates conventional phenomena in the vision of emptiness, the mind that comprehends space sees an absence that is the mere lack of obstructive contact. In the same way, that wisdom sees a mere elimination or a mere nonexistence of conventional phenomena in its field of vision. If conventional phenomena existed in that field of vision that realizes emptiness, they would have to be ultimately established. This is because if some conventional phenomenon existed in the vision of emptiness by those two reasoning consciousnesses [inferential and direct realizations of emptiness], then those two reasoning consciousnesses would not be minds that realize that there is nothing to find at the conclusion of ultimate analysis; they would have to be minds that realize that something is found at the conclusion of analysis. In that case, because what is found is a conventional phenomenon, that conventional phenomenon would withstand analysis by reasoning that analyzes the ultimate. Therefore it would be truly established. If even emptiness existed in the field of vision of the mode of being of emptiness itself, it would be truly established, like the conventional phenomenon that would be found.

Someone might object, "The reality of a sprout, for example, exists in the field of vision of a reasoning consciousness that analyzes the reality of the sprout. Therefore it should be ultimately established." If something is ultimately established, it must be established for a reasoning consciousness that analyzes the ultimate. However, if something is established for a reasoning consciousness that analyzes the ultimate, it does not have to be ultimately established. The reason for that is that the reasoning consciousness itself analyzes whether or not something is ultimately established. Thus, if something like a sprout were ultimately established, it would have to be ultimately established by a reasoning consciousness. [323] Although the reality of the sprout is found by the reasoning consciousness, it is found in that way by analyzing whether the sprout ultimately exists; it is not found by analyzing whether the reality of the sprout ultimately exists. Therefore the reality of the sprout does not become ultimately established. Thus, although being established by a reasoning consciousness that analyzes the ultimate exists, to be established as withstanding analysis by such a reasoning consciousness is not different from being truly established. Therefore it does not exist even conventionally.

This object of negation in the face of reasoning is set forth clearly in such works as the *Blaze of Reasoning* and *Illumination of the Middle Way*. The *Blaze of Reasoning* says:

> Someone might say, "The ultimate is beyond all forms of intellect, but the negation of the entityness of things is the object of language. Therefore is it not the case that there is no such negation?" The ultimate is of two types . . . What is called *mundane wisdom* has elaborations. Here, because it [the term *ultimately*] qualifies the thesis, there is no fault.[667]

The proponents of true existence would say that if the four elements do not ultimately exist for the Madhyamaka school, this contradicts their own assertion, it is undermined by direct perception, and it is underminded by what is known in the world. The passage above comes at the point of [Bhāviveka] responding to such an objection, saying that in this context, the statement "the four elements do not ultimately exist" means that they do not exist in the face of the reasoning consciousness that analyzes the ultimate; because it refers to their not being established by that, the faults stated earlier do not apply. This is a very clear statement of how the object of negation for reasoning is identified.

Illumination of the Middle Way says, "All the cognitions arisen from hearing, thinking, and meditating on the perfect truth . . . to say 'not ultimately produced' is explaining that a correct consciousness does not establish them as produced."[668] By saying that production and so forth are not ultimately established because they do not exist in the vision of reality of the reasoning consciousnesses of hearing, thinking, and meditation, this passage is also indicating the object of negation for reasoning. This object of negation for reasoning is merely something superimposed by tenets. Therefore the mind that apprehends it is found in persons whose minds have been affected by tenets [that is, studied philosophy]; it does not exist in the minds of other living beings whose minds have not been affected by tenets, such as birds and deer. It must be posited as the artificial conception of true existence.

The second object of negation in this system is the object of negation that is the apprehended object of the innate conception of true existence in which the ultimate is taken to be that which is established from the side of the object's own unique mode of subsistence, one that is not posited by the power of simply appearing to a nondefective awareness. This is not clearly set forth in texts that are Svātantrika sources; however, it is implied by what is explicitly said about the meaning of conventional existence in *Illumination of the Middle Way*. The opposite of that meaning of conventional existence indicates what the ultimate existence of the object of negation would be like, because the opposite of conventional existence must be posited as ultimate establishment. [324] Thus *Illumination of the Middle Way* says, "They [conventional appearances] arise through the power of the fructification of the predispositions of beginningless error. They are displayed to all living beings as if the nature of things were real. Therefore, by the power of their minds, all the natures of false things are said to only exist conventionally."[669] The first two sentences of this passage, from "They arise" through "things were real," indicate that things such as form appear to sentient beings by the power of predispositions for the conception of true existence as if they were true, although they are not true. Therefore such a conception of true existence is innate. The passage from "Therefore, by the power of their minds" to "only exist conventionally" is explicitly indicating that the meaning of *existing conventionally* is to exist as merely posited by the power of appearing to the nondefective awareness, both conceptual and nonconceptual, of those living beings. The passage is implicitly indicating that being established from the side of the object's own unique mode of subsistence, one that is not posited by the power of appearing to a nondefective awareness, is the measure of being truly established.

The *minds* in the phrase "posited by the power of the minds of those living beings" are conceptual and nonconceptual. Regarding the nonconceptual mind, there are the valid sense consciousnesses and so forth. The awareness that perceives true establishment under the influence of delusion, the conception of true existence, is posited as conceptual; it is not the nonconceptual sense consciousnesses. Śāntarakṣita's *Commentary on Distinguishing the Two Truths* says, "The text states, 'It is said that true production and so forth do not appear.' Someone might ask, 'If it does not appear, how is it superimposed?' It states, 'It is merely superimposed spontaneously or based on tenets.'"[670] This statement that true establishment does not appear to the sense consciousnesses rests on the important assertion in this system that the sense consciousnesses are not polluted by predispositions of the conception of true existence.

Due to the falsity that is the difference between the mode of appearance and the mode of being of something like a pot, this Svātantrika Madhyamaka system asserts that things appear to truly exist in their mode of appearance. Furthermore, they appear to truly exist to both conceptual and nonconceptual consciousnesses. Thus, in this system, there is also the assertion that the object of negation, true establishment, does appear to the sense consciousnesses. Therefore, in this system, establishment from the side of the object's unique mode of subsistence, one that is not posited by the power of appearing to a nondefective awareness, is the referent object of the innate conception of true existence and is the primary object of negation of the reasoning that analyzes the ultimate. [325]

This can be explained in terms of a magician's illusion. When the basis of conjuring, such as a pebble or a stick, is conjured by a magician into a horse or an elephant, there are three ways in which it appears: with appearance but without belief, with both appearance and belief, and with neither appearance nor belief. Regarding the first, for the magician himself, the pebble or stick appears as a horse or an elephant, but he does not believe that it is. In the same way, for common beings who have realized emptiness, things appear as if they were truly established, but they do not believe that they are. Regarding the second, to the audience whose eyes are affected by the magician's mantra and substances and who have never seen or heard of illusion before, the pebble or stick appears as a horse or an elephant, and they believe that it is. In the same way, for ordinary people who have not realized emptiness, things appear to be truly established and they believe that they are truly established. Regarding the third, for those whose eyes have not been affected by the magician's mantra and substances, the stick or pebble neither appears as a horse or elephant nor do they believe that it is. In the same way, to the wisdom that knows the modes, which is not polluted by ignorance, things do not appear to be truly established, nor are they believed to be.

Furthermore, for the magician, the basis of conjuring merely appears to be a horse and elephant through the power of his awareness being affected by the substance and mantra; it does not appear to be a horse or elephant from the side of the mode of subsistence of the pebble or stick without depending on such an awareness. For the audience whose eyes have been affected, the appearance as a horse or elephant appears from the start to be a real horse or elephant on that basis of appearance, without being posited by the power of an internal awareness. It appears to be standing there occupying the place, and they apprehend it in the way that it appears. In the same way, any phenomenon that appears to ordinary sentient beings appears as if it is something that exists from the side of the object's own mode of subsistence without depending on being posited by the power of the mind. Because belief arises in accordance with that appearance, awarenesses to which that appears are posited as being mistaken consciousnesses and as having the perception of true existence. Consciousnesses that conceive of phenomena as they appear are called *mistaken consciousnesses* and *conceptions of true existence*. The *Ornament of the Middle Way* says:

> Aspects that are apparitions appear
> through the fructification of predispositions.
> Yet because they are mistaken, they are like illusions.[671]

In this Svātantrika Madhyamaka system, the example of the magician's illusion is praised as a way to understand how being posited and not being posited by the power of awareness differ. The appearance of the basis of conjuring, the pebble or stick, as a horse or elephant is posited by the power of awareness. However, there is no contradiction that it appears as a horse or elephant from the side of the basis of conjuring, the pebble or stick. In the same way, for all phenomena, there is a convergence of being posited by the power of awareness and being established from the side of the object. The illusory horse or elephant is praised as an example of that. Such a conception of true existence has arisen from time without beginning in the minds of sentient beings such as birds and deer, whose minds have not been affected by tenets, without needing to think about reasons. It is called the innate conception of true existence. [326]

Therefore any phenomenon whatsoever is like an illusion, appearing to be true even though not even one is truly established. *Nondefective awareness* refers to a consciousness that is not mistaken in the sense of being polluted by adventitious causes of error. "Posited by the power of appearing to a nondefective awareness" means every phenomenon is posited by the power of a unique awareness—one that is not polluted by adventitious causes of error—that acts to establish it. For example, something like form is posited by a unique awareness that establishes it—that is, it is posited by the power of an eye consciousness apprehending form that is nonmistaken with respect to an object of engagement that is intrinsically real. This is the case up to a mental consciousness that is nonmistaken with respect to its own specific object among the objects included in the category of phenomena source.

This system asserts that the first wheel of Dharma explained in the *Explanation of the Intention* is of provisional meaning and that the final wheel is of definitive meaning. When "no production" and so forth is stated in a sūtra of the middle wheel, like the *Heart Sūtra*, because the qualification "ultimately" is not specifically added to the object of negation, it is considered a sūtra of provisional meaning. When the qualification "ultimately" is specifically added to the object of negation in a sūtra, such as the *Perfection of Wisdom in One Hundred Thousand Stanzas*, it is asserted to be a sūtra of definitive meaning. Thus they assert that the middle wheel has both provisional and definitive elements.

Sautrāntika-Svātantrika Madhyamaka

It has already been explained that the founder of Sautrāntika-Svātantrika Madhyamaka is Bhāviveka, who composed such works as the *Lamp of Wisdom*, a commentary on *Root Verses on the Middle Way*. He found fault with each of the consequences used by Buddhapālita in the context of refuting production from the four extremes, giving extensive refutations. He refuted the Cittamātra assertions that the imaginary is not established by means of its own character, that there is a foundation consciousness, and that there is reflexive awareness. Having done so, he blazed the trail of Sautrāntika-Svātantrika Madhyamaka, asserting that phenomena are intrinsically established, that phenomena are established by way of their own character conventionally, and that external objects exist.

Bhāviveka's follower Avalokitavrata lived during the seventh century and composed an extensive commentary on the *Lamp of Wisdom*, where he set forth various non-Buddhist and Buddhist assertions. Another of his followers, Jñānagarbha, was born in the seventh century in Oḍiviśa. He composed both *Distinguishing the Two Truths* and its autocommentary, upholding the tradition of Bhāviveka well. This master is said to have been the teacher of the great abbot Śāntarakṣita.

In this system, they assert the existence of external objects and do not assert the existence of the foundation consciousness and the afflicted mental consciousness. Specific Madhyamaka works by Nāgārjuna and his heir Āryadeva do not clearly explain how external objects exist or do not exist conventionally. [327] However, Bhāviveka asserts that external objects exist conventionally and that sense consciousnesses do not apprehend external objects such as form and sound without aspects; they are only able to apprehend them from the perspective of having aspects. He extensively refutes the Cittamātra assertion that the sense consciousnesses and their objects, such as form and sound, are the same nature, asserting that [objects and apprehending consciousnesses] are cause and effect and hence sequential. The *Blaze of Reasoning* says:

> The sūtra passage cited by Cittamātra, "because a creator and a consumer are refuted," was stated to dispel the imputation by the tīrthikas that there is a creator and a consumer that is different from consciousness. The buddhas and bodhisattvas set forth "mind only" (*cittamātra*), but they did not do so in order to dispel external objects.[672]

And that same text says:

> [The Cittamātra position] is undermined by the accepted scriptures because it contradicts the scriptures that say that the eye consciousness arises in dependence on the eye and form. It is undermined by common knowledge because in the world it is known that a consciousness, such as that of the eye, is not produced without an object, such as form. Therefore it is undermined by common knowledge.[673]

Such statements also appear at length in his *Lamp of Wisdom*.

Regarding the meaning of those passages cited above, the statement from a sūtra that all the worlds and their inhabitants are only of the nature of consciousness was stated in that way to refute the existence of an eternal and self-arisen creator of the world that is different from consciousness, as postulated by the tīrthikas. The statement was not set forth to refute external objects. Even a statement that literally says "external objects do not exist" simply means that they do not ultimately exist. Therefore that external objects do not exist is not the meaning of any sūtra. If external objects that are a different entity than consciousness did not exist, it would contradict the passage from the sūtra that one has accepted, which says that the eye consciousness arises in dependence on the eye and form. It also contradicts what is well known in the world, that without external objects such as form, an eye consciousness that apprehends it is not produced. Therefore such passages are explaining that this is not tenable.

They also do not accept reflexive awareness. Cittamātra asserts that there are two factors in consciousnesses—the factor that appears as the object and the factor that perceives itself—referring to the former as the *apprehended aspect* and the latter as *reflexive awareness*, and they assert that they are the same nature. [328] For example, when a crystal is next to something colorful, there are two factors for the consciousness that perceives it: the factor of the crystal's own clear nature and the factor produced as having the aspect of the nearby color. Although there are two, it is asserted that it is as if they were a single entity. No matter how much reflexive awareness is analyzed by this system, apart from this awareness of another phenomenon, there is no appearance of subject and object, and the awareness itself does not receive the designation of object or subject. When a crystal is next to something colorful, its clear nature changes, and it is produced in the aspect of that color; when it is apart from the color, it becomes only clear. For consciousness, because the aspect of its clear nature never appears separately, there is no similarity between the example and the meaning. Therefore reflexive awareness is refuted. Regarding these points, the *Essence of the Middle Way* says:

> If one asserts that the appearance as the object
> is the object of observation of the mind,
> apart from the appearance as the object,
> what other nature of the mind is there?[674]

The *Blaze of Reasoning* says, "For us, the nature of consciousness is to produce the perception of objects, such as form. Apart from seeing the object, it does not perceive itself. If there is a second nature of consciousness other than the perception of the object, please show us what it is."[675] And Jñānagarbha's *Distinguishing the Two Truths* says, "Because reflexive awareness is not correct."[676] One can infer [their position] from what appears in statements such as these.

They also do not accept the foundation consciousness and the afflicted mental consciousness. If one accepts the foundation consciousness, one would have to accept that there are no external objects apart from what just appears as form, sound, and so forth through the fructification of predispositions on the foundation consciousness, and that is not tenable. They assert that the mental consciousness takes rebirth and that it is the referent of the person; they do not assert a foundation consciousness and afflicted mental consciousness that is different in nature from the six operative consciousnesses. Thus the *Blaze of Reasoning* says, "On the conventional level, we explicitly apply the term *self* to consciousness. Because consciousness takes rebirth, it is the *self*. It is thus designated to the body and the collection of sense faculties."[677] The same text says, "The three various things called *fructification*, *thought of 'I,'* and *awareness* that you have imputed as being produced from the transformations of consciousness are not asserted by us."[678] [329] This is saying that some types of consciousness at times serve as the foundation of saṃsāra and nirvāṇa and are concomitant with the view of the perishable collection; the foundation consciousness and the afflicted mental consciousness are not tenable.

Their assertion of the subtle and coarse selflessness of persons is like that of Vaibhāṣika. They assert that the emptiness of true establishment and the ultimate truth are the subtle selflessness of phenomena. They assert that all phenomena are established by way of their own character conventionally and are established from the side of their own basis of designation.

Yogācāra-Svātantrika Madhyamaka

The founder of Yogācāra-Svātantrika Madhyamaka was Śāntarakṣita. It is explained that he lived in the eighth century in Bengal, the son of Vihāradhara, the king of Sahor. He composed the *Ornament of the Middle Way* and its commentary, which sets forth the basis, path, and fruition of Yogācāra-Svātantrika Madhyamaka, thereby founding the Yogācāra-Svātantrika Madhyamaka school of tenets. His most famous work is the

Compendium of Principles, which extensively sets forth and analyzes the assertions of principles by the non-Buddhist and Buddhist schools of India.

The great upholder of the philosophical tradition of Śāntarakṣita was his direct disciple Kamalaśīla, who also lived in the eighth century. He composed *Illumination of the Middle Way* and upheld well the tradition of Yogācāra-Svātantrika Madhyamaka. His own texts included such works as the three *Stages of Meditation*, the *Proof of the Lack of Intrinsic Nature*, the *Commentary on the Ornament of the Middle Way*,[679] and the *Commentary on the Compendium of Principles*. Other works that delineate the view in accordance with the system of Śāntarakṣita include Haribhadra's *Illumination of the Ornament of Realizations*, *Commentary on the Perfection of Wisdom in Twenty-Five Thousand Stanzas in Eight Chapters*, and *Commentary on the Verse Summary of the Precious Qualities*; Buddhajñānapāda's works on the perfection of wisdom; and Abhayākaragupta's *Moonlight of Essential Points* and *Ornament of the Sage's Thought*.

In the Yogācāra-Svātantrika Madhyamaka system, although they assert reflexive awareness, they do not assert external objects, the foundation consciousness, and the afflicted mental consciousness. Regarding how they accept reflexive awareness, the *Commentary on the Ornament of the Middle Way* says, "Therefore the nature that illuminates itself without relying on another illuminator is called *reflexive awareness of consciousness*."[680] [330] They assert that the mental consciousness is the referent of the person. Because they do not assert that multiple consciousnesses of the same type can be manifestly produced simultaneously, they do not accept a foundation consciousness that is a different entity from the six operative consciousnesses. They also do not assert the afflicted mental consciousness.

In this system, unlike in Sautrāntika-Svātantrika Madhyamaka, not only do they assert that the lack of external objects is the meaning of the sūtra, they accept it as a tenet of their own system. In the *Sixty Stanzas on Reasoning* Nāgārjuna says:

> What is explained to be the great elements and so forth
> are completely included in consciousness.[681]

They assert that this passage is teaching that such things as the elements and the elemental evolutes are consciousness that merely appear as those phenomena and that therefore all of them are the same entity as the consciousness that apprehends them. In this way they assert that that mode of the nonexistence of external objects is Nāgārjuna's intention in making this statement.

In this system, one first determines the selflessness of persons and then determines that reality of nonduality, which is the lack of subject and object being different entities. After that, a person of especially great awareness and effort sees that there is not even a particle that it is ultimately established, and therefore they come to understand the middle path that is free from all extremes. That is, they assert that there are three stages in the determination of reality. This mode is described in this way in the *Ornament of the Middle Way*, which says:

> In dependence on mind only,
> one should understand that there are no external things.
> In dependence on this,
> one should understand that it also is without self.[682]

Haribhadra's *Clear Meaning Commentary* says on this point, "By meditating on the fact that there is no self because it lacks production and disintegration, one completely discards attachment to the self. Then one correctly sees that dependent arisings such as the aggregates that lack that [self] have the quality of production and disintegration. Because one determines that blue and the awareness of it are certain to be observed simultaneously, there is mind only."[683] Thus, as in Cittamātra, they assert conventionally that external objects do not exist and that all phenomena are of the nature of consciousness. [331] Although this system is similar to Cittamātra, they do not assert even conventionally that consciousness is truly established or that the reality of nonduality is truly established.

Their assertion of the subtle and coarse selflessness of persons is like that of Vaibhāṣika. Regarding the selflessness of phenomena, they assert that the nonduality of apprehended and apprehender and the lack of external objects is the coarse selflessness of phenomena, and that the emptiness of true establishment, lack of true existence, and the ultimate truth are the subtle selflessness of phenomena. Because they assert that all phenomena are established by way of their own character conventionally, in their own system they do not describe them as mere imputations by thought and merely posited by names and terms.

This is just a summary of how the tenets of this system are asserted. The presentation of the two truths in the Svātantrika system and what emanates from that—that is to say, how they delineate reality—will be explained in the fourth volume of *Science and Philosophy in the Indian Buddhist Classics*.

PRĀSAṄGIKA MADHYAMAKA

As was explained above, the founder of Prāsaṅgika Madhyamaka is Candrakīrti. He lived in the seventh century and composed *Clear Words*, a commentary on *Root Verses on the Middle Way*. At that time Buddhapālita had commented on the passages in *Root Verses on the Middle Way* that refute production from the four extremes, such as the statement "not from self and not from other." In his commentary on the *Root Verses*, the *Lamp of Wisdom*, Bhāviveka set forth many faults with Buddhapālita's argument. [Candrakīrti] then said that those faults did not apply to Buddhapālita, that Buddhapālita did not assert the use of autonomous syllogisms, and he proved that it is not suitable for a Mādhyamika to accept autonomous syllogisms, setting forth many points that undermined accepting them. He thus founded the Prāsaṅgika Madhyamaka school. His independent work *Entering the Middle Way* and its autocommentary extensively delineate a selflessness of persons and phenomena that is unshared with Svātantrika and other schools.

Furthermore, as was also explained above, this master composed commentaries on the works of Nāgārjuna, such as *Sixty Stanzas on Reasoning* and *Seventy Stanzas on Emptiness*, as well as a commentary on Āryadeva's *Four Hundred Verses*. Śāntideva was a follower of Candrakīrti and a great upholder of his tradition. He lived in the eighth century, and his most famous works are *Entering the Bodhisattva Way* and the *Compendium of Training*. In his own works, he upheld the Madhyamaka tradition of Candrakīrti well. [332] In addition, such scholars as Āryaśūra and Nāgasena, and later Prajñākaramati, Maitripa, and Atiśa, must be counted as masters who accepted the Prāsaṅgika view.

The Prāsaṅgika school is defined as the philosophical school that propounds that there is no entityness and that does not assert that things are established by way of their own intrinsic character even conventionally. It is called Prāsaṅgika Madhyamaka because, without accepting autonomous syllogisms, it accepts reasonings that are known to others to create the view for the opponent, and it primarily states consequences (*prasaṅga*) to demonstrate internal contradictions to the proponents of true existence. *Clear Words* says, "This statement mentions the similar example that is known to others and is concordant with the probandum and the proof."[684] And the same text says, "Thus the master... for the most part dispelled the position of the other through using consequences only."[685]

The unique feature of this system is that no person or phenomenon is intrinsically established in any way, yet all categories of actions and agents are possible. The ultimate root of the many unique ways of describing the world in this system is that it does not accept that persons or phenomena are established by way of their own intrinsic character even conventionally.

Entering the Middle Way says, "Know that that which has the meaning of emptiness is the definitive meaning."[686] Regarding provisional and definitive sūtras, this passage is saying that they are differentiated by whether they explicitly set forth the profound emptiness of persons and phenomena. Therefore this system asserts that sūtras in the first wheel that teach that all conditioned phenomena are impermanent are sūtras of provisional meaning, and within that wheel, sūtras that teach that all phenomena lack true existence are sūtras of definitive meaning. [333] Because the sūtras of the middle wheel, the wheel of no characteristic, prove with countless types of reasonings that phenomena are not established from their own side, they are sūtras of definitive meaning. Because the sūtra *Explanation of the Intention* of the final wheel teaches the three natures—the dependent, the consummate, and the imaginary—differentiating them into what is and is not truly established in a way that accords with the assertions of Cittamātra, it is asserted to be a sūtra of provisional meaning.

The three natures that are explained in the *Explanation of the Intention* are key elements of the Cittamātra system. However, there is a unique way of positing the three natures in the Madhyamaka system, according to what appears in the "Questions of Maitreya" chapter in the *Perfection of Wisdom in Twenty Thousand Verses*. It is set forth in the *Autocommentary on Entering the Middle Way*:

> A snake is an imaginary dependent arising in relation to a coiled rope because it does not exist there. In relation to a real snake, it is established as real because it is not imaginary. In the same way, intrinsic nature is imaginary in relation to conditioned depen-

dent phenomena. Thus Nāgārjuna's *Root Verses on the Middle Way* [in verse 15.2] says:

> Intrinsic nature is not fabricated
> and does not depend on another.

Entityness is not something created. That which is imputed to apprehended dependent arisings, reflection-like creations, are real in the sphere of a buddha because they are not imaginary. Because he understands reality through directly perceiving the true nature alone, without touching created things, he is called a *buddha*. Thus, having understood the three natures—the imaginary, the dependent, and the consummate—in that way, one should explain the intention of the sūtra. Regarding apprehended and apprehender, nothing exists apart from the dependent. Therefore consider how those two are imagined in the dependent. I have said enough.[687]

This is saying that these conventional phenomena as they appear are the *dependent*. The factor that is superimposed as the mode of being onto the dependent is the *imaginary*. The lack of those dependent conventional phenomena being intrinsically established is the *consummate*.

They assert that the lack of a self-sufficient and substantially existent person is the *coarse selflessness of persons*, the lack of an intrinsically established person is the *subtle selflessness of persons*, and the lack of true existence in the basis of designation, such as the aggregates, is the *subtle selflessness of phenomena*. [334] The difference between the two subtle types of selflessness is not from the perspective of the object of negation; it is from the perspective of the basis that is empty. *Entering the Middle Way* says:

> In order to liberate wandering beings, this selflessness
> is said to be two types, divided into phenomena and
> persons.[688]

This is saying that the refutation of true establishment, the object of negation, in terms of the basis of the person is posited as the subtle selflessness of persons and the refutation of that in terms of the basis of the aggregates and so forth is posited as the subtle selflessness of phenomena. They assert that there is no difference in subtlety between the selflessness of persons and phenomena and that both of those are the final mode of being.

In the Prāsaṅgika Madhyamaka system, there is nothing that is established by way of its own character in any way, and yet both a cause and its effect and an action and its agent can be posited without the least confusion. Indeed, not only are the two not contradictory, they assist each other. From that perspective, this system has many features that are unshared with Svātantrika and the other Buddhist schools. If one carefully analyzes Candrakīrti's *Clear Words* and his *Entering the Middle Way* and its autocommentary, one can understand these features in greater detail. Here are some of the most important among these positions not shared with other schools of tenets: (1) their way of positing dependent arising and the conventional through explaining the meaning of emptiness to be dependent arising, (2) their unique position that one must accept external objects while also accepting the existence of consciousness, (3) their unique way of refuting a foundation consciousness that is a different entity than the six collections of consciousness, (4) their unique way of explaining that, even though there is no foundation consciousness, the connection of actions and their effects is tenable from the point of positing the disintegrated state as an impermanent thing, (5) their unique way of positing the three times based on their view of the disintegrated state, (6) their unique way of refuting reflexive awareness, and (7) their unique way of refuting that the view of reality is to be produced in the opponent through autonomous syllogisms. From among these, a few will be explained here. The others will be explained in volume 4 of this series.

The first of these is their unique position that the existence of external objects must be accepted. In general, both Vaibhāṣika and Sautrāntika assert that when the basis of composition of a coarse form is searched for and analyzed, dimensionless subtle particles are found; they apply the terms *external form* and *external object* to the forms that are established by those partless particles acting as the basis of composition. Both Cittamātra and Yogācāra-Svātantrika Madhyamaka refute external objects with many reasonings. [335] Although Prāsaṅgika Madhyamaka accepts the existence of external objects in general, it does not assert that external objects are established through the accumulation of partless particles, like the Vaibhāṣika do. The proponents of true existence, for whatever phenomenon is posited, are not satisfied with its being merely a conventional designation. They search for the designated object and simply posit it as real.

Due to this, Prāsaṅgika asserts that although neither external objects nor consciousnesses that are established by way of their own character exist, according to unanalyzed conventions, external objects as well as consciousnesses do exist; conventions such as mountains and forests, when posited as they are known to the world, are not undermined by any valid means of knowledge. Also, in the Perfection of Wisdom sūtras it is said that both objects and consciousnesses equally lack intrinsic nature, and in the Abhidharma it is said that they both equally exist. Therefore they assert that it is not correct to make a distinction of existence and nonexistence between objects and consciousnesses in terms of either the conventional or the ultimate. The *Autocommentary on Entering the Middle Way* says:

> When the nonexistence of form is understood by reasoning, one must understand that the mind also does not exist because the existence of both is untenable. Also, when one understands that the mind exists, one must understand that form also exists because both are known to the world.[689]

That same text also says:

> Regarding the aggregates, form and so on, the Abhidharma says that all five are similar from the perspective of their division into, say, specific characteristics and general characteristics. In the Perfection of Wisdom, all five are similar in being refuted because it says, "Subhūti, form is empty of intrinsic nature . . . [up to] consciousness."[690]

The existence of external objects is based on the fact that they are not established by way of their own character. Because establishment by way of its own character is refuted, the existence of such things as forms—which are different entities from the consciousness that apprehends them, as is known in the conventions of the world—is established. Because they are established, the existence of external objects is established.

Turning to the unique way that this system posits dependent arising and the conventional, although not even a particle of a phenomenon is established by way of its own character, in this system they can accept that all agents and actions, such as karmic effects, are tenable—without needing to simply relegate it to the perspective of the other person. Furthermore, simply inducing ascertainment of the dependent arising of phenomena causes one's ascertainment of their lack of intrinsic nature to grow. In this way, emptiness and dependent arising come to the aid of each other. [336] By reason of something being empty, that it is dependently established is unambiguous. Because something is dependently established, it is not established by means of its own entity. Therefore being empty establishes that something is a mere appearance, and being a mere appearance establishes that it is empty of its own entity. This means that appearance and emptiness are not contradictory. Because Prāsaṅgika Madhyamaka accepts that phenomena are not independently or intrinsically established, it is most tenable for them to present ultimate truths. And because they accept that the way that they are validly established is simply that they are established in dependence on each other, it is most tenable for them to present conventional truths. This will be explained more fully in volume 4 of this series.

Furthermore, in this system it is asserted that although a long time passes after karmic actions have ceased before their effects arise, it is possible to posit the relationship of actions and effects without such things as a foundation consciousness, inexhaustibility (*avipraṇāśa*), and acquisition (*prāpti*), even conventionally. One might ask in what way the tenability of the connection between actions and effects is unique in this system. In general, although a virtuous or nonvirtuous action and its effects are separated by a long period of time, the effects, such as happiness and suffering, arise without being exhausted. All the higher and lower Buddhist schools of tenets assert this. *Root Verses on the Middle Way* says:

> If it remains until the time of fruition,
> that action would be permanent.
> If it stops, then having stopped,
> how could it produce an effect?[691]

Someone raises this objection: "If the action remained up to the moment before the fruition of the effect, it would be permanent. Because something that is permanent cannot produce an effect, it is not tenable for there to be the connection of an effect arising from an action. And if that action is destroyed in the second moment of its activity, no action would exist up to the moment of the fruition of the effect. Given that it is not tenable that the disintegrated state of an action is a functioning thing, how does an effect arise from an action?" Cittamātra Following Scripture would dispel this objection by saying that there is no fault because at the time of the disintegration of the action, the predisposition of the action and the foundation consciousness, the basis of infusing that keeps predispositions inexhaustible, exists. The way the objection would be dispelled by Vaibhāṣika has already been explained. Sautrāntika would dispel the objection from the perspective of accepting that although the action has already disintegrated, the continuum of consciousness—the referent of the person that is the place of infusing the predispositions of those actions—continues to exist. Regarding the Prāsaṅgika Madhyamaka position, *Entering the Middle Way* says:

> Because it does not intrinsically cease,
> it has the capacity, although there is no foundation consciousness.
> In some, although the action ceased long ago,
> one should know that the effect arises properly.[692] [337]

They assert that it is not feasible for something that arises in dependence on causes and conditions to have an intrinsically established cessation. Therefore, although such things as the foundation consciousness do not exist, it is suitable for the disintegrated state of an action to be a functioning thing. And even though the action in the continuum of consciousness of some person ceased long ago, the effect of happiness or suffering arises from the continuum of the ceased action, without those effects becoming confused. If actions and their effects were intrinsically established, they would not depend on other causes and conditions. If an action ceased intrinsically, then after the cessation of the action, it would have no capacity whatsoever. There are such problems.

In brief, because actions are not intrinsically established, the disintegrated state of an action can be posited as being established based on its cause. Therefore the disintegrated state connects the action and effect; the "I" that is merely designated in dependence on the aggregates is posited as the basis of infusing predispositions that is continuous, and the consciousness is posited as the basis of infusing that is occasional. Thus a foundation consciousness is not needed as the basis for the infusing of predispositions of actions. Having searched for the designated object among the aggregates, even the person does not need to be found; therefore they do not assert that the foundation consciousness is the referent of the person. They do not assert a foundation consciousness because it is not possible for something to be established by way of its own intrinsic character. For this reason, they posit the mere "I" that is imputed by thought as the basis for the infusing of predispositions—there is no point in accepting the foundation consciousness.

In this system, the disintegrated state is asserted to be a functioning thing. In Sautrāntika, Cittamātra, and Svātantrika, when the designated object of any phenomenon is searched for, it is asserted that it must be found. For example, when a sprout disintegrates, everything that is part of the sprout ceases; it does not obtain the status of something else, such as a pot. The parts or the collection [of the parts] of such things as pots are not an instance of any disintegrated state. Therefore, for these other schools, what is called the *disintegrated state* is asserted to be a nonimplicative negation, the factor of the mere cessation of another thing, and it is not asserted to be a functioning thing. This has already been discussed in the first volume of *Science and Philosophy in the Indian Buddhist Classics* in the context of the three times in chapter 18. In the Prāsaṅgika system, however, it is asserted that when the designated object is searched for, no phenomenon is found. For example, there is nothing to be posited as the referent of the person—not the five aggregates of the person individually, their collection, or anything that is a different entity from those two. However, it is not contradictory for that which is posited as the person in dependence on its aggregates to be a functioning thing. In the same way, regarding the disintegrated state, neither the thing that is disintegrating nor something of the same type is suitable to be posited as its instance. However, because it is produced in dependence on the thing that is disintegrating, it is asserted to be a functioning thing.

That the disintegrated state is a functioning thing is set forth in scripture. The *Ten Levels Sūtra* says, "Death is two activities coming together: it destroys that which is composed, and it acts as a cause of continuing ignorance."[693] [338] The same text says, "The statement 'Through the condition of birth, there is aging and death' means that the condition of birth is the continuation and support of aging and death."[694] This is saying that death is produced by causes and produces its own effect. Death is the disintegrated state of a being that was born, and so a sentient being's disintegrated state has both its own causes and its own effects. Therefore a sentient being's disintegrated state is established as a functioning thing.

That the disintegrated state is a functioning thing is also established by reasoning. Candrakīrti's commentary on *Sixty Stanzas on Reasoning* says, "It would then be logical for the lamp to become no more, without the exhaustion of the oil and the wick. This, however, is not the case. Therefore there is no intrinsically real cessation."[695] This is saying that the exhaustion of the butter and the wick is said to be the cause of the extinguishment of the butter lamp's flame. Therefore the disintegrated state of a continuum of fire is proven to be a functioning thing. Based on this, one can understand that a functioning thing in the first moment, although it disintegrates in the second moment, is a functioning thing.

Furthermore, if disintegration has a cause, then the disintegrated state must also have a cause. Otherwise, there would be the fault of the absurd consequence that production would have a cause and the state of having been produced would not have a cause. If one differentiates the disintegrated state and disintegration based on whether they have a cause, then one would also have to differentiate production and having been produced, because otherwise it would be undermined by the reasoning of equality.

This system asserts that the disintegrated state is disintegration; therefore it is able to posit that things not remaining for a second moment is the disintegrated state. If a thing that does not remain for a second moment is a functioning thing, then a thing that has not remained for a second moment must also be a functioning thing because both are similar in that they are produced by causes.

This system does not posit something like the disintegrated state of a sprout to be a functioning thing upon having searched for the object designated. It posits the disintegrated state as a functioning thing that is produced in dependence on another functioning thing that is disintegrating conventionally. *Root Verses on the Middle Way* says, "Things and nonthings are conditioned."[696] This is saying that a thing like a butter lamp and the nonthing of the butter lamp—that is, its disintegrated state—are both conditioned.

Therefore both disintegrated states and nondisintegrated states are similar in being functioning things. A causal relationship of invariability that is intrinsically real is lacking even for a nondisintegrated state. As for a causal relationship of invariability that is posited merely on the conventional level, this is present in a disintegrated state as well. [339]

In brief, the disintegrated state being a functioning thing rests also on the fact that nothing is intrinsically established. By refuting that it is intrinsically established, it is established as a functioning thing that is merely nominally and imputedly existent, without existing from its own side. By establishing that, then the disintegrated state of a sprout—without being a nonimplicative negation that is the mere opposite of the entity of the sprout that existed earlier—is proven to be a functioning thing that is merely posited having been designated with a name, taking that very nonimplicative negation to be the basis of designation. Whatever causes and conditions that have become the cause of the disintegration of a sprout establishes it as a thing that was produced.

Based on this explanation that the disintegrated state is a functioning thing, this Prāsaṅgika system has a unique way of presenting the three times. The *past*, for instance, consists of the transformation of a cause that becomes an entity that retains its continuity. It is not simply the cessation of a present moment. That factor that is not produced for the time being, because the cause to produce a different thing exists but the conditions are not complete, is posited as the *future*. That which has been produced and has not ceased, without being either of those [the past and the future], is posited as the *present*. Therefore, unlike the other systems, they assert that all three times are functioning things produced by causes and conditions. Thus the *Commentary on Sixty Stanzas on Reasoning* says:

> Because it is possible for the nonexistent to be a cause, it is not reasonable to say, "The nonexistent is not suitable as a cause." You might say that when it is analyzed with reasoning, it is impossible for it to be a cause, but that is not the case, because the things of the world are not to be analyzed and then accepted; it is just the way the world is. In the world it is said that the nonexistent is a cause. People say, "Because there was no water, the grain was ruined," and, "Because there was no food, my child died." In that way, because there was no water and no food, the grain was ruined, and the child perished.[697]

This is saying that even by the measure of what is known in the world, running out of water is cause for grain to be destroyed, and having no food is the cause of the death of a child. It is said that the disintegrated state must be accepted as a cause in their own system just as it is known to be in the world.

The future is also a functioning thing. That same text says, "The lack of the condition of the future serves as a cause of something not being produced. If it is not the case that the condition is lacking, it will definitely be produced."[698] When the wick of a butter lamp is exhausted, the fact that the conditions for producing a similar type of butter lamp later are incomplete is the cause for a similar type of butter lamp not being produced in the future. Therefore, if such causes are not incomplete, that future is produced. Based on those reasons, the future is also asserted to be a functioning thing. [340]

It is most tenable that although nothing exists intrinsically, things exist from the perspective of depending on others and being designations, without being utterly nonexistent. Therefore one must distinguish between existence and intrinsic existence and also nonexistence and intrinsic nonexistence—that is, between the two types of existence and the two types of nonexistence. *Clear Words* says, "We do not say, 'Actions, agents, and effects do not exist.' What do we posit? We say, 'These do not exist intrinsically.'"[699] And the *Autocommentary on Entering the Middle Way* says, "Understanding the descriptions of the causes and effects of a reflection that does not intrinsically exist, since such things as forms and feelings that are not different from causes and effects are observed to be something that merely exists, what wise person would determine that they have intrinsic existence? Therefore, although they are observed to exist, they are not intrinsically produced."[700]

In general, for something to conventionally exist, three factors must be complete: (1) it is known to a conventional consciousness, (2) how it is known is not undermined by other conventional valid means of knowledge, and (3) it is not undermined by reasoning that analyzes reality. All the other schools assert that the extreme of nonexistence is dispelled by appearance and the extreme of existence is dispelled by emptiness. However, there are many unique assertions of the Prāsaṅgika. For them, the way that the extreme of existence is dispelled is by appearance: whenever something dependently arisen appears, the lack of intrinsic existence vividly appears.

The way that the extreme of nonexistence is dispelled is by emptiness: whatever appears, the very appearance of the absence of intrinsic existence of a phenomenon causes it to vividly appear as a mere imputation by thought.

In commenting on the thought of Ārya Nāgārjuna, Candrakīrti himself described this Prāsaṅgika Madhyamaka system as distinctly superior to other systems. The *Autocommentary on Entering the Middle Way* says:

> This is a system in which the doctrine of emptiness, expressed through responses to objections, does not appear in other treatises. We ask scholars to be certain of that. Therefore one should know that whoever says "Whatever the Sautrāntika say is ultimate in their system, Madhyamaka asserts to be conventional" is only saying that they have misunderstood the reality of the meaning of *Root Verses on the Middle Way*. Those who think that "What Vaibhāṣika says is ultimate, Madhyamaka asserts to be conventional" have only misunderstood the reality of the meaning of the treatise. [341] This is because it is not correct that supramundane phenomena are similar to mundane phenomena. This system is unique. Scholars, be certain of this. For that reason, those who do not understand the thought of the master [Nāgārjuna], who are frightened by ascertaining just his words without having ascertained the reality of their meaning, completely abandon supramundane phenomena. Therefore, in order to set forth without error the reality of the meaning of [Nāgārjuna's] treatise, I have composed this entrance to *Root Verses on the Middle Way*.[701]

This is understood from what he clearly states together with the reasons. This system's presentation of the two truths and, extending from that, how they delineate reality, will be explained in volume 4 of this series.

This Madhyamaka tradition, delineated by the protector Nāgārjuna, represents the tradition of the profound middle way, where emptiness—the mode of being in which phenomena lack even a particle that is intrinsically established—is explained to be the reality of dependent arising. It was elucidated by Candrakīrti in a way that differentiates it from the other Madhyamaka schools as well as the proponents of true existence. It is hailed by all Tibetan Mādhyamikas as the apex of all the Indian Buddhist schools of thought. The tradition of upholding this system remains alive to the present day. This concludes the presentation of the Madhyamaka school, based on treating the Prāsaṅgika Madhyamaka system as foremost. [342]

15

Conclusion

HAVING PROVIDED just a rough explanation of the philosophies of the non-Buddhist and Buddhist schools of ancient India in general and the four Buddhist schools of tenets in particular, it is now time to conclude. To summarize, regarding the term *tenets* in general: based on the perceptions of the natural awareness of a particular person, at the conclusion of investigating and analyzing the method to achieve happiness and dispel suffering in this lifetime or the next, [that person's tenets] would be posited as the viewpoint from which they decide whether a philosophical truth is correct or incorrect. All four schools of Buddhist tenets are similar in being free from the two extremes of permanence and annihilation, from the perspective of their respective systems, and in asserting that they present the truth in accordance with objects' mode of being. However, because they have different presentations of the basis and different ways of asserting their views, it is obvious that they identify what it means to fall to the extremes of permanence and annihilation differently.

In general, if one considers what is shared among the Buddhist schools of tenets, the conception of the person as permanent, partless, and independent is the *view of permanence*. Because they do not accept that, they are free from the view of permanence. To not accept that happiness and suffering are effects that arise without confusion from virtuous and sinful actions is the *view of annihilation*. Because all Buddhist schools accept that actions and their effects cannot be confused, they assert that they are free from the extreme of annihilation.

Roughly speaking, each tenet system abandons the two extremes according to their unique views as follows. The Vaibhāṣika say that because they assert that when an effect is produced, its cause ceases, they abandon the extreme of permanence, and because they accept that an effect arises immediately after its cause, they abandon the extreme of annihilation. The Sautrāntika say that because they assert that conditioned phenomena operate continuously, they abandon the extreme of annihilation, and because they nonetheless accept that those conditioned phenomena disintegrate each moment, they are free from the extreme of permanence. The Cittamātra say that because they assert that the imaginary is not truly established, they abandon the extreme of permanence, and because they accept that the dependent and the consummate are truly established, they abandon the extreme of annihilation. Madhyamaka says that because they assert that all phenomena conventionally exist, they are free from the extreme of annihilation, and because they prove that they do not exist ultimately, they are free from the extreme of permanence.

Turning to their unshared assertions, the proponents of the non-Buddhist and Buddhist philosophical schools of India composed extensive analyses and refutations, using many types of reasoning. Each takes their own system's tenets as valid and true, as determined with correct reasoning. [343] When one analyzes the assertions that other schools of tenets have proven with reasoning, not only are many of them shared with the tenets of one's own school, but as has been stated by many scholars of the past, a great many of the assertions and arguments of other schools become like the steps of a ladder leading gradually to the profound philosophy of one's own school. In general, the non-Buddhist and Buddhist traditions of philosophical tenets were founded by wise masters in accordance with the intellect of a great many disciples.

When one considers this, one can understand the statement in Śāntideva's *Entering the Bodhisattva Way* in which he says that lower positions are undermined and outshone by higher views. He says:

> Ordinary worldly people
> are undermined by worldly yogins,
> and those yogins are undermined
> by those who are higher due to a difference in awareness.[702]

This stanza is saying that what is accepted by ordinary worldly people—such as those whose minds have not been affected by tenets and those who assert that partless subtle particles, partless moments of consciousness, and mere things are true—is undermined by the intelligence of worldly yogins who realize that all phenomena lack intrinsic existence. Even among yogins who have attained the union of serenity and insight, the realization that all phenomena lack intrinsic existence, due to a difference in superiority of various yogins' intelligence, the higher outshines the lower. For example, the permanent things that are accepted by non-Buddhists are undermined by the reasoning of the lower Buddhist schools of tenets that proves that permanent things do not exist. The partless subtle particles that are accepted by the two śrāvaka schools are undermined by the reasoning of Cittamātra and other schools that refutes the existence of partless subtle particles. The truly established consciousness that is accepted by Cittamātra is undermined by the reasoning of Madhyamaka that refutes true establishment. In this way one understands that the unshared positions of the former are refuted by the reasoning of the latter.

To summarize, the tīrthikas, for example, emphasize and prove the existence of a permanent, partless, independent self. This is refuted by the Buddhist sūtras and treatises in general and by the various reasonings of all the earlier and later scholars of the higher and lower Buddhist schools of tenets. A series of tīrthika scholars of logic and epistemology who propounded that the Vedas are valid held the view that expressions and thoughts operate by way of what is established in the object itself [rather than through exclusion], and they composed many refutations and assertions [in support of that]. [344] The Buddhist logician Dignāga delineated an extensive presentation of the exclusion of what is other and refuted this tīrthika view. A succession of Buddhist scholars, such as Dharmakīrti and his heirs and Śāntarakṣita, greatly clarified the system that propounds the exclusion of what is other through debate, responding to debate, and rebuttal. To illustrate this among the Buddhist schools of tenets, Vaibhāṣika asserts that the disintegration of conditioned phenomena depends on a cause that is a different entity that arises later. Sautrāntika and so forth refute this with reasoning, arguing that conditioned phenomena have a nature to disintegrate from their own causes. Also, some Vaibhāṣika accept the existence of an inexpressible self; many Madhyamaka and Cittamātra scholars such as Vasubandhu and Candrakīrti set forth extensive reasonings that undermine this assertion. Also, proponents of true existence assert that external objects that are composites of partless particles are truly established; such scholars as Vasubandhu set forth many types of reasonings that refute partlessness and expressed the faults of that position. And Vaibhāṣika asserts that sense consciousnesses comprehend their object nakedly, without an aspect; such scholars as Śāntarakṣita set forth many reasonings that undermine this. The Cittamātra scholars do not assert external objects and prove with various reasonings that the dependent and consummate natures are truly established, and in addition to that, Cittamātra Following Scripture asserts the existence of the foundation consciousness and the afflicted mental consciousness. Such scholars as Bhāviveka and Candrakīrti set forth extensive reasonings undermining that. Moreover, the proponents of true existence assert that dependently arisen phenomena are truly established; Nāgārjuna refuted that with limitless arguments in his collections of Madhyamaka reasoning, and the great Madhyamaka masters who followed him expanded on those refutations. Within Madhyamaka, such figures as the Svātantrika scholar Bhāviveka accepted reasons that are established from their own side. The works of the Prāsaṅgika scholar Candrakīrti refute this extensively with many subtle and detailed arguments. Illustrated in this way, between the non-Buddhists and the Buddhists, and even among the Buddhists such as Vaibhāṣika and Sautrāntika, many unshared assertions of the former are undermined by the correct arguments of the latter. This is implied in Nāgārjuna's *Five Stages*, which says:

> The perfect Buddha described this method
> as being like the steps of a ladder.[703]

Kamalaśīla's second *Stages of Meditation* says, "All the words of the Bhagavan are well spoken. Directly or indirectly, they illuminate reality directly or they flow to reality. If one understands reality, then just as the coming of light clears away darkness, one becomes free from all of the nets of views."[704] [345] In accordance with the explicit intention of such teachings, just as in the world one proceeds up a ladder by means of ascending from the lower rungs to the higher rungs, in the same way, the many positions delineated with reasoning by the lower schools of tenets become the means of understanding the view of the higher schools.

For example, the assertions of the tīrthikas are superior to those of an ordinary person who does not analyze at all whether the self exists. Furthermore, many of their methods of analysis and their presentations of logical reasoning served as the foundation for the spread of Buddhist logic. Many of their descriptions of mental states—such as ways to achieve one-pointed samādhi as a means of pacifying the manifest affliction of attachment to the qualities of the desire realm—are shared with the proponents of Buddhist tenets.

The permanent self propounded by the tīrthikas and, refuting that, the impermanent person propounded by Vaibhāṣika are a means for Sautrāntika to understand that the person is imputedly existent and not substantially existent—in the sense of being a freestanding thing that can be apprehended as a substance separate from the aggregates. Understanding this Sautrāntika assertion about the person and that the relation between the object of expression and the expression is imputedly existent and not a functioning thing is a means for Cittamātra to know how to present actions and agents—without any phenomena being established on the basis of their names through their own mode of subsistence. Understanding that Cittamātra posits phenomena in that way is a means for Svātantrika Madhyamaka to understand how to posit phenomena—without their having a mode of subsistence that is not posited by the power of appearing to the mind. Understanding that Svātantrika Madhyamaka posits phenomena in that way is a means for Prāsaṅgika Madhyamaka to understand how to posit all phenomena as not being established as their own mode of subsistence.

Thus, between these non-Buddhist and Buddhist schools of tenets, the latter school is more profound than the former. However, through a careful analysis based on the philosophy of the lower, the higher only becomes more profound. This way in which Buddhist schools of tenets are like the steps of a ladder, from the former to the latter, can be illustrated with an example. All the proponents of Buddhist tenets accept that conditioned phenomena are like illusions. However, the latter school is more profound than the former in the way that they use the example of a magician's illusion. Vaibhāṣika uses the example of the impermance of continuity or coarse impermanence in the sense that, just as the illusory horse or elephant exists at the time of the magician's illusion but becomes nonexistent when the illusion dissolves, so the body and possessions of this life must come to an end at death.

Sautrāntika uses the illusion as an example of subtle impermanence in that, because the magician's illusions change from moment to moment, they have the quality of disintegrating upon being produced, without depending on another cause that arises later. [346] Cittamātra uses the example to show that just as the horse or elephant does not exist from the side of the pebble or stick that is the basis of conjuring but is merely the factor that appears to a consciousness affected by the mantra and substance, so such things as forms and sounds are merely factors that appear to an internal consciousness without being established as external objects. Madhyamaka uses the illusion as an example of the fact that, apart from merely being posited by the power of appearing to the mind, phenomena are not truly established. However, there is a difference between the different Madhyamaka subschools. Because Svātantrika asserts that phenomena are established from the side of their basis of designation, in the context of the example, the illusory horse or elephant must appear from the side of the basis of conjuring. They assert that if they did not appear in that way, there would be the fault that even in a place where there was no basis of conjuring, the illusion would appear due only to the eyes being affected by the mantra and substance.

Prāsaṅgika uses the example to show that just as the illusion conjured by the magician is not a horse or elephant yet appears to be, so for phenomena such as the person, when one searches for some nature that is established from the object's own side, there is nothing to be found despite it appearing to be established from its own side. The appearance of the illusory horse or elephant is not due to that appearance being established from its own side but is due to whether the mind imputes it to be a horse or an elephant. For example, due to the thought apprehending the horns of a rabbit, the horns of a rabbit are apprehended, but something else that does not exist, such as the son of a barren woman, is not apprehended. In the same way, they assert that whether the object exists or not, it is imputed by the mind. Furthermore, they assert that if the horse or elephant appeared from the side of the pebble or stick, there would be the fault that the appearance of the horse or elephant would have to be produced even for a member of the audience whose eyes were not affected [by the mantra or substance]. As this illustration shows, there are many topics in the philosophies of non-Buddhists and Buddhists that contain major differences, with the views of the latter schools emerging as more profound when compared to the views of the former.

Turning to the view of no-self, as it is said in the sūtras and the eloquent explanations of Nāgārjuna and Asaṅga, compared to the latter levels of selflessness, the former are easy to understand and serve as a means of entering into the latter. These levels of selflessness are: the lack of a self that is permanent, partless, and independent; the selflessness that is the lack of being self-sufficient and substantially existent; the reality that is the lack of external objects that are a different entity from internal consciousness; the lack of an ultimately existent entity, although all phenomena exist by way of their own character; and all phenomena lack even a particle that is established by way of its own character even conventionally, yet it is possible to present all categories, such as cause and effect. For some people, having been taught the view of the lower schools of tenets, if they are led gradually higher, such progression becomes meaningful. Otherwise, if they are taught the highest view from the start, far from it being beneficial, it could cause great harm. Therefore one will gain the certainty of conviction that these various traditions of tenets that were created by the great masters with discernment and with the intention to benefit others are solely a source of benefit and happiness for disciples of a variety of capacities and interests. [347]

Thus, gathered here and organized in a special way are descriptions of reality as well as many important philosophical topics found in the classical Buddhist sources, the scriptures of the Conquerer Śakyamuni, and in particular the treatises of the great Buddhist philosophers of ancient India that were translated into Tibetan.

This completes the first of two philosophy volumes, presenting the non-Buddhist and Buddhist schools of tenets, and the third volume overall in the four-volume series *Science and Philosophy in the Indian Buddhist Classics*.

Notes

Abbreviations

Toh The Tohoku Catalogue. *A Complete Catalogue of the Tibetan Buddhist Canons.* Sendai, Japan: Tohoku Imperial University, 1934.

Pd The comparative editions of the Tibetan canons, the Kangyur and Tengyur, referred to in Tibetan as *Dpe bsdur ma*, published between 2006 and 2009 in Beijing by the Tibetan Tripiṭaka Collation Bureau (Bka' bstan dpe sdur khang) of the China Tibetology Research Center (Krung go'i bod rig pa zhib 'jug ste gnas).

1. Atiśa Dīpaṅkaraśrījñāna, *Madhyamakopadeśa*, T 3930, 112a7.
2. For a fuller discussion, see the translator's introduction in Changkya Rölpai Dorjé, *Beautiful Adornment of Mount Meru*, 8–13.
3. *Grub mtha' chen mo*. For a translation of and detailed commentary on the verse version of Jamyang Shepa's text, see Hopkins, *Maps of the Profound*.
4. *Lcang skya grub mtha*. For a full translation, see Changkya, *Beautiful Adornment*.
5. For a full translation by Geshé Lhundub Sopa et al., see Thuken, *Crystal Mirror*.
6. An English translation by Sara Boin-Webb was published by the University of Hawai'i Press in 2013.
7. *Vinayavibhaṅga*, chap. 7. Toh 3, 111b, Pd 5:275.
8. Wheeler 1968, 76.
9. Bhāviveka, *Tarkajvālā*, chap. 9. Toh 3856, 299a, Pd 58:727.
10. *Viśeṣastavaṭīkā*. Toh 1110, 27a, Pd 1:66.
11. *Madhyamakāvatārabhāṣya*, chap. 6. Toh 3862, 294a, Pd 60:778.
12. *Tarkajvālā*, chap. 9. Toh 3856, 277b, Pd 58:675.
13. *Śrīmad Bhāgavatam*, canto 3, chap. 21, v. 32ff.
14. *Vinayavastu*, chap. 2. Toh 1, *ka*:32a, Pd 1:53.
15. This is clear, for example, in Üpa Losal's *Treasury of Explanations of Tenets*, 258.
16. Regarding how the seven books of the Abhidharma are counted, there are two different systems: the system of the noble Theravāda and the system of the *Abhidharmakośa*, which is based on the *Mahāvibhāṣā*. On this, see the translator's introduction in Chim Jampaiyang, *Ornament of Abhidharma*, 5. The seven are also listed on page 239.

17. *Great Exegesis of the Abhidharma*, 10:910.
18. Potter 1970–2019, 7:112.
19. In the footnote in Potter 1970–2019, 7:511, it says that this is what was explained by the French scholar Étienne Lamotte. Kaniṣka, the great emperor of the Kuṣāṇa empire, ruled northwestern India and parts of Central Asia circa 127–50 CE.
20. The status of other works composed by this scholar will be explained in the chapter on the tenets of Sautrāntika. In Tāranātha's *Rgya gar chos 'byung* (codex version, p. 79), in accordance with the explanation that he was a contemporary of the emperor Kaniṣka, it is clear that it was the period of the scholar Śūra. In Changkya's *Beautiful Adornment* (p. 141), it says, "Among the early scholars, masters such as Kumāralāta, Śrīlāta, and Bhadantalāta are well known." Üpa Losal's *Tenets* (p. 75) explains that this system split off from the Sarvāstivāda.
21. *Laṅkāvatāra Sūtra*, chap. 3. Toh 107, 123b, Pd 49:307.
22. These explanations are based on what appear in Changkya's *Beautiful Adornment*, 74.
23. *Abhisamayālaṃkāraṭīkā-prasphuṭapadā*. Toh 3796, 75a, Pd 52:880.
24. For example, Üpa Losal's *Tenets* says (p. 6), "Assertions about their respective objects of knowledge by proponents of textual traditions are tenets. View, assertion, vehicle, and tenets are synonyms."
25. Prajñāvarman, *Viśeṣastavaṭīkā*. Toh 1110, 32a, Pd 1:78.
26. *Prajñāpradīpaṭīkā*, chap. 1. Toh 3859, 15b, Pd 58:893.
27. This appears in Changkya's *Beautiful Adornment*, 74. It also appears in such works as Tsongkhapa's *Great Treatise on the Stages of the Path to Enlightenment*.
28. *Sarvayānālokaviśeṣabhāṣya*. Toh 3907, 306a, Pd 63:1871.
29. *Abhidharmakośaṭīkopayikā*, chap. 1. Toh 4094, 83b, Pd 82:952.
30. *Sāgaranāgarājaparipṛcchāsūtra*. Toh 154, 205b, Pd 58:540.
31. *Mahāyānasūtrālaṃkāra*. Toh 4020, 31b, Pd 70:873.
32. *Bodhisattvabhūmi*. Toh 4037, 146a, Pd 73:884.
33. *Pramāṇavārttika*, 2.191. Toh 4210, 114b, Pd 97:517.
34. *Madhyamakāvatāra*, 6.118. Toh 3861, 210a, Pd 60:575.
35. *Samādhirāja Sūtra*, chap. 19. Toh 127, 69b, Pd 55:167.
36. *Catuḥśataka*, 9.9. Toh 3846, 9b, Pd 57:800.
37. In 1968, an Indian publisher called Bauddha Bhārati gathered many Sanskrit manuscripts of this text from Jaina libraries and published an edition. In that compilation, the six sections on the analysis of the self were made into one called "Analysis of the Self" (*Ātmaparīkṣā*). The analyses of the general and specific meaning of words were treated separately, making twenty-six analyses.
38. For more on the general structure and content of the most famous tenets texts, such as those of Üpa Losal, Taktsang Lotsāwa, and the omniscient Jamyang Shepa, see the translator's introduction to Changkya, *Beautiful Adornment*.
39. *Vinayavastu*. Toh 1, *ga*:77b, Pd 3:666.
40. *Vinayavastu*. Toh 1, *ka*:23b, Pd 1:53.

41. *Vinayavastuṭīkā*. Toh 4113, 196b, Pd 87:530.
42. *Madhyamakaratnapradīpa*. Toh 3854, 262b, Pd 6:238.
43. *Brahmajāla Sūtra*. Toh 352, 84b, Pd 76:238.
44. *Tarkajvālā*, chap. 11. Toh 3856, 325b, Pd 58:793.
45. *Laṅkāvatāra Sūtra*, chap. 3. Toh 107, 128b, Pd 69:1327.
46. Jñānavajra, *Ornament for the Essence of the Tathāgata* (*Tathāgatahṛdayālaṃkāra*). Toh 4019, 213a, Pd 70:513. Ngawang Palden, *Notes on Tenets* (Lokāyata chapter), 53.
47. *Tarkajvālā*, chap. 9. Toh 3856, 278a, Pd 58:676.
48. *Jñānasārasamuccayanibandhana*. Toh 3852, 111a, Pd 57:864.
49. *Madhyamakaratnapradīpa*. Toh 3854, 262b, Pd 57:1495.
50. *Tattvabhāvanāmukhāgamavṛtti*. Toh 1866, 111a, Pd 21:1136.
51. *Tarkajvālā*, chap. 3. Toh 3856, 128b, Pd 58:315.
52. *Tarkajvālā*, chap. 9. Toh 3856, 271b, Pd 58:659.
53. *Tarkajvālā*, chap. 9. Toh 3856, 274b, Pd 58:668.
54. Puṇḍarīka, *Vimalaprabhā*, chap. 1. Toh 1347, 75a, Pd 6:410. These are listed in the same way in the second and third chapters of the *Vimalaprabhā*.
55. *Jñānasārasamuccaya*, verses 12–16. Toh 3851, 27a, Pd 57:857.
56. The Vaiśeṣika who regard time as the cause are indicated by the words "and so forth" in the verse above.
57. See Changkya, *Beautiful Adornment*, 78.
58. Üpa Losal, *Treasury of Explanations of Tenets*, 254
59. For example, Üpa Losal, *Treasury of Explanations of Tenets*, 252, says, "The tīrthika have five schools of logic, divided into one annihilationist and four eternalists; their assertions are set forth."
60. Changkya, *Beautiful Adornment*, 78.
61. Nicholson 2013, 2–4.
62. *Śvetāśvatara Upaniṣad* 5.2.
63. Potter 1970–2019, 4:3–9.
64. Īśvarakṛṣṇa, *Īśvarakṛṣṇatantra*, v. 70. This text was translated into Tibetan by Thupten Chokdrup (Thub bstan mchog grub) in 1974.
65. *Yogasūtrabhāṣya*.
66. Vijñānabhikṣu, *Sāṅkhyadarśana*.
67. Potter 1970–2019, 4:15.
68. *Pramāṇasamuccayasvavṛtti*, chap. 1. Toh 4204, 23b, Pd 97:79.
69. Joshi, *Sāṅkhyayogadarśana kā jñoddhāra*, 13.
70. Joshi, *Sāṅkhyayogadarśana kā jñoddhāra*, 48.
71. Joshi, *Sāṅkhyayogadarśana kā jñoddhāra*, 49.
72. *Tarkajvālā*, chap. 6. Toh 3856, 230b, Pd 58:561.
73. *Jñānasārasamuccayanibandhana*. Toh 3852, 38a, Pd 57:881.
74. Üpa Losal, *Treasury of Explanations of Tenets*, 256.
75. *Tattvasaṅgrahapañjikā*, chap. 1. Toh 4267, 147a, Pd 107:388.
76. *Tattvasaṅgrahapañjikā*, chap. 3. Toh 4267, 179a, Pd 107:468.

77. *Tattvasaṅgrahapañjikā*, chap. 3. Toh 4267, 179a, Pd 107:468.
78. Üpa Losal, *Treasury of Explanations of Tenets*, 271.
79. *Mahāparinirvāṇasūtra*. Toh 119, 278b, Pd 53:646.
80. Īśvarakṛṣṇa, *Īśvarakṛṣṇatantra*, verse 3.
81. *Sarvadarśanasaṅgraha*, English translation, pp. 21–23.
82. The sixth chapter of the *Tarkajvālā* (Toh 3856, 233a) says, "The Sāṅkhya tenet is this: '[Individual] puruṣas abide in each body of individual gods, demigods, humans, and animals, and all these puruṣas again pervade all [beings].'"
83. *Madhyamakāvatārabhāṣya*, chap. 6. Toh 3862, 239a.
84. *Madhyamakāvatāra*, 6.121. Toh 3861, 210a, Pd 60:532.
85. *Madhyamakahṛdaya*, 6.1. Toh 3855, 24b, Pd 58:57.
86. Kamalaśīla, *Tattvasaṅgrahapañjikā*, chap. 1. Toh 4267, 141b, Pd 107:375.
87. Bhāviveka, *Tarkajvālā*, chap. 6. Toh 3856, 227b, Pd 58:553.
88. Īśvarakṛṣṇa, *Īśvarakṛṣṇatantra*, verse 23.
89. Kamalaśīla, *Tattvasaṅgrahapañjikā*, chap. 6. Toh 4267, 147a, Pd 107:388.
90. Bhāviveka, *Tarkajvālā*, chap. 6. Toh 3856, 230a, Pd 58:560.
91. Īśvarakṛṣṇa, *Īśvarakṛṣṇatantra*, verse 24.
92. Bhāviveka, *Tarkajvālā*, chap. 3. Toh 3856, 89b, Pd 57:222.
93. Īśvarakṛṣṇa, *Īśvarakṛṣṇatantra*, verse 26.
94. Bhāviveka, *Tarkajvālā*, chap. 6. Toh 3856, 228a, Pd 58:555.
95. Īśvarakṛṣṇa, *Īśvarakṛṣṇatantra*, verse 26.
96. *Abhidharmakośaṭīkā-lakṣaṇānusāriṇī*, chap. 2. Toh 4093, 107b, Pd 81:266.
97. Bhāviveka, *Tarkajvālā*, chap. 6. Toh 3856, 228a, Pd 58:555.
98. Īśvarakṛṣṇa, *Īśvarakṛṣṇatantra*, verse 27.
99. Bhāviveka, *Tarkajvālā*, chap. 6. Toh 3856, 228a, 228a, Pd 58:555.
100. Kamalaśīla, *Tattvasaṅgrahapañjikā*, chap. 6. Toh 4267, 147a, Pd 107:388.
101. Bhāviveka, *Tarkajvālā*, chap. 6. Toh 3856, 228a, Pd 58:555.
102. Śāntarakṣita, *Madhyamakālaṃkāravṛtti*. Toh 3885, 80a, Pd 62:966.
103. Īśvarakṛṣṇa, *Īśvarakṛṣṇatantra*, verse 10.
104. It is explained slightly differently in Candrakīrti's *Madhyamakāvaṭārabhāṣya* and Jayānanda's *Madhyamakāvatāraṭīkā*.
105. Īśvarakṛṣṇa, *Īśvarakṛṣṇatantra*, verse 22.
106. *Prajñāpradīpaṭīkā*, chap. 2. Toh 3859, 139a, Pd 58:1200.
107. Īśvarakṛṣṇa, *Īśvarakṛṣṇatantra*, verse 59.
108. Īśvarakṛṣṇa, *Īśvarakṛṣṇatantra*, verse 23.
109. Īśvarakṛṣṇa, *Īśvarakṛṣṇatantra*, verse 28.
110. Īśvarakṛṣṇa, *Īśvarakṛṣṇatantra*, verse 33.
111. Īśvarakṛṣṇa, *Īśvarakṛṣṇatantra*, verse 30.
112. Īśvarakṛṣṇa, *Īśvarakṛṣṇatantra*, verse 4.
113. *Nyāyabindupūrvapakṣasaṅkṣipti*. Toh 4232, 92a, Pd 105:258.
114. Kapila, *Sāṅkhyasūtra*, 1.89.
115. *Yuktidīpikā*, 5.
116. *Nyāyamañjarī*, 100.

117. *Pramāṇasamuccayavṛtti*, chap. 1. Toh 4204, 21a, Pd 97:6.
118. Īśvarakṛṣṇa, *Īśvarakṛṣṇatantra*, verse 5.
119. Kapila, *Sāṅkhyasūtra*, 1.100.
120. *Pramāṇasamuccaya*, chap. 2. Toh 4203, 5b, Pd 97:11.
121. Kamalaśīla, *Nyāyabindupūrvapakṣasaṅkṣipti*. Toh 4232, 95a, Pd 107:266.
122. Īśvarakṛṣṇa, *Īśvarakṛṣṇatantra*, verse 5.
123. Kapila, *Sāṅkhyasūtra*, 1.101.
124. Īśvarakṛṣṇa, *Īśvarakṛṣṇatantra*, verse 5.
125. Īśvarakṛṣṇa, *Īśvarakṛṣṇatantra*, verse 6.
126. Dignāga, *Pramāṇasamuccayavṛtti*, chap. 3. Toh 4204, 54a, Pd 97:155.
127. Kamalaśīla, *Nyāyabindupūrvapakṣasaṅkṣipti*. Toh 4232, 95a, Pd 105:266.
128. Īśvarakṛṣṇa, *Īśvarakṛṣṇatantra*, verse 8.
129. Īśvarakṛṣṇa, *Īśvarakṛṣṇatantra*, verse 15.
130. *Tattvasaṅgrahapañjikā*, chap. 1. Toh 4267, 150b, Pd 107:397.
131. *Tattvasaṅgrahapañjikā*, chap. 1. Toh 4267, 150b, Pd 107:397.
132. *Tattvasaṅgrahapañjikā*, chap. 1. Toh 4267, 151a, Pd 107:398.
133. *Tattvasaṅgrahapañjikā*, chap. 1. Toh 4267, 150b, Pd 107:398.
134. *Tattvasaṅgrahapañjikā*, chap. 1. Toh 4267, 151a, Pd 107:399.
135. Īśvarakṛṣṇa, *Īśvarakṛṣṇatantra*, verse 9.
136. Īśvarakṛṣṇa, *Īśvarakṛṣṇatantra*, verse 7.
137. *Tattvasaṅgrahapañjikā*, chap. 5. Toh 4267, 257a, Pd 107:669.
138. *Devātiśayastotraṭīkā*. Toh 1113, 55b, Pd 1:147. Also, N. K. Devaraja's *Bhāratīya Darśana* (p. 321) explains that Kāṇāda are so called because they eat particles of grains left on others' harvested fields. Several modern researchers on ancient Indian philosophy explain why the Vaiśeṣika are called the "Owls" (*aulūkya*). For example, the twentieth-century Indian scholar Harendra Prasad Sinha says in his *Bhāratīya Darśana kī Rūparekhā*, "Based on the fact that the name 'Kaṇāda' is based on 'Ulūka,' Vaiśeṣika philosophy also has the names Grain-Eaters' (Kāṇāda) philosophy and the Owls' (Aulūkya) philosophy."
139. Bhāviveka, *Tarkajvālā*, chap. 7. Toh 3856, 249b, Pd 58:608.
140. *Tarkajvālā*, chap. 7. Toh 3856, 249b, Pd 58:608.
141. Jamyang Shepa, *Great Exposition of Tenets*, 126. Also, regarding the dates of the sage Kaṇāda, the twentieth-century Indian philosopher Dharmendra Nath Shastri explains in his *Critique of Indian Realism* that, according to the Chinese scholar Jizang's commentary on Āryadeva's *Śataśāstra*, he appeared about eight hundred years before Śākyamuni Buddha. Some Indian historians explain that he appeared around the early fourth century BCE. There appear to be a variety of explanations.
142. Potter 1970–2019, 2:7.
143. Chomden Rikpai Raldri, *Flower Adorning Tenets*, 24b.
144. *Vaiśeṣikasūtra* 1.1.3.
145. *Tattvasaṅgrahapañjikā*, chap. 15. Toh 4267, 261b, Pd 107:679.
146. *Tarkajvālā*, chap. 7. Toh 3856, 243a, Pd 58:592.

147. *Tattvasaṅgrahapañjikā*, chap. 15. Toh 4267, 257b, Pd 107:669.
148. Bhāviveka, *Tarkajvālā*, chap. 7. Toh 3856, 242b, Pd 58:590.
149. Kamalaśīla, *Tattvasaṅgrahapañjikā*, chap. 15. Toh 4267, 270b, Pd 107:702.
150. *Tattvasaṅgrahapañjikā*, chap. 6. Toh 4267, 192a, Pd 107:501.
151. Candrakīrti, *Madhyamakāvatārabhāṣya*, chap. 6. Toh 3862, 240a.
152. Bhāviveka, *Tarkajvālā*, chap. 7. Toh 3856, 242b, Pd 58:591.
153. Kamalaśīla, *Tattvasaṅgrahapañjikā*, chap. 16. Toh 4267, 273a, Pd 107:710.
154. Kamalaśīla, *Tattvasaṅgrahapañjikā*, chap. 16. Toh 4267, 273b, Pd 107:711.
155. Kamalaśīla, *Tattvasaṅgrahapañjikā*, chap. 16. Toh 4267, 273b, Pd 107:711.
156. Kamalaśīla, *Tattvasaṅgrahapañjikā*, chap. 16. Toh 4267, 273b, Pd 107:712.
157. Śāntarakṣita, *Tattvasaṅgraha*, 6.15. Toh 4266, 25a, Pd 107:62.
158. Kamalaśīla, *Tattvasaṅgrahapañjikā*, chap. 16, Toh 4267, 285a, Pd 107:740.
159. Kamalaśīla, *Tattvasaṅgrahapañjikā*, chap. 16, Toh 4267, 285a, Pd 107:740.
160. *Madhyamakāvatārabhāṣya*, chap. 6. Toh 3862, 294a, Pd 60:779.
161. This is according to Kamalaśīla's *Tattvasaṅgrahapañjikā*. Candrakīrti's *Madhyamakāvatārabhāṣya* offers a slightly different explanation.
162. Kamalaśīla, *Tattvasaṅgrahapañjikā*, chap. 17. Toh 4267, 287b, Pd 107:747.
163. Kamalaśīla, *Tattvasaṅgrahapañjikā*, chap. 18. Toh 4267, 290a, Pd 107:745.
164. Bhāviveka, *Tarkajvālā*, chap. 3. Toh 3856, 89b, Pd 58:222.
165. Bhāviveka, *Tarkajvālā*, chap. 7. Toh 3856, 243a, Pd 58:592.
166. Bhāviveka, *Tarkajvālā*, chap. 7. Toh 3856, 242b, Pd 58:591.
167. Bhāviveka, *Tarkajvālā*, chap. 7. Toh 3856, 243a, Pd 58:592.
168. Candramati's *Daśapadārthaśāstra* is extant only in Chinese. A summary of this treatise appears in Potter 1970–2019, 2:274–81.
169. Here, the Vaiśeṣika explanations of how coarse form is produced from permanent particles are drawn from what appears in Jamyang Shepa's *Great Exposition of Tenets* (pp. 210–12), citing the *Tattvasaṅgraha* and its commentary, and, especially, the quotations that Avalokitavrata provides in the *Prajñāpradīpaṭīkā* just before the end of his exposition of Vaiśeṣika assertions.
170. Avalokitavrata, *Prajñāpradīpaṭīkā*, chap. 1. Toh 3859, 93a, Pd 58:1109.
171. Avalokitavrata, *Prajñāpradīpaṭīkā*, chap. 1. Toh 3859, 93a, Pd 58:1092.
172. *Pramāṇasamuccaya*, chap. 1. Toh 4203, 2b, Pd 97:5.
173. This way of dividing direction perception into six based on relation is from Jamyang Shepa's *Great Exposition of Tenets* (p. 191).
174. *Pramāṇasamuccaya*, chap. 2. Toh 4203, 5a, Pd 97:10.
175. Dignāga, *Pramāṇasamuccayavṛtti*, chap. 3. Toh 4204, 59a, Pd 97:167.
176. Dharmakīrti, *Pramāṇavārttika*, 2.10. Toh 4210, 108a, Pd 97:501.
177. The Vaiśeṣika proofs for the permanent ātman arranged here are collected from the seventh chapter ("Ātmaparīkṣā") of Śāntarakṣita's *Tattvasaṅgraha* and Kamalaśīla's *Tattvasaṅgrahapañjikā*. In that chapter, the syllogisms formulated by Nyāya-Vaiśeṣika masters such as Aviddhakarṇa, Śaṅkarapati, and Bhāvivikta are quoted and refuted. For Kamalaśīla's discussion, see Pd 65:504–8.
178. Kamalaśīla, *Tattvasaṅgrahapañjikā*, chap. 15. Toh 4267, 258b, Pd 107:672.
179. Śāntarakṣita, *Tattvasaṅgraha*, 15.73. Toh 4266, 24a, Pd 107:59.

180. Kamalaśīla, *Tattvasaṅgrahapañjikā*, chap. 16. Toh 4267, 271a, Pd 107:704.
181. Kamalaśīla, *Tattvasaṅgrahapañjikā*, chap. 15. Toh 4267, 259b, Pd 107:675.
182. The claim that Gautama and Akṣapāda were different persons appears in Vidyabhusana's *A History of Indian Logic* (p. 17). Also, Mādhava's tenets text, the *Sarvadarśanasaṅgraha*, uses the phrase "view of the followers of Akṣapāda" in the Vaiśeṣika chapter to refer to Nyāya. However, in *Bharatiya Darshan Parichay* (vol. 1, p. 4) the Indian scholar Hari Mohan Jha notes that many Indian texts call the *Nyāya Sūtra* the *Sūtra of Akṣapāda*.
183. For example, Khedrup Jé's *Ocean of Reasoning* (p. 121) says, "The followers of the brahmin Akṣapāda are the Naiyāyika. Because they follow the rishi Kaṇāda, they are the Kāṇāda. Because they take on the conduct of owls, they are the Owl followers, or the Vaiśeṣika."
184. The Sanskrit edition of the *Laṅkāvatāra*, p. 122. According to Vidyabhusana's *A History of Indian Logic* (p. 16), many modern historians assert that the *Nyāya Sūtra* was initially committed to writing in the second century and that its author, the rishi Gautama, also lived in the second century.
185. *Devātiśayastotraṭīkā*. Toh 1113, 55b, Pd 1:147. Hari Mohan Jha's *Bharatiya Darshan Parichay* (vol. 1, p. 9) says that Akṣapāda is an epithet of Gautama and that, when he was writing the treatise on Nyāya, because his mind was focused on the meaning of the text, he was not aware of what was ahead of him. One day, while analyzing the meaning of the treatise, he fell into a well, so Īśvara put eyes on the rishi's feet. Thus he is known as Akṣapāda, "one whose eyes are on his feet."
186. According to Vācaspati Miśra's *Nyāyasūcīnibandha* (p. 14), the current *Nyāya Sūtra* consists of five books, ten chapters, eighty-four sections, and 8,385 syllables.
187. *Pramāṇaviniścayaṭīkā*. Toh 207a, Pd 104:519.
188. Kamalaśīla, *Tattvasaṅgrahapañjikā*, chap. 7. Toh 4267, 193a, Pd 107:504–7.
189. Chomden Rikpai Raldri, *A Flower Adorning Tenets*, 29a. The manuscript of this text is from the Temple of the Sixteen Arhats at Drepung Monastery and was transcribed and published in Tibet in 2006.
190. *Nyāya Sūtra*, book 1, chap. 1, sūtra 1.
191. *Sarvayānālokaviśeṣabhāṣya*. Toh 3907, 307a, Pd 63:1873.
192. *Vaidalyaprakaraṇa*. Toh 3826, 102b, 57:274.
193. Kamalaśīla, *Nyāyabindupūrvapakṣasaṅkṣipti*. Toh 4232, 92a, Pd 105:258.
194. Bhāviveka, *Tarkajvālā*, chap. 7. Toh 3856, 242b, Pd 58:591.
195. Dignāga, *Pramāṇasamuccaya*, chap. 1. Toh 4203, 2b, Pd 97:5.
196. Śāntarakṣita, *Tattvasaṅgraha*, 23.40. Toh 4266, 56a, Pd 107:138.
197. *Nyāya Sūtra*, book 1, chap. 1, sūtra 7–8.
198. Dignāga, *Pramāṇasamuccaya*, chap. 2. Toh 4203, 5a, Pd 97:10.
199. Gautama, *Nyāyasūtra* (book 1, chap. 2, sūtra 4), lists five kinds of pseudo-reasons. There, the fifth kind of pseudo-reason is called *atītakāla*—that is, a mistimed reason or that of confused time. The illustrations of each kind of pseudo-reason appear in the *Nyāyabhāṣya* by Vātsyāyana.
200. *Ratnamālā*, verses 13–15. Toh 3901, 67b, Pd 63:1038.

201. Bhāviveka, *Tarkajvālā*, chap. 9. Toh 3856, 299a, Pd 58:727.
202. Bhāviveka, *Tarkajvālā*, chap. 9. Toh 3856, 299a, Pd 58:727.
203. Bhāviveka, *Tarkajvālā*, chap. 9. Toh 3856, 299a, Pd 58:727.
204. *Tattvasaṅgraha*, 8.1–2. Toh 4266, 9b, Pd 107:23.
205. *Nyāyabindupūrvapakṣasaṅkṣipti*. Toh 4232, 92b, Pd 105:260.
206. Kamalaśīla, *Nyāyabindupūrvapakṣasaṅkṣipti*. Toh 4232, 92a, Pd 105:258.
207. Dignāga, *Pramāṇasamuccayasvavṛtti*. Toh 4204, 25a, Pd 97:83.
208. Kamalaśīla, *Nyāyabindupūrvapakṣasaṅkṣipti*. Toh 4232, 92a, Pd 105:259.
209. Dignāga, *Pramāṇasamuccayasvavṛtti*. Toh 4204, 39a, Pd 97:118.
210. Kamalaśīla, *Tattvasaṅgrahapañjikā*, chap. 23. Toh 4267, 41a, Pd 107:1088. The definitions of verbal valid knowledge and its divisions are clearly explained in Śabarasvāmin's *Explanation of Mīmāṃsā* (*Mīmāṃsābhāṣya*).
211. In his chapter on *apoha* in his *Ślokavārttika*, Kumārila refutes Dignāga's idea of "exclusion of others" (*anyāpoha*), finding these faults: It would follow that understanding tree and non-tree would be mutually dependent. Because "object of knowledge" has no object to exclude, the term does not have an object of exclusion. It follows that if the word "pot" expresses the opposite of what is not itself, then because all words are similar in expressing exclusion, they would be synonymous. Dharmakīrti responds to each of those. This will be explained in volume 4.
212. Śāntarakṣita, *Tattvasaṅgraha*, 23.94. Toh 4266, 58a, Pd 107:143.
213. Kamalaśīla, *Tattvasaṅgrahapañjikā*, chap. 24. Toh 4267, 53b, Pd 107:1118.
214. Śāntarakṣita, *Tattvasaṅgraha*, 24.158. Toh 4266, 60a, Pd 107:148.
215. *Tattvasaṅgraha*, 24.161. Toh 4266, 60b, Pd 107:149.
216. Bhāviveka, *Madhyamakahṛdaya*, 9.2. Toh 3855, 31b, Pd 58:74.
217. Bhāviveka, *Madhyamakahṛdaya*, 9.3. Toh 3855, 31b, Pd 58:74.
218. Dharmakīrti, *Pramāṇavārttika*, 1.318. Toh 4210, 106b, Pd 97:498.
219. *Ślokavārttika*, verse 236, p. 512.
220. *Tattvasaṅgraha*, 8.8. Toh 4266, 10a, Pd 107:24.
221. This was composed by the rishi Agniveśa and compiled by Caraka. Book 1, 11.17, p. 255.
222. Agniveśa, *Carakasaṃhitā*, book 1, 11.20, p. 257.
223. Agniveśa, *Carakasaṃhitā*, book 1, 11.21–22, p. 257.
224. Agniveśa, *Carakasaṃhitā*, book 1, 11.19, p. 257.
225. Agniveśa, *Carakasaṃhitā*, book 1, 11.23, p. 257.
226. Kamalaśīla, *Nyāyabindupūrvapakṣasaṅkṣipti*. Toh 4232, 92a, Pd 105:259.
227. Kamalaśīla, *Tattvasaṅgrahapañjikā*, chap. 24. Toh 4267, 68a, Pd 107:1155.
228. Kamalaśīla, *Tattvasaṅgrahapañjikā*, chap. 24. Toh 4267, 68b, Pd 107:1155.
229. Kamalaśīla, *Tattvasaṅgrahapañjikā*, chap. 24. Toh 4267, 69a, Pd 107:1157.
230. Kamalaśīla, *Tattvasaṅgrahapañjikā*, chap. 24. Toh 4267, 69b, Pd 107:1157.
231. Kamalaśīla, *Tattvasaṅgrahapañjikā*, chap. 24. Toh 4267, 68b, Pd 107:1157.
232. Agniveśa, *Carakasaṃhitā*, book 1, 11.30, p. 261.
233. *Tarkajvālā*, 8. Toh 3856, 28a, Pd 58:66. This verse ("When the space in a pot is

covered with dust and smoke, everything else is not like that. In the same way, happiness and so forth do not exist in the Ātman.") appears to be the same as *Gauḍapādakārikā* 3.5.

234. Modern researchers explain that Vedāntin and Aupaniṣada (literally "Secretist," *gsang ba pa*) are synonyms. While many Tibetan authors of tenets texts speak of the two separately, Chomden Rikpai Raldri's *Flower Adorning Tenets* says the two are synonyms, referring to "Vedāntin Secretists" (p. 41b).
235. *Jñānasārasamuccaya.* Toh 3851, 27, Pd 57:852.
236. *Jñānasārasamuccayanibandhana.* Toh 3852, 39b, Pd 57:884.
237. Bhāviveka, *Tarkajvālā*, chap. 8. Toh 3856, 251a, Pd 57:611.
238. Śāntarakṣita, *Tattvasaṅgraha*, 6.1. Toh 4266, 7b, Pd 107:17.
239. Bhāviveka, *Madhyamakahṛdaya*, 8.16–17. Toh 3855, 28a, Pd 58:66.
240. Gauḍapāda, *Gauḍapādakārikā*, 4.87.
241. Gauḍapāda, *Gauḍapādakārikā*, 4.87.
242. Gauḍapāda, *Gauḍapādakārikā*, 4.88.
243. Gauḍapāda, *Gauḍapādakārikā*, 3.3–4 and 3.6.
244. Gauḍapāda, *Gauḍapādakārikā*, 3.8.
245. Gauḍapāda, *Gauḍapādakārikā*, 2.17–20.
246. Gauḍapāda, *Gauḍapādakārikā*, 3.30–32.
247. *Madhyamakālaṃkāravṛtti.* Toh 3885, 80b, Pd 62:966.
248. See the explanation of the six valid means of knowledge in the Mīmāṃsā chapter above on pages 166–69.
249. Gauḍapāda, *Gauḍapādakārikā*, 1.12. Here, "the fourth one" should be understood as the fourth state, nondual ultimate consciousness.
250. When Bhāviveka refutes Vedānta in the eighth chapter of his *Tarkajvālā* (Toh 3856, 270a, Pd 58:657), he urges them, "If you take pleasure in this ambrosia of reality, then definitely discard this baseless false upholding of a nonexistent ātman as agent and enjoyer; it obstructs right view." To this, the opponent answers, "If our ātman and your anātman are similar, then your and our tenets are similar." [Bhāviveka responds:] "That is not so." Also, from Bhāviveka's reply that the tenets of Madhyamaka and Vedānta are not similar, it can be inferred that the followers of the Upaniṣads' argument for the nonproduction of internal and external phenomena partially resembles Madhyamaka reasoning.
251. Like Bhāviveka's *Tarkajvālā*, at the conclusion of Śāntarakṣita's autocommentary on his *Madhyamakālaṃkāra* (Toh 3885, 80a, Pd 69:966) he explains how the Madhyamaka emptiness of nonproduction and the Vedānta assertion differ. He also explains their difference from Vijñaptivāda, saying, "Thus all views, such as the ātman, to which the tīrthikas are attached, are called trifling emptiness."
252. See Muniśrī Pramāṇasāgara's *Jain Dharma aur Darśan*, p. 40, and Jagadish Candra Mishra's *Bhāratīya Darśan*, p. 210. See also Prajñāvarman, *Viśeṣastavaṭīkā*, Toh 4113, 28a, Pd 1:69.

253. See Muniśrī Pramāṇasāgara's *Jain Dharma aur Darśan*, p. 40, and Jagadish Candra Mishra's *Bhāratīya Darśan*, p. 210.
254. *Tattvārthasūtra*, chap. 1, sūtra 4.
255. *Tarkajvālā*, chap. 3. Toh 3856, 90a, Pd 58:223.
256. Chomden Rikpai Raldri, *A Flower Adorning Tenets*, 51a.
257. *Viśeṣastava*, verse 46. Toh 1109, 3b, Pd 1:7.
258. *Tarkajvālā*, chap. 3. Toh 3856, 90a, Pd 58:223.
259. Bhāviveka, *Tarkajvālā*, chap. 3. Toh 3856, 90a, Pd 58:224.
260. Bhāviveka, *Tarkajvālā*, chap. 3. Toh 3856, 90b, Pd 58:224.
261. Bhāviveka, *Tarkajvālā*, chap. 3. Toh 3856, 90b, Pd 58:224.
262. Bhāviveka, *Tarkajvālā*, chap. 3. Toh 3856, 90b, Pd 58:224.
263. Bhāviveka, *Tarkajvālā*, chap. 3. Toh 3856, 90b, Pd 58:224.
264. *Tattvārthasūtra*, chap. 5, sūtra 23.
265. *Tattvārthasūtra*, chap. 5, sūtra 18.
266. *Tattvārthasūtra*, chap. 5, sūtra 22.
267. This is known from, for example, the Jaina master Kundakunda's *Essence of the Five Existents* (*Pañcāstikāyasāra*).
268. *Tattvārthasūtra*, chap. 5, sūtra 37.
269. *Tattvasaṅgrahapañjikā*. Toh 27, 217a, Pd 107:564.
270. Umāsvāti, *Tattvārthasūtra*, chap. 3, sūtra 1.
271. *Tattvārthasūtra*, chap. 1, sūtra 6.
272. Kamalaśīla's *Tattvasaṅgrahapañjikā* (Toh 4267, 24b) says, "'Otherwise' means a reason is not correct without what is to be established. It means that a reason exists only in what is to be established."
273. *Tarkajvālā*, chap. 9. Toh 3856, 313b, Pd 58:763.
274. *Tarkajvālā*, chap. 9. Toh 3856, 311a, Pd 58:757.
275. *Madhyamakālaṃkārapañjikā*. Toh 3886, 99b, Pd 62:1019.
276. *Jñānasārasamuccayanibandhana*. Toh 3852, 39b, Pd 57:885.
277. *Prajñāpradīpaṭīkā*, chap. 2. Toh 3859, 121b, Pd 58:1156.
278. *Tattvasaṅgraha*, 26.7. Toh 4266, 68a, Pd 107:168.
279. *Abhiniṣkramaṇasūtra*. Toh 301, 5b, Pd 72:13.
280. *Prajñāpradīpaṭīkā*, chap. 2. Toh 3859, 112a, Pd 58:1135.
281. *Jñānasārasamuccayanibandhana*. Toh 3852, 39b, Pd 57:885.
282. Üpa Losal, *Treasury of Explanations of Tenets*, 256.
283. Kamalaśīla, *Tattvasaṅgrahapañjikā*. Toh 4267, 181a, Pd 107:473.
284. Bodhibhadra, *Jñānasārasamuccayanibandhana*. Toh 3852, 40a, Pd 57:885.
285. *Laṅkāvatārasūtra*, chap. 6. Toh 107, 256b Pd 49:660.
286. *Yogācārabhūmi*, chap. 7. Toh 4035, 75b, Pd 72:851.
287. Chomden Rikpai Raldri, *A Flower Adorning Tenets*, 8a.
288. *Skhalitapramathanayuktihetusiddhi*, verses 10–11. Toh 3847, 19b, Pd 57:827.
289. *Tarkajvālā*, chap. 3. Toh 3856, 103b, Pd 58:254.
290. *Prajñāpradīpaṭīkā*, chap. 1. Toh 3859, 115a, Pd 58:1142.
291. *Madhyamakāvatārabhāṣya*, chap. 6. Toh 3862, 285a, Pd 60:756.

292. *Tattvasaṅgrahapañjikā*, chap. 28. Toh 4267, 90a.
293. *Madhyamakahṛdaya*, 3.192. Toh 3855, 10b, Pd 58:25.
294. *Madhyamakahṛdaya*, 3.209. Toh 3855, 107b.
295. *Pramāṇavārttikālaṃkāra*, chap. 2. Toh 4221, 46b, Pd 99:879.
296. Bṛhaspati, *Bārhaspatya Sūtra*, 39.
297. Kalyāṇamitra, *Vinayavastuṭīkā*, chap. 2. Toh 4113, 197, Pd 87:530.
298. *Vinayavastu*. Toh 1, *ka*:24a, Pd 1:54.
299. This stanza is from a quotation in Candrakīrti's *Madhyamakāvatārabhāṣya*, chap. 6. Toh 3862, 285a, Pd 60:757.
300. Bṛhaspati, *Bārhaspatya Sūtra*, 15.
301. Bṛhaspati, *Bārhaspatya Sūtra*, 25.
302. This stanza is from a quotation in Candrakīrti's *Madhyamakāvatārabhāṣya*, chap. 6. Toh 3862, 176b, Pd 60:757.
303. Bṛhaspati, *Bārhaspatya Sūtra*, 6.
304. Bṛhaspati, *Bārhaspatya Sūtra*, 19.
305. *Tathāgatahṛdayālaṃkāra*, chap. 7. Toh 4019, 261b, Pd 70:632.
306. *Pramāṇavārttikaṭīkā*, chap. 1. Toh 4220, 37b, Pd 48:1042.
307. *Pramāṇavārttikālaṃkāra*, chap. 1. Toh 4221, 121a, Pd 99:1060.
308. Bṛhaspati, *Bārhaspatya Sūtra*, 35.
309. *Nyāyabindupūrvapakṣasaṅkṣipti*. Toh 4232, 97b, Pd 105:272.
310. Prajñākaragupta, *Pramāṇavārttikālaṃkāra*, chap. 4. Toh 422, 149b, Pd 100:374.
311. *Prajñāpradīpaṭīkā*, chap. 2. Toh 3859, 112a, Pd 58:1135.
312. Bṛhaspati, *Bārhaspatya Sūtra*, 44.
313. Bṛhaspati, *Bārhaspatya Sūtra*, 43.
314. *Vinayavastu*. Toh 1, *ka*:24a, 1:54.
315. *Prajñāpradīpaṭīkā*, chap. 16. Toh 3859, 334b, Pd 59:838.
316. Bṛhaspati, *Bārhaspatya Sūtra*, 46.
317. *Vinayavastu*. Toh 1, *ka*:23b, Pd 1:53.
318. *Vinayavastuṭīkā*. Toh 4113, 196a, Pd 87:529.
319. *Vinayavastu*. Toh 1, *ka*:23b, Pd 1:54.
320. Kalyāṇamitra, *Vinayavastuṭīkā*. Toh 4113, 197b, Pd 87:531.
321. Bṛhaspati, *Bārhaspatya Sūtra*, 41.
322. Bṛhaspati, *Bārhaspatya Sūtra*, 42.
323. *Pramāṇavārttika*, 2.34. Toh 4210, 108, Pd 87:503.
324. Bṛhaspati, *Bārhaspatya Sūtra*, 39.
325. *Prajñāpradīpaṭīkā*, chap. 16. Toh 3859, 334b, Pd 59:1100.
326. *Pramāṇaparīkṣā*. Toh 4249, 235b, Pd 106:634.
327. Bṛhaspati, *Bārhaspatya Sūtra*, 13–14.
328. That this is mentioned in Üpa Losal's *Tenets* was stated above.
329. *Science and Philosophy in the Indian Buddhist Classics, vol. 1: The Physical World*, 1.
330. *Laṅkāvatārasūtra*. Toh 107, 203b, Pd 49:534.

331. *Ratnāvalī*, 4.94–96. Toh 4158, 121b, Pd 96:324.
332. *Catuḥśataka*, 8.15. Toh 3846, 9b, Pd 57:801.
333. The text of the Tibetan translation of the *Mahāvibhāṣā* became dispersed during the upheaval of the Cultural Revolution. Because it is now incomplete, these verses have not been identified. However, they are quoted in many Tibetan texts—for example, Butön's *History of the Dharma*, 115, and Yongzin Yeshé Gyaltsen's *History of the Excellent Dharma and Vinaya*, 38a. It is also quoted in Longchenpa's *Treasury of Tenets*.
334. *Vinayakṣudrakavastu*. Toh 6, *da*, 323b.
335. For example, the names of four schools of tenets appear clearly in such works as the *Hevajra Tantra in Two Sections*, the *Kālacakra Tantra*, and the *Vajrārali Tantra*.
336. *Hevajrapiṇḍārthaṭīkā*, chap. 1. Toh 1180, 3a, Pd 1:759.
337. *Pradarśanānumatoddeśaparīkṣā*, chap. 1. 22b, Pd 12:570.
338. *Ratnāvalī*, 4.90. Toh 4158, 121b; Pd 96:324.
339. *Viśeṣastava*. Toh 1109, 3a, Pd 1:5.
340. Bhāviveka, *Tarkajvālā*, chap. 4. Toh 3856, 148a, Pd 58:361.
341. Bhāviveka, *Tarkajvālā*, chap. 4. Toh 3856, 149b, Pd 58:364.
342. Bhāviveka, *Tarkajvālā*, chap. 4. Toh 3856, 149b, Pd 58:365.
343. *Nikāyabhedopadeśanasaṅgraha*. Toh 4140, 154b3, Pd 93:1166. In the *Great Tenets* (pp. 260–73), discussing how the eighteen schools were divided, Jamyang Shepa sets forth each of the different individual systems for dividing them from four major schools, from one major school, and from three major schools. Regarding the first, he sets forth two systems: Vinītadeva's system of dividing them, set forth above, and the way it is explained in the text called *Bhikṣuvarśāgrapṛcchā* attributed to Padmasambhava. The way of dividing them from one major school is the system of Śākyaprabha, which takes only the Sarvāstivāda to be the main school. Dividing them from three are the three ways set forth in the passage from the *Blaze of Reasoning* cited above. Jamyang Shepa's description is quite detailed.
344. Śākyaprabha, *Prabhāvatī*. Toh 4125. From the commentary on the *Śrāmaṇerakārikā*, 160b.
345. Bhāviveka, *Tarkajvālā*, chap. 4. Toh 3856, 148a, Pd 58:361.
346. At the top of a stone pillar with a lion capital from the first century discovered in Mathura, there is an inscription about offering the place and property to a Sarvāstivāda monastery and to a group of monks. This is clear from a book called *Mathura Inscriptions* by the modern German scholar Klaus Janert. In our own [Tibetan] texts on tenets, there are three divisions of the Vaibhāṣika: the Magadha Vaibhāṣika, the Aparāntaka, and the Kashmiri Vaibhāṣika. However, it seems likely that is based for the most part on how the tenets of the Sarvāstivāda gradually spread from Magadha.
347. Potter 1970–2019, 7:100.
348. These figures do not appear in one place in his travel journal; they are gathered from throughout the text.

349. Potter 1970–2019, 8:25.
350. Üpa Losal, *Treasury of Explanations of the Tenet Systems*, 257.
351. *Sphuṭārthābhidharmakośavyākhyā*, chap. 1. Toh 4092, 9a, Pd 80:21.
352. Yaśomitra, *Sphuṭārthābhidharmakośavyākhyā*, chap. 1. Toh 4092, 7a, Pd 80:17.
353. Potter 1970–2019, 7:102.
354. The text was translated in its entirety in modern times from the Chinese by the Chinese translator Losang Chöpak, or Fazun, between 1945 and 1949. During the upheaval of the Cultural Revolution some parts of the Tibetan translation of the text became dispersed. Copied from a manuscript received by His Holiness the Dalai Lama, a scanned version of the complete edition is now available both inside and outside Tibet. The missing parts of the text are being translated into Tibetan in Taiwan, according to the wishes of His Holiness the Dalai Lama.
355. A summary of the presentation of mental factors in the twelfth-century Theravāda text *Compendium of Abhidhamma* appears in chapter 14 of *Science and Philosophy in the Indian Buddhist Classics, vol. 2: The Mind.*
356. *Jñānasārasamuccayanibandhana*. Toh 3852, 42a, Pd 57:891.
357. *Sphuṭārthābhidharmakośavyākhyā*, chap. 8. Toh 4092, 311b, Pd 80:1597.
358. According to the *Great Exegesis* (3:693, fascicle 70), "The four great Sarvāstivāda masters present the three times differently. The monk Dharmatrāta says that they are different things. The monk Ghoṣaka says that they are different characteristics. The monk Vasumitra says that they are different states. The monk Buddhadeva says that they are different from each other." Their assertions are set forth in detail in *Science and Philosophy in the Indian Buddhist Classics, vol. 1: The Physical World.*
359. *Abhidharmakośabhāṣya*, chap. 5. Toh 4090, 239a, Pd 79:586. This is set forth in the first volume of *Science and Philosophy in Indian Buddhist Classics*.
360. Vasubandhu, *Abhidharmakośa*, 1.19. Toh 4089, 2b, Pd 97:5.
361. *Lakṣaṇānusāriṇī*, chap. 1. Toh 4093, 13a, Pd 81:30.
362. *Abhidharmamahāvibhāṣā*, 6:939, fascicle 127.
363. Yaśomitra, *Sphuṭārthābhidharmakośavyākhyā*, chap. 1. Toh 4092, 236a, Pd 80:555.
364. Pūrṇavardhana, *Lakṣaṇānusāriṇī*, chap. 1. Toh 4093, 31b, Pd 81:76.
365. The description of Kaurukullaka, Avantaka, and Vātsīputrīya as divisions of Sāṃmitīya following Vinītadeva's *Compendium Setting Forth the Different Sects* and a different explanation from Bhāviveka's *Blaze of Reasoning* have already been set forth above in the section on how the eighteen schools are divided. See pp. 229–36.
366. Āryadeva, *Jñānasārasamuccaya*, verse 21. Toh 3851, 27a, Pd 57:853.
367. *Sugatamatavibhaṅgakārikā*, verse 1. Toh 3899, 7b, Pd 63: 884.
368. Kātyāyanīputra, *Jñānaprasthāna*, 1:1358, fascicle 20.
369. Vasubandhu, *Abhidharmakośa*, 1.19. Toh 4089, 2b, Pd 97:5.
370. *Abhidharmakośabhāṣya*, chap. 2. Toh 4090, 63a, Pd 79:157.
371. *Abhidharmasamuccayabhāṣya*, chap. 1. Toh 4054, 143b, Pd 76:1328.

372. Vasubandhu, *Abhidharmakośa*, 1.11. Toh 4089, 2a, Pd 79:4.
373. *Abhidharmamahāvibhāṣā*, 7:347, fascicle 136.
374. *Abhidharmamahāvibhāṣā*, 7:354, fascicle 136.
375. *Abhidharmamahāvibhāṣā*, 3:545, fascicle 73.
376. *Bāhyārthasiddhi*, verse 56. Toh 4244, 191b, Pd 106:514.
377. *Science and Philosophy in the Indian Buddhist Classics*, vol. 1, 125–40.
378. *Science and Philosophy in the Indian Buddhist Classics*, vol. 2, 175–79.
379. Vasubandhu, *Abhidharmakośa*, 2.35. Toh 4089, 5a, Pd 79:11.
380. *Abhidharmakośaṭīkopayikā*, chap. 1. Toh 4094, 8b, Pd 82:14. In the *Dense Array Sūtra* (Toh 110, 45b, Pd 50:104) there is a passage that is similar to that from the *Sūtra of the Nun Dharmadinnā*:

    When the life force, heat, and consciousness
    leave the body,
    the abandoned body
    is like a log, without feeling.

381. Vasubandhu, *Abhidharmakośabhāṣya*, chap. 2. Toh 4090, 79a, Pd 79:196.
382. Kātyāyanīputra, *Jñānaprasthāna*, 1:117, fascicle 2.
383. *Abhidharmamahāvibhāṣā*, 3:664, fascicle 76.
384. Vasubandhu, *Abhidharmakośabhāṣya*, chap. 2. Toh 4090, 80b, Pd 79:202.
385. Vasubandhu, *Abhidharmakośabhāṣya*, chap. 2. Toh 4090, 81a, Pd 79:201.
386. Vasubandhu, *Abhidharmakośabhāṣya*, chap. 2. Toh 4090.
387. Yaśomitra, *Sphuṭārthābhidharmakośavyākhyā*, chap. 2. Toh 4092, 158b, Pd 80:378.
388. Vasubandhu, *Abhidharmakośabhāṣya*, chap. 2. Toh 4090, 83a, Pd 79:206.
389. *Tarkajvālā*, chap. 4. Toh 3856, 152a, Pd 58:378.
390. *Sugatamatavibhaṅgabhāṣya*. Toh 3900, 8b, Pd 63:883.
391. Vasubandhu, *Abhidharmakośabhāṣya*, chap. 4. Toh 4090, 166b, Pd 79:410.
392. *Lakṣaṇānusāriṇī*, chap. 4. Toh 4093, 4a, Pd 81:925.
393. *Tarkajvālā*, chap. 4. Toh 3856, 152b, Pd 58:377.
394. *Lakṣaṇānusāriṇī*, chap. 4. Toh 4093, 5a, Pd 81:927.
395. *Lakṣaṇānusāriṇī*, chap. 4. Toh 4093, 4b, Pd 81:925.
396. *Lakṣaṇānusāriṇī*, chap. 4. Toh 4093, 4a, Pd 81:925.
397. *Abhidharmakośabhāṣya*, chap. 2. Toh 4090, 84b, Pd 72:210.
398. *Jñānasārasamuccayanibandhana*. Toh 3852, 41b, Pd 57:890.
399. Vasubandhu, *Abhidharmakośa*, 2.49. Toh 4089, 5b, Pd 79:12.
400. Vasubandhu, *Abhidharmakośabhāṣya*, chap. 2. Toh 4090, 86a, Pd 79:214.
401. *Lakṣaṇānusāriṇī*, chap. 2. Toh 4093, 199b, Pd 81:503.
402. Vasubandhu, *Abhidharmakośabhāṣya*, chap. 2. Toh 4090, 86b, Pd 79:215.
403. Vasubandhu, *Abhidharmakośa*, 2.35. Toh 4089, 6a, Pd 79:13.
404. Vasubandhu, *Abhidharmakośabhāṣya*, chap. 2. Toh 4090, 91a, Pd 79:226.
405. Vasubandhu, *Abhidharmakośabhāṣya*, chap. 2. Toh 4090, 91b, Pd 79:227.
406. Vasubandhu, *Abhidharmakośabhāṣya*, chap. 2. Toh 4090, 92a, Pd 79:228.

407. *Sphuṭārthābhidharmakośavyākhyā*, chap. 2. Toh 4092, 174a, Pd 80:415.
408. *Abhidharmakośavṛttimarmadīpa*, chap. 2. Toh 4095, 121b, Pd 82:1063.
409. *Abhidharmamahāvibhāṣā*, 7:166, fascicle 131.
410. Vasubandhu, *Abhidharmakośa*, 2.62. Toh 4089, 6a, Pd 79:13.
411. Vasubandhu, *Abhidharmakośa*, 2.64. Toh 4089, 6b, Pd 79:14.
412. Vasubandhu, *Abhidharmakośabhāṣya*, chap. 2, Toh 4090, 93a, Pd 79:231.
413. Vasubandhu, *Abhidharmakośa*, 2.56. Toh 4089, 6a, Pd 79:13.
414. Vasubandhu, *Abhidharmakośabhāṣya*, chap. 2. Toh 4090, 96b, Pd 79:240.
415. Vasubandhu, *Abhidharmakośabhāṣya*, chap. 2. Toh 4090, 97b, Pd 79:241.
416. Vasubandhu, *Abhidharmakośabhāṣya*, chap. 2. Toh 4090, 97b, Pd 79:241.
417. Vasubandhu, *Abhidharmakośa*, 2.58. Toh 4089, 6a, Pd 79:13.
418. Vasubandhu, *Abhidharmakośabhāṣya*, chap. 2. Toh 4090, 97a, Pd 79:241.
419. *Abhidharmamahāvibhāṣā*, 5:721, fascicle 108.
420. *Abhidharmamahāvibhāṣā*, 2:161, fascicle 3.
421. *Nyāyabindupūrvapakṣasaṅkṣipti*. Toh 4232, 92b, Pd 105:259.
422. *Abhidharmamahāvibhāṣā*, 3:425, fascicle 71.
423. *Abhidharmamahāvibhāṣā*, 3:443, fascicle 71.
424. Vasubandhu, *Abhidharmakośa*, 1.42. Toh 4089, 3b, Pd 79:7.
425. *Sugatamatavibhaṅgakārikā*, verse 2. Toh 3899, 76, Pd 63:884.
426. *Sugatamatavibhaṅgabhāṣya*.Toh 3900, 38b, Pd 63:961.
427. Üpa Losal, *Treasury of Explanations of Tenets*, 383.
428. Chomden Rikpai Raldri, *A Flower Adorning Tenets*, 97a and 51a.
429. *Jñānasārasamuccayanibandhana*. Toh 3852, 42b, Pd 57:892.
430. Although not found in Xuanzang's travel journal in the Tibetan translation by the translator Gung Gönpo Kyab, the passage is found in the twelfth fascicle of the Chinese version. T.51.2087.942a10–20.
431. Chinese Electronic Canon (CBETA). The *Notes on the Proof of Consciousness Only* (*Cheng weishi lun shu ji*; T 43, no. 1830) by the Chinese monk Kuiji says, "The sun of the north, Kumāralāta, composed the *Nine Hundred* and the *Garland of Examples*." In Jizang's *Commentary on the Verses on the Middle Way* (*Zhongguan lun shu*; T 42, no. 1824), it says, "Kumāralāta composed the *Rising of the Sun*." Dunlin's *Commentary on the Treasury of Abhidharma* (*Jushesong shu ji*; X 53, no. 0841) says, "Kumāralāta composed the *Garland of Examples*, the *Garland of Obscuration*, and the *Clarifier*." Because these works are not included in the Chinese canon, it appears that they were not translated into Chinese.
432. This is according to what appears in Üpa Losal, *Treasury of Explanations of Tenets*, 258.
433. Yaśomitra, *Sphuṭārthābhidharmakośavyākhyā*, chap. 1. Toh 4092, 9b, Pd 80:21.
434. *Ratnakaraṇḍodghāṭa*. Toh 3930, 112b, Pd 64:327.
435. These two lines are cited by Sakya Paṇḍita in his *Commentary on the Treasury of Valid Knowledge and Reasoning*, p. 59.
436. *Jñānasārasamuccayanibandhana*. Toh 3852, 42b, Pd 57:892.

437. *Jñānasārasamuccayanibandhana*. Toh 3852, 42b, Pd 57:892. In accordance with this, Chomden Rikpai Raldri's *Flower Adorning the Tenets* (96a) says, "They accept literally and propound such sūtras as the *Six-Door Dhāraṇī* (*Ṣaṇmukhadhāraṇī*), the [*Prayer of*] *Good Conduct* (*Bhadracaryāpraṇidhāna*), the *Single Verse* (*Ekagāthā*), the *Four Verses* (*Caturgāthā*), the *Two Verse Dhāraṇī* (*Gāthādvayadhāraṇī*), the *Extensive Sport* (*Lalitavistara*), the *Four Factors* (*Caturdharmaka*), and the *Ten Levels* (*Daśabhūmika*). Therefore they are called Sautrāntika. Because they are skilled in setting forth phenomena through examples, they are called Dārṣṭāntika." Many statements like this appear in tenets texts composed by Tibetan scholars.
438. *Jñānasārasamuccaya*, verse 23. Toh 3851, 27, Pd 57:853.
439. *Sugatamatavibhaṅgakārikā*, verse 2. Toh 3899, 7b, Pd 63:884.
440. The reason why Sautrāntika does not accept that nonrevelatory form is actual form, as well as the sources for that, is explained in the first volume of *Science and Philosophy in the Indian Buddhist Classics*, 88–89.
441. *Pramāṇavārttika*, 3.3. Toh 4210, 118b, Pd 97:526.
442. *Pramāṇavārttika*, 1.87–88. Toh 4210, 98a, Pd 97:477.
443. *Pramāṇavārttika*, 3.51. Toh 4210, 120b, Pd 97:530.
444. *Pramāṇavārttika*, 3.2. Toh 4210, 118b, Pd 97:530.
445. *Pramāṇavārttika*, 3.11. Toh 4210, 119b, Pd 97:526.
446. *Pramāṇavārttika*, 1.87–88. Toh 4210, 98a, Pd 97:477.
447. *Pramāṇavārttika*, 1.121. Toh 4210, 99a, Pd 97: 480.
448. *Pramāṇavārttika*, 1.77. Toh 4210, 97a, Pd 97:476.
449. *Pramāṇavārttika*, 1.195. Toh 4210, 102a, Pd 97:486.
450. *Pramāṇaviniścaya*, chap. 2. Toh 4211, 179b, Pd 97:677.
451. *Kṣaṇabhaṅgasiddhi*. Toh 4253, 253b, Pd 106:691.
452. Dharmottara, *Kṣaṇabhaṅgasiddhi*. Toh 4253, 253b, Pd 106:692.
453. *Pramāṇavārttikālaṃkāra*, chap. 4. Toh 4221, 276b, Pd 100:695.
454. Dharmakīrti, *Pramāṇavārttika*, 2.205. Toh 4210, 115a, Pd 97:518.
455. *Science and Philosophy in the Buddhist Classics*, vol. 1, chap. 13, esp. pp. 179–89, "Negation and Affirmation."
456. Dharmakīrti, *Pramāṇavārttika*, 1.106. Toh 4210, 98b, Pd 97:479.
457. Vasubandhu, *Abhidharmakośa*, 3.30–31. Toh 4089, 8b, Pd 79:17.
458. *Abhidharmakośabhāṣya*, chap. 3. Toh 4090, 134b, Pd 79:332.
459. *Abhidharmakośabhāṣya*, chap. 3. Toh 4090, 134b, Pd 79:332.
460. *Abhidharmakośabhāṣya*, chap. 3. Toh 4090, 134b, Pd 79:332.
461. *Abhidharmakośabhāṣya*, chap. 3. Toh 4090, 134b, Pd 79:332.
462. *Abhidharmakośabhāṣya*, chap. 3. Toh 4090, 135a, Pd 79:332.
463. *Abhidharmakośabhāṣya*, chap. 3. Toh 4090, 135a, Pd 79:332.
464. *Abhidharmakośabhāṣya*, chap. 3. Toh 4090, 135a, Pd 79:332.
465. *Abhidharmakośabhāṣya*, chap. 3. Toh 4090, 135a, Pd 79:333.
466. *Abhidharmakośabhāṣya*, chap. 3. Toh 4090, 135a, Pd 79:333.
467. *Abhidharmakośabhāṣya*, chap. 3. Toh 4090, 135a, Pd 79:333.

468. *Abhidharmakośabhāṣya*, chap. 3. Toh 4090, 135a, Pd 79:333.
469. *Abhidharmakośabhāṣya*, chap. 3. Toh 4090, 135b, Pd 79:333.
470. *Abhidharmakośabhāṣya*, chap. 3. Toh 4090, 135b, Pd 79:334.
471. *Abhidharmakośabhāṣya*, chap. 3. Toh 4090, 135b, Pd 79:334.
472. *Abhidharmakośabhāṣya*, chap. 3. Toh 4090, 135b, Pd 79:334.
473. *Abhidharmakośabhāṣya*, chap. 3. Toh 4090, 136a, Pd 79:334.
474. *Abhidharmakośabhāṣya*, chap. 3. Toh 4090, 136a, Pd 79:335.
475. *Abhidharmakośabhāṣya*, chap. 3. Toh 4090, 133a, Pd 79:328.
476. *Abhidharmakośaṭīkā-lakṣaṇānusāriṇī*, chap. 2. Toh 4093, 308a, Pd 81:766.
477. *Abhidharmakośabhāṣya*, chap. 3. Toh 4090, 133a, Pd 79:328.
478. *Pramāṇavārttika*, 3.246. Toh 4210, 127b, Pd 97:548.
479. *Sambandhaparīkṣāṭīkā*. Toh 4236, 17b, Pd 106:42.
480. *Bāhyārthasiddhi*, verse 56. Toh 4244, 191b, Pd 106:514. See chapter 15 of *Science and Philosophy in the Indian Buddhist Classics, vol. 1: The Physical World*.
481. *Bāhyārthasiddhi*, verses 2–3. Toh 4244, 189b, Pd 106:509.
482. *Bāhyārthasiddhi*, verses 4–5. Toh 4244, 189b, Pd 106:509.
483. *Bāhyārthasiddhi*, verse 6. Toh 4244, 189b, Pd 106:510.
484. *Bāhyārthasiddhi*, verse 30. Toh 4244, 190b, Pd 106:512.
485. *Bāhyārthasiddhi*, verse 125. Toh 4244, 194a, Pd 106:520.
486. *Bāhyārthasiddhi*, verse 106. Toh 4244,193a, Pd 106:518.
487. *Sugatamatavibhaṅgakārikā*. Toh 3899, 53a, Pd 63:997. In Changkya's *Beautiful Adornment* (p. 158) the passage appears differently:

    The internal perceiver is other,
    and the external appearance is also other than that.
    That which is illuminated and that which illuminates
    are not the same, like a butter lamp [and what it illuminates].

488. *Pramāṇasamuccaya*. Toh 4203, 2a, Pd 108:92.
489. *Pramāṇavārttika*, 3.249. Toh 4210, 128a, Pd 97:548.
490. Although this passage is often cited in Indian texts on valid knowledge, the sūtra that is its source has not been clearly identified.
491. Dharmakīrti, *Pramāṇavārttika*, 3.239. Toh 4210, 127b, Pd 97:547.
492. Dharmakīrti, *Pramāṇavārttika*, 3.243. Toh 4210, 127b, Pd 97:547.
493. Dharmakīrti, *Pramāṇavārttika*, 3.244. Toh 4210, 127b, Pd 97:547.
494. Sakya Paṇḍita's *Commentary on the Treasury of Valid Knowledge and Reasoning* (section 3, p. 271) says that the first system is that of the author of the *Ornament of the Exposition of Valid Knowledge* [Prajñākaragupta], the second is that of the great brahmin Śaṅkarānanda, and the third is the system of Dharmottara. From among these three, he says that for himself, the system of the great brahmin is correct: "What I have found from my abbot about the view of Śaṅkarānanda is that it alone is seen to be correct." Here, "my abbot" must be the Kashmiri paṇḍita Śākyaśrībhadra.
495. Although this assertion is something that is well known in the oral tradition

of scholars, many scholars have noted that it does not appear clearly in the Tibetan translations of Prajñākaragupta's works. For example, in *Eliminating Confusion: An Ornament for the Seven Texts on Valid Knowledge*, Khedrup Jé says, "'The assertion of the author of the *Ornament of the Exposition of Valid Knowledge* is that at the beginning sense direct perception leads and at the end mental direct perception concludes; sense direct perception and mental direct perception alternate.' This statement is merely something that is well known to scholars; it does not appear in the Tibetan translation of any text related to the *Ornament*."

496. Similar to the previous note, Khedrup Jé, in his *Dispelling Confusion*, says (p. 152), "The statement 'This is the assertion of the great brahmin" is just something well known to earlier scholars. There is no source for it in any of the Tibetan translations of the brahmin's works, and [Sakya Paṇḍita's] *Treasury of Valid Knowledge and Reasoning* clearly agrees with this."
497. *Nyāyabinduṭīkā*. Toh 4231, 43a, Pd 105:120.
498. Dharmakīrti, *Pramāṇavārttika*, 3.256. Toh 4210, 128a, Pd 97:549.
499. For example, as the later Buddhist scholar of valid knowledge Jetāri says in his *Logic for the Childish* (*Bālāvatāratarka*, chap. 1; Toh 4263, 327a, Pd 106:905), "Direct perception that has the nature of the mind is asserted to be a valid means of knowledge when the activity of the eye and so forth are completed." That is, he is explaining that it must be posited at the conclusion of the sequence of sense direct perception. In *Language of Logic* (*Tarkabhāṣā*, Toh 4264, 342b, Pd 106:948) Mokṣākaragupta, in accordance with Dharmottara, explains the very short duration of mental direct perception and the need that it be proven with scripture. In Tibet, the scholars of valid knowledge in the system of Ngok Lotsāwa and the majority of Ganden scholars of valid knowledge, such as Gyaltsab Jé, present Dharmottara's system as their own.
500. *Jñānasārasamuccayanibandhana*. Toh 3852, 42a, Pd 57:891.
501. Bodhibhadra, *Jñānasārasamuccayanibandhana*. Toh 3852, 43a, Pd 57:891.
502. *Pramāṇavārttika*, 3.247. Toh 4210, 127b, Pd 97:548.
503. *Pramāṇavārttika*, 3.224. Toh 4210, 127a, Pd 97:546.
504. Regarding the prophecies of Asaṅga, the *Mañjuśrī Root Tantra* (Toh 543, 309a, Pd 88:880) says:

> A monk named Asaṅga,
> skilled in the meaning of the treatises,
> will distinguish the many elements of the sūtras
> into the definitive meaning and the provisional meaning.

And the *Commentary on Explanation of the Intention* (Toh 3981, 31a, Pd 68:73) [traditionally attributed to Asaṅga] says, "Nine hundred years passed after the Buddha had passed into nirvāṇa." A brief version of the best-known account of Asaṅga's life appears in Butön's *History of the Dharma*, 152–53.

505. Maitreya, *Ornament of the Mahāyāna Sūtras* (*Mahāyānasutrālaṃkāra*), 2.1. Toh 4020, 2a, Pd 70:806.

506. *Madhyamakāloka*. Toh 3887, 145b, Pd 62:1143.
507. Jamyang Shepai Dorjé, *Great Exposition of Tenets*, 326.
508. *Guhyārthapiṇḍārthavyākhyā*, traditionally ascribed to Vasubandhu. Apart from some fragments, a complete translation of this text does not exist in our Tengyur. At present, the original Sanskrit text has not been found.
509. Tibetan scholars have different ways of explaining how the intentions of the Five Books of Maitreya are categorized as Madhyamaka or Cittamātra. For example, the Sakya master Rendawa explains that all five are Cittamātra, whereas Tsongkhapa and his heirs explain that *Ornament of Realizations* and the *Sublime Continuum* are Madhyamaka and the other three are Cittamātra. Shentongpas—the proponents of other-emptiness, such as Dölpopa—explain that the intention of all five is the system of the other-emptiness of the so-called Great Madhyamaka, which they say is a Yogācāra system that is different from Cittamātra.
510. According to later research, there is a question as to whether what is known to us as Asaṅga's commentary on the *Sublime Continuum* is by Asaṅga. In what exists today in Chinese, the name of the author has been reconstructed as *Sāramati, which may point here to the prolific commentator Sthiramati.
511. *Daśabhūmikasūtra*, chap. 31 of the *Flower Garland Sūtra*. Toh 44, 220b, Pd 36:471.
512. *Laṅkāvatāra Sūtra*. Toh 107,168b, Pd 49:413.
513. *Bodhisattvayogacaryācatuḥśataka*, normally referred to as just *Four Hundred Verses* (*Catuḥśataka*). Tibetan scholars who are proponents of other-emptiness distinguish Cittamātra from Yogācāra. For these scholars, Asaṅga and his brother Vasubandhu are not Cittamātra, they are Yogācārin, and the view of nonduality delineated by them is more profound than the view of emptiness set forth in, for instance, the six works of Nāgārjuna's Collection of Reasoning. Such an explanation is an exception, however.
514. *Sarvayānālokaviśeṣabhāṣya*. Toh 3907, 308b, Pd 63:1876.
515. *Sarvayānālokaviśeṣabhāṣya*. Toh 3907, 310b, Pd 63:1883.
516. *Jñānasārasamuccayanibandhana*. Toh 3852, 43b, Pd 57:895. Here, due to the fact that Dignāga and Asaṅga assert six collections of consciousness and eight collections of consciousness, respectively, it seems that the statement that the former says that there is an aspect and the latter says that there is no aspect must refer to their being True and False Aspectarians. Otherwise, if it refers to Asaṅga's own system asserting that consciousness has no aspect, this would obviously be a significant point to be investigated. In addition, it is possible that the difference between the existence or nonexistence of an aspect here implies the need to differentiate them from the point of view of not asserting in their own system that the aspect of the apprehended and the aspect of the apprehender for the mind are two different entities. In that case, one would need to analyze whether something like this is the source for the statement made by some Tibetan scholars that Dignāga's own system asserted reflexive awareness and Asaṅga and his brother Vasubandhu did not. Regardless, the

division of Cittamātra into True and False Aspectarian is stated clearly in many early Buddhist texts and especially in many Indian and Tibetan texts on tenets.

517. Āryadeva, *Jñānasārasamuccaya*, verse 24. Toh 3851, 26b, Pd 57:853.

518. Jetāri, *Sugatamatavibhaṅgakārikā*, verse 6. Toh 3899, 8a, Pd 63:885. The commentary to this says, "That which has parts does not exist. / There are also no particles." *Sugatamatavibhaṅgabhāṣya*. Toh 3900, 40b.

519. *Mahāyānasaṅgraha*. Toh 4048, 13a, Pd 76:30.

520. *Trisvabhāvanirdeśa*, verse 2. Toh 4058, 10a, Pd 77:29.

521. Vasubandhu, *Trisvabhāvanirdeśa*, verse 27. Toh 4058, 10a, Pd 77:31.

522. *Trisvabhāvanirdeśa*, verses 22–26. Toh 4058, 11a, Pd 77:31.

523. *Triṃśikā*, verse 22. Toh 4055, 2b, Pd 77:5. In Sthiramati's explanation of the *Thirty Verses*, in a statement that transitions to the teaching on the three natures, he says, "If these are mere cognition, how does it not contradict the sūtra?" That is, if all phenomena are mere cognitions, their three natures—the dependent, the imaginary, and the consummate—that are stated in the sūtra do not contradict their being mere cognition. Dispelling that objection, he appears to comment on the intention of the sūtra.

524. *Madhyāntavibhāga*, verses 1–2. Toh 4021, 40b, Pd 70:902.

525. Asaṅga, *Mahāyānasaṅgraha*. Toh 4048, 16a, Pd 76:38.

526. *Saṃdhinirmocanasūtra*, chap. 7. Toh 106, 22b, Pd 49:52.

527. *Saṃdhinirmocanasūtra*, chap. 7. Toh 106, 22b, Pd 49:52.

528. For example, when Candrakīrti in his *Entering the Middle Way* (6.47) identifies the dependent in the Vijñaptika system, he describes it as having these three qualities. Toh 3861, 206b, Pd 60:524.

529. Asaṅga, *Mahāyānasaṅgraha*. Toh 4048, 16a, Pd 76:38.

530. Maitreya, *Madhyāntavibhāga*, 1.14. Toh 4021, 40b, Pd 70:903.

531. *Saṃdhinirmocanasūtra*, chap. 7. Toh 106, 24a, Pd 49:54.

532. Asaṅga, *Mahāyānasaṅgraha*. Toh 4048, 16a, Pd 76:38.

533. *Saṃdhinirmocanasūtra*, chap. 7. Toh 106, 17a, Pd 49:39.

534. *Saṃdhinirmocanasūtra*, chap. 7. Toh 106, 17a, Pd 49:39.

535. *Saṃdhinirmocanasūtra*, chap. 7. Toh 106, 17a, Pd 49:40.

536. *Udānavarga*, 31.9. Toh 326, 243a, Pd 83:83.

537. *Mahāyānasaṅgrahabhāṣya*. Toh 4050, 145b, Pd 76:376.

538. *Pañcakramaṭīkā*. Toh 1842, 240a, Pd 19:636.

539. *Jñānasārasamuccayanibandhana*. Toh 3852, 43b, Pd 57:897.

540. The Chinese Yogācāra tradition established by Xuanzang was based on the *Proof of Consciousness Only* (*Cheng weishi lun*, **Vijñaptimātratāsiddhi*), an anthology that presented Vasubandhu's *Thirty Verses* in the context of ten of its Indian commentaries, privileging the reading of Dharmapāla.

541. *Jieshenmijing shu* (**Saṃdhigambhīranirmocanasūtraṭīkā*), chap. 4. Toh 4016, 214b, Pd 68:510.

542. *Pitāputrasamāgamasūtra*, chap. 26. Toh 60, 133a, Pd 42:319.

543. Vasubandhu, *Abhidharmakośabhāṣya*, chap. 1. Toh 4090, 33b, Pd 79:83.

544. *Catuḥśatakaṭīkā*, chap. 11. Toh 3865, 180a, Pd 60:1357.
545. *Pañcakramaṭīkā*. Toh 1842, 240a, Pd 19:72.
546. *Jieshenmijing shu*, chap. 4. Toh 4016, 214b, Pd 68:511.
547. *Saṃdhinirmocanasūtra*, chap. 5. Toh 106, 13b, Pd 49:31.
548. *Ghanavyūhasūtra*, chap. 7. Toh 110, 37b, Pd 50:84.
549. *Laṅkāvatārasūtra*, chap. 6. Toh 107, 142b, Pd 49:352.
550. Asaṅga, *Mahāyānasaṅgraha*. Toh 4048, 3b, Pd 76:7. The *Abhidharma Sūtra* is not in the Tibetan canon. It is known through citations like the one here.
551. *Triṃśikā*, verses 3–4. Toh 4055, 1a, Pd 77:3.
552. *Triṃśikābhāṣya*. Toh 4064, 149b, Pd 77:397.
553. *Pratītyasamutpādādivibhaṅgabhāṣyanirdeśa*. Toh 3995, 22a, Pd 66:1046.
554. Asaṅga, *Mahāyānasaṅgraha*. Toh 4048, 5a, Pd 76:10.
555. Asaṅga, *Viniścayasaṅgrahaṇī*. Toh 4038, 2a, Pd 74:4.
556. *Abhidharmasamuccayavyākhyā*, chap. 1. Toh 4054, 134a, Pd 76:1306.
557. The fifteen cognizances are discussed beginning on page 350.
558. *Mahāyānasaṅgrahopanibandhana*. Toh 4051, 203b, Pd 76:535.
559. *Vivṛtagūhyārthapiṇḍavyākhyā*. Toh 4052, 328a, Pd 76:861.
560. Asaṅga, *Mahāyānasaṅgraha*. Toh 4048, 6b, Pd 76:13.
561. *Vivṛtagūhyārthapiṇḍavyākhyā*. Toh 4052, 328a, Pd 76:862.
562. Asaṅga, *Mahāyānasaṅgraha*. Toh 4048, 7a, Pd 76:16.
563. Asaṅga, *Mahāyānasaṅgraha*. Toh 4048, 12a, Pd 76:27.
564. Asaṅga, *Mahāyānasaṅgraha*. Toh 4048, 13a, Pd 76:31.
565. *Mahāyānasaṅgrahabhāṣya*. Toh 4050, 143b, Pd 76:370.
566. Asaṅga, *Mahāyānasaṅgraha*. Toh 4048, 12a, Pd 76:28.
567. Asaṅga, *Mahāyānasaṅgraha*. Toh 4048, 12b, Pd 76:29.
568. Vasubandhu, *Triṃśikā*, verses 5–7. Toh 4055, 1a, Pd 77:3.
569. *Triṃśikāvijñaptibhāṣya*. Toh 4064, 152b, Pd 77:404.
570. *Triṃśikāvijñaptibhāṣya*. Toh 4064, 153a, Pd 77:404.
571. *Ghanavyūhasūtra*. Toh 110, 45b, Pd 50:104.
572. *Laṅkāvatārasūtra*. Toh 107, 267b, Pd 49:410.
573. Asaṅga, *Mahāyānasaṅgraha*. Toh 4048, 4a, Pd 76:8.
574. Asaṅga, *Mahāyānasaṅgraha*. Toh 4048, 4a, Pd 76:8.
575. Asaṅga, *Mahāyānasaṅgraha*. Toh 4048, 4a, Pd 76:8.
576. Asaṅga, *Mahāyānasaṅgraha*. Toh 4048, 4a, Pd 76:8.
577. Asaṅga, *Mahāyānasaṅgraha*. Toh 4048, 4a, Pd 76:8.
578. Asaṅga, *Mahāyānasaṅgraha*. Toh 4048, 4a, Pd 76:8.
579. Asaṅga, *Mahāyānasaṅgraha*. Toh 4048, 13b, Pd 76:32.
580. *Daśabhūmikasūtra*. Toh 44, 220b, Pd 36:471.
581. *Saṃdhinirmocanasūtra*, chap. 8. Toh 106, 27a, Pd 49:62.
582. Asaṅga, *Mahāyānasaṅgraha*. Toh 4048, 14a, Pd 76:33.
583. Vasubandhu, *Triṃśikā*, verses 1–2. Toh 4055, 1a, Pd 77:3.
584. Vasubandhu, *Viṃśikā*, verse 1. Toh 4056, 3a, Pd 77:8.
585. Vasubandhu, *Viṃśikā*, verse 8. Toh 4056, 3b, Pd 77:9.

586. Vasubandhu, *Viṃśikā*, verse 9. Toh 4056, 3b, Pd 77:9.
587. Vasubandhu, *Viṃśikāvṛtti*. Toh 4057, 6a, Pd 77:12.
588. Vasubandhu, *Viṃśikā*, verse 12. Toh 4056, 3b, Pd 77:9.
589. Tibetan scholars hold diverse views on whether Dignāga and his heirs accept the foundation consciousness. In the works of Dignāga that are currently extant, no explanation of the foundation consciousness, explicit or implicit, appears. In addition, at the point in his *Investigation of the Support* and its autocommentary where he explains the observed object condition and the dominant condition of sense consciousnesses in terms of potencies or predispositions, if he accepted the foundation consciousness, he certainly would have discussed it there. However, not even the slightest mention appears in these texts. The statement in the *Explanation of the Compendium on the Essence of Wisdom* that Dignāga accepted that there are six collections of consciousness is certainly true. And in both his *Exposition of Valid Knowledge* and *Ascertainment of Valid Knowledge*, Dharmakīrti proves with extensive reasonings how phenomena are established as cognition only. However, he appears to use the explanation of only six collections of consciousness as the basis of his system rather than in terms of the foundation consciousness. Similarly, when explaining his own system in the *Proof of Other Minds* and its autocommentary, if he accepted the foundation consciousness, then a commentary explaining that the minds of different persons are established from the perspective of different foundation consciousnesses would have to clearly appear. However, such commentary does not appear, either explicitly or implicitly. Furthermore, in the chapter on direct perception in the *Exposition of Valid Knowledge* (3.520), the statement "It does not arise from something other than the foundation" is the only time that the word *foundation* even appears. Whether he had in mind something like the explanation of an unclear fruitional consciousness whose nature is neutral but undefiled and very stable, such as that asserted by Cittamātra Following Scripture, is obviously something to be analyzed.
590. Dignāga, *Ālambanaparīkṣāvṛtti*. Toh 4206, 86a, Pd 97:432.
591. Dignāga, *Ālambanaparīkṣāvṛtti*. Toh 4206, 86a, Pd 97:433.
592. Dignāga, *Ālambanaparīkṣā*, verses 6–7. Toh 4205, 86a, Pd 97:431.
593. Dignāga, *Ālambanaparīkṣā*, verse 7. Toh 4205, 86a, Pd 97:431.
594. Dignāga, *Ālambanaparīkṣā*, verse 7. Toh 4205, 86a, Pd 97:431.
595. Dignāga, *Ālambanaparīkṣāvṛtti*. Toh 4206, 87a, Pd 97:435.
596. Dharmakīrti, *Pramāṇaviniścaya*. Toh 4211, 166a, Pd 97:645.
597. *Pramāṇaviniścayaṭīkā*, chap. 2. Toh 4229, 163a, Pd 104:1152.
598. For example, this statement can be found in Jamyang Shepai Dorjé's *Great Exposition of Tenets*, p. 236.
599. *Pramāṇaviniścayaṭīkā*, chap. 1. Toh 4229, 157b, Pd 104:1138.
600. *Pramāṇaviniścayaṭīkā*, chap. 1. Toh 4229, 157b, Pd 104:1138.
601. *Madhyamakālaṃkāravṛtti*. Toh 3885, 62b, Pd 62:922.
602. *Madhyamakālaṃkārapañjikā*. Toh 3886, 98a, Pd 62:1015.
603. Śāntarakṣita, *Madhyamakālaṃkāra*, verse 31. Toh 3884, 54a, Pd 62:898.

604. Śāntarakṣita, *Madhyamakālaṃkāravṛtti*. Toh 3885, 63a, Pd 62:922.
605. Śāntarakṣita, *Madhyamakālaṃkāravṛtti*. Toh 3885, 63a, Pd 62:922.
606. *Madhyamakālaṃkāra*, verse 31. Toh 3884, 54a, Pd 62:898.
607. *Ratnamālā*, verse 74. Toh 3901, 69b, Pd 63:1042.
608. *Sugatamatavibhaṅgabhāṣya*. Toh 3900, 59b, Pd 63:1012.
609. Śāntarakṣita, *Madhyamakālaṃkāravṛtti*. Toh 3885, 65b, Pd 69:929.
610. *Sugatamatavibhaṅgabhāṣya*. Toh 3900, 54b, Pd 63:999.
611. Dharmakīrti, *Pramāṇavārttika*, 3.200. Toh 4210, 126a, Pd 97:544.
612. *Pramāṇaviniścaya*, chap. 1. Toh 4211, 167a, Pd 97:647.
613. Dharmakīrti, *Pramāṇavārttika*, 3.392. Toh 4210, 133b, Pd 97:561.
614. In Avalokitavrata's *Commentary on the Lamp of Wisdom* (*Prajñāpradīpaṭīkā*, chap. 1. Toh 3859, 5b, Pd 58:868), it says that the commentary on the *Root Verses on the Middle Way* called *Akutobhayā* is the author's own commentary. However, scholars disagree on whether or not it is an autocommentary.
615. *Laṅkāvatārasūtra*, chap. 8. Toh 107, 165b, Pd 49:406. Two prophecies—this prophecy from the *Laṅkāvatāra Sūtra* and one in the *Great Cloud Sūtra* (*Mahāmeghasūtra*)—are cited both by Bhāviveka in his *Lamp of Wisdom* and by Candrakīrti in his *Clear Words*.
616. *Prajñāpradīpaṭīkā*, chap. 1. Toh 3859, 7b, Pd 58:873.
617. *Madhyamakāloka*. Toh 3887, 149a, Pd 62:1153.
618. *Akṣayamatinirdeśasūtra*, chap. 6. Toh 175, 150a, Pd 68:373.
619. *Prasannapadā*, chap. 1. Toh 3860, 13b, Pd 60:30.
620. This is stated clearly in Tsongkhapa's *Ocean of Reasoning*, 5b.
621. *Prasannapadā*, chap. 1. Toh 3860, 2b, Pd 60:4. "I pay homage to him who is fully enlightened, the best of preachers, who taught dependent origination, which is without cessation or origination, annihilation or the eternal, neither singular nor manifold, without coming or going, for the cessation of all elaboration and the ultimate good."
622. Nāgārjuna, *Mūlamadhyamakakārikā*, 1.6–9. Toh 3824, 1a, Pd 57:3.
623. This is stated clearly in, for example, Tsongkhapa's *Ocean of Reasoning*, 22b.
624. *Abodhabodhakanāmaprakaraṇa*. Toh 3838, 149b, Pd 57:413.
625. Nāgārjuna, *Mūlamadhyamakakārikā*, 1.5. Toh 3824, 1b, Pd 57:3.
626. Nāgārjuna, *Vigrahavyāvartanī*, verse 1. Toh 3828, 27a, Pd 57:74.
627. Nāgārjuna, *Mūlamadhyamakakārikā*, 7.34. Toh 3824, 5b, Pd 57:13.
628. These exact words are not found in a sūtra in the Kangyur, but they are cited in Candrakīrti's *Clear Words* (*Prasannapadā*, Toh 3860, 48b, Pd 60:117).
629. *Śūnyatāsaptatikārikā*, verse 1. Toh 3827, 24a, Pd 57:67.
630. Nāgārjuna, *Yuktiṣaṣṭikākārika*, verse 5. Toh 3825, 20a, Pd 57:51.
631. Nāgārjuna, *Yuktiṣaṣṭikākārika*, verse 5. Toh 3825, 20a, Pd 57:61.
632. Candrakīrti, *Yuktiṣaṣṭikāvṛtti*. Toh 3864, 2b, Pd 60:930.
633. Candrakīrti, *Yuktiṣaṣṭikāvṛtti*. Toh 3864, 2a, Pd 60:936.
634. This work called *Proof for Entering into the Three Natures* (*Svabhāvatrayapraveśasiddhi*) sets forth the three natures, the foundation consciousness, and the afflicted mental consciousness of the Cittamātra system, and both its

subject matter and its language are very similar to the work by Vasubandhu called *Setting Forth the Three Natures* (*Trisvabhāvanirdeśa*). Since Nāgārjuna predates Vasubandhu, it is unlikely this is a work of Nāgārjuna.

635. In Chinese translation there is a work called the *Twelve Gates* (*Shier men lun*, Taishō 1568), which has twelve sections: (1) dependent arising, (2) production and nonproduction from the self, (3) conditions, (4) the nature of conditioned phenomena, (5) what is and is not the defined, (6) same and different, (7) existence and nonexistence, (8) intrinsic nature, (9) cause and effect, (10) agency, (11) the three times, and (12) birth. This work is also said to have an autocommentary. Also in Chinese translation is a treatise called the *One [Hundred] Verses* (*Yishu lujia lun*, Taishō 1573) and the *Instructions on the Perfection of Wisdom* (*Dazhidu lun*, Taishō 1509), the latter the size of a full volume, both said to have been composed by Nāgārjuna. However, because none of the many Indian commentators on Nāgārjuna cites this latter text, its authorship remains something to be examined. Also among the works by Nāgārjuna in the Tengyur are tantric texts such as the *Five Stages* (*Pañcakrama*) and the *Condensed Sādhana* (*Piṇḍīkṛtasādhana*) and the *Commentary on the Awakening Mind* (*Bodhicittavivaraṇa*).

636. *Mūlamadhyamakakārikā*, 15.1. Toh 3824, 8b, Pd 57:20.

637. Candrakīrti, *Yuktiṣaṣṭikāvṛtti*, verse 53. Toh 3864, 21a, Pd 57:53

638. Nāgārjuna, *Ratnāvalī*, 1.63. Toh 4158, 109a, Pd 96:264.

639. Candrakīrti, *Yuktiṣaṣṭikāvṛtti*, verse 60. Toh 3864, 22a, Pd 57:56.

640. *Anavataptanāgarājaparipṛcchāsūtra*. Toh 156, 230b, Pd 58:598.

641. Nāgārjuna, *Mūlamadhyamakakārikā*, 18.9. Toh 3824, 11a, Pd 57:26.

642. Nāgārjuna, *Mūlamadhyamakakārikā*, 24.18. Toh 3824, 15a, Pd 57:36. At that point in the text, Nāgārjuna identifies the purpose, nature, and meaning of emptiness.

643. Nāgārjuna, *Mūlamadhyamakakārikā*, 18.10. Toh 3824, 11a, Pd 57:26.

644. Nāgārjuna, *Mūlamadhyamakakārikā*, 24.18–19. Toh 3824, 15a, Pd 57:37.

645. The *Compendium on the Essence of Wisdom* explicitly sets forth the assertions of all four schools of Buddhist tenets. Because there is an explicit statement of the Yogācāra assertions that external objects do not exist and nondual consciousness truly exists, there are some who doubt whether this text was in fact composed by Āryadeva, whose generally accepted dates predate the composition of the Yogācāra treatises.

646. *Prasannapadā*, chap. 1. Toh 3860, 6a, Pd 60:13.

647. *Tarkajvālā*, chap. 11. Toh 3856, 329a, Pd 58:802.

648. Nāgārjuna, *Mūlamadhyamakakārikā*, 15.11. Toh 3824, 9a, Pd 57:21.

649. Prāsaṅgika Madhyamaka and Svātantrika Madhyamaka appear to be terms that are known to Tibetan scholars. The terms appear in a statement by the translator Patsab Nyima Drak, an eleventh-century Buddhist scholar who translated Candrakīrti's *Entering the Middle Way* into Tibetan. In Patsab Lotsāwa's *Commentary on Root Verses on the Middle Way* (p. 3b), he writes, "Buddhapālita

wrote first and interpreted it [the treatise] in terms of consequences." And, "After Buddhapālita, Bhavyakīrti composed the *Lamp of Wisdom*, criticizing the earlier consequences and commenting with autonomous [syllogisms]. After that, Candrakīrti criticized autonomous [syllogisms] and defended the text of Buddhapālita, commenting with consequences." That same text goes on to say (p. 7a), "A response to this critique was made by the Mādhyamika who propound autonomous assertions and express their positions in autonomous syllogisms. Candrakīrti refuted those who accept the idea of autonomous syllogisms. Candrakīrti's own assertion was that the intention of Nāgārjuna is that Madhyamaka uses consequences." Also, that same text says (p. 10b), "Regarding the eighth point, setting forth the presentation of Candrakīrti's own position that the intention of the master Nāgārjuna is Prāsaṅgika, there are two." This can be understood from many such examples. Therefore Tsongkhapa in his *Great Treatise on the Stages of the Path* (p. 573) said, "The use of the terms Prāsaṅgika and Svātantrika for Madhyamaka by scholars of the Snowy Range during the latter dissemination of the Dharma accords with the *Clear Words*. Therefore I do not believe it is fabricated." This statement seems to hit the mark.

650. Such as Rongzom Paṇḍita (1012–88) and Taktsang Lotsāwa (1404–77).

651. Tibetan Mādhyamikas agreed on the division of the Madhyamaka of India into Prāsaṅgika and Svātantrika. However, they did not agree on the factors that separated Prāsaṅgika and Svātantrika. Many said that the two types of Madhyamaka had no difference in view. In the commentary on *Root Verses on the Middle Way* called *Ornament of Reason* by Patsab Lotsāwa's direct disciple Maja Jangchup Tsöndrü, this statement makes clear that the difference between Prāsaṅgika and Svātantrika is whether they assert that things are established by way of their own character: "According to what was explained earlier, because production is not tenable even conventionally when analyzed in terms of the four extremes, although no intrinsic production as postulated by Svātantrika exists, things merely appear to be produced in dependence on causes and conditions to those whose eye of the intellect has been damaged by the myodesopsia of ignorance. Because their conventional continuity is not severed, they arise dependently conventionally." Tsongkhapa and his heirs explain it in the same way.

652. *Tattvadaśaka*, verse 2. Toh 2236, 113a, Pd 26:320.

653. *Tattvadaśakaṭīkā*. Toh 2254, 164b, Pd 26:491.

654. *Tarkajvālā*, chap. 3. Toh 3856, 59b, Pd 58:149.

655. *Tarkajvālā*, chap. 3. Toh 3856, 60b, Pd 58:152.

656. *Tarkajvālā*, chap. 3. Toh 3856, 59b, Pd 58:149.

657. Bhāviveka, *Prajñāpradīpa*, chap. 13. Toh 3853, 147b, Pd 57:1165.

658. *Amarakośa*. Toh 4299, 207a, Pd 110:642.

659. *Prajñāpradīpa*, chap. 15. Toh 3853, 242a, Pd 57:1410.

660. In his *Essence of Eloquence* (p. 54b), Tsongkhapa says, "This explanation of the

meaning of the existence and nonexistence of the entityness of character set forth in the *Explanation of the Intention* is the clearest source by this master that things are established by way of their own character conventionally."

661. *Madhyamakāvatārabhāṣya*, chap. 6. Toh 3862, 258a, Pd 60:692.
662. *Tattvasaṅgraha*, 7.33. Toh 4266, 9a, Pd 107:22.
663. Śāntarakṣita, *Madhyamakālaṃkāravṛtti*. Toh 3885, 72a, Pd 62:945.
664. Kamalaśīla, *Madhyamakāloka*. Toh 3887, 151b, Pd 62:1157.
665. *Brahmaviśeṣacintiparipṛcchāsūtra*. Toh 160, 65a, Pd 69:161.
666. *Prajñāpāramitāsañcayagāthā*. Toh 13, 12.8–9.
667. Bhāviveka, *Tarkajvālā*, chap. 3. Toh 3856, 60b, Pd 58:152.
668. Kamalaśīla, *Madhyamakāloka*. Toh 3887, 229b, Pd 62:1350.
669. Kamalaśīla, *Madhyamakāloka*. Toh 3887, 228b, Pd 62:1348.
670. *Satyadvayavibhaṅgapañjikā*. Toh 3883, 24a, Pd 62:815.
671. Śāntarakṣita, *Madhyamakālaṃkāra*, verse 43. Toh 3884, 54b, Pd 62:899.
672. Bhāviveka, *Tarkajvālā*, chap. 5. Toh 3856, 207b, Pd 58:505.
673. Bhāviveka, *Tarkajvālā*, chap. 5. Toh 3856, 204b, Pd 58:498.
674. Bhāviveka, *Madhyamakahṛdaya*, 5.18. Toh 3855, 20b, Pd 58:48.
675. Bhāviveka, *Tarkajvālā*, chap. 5. Toh 3856, 205a, Pd 58:500.
676. *Satyadvayavibhaṅga*, verse 6. Toh 3881, 1a, Pd 62:756.
677. Bhāviveka, *Tarkajvālā*, chap. 3. Toh 3856, 80b, Pd 58:200.
678. Bhāviveka, *Tarkajvālā*, chap. 5. Toh 3856, 213a, Pd 58:518.
679. Because some statements in this treatise disagree with the *Ornament of the Middle Way*, there is disagreement as to whether it was composed by Kamalaśīla.
680. Śāntarakṣita, *Madhyamakālaṃkāravṛtti*. Toh 3885, 60b, Pd 62:917.
681. Nāgārjuna, *Yuktiṣaṣṭikākārikā*, verse 34. Toh 3825, 21b, Pd 57:54.
682. Śāntarakṣita, *Madhyamakālaṃkāra*, verse 92. Toh 3884, 56a, Pd 62:903.
683. *Abhisamayālaṃkāraṭīkā-Prasphuṭapadā*. Toh 3793, 124b7.
684. Candrakīrti, *Prasannapadā*, chap. 1. Toh 3860, 7a, Pd 60:15.
685. Candrakīrti, *Prasannapadā*, chap. 1. Toh 3860, 8a, Pd 60:18.
686. Candrakīrti, *Madhyamakāvatāra*, 6.97. Toh 3861, 209a, Pd 60:572.
687. Candrakīrti, *Madhyamakāvatārabhāṣya*, chap. 6. Toh 3862, 282b, Pd 60:751.
688. Candrakīrti, *Madhyamakāvatāra*, 6.179. Toh 3861, 213a, Pd 60:582.
689. Candrakīrti, *Madhyamakāvatārabhāṣya*, chap. 6. Toh 3862, 280a, Pd 60:744.
690. Candrakīrti, *Madhyamakāvatārabhāṣya*, chap. 6. Toh 3862, 280a, Pd 60:744.
691. Nāgārjuna, *Mūlamadhyamakakārikā*, 17.6. Toh 3824, 9b, Pd 57:23.
692. Candrakīrti, *Madhyamakāvatāra*, 6.39. Toh 3861, 206a, Pd 60:523.
693. *Daśabhūmikasūtra*. Toh 44, 221b, Pd 36:473.
694. *Daśabhūmikasūtra*. Toh 44, 221b, Pd 36:474.
695. *Yuktiṣaṣṭikāvṛtti*. Toh 3864, 15b, Pd 60:967.
696. Nāgārjuna, *Mūlamadhyamakakārikā*, 25.13. Toh 3824, 16b, Pd 57:40.
697. Candrakīrti, *Yuktiṣaṣṭikāvṛtti*. Toh 3864, 16a, Pd 60:969.
698. Candrakīrti, *Yuktiṣaṣṭikāvṛtti*. Toh 3864, 15b, Pd 60:968.
699. Candrakīrti, *Prasannapadā*, chap. 17. Toh 3860, 109a, Pd 60:272.

700. Candrakīrti, *Madhyamakāvatārabhāṣya*, chap. 6. Toh 3862, 259b, Pd 60:695.
701. Candrakīrti, *Madhyamakāvatārabhāṣya*. Toh 3862, 347b, Pd 60:905.
702. *Bodhicaryāvatāra*, 9.4. Toh 3871, 31a, Pd 67:1017.
703. *Pañcakrama*, 1.2. Toh 1802, 45a, Pd 18:129.
704. *Bhāvanākrama II*. Toh 3916, 48a, Pd 64:135.

Glossary

Abhidharma (*chos mngon pa*). Often translated as "knowledge," "higher knowledge," or "phenomenology," the portion of Buddhist literature that deals with what would be termed psychology, epistemology, cosmology, and soteriology. The term also refers to the Abhidharma Piṭaka, that portion of the three scriptural collections where works on these topics are gathered.

acquisition (*prāpti, thob pa*). A nonassociated compositional factor that allows one to maintain that which has been acquired by the mind.

activity (*karman, las*). One of the six categories of the Vaiśeṣika school, *activity* is that which has a nature of movement, like walking, and is of five types. In the other Indian schools, it refers most often to "the law of karma," which says that conditions in the present are the result of actions performed in the past and that actions performed in the present will affect the future, including future lives.

afflicted mental consciousness (*kliṣṭamanas, nyon yid*). For the Yogācāra school that asserts the existence of eight consciousnesses, this is counted as the seventh consciousness. It is a form of the mental consciousness that takes the foundational consciousness as its object and mistakenly regards it as a permanent self.

afflictions (*kleśa, nyon mongs*). Negative mental states that motivate nonvirtuous actions, which in turn fructify as feelings of pain and as rebirth in the lower realms. Among lists of primary and secondary afflictions, desire, hatred, and ignorance are particularly important.

aggregates (*skandha, phung po*). In Buddhism, the five impermanent "heaps" or physical and mental components that serve as the basis of designation of the person and among which a self is not found. The five are form (*rūpa, gzugs*), feeling (*vedanā, tshor ba*), discrimination (*saṃjñā, 'du shes*), compositional factors (*saṃskāra, 'du byed*), and consciousness (*vijñāna, rnam shes*).

appearing object (*pratibhāsaviṣaya, snang yul*). That which appears to a consciousness. In the case of a nonconceptual sense consciousness, it is the object itself. In the case of a conceptual consciousness, it is a mental image of the object, which can be mistaken for the object itself.

arhat (*bgra bcom pa*). In Sanskrit, a "worthy one," rendered in Tibetan as "foe destroyer," a person who has destroyed all causes for future rebirth and will enter nirvāṇa upon their death. In the Mahāyāna, the achievement of the śrāvaka or pratyekabuddha who becomes an arhat is contrasted with that of a bodhisattva who becomes a buddha.

aspect (*ākāra, rnam pa*). Also translated as "image," an element of sense experience accepted by some Buddhist schools but not others. It refers to the image that is projected by the object onto the consciousness that perceives it.

Āstika (*yod par smra ba*). Literally "those who say 'yes,'" a term for schools that accept the Vedas as a valid source of knowledge—hence, the Hindu schools.

atheistic Sāṅkhya (*nirīśvara-sāṅkhya, grangs can lha med pa*). The branch of Sāṅkhya that does not assert the existence of a creator deity (Īśvara), holding instead that worldly abodes, bodies, resources, and so forth directly or indirectly arise only from the primary nature and that afterward, having dissolved only into the primary nature, liberation is attained.

autonomous proof (**svatantra-anumāna, rang rgyud kyi gtan tshigs*). A proof or argument that satisfies the three conditions and proves the thesis of a syllogism. In Madhyamaka, this is a point of contention between Svātantrika and Prāsaṅgika, with Prāsaṅgika arguing that the use of such autonomous reasons is inappropriate for a Mādhyamika, who must instead rely on consequences (*prasaṅga*) when debating with an opponent.

basis of designation (*prajñaptivastu, gdags pa'i gzhi*). Also "basis of imputation." Any permanent or impermanent object to which qualities and attributes are imputed.

category (*padārtha, tshig gi don*). In the Vaiśeṣika school, all objects of knowledge are included in the six categories: substance, quality, activity, universal, particularity, and inherence. Some later masters in the lineage of this school of tenets add a seventh: nonexistence (*abhāva, dngos med*). In Nyāya, there are the sixteen categories of logic.

condition (*pratyaya, rkyen*). Technically a synonym of *cause* (*hetu*) but generally used to refer to secondary factors involved in the production of a particular phenomenon, assisting causes in the creation of effects.

conditioned phenomenon (*saṃskṛtadharma, 'dus byas kyi chos*). A phenomenon conditioned by production, abiding, and disintegration and therefore impermanent.

conqueror (*jina, rgyal ba*). An epithet used in both Jainism and Buddhism to refer to their enlightened founder as well as enlightened teachers of the past.

consciousness (*vijñāna, rnam par shes pa*). Defined in Buddhism as that which is "clear and knowing," variously enumerated in the Buddhist schools, but most often as six: eye consciousness, ear consciousness, nose consciousness, tongue consciousness, body consciousness, and mental consciousness. It may be either conceptual (as in the case of thought) or nonconceptual (as in the case of sense experience). It is a synonym of *mind* and *awareness*. In Cittamātra there are eight, adding the afflicted mental consciousness and the foundation consciousness.

consequence (*prasaṅga, thal 'gyur*). Also translated as "logical consequence" or "absurd consequence," an argument designed to draw out a fallacy and hence dispel a wrong view held by an opponent. A consequence can be valid without the two parties in a debate having a shared understanding of the topic in question.

constituent (*dhātu, khams*). In Buddhism, any of the eighteen constituents that together constitute phenomena: the six objects (forms, sounds, smells, tastes, objects of touch, and phenomena), the six sense faculties (eye, ear, nose, tongue, body, and mind), and the six consciousnesses (eye consciousness, ear consciousness, nose consciousness, tongue consciousness, body consciousness, and mental consciousness).

consummate nature (*parinispanna, yongs grub kyi mtshan nyid*). In Cittamātra, one of the *three natures* (together with the imaginary nature and the dependent nature). The consummate nature is the ultimate truth and emptiness for this school, referring to the absence of an object being a different entity from the consciousness that perceives it.

conventional truths (*saṃvṛtisatya, kun rdzob bden pa*). The Buddhist schools divide all phenomena into the two truths: conventional truths and ultimate truths, with each school defining the terms differently. However, conventional truths generally refer to the objects of the world as experienced by ordinary people, which upon analysis are found to contain some element of falsity.

correct sign (*samyagliṅga, rtags yang dag*). Also called a "correct reason," an element of a syllogism, after the subject and predicate (property of position), providing the reason why the thesis (the subject and predicate) is correct. To be correct, a sign must be coextensive with the property of the position. For a Buddhist, a correct reason is that which possesses the three modes.

definitive meaning (*nītārtha, nges pa'i don*). A term used in the interpretation of statements of the Buddha, most often referring to statements that he made that represent his own view as opposed to statements that he made for a particular purpose or audience (*see* provisional meaning). In Prāsaṅgika, the term refers to any statement in a sūtra whose referent is emptiness, the ultimate truth.

dependent arising (*pratītyasamutpāda, rten 'byung*). In Buddhism a term with two meanings. The first is a twelvefold sequence of causation that describes the process of rebirth, beginning with ignorance and ending with aging and death. More generally, it refers to the fact that effects arise in dependence on their causes. In Madhyamaka, it is seen as a proof of emptiness in the sense that nothing arises independently, but everything arises dependently, with effects depending on their causes, wholes depending on their parts, and all phenomena depending on the consciousness that perceives them.

dependent nature (*paratantra, gzhan dbang gi mtshan nyid*). In Cittamātra, one of the *three natures* (together with the imaginary nature and the consummate nature). *Dependent natures* are impermanent phenomena produced by, and thus dependent upon, causes and conditions, including past karma or, in the language of the school, predispositions (*vāsanā*).

direct perception (*pratyakṣa, mngon sum*). A term with different meanings in different schools. For example, in Vaiśeṣika, Nyāya, and Mīmāṃsā, it is a material relation established from the conjunction of *ātman*, sense faculty, mind, and object. In the Buddhist schools, direct perception is one of two valid means of knowledge (*pramāṇa*), together with inference. It is a mind that perceives its object accurately and directly without the presence of conception or thought.

discrimination (*saṃjñā, 'du shes*). Also translated as "discernment" and "recognition," the third of the five aggregates. It is a mental factor that identifies the distinguishing marks of an object, allowing the mind to distinguish among different objects.

disintegrated state (*vināśa, zhig pa*). The state of an impermanent phenomenon after it has disintegrated or ceased, with Prāsaṅgika arguing that it continues to exist as a functioning thing rather than a permanent state of absence, thus ensuring that karmic deeds performed in the past can produce their effects in the future.

ego (*ahaṃkāra, nga rgyal*). In the Sāṅkhya school, one of the twenty-five principles, the overt pride that clings to such things as having a good lineage and abundant wealth.

elaboration (*prapañca, spros pa*). The tendency of ignorance to imagine, elaborate, or superimpose false qualities onto the objects of experience, resulting in misperception and an increase in the afflictions.

emptiness (*śūnyatā, stong pa nyid*). A term particularly associated with the Madhyamaka school, where it is the ultimate truth, described as the absence of intrinsic qualities that are falsely ascribed to phenomena.

environment and inhabitants (*sattva-bhājana-loka, snod bcud*). A term used to refer to the physical world (environment) and the sentient beings who inhabit that world (inhabitants).

exclusion (*anyāpoha, gzhan sel*). The object comprehended by thought, which operates not by cognizing the object directly but by excluding everything that is not the object, creating a generic image. Also referred to as an "isolate."

existence of effects in their causes (*satkārya, 'bras yod*). The assertion of the Sāṅkhya school that effects preexist in their causes. The *Sāṅkhyakārikā* provides five proofs in support of this position.

extensive foundation (*mahābhūmika, sa chen po pa*). In Buddhism, a rubric for dividing the forty-six mental factors (*caitta*) into six "extensive foundations" or categories: mind, the virtues, the nonvirtues, the great afflictions, the small afflictions, and the indefinite.

False Aspectarians (*alīkākāravāda, rnam rdzun pa*). In the Cittamātra school, those who assert that the "aspect" cast by an object and cognized by a sense consciousness is "false" in the sense that it is polluted by ignorance and thus is not an accurate image of the sense object.

five action faculties (*karmendriya, las kyi dbang po*). In the Sāṅkhya school, five of the twenty-five principles: speech (*vāc, ngag*), hand (*pāṇi, lag pa*), foot (*pāda, rkang pa*), anus (*pāyu, rkub*), and sexual organ (*upastha, 'doms*). They are called the *action faculties* because they control actions such as speaking words and taking things.

five coarse elements (*bhūta, 'byung ba*). In the Sāṅkhya school, five of the twenty-five principles: earth (*pṛthivī, sa*), water (*āpas, chu*), fire (*tejas, me*), wind (*vāyu, rlung*), and space (*ākāśa, nam mkha'*). Unlike the five subtle elements, the five coarse elements have many different natures, such as being peaceful and wrathful.

five sense faculties (*buddhīndriya, blo'i dbang po*). In the Sāṅkhya school, five of the twenty-five principles: eye (*cakṣus, mig*), ear (*śrotra, rna ba*), nose (*ghrāṇa, sna*), tongue (*rasana, lce*), and body (*sparśana, pags pa*). They cognize their own objects such as form, they engage with their objects before intellect does, and they are the doors through which the sense consciousnesses engage with objects.

five subtle elements (*tanmātra, de tsam*). In the Sāṅkhya school, five of the twenty-five principles: form (*rūpa, gzugs*), sound (*śabda, sgra*), smell (*gandha, dri*), taste (*rasa, ro*), and object of touch (*sparśa, reg bya*). These evolve into the five coarse elements.

foundation consciousness (*ālayavijñāna, kun gzhi rnam shes*). For the Cittamātra school that asserts that there are eight consciousnesses, the two in addition to the standard six are the afflicted mental consciousness and the foundation consciousness. The foundation consciousness is the repository of karmic seeds or predispositions, which it carries from moment to moment and from lifetime to lifetime. The afflicted mental consciousness mistakes it for a self.

four seals (*caturmudrā, phyag rgya bzhi*). Four assertions that determine whether a philosophical school or doctrine is Buddhist: (1) all products are impermanent, (2) all contaminated things are suffering, (3) all phenomena are without self, and (4) nirvāṇa is peace.

generality (*sāmānya, spyi*). In Buddhist epistemology, a technical term referring to the appearing object of a conceptual consciousness, created through exclusion (*apoha*), lacking the specific characteristics of the actual impermanent object.

generally characterized (*sāmānyalakṣaṇa, spyi mtshan*). In the Sautrāntika school, those phenomena that are not produced by causes and conditions and that are incapable of producing effects. Such phenomena are permanent and are conceptual constructs that do not appear to direct perception, appearing only to thought. In Sautrāntika, such phenomena are conventional truths.

hidden phenomenon (*parokṣa, lkog 'gyur*). An object that cannot be directly perceived with the senses and therefore must be known through inference.

imaginary nature (*parikalpita, kun btags kyi mtshan nyid*). In Cittamātra, one of the *three natures* (together with the dependent nature and the consummate nature). Imaginary natures are objects that appear falsely to sense consciousnesses as separate from the consciousness perceiving them and appear falsely to mental consciousnesses as naturally being the basis of their names.

implicative negation (*paryudāsapratiṣedha, ma yin dgag*). Also translated as "affirming negative," a form of negation that implies the existence of a positive phenomenon.

imputed existent (*prajñaptisat, btags yod*). In Buddhism, something presumed to exist based on the superimposition of a concept onto a phenomenon, such as imputing the person to the mind and body.

inexpressible person (*avācyapudgala, brjod med kyi gang zag*). The person that is asserted to exist by the Vātsīputrīya school of Buddhism, which is neither permanent nor impermanent, is neither the same as nor different from the five aggregates, and carries the effects of past actions from lifetime to lifetime.

inference (*anumāna, rjes dpag*). Understanding a thesis concerning a "hidden object" based on (1) the previous understanding that the sign or reason (*liṅga*) is a property of the position (*pakṣadharma*) or the subject (*dharmin*) and (2) understanding the pervasion (*vyāpti*) between the reason and the predicate of the thesis. In the Buddhist schools, inference is one of two valid means of knowledge (*pramāṇa*), together with direct perception.

influx (*āsrava, zag pa*). A term used in both Jainism and Buddhism. In Jainism, it is the positive and negative karma that flows in as a result of the performance of actions and that binds the soul. The bondage (*bandha*) of the soul to karma prevents liberation. In Buddhism, it refers to various contaminants of the mind.

inherence (*samavāya, 'du ba*). One of the six categories of the Vaiśeṣika school, inherence is that which serves as the object apprehended by a consciousness that, having observed the supporting and supported qualities of a single object, thinks, "This has that."

intellect (*buddhi, blo*) or the great one (*mahat, chen po*). In the Sāṅkhya school, one of the twenty-five principles. It has the characteristics of determining or ascertaining objects. It has eight features. Four are related to *sattva*, which has the qualities of virtue (*dharma*), knowledge (*jñāna*), nonattachment (*virāga*), and might (*aiśvarya*). The other four are related to *tamas*, which has the opposite qualities: nonvirtue, nonknowledge, attachment, and nonmight. In other schools, the term tends to be a synonym for *vijñāna* and *manas*.

intrinsic nature (*svabhāva, rang bzhin*). Also translated as "inherent existence," in Prāsaṅgika, that quality falsely perceived and believed to be present in all phenomena. The lack or absence of intrinsic nature is emptiness.

isolation (*kaivalya, nyag gcig gnas pa*). In the Sāṅkhya school, when the primordial nature (*prakṛti*) becomes unmanifest and *puruṣa* abides in the state of isolation, liberation is attained.

liberation (*mokṣa, thar pa*). A term for permanent freedom from rebirth widely used among the schools of Indian philosophy.

manifest (*vyakta, gsal ba*). In the Sāṅkhya school, the twenty-three principles other than the primordial nature and *puruṣa* are asserted to be conventional or false since they become manifest as sense objects and are without essence, like a magician's illusion. They are caused, produced, impermanent, not pervasive, the supported, many, have a nature of dissolution, are active, have parts, and are dependent.

mental consciousness (*manovijñāna, yid kyi rnam shes*). In Buddhism, the sixth of the six consciousnesses, in addition to the five sense consciousnesses. It is the primary organ of thought but is also capable of direct perception. It does not have a physical sense organ but instead arises in dependence on its object and the presence of a prior moment of consciousness.

mental direct perception (*mānasapratyakṣa, yid mngon*). The direct perception of an object with the mental consciousness, without the presence or interference of conceptions or thoughts. In Sautrāntika, it is immediately preceded by a sense direct perception and apprehends the object of that sense perception, which is not different in type but is different in entity.

mental factors (*caitta, sems 'byung*). Secondary consciousnesses that accompany a primary consciousness such that when the primary consciousness or main mind cognizes an object, the concomitant mental factors cognize the object's attributes. In Vaibhāṣika, there are forty-six mental factors that accompany the main mind. They are divided into six categories: the extensive foundation (*mahābhūmika*) of mind, the extensive foundation of the virtues, the extensive foundation of the great afflictions, the extensive foundation of the nonvirtues, the foundation of the small afflictions, and the indefinite.

middle path (*madhyamā pratipad, dbu ma'i lam*). In Buddhism, a term with multiple meanings, referring initially to the path set forth by the Buddha between the extremes of self-indulgence and self-mortification. The term has a more philosophical sense as the middle path between the extreme of permanence/existence and the extreme of annihilation/nonexistence, with the two extremes variously defined by the Buddhist schools.

mind (*citta, sems*). In Buddhism, a general term for the seat of mental activity, in this sense a synonym of consciousness (*vijñāna*) and awareness (*buddhi*). In the context of "minds and mental factors" (*citta-caitta*) of the Vaibhāṣika school, it refers to the "main minds"—that is, any of the six consciousnesses, as opposed to the mental factors that accompany them.

mind (*manas, yid*). In the Sāṅkhya school, it has the nature of both sense and action organs and has the characteristic of conceptualizing. In the Buddhist schools, it refers to the mental consciousness (*manovijñāna*) among the six consciousnesses.

momentary (*kṣaṇika, skad cig ma*). That which is impermanent, being produced and then disintegrating in the next moment.

Nāstika (*med par smra ba*). Literally "those who say 'no,'" a term for those schools that do not accept the Vedas as a valid source of knowledge—for example, the Buddhists and the Jains.

no entityness (*niḥsvabhāvatā, ngo bo nyid med pa*). A term used both in Cittamātra and Madhyamaka. In Cittamātra, it refers to three different absences of entityness, one for each of the three natures. In Madhyamaka, it is a synonym for emptiness.

nonexistence (*abhāva, dngos med*). In later Vaiśeṣika, the seventh category, defined as the object of valid knowledge that perceives the absence of real existence. It has four kinds: prior nonexistence (*prāgabhāva*), nonexistence through disintegration (*pradhvaṃsābhāva*), utter nonexistence (*atyantābhāva*), and mutual nonexistence (*anyonyābhāva*).

nonassociated compositional factor (*viprayuktasaṃskāra, ldan min 'du byed*). A category in the Buddhist Abhidharma that includes all impermanent phenomena that are not classified as form, mind, or mental factors. The category includes such things as the absorption of cessation (*nirodhasamāpatti*), the life force, groups of letters, and time.

nonimplicative negation (*prasajyapratiṣedha, med dgag*). Also translated as "nonaffirming negative," a form of negation that does not imply the existence of a positive phenomenon.

nonrevelatory form (*avijñaptirūpa, rnam par rig byed ma yin pa'i gzugs*). In Vaibhāṣika, a particular form of subtle matter that resides in the body and provides the connection between actions and their effects as well as the means by which various mental acts, such as the taking of vows, persist over time.

nonsoul (*ajīva, srog min*). A term used in Jainism to refer to unconscious substances. It is fivefold: matter (*pudgala*), bondage (*bandha*), motion (*dharma*), rest (*adharma*), and time (*kāla*). The substance of matter is physical, while the others do not have form.

object of apprehension (*grāhyaviṣaya, gzung yul*). The object of a consciousness, regardless of whether the consciousness is direct perception or a thought consciousness.

particularity (*viśeṣa, bye brag*). In the Vaiśeṣika school, particularity or difference is a quality that serves as the cause for understanding that its basis is different from something else. In other schools, it refers to an instance of a general category.

person (*pudgala, gang zag / puruṣa, skyes bu*). The term *pudgala* is used in the Indian schools to refer to the agent of actions in the ordinary sense. In Jainism, *pudgala* does not mean "person" but instead "matter." The term *puruṣa* refers to the conscious self and thus can also be translated as "self." In Sāṅkhya, it is an entity that is completely devoid of change, the only one of the twenty-five principles that is not matter. It is unborn, permanent, and unitary but is not the creator of transformations. When *puruṣa* is used to refer to the deity or the eternal self, it is often translated as "supreme person."

pervasion (*vyāpti, khyab pa*). In the context of a syllogism, *pervasion* refers to the relationship between the predicate and the reason, such that whatever is the reason is necessarily the predicate and whatever is not the predicate is necessarily not the reason.

pratyekabuddha (*rang rgyal*). Sometimes translated as "solitary enlightened one," a Buddhist practitioner who achieves the nirvāṇa of an arhat without depending on the teachings of a buddha in their final lifetime. In the Mahāyāna, the path referred to as the Pratyekabuddhayāna is one of the three vehicles, together with the Śrāvakayāna and the Bodhisattvayāna.

predisposition (*vāsanā, bag chags*). Also translated as "latency." For the Cittamātra school that asserts that there are eight consciousnesses, the foundation consciousness is the repository for predispositions, the seeds created by past actions. These are deposited or imprinted on the foundation consciousness by virtuous, nonvirtuous, or neutral activities of body, speech, or mind, later fructifying as experience.

primary nature (*pradhāna, spyi gtso bo*). Also called the *primordial nature* (*prakṛti, rang bzhin*), in the Sāṅkhya school, it is the eternal and unitary cause of the world and its various transformations. It is unconscious matter that is only a cause and is never an effect or transformation. It is unmanifest and pervades all the objects of knowledge. Its three qualities (*sattva, rajas*, and *tamas*), which are in equilibrium when unmanifest, pervade all its manifest transformations.

primordial nature (*prakṛti, rang bzhin*). *See* primary nature.

principle (*tattva, de nyid*). A term for ultimate constituents in the Sāṅkhya and Jaina schools. They consider the world to consist of twenty-five and seven principles, respectively.

probandum (*sādhya, bsgrub bya*). Also translated as "thesis." The combination of the subject and the predicate of a syllogism that is to be proved by the sign (*liṅga*) or reason (*hetu*).

property of the position (*pakṣadharma, phyogs chos*). One of three criteria for a valid reason, that it must be an attribute of the subject.

provisional meaning (*neyārtha, drang ba'i don*). A term used in the interpretation of statements of the Buddha, most often referring to statements that he made for a particular purpose or audience and do not represent his own view (*see* definitive meaning). In Prāsaṅgika, the term refers to any statement in a sūtra whose referent is not emptiness, the ultimate truth.

pseudo reason (*hetvābhāsa, rtags ltar snang*). A sign or reason in which the relation between the sign and the predicate is not established, is uncertain, or is doubtful.

quality (*guṇa, yon tan*). One of the six categories of the Vaiśeṣika school. It is that which depends on a substance, does not possess another quality, is not the cause of conjunction and separation, and is independent. There are twenty-four qualities.

reflexive awareness (*svasaṃvedana, rang rig*). A form of direct perception, accepted by some Buddhist schools but rejected by others, that directly perceives an outward-facing consciousness that is perceiving its own object. According to the schools that accept it, reflexive awareness is what allows for memory of subjective experience.

rishi (*ṛṣi, drang srong*). Often translated as "sage," a term more commonly used to refer to Hindu luminaries.

self (*ātman, bdag*). The element that resides within the mind and body that travels from lifetime to lifetime, carrying past karma. It is often described as permanent, partless, and independent. Such a self is generally accepted by most of the non-Buddhist Indian schools and is rejected by the Buddhist schools.

selflessness of persons (*pudgalanairātmya, gang zag gi bdag med*). In Buddhism, the lack of self (*ātman*) among the various physical and mental elements that together constitute the person. It is variously defined by the Buddhist schools.

selflessness of phenomena (*dharmanairātmya, chos kyi bdag med*). In Buddhism, the lack of self (*ātman*) among all phenomena apart from the various physical and mental elements that together constitute the person. It is variously defined by the Buddhist schools.

sense consciousness (*indriyajñāna*, *dbang shes*). The five sense consciousnesses (of the eye, ear, nose, tongue, and body) plus the mental sense consciousness. Each arises in dependence on its two "sources" (*āyatana*): its respective object and its respective sense faculty. For the mental consciousness, the "sense faculty" is not a material sense organ but a previous moment of consciousness.

sense direct perception (*indriyapratyakṣa*, *dbang mngon*). The direct perception of a sense object with a sense consciousness, without the presence or interference of conceptions or thoughts.

sense faculty (*indriya*, *dbang po*). Also translated as "sense organ" and "sense power," the subtle material sense organs located in the eye, ear, nose, tongue, and throughout the body, functioning as the internal support of their respective sense consciousnesses. The mental sense faculty is not a physical organ but a previous moment of consciousness.

sentient being (*sattva*, *sems can*). A being that has consciousness and, according to the schools that accept rebirth, is subject to rebirth. The Indian schools differ on which forms of life have consciousness, with Buddhism naming gods, demigods, humans, animals, ghosts, and denizens of hell.

sign (*liṅga*, *rtags*). Also translated as "reason" or "mark." The evidence or reason posited in a syllogism to prove that the predicate is a property of the subject. In a valid syllogism, there must be pervasion between the sign and the predicate.

soul (*jīva*, *srog*). Also translated as "life force," a term used in Jainism (where it is one of the seven principles) as a synonym for the self, which goes from lifetime to lifetime and which is liberated from rebirth.

source (*āyatana*, *skye mched*). In Buddhism, any of the twelve sources of consciousness: the six objects—forms, sounds, smell, tastes, objects of touch, and phenomena (also known as "mental objects")—and the six sense faculties: of the eye, ear, nose, tongue, body, and mind.

specifically characterized (*svalakṣaṇa*, *rang mtshan*). Also translated as "unique particular," those phenomena that have defining characteristics unique to them that distinguish them from other phenomena. In the Sautrāntika school, those phenomena that are produced by causes and conditions and that are capable of producing effects. Such phenomena have their own specific as well as the more general characteristics of all conditioned things, such as impermanence. In Sautrāntika, such phenomena are ultimate truths and appear to direct perception. Whether phenomena are established by way of their own specific characteristics conventionally is one of the questions that separates Svātantrika and Prāsaṅgika.

śrāvaka (*nyan thos*). Literally "listener," a general term for a monastic disciple of the Buddha. In the Mahāyāna, it refers to someone who seeks the nirvāṇa of the arhat, with their path referred to as the Śrāvakayāna, one of the three vehicles, together with the Pratyekabuddhayāna and the Bodhisattvayāna.

stoppage (*saṃvara, sdom pa*). In Jainism, the blockage of the influx of karma through various practices, including meditation and asceticism, in order to bring about the extinction (*nirjarā*) of all karma.

subject. A term used to render two different terms in Indian philosophy. The first is *dharmin* (*chos can*), meaning "attribute possessor" and refers to the subject or topic of a formal argument. The second is *viṣayin* (*yul can*), meaning "object possessor," referring to a consciousness that has an object.

subsequent cognition (*paricchinnajñāna, bcad shes*). A cognition that follows upon a direct perception, typically by a sense consciousness, cognizing and sometimes forming judgments about that which has been perceived.

substance (*dravya, rdzas*). One of the six categories of the Vaiśeṣika school, *substance* is defined as a phenomenon that has three features—possessing activities, possessing qualities, and being the cause for inherence. When it is divided, there are nine: earth (*pṛthivī*), water (*āpas*), fire (*tejas*), wind (*vāyu*), space (*ākāśa*), time (*kāla*), direction (*diś*), self (*ātman*), and mind (*manas*).

substantial existent (*dravyasat, rdzas yod*). In Buddhism, a phenomenon whose comprehension does not depend on understanding something other than it.

subtle particle (*paramāṇu, rdul phran*). The smallest discrete unit of matter, variously defined by the Indian philosophical schools. For example, in the Vaiśeṣika school, the particles of the four elements are permanent, while coarse things, which are accumulations of those particles, are impermanent.

superimposition (*samāropa, sgro btags*). Also translated as "reification" and "exaggeration," the imagination or acceptance of the existence of something that does not exist.

supersensory knowledge (*abhijñā, mngon shes*). Certain supernormal powers said to be side effects of achieving deep states of meditative concentration, using either Buddhist or non-Buddhist techniques. The powers are often listed as five: (1) various magical powers such as the ability to fly, (2) the "divine eye" that allows one to see at great distances, (3) the "divine ear" that allows one to hear at great distances, (4) the ability to know the thoughts of others, (5) the ability to remember former lives.

sūtra (*mdo*). Often translated as "discourse," the term more literally means "aphorism," and thus a collection of aphorisms, often in verse. In the philosophical context, these are often the teachings of a founder, which are later elaborated in commentaries. In Buddhism, a sūtra is a discourse delivered by the Buddha or by another person with his sanction. The term also refers to the Sūtra Piṭaka, that portion of the three scriptural collections in which those discourses are gathered.

syllogism (*prayoga, sbyor ba*). A logical statement consisting of a thesis, sign, and example. In order to be correct, the reason must have the "three modes" (*trairūpya, rtags kyi tshul gsum*): (1) the sign (or reason) must be a property or attribute of the position, that is, of the subject (*pakṣadharma*), (2) there must be pervasion (*vyāpti*) in the sense that whatever is the sign is necessarily the predicate, such that the presence of the sign entails the presence of the predicate, and (3) there must be negative pervasion in the sense that whatever is not the predicate is not the sign—that is, the absence of the predicate entails the absence of the sign.

tenet (*siddhānta, grub mtha'*). A philosophical position of any of the Indian schools, whether Buddhist or non-Buddhist.

theistic Sāṅkhya (*seśvarasāṅkhya, grangs can lhar bcas pa*). The branch of Saṅkhya that holds that although cause and effect have the same nature, transformation occurs through the control of the deity Īśvara, who in dependence on the primary nature is the creator of effects.

thing (*vastu/bhāva, dngos po*). A term sometimes used to refer to any phenomenon but especially used to refer to an impermanent phenomenon that is produced by causes and conditions and that is able to perform a function.

three modes (*trairūpya, rtags kyi tshul gsum*). The three elements of a valid argument: (1) the sign or reason is an attribute of the subject, (2) the presence of the sign entails the presence of the predicate, and (3) the absence of the predicate entails the absence of the sign. The latter two modes are called the *positive pervasion* and the *negative pervasion*, respectively.

three natures (*trisvabhāva, rang bzhin gsum / mtshan nyid gsum*). In Cittamātra, the primary rubric for classifying the objects of experience: the imaginary nature, the dependent nature, and the consummate nature.

three qualities (*triguṇa, yon tan gsum*). In the Sāṅkhya school, the three natures of the primary nature (*pradhāna*): *rajas* (mobility), *tamas* (darkness), and *sattva* (lightness). When the three qualities lose their equilibrium, the quality that is predominant becomes manifest and creates transformations. *Rajas* (*rdul*) causes suffering, *tamas* (*mun pa*) causes delusion, and *sattva* (*snying stobs*) causes pleasure.

three scriptural collections (*tripiṭaka, sde snod gsum*). Often translated as the "three baskets," the traditional division of the Buddhist canon into Sūtra, Vinaya, and Abhidharma.

tīrthika (*mu stegs pa*). A term used in Buddhist texts to describe adherents of non-Buddhist schools of Indian philosophy and practice.

True Aspectarians (*satyākāravādin, rnam bden pa*). In the Cittamātra school, those who assert that the "aspect" cast by an object and cognized by a sense consciousness is "true" in the sense that it is an accurate image of the sense object. The True Aspectarians are further divided into three: Nonpluralist, Half-Eggist, and Proponent of an Equal Number of Subjects and Objects.

two truths (*satyadvaya, bden pa gnyis*). The Buddhist schools divide all phenomena into the two truths—conventional truths and ultimate truths—with each school defining the terms differently. However, conventional truths generally refer to the objects of the world as typically experienced, containing some element of falsity. Ultimate truths are objects of consciousness that when directly perceived lead to liberation from rebirth.

ultimate truth (*paramārthasatya, don dam bden pa*). The true nature of reality as defined by a particular school, and the object of the wisdom that leads to liberation as understood by that school. Thus in Vedānta it is *ātman* and Brahman, in Madhyamaka it is emptiness (*śūnyatā*), and so forth. *See also* two truths.

unconditioned phenomenon (*asaṃskṛtadharma, 'dus ma byas kyi chos*). A phenomenon that is permanent in the sense that it lacks, and hence is not conditioned by, the three characteristics of arising, abiding, and disintegration.

universal (*sāmānya, spyi*). One of the six categories of the Vaiśeṣika school, a *universal* is defined as that which serves as the cause for the attribution of common terms or concepts to things that instantiate a quality. It has two kinds, pervasive universal and partial universal, also called, respectively, supreme universal and nonsupreme universal. In the Indian schools more generally, a universal is an abstract object of thought that encompasses all its actual instances.

unmanifest (*avyakta, gsal ba min pa*). In the Sāṅkhya school, the primary/primordial nature when its three natures (*sattva, rajas, tamas*) are in equilibrium, does not transform into other evolutes, and remains unmanifest.

Veda (*rig byed*). Literally "knowledge," the sacred scriptures of Hinduism. In some cases, the term is used to refer only to the *Ṛg Veda*. In other cases, it is used to refer to the entire Vedic corpus, including the four Vedas (Ṛg, Yajur, Sāma, and Atharva), and its four parts: the Saṃhitā, Brāhmaṇa, Āraṇyaka, and Upaniṣad.

verbal testimony (*āgama, lung*). A term used to refer both to expressive speech, or valid words, and to valid awareness produced in dependence on hearing such speech. Buddhist and Hindu schools disagree as to whether verbal testimony is a valid source of knowledge (*pramāṇa*), with the Hindu schools claiming that the Vedas are a form of verbal testimony that is valid and the Buddhists denying that they are. Other terms for verbal testimony as a valid means of knowledge are *śrutajñāna* (scriptural knowledge), and *śabda* (speech).

Vinaya (*'dul ba*). Literally "discipline," in the sense of the monastic code. The term also refers to the Vinaya Piṭaka, that portion of the three scriptural collections that deals with monastic life.

wheel of the Dharma (*dharmacakra, chos kyi 'khor lo*). A general term for the teachings of the Buddha, used in the Yogācāra school and specifically the *Saṃdhinirmocana Sūtra* to refer to three categories of the Buddha's teachings: the "wheel of the four truths," used to refer to the Buddha's teachings to those who seek to attain the state of an arhat; the "wheel of signlessness," used to refer to the Buddha's teachings of emptiness, especially in the Perfection of Wisdom sūtras; and "the wheel of good discrimination," used to refer to the teachings in the *Saṃdhinirmocana Sūtra*, where what exists and what does not exist are clearly distinguished. The term as used in later works includes other sūtras in the third wheel.

yogic direct perception (*yogipratyakṣa, rnal 'byor mngon sum*). One of the three forms of direct perception (together with sense direct perception and mental direct perception). It is the direct perception of reality after attaining a particular level of concentration.

Bibliographic Note

THERE HAVE BEEN centuries of scholarship on classical Indian philosophy, first in India and later around the world. In English, some of the first serious work on Indian philosophy, often in unacknowledged collaboration with Indian scholars, was published by officers of the East India Company in journals like *Asiatic Researches* and *Journal of the Asiatic Society of Bengal*. Among many notable Sanskrit scholars was Henry Thomas Colebrooke (1765–1837), whose essays on Hindu and Jaina philosophy were published posthumously in 1858 as *Essays on the Religion and Philosophy of the Hindus*.

This is simply to illustrate that there has been over two centuries of scholarship on Indian philosophy in English alone, not to mention the work published in French and German, and since the late nineteenth century, in Hindi and Japanese and, more recently, in Chinese and Korean. In the domain of modern scholarship, there are today hundreds of monographs and thousands of articles on the topics discussed in this volume. This does not include the vast commentarial literature in Pāli, Sanskrit, Chinese, and Tibetan, only a tiny fraction of which is cited in these pages.

All of this is to say that referencing the relevant scholarship on Indian philosophy would have added many hundreds of additional footnotes to the hundreds already here. We therefore will mention just a few sources, which will lead the interested reader to the relevant scholarship on the Indian schools and their philosophies.

In the first half of the twentieth century, the major English-language survey was Surendranath Dasgupta's *History of Indian Philosophy*, published in five volumes between 1922 and 1925. Its primary focus is the Hindu schools, although chapters are devoted to both Jainism and Buddhism. Beginning in 1970 Karl Potter began publishing his *Encyclopedia of Indian Philosophies* with volumes devoted to all the major Indian schools, composed of essays and bibliographies by the leading Anglophone scholars on each school. It eventually encompassed twenty-five volumes, many of which are devoted to Buddhism, and remains an essential resource. The first section of the Vaibhāṣika chapter of the present volume is devoted to the early schools of Indian Buddhism. The standard work on these schools remains André Bareau's 1955 *Les sects bouddhique de Petit Véhicule*, published in English as *The Buddhist Sects of the Small Vehicle*. Among the large Tibetan genre of texts on Indian philosophical tenets, one of the most famous works, and one praised by His Holiness in his introduction to the present volume, is *Beautiful Adornment of Mount Meru* by Changkya Rölpai Dorjé (1717–86). Many of the technical terms, authors, and texts mentioned in this volume are the subject of their own entries in *The Princeton Dictionary of Buddhism* by Robert Buswell and Donald Lopez. For the most current scholarship, the best resource is the online *Stanford Encyclopedia of Philosophy*, where there are entries on many of the authors, texts, and topics discussed in these pages, each with an extensive bibliography.

Bibliography of Works Cited

Canonical Buddhist Scripture (Kangyur)

Analysis of the Vinaya. Vinayavibhaṅga. 'Dul ba lung rnam 'byed. Toh 3, Vinaya, *ca.*

Brahmā's Net Sūtra. Brahmajālasūtra. Tshangs pa'i dra ba'i mdo. Toh 352, Sūtra, *a.*

Chapters on the Fine Points of the Vinaya. Vinayakṣudrakavastu. 'Dul ba lung phran tshegs. Toh 6, Vinaya, *da.*

Chapters on the Vinaya. Vinayavastu. 'Dul ba lung gzhi. Toh 1, Vinaya, *ka, kha, ga,* and *nga.*

Collection of Aphorisms. Udānavarga. Ched du brjod pa'i tshoms. Toh 326, Sūtra, *sa.*

Dense Array Sūtra. Ghanavyūhasūtra. Rgyan stug po bkod pa'i mdo. Toh 110, Sūtra, *cha.*

Descent into Laṅkā Sūtra. Laṅkāvatārasūtra. Lang kar gshegs pa'i mdo. Toh 107, Sūtra, *ca.*

Entering the Two Truths Sūtra. Saṃvṛtiparamārthasatyanirdeśasūtra. Bden pa gnyis la 'jug pa'i mdo. Toh 179, Sūtra, *ma.*

Explanation of the Intention. Saṃdhinirmocanasūtra. Dgongs pa nges par 'grel pa'i mdo. Toh 106, Sūtra, *ca.*

Flower Garland Sūtra. Avataṃsakasūtra. Phal po che'i mdo. Toh 44, Avataṃsaka, *ka, kha, ga,* and *a.*

Going Forth Sūtra. Abhiniṣkramaṇasūtra. Mngon par 'byung ba'i mdo. Toh 301, Sūtra, *sa.*

Great Cloud Sūtra. Mahāmeghasūtra. Sprin chen po'i mdo. Toh 232, Sūtra, *wa.*

Great Discourse on the Final Nirvāṇa. Mahāparinirvāṇasūtra. Yongs su mya ngan las 'das pa'i mdo. Toh 119, Sūtra, *ta.*

Great Drum Sūtra. Mahābherīhārakaparivarta. Rnga bo che chen po'i le'u. Toh 222, Sūtra, *dza.*

King of Samādhis Sūtra. Samādhirājasūtra. Ting nge 'dzin gyi rgyal po'i mdo. Toh 127, Sūtra, *da.*

Mañjuśrī Root Tantra. Mañjuśrīmūlatantra. 'Jam dpal rtsa rgyud. Toh 543, Tantra, *na.*

Meeting of Father and Son Sūtra. Pitāputrasamāgamasūtra. Yab sras mjal ba'i mdo. Toh 60, Ratnakuṭa, *nga.*

Perfection of Wisdom in Eighteen Thousand Stanzas. Aṣṭādaśasāhasrikāprajñāpāramitāsūtra. Shes rab kyi pha rol tu phyin pa khri brgyad stong pa. Toh 10. Prajñāpāramitā, *ga.*

Questions of Brahmaviseśacinti. Brahmaviśeṣacintiparipṛcchāsūtra. Tshangs pa khyad par sems kyis zhus pa'i mdo. Toh 160, Sūtra *ba.*

Questions of King Dhāraṇīśvara. Dhāraṇīśvararājaparipṛcchā. Gsungs kyi dbang phyug rgyal pos zhus pa. Also known as the *Tathāgatamahākaruṇānirdeśa.* Toh 147, Sūtra, *pa.*

Questions of the Nāga King Anavatapta. Anavataptanāgarājaparipṛcchāsūtra. Klu'i rgyal po ma dros pas zhus pa'i mdo. Toh 156, Sūtra, *pha.*

Questions of the Nāga King Sāgara. Sāgaranāgarājaparipṛcchāsūtra. Klu'i rgyal po rgya mtshos zhus pa'i mdo. Toh 154. Sūtra, *pha.*

Teaching of Akṣayamati Sūtra. Akṣayamatinirdeśasūtra. Blo gros mi zad pas bstan pa'i mdo. Toh 175, Sūtra, *ma.*

Ten Levels Sūtra. Daśabhūmikasūtra. Sa bcu pa'i mdo. Toh 44, Avataṃsaka, *kha.* This sūtra is chapter 31 of the *Flower Garland Sūtra* collection.

Canonical Buddhist Treatises (Tengyur)

Abhayākaragupta (twelfth century). *Moonlight of Essential Points: A Commentary on the Perfection of Wisdom in Eight Thousand Stanzas. Aṣṭasāhasrikāprajñāpāramitāvṛttimarmakaumudī. Shes rab kyi pha rol tu phyin pa brgyad stong pa'i 'grel pa gnad kyi zla ba'i 'od.* Toh 3805. Prajñāpāramita, *da.*

———. *Ornament of the Sage's Thought. Munimatālaṃkāra. Thub pa'i dgongs pa'i rgyan.* Toh 3903, Madhyamaka, *a.*

Amarasiṃha (ca. twelfth century). *Amara's Treasury. Amarakośa.'Chi ba med pa'i mdzod* (*Mngon brjod 'chi med mdzod*). Toh 4299, Śabdavidyā, *se.*

Āryadeva (ca. second century). *Commentary on the Measure of What Is at Hand. Hastavālavṛtti. Lag pa'i tshad kyi 'grel pa.* Toh 3849, Madhyamaka, *tsha.*

———. *Compendium on the Essence of Wisdom. Jñānasārasamuccaya. Ye shes snying po kun las btus pa.* Toh 3851, Madhyamaka, *tsha.*

———. *Destruction of Errors about Madhyamaka. Madhyamakabhramaghāta. Dbu ma 'khrul pa 'joms pa.* Toh 3850, Madhyamaka, *tsha.*

———. *Establishing Proofs That Refute Mistaken Views. Skhalitapramathanayuktihetusiddhi. 'Khrul pa bzlog pa'i rigs pa gtan tshigs grub pa.* Toh 3847, Madhyamaka, *tsha.*

———. *Four Hundred Verses. Catuḥśataka. Bstan bcos bzhi brgya pa.* Toh 3846, Madhyamaka, *tsha.*

———. *Hundred Verse Treatise. Śatakaśāstra. Bailun ben,* Taishō 1569.

———. *Measure of What Is at Hand. Hastavālaprakaraṇakārikā. Lag pa'i tshad kyi tshig le'ur.* Toh 3848, Madhyamaka, *tsha.*

———. *Parts of the Constituents. Hastavālanāmaprakaraṇa. Cha shas kyi yan lag ces bya ba'i rab tu byed pa.* Toh 3844, Madhyamaka, *tsa.*

Asaṅga (fourth century). *Bodhisattva Levels. Bodhisattvabhūmi. Byang chub sems dpa'i sa.* Toh 4037, Cittamātra, *wi.*

———. *Commentary on Explanation of the Intention. Saṃdhinirmocanabhāṣya. Dgongs pa nges par 'grel pa'i rnam par bshad pa.* Toh 3981, Sūtra commentary, *ngi.*
———. *Compendium of Abhidharma. Abhidharmasamuccaya. Chos mngon pa kun las btus pa.* Toh 4049, Cittamātra, *ri.*
———. *Compendium of Ascertainments. Viniścayasaṅgrahaṇī* [*or Nirṇayasaṅgraha*]. *Rnam par gtan la dbab pa bsdu ba.* Toh 4038, Cittamātra, *zhi, zi.*
———. *Compendium of the Mahāyāna. Mahāyānasaṅgraha. Theg pa chen po bsdus pa.* Toh 4048, Cittamātra, *ri.*
———. *Yogācāra Levels. Yogācārabhūmi. Rnal 'byor spyod pa'i sa.* Toh 4035, Cittamātra, *tshi.*
Asvabhāva (d.u.). *Explanation of the Compendium of the Mahāyāna. Mahāyānasaṅgrahopanibandhana. Theg pa chen po bsdus pa'i bshad sbyar.* Toh 4051, Cittamātra, *ri.*
Atiśa Dipaṃkaraśrījñāna (982–1054). *Entry to the Two Truths. Satyadvayāvatāra. Bden pa gnyis la 'jug pa.* Toh 3903, Madhyamaka, *a.*
———. *Lamp for the Path to Enlightenment. Bodhipathapradīpa. Byang chub lam gyi sgron ma.* Toh 3947, Madhyamaka, *khi.*
———. *An Open Casket of Jewels: Instructions on the Middle Way. Ratnakaraṇḍodghāṭa-nāma-madhyamakopadeśa. Dbu ma'i man ngag rin po che'i za ma tog kha phye ba.* Toh 3930, Madhyamaka, *ki.*
Avalokitavrata (late sixth to early seventh century). *Commentary on the Lamp of Wisdom. Prajñāpradīpaṭīkā. Shes rab sgron ma rgya cher 'grel pa.* Toh 3859, Madhyamaka, *wa, zha, za.*
Bhāviveka (sixth century). *Blaze of Reasoning. Tarkajvālā. Rtog ge 'bar ba.* Toh 3856, Madhyamaka, *dza.*
_____. *Essence of the Middle Way. Madhyamakahṛdaya. Dbu ma snying po.* Toh 3855, Madhyamaka, *dza.*
_____. *Lamp of Wisdom: Commentary on Verses on the Middle Way. Prajñāpradīpamūlamadhyamakavṛtti. Dbu ma rtsa ba'i 'grel pa shes rab sgron ma.* Toh 3853, Madhyamaka, *tsha.*
Bhāviveka (the Lesser, d.u.). *Jewel Lamp of the Middle Way. Madhyamakaratnapradīpa. Dbu ma rin po che sgron ma.* Toh 3854, Madhyamaka, *tsha.*
Bodhibhadra (ca. eighth century). *Explanation of the Compendium on the Essence of Wisdom. Jñānasārasamuccayanibandhana. Ye shes snying po kun las btus pa'i bshad sbyar.* Toh 3852, Madhyamaka, *tsha.*
Buddhapālita (late fifth to early sixth century). *Buddhapālita's Commentary on Root Verses on the Middle Way. Buddhapālitamūlamadhyamakavṛtti. Rtsa she 'grel pa buddha pā li ta.* Toh 3842, Madhyamaka, *tsa.*
Candrahari (twelfth century). *Jewel Garland. Ratnamālā. Rin po che phreng ba.* Toh 3901, Madhyamaka, *a.*
Candrakīrti (seventh century). *Autocommentary on Entering the Middle Way. Madhyamakāvatārabhāṣya. Dbu ma la 'jug pa'i bshad.* Toh 3862, Madhyamaka, *'a.*

———. *Commentary on Seventy Stanzas on Emptiness. Śūnyatāsaptativṛtti. Stong nyid bdun cu pa'i 'grel pa.* Toh 3867, Madhyamaka, *ya.*

———. *Commentary on Sixty Stanzas on Reasoning. Yuktiṣaṣṭikāvṛtti. Rigs pa drug cu pa'i 'grel pa.* Toh 3864, Madhyamaka, *ya.*

———. *Clear Words: A Commentary on Root Verses on the Middle Way. Mūlamadhyamakavṛtti-Prasannapadā. Dbu ma rtsa ba'i 'grel pa tshig gsal ba.* Toh 3860, Madhyamaka, *'a.*

———. *Entering the Middle Way. Madhyamakāvatāra. Dbu ma la 'jug pa.* Toh 3861, Madhyamaka, *'a.*

———. *Extensive Commentary on the Four Hundred Verses. Catuḥśatakaṭīkā. Bzhi brgya pa'i rgya cher 'grel pa.* Toh 3865, Madhyamaka, *ya.*

Dharmakīrti (seventh century). *Analysis of Relations. Sambandhaparīkṣā. 'Brel pa brtag pa.* Toh 4214, Pramāṇa, *ce.*

———. *Ascertainment of Valid Knowledge. Pramāṇaviniścaya. Tshad ma rnam par nges pa.* Toh 4211, Pramāṇa, *ce.*

———. *Drop of Reasoning. Nyāyabindu. Rigs pa'i thigs pa.* Toh 4212, Pramāṇa, *ce.*

———. *Drop of Reasons. Hetubindu. Gtan tshigs kyi thigs pa.* Toh 4123, Pramāṇa, *ce.*

———. *Exposition of Valid Knowledge. Pramāṇavārttika. Tshad ma rnam 'grel.* Toh 4210, Pramāṇa, *ce.*

———. *Principles of Debate. Vādanyāya. Rtsod pa'i rigs.* Toh 4218, Pramāṇa, *ce.*

———. *Proving Others' Minds. Saṃtānāntarasiddhi. Rgyud gzhan grub pa.* Toh 4219, Pramāṇa, *ce.*

Dharmamitra (ca. ninth century). *Clear Words: Commentary on the Ornament of Realizations. Abhisamayālaṃkāraṭīkā-Prasphuṭapadā. Mngon par rtogs pa'i rgyan gyi'grel bshad tshig rab tu gsal ba.* Toh 3796, Prajñāpāramitā, *nya.*

Dharmottara (ca. eighth century). *Commentary on Ascertainment of Valid Knowledge. Tshad ma rnam par nges pa'i 'grel bshad. Pramāṇaviniścayaṭīkā.* Toh 4229, Pramāṇa, *dze.*

———. *Examination of Valid Knowledge. Pramāṇaparīkṣā. Tshad ma brtag pa.* Toh 4249, Pramāṇa, *zhe.*

———. *Proof of Momentariness. Skad cig ma 'jig pa grub pa. Kṣaṇabhaṅgasiddhi.* Toh 4253, Pramāṇa, *zhe.*

———. *Vast Commentary on the Drop of Reasoning. Nyāyabinduṭīkā. Rigs thigs rgya cher 'grel pa.* Toh 4231, Pramāṇa, *we.*

Dignāga (sixth century). *Autocommentary on Compendium of Valid Knowledge. Pramāṇasamuccayavṛtti. Tshad ma kun las btus pa'i 'grel pa.* Toh 4204, Pramāṇa, *ce.*

———. *Commentary on Investigation of the Support. Ālambanaparīkṣāvṛtti. Migs pa rtags pa'i 'grel pa.* Toh 4206, Pramāṇa, *ce.*

———. *Commentary on the Treasury of Abhidharma: Lamp for the Essential Points. Abhidharmakośavṛttimarmadīpa. Chos mngon pa'i mdzod kyi 'grel pa gnad kyi sgron me.* Toh 4095, Abhidharma, *nyu.*

———. *Compendium of Valid Knowledge. Pramāṇasamuccaya. Tshad ma kun las btus pa.* Toh 4203, Pramāṇa, *ce.*

———. *Investigation of the Support. Ālambanaparīkṣā. Migs pa rtags pa.* Toh 4205, Pramāṇa, *ce.*

Guṇaprabha (seventh century) *Vinayasūtra. 'Dul ba'i mdo.* Toh 4115, Vinaya, *dzu.*

Haribhadra (late eighth century). *Commentary on the Explanation of the Perfection of Wisdom Treatise Called Ornament for Realizations (Clear Meaning Commentary). Abhisamayālaṃkāranāmaprajñāpāramitopadeśavṛtti (Sphuṭārthā). Shes rab kyi pha rol tu phyin pa'i man ngag gi bstan bcos mngon par rtogs bcos mngon par rtogs pa'i rgyan zhes bya ba'i 'grel pa, ('Grel pa don gsal).* Toh 3793, Prajñāpāramitā, *ja.*

———. *Commentary on the Perfection of Wisdom in Twenty-Five Thousand Stanzas. Pañcaviṃśatisāhasrikāprajñāpāramitā. Shes rab kyi pha rol tu phyin pa stong phrag nyi shu lnga pa.* Toh 3790, Prajñāpāramitā, ga.

———. *Commentary on the Verse Summary of the Precious Qualities. Ratnaguṇasañcayagathānāmapañjikā. Yon tan rin po che sdud pa'i tshigs su bcad pa'i dka' 'grel.* Toh 3792, Prajñāparamitā, *ja.*

———. *Illumination of the Ornament of Realizations. Abhisamayālaṃkārāloka. Mngon par rtogs pa'i rgyan gyi snang ba.* Toh 3791, Prajñāpāramitā, *cha.*

Jetāri (tenth century). *Commentary on Distinguishing the Sugata's Texts. Sugatamatavibhaṅgabhāṣya. Bde bar gshegs pa gzhung rnam par 'byed pa'i bshad pa.* Toh 3900, Madhyamaka, *a.*

———. *Logic for the Childish. Bālāvatāratarka. Byis pa 'jug pa'i rtog ge.* Toh 4263, Pramāṇa, *zhe.*

———. *Verses on Distinguishing the Sugata's Texts. Sugatamatavibhaṅgakārikā. Bde bar gshegs pa gzhung rnam par 'byed pa'i tshig le'ur byas pa.* Toh 3899, Madhyamaka, *a.*

Jñānagarbha (ca. eighth century). *Distinguishing the Two Truths. Satyadvayavibhaṅgakārikā. Bden pa gnyis rnam par 'byed pa'i tshig le'ur byas pa.* Toh 3881, Madhyamaka, *sa.*

Jñānaśrībhadra (eleventh century). *Commentary on the Ascertainment of Valid Knowledge. (Pramāṇaviniścayaṭīkā) Tshad ma rnam par nges pa'i 'grel bshad.* Toh 4228, Pramāṇa, *tshe.*

Jñānavajra (twelfth century). *Ornament for the Essence of the Tathāgata: A Commentary on the Descent into Laṅkā. Laṅkāvatārasūtravṛtti-tathāgatahṛdayālaṃkāra. Lang kar gshes pa'i mdo 'grel pa de bzhin gshegs pa'i snying po.* Toh 4019, Sūtra Commentary, *pi.*

Kalyāṇamitra (ca. ninth century). *Commentary on the Chapters on the Vinaya. Vinayavastuṭīkā. 'Dul ba gzhi'i rgya cher 'grel pa.* Toh 4113, Vinaya, *tsu.*

Kamalaśīla (eighth century). *Commentary on the Compendium of Principles. Tattvasaṅgrahapañjikā. De kho na nyid bsdus pa'i dka' 'grel.* Toh 4267, Pramāṇa, *ze, 'e.*

———. *Commentary on the Difficult Points of the Ornament of the Middle Way. Madhyamakālaṃkārapañjikā. Dbu ma rgyan gyi dka' 'grel.* Toh 3886, Madhyamaka, *sa.*

———. *Illumination of the Middle Way. Madhyamakāloka. Dbu ma snang ba.* Toh 3887, Madhyamaka, *sa.*

———. *Stages of Meditation*, second. *Bhāvanākrama (II). Bsgom rim bar pa.* Toh 3916, Madhyamaka, *ki.*

———. *Summary of the Opponents' Positions in the Drop of Reasoning. Nyāyabindupūrvapakṣasaṅkṣipti. Rigs pa'i thigs pa'i phyogs snga ma mdor bsdus pa.* Toh 4232, Pramāṇa, *we.*

Lakṣmī (eighth century). *Commentary on the Five Stages. Pañcakramaṭīkā. Rim lnga'i 'grel pa.* Toh 1842, Tantra, *chi.*

Maitreya (fourth century). *Distinguishing the Middle from the Extremes. Madhyāntavibhāga. Dbus mtha' rnam 'byed.* Toh 4021, Cittamātra, *phi.*

———. *Distinguishing Phenomena from Suchness. Dharmadharmatāvibhāga. Chos dang chos nyid rnam 'by*ed. Toh 4022, Cittamātra, *phi.*

———. *Ornament of the Mahāyāna Sūtras. Mahāyānasūtrālaṃkāra. Dbus mtha' rnam 'byed.* Toh 4020, Cittamātra, *phi.*

———. *Sublime Continuum of the Mahāyāna. Mahāyānottaratantraśāstra. Theg pa chen po'i rgyud bla ma'i bstan bcos.* Toh 4024, Cittamātra, *phi.*

Maitri Advayavajra / Maitrīpāda (tenth century). *Ten Verses on Reality. Tattvadaśaka. De kho na nyid bcu pa.* Toh 2236, Tantra, *wi.*

Mañjughoṣha Narendrakīrti (d.u.). *Brief Explication of the Assertions of Our Own View. Pradarśanānumatoddeśaparīkṣā. Rang gi lta ba'i 'dod pa mdor bstan pa yongs su brtag.* This text is not found in the Derge edition. Narthang Tengyur, Sūtra Commentary, *pu.*

Mokṣākaragupta (ca. eleventh to twelfth century). *Language of Logic. Tarkabhāṣā. Rtog ge'i skad.* Toh 4264, Pramāṇa, *zhe.*

Nāgārjuna (second century CE). *Chapter on the Essence of Dependent Arising. Pratītyasamutpādahṛdayakārikā.* Toh 3836. *Rten cing 'grel bar 'byung ba'i snying po'i tshig le'ur.* Toh 3836, Madhyamaka, *tsa.*

———. *Chapter on Understanding What Is Not Understood. Abodhabodhakanāmaprakaraṇa. Ma rtogs pa rtogs par byed pa'i rab byed.* Toh 3838, Madhyamaka, *tsa.*

———. *Commentary on Chapter on the Essence of Dependent Arising. Pratītyasamutpādahṛdayavyākhyāna. Rten cing 'grel bar 'byung ba'i snying po'i rnam par bshad pa.* Toh 3837, Madhyamaka, *tsa.*

———. *Compendium of Sūtras. Sūtrasamuccaya. Mdo kun las bstod pa.* Toh 3934, Madhyamaka, *ki.*

———. *Discourse on the Dream. Svapnacintāmaṇiparikathā. Rmi lam yid bzhin no bu'i gtam.* Toh 4160, Lekha, *ge.*

———. *Finely Woven. Vaidalyasūtra. Zhib mo rnam par 'thag pa'i mdo.* Toh 3826, Madhyamaka, *tsa.*

———. *Finely Woven Treatise. Vaidalyaprakaraṇa. Zhib mo rnam par 'thag pa'i rab tu byed pa.* Toh 3830, Madhyamaka, *tsa.*

———. *Five Stages. Pañcakrama. Rim pa lnga pa.* Toh 1802, Tantra, *ngi.*

———. *Letter to a Friend. Suhṛllekha. Bshes pa'i spring yig.* Toh 4182, Lekha, *nge.*

———. *Praise of the Inconceivable. Acintyastava. Bsam gyis mi khyab par bstod pa.* Toh 1128. Stotra, *ka.*

———. *Precious Garland. Ratnāvalī. Rin chen phreng ba.* Toh 4158, Lekha, *ge.*

———. *Proof for Entering into the Three Natures. Svabhāvatrayapraveśasiddhi. Rang bzhin gsum la 'jug pa'i grub pa.* Toh 3843. Madhyamaka, *tsa.*

———. *Refutation of Objections.. Vigrahavyāvartanī. Rtsod pa bzlog pa.* Toh 3828, Madhyamaka, *tsa.*

———. *Refutation of Objections Commentary. Vigrahavyāvartanīvṛtti. rtsod pa bzlog pa'i 'grel pa.* Toh 3832, Madhyamaka, *tsa.*

———. *Root Verses on the Middle Way [called Wisdom]. Mūlamadhyamakakārikā. Dbu ma rtsa ba'i tshig le'ur byas pa shes rab.* Toh 3824, Madhyamaka, *tsa.*

———. *Seventy Stanzas on Emptiness. Śūnyatāsaptatikārikā. Stong pa nyid bdun cu pa'i tshig le'ur byas pa.* Toh 3827, Madhyamaka, *tsa.*

———. *Sixty Stanzas on Reasoning. Yuktiṣaṣṭikākārikā. Rigs pa drug cu pa'i tshig le'ur byas pa.* Toh 3825, Madhyamaka, *tsa.*

———. *Transferring to Another Existence. Bhavasaṅkrānti. Srid pa 'pho ba.* Toh 3840, Madhyamaka, *tsa.*

———. *Twenty Verses on the Mahāyāna. Mahāyānaviṃśikā. Theg pa chen po nyi shu pa.* Toh 3833, Madhyamaka, *tsa.*

Prajñākaragupta (tenth century). *Ornament of the Exposition of Valid Knowledge. Pramāṇavārttikālaṃkāra. Tshad ma rnam 'grel gyi rgyan.* Toh 4221, Pramāṇa, *te.*

Prajñākaramati (tenth century). *Commentary on the Difficult Points of Entering the Bodhisattva Way. Bodhicaryāvatārapañjikā. Byang chub kyi spyod pa la 'jug pa'i dka' 'grel.* Toh 3872, Madhyamaka, *la.*

Prajñāvarman (ca. eighth century). *Commentary on Praise of the Exalted. Viśeṣastavaṭīkā. Khyad par 'phags bstod kyi rgya cher bshad pa.* Toh 1110, Stotra, *ka.*

———. *Commentary on Praise of the One More Perfect Than the Gods. Devātiśaya-stotraṭīkā. Lha las phul du byung bar bstod pa'i rgya cher 'grel pa.* Toh 1113, Stotra, *ka.*

Puṇḍarīka (eleventh century). *Stainless Light: A Commentary on the Kālacakra Tantra. Laghukālacakratantrarājaṭīkā-Vimalaprabhā. Bsdus pa'i rgyud kyi rgyal po dus kyi 'khor lo 'grel bshad dri med 'od.* Toh 1347, Tantra, *tha.*

Pūrṇavardhana (ca. eighth century). *Investigating Characteristics: A Commentary on the Treasury of Abhidharma. Abhidharmakośaṭīkā-Lakṣaṇānusāriṇī. Chos mngon pa'i mdzod kyi 'grel bshad mtshan nyid kyi rjes su 'brang ba.* Toh 4093, Abhidharma, *cu.*

Sahajavajra (tenth century). *Commentary on the Ten Verses on Reality. Tattva-daśakaṭīkā. De kho na nyid bcu pa'i rgya cher 'grel pa.* Toh 2254, Tantra, *wi.*

Śākyabuddhi (ca. late seventh or early eighth century). *Commentary on the Exposition of Valid Knowledge. Pramāṇavārttikaṭīkā. Tshad ma rnam 'grel gyi 'grel bshad.* Toh 4220, Pramāṇa, *je.*

Śākyaprabha (ca. eighth century). *Luminous Vinaya. Prabhāvatī. 'Dul ba 'od ldan.* Toh 4125, Vinaya, *shu.*

Śamathadeva (d.u.). *Salient Points Commentary to the Treasury of Abhidharma.*

Abhidharmakośaṭīkopayikā. Chos mngon pa'i mdzod kyi 'grel bshad nye bar mkho ba. Toh 4094, Abhidharma, *nyu.*

Saṅghabhadra (fifth century). *Treatise on Conforming to Reasoning in the Abhidharma. Abhidharmanyāyānusāra. Apidamo shunzhengli lun.* Taishō 1562.

Śāntarakṣita (725–88). *Commentary on the Difficult Points of Distinguishing the Two Truths. Satyadvayavibhaṅgapañjikā. Bden gnyis dka' 'grel.* Toh 3883, Madhyamaka, *sa.*

———. *Commentary on the Ornament of the Middle Way. Madhyamakālaṃkāravṛtti. Dbu ma'i rgyan gyi 'grel ba.* Toh 3885, Madhyamaka, *sa.*

———. *Compendium of Principles. Tattvasaṅgraha. De kho na nyid bsdus pa.* Toh 4266, Pramāṇa, *ze.*

———. *Ornament of the Middle Way. Madhyamakālaṃkāra. Dbu ma rgyan.* Toh 3884, Madhyamaka, *sa.*

Śāntideva (eighth century). *Compendium of Training. Śikṣāsamuccaya. Bslab pa kun las btus pa.* Toh 3940, Madhyamaka, *khi.*

———. *Entering the Bodhisattva Way. Bodhicaryāvatāra. Byang chub sems dpa'i spyod pa la 'jug pa.* Toh 3871, Madhyamaka, *la.*

Sthirmati (ca. sixth century). *Commentary on the Thirty Verses. Triṃśikābhāṣya. Sum cu pa'i bshad pa.* Toh 4064, Cittamātra, *shi.*

Śubhagupta (ca. eighth century). *Proof of External Objects. Bāhyārthasiddhi. Phyi rol gyi don grub pa.* Toh 4244, Pramāṇa, *zhe.*

Subhūtighoṣa (eighth century). *Detailed Explanation Illuminating All the Vehicles. Sarvayānālokaviśeṣabhāṣya. Theg pa thams cad snang bar byed pa'i bye brag tu bshad pa.* Toh 3907, Madhyamaka, *a.*

Udbhaṭasiddhasvāmin (ca. late third or early fourth century). *Praise of the Exalted. Viśeṣastava. Khyad par du 'phags pa'i bstod pa.* Toh 1109, Stotra, *ka.*

Vajragarbha (ca. tenth to eleventh century). *Commentary on the Condensation of the Hevajra Tantra. Hevajrapiṇḍārthaṭīkā. Kye'i rdo rje bsdus pa'i don gyi rgya cher 'brel pa.* Toh 1180, Tantra, *ka.*

Vasubandhu (fourth or fifth century). *Autocommentary on the Treasury of Abhidharma. Abhidharmakośabhāṣya. Chos mngon pa'i mdzod kyi bshad pa.* Toh 4090, Abhidharma, *ku, khu.*

———. *Commentary on the Compendium of the Mahāyāna. Mahāyānasaṅgrahabhāṣya. Theg pa chen po bsdus pa'i 'grel pa.* Toh 4050, Cittamātra, *ri.*

———. *Commentary on Distinguishing the Middle from Extremes. Madhyāntavibhāgabhāṣya. Dbus dang mtha' rnam par 'byed pa'i 'grel pa.* Toh 4027, Cittamātra, *bi.*

———. *Commentary on Distinguishing Phenomena and Suchness. Dharmadharmatāvibhaṅgavṛtti. Chos dang chos nyid rnam par 'byed pa'i 'grel pa.* Toh 4028, Cittmātra, *bi.*

———. *Commentary on Ornament of the Sūtras. Sūtrālaṃkārabhāṣya. Mdo sde rgyan gyi bshad pa.* Toh 4026, Cittamātra, *phi.*

———. *Commentary on the Teaching of Akṣayamati. Akṣayamatinirdeśaṭīkā. Blo gros mi zad pas bstan pa'i rgya cher 'grel pa.* T 3994, Sūtra Commentary, *ngi.*

———. *Commentary on the Ten Levels Sūtra. Daśabhūmivyākhyāna. Sa bcu pa'i rnam par bshad pa.* Toh 3993, Sūtra Commentary, *ngi.*

———. *Commentary on the Twenty Verses. Viṃśikāvṛtti. Nyi shu pa'i 'grel pa.* Toh 4057, Cittamātra, *shi.*

———. *Condensed Explanation Revealing the Secret Meaning. Vivṛtagūhyārtha-piṇḍavyākhyā. Don gsang rnam par phye ba.* Toh 4052, Cittamātra, *ri.*

———. *Explanation of the First Dependent Origination and Its Divisions. Pratītyasamutpādādivibhaṅgabhāṣya. Rten cing 'brel bar 'byung ba'i rnam par dbye ba bshad pa.* Toh 3995, Sūtra Commentary, *chi.*

———. *Exposition of the Three Natures. Trisvabhāvanirdeśa. Rang bzhin gsum nges par bstan pa.* Toh 4058, Cittamātra, *shi.*

———. *Principles of Exegesis. Vyākhyāyukti. Rnam par bshad pa'i rigs pa.* Toh 4061, Cittamātra, *shi.*

———. *Thirty Verses. Triṃśikā. Sum cu pa'i tshig le'ur byas pa.* Toh 4055, Cittamātra, *shi.*

———. *Treasury of Abhidharma. Abhidharmakośa. Chos mngon pa'i mdzod.* Toh 4089, Abhidharma, *ku.*

———. *Treatise on the Five Aggregates. Pañcaskandhaprakaraṇa. Phung po lnga'i rab byed.* Toh 4059, Cittamātra, *shi.*

———. *Treatise Proving Actions. Karmasiddhiprakaraṇa. Las grub pa'i rab tu byed pa.* Toh 4062, Cittamātra, *shi.*

———. *Twenty Verses. Viṃśikā. Nyi shu pa.* Toh 4056, Cittamātra, *shi.*

Vasumitra (second century). *Wheel Setting Forth the Differences of the Systems. Samayabhedoparacanacakra. Gzhung lugs kyi bye brag bkod pa'i 'khor lo.* Toh 4138, Vinaya, *su.*

Vinītadeva (early eighth century). *Compendium Setting Forth the Different Sects, Wheel for Reading the Sequence of the Systems. Samayabhedoparacanacakre-Nikāyabhedopadeśanasaṅgraha. Gzhung tha dad pa rim par bklag pa'i 'khor lo las sde pa tha dad pa bstan pa bsdus pa.* Toh 4140, Vinaya, *su.*

———. *Extensive Commentary on [Dharmakīrti's] Analysis of Relations. Sambandha-parīkṣāṭīkā. 'Brel pa brtag pa'i rgya cher bshad pa.* Toh 4236, Pramāṇa, *zhe.*

Vitapāda (ca. tenth to eleventh century). *Commentary on [Jñānagarbha's] Oral Teaching on Meditation on Reality. Tattvabhāvanāmukhāgamavṛtti. De kho na nyid sgom pa zhal gyi lung gi 'grel pa.* Toh 1866, Tantra, *di.*

Wŏnch'ŭk (Wen tshegs, 613–96 CE). *Commentary to the Explanation of the Intention Sūtra. Saṃdhinirmocanasūtraṭīkā. Dgongs 'grel gyi mdo'i rgya cher 'grel.* Toh 4016, Sūtra, *thi.*

———. *Extensive Commentary on the Explanation of the Intention Sūtra. Jieshenmijing shu. Dgongs pa zab mo nges par 'grel pa'i mdo rgya cher 'grel pa.* Toh 4016, Sūtra Commentary, *ti.*

Yaśomitra/Jinaputra (ca. eighth century). *Clarifying the Meaning: A Commentary on the Treasury of Abhidharma. Sphuṭārthābhidharmakośavyākhyā / Abhidharmakośaṭīkā. Chos mngon pa'i mdzod kyi 'grel bshad don gsal / Chos mngon pa'i mdzod kyi 'grel bshad.* Toh 4092, Abhidharma, *gu, ngu.*

———. *Elucidation of the Compendium of Abhidharma. Abhidharmasamuccayavyākhyā. Mngon pa kun las btus pa'i rnam par bshad pa.* Toh 4054, Cittamātra, *li.*

Other Works

Agniveśa (compiled by Caraka during the second century). *Compendium of Caraka. Carakasaṃhitā.* Translated into Tibetan by Dr. Lobsang Tenzin and Shastri Lobsang Norbu. Varanasi: Institute of Higher Tibetan Studies, 2006.

Akalaṅka (fifth century). *Ascertainment of Reasoning. Nyāyaviniścaya.*

———. *Compendium of Valid Knowledge. Pramāṇasaṅgraha.*

Akṣapāda. *See* Gautama.

Anonymous (twelfth century). *Compendium of Ahirbudhnya. Ahirbudhnyasaṃhitā.*

Anonymous. *Yuktidīpikā.*

Bareau, André. *The Buddhist Schools of the Small Vehicle.* Translated from the French by Sara Boin-Webb. Honolulu: The University of Hawai'i Press, 2013.

Bṛhaspati. *Sūtra of Bṛhaspati. Bārhaspatya Sūtra.*

Butön Rinchen Drup (Bu ston Rin chen grub, 1290–1364). *History of the Dharma: A Treasury of the Jewels of Scripture. Chos 'byung gsung rab rin po che'i mdzod.* Codex form.

Candramati, Vaiśeṣika (fifth century). *Daśapadārthaśāstra.*

Changkya Rölpai Dorjé (Lcang skya rol pa'i rdo rje, 1717–86). *Clear Presentation of Tenets, an Elegant Ornament of the Meru of the Sage's Teachings. Grub mtha'i rnam par bzhag pa gsal bar bshad pa thub bstan lhun po'i mdzes rgyan.* Bod kyi gtsug lag gces btus 24. New Delhi: Institute of Tibetan Classics, 2012. Citations, unless otherwise specified, are of the English translation: *Beautiful Adornment of Mount Meru: A Presentation of Classical Indian Philosophy.* Translated by Donald S. Lopez Jr. The Library of Tibetan Classics 24. Somerville, MA: Wisdom Publications, 2019.

Chapa Chökyi Sengé (Phwya pa chos kyi seng ge, 1109–69). *Dispelling Confusion about Valid Knowledge. Tshad ma yid kyi mun sel.* Bka' gtams gsung 'bum phyogs bsgrigs theng dang po 9. Chengdu: Si khron mi rigs dpe skrun khang nas dpe rnying bris ma la dpar bshus, 2006.

———. *A Summary of Presentations of Non-Buddhist and Buddhist Tenets. Phyi nang gi grub mtha'i rnam bzhag bsdus pa.*

Chekawa Yeshé Dorjé ('Chad kha ba ye shes rdo rje, 1101–75). *Tenets. Grub mtha'.*

Chim Jampaiyang (Mchims 'Jam pa'i dbyangs, ca. 1245–1325). *Ornament of Abhidharma. Mdzod 'grel mngon pa'i rgyan.* See translation: *Ornament of Abhidharma: A Commentary on Vasubandhu's Abhidharmakośa.* Translated by Ian James Coghlan. The Library of Tibetan Classics 23. Somerville, MA: Wisdom Publications, 2018.

Chomden Rikpai Raldri (Bcom ldan rigs pa'i ral gri, 1227–1307). *A Flower Adorning Tenets. Grub mtha' rgyan gyi me tog.* Collected Works, vol. *ca*. Lhasa: Bod 'bras spung gnas bcu lha khang gi phyag dpe las bshus, 2006.

Dasgupta, Surendranath. *A History of Indian Philosophy*, 5 vols. Cambridge: Cambridge University Press, 1922–25.

Devaraja, N. K. ed. *Indian Philosophy. Bhāratīya Darśana*. Lucknow: Uttara Pradeśa Hindī Grantha Akādamī, 1975.

Drakar Losang Palden (Brag dkar Blo bzang dpal ldan, 1866–1928). *Lamp Illuminating Jewels: A Summary of the Essentials of Tenets. Grub mtha'i gnad bsdus rin chen gsal ba'i sgrom me.*

Dunlin (d.u.). *Commentary on the Treasury of Abhidharma. Jushesong shu ji.* Xuzangjing 53, CBETA 0841.

Gaṅgeśa (fourteenth century). *Wish-Granting Jewel of Reality. Tattvacintāmaṇi.*

Gauḍapāda (sixth century). *Verses of Gauḍapāda. Gauḍapādakārikā.*

Gautama (second century). *Aphorisms on Reasoning. Nyāyasūtra.* A.k.a. *Sūtra of Akṣapāda. Akṣapādasūtra.*

Gendun Gyatso, Second Dalai Lama (Dge 'dun rgya mtsho, 1476–1542). *Ship That Sails the Ocean of Tenets. Grub mtha' rgya mtshor 'jug pa'i gru gzings.*

Great Exegesis of the Abhidharma. Abhidharmamahāvibhāṣā, also known as *Mahāvibhāṣā. Chos mngon pa bye brag bshad pa chen po.* Translated from Chinese between 1945 and 1949 by the Chinese translator Blo bzang chos 'phags, or Fazun. Manuscript of the Dga' ldan pho brang library. Beijing: Krung go'i bod rig pa'i dpe skrun khang, 2011.

Hopkins, Jeffrey. *Maps of the Profound: Jam-yang-shay-ba's Great Exposition of Buddhist and Non-Buddhist Views on the Nature of Reality.* Ithaca, NY: Snow Lion Publications, 2003.

Īśvarakṛṣṇa (fifth century). *Īśvarakṛṣṇa's Tantra* (*Īśvarakṛṣṇatantra*) or *Verses of Sāṅkhya* (*Sāṅkhyakārikā*). Varanasi ed. Translated into Tibetan in 1974 by Thub bstan mchog grub.

Jagadish Candra Mishra. *Bhāratīya Darśan.* Varanasi: Chaukhamba Surbharati Prakashan, 2016.

Jaina master Umāsvāti (third century). *Tattvārthasūtra.*

Jamyang Shepai Dorjé ('Jam dbyang bzhad pa'i rdo rje, 1648–1721). *Great Exposition of Tenets. Grub mtha' chen mo.* Taiwan edition.

Jayanta Bhaṭṭa (ninth century). *Blossoms of Reasoning. Nyāyamañjarī.*

Jha, Hari Mohan. *Bharatiya Darshan Parichay*, vol. 1.

Jizang (549–623 CE). *Commentary on the Verses on the Middle Way. Zhongguan lun shu.* Taishō 42, CBETA 1824.

Joshi, Hari Shankar. *Sāṅkhyayogadarśana kā jñoddhāra*, 1965.

Kapila (eighth century BCE). *Sāṅkhyasūtra.*

Kātyāyanīputra (second to first century BCE). *Establishment of Knowledge. Jñānaprasthāna*, vol. 1. Translated from Chinese between 1945 and 1949 by the

Chinese translator Blo bzang chos 'phags or Fazun. Manuscript of the Dga' ldan pho brang library. Beijing: Krung go'i bod rig pa'i dpe skrun khang, 2011.

Kawa Paltsek (Ska ba dpal brtsegs, eighth century). *Explanation of the Stages of Views. Lta ba'i rim pa bshad pa.*

Khedrup Jé Gelek Palsang (Mkhas grub rje Dge legs dpal bzang po, 1385–1438). *Dispelling Confusion: An Ornament for the Seven Texts on Valid Knowledge. Tshad ma sde bdun gyi rgyan yid kyi mun sel.* Bod kyi gtsug lag gces btus 21. New Delhi: Institute of Tibetan Classics, 2006.

———. *Ocean of Reasoning: An Extensive Commentary on Exposition of Valid Cognition. Tshad ma rnam 'grel gyi rgya cher bshad pa rigs pa'i rgya mtsho.*

Könchok Jikmé Wangpo (Dkon mchog 'jigs med dpang po, 1728–91). *Jewel Rosary of Tenets. Grub pa'i mtha'i rnam par bzhag pa rin po che'i phreng ba.* New Delhi: Ngawang Gelek Demo, 1972.

Kuiji (632–82). *Notes on the Proof of Consciousness Only. Cheng weishi lun shu ji.* Taishō 43, CBETA 1830.

Kumārila Bhaṭṭa (seventh century). *Commentary in Verse. Ślokavārttika.*

———. *Commentary on Ritual Practice. Tantravārttika.*

———. *Small Commentary. Ṭupṭīkā.*

Kundakunda (ca. first or early second century CE). *Essence of the Five Existents. Pañcāstikāyasāra.*

Laṅkāvatāra Sūtra. Sanskrit edition.

Lokāyata Sūtra. See Bṛhaspati, *Bārhaspatya Sūtra.*

Longchenpa (Klong chen pa, 1308–64). *Wish-Fulfilling Treasury of Tenets. Yid bzhin mdzod kyi grub mtha' bsdus pa.*

Mādhava (a.k.a. Vidyāraṇya, thirteenth century). *Compendium of All Views. Sarvadarśanasaṅgraha.*

Mahāvibhāṣā. See *Great Exegesis of the Abhidharma.*

Maja Jangchup Tsöndrü (Rma bya byang chub brtson 'grus, d. 1185). *Ornament of Reasoning: Commentary on Root Verses on the Middle Way. Rtsa she'i 'grel pa 'thad pa'i rgyan.*

Mallavādin (eighth century). *Wheel of Perspectives. Nayacakra.*

Maṇḍana Miśra (eighth century). *Ordered Explanation of Mīmāṃsā. Mīmāṃsānukramaṇī.*

Māṭhara's Commentary. Māṭharavṛtti.

Mipham, Ju ('Ju Mi pham, 1845–1912). *Collection of Tenets: A Wish Granting Treasury. Yid bzhin mdzod kyi grub mtha' bsdus pa.*

Muniśrī Pramāṇasāgara. *Jain Dharma aur Darśan.*

Murāri Miśra (twelfth century). *Eleven Chapters. Ekādaśādyadhikaraṇa.*

———. *Eyes of the Threefold Law. Tripādīnītinayana.*

Ngawang Palden, Chöjé (Ngag dbang dpal ldan, Chos rje, b. 1797). *Notes on [Jamyang Shepa's Great] Tenets. Grub mtha'i mchan.* Codex edition. Mundgod: Gomang Publishing House, 2007.

Nicholson, Andrew. *Unifying Hinduism: Philosophy and Identity in Indian Intellectual History*. New York: Columbia University Press, 2013.
Pārthasārathi Miśra (eleventh century). *Jewel of the Doctrine. Tantraratna.*
———. *Lamp on the Treatise. Śāstradīpikā.*
Patsab Nyima Drak (Pa tshab nyi ma grags, b. 1055). *Commentary on the Root Verses on the Middle Way. Rtsa she'i 'grel pa.*
Points of Controversy. Kathāvatthu. Gtam gyi gzhi. Pali canon, Abhidhamma Piṭaka.
Potter, Karl, ed. *Encyclopedia of Indian Philosophies*. 25 vols. Delhi: Motilal Banarsidass, 1970–2019.
Praśastapāda (sixth century). *Compendium of Categories. Padārthadharmasaṅgraha.*
Pūjyapāda (sixth century). *Proof of All Meanings. Sarvārthasiddhi.*
Rongzom Paṇḍita Chökyi Sangpo (Rong zom Chos kyi bzang po, 1012–88). *Memoranda on Various Views and Tenets. Lta ba dang grub mtha' sna tshogs pa brjed byang du bgyis pa.*
Śabarasvāmin (a.k.a. Ādityasena, sixth century). *Commentary of Śabara. Śābarabhāṣya.*
———. *Explanation of Mīmāṃsā. Mīmāṃsābhāṣya.*
Sakya Paṇḍita (Sa skya Paṇḍi ta, 1182–1251). *Classification of Tenets. Grub mtha' rnam 'byed.*
———. *Commentary on the Treasury of Valid Knowledge and Reasoning. Tshad ma rigs gter 'grel pa.* Sa skya'i gsung rab dpe bdur ma 17.
———. *Entranceway to Wisdom. Mkhas pa la 'jug pa'i sgo.* Sa skya'i gsung rab dpe bdur ma 18.
———. *Excellent Discourse on the Systems. Gzhung lugs legs par bshad pa.*
Samantabhadra (second century). *Investigation of Authority. Āptamīmāṃsā.*
Śaṅkarācārya (eighth century). *Commentary on the Brahmasūtra. Brahmasūtrabhāṣya.*
Siddhasena Divākara (fifth century). *Introduction to Reasoning. Nyāyāvatāra.*
———. *Sūtra of the Noble-Minded. Sanmatisūtra.*
Sinha, Harendra Prasad. *Bhāratīya Darśana kī Rūparekhā.*
Śrīdhara (tenth century). *Deer of Reasoning. Nyāyakandalī.*
Sūtra of Akṣapāda. See under Gautama.
Taktsang Lotsāwa (Stag tshang lo tsā ba, 1404–77). *Complete Knowledge of Tenets. Grub mtha' kun shes kyi rtsa ba.*
Tāranātha (1575–1634). *History of Indian Buddhism. Rgya gar chos 'byung.*
Thuken Losang Chökyi Nyima (Thu'u bkwan Blo bzang chos kyi nyi ma, 1737–1802). *Crystal Mirror of Philosophical Systems. Grub mtha' shel gyi me long.* See translation: *The Crystal Mirror of Philosophical Systems: A Tibetan Study of Asian Religious Thought.* Translated by Geshé Lhundub Sopa et al. Edited by Roger R. Jackson. The Library of Tibetan Classics 25. Boston: Wisdom Publications, 2009.
Tsongkhapa (Tsong kha pa, 1357–1419). *Essence of Eloquence. Legs bshad snying po.* Collected Works, vol. *pha*. Kumbum edition.

———. *Great Treatise on the Stages of the Path to Enlightenment. Byang chub lam rim chen mo*. Collected Works, vol. *pa*. Kumbum edition.

———. *Ocean of Reasoning: Explanation of the Root Verses on the Middle Way. Rje'i gsung 'bum*. Collected Works, vol. *ba*. Kumbum edition.

Udayana (eleventh century). *Garland of Moonbeams. Kiraṇāvalī*.

———. *Purification of the Notes on the Meaning. Tātparyaṭīkāpariśuddhi*.

Uddyotakara (sixth century). *Commentary on Nyāya. Nyāyavārttika*.

Umāsvāti (second century). *Sūtra on the Meaning of the Principles. Tattvārthasūtra*.

Üpa Losal (Dbus pa blo gsal, thirteenth century). *A Treasury of Explanations of Tenets. Grub pa'i mtha' rnam par bshad pa'i mdzod*. Bod kyi bcu phrag mdzod chen mo las sa skya'i gsung rab 10. Xining: Mi rigs dpe skrun khang dang mtsho sngon mi rigs dpe skrun khang, 2004.

Vācaspati Miśra (tenth century). *Nyāyasūcīnibandha*.

———. *Notes on the Meaning of the Commentary on the Nyāya Sūtra. Nyāyavārttikatātparyaṭīkā*.

Vātsyāyana (fifth century). *Extensive Explanation on the Nyāya Sūtra. Nyāyabhāṣya*.

Verses of Sāṅkhya. See under Īśvarakṛṣṇa.

Vidyabhusana, Satis Chandra. *A History of Indian Logic: Ancient, Medieval, and Modern Schools*. Delhi: Motilal Banarsidass, 1988.

Vidyāraṇya. *See* Mādhava.

Vijñānabhikṣu (late sixteenth century). *Sāṅkhyadarśana*.

Viṣṇu. *Examination of Īśvara. Īśvaramīmāṃsā*.

Vyāsa. *Commentary on the Yoga Sūtra. Yogasūtrabhāṣya*.

Wheeler, Mortimer. *The Indus Civilization*. Cambridge History of India. Cambridge: Cambridge University Press, 1968.

Xuanzang (602–64). *Travel Journal of Xuanzang of the Tang*. Translated by the Mongolian translator Gung mgon po skyabs. Published by the Library of Tibetan Works and Archives, Dharamsala.

Yeshé Dé (Ye shes sde, ninth century) *An Explanation of Different Views. Lta ba'i khyad par bshad pa*.

Yeshé Gyaltsen, Yongzin (Ye shes rgyal mtshan, 1713–93). *History of the Excellent Dharma and Vinaya. Dam pa'i chos 'dul ba'i byung tshul*. Collected Works (xylograph form), vol. *ja*.

Index

I

U

About the Authors

HIS HOLINESS THE DALAI LAMA is the spiritual leader of the Tibetan people, a Nobel Peace Prize recipient, and a beacon of inspiration for Buddhists and non-Buddhists alike. He is admired also for his more than four decades of systematic dialogues with scientists exploring ways to developing new evidence-based approaches to alleviation of suffering and promoting human flourishing. He is the co-founder of the Mind and Life Institute and has helped to revolutionize traditional Tibetan monastic curriculum by incorporating the teaching of modern science. He is a great champion of the great Indian Nalanda tradition of science, philosophy, and wisdom practices.

THUPTEN JINPA is a well-known Buddhist scholar and has been the principal English-language translator for His Holiness the Dalai Lama for more than three decades. A former monk and a Geshe Lharampa, he also holds a BA in philosophy and a PhD in religious studies, both from Cambridge University. He is the author and translator of many books and teaches at McGill University in Montreal.

DONALD S. LOPEZ JR. is the Arthur E. Link Distinguished University Professor of Buddhist and Tibetan Studies at the University of Michigan. He was elected to the American Academy of Arts and Sciences in 2000.

HYOUNG SEOK HAM is an assistant professor in the Department of Philosophy at Chonnam National University in Gwangju, South Korea.

What to Read Next from the Dalai Lama

Buddhism
One Teacher, Many Traditions

The Compassionate Life

Ecology, Ethics, and Interdependence
The Dalai Lama in Conversation with Leading Thinkers on Climate Change

Essence of the Heart Sutra
The Dalai Lama's Heart of Wisdom Teachings

The Essence of Tsongkhapa's Teachings
The Dalai Lama on the Three Principal Aspects of the Path

The Good Heart
A Buddhist Perspective on the Teachings of Jesus

Imagine All the People
A Conversation with the Dalai Lama on Money, Politics, and Life as It Could Be

Kalachakra Tantra
Rite of Initiation

The Library of Wisdom and Compassion series:

1. **Approaching the Buddhist Path**
2. **The Foundation of Buddhist Practice**
3. **Saṃsāra, Nirvāṇa, and Buddha Nature**
4. **Following in the Buddha's Footsteps**
5. **In Praise of Great Compassion**
6. **Courageous Compassion**
7. **Searching for the Self**
8. **Realizing the Profound View**

The Life of My Teacher
A Biography of Kyabjé Ling Rinpoché

Meditation on the Nature of Mind

The Middle Way
Faith Grounded in Reason

Mind in Comfort and Ease
The Vision of Enlightenment in the Great Perfection

MindScience
An East-West Dialogue

Opening the Eye of New Awareness

Practicing Wisdom
The Perfection of Shantideva's Bodhisattva Way

Science and Philosophy in the Indian Buddhist Classics
Volume 1: The Physical World

Science and Philosophy in the Indian Buddhist Classics
Volume 2: The Mind

Sleeping, Dreaming, and Dying
An Exploration of Consciousness

The Wheel of Life
Buddhist Perspectives on Cause and Effect

The World of Tibetan Buddhism
An Overview of Its Philosophy and Practice

About Wisdom Publications

Wisdom Publications is the leading publisher of classic and contemporary Buddhist books and practical works on mindfulness. To learn more about us or to explore our other books, please visit our website at wisdomexperience.org or contact us at the address below.

Wisdom Publications
199 Elm Street
Somerville, MA 02144 USA

We are a 501(c)(3) organization, and donations in support of our mission are tax deductible.

Wisdom Publications is affiliated with the Foundation for the Preservation of the Mahayana Tradition (FPMT).